Security and Human Rights

edited by

Benjamin J Goold

and

Liora Lazarus

·HART·
PUBLISHING

OXFORD AND PORTLAND, OREGON
2007

Published in North America (US and Canada) by
Hart Publishing
c/o International Specialized Book Services
920 NE 58th Avenue, Suite 300
Portland, OR 97213-3786
USA
Tel: +1 503 287 3093 or toll-free: (1) 800 944 6190
Fax: +1 503 280 8832
E-mail: orders@isbs.com
Website: www.isbs.com

Hart Publishing, 16C Worcester Place, OX1 2JW
Telephone: +44 (0)1865 517530 Fax: +44 (0)1865 510710
E-mail: mail@hartpub.co.uk
Website: http://www.hartpub.co.uk

British Library Cataloguing in Publication Data
Data Available

ISBN-13: 978-1-84113-608-0 (paperback)

Typeset by Hope Services (Abingdon) Ltd.
Printed and bound in Great Britain by
TJ International Ltd, Padstow, Cornwall

Foreword

This collection of essays, scrutinising the relationship between security and human rights from a multidisciplinary perspective, could not have come at a more opportune moment. The political interest in security and human rights, and in crime and disorder, has never been more intense. Much of this attention has very direct effects upon the rights of defendants and the interests of the victims of crime. It seems to me that this key place, where the rights of these two groups bisect, is a touchstone for the quality of criminal justice and its moral heart. And this is particularly critical, particularly stark, in cases involving allegations of terrorist activity, where the victim may not be simply private but also in a real sense public—where the victim is, and is intended to be, the community as a whole: all of us and all of our institutions.

It is often said that the pendulum has swung too far in favour of defendants. Too many due process restraints are Victorian in culture. They are no longer relevant. They are too restrictive and hamper the search for justice. Much is made of the revived jurisdiction on abuse of process and some of its wilder manifestations. Obviously the prosecuting authority finds itself at the heart of this debate. That is as it should be and I welcome our being there.

Of course we have our own view of the appropriate balance between defendants and the victims of crime in a criminal trial. Just as we have our own view of the appropriate relationship between the State and those against whom it determines to apply punitive criminal sanctions. And I understand, as do all criminal lawyers, that in no place is this relationship more sensitive than in cases where it is alleged the defendants have set out to attack the State itself, often hoping to destroy its values and its institutions by deliberately targeting its most vulnerable members.

So we need to start by being clear that the threat posed by terrorism is real and serious. It is also necessary to be clear that the precise category of threat which we face is actually new. Of course terrorism isn't a new phenomenon. But this form is a little different.

Terrorists today will use indiscriminate violence. They seek, as a deliberate tactic, mass civilian casualties, of the most vulnerable people they can find. They target individuals, institutions, communities and nations, trying to set people against each other. This is all calculated and deliberate. It can also, if we are not careful, be strikingly successful.

Moreover, the terrorist threat comes with global dimensions. It is no longer purely a domestic problem. Its causes are no longer restricted to one state. This means those causes may be a long way beyond our control. We may be dependent on the whims of foreign electorates.

But I also believe it is critical that we understand that this new form of terrorism carries another more subtle, perhaps equally pernicious risk: it might encourage a fear-driven and inappropriate response. By that I mean it can tempt us to abandon our values. I think it important to understand that this is one of its primary purposes. Understanding this will help us to resist the dangerous temptation to succumb, as will a determination to judge the threat itself with care, and obviously not to underestimate it, obviously. Only a fool would do that.

Terrorism is designed to put pressure on some of our most cherished beliefs and institutions. So it demands a proactive and comprehensive response on the part of law enforcement agencies. But this should be a response whose fundamental effect is to protect those beliefs and institutions. Not to undermine them. We must protect ourselves from these atrocious crimes without abandoning our traditions of freedom.

Our criminal justice response to terrorism must be proportionate and grounded in due process and the rule of law. So, although a development in the role of the security services and the police is essential and desirable in this context, I believe an abandonment of Article 6 fair trial protections in the face of terrorism would represent an abject surrender to nihilism. It would represent defeat.

The rhetoric around the 'War on Terror' illustrates the risks nicely. London is not a battlefield. The innocents who were murdered on 7 July 2005 were not victims of war. And the men who killed them were not, as in their vanity they claimed on their ludicrous videos, 'soldiers'. They were criminals. They were fantasists. We need to be very clear about this. On the streets of London, there is no such thing as a 'war on terror', just as there can be no such thing as a 'war on drugs'. The fight against terrorism on the streets of Britain is not a war. It is the prevention of crime, the enforcement of our laws and the winning of justice for those damaged by their infringement.

Acts of unlawful violence are proscribed by the criminal law. They are criminal offences. We should hold it as an article of faith that crimes of terrorism are dealt with by criminal justice. And we should start by acknowledging the view that a culture of legislative restraint in the area of terrorist crime is central to the existence of an efficient and human rights compatible process.

We wouldn't get far in promoting a civilising culture of respect for rights amongst and between citizens if we set about undermining fair trials in the simple pursuit of greater numbers of inevitably less safe convictions. On the contrary, it is obvious that the process of winning convictions ought to be in keeping with a consensual rule of law and not detached from it. Otherwise we sacrifice fundamental values critical to the maintenance of the rule of law—upon which everything else depends.

Sometimes it is important to restate the obvious: the complexities of modern society are such that there is unlikely to be an end to the use of violence for political ends any time soon. Perhaps all we have at our disposal are different methods of managing this ugly phenomenon. But it is self evident that the means we choose must be far-sighted. Because every time a conviction is achieved, it can only be sustained and built upon by ensuring that it is fair—and therefore safe from being overturned on appeal. Equally that it enjoys the widest public confidence. People must be able to trust the decisions of the Courts.

Ultimately, this means sustaining an approach to the prosecution of these crimes that is founded in reason and which welcomes the shield against injustice which due process rules provide. A similar tone may be found in United States constitutional writing, which emphasises that 'implicit in the provisions and tone of the constitution are the values of a more mature society, which relies on moral persuasion rather than force; on example rather than coercion'.[1] These are civilising qualities in the State and criminal lawyers should celebrate them. We should never be defensive about them.

So, how should the criminal justice system respond to the terrorist threat? In answering this question, we need to deal with a number of issues: the importance of the Human Rights Act 1998; the role of lawyers; legislation and evidence; and finally, community relations. But more generally, we need to avoid a response to terrorism that is based only on fear and suspicion. This kind of climate has no room for the rule of law. Indeed it encourages the opposite.

In the United Kingdom, our institutions are strong, and our liberal values are intact. We continue to have a Constitution and laws that protect rather than oppress us. And our enduring criminal law framework, underpinned by the European Convention on Human Rights, properly directs us towards justice and due process, towards fair procedures and evidence-driven policing. So in fighting terrorism, we shouldn't make exceptions to the rule of law; we should use the strength inherent within it.

Critical to this is that individual rights and national security are not seen as being mutually exclusive. As many of the authors in this timely volume point out, this is not a zero-sum game. Improvements to national security do not have to come at the expense of rights. As the title of this collection has it: security and human rights. Not security or human rights.

So where does all this leave us as lawyers, as politicians, as intellectuals? What is our specific response to the threats to our security, and the strains that those threats are putting on our Constitution? As a lawyer myself, I think it is vital that we work to convince the public of the importance of our traditional values of justice. We need to reveal again their centrality to our way of life, especially in the face of terrorist threats. We need to preach more widely than to the converted. We need, all of us, to be advocates for the view that human rights do matter. That far from undermining our national security, they are a critical part of it.

There is clear room for security and rights. And it is our duty to protect both.

Ken Macdonald QC
Director of Public Prosecutions
London
February 2007

---

[1] *S v Makwanyane and Another CCT3/94* paragraph 222 (per Justice Langa).

Acknowledgments

This book arose out of the Oxford Colloquium on Security and Human Rights, which was held on 16–17 March 2006. We are extremely grateful to all of those who took part, both for their support of the project and for their contributions to the Colloquium and this book. We are also deeply indebted to Sarah McCosker for her research assistance, organisational skills and good humour throughout. In addition, thanks must go to Tamson Pietsch, who helped everything to run smoothly during the Colloquium, and to Lisa Gourd, for her meticulous and patient copyediting in the months that followed. Finally, we would like to say thank you to the British Academy and the Oxford University Faculty of Law for their generous financial support of the Colloquium and the publication of this book, and to Richard Hart for his unwavering confidence from the very beginning.

Benjamin J Goold and Liora Lazarus
Oxford
December 2006

Contents

List of Contributors

Andrew Ashworth is Vinerian Professor of English Law and Fellow of All Soul's College, University of Oxford.

Didier Bigo is Professor of International Relations at the Institut d'Etudes Politiques de Paris.

David Dyzenhaus is Professor of Law and Philosophy, University of Toronto.

Sandra Fredman is Professor of Law and Fellow of Exeter College, University of Oxford.

Benjamin J Goold is Fellow and Tutor in Law at Somerville College, University of Oxford.

Elspeth Guild is Professor of European Migration Law at Radboud University, Nijmegen and a partner at the London law firm Kingsley Napley.

Bernard E Harcourt is Professor of Law and Faculty Director of Academic Affairs at the University of Chicago.

Liora Lazarus is Fellow and Tutor in Law at St Anne's College, University of Oxford.

Ian Loader is Professor of Criminology and Director of the Centre for Criminology, University of Oxford.

S Neil MacFarlane is Lester B Pearson Professor of International Relations and Fellow of St Anne's College, University of Oxford

C H Powell is Senior Lecturer in Law at the University of Cape Town.

Victor V Ramraj is Associate Professor at the Faculty of Law, National University of Singapore.

Kent Roach is Professor of Law and Criminology at the University of Toronto.

Shlomit Wallerstein is Lecturer in Law at St Peter's College, University of Oxford.

Jennifer M Welsh is Lecturer in International Relations and Fellow of Somerville College, University of Oxford.

Lucia Zedner is Professor in Criminal Justice and Fellow of Corpus Christi College, University of Oxford.

List of Colloquium Participants

The Oxford Colloquium on Security and Human Rights (16–17 March 2006) was organised in an effort to encourage more interdisciplinary thinking about the relationship between security and human rights. For this purpose, it brought together academics and practitioners from the related fields of criminal justice, public law, international law and international relations.

The Colloquium was supported by the Law Faculty of the University of Oxford and the British Academy, and was hosted by St Anne's College.

The following people were participants:

Mr Dapo Akande
Professor Andrew Ashworth
Professor Didier Bigo
Professor David Dyzenhaus
Professor Sandra Fredman
Dr Benjamin Goold
Professor Elspeth Guild
Professor Bernard Harcourt
Dr Gary Hart
Mr Richard Hart
Mr Murray Hunt
Dr Liora Lazarus
Professor Ian Loader
Professor Vaughan Lowe
Mr Ken Macdonald QC
Professor Neil MacFarlane
Ms Sarah McCosker
Ms Cathy Powell
Professor Victor V Ramraj
Professor Kent Roach
Mr David Rose
Mr Roger Smith
Dr Shlomit Wallerstein
Dr Jennifer Welsh
Professor Lucia Zedner

Abbreviations

ACLU	American Civil Liberties Union
ASBO	anti-social behaviour order (UK)
AU	African Union
CAPPS	Computer Assisted Passenger Pre-screening System (USA)
CCTV	closed-circuit television
CERD	Committee on the Elimination of Racial Discrimination (UN)
CHS	Commission on Human Security
CIA	Central Intelligence Agency (USA)
CODIS	Combined DNA Indexing System (USA)
CTC	Counter-terrorism Committee (UN)
DARPA	Defence Advanced Research Projects Agency (USA)
ECHR	European Convention for the Protection of Human Rights and Fundamental Freedoms, or European Convention on Human Rights (1950)
ECtHR	European Court of Human Rights
ECOSOC	Economic and Social Council (UN)
ECOWAS	Economic Community of West African States
ESC	European Social Charter
ETA	Basque Homeland and Freedom group
EU	European Union
FAA	Federal Aviation Administration (USA)
FBI	Federal Bureau of Investigations
FCC	Federal Constitutional Court (Germany)
GA	General Assembly (UN)
HRA	Human Rights Act (1998) (UK)
ICCPR	International Covenant on Civil and Political Rights (1976)
ICESCR	International Covenant for Economic, Social and Cultural Rights
ICISS	International Commission on Intervention and State Sovereignty
ICJ	International Court of Justice
ICTY	International Criminal Tribunal for the Former Yugoslavia
IOCA	Interception of Communications Act (1985) (UK)
ISC	Intelligence and Security Committee (UK)
JCHR	Joint Committee on Human Rights (UK)
JTAC	Joint Terrorism Analysis Centre
NATO	North Atlantic Treaty Organization

NDNAD	National DNA Database (UK)
NGO	non-governmental organisation
NYPD	New York City Police Department
OAU	Organisation of African Unity
P5	Permanent Five (UN)
PIRA	Provisional Irish Republican Army
R2P	'Responsibility to Protect'
RCAG	Rail Commuters Action Group (South Africa)
RIPA	Regulation of Investigatory Powers Act (2000) (UK)
RSHO	risk of sexual harm order (UK)
SC	Security Council (UN)
SCR	Security Council Resolution (UN)
SIAC	Special Immigration Appeals Commission (UK)
TIA	Total Information Awareness (USA)
UDHR	Universal Declaration of Human Rights
UN	United Nations
UNDP	United Nations Development Programme
UNGA	United Nations General Assembly
UNICEF	United Nations Children's Fund
UNOSOM	UN Operation in Somalia
UNITAF	Unified Task Force (Somalia)
UNSG	United Nations Secretary-General
USA PATRIOT Act	Uniting and Strengthening America by Providing Appropriate Tools Required to Intercept and Obstruct Terrorism Act (2001) (USA)
WMD	weapons of mass destruction

Table of Cases

European Court of Justice and Court of First of Instance

Germany

United Kingdom

United Nations Human Rights Committee

United States of America

Table of Legislation

Recommendations

Germany

Hungary

India

International

Israel

South Africa

United Kingdom

Statutory Instruments

United States of America

Constitution

It is the liberals, then, who count. They are, as it might be, the canaries in the sulphurous mineshaft of modern democracy.

—Tony Judt, 'Bush's Useful Idiots', *London Review of Books*, 21 September 2006

1

Introduction
Security and Human Rights: The Search
for a Language of Reconciliation

LIORA LAZARUS and BENJAMIN J GOOLD

THE ATTAINMENT OF security and the protection of human rights are not necessarily antithetical, either as a matter of fact or principle. Nevertheless, since 9/11 the words 'security' and 'human rights' have, in the collective imagination, now come to connote an almost insuperable opposition. Anyone who engages in the debate over security and human rights is almost immediately confronted by this dichotomy, tacit in the political call for a 'new balance' and explicit in newspaper editorials calling for the retreat from human rights. Prompted by the urgency or supposed 'exceptionalism' of our times, politicians, judges and intellectuals are all addressing the central dilemma of this dichotomy: how are we to protect freedom (through security) without denying its essence (by violating human rights)? For liberals, the search for a new language of reconciliation between security and human rights has arguably become one of their most urgent intellectual challenges. Indeed, there is a growing sense in the academy internationally that the stakes of the thoughts and arguments on this question have been raised.[1]

The challenge of how best to safeguard freedom and democracy without squandering them is not simply a product of the threats arising out of 9/11 (or perceptions of them). It is a challenge that has always existed at the centre of the liberal democratic enterprise. It is this pursuit that animates democratic politics, and the tension that spurs its philosophical refinement. Moreover, if we are to remain squarely within the liberal democratic tradition, many would argue that security

---

[1] This is no less the case for the contributors to this volume, who came together at the Oxford Colloquium on Security and Human Rights on 16 and 17 March 2006. Drawn from a variety of disciplinary perspectives—legal theory, criminology, criminal law, constitutional law, international law and international relations, as well as government and legal practice—these contributors were able to bring a range of views to bear on the question of how best to resolve the tension between security and the protection of human rights.

and human rights *must* be reconciled.[2] National and individual security strikes at the heart of sovereignty: the capacity to maintain security, and demonstrably so, is a litmus test of the functionality of the modern state.

From both Lockean and Kantian perspectives, what distinguishes a liberal democracy from a totalitarian state is that the attainment of security through the exercise of democratic sovereignty is justified ultimately by the pursuit of liberty (which itself cannot be exercised in conditions of grave insecurity).[3] Human rights, as positive articulations of the constituents of liberty, are the benchmark by which liberal democracies are judged. Constitutions, parliaments and courts act to protect them and to constrain the executive's overweening assertions of authority. Security as the precondition for liberty, and human rights as the constituents of liberty, are thus both inherent parts of the broader liberal democratic project:

> [W]e must find ways of reconciling security with liberty, since the success of one helps the other. The choice between security and liberty is a false choice . . . Our history has shown us that insecurity threatens liberty. Yet if our liberties are curtailed, we lose the values that we are struggling to defend.[4]

Given the evident relationship between the maintenance of security and the preservation of rights within the liberal tradition, we might well ask why a language of reconciliation has become so politically elusive. If it is not the case that the pursuit of security and respect for human rights are necessarily irreconcilable, is the tension between the two a product of our collective inability to agree on a set of assumptions, terms and rules for discussion? Or have the rules of the game, or at least the rules of the debate, really changed?

I. SECURITY, RIGHTS AND THE 'NEW NORMALCY'

> A time of terror may not be the ideal moment to trifle with the most time-tested postulates of government under law. It is certainly not a good time to dispense lightly with bedrock principles of our constitutional system.[5]

Despite the wisdom of Katyal and Tribe's warning, the claim that 9/11 ushered in an era of ongoing emergency that demands fundamental political, legal and constitutional reordering has acquired a seemingly irresistible currency. We are, it is said, in a continuing 'state of exception',[6] the end of which, due to the nature of

---

[2] Tesón, FR, 'Liberal Security' in R Ashby Wilson (ed), *Human Rights in the 'War on Terror'* (Cambridge, Cambridge University Press, 2005) 57; Luban, D, 'Eight Fallacies about Liberty and Security' in R Ashby Wilson (ed), *Human Rights in the 'War on Terror'* (Cambridge, Cambridge University Press, 2005) 242, 245.

[3] Tesón (2005) 60.

[4] National Commission on Terrorist Attacks upon the United States (9/11 Commission), *Report* (2004), available at http://www.9-11commission.gov/?report/?index.htm, 395.

[5] Katyal, NK and Tribe, LH, 'Waging War, Deciding Guilt: Trying the Military Tribunals' (2002) *Yale Law Journal* 1111, 1259.

[6] For an argument that the 'state of exception' is a standing constituent of liberal regimes and thus always a part of the 'normal', see Agamben, G, *The State of Exception* (Chicago, University of Chicago Press, 2005).

the super-terrorist threat,[7] we cannot identify. In short, what was previously viewed as the exception, a time of unprecedented crisis calling for appropriately exceptional measures, has now become the norm. The claim is not the preserve of only neo-conservative US politicians, such as Vice President Dick Cheney, who argue that 'emergency is the "new normalcy" '.[8] Supposedly left-wing European leaders also argue that the 'rules of the game have changed'.[9] Similarly, the idea that we are facing the 'normalization of emergency conditions'[10] and that the 'age of terror' calls for unprecedented measures is now taken increasingly seriously within the academy across an ever-extending range of the political spectrum.[11] Even those more sceptical of these exceptionalist claims recognise that 'there seems to be a general acceptance in the wake of the terrorist attacks of September 11, 2001 that some adjustment in our scheme of civil liberties is inevitable'.[12]

Such is the currency of these propositions that previously marginal arguments have become plausible, while positions that formerly attracted a broad political consensus have come to be seen as naïve or passé. In this environment, Michael Ignatieff's promotion of 'lesser evils',[13] Alan Dershowitz's support for the legal regulation of torture,[14] Oren Gross's endorsement of transparent illegality[15] and Bruce Ackerman's endorsement of 'suspicionless' preventative detention under an 'emergency constitution'[16] have become the central arguments with which we must engage.

Whereas 10 years ago such arguments might have settled at the fringes of scholastic debate, the shoe is now very much on the other foot: constitutional and international human rights once claimed a privileged moral status, their limitation always requiring justification; but claims to security now appear to receive less

---

[7] 'Super-terrorism' is characterised as terrorism that has global aims, an 'apocalyptic' ideology, 'war-like' means and with which political negotiation is impossible: Freeman, M, 'Order, Rights and Threats: Terrorism and Global Justice' in R Ashby Wilson (ed), *Human Rights in the 'War on Terror'* (Cambridge, Cambridge University Press, 2005) 37, 38.

[8] Remarks to the Republican Governors Association, Washington, DC, on 25 October 2001, available at http://www.whitehouse.gov/?vicepresident/?news-speeches/?speeches/?text/?vp20011025.html. Repeated in an interview to the television programme *60 Minutes II* on 14 November 2001, available at http://www.whitehouse.gov/?vicepresident/?news-speeches/?speeches/?vp20011114.html.

[9] See UK Prime Minister's Press Conference, 5 August 2005, available at http://www.number-10.gov.uk/?output/?Page8041.asp.

[10] Ackerman, B, 'The Emergency Constitution' (2004) 113 *Yale Law Journal* 1029, 1043.

[11] The responses to this perceived condition are, however, quite varied. See, inter alia: Ackerman (2004); Gross, O, 'Chaos and Rules: Should Responses to Violent Crises Always be Constitutional?' (2003) 112 *Yale Law Journal* 1011; Ignatieff, M, *The Lesser Evil: Politics in an Age of Terror* (Princeton, Princeton University Press, 2004); Cole, D, 'The Priority of Morality: The Emergency Constitution's Blind Spot' (2004) 113 *Yale Law Journal* 173; Tribe, LH and Gudridge, PO, 'The Anti-emergency Constitution' (2004) 113 *Yale Law Journal* 1801.

[12] Waldron, J, 'Security and Liberty: The Image of Balance' (2003) 11(2) *The Journal of Political Philosophy* 191.

[13] Ignatieff (2004).

[14] Dershowitz, A, 'Tortured Reasoning' in S Levinson (ed), *Torture: A Collection* (Oxford, Oxford University Press, 2004) 14.

[15] Gross (2003).

[16] Ackerman (2004), but see now amended proposals in Ackerman, B, *Before the Next Attack: Preserving Civil Liberties in an Age of Terrorism* (Hartford, Yale University Press, 2006).

scrutiny than the assertion of rights that may restrict measures in its pursuit. Whatever the empirical merits of the argument that we have entered an 'age of exception'—and it is far from clear how one would ever prove this—one thing is becoming apparent: the claim is shifting the foundations of political and constitutional debate. It has become the tacit challenge against which we must formulate our propositions.

As a consequence of the status of the perpetual emergency claim and statements about the uniqueness of our present conditions, those who claim that we already have the structures and institutions in place to deal with the threat at hand[17] risk being accused of a blind adherence to absolutism, perfection or idealism.[18] According to Ignatieff, for example,

> the belief that our existing rights and guarantees should never be suspended is a piece of moral perfectionism . . . To claim that there are no lesser evil choices to be made is to take refuge in the illusion that the threat of terrorism is exaggerated.[19]

Whereas in the past those concerned with questions of security within liberal democracies may have stopped short of calling for the suspension of rights altogether, in the current climate the idea that certain human rights can be 'turned off' when necessary has come to be regarded by many as a thoroughly reasonable reaction to the dangers allegedly faced by democratic societies. In effect, the exceptionalism argument has become pivotal, so much so that liberals and human rights organisations must either rebut claims that our conditions are unique, or respond to these supposedly exceptional conditions by adjusting our institutions, practices, procedures and laws:

> The season for talk of leaving the Constitution behind, while we grit our teeth and do what must be done in times of grave peril—the season for talk of saving the Constitution from the distortions wrought by sheer necessity, while we save ourselves from the dangers of genuine fidelity to the Constitution—is upon us.[20]

For many, then, the search for reconciliation between security and human rights is really a search for a language that can claim a purchase on the political, legal and popular imaginations within the existing climate of exceptionalism: a language that engages with the assertion of exceptionalism and the claims of unique crisis, while blunting its worst implications.

Of course, the currency of the exceptionalism claim has deeper social and political roots than the iconic collapse of the New York World Trade Center towers. Two factors in particular underpin the social receptivity of the claim to exceptionalism. The first of these relates to what David Garland and others within the realm of criminal justice have referred to as the emergence of a 'culture of

[17] See for example, Luban (2005); and Goldstone, R, 'The Tension between Combating Terrorism and Protecting Civil Liberties' in R Ashby Wilson (ed), *Human Rights in the 'War on Terror'* (Cambridge, Cambridge University Press, 2005) 242, 249.
[18] See Gross on those who conduct 'business as usual': Gross (2003).
[19] Ignatieff (2004) vii.
[20] Tribe and Gudridge (2004).

control'.[21] According to these writers, late modern states are increasingly characterised by aspirations towards 'public protection', the 'containment of danger' and
the 'management of risk', all of which arise out of a perceived and politically
exploited condition of social 'insecurity'.[22]

During the late 1980s and throughout the 1990s, as governments began to shift
attention away from the elimination of crime—a problem that they had come to
regard as insoluble—to strategies aimed at its management and containment, a
new discourse emerged about the role of the state. Instead of presenting themselves as primarily responsible for addressing the problem of crime, states instead
began focusing on making people feel safer and more secure while also arguing
that responsibility for such security had to be shared with institutions and organisations outside of the state realm. Within political discourse, fear of crime and
questions of insecurity were elevated in status, so that the pursuit of 'security'—a
term often invoked but rarely defined by politicians—became an overriding social
aim.

Insofar as this shift coincided with a gradual surrendering by states of primary
responsibility for other important public matters (such as health, transport and
education), it contributed to the emergence of a new, neo-liberal conception
of government. No longer is the state the unquestioned provider or guarantor of
public services or certain accepted social rights, but rather it is one player amongst
many. Whether this change was the product of the state's awareness of its own
impotence—its inability to 'solve' the problem of crime and other social ills—or
an inevitable product of wider changes in governance brought on by the forces of
late modernity is open to discussion. Regardless of the reasons behind the shift, the
move to disperse responsibility for society's problems usefully freed politicians
from having to answer for many of the failures of modern government. At the
same time, however, the admission that the state could no longer be the primary
provider of security, despite the political elevation of this aim, also threatened to
undermine state legitimacy.

It is in this complex and contradictory neo-liberal political environment that
Western political responses to the attacks of 9/11 need to be read. In countries like
the United States and the United Kingdom, the threat of super-terrorism starkly
exposed the limits of the state's capacity to provide security for its citizens. But
equally, this threat presented governments with a novel opportunity to develop
new and powerful rhetorical arguments, in particular the claim to exceptionalism,
in favour of increased state power. Seen in this light, the popularity of exceptionalism is a product of a social transformation whereby the legitimacy of late-
modern states has become increasingly bound up with their role as the guarantor

---

[21] Garland, D, *The Culture of Control* (Oxford, Oxford University Press, 2001). See also: Simon, J,
'"Entitlement to Cruelty": Neo-liberalism and the Punitive Mentality in the United States' in
K Stenson and R Sullivan (eds), *Crime, Risk, and Justice: The Politics of Crime Control in Liberal
Democracies* (Portland, Willan Publishing, 2001) 125–43; and O'Malley, P, 'Volatile and Contradictory
Punishment' (1999) 3(2) *Theoretical Criminology* 175–96.

[22] Garland (2001).

of security and with a politics of security that seeks both to allay and exploit communal feelings of insecurity and fear.

The second factor underpinning the apparent effectiveness of the exceptionalism argument relates to what we term the 'politics of rights scepticism'. Alongside the rise of human rights discourse since 1945 and its seeming international ubiquity after the end of the Cold War,[23] there has been a strong philosophical scepticism of the moral foundation of human rights claims and considerable political controversy regarding their judicial and constitutional protection.[24] Although human rights have been the benchmark of the liberal democratic ideal, there are deep controversies as to how they should be realised, under what institutional conditions they should be pursued, and which specific rights may be branded as sufficiently fundamental to trump majoritarian desires.

Rights-sceptic arguments are the product variously of republican criticisms of the constitutional and political legitimacy of judicial review;[25] pragmatic empiricist, post-modern and conservative rejections of the idealist pretensions of enlightenment rationalism;[26] socialist and communitarian objections to the egoistic individualism and atomistic legalism to which rights give rise; left-wing suspicion, particularly in the United Kingdom, of the elite judiciary;[27] and critical pragmatic arguments regarding the emancipatory potential of human rights discourse.[28] This complex amalgam of political, philosophical and pragmatic objections to human rights has generated a debate internal to rights discourse that has made it particularly vulnerable to the competing and increasingly powerful discourse of security.

In essence, then, two divides need to be bridged if we are to find some way of reconciling the pursuit of security with a respect for fundamental human rights.

---

[23] Freeman, M, *Human Rights: An Interdisciplinary Approach* (Cambridge, Polity, 2002) ch 3.

[24] Douzinas, C, *The End of Human Rights* (Oxford, Hart Publishing, 2000) 1; Campbell, T, Ewing, KD and Tomkins, A, *Sceptical Essays on Human Rights* (Oxford, Oxford University Press, 2001). See also Lazarus, L, *Contrasting Prisoners' Rights* (Oxford, Oxford University Press, 2004) 163–8.

[25] Kramer, LD, *The People Themselves: Popular Constitutionalism and Judicial Review* (Oxford, Oxford University Press, 2004); Waldron, J, *Law and Disagreement* (Oxford, Oxford University Press, 1999); Bellamy, R, 'Constitutive Citizenship versus Constitutional Rights: Republican Reflections on the EU Charter and the Human Rights Act' in T Campbell, KD Ewing and A Tomkins (eds), *Sceptical Essays on Human Rights* (Oxford, Oxford University Press, 2001); Tomkins, A, *Our Republican Constitution* (Oxford, Hart Publishing, 2005).

[26] Minogue, K, 'What is Wrong with Rights' in C Harlow (ed), *Public Law and Politics* (London, Sweet & Maxwell, 1986) 209, 209–12; Gray, J, *Enlightenment's Wake: Politics and Culture at the Close of the Modern Age* (London, Routledge, 1995) 172–3; Ryan, A, 'The British, the Americans, and Rights' in M Lacey and K Haakonssen (eds), *A Culture of Rights* (Cambridge, Cambridge University Press, 1991) 375–95; Loughlin, M, 'Rights, Democracy, and Law' in T Campbell, KD Ewing and A Tomkins (eds), *Sceptical Essays on Human Rights* (Oxford, Oxford University Press, 2001); Gearty, C, *Can Human Rights Survive* (Cambridge, Cambridge University Press, 2006) ch 2; Klug, F, *Values for a Godless Age* (London, Penguin, 2000) 154; Douzinas (2000).

[27] Griffiths, J, *The Politics of the Judiciary*, 4th edn (London, Fontana, 1991); Griffiths, J, 'The Political Constitution' (1979) 42 *MLR* 1; Ewing, K and Gearty, C, *Freedom under Thatcher: Civil Liberties in Modern Britain* (Oxford, Clarendon Press, 1990) ch 8; Ewing, K and Gearty, C, *The Struggle for Civil Liberties* (Oxford, Oxford University Press, 2000) ch 8.

[28] Kennedy, D, 'The International Human Rights Movement: Part of the Problem?' (2001) 3 *European Human Rights Law Review* 245.

On the one hand, we must critically engage with the politics of security
ʕ modern states—a politics in which appeals to security are increasingly uₗ
governments and politicians as a rhetorical device for the expansion oɬ
power. This necessitates the development of an understanding and critique oɾ the
conditions in which security discourse—and its displacement of liberal values
and human rights—occurs. As a number of authors observe in this volume,
although much of the current debate over security can be traced to the events of
9/11, many of the arguments and policies that have emerged over the past five
years have their origins in longstanding political and social trends. Looked at in
this way, the preoccupation with security is best understood as a cipher for a range
of diverse concerns, and as such it is crucial that we retain a meta- or sociological
perspective on the apparent conflict between rights and security. We must in other
words engage with the social phenomenon of security, the social conditions in
which security discourse exists and the philosophical foundations of security
claims.

Equally, however, we must also address deeper philosophical concerns that
strike at the very heart of the human rights project. For it is not so much that security and rights have to be reconciled per se, but rather that the present concern
with collective security and the persistent claim to exceptionalism have exposed
and heightened a number of fundamental tensions that are inherent to modern
liberal democracies. In broaching the question of how to reconcile security and
human rights, we are in effect also asking how to balance between the individual
and the collective, between the political and the legal, and between political sovereignty and the rule of law. Thus, the pursuit of the mutual attainment of security
and human rights since 9/11 has provoked a re-engagement with questions that
are central to democratic orders and has peeled back any veneer of political consensus that may have surrounded them. The current fight is then not only about
security and rights, it is also about the essential institutional, procedural and substantive principles that we think a legitimate democracy ought to have. Clearly,
conservatives, civic republicans, communitarians and classical liberals will all have
different answers to what constitutes legitimacy in this context.

In developing a defence of human rights, if we are unable to be clear about why
the rule of law matters and why rights are worthy of respect—regardless of the
threats of terrorism—then it is unlikely that liberals will be able to resist arguments
aimed at curtailing legal safeguards in the name of security or assuaging the fears
of the majority. In this pursuit, it is not safe merely to fall back on previously
accepted political presumptions. Given the broader context in which this debate is
occurring, defenders of rights are correct to be wary of baldly asserting concepts
that, in these times, have become question-begging. We have to find new ways of
articulating established beliefs and must engage in new theoretical discussion with
a sharpened agenda. As Conor Gearty argues,

> without a reworking of what the term 'human rights' means today, designed to give
> it contemporary intellectual confidence, some theoretical zest, then the time might
> come when firing the human rights argument will be greeted neither with warmth

nor dismay but rather with blank indifference, or (which is worse) mute incompre-
hension: whatever can that term mean?[29]

In other words, if we are properly to defend human rights, we need fully to engage
with them.

In attempting to re-enter and realign the debate in this way it is important also
to recognise that there are disciplinary as well as political and philosophical divides
that must be overcome. Within the academy, different disciplines have developed
their own responses to the challenges of security in the years since 9/11, often with
little knowledge of or reference to the responses of related fields. While all of these
responses, from human rights scholars and practitioners, international lawyers,
international relations scholars and criminologists, are important and legitimate,
the absence of a shared language, or even a commonly held understanding of the
challenge, has perhaps undermined the effectiveness of the liberal response. Partly,
this is because of the variance in the questions or pursuits that different disciplines
hold as legitimate.

For legal scholars, the defence of the rule of law, legal institutions, the integrity
of legal rules and the specificity of rights reasoning feature foremost. For sociolo-
gists, criminologists and international relations scholars, on the other hand, questions of the effectiveness of human rights discourse and policy or underlying
changes in the social and political landscape may hold centre stage. Hence, this
book brings together those disciplines at the forefront of the conflict between
rights and security. By encouraging interdisciplinary communication, it is hoped
that we can not only learn from each other and gain greater insight into this conflict, but also ensure that we are able both to critique security whilst fully engaging
with human rights and to find a collective strategy that is expansive and coherent.
While certain disciplines may naturally favour an engagement with either rights or
security, it is important that the two approaches overlap. If we are to develop a language of reconciliation between security and human rights—or even simply think
about them effectively—then it is important to ensure that those involved in these
different debates are aware of each other and to work to enhance the analysis that
takes place at the margins and in the overlap between the two.

II. ENGAGING SECURITY

1. A Sociology of Security

When attempting to find a language of reconciliation between security and human
rights, or, put another way, when searching for some basis upon which liberals can
engage with those who promote the pursuit of security, it is important to return to
the question of what is actually at stake. Just as those in favour of increased security and restricting certain rights continue to critique the 'human rights project',

---

[29] Gearty (2006) 20.

so too must liberal scholars and rights advocates continue to scrutinise the claims of the security lobby. Although many accounts of the tension between rights and security rightly focus on definitions of torture, the serious dangers of preventative detention and the requirements of a fair trial, the current concern with security must also be seen in terms of longstanding and potentially disturbing structural changes that are taking place in modern society. This volume contains a number of contributions that seek to engage with the claims of the security lobby and to place them within a broader sociological critique.

Ian Loader argues in his chapter that it is important to keep sight of what he refers to as the 'cultural lives' of security and rights. He seeks to uncover the social and political conditions that enable the rhetoric of security to override the rhetoric of rights. In particular, Loader examines three examples from English criminal justice politics that pre-date 9/11: miscarriages of justice, public responses to closed-circuit television (CCTV) and the rise of 'anti-social behaviour orders' (ASBOs), which are designed to sidestep established procedural protections. By identifying and examining some of the key rhetorical strategies that have been employed by politicians and others, Loader reveals how they are able to 'mobilise a populist appeal to the idea of security, while presenting rights claims as the concern of remote special interest groups willing to play fast and loose with the safety of their co-citizens'.[30] Part of the story rests, Loader suspects, in the general distaste for rights within certain cultures (notably English culture), as well as a political concern that rights undermine collective values by insisting on a division between individuals on the one hand and their communities on the other hand. Aside from the fact that one of Loader's stated aims is to encourage deeper investigation into the question of how best to advance human rights in this environment, he also contributes to the larger discussion on reconciliation by arguing that such rights must be situated within a 'solidaristic and egalitarian practice of security'. Security, in the sense that Loader views it, is a central value of the good society—and therefore also rights-regarding.

Like Loader, Benjamin Goold highlights the larger social and political implications of the current drive towards more security. He argues that it is important for us to resist many of these demands—in particular the claim that more and better state surveillance is needed—if we are to preserve our existing concepts of privacy or at least retain some measure of control over the way in which we construct and develop our identities. For Goold, 9/11 is significant because it provides the ongoing expansion of state surveillance in countries like the United States and the United Kingdom with a new, seemingly irrefutable justification, namely the pursuit of security. As a consequence, traditional notions of identity based on narrative understandings of personal development are now under serious threat from an emergent administrative form, the 'categorical identity'. Although this shift may be less obviously alarming than calls for use of torture or the suspension of the right to a fair trial, it is nonetheless deeply problematic. In particular, Goold's

---

[30] I Loader in this volume, p 27.

analysis suggests that the widespread expansion in surveillance that is currently being driven by the rhetoric of security has amplified various underlying, ongoing sociological changes that have made the public increasingly willing to surrender their privacy and submit to demands for greater state power.

In essence, what unites Loader and Goold is an appeal for perspective on the current preoccupation with security and a call for a more textured external critique that recognises that the apparent conflict between security and rights has its origins in deep social and political changes that pre-date 9/11. Whereas Loader points to the broader social and political contexts that shape the cultural lives of security and rights, Goold also asks us to look beyond the immediate dangers of security to larger developments in the role of surveillance in modern democratic states. To a lesser extent, both authors also share a willingness to engage with the practical claims of security, suggesting that the way forward to reconciliation may involve a mixture of approaches, some legal and political, others rhetorical. While not going so far as to endorse a pragmatic response to the politics of security, the chapters by Loader and Goold argue that if liberals are to play an effective part in the public debate over the future of human rights, we must engage with the broader context in which security is being pursued and develop a robust 'sociology of security'.

2. Exploiting the Language of Risk

If liberals are to resist the worst excesses of security, or at least to be able to respond to its demands, then it is also unavoidable that they will have to engage with the language of risk. One way in which this can be done is, as Bernard Harcourt does in this volume with respect to racial profiling, to test the effectiveness of new counter-terrorism and security measures on their own terms. Harcourt thus turns the rhetoric of security back upon itself, demanding proof that rights-restricting policies or programmes will in fact provide more security. In contrast to liberals who have refused in the past to countenance profiling because of the strong belief that such techniques are by definition discriminatory and therefore simply wrong, Harcourt instead demands that advocates of such methods prove that they in fact work to reduce the threat of terrorism. As he notes, since 9/11 the racial profiling of Muslim men has been advocated by a range of commentators and law enforcement agencies, despite the fact that there 'is no empirical evidence whatsoever, nor a solid theoretical reason why racial profiling would be an effective measure—rather than a counterproductive step resulting in detrimental substitutions and increased terrorist attacks'.[31] More disturbingly, Harcourt argues that, far from deterring terrorists, profiling may in fact undermine the legitimacy of other anti-terrorism measures and, crucially, 'encourage the recruitment of terrorists from outside the core profile and the substitution of other terrorist acts'.[32]

[31] B Harcourt in this volume, p 75 (3 in original file).
[32] *Ibid*, p 95 (29).

Is Harcourt's strategy one that defenders of human rights need to adopt if they are to counter the claims of those obsessed with security? In other words, should they be prepared to 'get their hands dirty' and participate in debates about the effectiveness of measures that may have serious implications for human rights? Certainly, Harcourt's approach represents a significant departure from that of many in Britain and Europe. Whereas US academics and human rights advocates have been ready to take a pragmatic approach to the preservation of rights, on the other side of the Atlantic there has been a distinct reticence to use such tools as economic modelling and statistical analysis. For those concerned to maintain the high ground, Harcourt's approach may be a step too far. There is always the danger that by accepting that effectiveness matters, we might be forced to concede that some new security measure that undermines rights, even torture, actually works and cannot therefore be resisted. Crucially, however, liberals need to think carefully about how best to balance the need to engage in certain debates while preserving some commitment to the idea of rights as trumps. If we do find that profiling 'works' and that it significantly reduces the risks of future attacks, do we risk being seen as hypocritical if we then fall back on more conventional, principled objections to such measures?

Like Harcourt, Lucia Zedner in this volume also engages with the language of risk, not for the purposes of using it as a critical tool but with a view to exposing some of the assumptions that drive the pursuit of security. According to Zedner, it is fundamentally important to remember that discussions of security and the limits of prevention are intimately bound up with perceptions of risk—perceptions that have been radically altered by the events of 9/11 and 7/7. Indeed, she argues that while we continue to focus our attention on the more obvious manifestations of the current obsession with security and anti-terrorism, there is a danger that too little attention is being paid to 'the degree to which the growing sophistication of actuarial tools and huge advances in computational power both enable and legitimate pre-emptive intervention'.[33] For Zedner, because it is impossible to separate these statistical tools from the political and policy choices that animate our conceptions of risk, it follows that pre-emptive measures designed to increase security can never be truly objective or divorced from our political concerns and values. By highlighting this connection and drawing together existing discourses on rights, risk and security, Zedner reveals one of the inherent dangers of the current focus on security: by using risk categories to impose restrictions on only targeted sections of the population, we minimise the likelihood that such responses will be accompanied by healthy political debate or 'invoke the natural political resistance generated by burdens that affect us all'.[34]

Taken together, the chapters by Harcourt and Zedner remind us that the emerging discourse of risk has not only provided a drive for much of the current obsession with security, but also fundamentally altered the way in which policy makers

[33] L Zedner in this volume, pp 260–61 (8–9 in original file).
[34] *Ibid*, p 272.

and governments assess the success or failure of new security measures. In our efforts to respond to curtailments or modifications of existing human rights, it is important to ensure that risk does not become the only lens through which concerns about security are viewed, or the only set of criteria that informs decision making about them. This is a point that is also made by Didier Bigo and Elspeth Guild, although for them the central challenge is to ensure that when risk is at the centre of any public debate about security, the language used to describe that risk—which inevitably structures the response to it—is accessible to all. Noting that it is difficult to imagine an average person being able to 'successfully navigate the overwhelming professional discourses surrounding the management of threats and not be under their "charm" ',[35] Bigo and Guild construct a powerful argument in favour of a common conception of risk, based in particular on the accepted norm of the reasonable person or 'man on the Clapham omnibus'. Fearing that undue reliance on a specialist conception of risk gives too much power and influence to the security industry, they argue that reference to a 'reasonable person' can act as an important 'reality check' against exceptional legal decision making. The general discussion of risk and security must, they argue, be moved away from a fixation on worst-case scenarios—typically favoured by governments and the security industry—to a discourse based on reasonable grounds for a reasonable person. By shifting the language of risk in this way, they argue, we are better able to protect the rule of law and to ensure that many, rather than a few, voices are heard in the security and human rights debate.

III. ENGAGING RIGHTS

A robust defence of rights needs to be situated within a critical appreciation of the limit of rights, an engagement with the constitutional controversies they present and an understanding of the particular political dilemmas to which they give rise when society is faced with grave threats. It is not enough to assert rights as a good in themselves by reference to metaphysical arguments that transcend social reality. Rights advocates must show how rights can work in practice, how the rule of law can be maintained, why the integrity of the law matters and how rights-regarding institutions can be shown to work even when facing our most perilous social challenges. Rights arguments need also to engage with the possibility of alternative conceptions of rights, law and legal institutions, as well as rights-sceptical challenges, if they are to have a contemporary currency. There is, however, a difference between critically engaging with such challenges and succumbing to their worst excesses, as Judt warns:

> The alacrity with which many of America's most prominent liberals have censored themselves in the name of the War on Terror, the enthusiasm with which they have invented ideological and moral cover for war and war crimes and proffered that

---

[35] D Bigo and E Guild in this volume, p 101 (4 in original file).

cover to their political enemies: all this is a bad sign. Liberal intellectuals used to be distinguished precisely by their efforts to think for themselves, rather than in the service of others. Intellectuals should not be smugly theorising endless war, much less confidently promoting and excusing it. They should be engaged in disturbing the peace—their own above all.[36]

Thus, intellectuals now have to walk a tightrope between being single-mindedly committed to rights to the point of dismissing issues of security, and providing the intellectual legitimation for proponents of the security lobby.

1. Politics, the Rule of Law and a Culture of Justification

Two central dichotomies—between politics and legality, and between pragmatism and idealism—exist within constitutional debate in 'times of crisis'.[37] This volume contains a number of contributions that seek to establish a middle ground between the polarities of pragmatic political responses to security threats and the idealistic preservation of legality. In doing this, these contributors help to resolve the background political and constitutional conflicts underpinning the tension between security and human rights, thereby identifying the conditions in which a language of reconciliation between these supposedly competing objectives might be achieved.

In his chapter, David Dyzenhaus asserts that the middle ground between legality and political sovereignty rests in the development of principles of judicial due deference grounded in a 'culture of justification'. Because common law principles of judicial review 'rest on the distinction between inappropriate merits or correctness review and appropriate review of legality'[38] they contain the possibility to check the legality of administrative action while also affording leeway and respect to administrative expertise. Hence, judicial deference to expert administrative tribunals that are set up to deal with sensitive security concerns, such as the Special Immigration Appeals Commission (SIAC) in the United Kingdom, is not a necessary violation of rule of law values. The test, however, lies in just how that judicial deference is exercised.

For Dyzenhaus, the overriding principle of the constitutional legitimacy of judicial review of security measures cannot be found exclusively in either liberal constitutionalism or democratic positivism but rather is situated in a distinct 'culture of justification'. This culture can be said to exist 'when a political order accepts that all official acts, all exercises of state power, are legal only on condition that they are justified by law, where law is understood in an expansive sense, that is, as including fundamental commitments such as those entailed by the principle of

---

[36] Judt, T, 'Bush's Useful Idiots' (2006) 28(18) *London Review of Books*, available at http://www.lrb.co.uk/v28/n18/judt01_.html.

[37] See the contribution by V V Ramraj in this volume.

[38] D Dyzenhaus in this volume, p 137 (22 in original file).

legality and respect for human rights'.[39] This onus of justification falls therefore on the legislature, the executive and the judiciary. In such a culture, judicial due deference to executive and legislative decisions is not only possible but necessary for the establishment of 'an effective principle of legality'. The 'very possibility of deferring is what makes evaluation of the quality of reasoning necessary, but that evaluation is of whether the decision-maker's reasons were good enough in a democratic society'.[40] In this way, Dyzenhaus seeks to 'reconcile the democratic urge to place the development of law in the hands of the representatives of the people with the liberal urge to ensure that such development does not interfere with the rights of the individual more than can be justified'.[41] To that extent, the resolution between security and human rights, for Dyzenhaus, rests on the possibility of 'deference as respect' as opposed to 'submissive deference'—and this type of judicial due deference can only function properly within an established culture of justification.

The culture of justification model need not apply only to municipal legal orders, or describe the rule of law in a municipal setting. Nor, as Cathy Powell argues in this volume, need it apply only to questions of judicial deference. As she demonstrates, a culture of justification can legitimately be said to form part of the 'institutional design of the international legal order'. This is because 'all law, including international law, entails the rule of law' and as a consequence 'requires that the law constrain those who wield power and hold them to account'.[42] On this basis, Powell critiques the increasing power of the United Nations Security Council in its anti-terrorism activities; the acquiescence of many states to this power; and the capacity of the Security Council to both make and enforce the laws for the international community, and to take and enforce its own executive decisions. She concludes provocatively that the international order is presently one based on a culture of authority, rather than on a culture in which such assertions of power are justified.

Victor Ramraj is sceptical of the culture of justification approach, however. He is concerned about Dyzenhaus and Hunt's optimistic approach to what he terms 'deferential standards of review', which he believes leave considerable latitude to the executive. He argues in his contribution that novel institutional design to deal with security questions can considerably dilute independent judicial oversight and that courts remain retrospective in their responses to emergency powers. These risks, he argues, are not necessarily lessened in a culture of justification. Ramraj is equally unconvinced, however, by pragmatic scepticism of the courts' capacity to stem exceptional powers effectively in the face of threats to national security. This pragmatism, he argues, is exemplified in the extra-legal measures argument of Oren Gross.[43]

---

[39] *Ibid*, p 137 (19 in original file).
[40] *Ibid*, p 141 (27 in original file).
[41] *Ibid*, p 138 (21 in original file).
[42] C H Powell in this volume, p 181.
[43] See: Gross (2003); Gross, O, 'Are Torture Warrants Warranted? Pragmatic Absolutism and Official Disobedience' (2004) 88 *Minn L Review* 1481; Gross, O, 'Stability and Flexibility: A Dicey

Gross's argument is that the 'highly deferential' judicial attitude in states of emergency results in a dilution of the rule of law and, worse, adds a 'veneer of legality' to extra-legal measures. In these circumstances, Gross has argued, it is better publicly to declare an action extra-legal when officials, in dealing with catastrophic cases, must 'go outside the constitutional order and violate accepted constitutional principles, rules and norms'.[44] The public must then decide whether retrospectively to approve of the action or to hold actors accountable through criminal prosecution. This, Gross has argued, establishes a bright line between extra-legal measures, used in 'truly exceptional situations', and the integrity of the rule of law. Against this view, Ramraj argues that the political strategy of promoting public admission of 'extra-legal measures' does not form an appropriate alternative because 'in the long term, it is likely to prolong the underlying conflict, compounding and perpetuating state abuses of power'.[45] In particular, it is likely that short-term actions taken in pursuit of security will alienate the very minorities that more fundamental political reforms should address.

In sum, while Ramraj accepts that both the 'culture of justification' and the 'extra-legal measures' approaches preserve the integrity of the rule of law while taking a pragmatic approach to the limits of judicial review, they 'nevertheless fail to provide a comprehensive theory that combines the virtues of legality with the pragmatism of a political response to emergencies'.[46] Instead, Ramraj argues that 'in a more complex conflict (or set of conflicts), such as the current "war on terror", it may be necessary to resort to multiple strategies, legal and political.'[47] Thus, he promotes an alternative, broad and multi-faceted political strategy that addresses 'the problem of minority alienation squarely both by entrenching rule of law protections (for instance, human rights and equality guarantees) and by reforming key institutions to build confidence'.[48]

Taken together, Dyzenhaus, Powell and Ramraj provide a broad and textured approach to the constitutional dilemmas, in both domestic and international contexts, that arise in times of crisis. Their chapters suggest a theoretical foundation for a language of reconciliation between security and human rights by providing a middle ground between the pragmatic political approaches to exceptional measures on the one hand and the strict adherence to the rule of law on the other hand. The culture of justification approach emphasises the quality of reasoning as the primary test for the legitimacy of legislative, executive and judicial action, and rests in a clear recognition of the necessity of dialogue between the constitutional actors who represent the political and the legal respectively. Although Ramraj is more sceptical of the assertion that the exercise of judicial deference can also be rights-regarding, his emphasis on political strategies that address the root causes

Business' in VV Ramraj, M Hor and K Roach (eds), *Global Anti-terrorism Law and Policy* (Cambridge, Cambridge University Press, 2005) 92.

[44] Gross (2005) 92.
[45] VV Ramraj in this volume, pp 196–7 (12 in original file).
[46] *Ibid*, p 186.
[47] *Ibid*, p 199 (14 in original file).
[48] *Ibid*, pp 198–9.

of terrorist threats is entirely complementary to the culture of justification approach.

2. The Limits and Dangers of Balancing

One now common approach to the task of reconciling security and human rights is to invoke metaphors of balance. Typically drawing on appeals to common sense and everyday reasoning, policy makers and governments have in recent years argued for a 'rebalancing' of the criminal justice system in favour of better security and more public protection, and fewer substantive and procedural rights-based restrictions on law enforcement. Prime Minister Tony Blair in a speech delivered in June 2006 declared that it is both right and necessary for governments to rebalance the criminal justice system 'in favour of the decent, law-abiding majority who play by the rules and think others should too', and to decide whose civil liberties should 'take priority' in a given situation.[49] Although the metaphor of balance is a tempting starting point for a language of reconciliation between security and human rights, it is not one that any of the authors in this book embrace. As both Andrew Ashworth and Lucia Zedner point out in this volume—in keeping with works by Dworkin and Waldron[50]—the argument for balancing not only lacks specificity and militates against any structured consideration of the value of rights, it naturally lends itself to the political rhetoric of greater security and to the curtailment of rights.

According to Ashworth, there is a danger that political discussions of balancing and proportionality can obscure genuine conflicts between the promotion of human rights and the pursuit of security. Rhetorical appeals for a rebalancing of the criminal justice system in favour of greater security and public protection assume not only that such an exercise is possible but that once balanced, the relationship between rights and security will be a stable one. For Ashworth, a more productive approach is to establish first a clear hierarchy of rights and then develop new modes of reasoning and discussion that acknowledge the fact that certain rights are more subject to the claims of security than others. Although he admits that the success of such an approach will largely depend on the extent to which decision-making bodies such as the courts are prepared to enter into a genuine dialogue with rights advocates and proponents of security, Ashworth's approach engages directly with those who question the idea of rights as trumps, as well as the notion that reconciling rights and security is simply a matter of reordering certain political priorities. Like Dyzenhaus, he also recognises the importance of establishing clear norms for the evaluation of evidence relating to perceived threats.

---

[49] Prime Minister Tony Blair, 'Our Nation's Future', Speech delivered in Bristol on 23 June 2006, available at http://www.pm.gov.uk/output/Page9737.asp.
[50] Dworkin, R, 'The Threat to Patriotism', *New York Review of Books*, 28 February 2002; Waldron (2003).

This insistence on structured engagement with the substance of human rights and the security claims posited in order to restrict them is important. As recent experiences have shown, there is a danger that zealous governments may overstate the risks of terrorism when attempting to garner public support for new security measures, legal reform or military action. By ensuring that there are clear, or at least identifiable, standards by which evidence for such actions can be judged by the judiciary and (where appropriate) the public at large, we improve the chances not only of there being a meaningful discussion between different sides of the security debate, but also that members of the executive can be held accountable for their actions. Equally, human rights cannot simply be held up as trumps without a clear and rigorous exposition of the exact protections to which such rights give rise and of the reasons such protections cannot be weakened in the face of security claims. There is, in short, an onus on all sides of the security and rights debate to make clear, structured and accessible arguments.

3. The Integrity of Law

Another question raised by a number of the authors in this volume is whether established criminal law principles and practices are capable of meeting the demands of security. Although these authors share similar concerns, their three chapters take quite different approaches to answering this question.

As Kent Roach reminds us in his contribution, there is ample evidence to suggest that the perception of perpetual crisis continues to generate exceptional national and international legal measures. Indeed, the detention of 'illegal combatants' at Guantanamo Bay, the broad powers incorporated into the US PATRIOT Act 2001, the indefinite detention powers of the UK Anti-terrorism, Crime and Security Act 2001 and the freezing of assets of those suspected of terrorism are all examples of this. Observing that 'trends in anti-terrorism laws, unlike trends in fashion, do not fade away',[51] Roach is keen to stress that because past measures and procedural reforms are rarely evaluated or repealed before new ones are instituted, there is a danger that misguided trends and presumptions will continue to exert influence on how we respond to terrorism. In addition, he notes that because many new anti-terrorism measures cut across different areas of the law—most notably criminal law and immigration law—there is a danger that the assembled 'bricolage' may hide the extent of the damage that is being done to fundamental legal principles. As a result, Roach argues that even though many new and proposed anti-terrorism measures—such as incitement offences based on the principles set out in UN Security Council Resolution 1624—may end up having a disproportionate and ultimately discriminatory effect on already suspect communities, they may also contribute to a more general erosion of the rule of law.

---

[51] K Roach in this volume, p 229 (4 in original file).

If Roach's chapter serves as an implied caution against expanding the existing law before we have had time to assess or even reflect on its implications, then Zedner sounds an even clearer warning. For Zedner, many of the legislative measures enacted in the United Kingdom in the aftermath of 9/11 and the London bombings represent an attempt on the part of the government to sidestep normal legal channels and rule of law safeguards. According to Zedner, pre-emptive measures such as control orders are dangerous because they typically circumvent established criminal law values, such as proportionality of sentence and the need for blameworthiness, by ensuring that assessments of risk and dangerousness are dealt with in the civil sphere. This not only leads to the imposition of restrictions that are prospective and often expressive in character, but also enables governments to avoid the sort of rigorous public or legislative debate that usually accompanies proposed expansions in the substantive criminal law.

In contrast to both Roach and Zedner, Shlomit Wallerstein presents a case for extending existing law in times of insecurity, arguing in her contribution that the state is entitled to use the law and other coercive measures in order to provide security for its citizens. Her claim, based on well-established principles of individual self-defence, is hardly novel, and politicians in a host of countries have become increasingly fond of referring to the state's right to defend itself. However, Wallerstein rightly notes that to date the claim has not been clearly or rigorously examined, in terms either of its foundation or of its possible implication for broader legal principles. Observing that the state 'is an artificial entity created for the purpose of securing its citizens', Wallerstein suggests that it is entirely appropriate for states—within limits and by reference to what is necessary and proportionate in the particular circumstances—to make use of substantive criminal law in their efforts to defend those who live within their borders. Although she acknowledges that extending the power of the state to criminalise activities has its dangers and may ultimately lead to a curtailment of civil liberties, she argues at the same time that it is nonetheless crucial to admit openly that the state is uniquely placed and therefore duty-bound to respond to terrorism and threats to individual security.

As all three of these authors demonstrate, the demands of security have serious implications for the integrity of the criminal law and for the extent to which adherence to established criminal law principles and procedures should restrain responses to terrorism and other serious threats. Just as liberals must engage with political and policy arguments that threaten to undermine established human rights, so too must they expose substantive changes to the criminal law to careful analysis and critique. Equally, however, they must insist that changes in the law are based on rigorous arguments for legal change rather then loose or expedient political or moral arguments. While all of this may mean that we have to enter dangerous territory and seriously consider alternative conceptions of the criminal law and established legal concepts and boundaries, failing to engage in this way risks greater marginalisation and, more worryingly, removes the possibility of influencing future reforms.

IV. SECURITY AS A RIGHT: THE RESOLUTION?

The present fixation with the balance between security and human rights tends to obscure the parallel development of the notion of security *as* a human right. As Neil MacFarlane argues in this volume, 'the evolution of the discourse on security may considerably enhance the capacity for international protection of the human rights of individuals and communities at risk from violence'.[52] Clearly, the United Nations Declaration of Human Rights and numerous other human rights conventions and constitutions around the world enunciate that 'everyone has the right to life, liberty and *security* of person'.[53] While this right has traditionally been understood in its negative sense as the security of the citizen from state action, it is progressively being developed as a positive right to state action in pursuit of the security of its citizens. In the international realm, the increasingly popular concept of 'human security' is moving the conception of international security away from its traditional association with sovereign military action between states, to one focused on the well-being of citizens within states. This international movement is also associated with a broadening acceptance that security is a precondition not only of human and economic development[54] but also of individuals' capacity to exercise their human rights to freedom and dignity.

The growing international emphasis on 'human security' is closely paralleled with the development of the 'responsibility to protect' doctrine. Recently endorsed in the 2005 UN World Summit Outcome Document, this doctrine recognises the responsibility of sovereign states to protect their own populations from genocide, war crimes and ethnic cleansing, and urges the international community to take collective action when states fail to fulfil this obligation.[55] These international developments are mirrored in jurisdictions across the world, including the United Kingdom, Canada, South Africa and India, where courts are increasingly imposing positive obligations on the state as a correlative of the individual's right to security.

So what are we to make of these developments? Is this the way in which the supposedly competing imperatives of security and human rights may be reconciled? Certainly, those seeking to achieve such a reconciliation may be tempted to use the concepts of human security, the right to security or the responsibility to protect both to temper the authoritarian overtones of the language of security, as well as to provide a potentially new legitimating framework for human rights in the face of widespread human rights scepticism. Four chapters in this volume explore this approach. Sandra Fredman and Liora Lazarus look at the development of the right

---

[52] N MacFarlane in this volume, p 348.

[53] Universal Declaration on Human Rights (1948), Art 3 (emphasis added).

[54] A point strongly made in the final report of the Commission on Human Security (CHS): UN Commission on Human Security, 'Human Security Now' (New York, May 2003), available at http://www.humansecurity-chs.org/finalreport/index.html.

[55] United Nations, '2005 Summit Outcome', General Assembly Document, A/60/L.1, 15 September 2005, arts 138 and 139.

to security in a range of domestic jurisdictions, while Neil McFarlane and Jennifer Welsh explore the international development of 'human security' and the 'responsibility to protect' doctrine.

Drawing on the work of Nussbaum and Sen,[56] Fredman proffers a compelling theoretical case for a conception of the right to security—as freedom from fear and want—that is embedded in a deeper understanding of human freedom. For Fredman, the right to security ought to incorporate 'the right to demand from the state the minimum resources necessary to fulfil one's capabilities'.[57] From this platform, Fredman critiques the judicial development of the right to security in Canada, South Africa and the United Kingdom, exposing how these judicial approaches reflect 'background understandings of choice and responsibility'.[58] She argues that courts should apply interpretive principles founded on the prevention of destitution and degradation and shaped by the pursuit of dignity, fairness and equality. For Fredman, the development of the right to security within the courts can only be successful if courts 'deepen their understanding of the ways in which positive rights and obligations interact'. In other words, it is essential to locate the right to security within 'a community with reciprocal benefits and responsibilities, rather than in the competitive arena of individualised rights-bearers'.[59]

The contribution by Lazarus is concerned with the tendency of domestic courts and a number of human rights instruments to ground a broadening array of constitutional rights in a meta-right to security. While acknowledging that recourse to a 'right to security' may presently be a useful tool for the achievement of a variety of political ends, Lazarus argues that its widening legal conceptualisation has the potential to 'undermine accepted understandings of the foundations of fundamental rights reasoning'.[60] She warns that if the right to security becomes the meta-principle upon which all other rights rest, this can also inadvertently legitimise security measures that encroach upon other human rights. There is therefore a difference in Lazarus' view between 'securing rights' and 'securitising rights'. Although tempted as a consequence to reject altogether the argument for a right to security, Lazarus opts rather to engage with the evident development of the right in a number of jurisdictions. Nevertheless, in contrast to Fredman's broader conception, she argues that courts must restrict the right to security to a narrow and distinctive right to be protected from 'critical and pervasive' threats of harm to person. It is, in her view, the role of courts to temper the rhetoric of 'securitising rights'.

The varying approaches of Fredman and Lazarus are echoed in the 'conceptual disagreement over the purview of human security' in the international realm.[61] As

---

[56] Nussbaum, M, *Women and Human Development* (Cambridge, Cambridge University Press, 2000); Sen, A, *Development as Freedom* (Oxford, Oxford University Press, 1999).

[57] S Fredman in this volume, p 323.

[58] *Ibid*, p 308.

[59] *Ibid*, p 323.

[60] L Lazarus in this volume, p 344.

[61] N McFarlane in this volume, p 352.

MacFarlane notes, two 'general clusters' of thought have developed, one arguing that poverty, famine and widespread disease represent a far graver threat to human security than physical violence, the other arguing that broadening the term 'human security' undermines its potential as an analytical and policy tool. This dispute has arisen, MacFarlane notes, because of the international competition for scarce resources, which has resulted in the development community's politically expedient emphasis on the economic dimension of security. Nevertheless, MacFarlane argues that both sides of the debate are unified in their attempt to 'privilege human beings in security discourse', a process he terms the 'humanisation of security'. This has in turn led to 'numerous normative and legal developments' on the international stage, not least the development of the idea that states internationally have the 'responsibility to protect' citizens both within their own jurisdictions and, collectively, in other states where there are grave threats of harm to individuals. These developments, argues MacFarlane, have fundamentally shifted the grounding principle of state sovereignty in the law of states, as well as the conception of the role of states in the defence of individual security. In MacFarlane's view, this reordering of the sovereignty principle is the most important consequence of the humanisation of security and has fundamental implications for the future development of international law and relations. Given the United States' growing recourse to the language of its 'responsibility to protect' citizens around the world, not to mention its use of this language to prompt the UN Security Council into action, MacFarlane is led to suggest that this shift in principles of sovereignty will not always be benign.

Jennifer Welsh is similarly wary. Her contribution traces the evolution of the 'responsibility to protect' doctrine up to its endorsement in the UN 2005 World Summit Outcome Document and critically analyses its implications. Welsh emphasises two important aspects of this development. First, she shows how the term 'responsibility to protect' has come to displace the language of 'humanitarian intervention'. Thus instead of expressing a 'right of intervention', states can now claim a 'responsibility to protect' individuals in other states where grave violations of human rights are occurring. Second, Welsh shows how the doctrine has been developed as a means to reconcile the traditional antipathy between human rights and state sovereignty in international law. This reconciliation has occurred, Welsh argues, by linking the 'very notion of sovereignty . . . more closely to the responsibility of states to their citizens'.[62] However, Welsh does not view this emphasis on responsibilities instead of rights that citizens can invoke as entirely unproblematic. Because ambiguity remains as to who should fulfil the responsibility to protect when states fail, and at what stage the responsibility transfers from the state in question to the international community at large, Welsh is sceptical as to whether the language of the UN Outcome Document has actually enhanced the capacity of international actors to challenge state sovereignty effectively. Moreover, Welsh demonstrates that the expression of the responsibility to protect

---

[62] J Welsh in this volume, p 366.

in the Outcome Document is weaker than that originally conceived by the International Commission on Intervention and State Sovereignty (ICISS) in 2001, and it in effect 'circumscribes the international community's obligation to protect individuals from massive human rights violations'.[63] Given these factors, argues Welsh, there is a danger that the language of the 'responsibility to protect' sets up false expectations, namely a belief on the part of people under persecution that 'outsiders' will honour their right to security by intervening when in fact the nature of the international responsibility to do so still is not clear.

Welsh and the other commentators in this section reveal some disquiet about the directions in which the right to security, human security and the 'responsibility to protect' are developing. These objections do not amount to a rejection of the central concepts; however, nor do they all move in the same direction. For Fredman, the right to security fails if it rests on an individualistic conception of human rights that is disconnected from a broader material understanding of human agency and the values of dignity and equality. For Lazarus, the risk of securitising rights leads her to argue for courts to develop a narrow conception of the right to security as a right to be free from 'critical and pervasive' threats of harm. While MacFarlane welcomes the humanisation of security, he is hesitant about the ramifications of associated shifts in the conceptions of sovereignty under the law of states. Finally, Welsh sounds a warning about the move from rights to responsibilities as a means of securing citizens and is concerned that the 2005 Outcome Document's expression of the 'responsibility to protect' doctrine represents a weakening of the international community's existing obligation to protect individuals' human rights.

CONCLUSION

Notwithstanding the intellectual and disciplinary diversity amongst the authors who feature in this volume, they are united by the desire to move the current debate over security and human rights forward. They are equally concerned to do this in a way that does not underestimate the importance of security or undermine the legitimacy of rights. Clearly, reconciling the interests of security with a respect for fundamental rights is no easy task, and while finding a language of reconciliation—or acknowledging security as a right—may help to bring the two sides of the debate closer together, it is unlikely to resolve all of the tensions that are identified in this book. We must accept that the conflict between security and rights is a fundamental and recurring problem that will always be a central challenge for the liberal democratic project, even in times of peace or after threats of imminent terrorist attack have receded. If we are to move forward, however, we must do more than simply recognise this truth: we must embrace it and continue to seek new ways of thinking about this conflict and of minimising the negative effects that an absolutist commitment to either security or rights may produce.

---

[63] J Welsh in this volume, p 363.

If liberal academics and intellectuals are to offer a way forward, they must as a matter of urgency find a language that can claim a purchase on the broader political imagination within conditions of crisis. If academics are blessed with the freedom to offer a critical reflective response to the conditions of our world, they might also reflect on their responsibility to develop critiques with which the wider world can engage. In short, intellectuals who can offer clarity, detachment and rigour on the relationship between rights and security—or even develop ways of reconciling them—cannot risk being marginalised in a time of supposed exception.

REFERENCES

Ackerman, B, 'The Emergency Constitution' (2004) 113 *Yale Law Journal* 1029.
—— *Before the Next Attack: Preserving Civil Liberties in an Age of Terrorism* (Hartford, Yale University Press, 2006).
Agamben, G, *The State of Exception* (Chicago, University of Chicago Press, 2005).
Bellamy, R, 'Constitutive Citizenship versus Constitutional Rights: Republican Reflections on the EU Charter and the Human Rights Act' in T Campbell, KD Ewing and A Tomkins (eds), *Sceptical Essays on Human Rights* (Oxford, Oxford University Press, 2001).
Blair, Prime Minister Tony, 'Our Nation's Future', Speech delivered in Bristol on 23 June 2006, available at http://www.pm.gov.uk/output/Page9737.asp.
Campbell, T, Ewing, KD and Tomkins, A, *Sceptical Essays on Human Rights* (Oxford, Oxford University Press, 2001).
Cole, D, 'The Priority of Morality: The Emergency Constitution's Blind Spot' (2004) 113 *Yale Law Journal* 173.
Dershowitz, A, 'Tortured Reasoning' in S Levinson (ed), *Torture: A Collection* (Oxford, Oxford University Press, 2004) 14.
Douzinas, C, *The End of Human Rights* (Oxford, Hart Publishing, 2000).
Dworkin, R, 'The Threat to Patriotism', *New York Review of Books*, 28 February 2002.
Ewing, K and Gearty, C, *Freedom under Thatcher: Civil Liberties in Modern Britain* (Oxford, Clarendon Press, 1990).
—— *The Struggle for Civil Liberties* (Oxford, Oxford University Press, 2000).
Freeman, M, *Human Rights: An Interdisciplinary Approach* (Cambridge, Polity, 2002).
—— 'Order, Rights and Threats: Terrorism and Global Justice' in R Ashby Wilson (ed), *Human Rights in the 'War on Terror'* (Cambridge, Cambridge University Press, 2005) 37.
Garland, D, *The Culture of Control* (Oxford, Oxford University Press, 2001).
Gearty, C, *Can Human Rights Survive* (Cambridge, Cambridge University Press, 2006).
Goldstone, R, 'The Tension between Combating Terrorism and Protecting Civil Liberties' in R Ashby Wilson (ed), *Human Rights in the 'War on Terror'* (Cambridge, Cambridge University Press, 2005) 242.
Gray, J, *Enlightenment's Wake: Politics and Culture at the Close of the Modern Age* (London, Routledge, 1995).
Griffiths, J, 'The Political Constitution' (1979) 42 *MLR* 1.
—— *The Politics of the Judiciary*, 4th edn (London, Fontana, 1991).
Gross, O, 'Chaos and Rules: Should Responses to Violent Crises Always be Constitutional?' (2003) 112 *Yale Law Journal* 1011.

Gross, O, 'Are Torture Warrants Warranted? Pragmatic Absolutism and Official Disobedience' (2004) 88 *Minn L Review* 1481.

—— 'Stability and Flexibility: A Dicey Business' in VV Ramraj, M Hor and K Roach (eds), *Global Anti-terrorism Law and Policy* (Cambridge, Cambridge University Press, 2005) 92.

Ignatieff, M, *The Lesser Evil: Politics in an Age of Terror* (Princeton, Princeton University Press, 2004).

Judt, T, 'Bush's Useful Idiots' (2006) 28(18) *London Review of Books*, available at http://www.lrb.co.uk/v28/n18/judt01_.html.

Katyal, NK and Tribe, LH, 'Waging War, Deciding Guilt: Trying the Military Tribunals' (2002) *Yale Law Journal* 1111.

Kennedy, D, 'The International Human Rights Movement: Part of the Problem?' (2001) 3 *European Human Rights Law Review* 245.

Klug, F, *Values for a Godless Age* (London, Penguin, 2000) 154.

Kramer, LD, *The People Themselves: Popular Constitutionalism and Judicial Review* (Oxford, Oxford University Press, 2004).

Lazarus, L, *Contrasting Prisoners' Rights* (Oxford, Oxford University Press, 2004) 163–8.

Loughlin, M, 'Rights, Democracy, and Law' in T Campbell, KD Ewing and A Tomkins (eds), *Sceptical Essays on Human Rights* (Oxford, Oxford University Press, 2001).

Luban, D, 'Eight Fallacies about Liberty and Security' in R Ashby Wilson (ed), *Human Rights in the 'War on Terror'* (Cambridge, Cambridge University Press, 2005) 242.

Minogue, K, 'What is Wrong with Rights' in C Harlow (ed), *Public Law and Politics* (London, Sweet & Maxwell, 1986) 209.

National Commission on Terrorist Attacks upon the United States (9/11 Commission), *Report* (2004), available at http://www.9-11commission.gov/report/index.htm.

Nussbaum, M, *Women and Human Development* (Cambridge, Cambridge University Press, 2000).

O'Malley, P, 'Volatile and Contradictory Punishment' (1999) 3(2) *Theoretical Criminology* 175–96.

Ryan, A, 'The British, the Americans, and Rights' in M Lacey and K Haakonssen (eds), *A Culture of Rights* (Cambridge, Cambridge University Press, 1991) 375.

Sen, A, *Development as Freedom* (Oxford, Oxford University Press, 1999).

Simon, J, ' "Entitlement to Cruelty": Neo-liberalism and the Punitive Mentality in the United States' in K Stenson and R Sullivan (eds), *Crime, Risk, and Justice: The Politics of Crime Control in Liberal Democracies* (Portland, Willan Publishing, 2001) 125.

Tesón, FR, 'Liberal Security' in R Ashby Wilson (ed), *Human Rights in the 'War on Terror'* (Cambridge, Cambridge University Press, 2005) 57.

Tomkins, A, *Our Republican Constitution* (Oxford, Hart Publishing, 2005).

Tribe, LH and Gudridge, PO, 'The Anti-emergency Constitution' (2004) 113 *Yale Law Journal* 1801.

United Nations, '2005 Summit Outcome', General Assembly Document, A/60/L.1, 15 September 2005.

United Nations Commission on Human Security, 'Human Security Now' (New York, May 2003), available at http://www.humansecurity-chs.org/finalreport/index.html.

Waldron, J, *Law and Disagreement* (Oxford, Oxford University Press, 1999).

—— 'Security and Liberty: The Image of Balance' (2003) 11(2) *The Journal of Political Philosophy* 191.

Part I

Engaging Security

2

The Cultural Lives of Security and Rights

IAN LOADER

INTRODUCTION

LIBERAL LEGAL AND political theorists often posit an antique and inescapable tension between the claims of security and those of liberty. They have consequently busied themselves, and quite properly so, with the task of analysing precisely the manner in which these goods clash and how one might strike the appropriate 'balance' between them, or else with seeking to protect rights protections from the consequentialist logic of the balance metaphor.[1] But this tension, along with the seemingly innocent notion that one should strive to balance them, also surfaces routinely within the *cultural lives* of security and rights—that is, within quotidian social and political struggles to champion the merits and press the claims of one or other of these competing social goods. In the course of these struggles, for reasons I want shortly to describe and reflect upon, appeals to security have a pronounced tendency to trump demands for the protection of individual rights.

In the English setting with which I am most familiar, and upon which I concentrate in this chapter, this has been apparent for some time—in the manner in which high-profile miscarriages of justice have been so easily 'handled'; in public responses to CCTV; in the ways in which certain legal protections have been sidestepped or cast aside in the battle against anti-social behaviour; in the refusal of certain elements of English culture and society to treat the European Convention on Human Rights (ECHR) and the Human Rights Act (HRA) 1998 as settled parts of legal architecture; and in many of the illiberal practices mobilised today in a bid to win a 'war' against international terrorism. What these examples reveal and share in common is a dynamic in which political, professional and media actors are able to mobilise a populist appeal to the idea of security, while presenting rights claims as the concern of remote special interest groups willing to play fast and loose with the safety of their co-citizens.

---

[1] Waldron, J, 'Security and Liberty: The Image of Balance' (2003) 2 *Journal of Political Philosophy* 191–210.

The impulse of human rights theorists and activists faced with this inhospitable climate is often to resort to first principles in order to assert the fundamental importance and primacy of rights *over* security and to defend the former *against* the encroaching—majoritarian and potentially tyrannous—imperatives of the latter. One can easily see why this move is made, and it is no part of my purpose to suggest that it is entirely wrong-headed or ought to be abandoned. I want nonetheless to chart a different course—one that I think is relatively unexplored in what remains a predominantly legal and philosophical discourse about human rights but which draws upon and extends work in criminology that is concerned with the social and cultural analysis of lay anxieties towards crime and their political articulation and effects.[2] I want, in particular, to lay some foundations for a cultural sociology of the meanings-in-use of rights and security in contemporary political and public culture and, in so doing, deepen our understanding of how and why the metaphor of balance either seems in practical contexts to do so little work, or else operates to privilege the claims of security. Before doing so, however, some prefatory remarks are in order about the focal concerns of this line of enquiry and the value of pursuing it.

Paying close hermeneutic attention to rights and security in the vernacular enables us first of all to explore the ways in which these goods, and the claims that are made or disputed in respect of them, are intimately and inescapably entangled with people's hopes, fears and fantasies concerning the trajectory of their own lives, and that of the political community which they inhabit. The things that people say about rights and security, and the sensibilities displayed towards each of them, thus need to be apprehended in terms of their (often deeply affective) intersections with matters of political subjectivity and collective identity, and the lines of affiliation and exclusion, recognition and non- or mis-recognition, responsibility and accountability, that people draw when such matters are up for dispute. It enables us, in the present case, to highlight certain key properties of the contemporary cultural politics of this terrain, drawing our attention to the deep allure of, and the anxieties and fantasies evoked by, appeals for and to security, and the reasons underpinning what appears to be a weak identification with, even distaste for, human rights within elements of English culture and society.

This hermeneutic approach enables us to discern, secondly, some of the cultural limits of a strategy that is commonly deployed to defend and extend human rights—one that insists upon a rather narrow legalistic assertion of the value of rights and their protection, and understands rights protection as a project that has,

---

[2] See for example: Sasson, T, *Crime Talk: How Citizens Construct a Social Problem* (New York, Aldine de Gruyter, 1995); Zedner, L, 'In Pursuit of the Vernacular: Comparing Law and Order Discourse in Britain and Germany' (1995) 4 *Social and Legal Studies* 517–34; Girling, E, Loader, I and Sparks, R, *Crime and Social Change in Middle England: Questions of Order in an English Town* (London, Routledge, 2000); Hope, T and Sparks, R (eds), *Crime, Risk and Insecurity: Law and Order in Everyday Life and Political Discourse* (London, Routledge, 2001); and Sparks, R, 'Ordinary Anxieties and States of Emergency: Statecraft and Spectatorship in the New Politics of Insecurity' in S Armstrong and L McAra (eds), *Perspectives on Punishment: The Contours of Control* (Oxford, Oxford University Press, 2006).

unfortunately but necessarily, to be defended or advanced by social movements or legal reform groups in the face of lay ignorance, indifference or disdain. Analysing the cultural lives of security and rights not only highlights the limitations of this mode of thinking about and pressing the claims of human rights. It also, for reasons I set out briefly in the conclusion to this chapter and develop more fully elsewhere,[3] leads one not to start with individual rights and defend them against the claims of security, but to try instead to articulate and defend an egalitarian, other-regarding and, in these senses, rights-conducive practice of security—what one may, rhetorically, call rescuing security from the 'security lobby'.[4]

This chapter is in this respect partly an attempt to theorise an intuition that I have long held and acted upon but which has never entirely ceased to trouble me. The intuition leads me to recognise that human rights are an indispensable part of any good society and ought to be defended as such. It at the same time leaves me rather uninspired by human rights theory and praxis and seldom minded to become a rights scholar or activist. This is troubling because I suspect that it is in some part the complacent sensibility of someone who belongs to a society that recognises the value of human rights and continues to afford its citizens a measure of rights protection—akin, if one likes, to the cosmopolitan Western academic who takes for granted the benefits of a stable national identity while decrying the value of national political communities. But I think my intuition towards rights also has something to do with the fact that they—like the liberalism with which they are most closely identified[5]—speak more to our fears and the way the state is negatively implicated in them, than to our political hopes and the way in which the state can be positively bound up with their realisation.[6] I have, I suppose, a predilection for thinking about and seeking to advance the latter, something that has prompted me to think about rights *through* the solidaristic lens of security.

It ought to be noted, thirdly, that what I propose here is an empirical project. It is impossible to get very far in making sense of the cultural lives of security and rights without bumping into empirical questions—questions that call for a style of enquiry comprised of close observation and depth interpretation best conducted *in situ*. This places me in the apparently paradoxical position of writing a largely theoretical paper in support of a project committed to the fine-grained interpretive analysis of the political and lay vernacular of rights and security, the struggles that occur between them and the matters that are deemed to be at issue when they do battle in the settings of everyday social relations and public life. Hence the rather speculative nature of much of what follows, which I think is best read as extending an invitation to others to incorporate a new dimension into the way in which we theorise and investigate the interplay between security and human rights.

---

[3] Loader, I and Walker, N, *Civilizing Security* (Cambridge, Cambridge University Press, 2007).

[4] See further *ibid*, ch 1.

[5] Walzer, M, 'On Negative Politics' in B Yack (ed), *Liberalism without Illusions: Essays on Liberal Theory and the Political Vision of Judith N Shklar* (Chicago, University of Chicago Press, 1996).

[6] Mulgan, G, *Good and Bad Power: The Ideals and Betrayals of Government* (Harmondsworth, Penguin, 2006).

I. SECURITY AS TRUMPS? SOME IDIOMS OF ENGLISH PUBLIC CULTURE

I want to begin by sketching out some recent examples of how the tension between security and rights has been articulated and addressed in the settings of English public life. My aim here is not to engage in any sort of detailed reconstruction of these conflicts—a task that stands well beyond the ambit of this chapter. Instead, I wish to outline what appear to be certain recurrent properties of the interplay between lay anxieties towards crime and in/security and their political articulation in a range of sites in which the claims of security and those of rights have clashed. The common thread that holds these examples together is the invocation of a logic of populist reason[7] that enables security and its surrogates (safety, order, protection, etc) to act as a trump whose imperatives have a marked propensity to prevail over the claims pressed by remote, liberal (and, it is commonly said, safe and secure) special interest groups on behalf of rights. Five such cases will suffice to demonstrate this logic at work. In each case they are best, or at least most provocatively, introduced by means of the idioms that are expressly mobilised or implicitly in play during the course of struggles to 'name' the problem and fix the appropriate response.[8]

1. 'No Smoke without Fire'

In the mid- to late 1980s, following several years marked by angry denial among government, the media and elements of the judiciary, several serious miscarriages of justice arising from the conflict in Northern Ireland were officially acknowledged and 'rectified'—notably the cases of the 'Birmingham Six' and 'Guildford Four'. These were followed, in turn, by a welter of cognate cases encompassing the convictions quashed against many of those prosecuted by the West Midlands Serious Crime Squad (which was disbanded in 1989), four men wrongly convicted of killing newspaper boy Carl Bridgewater, the 'Cardiff Three', the 'Tottenham Three' (wrongly convicted of murdering PC Keith Blakelock during the 1985 urban disorders), and Stephen Kiszko.

---

[7] Laclau, E, *On Populist Reason* (London, Verso, 2005).

[8] The descriptive and interpretive focus of what follows is the cultural politics of security and rights in England. Two things need briefly to be said about this. First, I can in the space available offer only a sketch of the dominant discourses and sensibilities that are in play. A fuller empirical account would need, inter alia, to attend to the ambiguities and nuances of prevailing dispositions; to the dominated forms of discourse with which they clash; to the visions of the good society that these competing dispositions inscribe or project; and to the outcomes of the contests between them. It should, secondly, be noted that this is a field that invites and would benefit from historical and comparative enquiry; the space of positions and dispositions on security and rights that one finds in contemporary English society needs to be located within the contours of the historical development of that society and may differ from the mentalities and sensibilities found in other jurisdictions in potentially telling ways. See, for example, Lazarus, L, *Contrasting Prisoners' Rights: A Comparative Examination of Britain and Germany* (Oxford, Oxford University Press, 2004).

These cases shared in common the unlawful prosecution and unsafe conviction of individuals who were either personally vulnerable or members of unpopular groups, in circumstances where the police exceeded their powers in the face of intense public pressure to 'get results' following criminal or terrorist outrage. In the opinion of Robert Reiner, these events 'profoundly shook public opinion', their victims becoming for a time household names.[9] The sense of crisis they occasioned forced the then Conservative government—for the second time in just over a decade—to set up a Royal Commission on Criminal Justice,[10] an instrument of rule that the Thatcher administration found distasteful and wished to consign to constitutional history. The death-knell of a police-centred, authoritarian law and order politics appeared to have been sounded.

Yet during the course of its deliberations, the Royal Commission's work came to be resituated within and overtaken by the altogether different sense of crisis that followed the murder of toddler James Bulger by two 10-year-old boys in February 1993 and the subsequent intense public debate about what the *Daily Express* chose to call 'lawless Britain'. In the face of demands for what has come within English political discourse to be called 'security', and in the midst of a febrile political atmosphere in which a weak government sought to underpin its faltering legitimacy by giving voice and effect to the demands for order of anxious, 'respectable' citizens, the Royal Commission's investigations into the general disregard for suspects' rights resulted instead in measures that, inter alia, curtailed the accused's right of silence.

I am not seeking to deny that the 'miscarriages of justice' cases have had important and beneficial consequences for police practice, or that they have shaken the faith that some elements of the populace once had in the police.[11] But events that appeared initially to have delivered a telling blow to the politics of law and order have in fact been all too easily 'managed' by those who were rather uncomfortable with the scathing criticism that rained down upon the police and who were always minded to feel—if not publicly say—that 'there is no smoke without fire'. As a result, the societal lessons that might have been properly learned from those events are at risk of being forgotten or buried in a context where, once more, the police are coming under intense pressure to defend 'our way of life' from those alien, dangerous others who have brought, or may yet bring, fear and carnage to 'our' towns and cities.

2. 'If You've Got Nothing to Hide, You've Got Nothing to Fear'

Closed-circuit television (CCTV) surveillance has within the short space of two decades become a commonplace feature of the urban landscape of the United

---

[9] Reiner, R, 'Policing a Postmodern Society' (1992) 55(6) *Modern Law Review* 761–81, 765.

[10] Home Office, *Royal Commission on Criminal Justice: Report*, Cm 2263 (London, Home Office, 1993).

[11] Loader, I and Mulcahy, A, *Policing and the Condition of England: Memory, Politics and Culture* (Oxford, Oxford University Press, 2003) ch 4.

Kingdom. It is now easily forgotten that the first such cameras were installed in retail outlets in 1967, on the London Underground in 1975 and in a public setting (the promenade in Bournemouth) for the first time in 1985. Today millions of pounds per year are spent on CCTV schemes in England and Wales, and cameras have become familiar sights in shopping malls, airports, workplaces, town and city centres, sports stadia, schools, hospitals, police stations, the road network and certain residential areas.[12] This rapid social and technological development, which has made the United Kingdom a candidate for the most surveilled society on earth, has been remarkable in part for the lack of public debate and degree of public acceptance of, even enthusiasm for, the onset of CCTV technology. One telling indicator of the lack of public debate is the absence of a discourse of 'balance' in this context: there are, it seems, no genuine rights being infringed by CCTV and thus nothing to be balanced. As that routinely deployed 'saying of the tribe' has it,[13] 'if you've got nothing to hide, you've got nothing to fear'.

One thus tends to encounter in this corner of the field of security politics a pattern of political and lay sensibilities that overwhelmingly holds CCTV cameras to be a positive crime and disorder controlling force, a mindset disposed either to promote or willingly to accede to the view that cameras are effective in this task. Against this, one is struck by the relative weakness—it is almost not too strong to say absence—of a critical discourse focusing on the effects of mass surveillance on human rights. (Compare the case of identity cards, which seem much more able to touch a nerve within popular English sentiment.) CCTV has, it seems, become a non-issue, certainly in respect of electoral politics but also within public life more generally.

It is true that certain instances of individuals being caught engaged in legal but embarrassing acts on camera (from sex to suicide) have caused offence and momentary uproar; that people continue to fret about the selling of camera footage to television companies and the attendant formation of a surveillance-entertainment culture; and that the largely middle-class 'road lobby' has become angry about speed cameras and active in defence of the 'freedoms' they are deemed to threaten. But these appear isolated and sporadic exceptions to a lay response that has remained steadfastly untroubled by CCTV. 'Big Brother' critiques have not managed to obtain much cultural or political purchase in the face of the 'obvious' benefits of surveillance technology, both actual and—in the context of an ongoing 'war' on terror—potential. If one doubts this, simply reflect for a moment on how difficult it currently is to launch a serious sustained debate on the regulation of CCTV, or imagine the incredulous laughter that is likely to greet the claim that British society has been too promiscuous in its deployment of cameras and that some of them ought reasonably to be taken down.

---

[12] See Goold, BJ, *CCTV and Policing: Public Area Surveillance and Police Practices in Britain* (Oxford, Oxford University Press, 2004) ch 1.

[13] Bourdieu, P, *The Logic of Practice* (Cambridge, Polity, 1990) 110.

3. The 'So-called' Human Rights Act

My third example concerns a piece of legislation that appears at first glance to represent a challenge to the depiction of the vernacular of security and rights presented thus far—namely, the enshrining within English law of the protections that the British government long ago signed up to under the European Convention on Human Rights. The enactment of the Human Rights Act 1998 appears to indicate the existence of powerful support for legally enforceable, government-constraining rights within British society—and its passage was indeed enthusiastically welcomed within legal and civil liberties circles. Yet subsequent reaction to what Conservative politicians have sometimes tellingly named the 'so-called' Human Rights Act indicates that this landmark legislation has not yet been embedded in a way that enables it confidently to function as such legislation is intended—as a series of protections for individuals, providing a frame for the conduct of political life that politics itself should not encroach upon. The Act *has*, in other words, ushered in a human rights politics whose terms of dispute are the proper province and legal meaning of its protections, but without entirely dispensing with a politics *of* human rights that refuses to treat the Act as a settled and legitimate pillar of Britain's legal and political architecture.[14]

One curious dimension of this has been the embarrassment that the New Labour parent appears to feel towards its human rights child. Not only is it rare to find governmental actors singing in praise of the Human Rights Act, or using it as a platform for the formation of a culture of human rights within British society; one has even of late witnessed government ministers leading, or at least feeding, what has at times become a tabloid frenzy against the allegedly absurd consequences of enshrining human rights protections in law.[15] The Act appears, in other words, to sit uneasily alongside a dominant political discourse that insists that, as a society, we have become preoccupied with rights at the perilous cost of neglecting a sense of mutual obligation and responsibility. At the very least, this is human rights protection by stealth—in the face of an environment judged to be inhospitable to a strong defence of its claims.

---

[14] This absence of a human rights 'settlement' may not be entirely negative in its consequences. The persistence of a politics of human rights does at least give rise to spaces of contestation within which rights claims and the idea of rights more broadly are routinely pressed, challenged and argued about, not only by lawyers in legal settings but by social movements in political ones. This broader conversation about rights may be less robust in jurisdictions where human rights have come to be taken for granted as part of the legal and political order. I am grateful to Neil Walker for this point.

[15] Britain's most popular mass circulation newspaper, *The Sun*, spent the summer of 2006 running a high-profile campaign against the Human Rights Act (1998) under the slogan 'Give Us Back Our Human Rights'. On 7 September it reported the success of this campaign in reflecting and mobilising popular opinion as follows: 'THOUSANDS of Sun readers have voted to scrap the Human Rights Act. Nearly 35,000 rang our You-the-Jury hotline within 24 hours to back our call for an end to the interests of killers, rapists and paedophiles coming ABOVE those of victims. The crazy legislation has led to many dangerous criminals being freed to re-offend. Others have used the barmy laws to gain perks and payouts.' See http://www.thesun.co.uk/article/0,,2-2006220181,00.html. This is but the latest instance of what has been an ongoing current of popular suspicion towards this legislation: see Lazarus (2004) 174.

There may, however, be something in the fact that the wider culture remains sceptical, perhaps even hostile. Part of the picture here is that strand of English conservative opinion that has come—in ignorance of the part that the British government played in creating the ECHR in the wake of World War II—to consider human rights as something 'foreign', a European (Union) imposition on the anti-rationalist and pragmatic traditions of English common law and its 'incidental and organic approach to rights and liberties'.[16] This sentiment seems never far from the surface of the mutterings one hears about clawing back or repealing the Act—desires that periodically take the form of explicit statements of political intent. This, in turn, often forms part of a sensibility that has become very attuned to counting the costs of a society in which individuals 'know their rights'—costs registered in terms of children beyond the control of parents, pupils defying their teachers and teenagers untouchable by police officers; by the advent of a compensation (or 'compo') culture in which individuals relate to one another and to public institutions as aggrieved, litigious rights-bearers; and by an ambient decline in levels of civility, trust and orderliness within the settings of everyday life.

4. 'You Wouldn't Think that if You Lived Round Here'

This refrain has today come to be voiced routinely within a further public contest in which the claims of security and liberty are pitted against each other—namely, the control of 'anti-social behaviour'. A spate of legislation has in the last several years been introduced to deal with forms of nuisance, harassment and provocation that may not in any strict legal sense be criminal but which are said to nonetheless blight the lives of many residents in economically and socially deprived neighbourhoods.[17]

The Crime and Disorder Act 1998 and the Anti-social Behaviour Act 2003 (the first time, incidentally, that the terms 'disorder' and 'anti-social behaviour' have appeared in the titles of primary legislation in the United Kingdom) have thus sought to remedy these seemingly endemic problems, as part of a strategy that tries to tackle low-level disorder by prosecuting perpetrators for provable infringements of criminal law. The Acts have done so, inter alia, by creating new civil orders ('anti-social behaviour orders' (ASBOs)), breach of which is a criminal offence punishable by imprisonment; by allowing local authorities and the police to use curfews and dispersal orders to curtail gatherings of teenagers; and by giving the police greater powers to impose summary penalties, thereby placing the burden on the accused to appeal against his or her 'police sentence'.[18]

---

[16] Lazarus (2004) 163.

[17] Burney, E, *Making People Behave: Anti-social Behaviour, Politics and Policy* (Cullompton, Willan, 2005); and see also the contribution by Lucia Zedner in this volume.

[18] In June 2006, in the first of series of lectures on 'Our Nation's Future', Prime Minister Tony Blair defended this strategy, arguing that the criminal justice process and its due process protections were a hangover from nineteenth-century liberal reformism and had left the criminal justice system unable to

Such assaults on the liberal principles and processes of criminal justice have not been without their critics. Lawyers, civil liberties groups, criminologists and journalists, as well as new campaign groups such as 'AsboConcern' and 'AsboWatch', have angrily and actively taken issue with the blurring of civil and criminal procedures and the disproportionate, zealous and largely central government-driven use of ASBOs (which often target the 'troubled' as well as the 'troubling'). Similar arguments have been marshalled against curfew and dispersal orders, resulting in a successful legal challenge by a teenage boy against one imposition of the former. And liberal critics have railed against the upsetting of due process that new mechanisms of summary police punishment have entailed.

Yet these protests, for the most part, have been—or at least have been dismissed as—the anguished cries of liberal, well-healed human rights elites. Their claims are, as such, routinely scorned and de-legitimated by (selected) victims of disorder—or media and political actors who claim to speak on their behalf—as those of a constituency whose sensibilities have been formed by the fact that they have never experienced 'anti-social behaviour', still less had to live with it on a daily basis, such that they 'really wouldn't think like that if they lived round here'.

The critics have, in short, been represented as part of the problem not only for seeking to protect protections that make it difficult to tackle anti-social behaviour effectively, but also for promulgating the very culture of rights—and its attendant lack of respect—that conduces to escalating levels of spitting, swearing, graffiti, vandalism and drunkenness in the first place. They form part of the 'liberal consensus' on criminal justice matters that has come to be seen across a large swathe of the political spectrum as having left vulnerable, law-abiding people frightened and powerless in the face of escalating public disorder—a consensus that the New Labour government has set itself to dismantle.

5. 'The Rules of the Game have Changed'

There exist several noteworthy parallels between recent governmental responses to anti-social behaviour (which claim that the 'rules of the game' must be changed and set out to do just that) and those illiberal practices that have been mobilised in the aftermath of 9/11 and 7/7 to defeat international terrorism (the agents of which have, in the opinion of Prime Minister Tony Blair, changed the 'rules of the game'). The first concerns the rhetorical coupling together of these two threats under the sign of 'security' (a term of recent coinage within British political discourse, and one whose genealogy and discursive effects would repay some careful attention). As Tony Blair has put it, 'people do see a link between antisocial

combat twenty-first-century crime and disorder: Blair, T, 'Our Nation's Future: The Criminal Justice System', lecture, 23 June 2006, available at http://www.number-10.gov.uk/?output/?Page9737.asp. I was among a number of criminologists and police professionals invited by the Prime Minister's Office to comment on this thesis in advance of the lecture being delivered; my critique of it can be found in Loader, I, 'Rebalancing the Criminal Justice System?', paper prepared for the Prime Minister's lecture series 'Our Nation's Future', June 2006, available at http://www.pm.gov.uk/?output/Page9701.asp.

behaviour in the area where they live and global terrorism. They feel a general sense of insecurity and we have to take account of it'.[19]

The second parallel concerns the legislative hyperactivity that has been apparent in both fields as 'taking account of insecurity' has come to assume centre stage in both governmental discourse and its legislative programme.[20] The third concerns the way in which the imperatives and urgency of the security agenda has been brought to the fore. In respect of both anti-social behaviour and the 'war' against international terror, a new political common sense informs us that to continue to insist on the primacy of human rights is to take a large and unjustifiable risk with people's quality of life, or even life itself.

I have already set out some of the practical manifestations of this logic in respect of anti-social behaviour, a context in which the figure of the 'law-abiding citizen' has come to loom rhetorically large. In justification of the measures taken against the second threat—such as the Anti-terrorism, Crime and Security Act 2001, the introduction of an offence of 'glorifying terrorism', and the failed attempt to give the police powers to detain terrorist suspects for 90 days—this common sense is reinforced, first by securitising claims about the 'unprecedented' scale and 'unknown' nature of the threat and, second, by the things that we are now engaged in a potentially long 'war' to defend—not only public safety, but 'freedom', 'democracy' and 'the rule of law', in short, 'our way of life'.[21] With the stakes set this high, human rights are all too easily represented as a dangerous gamble that would be foolhardy to contemplate—notwithstanding their status as one of the things 'we' are fighting to save at home and have dispatched troops to try to install and instil abroad. When rights are discursively made to carry such risks, it is little wonder that security so often trumps them.

II. SEDUCTIONS OF SECURITY?

How then can we begin to make sense of this vernacular of security and rights, which has a marked propensity to privilege the claims of the former in ways that sideline human rights discourse and practice? What are the seductions of a notion of security that appears carelessly to disregard rights in the ways that I have described? In order to answer these questions, we need to reconstruct the idea—even fantasy—of security that is often at play in these political struggles with rights, and which appears to have a 'paleo-symbolic'—that is to say, affectively compelling but pre-conscious and difficult to articulate[22]—allure within English

---

[19] *The Independent*, 13 November 2004.

[20] Loader, I, 'Fall of the "Platonic Guardians": Liberalism, Criminology and Political Responses to Crime in England and Wales' (2006) 46(4) *British Journal of Criminology* 561–86.

[21] Johnson, R, 'Defending Ways of Life' (2002) 19(4) *Theory, Culture and Society* 211–31; Tsoukala, A, 'Defining the Terrorist Threat in the Post-11 September Era' in D Bigo (ed), *Illiberal Practices in Liberal Regimes* (Paris, L'Harmattan, 2006).

[22] Gouldner, A, *The Dialectic of Ideology and Technology* (London, Macmillan, 1976).

society. Such an exercise in creative reconstruction yields the following four elements.

One can say first that security, or at least a particular projection of what it may mean, appeals because it connects with people's deeply held worries and anxieties about the condition and trajectory of the current world and, at the same time, with their aspirations and fantasies about what that world may or should become. Security, in other words, speaks simultaneously to the best and worst of possible worlds. For many citizens, though in ways that are conditioned by and vary along axes of division such as class, gender, ethnicity and sexuality, rights do not seem to engage the passions in quite the same way. When one couples the capacity of security to provoke fear and whet appetites in this visceral fashion, with the fact that the imagined and projected condition of security tends to remain beyond reach— it is 'more within us as a yearning, than without us as a fact', as Ericson and Haggerty have nicely put it[23]—it becomes easy to grasp the often self-reinforcing spirals of anxiety, investment, disappointment and reinvestment that flow from the efforts of government and indeed market actors to provide security in the terms in which it is demanded.

The appeal to security possesses, secondly, an intimate and affective connection to notions of collective (national) belonging and their attendant forms of cultural and political subjectivity. Security demands are, as such, entangled in the production and reproduction of a 'we' whose territory, or values, or capacity for self-determination is felt to be under threat—either from without or from 'enemies within'. When this threatened 'way of life' is taken to encompass notions such as rights and the rule of law, these are often, paradoxically, invoked at the same time as they are chipped away in the name of their protection. Yet rights remain in the main poorly able to attract or mobilise this sort of collective, passionate sentiment. By contrast, security discourse and practices repeatedly invoke a binary logic of us/them, inside/outside, here/there, order/entropy—which polarises issues and populations (as in George W Bush's 'you' are either 'for us' or 'against us'); places sceptics about security and defenders of rights on the wrong (apparently treacherous) side of these binary lines; and mobilises an always potentially illiberal, parochial and xenophobic conception of the political community to be protected.

The seductions of security thus conceived are bound up, thirdly, with forms of often unconditional identification with a strong, sovereign authority, which is posited and looked to as the source of protection. When mobilised by state actors, this claim tends to call forth a sense of urgency and imperatives (rather than hard choices and trade-offs) and a need for the speedy, unhindered hand of executive authority. This sense of necessity is coupled with an impatience with the restraints and seeming indecisiveness occasioned by democratic debate, judicial scrutiny and rights. Security here easily becomes a pervasive discourse and practice—one that tends to colonise government and public life and to legitimate its own authority by making a necessity of the coercive force that it alone is capable of wielding.

---

[23] Ericson, R and Haggerty, K, *Policing the Risk Society* (Oxford, Oxford University Press, 1997) 99.

But one also encounters here what Paul Gilroy calls 'a passion for authoritarianism'[24]—a strand of English sentiment that responds to the fear of crime and violence by eagerly seeking solace in the omnipotent Leviathan—to the extent that sometimes there appears to be a willingness to meld one's individual autonomy and identity with that of the state. And once the strong state has been so deeply invested in as the solution to the problem of insecurity, little cognitive or affective space remains for the idea that someone might reasonably require protection from it.

What this amounts to, finally, is security as an expression of what Patchen Markell refers to as 'the desire for sovereign agency'[25]—a conception of security that sees people invest in the impossible promise of eliminating (rather than managing or finding resources for living with) risk, that dreams of individuals or communities becoming masters of their own fate. The seduction, at a paleo-symbolic level, of security thus conceived rests on the fantasy of being able to secure oneself in isolation from, with little regard for, or at the expense of, the security of others. It is security as individual or collective self-realisation—a form and fantasy of security practice that denies its irreducibly social dimensions[26] and refuses to acknowledge the mutual uncertainty, vulnerability and dependency that flows inescapably from 'the activity of living and interacting with other people'.[27] It is a conception of security that makes little room for and appears to have little need of the idea and practice of human rights.

III. DISTASTE FOR RIGHTS?

My efforts to reconstruct creatively the idea of security that is expressly or implicitly in play within many current debates about its relationship to rights may go some way towards explaining why the idea of rights is so often and easily marginalised in the forums in which it clashes with the promises of security. But we still have to pinpoint more exactly the alleged properties of rights that enable them to be so routinely and carelessly disregarded within English public culture. This is not, as mentioned, a culture in which rights are wholly unrecognised or unprotected. Far from it. But it is nonetheless hard to sustain the converse claim that Britain enjoys a strong and deeply embedded human rights culture.[28] We are thus confronted with the following question: if human rights represent a minimum core of standards that underpins any viable conception of the good society, as some have claimed,[29] or if they are the closest that secular Western culture today comes to an article of faith, then why does one encounter, within the English set-

---

[24] Gilroy, P, *After Empire: Melancholia or Convivial Culture?* (London, Routledge, 2004).
[25] Markell, P, *Bound by Recognition* (Princeton, Princeton University Press, 2003) 22.
[26] Loader and Walker (2007) ch 6.
[27] Markell (2003) 7.
[28] Lazarus (2004) ch 6.
[29] See, for example, Ignatieff, M, *Human Rights as Politics and Idolatry* (Princeton, Princeton University Press, 2001).

ting that is my concern here, so many agnostics and atheists—such a strong strand of weak identification with, even distaste for, the idea and practice of human rights? I think the answer can be found in the following interlocking properties that have come, culturally, to be attached to the idea of rights.

Rights have come to be thought of, first, as 'getting in the way of' and unduly constraining that which is deemed necessary to protect 'us' from disorderly, criminal or terrorist activity. To insist upon rights in the face of these dangers is to urge delay when speed is needed, to tie the hands of the police when they need all the powers that can be put at their disposal, to curb authority when its less fettered exercise is so obviously called for. It is, in a nutshell, to gamble with people's safety. One sees variants of this position whenever rights and security currently clash culturally and politically. The ultimate logic of this position leads its proponents to invoke a rights claim of their own, the force of which is felt to be undeniable: what about our right, as law-abiding citizens, to live in peace, free of crime, disorder and violation? This of course is the right to trump all rights: a right to security.[30]

Rights appear in the vernacular, secondly, not as a collective accomplishment, the outcome of a long historical struggle to wrest freedoms from the powerful and curb the power of the state, nor as something that 'we' enjoy and which constitutes us as a political community. They are rather cast today, even by their defenders, as individual protections that we each enjoy *qua* individuals as a token of the equal concern and respect to which we are all in liberal societies entitled.[31] The cultural translation of this in times of insecurity, however, conceives of rights as protections for others, rights that I, as a law-abiding citizen, have no pressing need either to use or defend.

The law-abiding can of course often be found resorting rhetorically to rights as an abstract claim—'I know my rights'. But rights seldom appear in the quotidian experience of such citizens in the form of concrete protections, as things that they need or that appear to be under threat in ways that pressingly matter. They can thus, as Dworkin pointed out in his discussion of illiberal responses to 9/11, be eroded, curtailed and chipped away by states without registering in any meaningful, experiential way in the everyday lives of the majority of citizens.[32] Rights as concrete protections are much more likely to be seen, from this vantage point, as protections that exist for dangerous, unworthy others, whether they be rowdy teenagers, criminals or terrorists. Tony Blair recently resorted to this type of formulation in defence of his failed attempt to persuade the British House of Commons to allow the police to detain terror suspects for 90 days.

There is, in short, no 'us' of rights. They are not ours to enjoy in common but rather dubious entitlements for 'them'—with the result on occasions that to make a rights claim is *prime facie* to bring oneself under a cloud of suspicion. And this, of course, is precisely the meaning (and effect) of that dangerous, complacent piece of doxic opinion that says, 'If you've got nothing to hide, you've got nothing

[30] See the contribution by Liora Lazarus in this volume.
[31] *Ibid.*
[32] Dworkin, R, 'The Threat to Patriotism' (2002) *New York Review of Books*, 28 February 2002.

to fear.' This disposition appears to leave its bearers lacking the motivation or resources to fret about, still less actively oppose, *any* extension of state power or creeping infringement of civil and political liberties.

A third closely related element of the vernacular distaste for rights has it that they are a conspiracy against common sense and practical wisdom, against the things that 'we' all know to be true. Rights on this view are not the common treasury of all but arcane claims defended by activists who inhabit the political fringes or interest groups that are securely located among the liberal elite. Prominent among those selected for political, media and lay opprobrium here are lawyers, journalists, professional activists and penal reformers, whose place in the economic and social hierarchy is deemed to permit them the luxury of insisting upon rights without having to live with the consequences of their actions, and who thus seem willing in the name of abstract principles to jeopardise the safety of those who are less able to insulate themselves from crime. Insofar as political responses to crime have since the early 1990s taken a 'populist turn' and gone into revolt against liberal-minded expertise,[33] they have tended to usher in, or give greater voice and credence to, just this sort of vernacular claim, which is resolutely hostile to those who would pour the cold water of human rights over the deep emotional satisfactions to be obtained from fantasies of absolute security.

CONCLUSIONS: A CASTLE BUILT ON SAND?

No topic—or approach to a topic—in the social sciences is its own justification, and this attempt to widen the field of vision regarding the interplay between rights and security is no exception. One might thus be tempted respond to my effort to grasp security and rights in the vernacular with a claim to the effect that this is interesting but of little lasting significance; or that it pales when set against the 'real' stuff of political, philosophical or legal analysis; or that it risks diverting attention from the pressing work of defending human rights from the forces that stand in the way of their extension or from those who wish to claw back such gains as have been made. So why, in the face of such possible objections, do I want to insist that an exploration of what I have called the cultural lives of security and rights is of some value? Why is it important that we seek to make sense of how rights and security are framed and fought over in the settings of everyday social relations and political life? I want, by way of conclusion, to return to my starting points and offer two brief responses to such quizzical or sceptical challenges.

Studying the vernacular of security and rights offers a clue, first of all, as to why human rights politics seems at present to assume an oppositional, defensive form—to be fighting a rearguard action in hostile terrain. In saying this, my aim is not to add to the pile of 'criminologies of catastrophe'[34] that take gloomy delight

---

[33] Loader (2006a).

[34] O'Malley, P, 'Criminologies of Catastrophe? Understanding Criminal Justice on the Edge of the New Millennium' (2000) 33 *Australian and New Zealand Journal of Criminology* 153–67.

in depicting civil liberties to be in historical retreat, or on the edge of radical dero-gation.[35] It is not the intention of this chapter to deny the significant advances that human rights have made in recent decades in the United Kingdom, or to disregard the powerful constituencies who now stand ready to defend them. But the present analysis does nonetheless offer reasons to think that these legal protections are not firmly located within what is often loosely called a human rights *culture*; they may even be necessary precisely because English society lacks such a culture.

Human rights may, in other words, be planted in some rather barren cultural soil or, to switch metaphors, be a castle built on sand. Their promotion and defence thus seem likely to continue to depend on a combination of social move-ments making rights claims as a form of recognition and liberal-minded profes-sionals and activists committed to human rights ideals. Both operate in the face of lay indifference, disdain and hostility, and are engaged in a project that always stands vulnerable to the seductive claims of strong rulers bearing the promise of security.

By addressing the place of rights and security in everyday and political life—by treating them, that is, as aspects of mundane culture—one is able to highlight the dynamics of struggles that in the English case give human rights a certain precari-ousness, but which in other comparative settings may conduce to different out-comes. One can, in so doing, also help to further what remains the barely visible but potentially important contribution that sociology can make to the analysis of human rights.[36]

The study of security and rights in the vernacular can help, secondly, to illumi-nate certain shortcomings in a theory and practice of rights that understands human rights as needing protection from the claims of security. Such defences, taking the individual as the basic unit of analysis and moral worth, hold human rights protections to be for individuals, who *qua* individuals require the protective capsule that rights offer against the unwarranted incursion of both other individ-uals and the state. Rights stand, as such, as the practical means of giving effect to the idea that individuals are entitled to equal concern and respect.[37] Yet this indi-vidualistic defence of the idea of individual rights is not only vulnerable, in the realm of practice, to the charges that we have seen are commonly levelled against it in liberal democratic settings today—that rights protect undeserving 'others' at the expense of 'my' security. It also, as a theoretical claim, disregards the forms of trust and abstract solidarity between strangers that provide the cultural conditions of possibility for rights by supplying the motivational force for creating and sus-taining a political community that recognises, protects and enforces them.[38]

---

[35] *Cf* Waddington, PAJ, 'Slippery Slopes and Civil Libertarian Pessimism' (2005) 15(3) *Policing & Society* 353–75.

[36] *Cf* Turner, BS, 'Outline of a Theory of Human Rights' in BS Turner (ed), *Citizenship and Social Theory* (London, Sage, 1993); Cohen, S, *States of Denial: Knowing about Atrocities and Suffering* (Cambridge, Polity, 2001); and Sjoberg, G, Gill, EA and Williams, N, 'A Sociology of Human Rights' (2001) 28(1) *Social Problems* 11–47.

[37] Dworkin, R, *Taking Rights Seriously* (Cambridge, MA, Harvard University Press, 1977).

[38] Canovan, M, *Nationhood and Political Theory* (London, Edward Elgar, 1996).

Rights may best be protected, in other words, when they come to be thought of and defended as goods that are valuable not 'for me' and 'for you' as individuals, but for 'us' as members of a political community that values and strives to uphold the rights of all of its members.[39] This, for reasons that Neil Walker and I have expanded upon much more fully elsewhere,[40] is why the second point of this brief enquiry is to encourage further investigation of the possibility that human rights can best be advanced—not only legally, but also as elements of culture—by situating them *within* a solidaristic and egalitarian practice of security.

REFERENCES

Blair, T, 'Our Nation's Future: The Criminal Justice System', lecture, 23 June 2006, available at http://www.number-10.gov.uk/output/Page9737.asp.

Bourdieu, P, *The Logic of Practice* (Cambridge, Polity, 1990).

Burney, E, *Making People Behave: Anti-social Behaviour, Politics and Policy* (Cullompton, Willan, 2005).

Canovan, M, *Nationhood and Political Theory* (London,Edward Elgar, 1996).

Cohen, S, *States of Denial: Knowing about Atrocities and Suffering* (Cambridge, Polity, 2001).

Dworkin, R, *Taking Rights Seriously* (Cambridge, MA, Harvard University Press, 1977).

—— 'The Threat to Patriotism' (2002) *New York Review of Books*, 28 February 2002.

Ericson, R and Haggerty, K, *Policing the Risk Society* (Oxford, Oxford University Press, 1997).

Gilroy, P, *After Empire: Melancholia or Convivial Culture?* (London, Routledge, 2004).

Girling, E, Loader, I and Sparks, R, *Crime and Social Change in Middle England: Questions of Order in an English Town* (London, Routledge, 2000).

Goold, BJ, *CCTV and Policing: Public Area Surveillance and Police Practices in Britain* (Oxford, Oxford University Press, 2004).

Gouldner, A, *The Dialectic of Ideology and Technology* (London, Macmillan, 1976).

Hope, T and Sparks, R (eds), *Crime, Risk and Insecurity: Law and Order in Everyday Life and Political Discourse* (London, Routledge, 2001).

Home Office, *Royal Commission on Criminal Justice: Report*, Cm 2263 (London, Home Office, 1993).

Ignatieff, M, *Human Rights as Politics and Idolatry* (Princeton, Princeton University Press, 2001).

Johnson, R, 'Defending Ways of Life' (2002) 19(4) *Theory, Culture and Society* 211–31.

Laclau, E, *On Populist Reason* (London, Verso, 2005).

Lazarus, L, *Contrasting Prisoners' Rights: A Comparative Examination of Britain and Germany* (Oxford, Oxford University Press, 2004).

Loader, I, 'Fall of the "Platonic Guardians": Liberalism, Criminology and Political Responses to Crime in England and Wales' (2006) 46(4) *British Journal of Criminology* 561–86.

---

[39] Taylor, C, 'Cross-Purposes: The Liberal-Communitarian Debate' in N Rosenblum (ed), *Liberalism and the Moral Life.*

[40] Loader and Walker (2007) chs 6–8.

—— 'Rebalancing the Criminal Justice System?', paper prepared for the Prime Minister lecture series 'Our Nation's Future', June 2006, available at http://www.pm.gov.uk/output/Page9701.asp.

Loader, I and Mulcahy, A, *Policing and the Condition of England: Memory, Politics and Culture* (Oxford, Oxford University Press, 2003).

Loader, I and Walker, N, *Civilizing Security* (Cambridge, Cambridge University Press, 2007).

Markell, P, *Bound by Recognition* (Princeton, Princeton University Press, 2003).

Mulgan, G, *Good and Bad Power: The Ideals and Betrayals of Government* (Harmondsworth, Penguin, 2006).

O'Malley, P, 'Criminologies of Catastrophe? Understanding Criminal Justice on the Edge of the New Millennium' (2000) 33 *Australian and New Zealand Journal of Criminology* 153–67.

Reiner, R, 'Policing a Postmodern Society' (1992) 55(6) *Modern Law Review* 761–81.

Sasson, T, *Crime Talk: How Citizens Construct a Social Problem* (New York, Aldine de Gruyter, 1995).

Sjoberg, G, Gill, EA and Williams, N, 'A Sociology of Human Rights' (2001) 28(1) *Social Problems* 11–47.

Sparks, R, 'Ordinary Anxieties and States of Emergency: Statecraft and Spectatorship in the New Politics of Insecurity' in S Armstrong and L McAra (eds), *Perspectives on Punishment: The Contours of Control* (Oxford, Oxford University Press, 2006).

Taylor, C, 'Cross-Purposes: The Liberal-Communitarian Debate' in N Rosenblum (ed), *Liberalism and the Moral Life* (Cambridge, MA, Harvard University Press, 1989).

Tsoukala, A, 'Defining the Terrorist Threat in the Post-11 September Era' in D Bigo (ed), *Illiberal Practices in Liberal Regimes* (Paris, L'Harmattan, 2006).

Turner, BS, 'Outline of a Theory of Human Rights' in BS Turner (ed), *Citizenship and Social Theory* (London, Sage, 1993).

Waddington, PAJ, 'Slippery Slopes and Civil Libertarian Pessimism' (2005) 15(3) *Policing & Society* 353–75.

Waldron, J, 'Security and Liberty: The Image of Balance' (2003) 2 *Journal of Political Philosophy* 191–210.

Walzer, M, 'On Negative Politics' in B Yack (ed), *Liberalism without Illusions: Essays on Liberal Theory and the Political Vision of Judith N Shklar* (Chicago, University of Chicago Press, 1996).

Zedner, L, 'In Pursuit of the Vernacular: Comparing Law and Order Discourse in Britain and Germany' (1995) 4 *Social and Legal Studies* 517–34.

3

Privacy, Identity and Security

BENJAMIN J GOOLD*

> Getting a list in a few seconds of anyone in the United States who subscribes to a Middle Eastern newspaper, watches Al-Jazeera, is between the ages of 20 and 35, and who travelled to Washington on the day of a major political demonstration is but a few clicks away. When a bureaucrat at the TIA (Total Information Awareness) or one of its successors performs such a search and you are named by the state, it is not just 'information' that has been gathered. The e-interpellation goes farther than the information separately considered—by the very act of naming you as a suspect (or 'person of interest') you have changed status in the eyes of others who know about this, and if you come to know or fear, in your eyes as well.
>
> P Galison and M Minow, 'Our Privacy, Ourselves'[1]

I N RECENT YEARS, events such as the attacks of 9/11 and London bombings of 7 July 2005 have given rise to major pieces of security legislation in countries like the United Kingdom and the United States. Enacted within months of each other, both the Anti-Terrorism, Crime and Security Act 2001 and the USA PATRIOT Act 2001 contain a range of provisions aimed at increasing the ability of the police, security services and other law enforcement agencies to detect and combat terrorist activities.[2] The enactment of these Acts, which have been hailed by politicians on both sides of the Atlantic as vital weapons in the 'war on terror', can be directly linked to recent large-scale terrorist events. However, many of the reforms ushered in by these pieces of legislation—although unusually bold and

* I would like to express my thanks to the participants at the Oxford Colloquium on Security and Human Rights for their comments on an earlier version of this chapter, and to Simon Cole, Lisa Gourd, Imogen Goold, Kevin Haggerty, Richard Jones, Simon Halliday, Mike Nellis, and Sophie Walker for their considerable help with subsequent drafts. Any remaining errors or omissions are my own.

[1] Galison, P and Minow, M, 'Our Privacy, Ourselves in the Age of Technological Intrusions' in R Ashby Wilson, *Human Rights in the 'War on Terror'* (Cambridge, Cambridge University Press, 2005) 282–83.

[2] Following a ruling by the House of Lords in *A and others v Secretary of State for the Home Department* [2004] UKHL 56 that the powers contained in Part 4 of the Anti-terrorism, Crime and Security Act 2001 were incompatible with the European Convention on Human Rights, Part 4 was repealed by the Prevention of Terrorism Act 2005. As a result, all measures contained within the Anti-Terrorism, Crime and Security Act 2001 now apply equally to nationals as well as non-nationals. The USA PATRIOT Act was renewed on 2 March 2006 by both Houses of Congress and subsequently signed into law by President George W Bush on 9 March 2006.

certainly unprecedented in terms of their scope—have largely been in keeping with established trends in the expansion of state power and the decline of privacy in the last years of the twentieth century. In particular, both Acts have led to a marked acceleration in the already rapid growth of existing surveillance networks in the United Kingdom and the United States. Moreover, the Acts have played a key role in breaking down barriers between various law enforcement agencies, as well as between state and non-state organisations—increasing the ease with which personal information can be exchanged.

Aside from significantly expanding the surveillance capacities of the state and creating new concerns for individual privacy, the Anti-Terrorism, Crime and Security and USA PATRIOT Acts have also weakened longstanding due process protections and the right to a fair trial. This general erosion of the rights of the majority brought about by these and subsequent Acts—although disturbing in and of itself—has been accompanied by a sustained attack on the freedoms of particular minorities, such as Middle Eastern and Muslim communities. Regardless of the intentions of the governments behind them, the provisions contained in these Acts represent a serious retreat from a commitment to human rights in general and a damaging attack on individual privacy in particular.

Privacy is protected as a right—albeit a qualified one—in both the United Kingdom and the United States, and measures that threaten to undermine individual expectations of privacy must therefore be taken extremely seriously.[3] A great deal has been written about the changing nature of surveillance and the extent to which 9/11 has contributed to the erosion of personal privacy in many Western democracies.[4] However, the aims and provisions of the Anti-terrorism, Crime and Security Act and the USA PATRIOT Act should also be seen as significant because they bring to the fore the complex dynamic between security, surveillance, privacy and the construction of identity. The fervour with which security has recently been pursued has not only led to more surveillance and less privacy in the United Kingdom and the United States, but also contributed to a major shift in the way in which personal identity is constructed and understood by both the state and individual citizens.

In this chapter, the relationship between security, surveillance, privacy and identity will be explored, both in the context of recent legislation such as the Anti-terrorism, Crime and Security Act and the USA PATRIOT Act, and also in the light of ongoing changes in the ways that personal information is gathered, processed and used. In particular, it will be argued that prevailing notions of privacy—and the legal frameworks that aim to protect privacy interests—are ill suited to defending individuals from an increasingly sophisticated array of sur-

---

[3] In the UK, privacy—as defined by Art 8 of the European Convention on Human Rights (ECHR)—is protected under the Human Rights Act 1998. In contrast, in the US privacy derives its status as a right from the First, Fourth, Ninth and Fourteenth Amendments to the Constitution. For a discussion of privacy rights in the US, see Alderman, E and Kennedy, C, *The Right to Privacy* (New York, Knopf, 1995); and Goold, B, 'Open to All? Regulating Open Street CCTV and the Case for "Symmetrical Surveillance"' (2006) 25(1) *Criminal Justice Ethics* 3–17.

[4] See, for example, Galison and Minow (2005).

veillance and data processing techniques that enable information to be acquired and shared at almost zero cost and that threaten to establish the 'categorical identity' as the primary means by which we are known—to the state and, more disturbingly, to each other.

I. REMOVING BARRIERS, REDUCING PRIVACY

Speaking immediately after the signing into law of the USA PATRIOT Act in October 2001, President George W Bush observed that the Act represents a significant step towards the greater integration of law enforcement and security agencies in the United States, in part because it removes many of the barriers to inter-agency communication that existed prior to the events of 9/11:

> This legislation gives . . . intelligence operations and criminal operations the chance to operate not on separate tracks, but to share vital information so necessary to disrupt a terrorist attack before it occurs. As of today, we're changing the laws governing information-sharing.[5]

The issue that Bush was referring to here is known generally in the United States as 'linkage blindness'[6] and is now recognised as the major reason behind the failure of the US intelligence services to predict the catastrophic events of 9/11.[7] In an effort to address this problem, the USA PATRIOT Act removed many of the barriers to communication between key agencies such as the Federal Bureau of Investigations (FBI) and the Central Intelligence Agency (CIA), while at the same time laying the foundations for the establishment of a new supervisory agency in the form of the Department of Homeland Security.[8] According to section 203(d)(1):

---

[5] 'President Signs Anti-terrorism Bill: Remarks by the President at Signing of the PATRIOT Act', The White House, 26 October 2001, quoted by Privacy International, 'Terrorism Profile: US' (3 October 2005), available at http://www.privacyinternational.org.

[6] According to Egger, linkage blindness typically arises when organisations fail to recognise areas of mutual interest or jurisdictional overlap and as a consequence duplicate work and refrain from sharing crucial information. See Egger, SA, *Serial Murder: An Elusive Phenomenon* (Westport, CT, Praeger, 1990); and Egger, SA, 'A Working Definition of Serial Murder and the Reduction of Linkage Blindness' (1984) 12 *Journal of Police Science and Administration* 348–57.

[7] In its report to Congress in December 2002, the Joint Inquiry into Intelligence Community Activities before and after the Terrorist Attacks of September 11 echoed earlier concerns about the problem of linkage blindness by stating in its conclusions (84):

> Serious problems in information sharing also persisted, prior to 9/11, between the Intelligence Community and non-Intelligence Community agencies. This included other federal agencies as well as state and local authorities. This lack of communication and collaboration deprived those other entities, as well as the Intelligence Community, of access to potentially valuable information in the 'war' against Bin Laden.

A full copy of the report is available at http://www.fas.org/irp/congress/2002_rpt/findings.html.

[8] For a detailed discussion of the provisions of the Act, see Doyle, C, 'USA Patriot Act: A Sketch', (Congressional Research Service report RS21203 for Congress, 2005); and Doyle, C, 'USA Patriot Act Sunset: A Sketch' (Congressional Research Service report RS21704 for Congress, 2005).

In general, notwithstanding any other provision of law, it shall be lawful for foreign intelligence or counterintelligence or foreign intelligence information obtained as part of a criminal investigation to be disclosed to any Federal law enforcement, intelligence, protective, immigration, national defense, or national security official in order to assist the official receiving that information in the performance of his official duties. Any Federal official who receives information pursuant to this provision may use that information only as is necessary in the conduct of that person's official duties subject to any limitations on the unauthorized disclosure of such information.

Before the USA PATRIOT Act, domestic and foreign intelligence gathering and surveillance activities had been deliberately kept separate, in part to ensure the accountability of the various agencies responsible for such tasks and in part to protect civil liberties.[9] These agencies have now been deliberately brought together with clear instructions to intensify their activities and share whatever information they uncover. However, the FBI, CIA, Department for Homeland Security and associated government officials have given little explicit consideration as to how this will affect the second half of the equation—the protection of civil liberties.

Although no equivalent to the Department for Homeland Security has yet been mooted for the United Kingdom, the Anti-Terrorism, Crime and Security Act also represents a concerted attempt to improve information gathering and intelligence sharing by the various agencies that are charged with the task of preventing terrorism and maintaining state security.[10] Prior to the events of 9/11, security services such as MI5 and MI6 had never been particularly well regulated, nor were their interactions with domestic law enforcement agencies formally constrained.[11] As a result, although there may have been concerns in some quarters about the accountability of these agencies and the extent to which Parliament was able effectively to monitor their activities, there were also few significant barriers to inter-agency co-operation and co-ordination.

Nevertheless, with the Anti-terrorism, Crime and Security Act the UK government sought to increase the already significant surveillance powers of the state by

---

[9] As Brian Hook observed in his testimony before the House Permanent Select Committee on Intelligence on 9 April 2003, in 1946 President Truman refused to place the CIA under the control of director of the FBI (who, at that time, was J Edgar Hoover) because he feared concentrating so much bureaucratic power in a single individual.

[10] While the current government has yet to argue for the establishment of an equivalent to the US Department of Homeland Security, in a recent speech to Demos, a London think tank, the Home Secretary John Reid suggested that there was a need for a US-style Minister for Homeland Security. For a report of the speech, see Tempest, M, 'Britain Facing "Most Sustained Threat since WWII" says Reid', *The Guardian*, 9 August 2006, available at http://politics.guardian.co.uk/terrorism/story/0,,1840482,00.html.

[11] A major exception to this general trend came with the enactment of the Regulation of Investigatory Powers Act (RIPA) in 2000. In addition to repealing the Interception of Communications Act 1985 (IOCA) and abolishing the post of IOCA Commissioner, RIPA created the position of the Interception of Communications Commissioner and replaced the Commissioners established under the Security Service Act 1989 and the Intelligence Services Act 1994 with a single combined Intelligence Services Commissioner. These two independent Commissioners oversee the activities of the Security Service (MI5) as well as other public bodies charged with protecting national security, such the Secret Intelligence Service (SIS) and the Government Communications Headquarters (GCHQ).

removing a number of formal restrictions on the use of personal information by the police and immigration services. For example, formerly, section 36 of the Immigration and Asylum Act 1999 required officials to destroy any fingerprints collected during the course of an investigation once that case had been resolved. Section 36 of the Anti-terrorism, Crime and Security Act has now removed this requirement. Through an amendment to the Police and Criminal Evidence Act 1984, section 92 of the Anti-terrorism, Crime and Security Act also gives the police the power to photograph suspected terrorists regardless of consent.

Significantly, the removal of these restrictions on the use of personal information has coincided with a renewed effort on the part of the government to expand the National DNA Database (NDNAD). Established in 1995 by the Forensic Science Service, the NDNAD currently contains over two million DNA samples, with some 500,000 new samples being added to the database every year.[12] Although NDNAD is already the largest such database in the world, recent legislation allowing the police to take DNA samples from anyone arrested on suspicion of a recordable offence—again, regardless of consent—is likely to lead to further significant growth in the number of samples held.[13] As the database expands, the use of genetic profiling by the police and other law enforcement agencies, in the context of both domestic crime and terrorism, is also likely to increase.[14] Coupled with compulsory identity cards that can be based on some form of biometric identifier, the NDNAD could conceivably provide the basis for a centralised identity register for the entire United Kingdom and could lead to further deliberate co-ordination between immigration and security policy.

Although the FBI's Combined DNA Indexing System (CODIS) contains fewer profiles than the NDNAD (in part because the vast majority of samples are taken from convicted prisoners), the collection of other forms of biometric data, such as fingerprints, has also become a priority for the Department of Homeland Security. At present, almost all non-US nationals are fingerprinted and photographed upon entry into the United States, and there are proposals for such measures to be extended to US citizens as well. The Department of State has explicitly drawn a link between the collection of such data and the successful maintenance of national security:

---

[12] According to recent Home Office estimates, the NDNAD will hold samples on over four million people—approximately 7% of the population—by 2008. This compares with a figure of some 700,000 samples when the current Labour government took office in 1997. See 'Freedom Fears as DNA Database Expands', *The Daily Telegraph,* 5 January 2006.

[13] According to s 10 of the Criminal Justice Act 2003, non-intimate DNA samples can be taken when an individual is in 'police detention in consequence of his arrest for a recordable offence' and provided that a sample of the same type and from the same part of the body has not already been taken (or, if it has been taken, has proved insufficient). For a discussion of the various legal and ethical issues raised by the creation of this database, see Williams, R, Johnson, P and Martin, P, 'Genetic Information and Crime Investigation' (University of Durham School of Applied Social Sciences, report, 2004); and GeneWatch UK, *The Police National DNA Database: Balancing Crime Detection, Human Rights and Privacy* (Buxton, GeneWatch UK, 2005).

[14] McCartney, C, 'Forensic DNA Sampling and the England and Wales National DNA Database: A Sceptical Approach' (2004) 12 *Critical Criminology* 157–78.

The use of these identifiers is an important link in US national security, because fin-gerprints taken will be compared with similarly collected fingerprints at US ports of entry under the US-VISIT program. This will verify identity to reduce use of stolen and counterfeit visas, and protect against possible use by terrorists or others who might represent a security risk to the US. These two important programs (collecting fingerprints for visa issuance and verifying travelers' fingerprints when they enter the United States) will make travel to the US safer for legitimate travelers, and also improve safety and national security for all Americans.[15]

There may be a danger in drawing too close a comparison between the US and UK responses to the events of 9/11, yet as the above examples make clear, the two gov-ernments have adopted a similar approach to improving state security. In each case, increasing the surveillance powers of the state and encouraging a greater degree of information sharing amongst state institutions have been seen as vital to increasing security and preventing future acts of domestic and international terrorism. Furthermore, both countries are now in the process of establishing comprehensive databases—based, for the moment at least, on the compulsory acquisition of biometric information from non-citizens and criminals. The UK and US governments expect these measures to improve their chances of identify-ing and apprehending potential terrorists—despite the amorphous nature of the threat and the lack of substantive evidence to suggest that surveillance systems, data matching and intelligence-led security measures actually help to prevent large-scale terrorist activities.[16]

In many respects, the fact that both countries have viewed the post-9/11 'secu-rity problem' in terms of information is unsurprising. Over the past 30 years the United States and the United Kingdom have grappled with a number of profound social changes—including increasingly diverse populations, increased mobility of citizens and the development of ever more flexible and efficient communications technologies—which have had a particularly significant effect on the ability of the state to provide security for its citizens.[17] These wide-reaching social and techno-logical developments have contributed to a transformation in the nature and pur-pose of surveillance. Whereas in the past maintaining order and security principally involved the control of physical bodies and the movements of citizens through the use of borders and documentation like passports and visas, the latter part of the twentieth century saw a shift in the provision of security from a static process that was generally fixed in time and space to a dynamic one that is inte-grated into what Lyon has referred to as 'a world of flows'.[18] Not only can citizens move freely and easily between towns, cities and even countries, but ideas and their more concrete manifestations in literature, images, propaganda, petitions, and so on, can travel at lightning speeds and reach unimaginably large numbers of

---

[15] For a copy of this statement, see http://travel.state.gov/visa/immigrants/info/info_1336.html.
[16] See the contribution by Bernard E Harcourt in this volume.
[17] See Garland, D, *The Culture of Control* (Oxford, Oxford University Press, 2001) ch 4; and Lyon, D, *Surveillance Society: Monitoring Everyday Life* (Buckingham, Open University Press, 2001) ch 6.
[18] Lyon (2001).

people. Maintaining order and security has therefore become an ever more complex enterprise that relies less on tracking physical bodies than on tracking the data trails that individuals leave behind.[19]

The challenges of securing an increasingly diverse population in an increasingly complex world did not appear out of the blue; but what makes 9/11 significant is that it marks the moment at which it became acceptable for governments to draw a direct and very public connection between the demand for security and the need for improved means of general surveillance, individual identification and social control.[20] As Levi and Wall have observed, since 9/11 the 'surveillance-society' model of security has become increasingly viewed as legitimate, with the result that there has been a considerable increase in the power of the state.[21] While formerly a degree of separation between those responsible for internal and external security was seen as essential to the preservation of democratic government, since 9/11 it has become standard practice in the United States and the United Kingdom to assume that breaking down the legal and institutional barriers between law enforcement and security agencies is both practical and necessary, resulting in the emergence of an all-embracing concept of 'national security'.[22]

The removal of these barriers has serious implications for individual privacy. As many civil libertarians and privacy advocates have argued, as the surveillance power of the state expands, the number of truly private spaces available for individuals necessarily contracts, with the result that it becomes increasingly difficult for citizens to 'keep things to themselves'.[23] Furthermore, as Galison and Minow have observed, because legislation such as the Anti-terrorism, Crime and Security Act and the USA PATRIOT Act helps to reinforce the view that it is worth sacrificing considerable amounts of privacy for the promise of security, it only exacerbates existing powerful anti-privacy trends in other areas of our social and economic lives:

---

[19] Lyon, D, 'Surveillance Studies: Understanding Visibility, Mobility and the Phenetic Fix' (2003) 1(1) *Surveillance and Society* 3.

[20] This point has also been made by the group Privacy International. See 'Increased Abuse of Data and Disregard for Protections' (Privacy International press statement, 9 August 2004), available at http://www.privacyinternational.org.

[21] Levi, M and Wall, DS, 'Technologies, Security, and Privacy in the Post-September 11 European Information Society' (2004) 31(2) *Journal of Law and Society* 203.

[22] This point is made clearly in a recent Department of Homeland Security press release: 'A critical obstacle to cooperation across the Federal government is to integrate data created by different agencies for different systems and different purposes.' See 'Secure Borders and Open Doors in the Information Age' (Department of Homeland Security fact sheet, 17 January 2006), available at http://www.dhs.gov/xnews/releases/press_release_0838.shtm.

   In many respects, this new idea of 'national security' closely resembles the German concepts of *Staatssicherheit* or *Staatsschutz.* I am indebted to Eric Topfler for the observation that one additional consequence of this all-embracing approach to security is the tactical, as well as organisational, convergence of the police and the military. As security becomes a more important part of the national agenda, not only do we see a sharing of information and the development of stronger organisational links between the police and the security services, but also domestic security bodies 'borrowing' weapons and tactics from the military and others more traditionally associated with external, international defence.

[23] See, for example, Stanley, J and Steinhardt, B, 'Bigger Monster, Weaker Chains: The Growth of an American Surveillance Society' (ACLU Technology and Liberty Program, 2003).

to attend to privacy in the design of technology, the articulation and ~ement of laws, and in the mechanisms of markets and politics produce down- ~rds spirals, reducing both the scope of experiential privacy and people's expectation of and hope for privacy.[24]

The idea that individuals should be able to retain control over certain types of information about themselves and their dealings—and determine who has access to that information—underpins a number of different conceptions of the right to privacy.[25] It is also an idea that has to varying degrees found support in both UK and US law. Yet while it is clear that the pursuit of security poses a threat to this aspect of privacy, in the remaining sections of this chapter it will be argued that there are deeper issues at stake than the loss of what we may call 'informational privacy'. Privacy, it will be argued, is not simply about the keeping of secrets or the restriction of access to information. Rather, it is also about maintaining a degree of control over one's identity—an endeavour that is by nature much more indefinable and fluid but also goes to the heart of what it is to be human/maintaining human dignity.

II. CHANGING NOTIONS OF IDENTITY: NARRATIVES AND CATEGORIES

One of the central challenges of the modern state has been to find ways in which to identify citizens.[26] Passports, identity cards and social security numbers all represent attempts to ensure that each individual is readily and unmistakably distinguishable from others. Without stable identities and reliable mechanisms for identification, it is difficult for states to exercise any hold over those who live within their borders, or to ensure that they are able to protect against internal and external threats.[27] At a more mundane level, reliable methods of identification are also essential to the running of anything other than the most minimal state. As Rose has observed, although individuals may at times resist, participation in modern society necessarily involves allowing oneself to be identified and, more crucially, classified:

It is impossible to participate in almost any contemporary practice without being prepared to demonstrate identity in ways that inescapably link individuation and

---

[24] Galison and Minow (2005) 258.

[25] For a defence of this particular view of privacy, see Fried, C, *An Anatomy of Values* (Cambridge, MA, Harvard University Press, 1970); and Parent, W, 'Privacy, Autonomy, and Self-Concept' (1983) 24 *American Philosophical Quarterly* 81–9. A critique of this approach to privacy, or at least Parent's account of it, can be found in DeCew, J, *In Pursuit of Privacy: Law, Ethics, and the Rise of Technology* (Ithaca, Cornell University Press, 1997).

[26] This problem has not been confined to the state but also confronts private organisations. In order to highlight the relationship between state security and surveillance, however, in this chapter the primary focus will be on states and their attempts to document the identity of individuals.

[27] See Higgs, E, 'The Rise of the Information State: The Development of Central State Surveillance of the Citizen in England, 1500–2000' (2001) 14(2) *Journal of Historical Sociology* 175–97; and Torpey, JC, *The Invention of the Passport: Surveillance, Citizenship and the State* (Cambridge, Cambridge University Press, 2000).

control. The modes of identification are multiple: computer-readable passports, driving licenses with unique identification codes, social insurance numbers, bank cards, credit cards . . . Each card identifies the bearer with a virtual identity—a database record storing personal details—whilst at the same time allowing access to various privileges.[28]

As anyone who has tried to open a bank account or obtain a licence to drive a car knows, it is almost impossible to live a normal life without some form of officially recognised identification document. Furthermore, we have come to accept that government agencies and private companies regularly obtain, keep and exchange information about us, often with a view to classifying us according to given sets of characteristics. For example, most people now regard it as normal and reasonable for the state to inquire about such things as an individual's employment status, level of income and marital status, particularly if that individual is seeking welfare subsidies, tax relief or some other kind of state benefit.[29] Equally, we willingly disclose information about our assets, financial liabilities and spending habits to banks in order to receive loans, mortgages and credit cards. Having to share personal information is widely understood to be one of the prices we pay in order to participate in society and enjoy many of the benefits that the modern state has to offer.

While most people may not feel particularly concerned about having to tell the government exactly how many children or other dependants they might have, or inform a bank of the amount of money they spent on loan repayments in the previous year, many are unaware of just how much the state and private sector companies actually know about them. In part, this is due to the fact that as we make more and more use of technologies like the mobile phone, credit cards and the internet, we leave behind us digital trails that may contain a wealth of personal information. If you shop online with any degree of regularity, you reveal not only your address but over time also various consumption preferences and possibly information about your creditworthiness. In addition, thanks to the spread of new and increasingly sophisticated surveillance techniques and technologies—such as CCTV cameras, internet cookies and computer spyware—many of our activities are now monitored without our knowledge and information collected without our consent.

This intensification in the level of state and private surveillance has had two distinct effects. First, in countries such as the United States and the United Kingdom, it has led to a significant reduction in levels of personal privacy and confidentiality. This is something that numerous commentators have drawn attention to in recent years, with the result that many contemporary critiques of surveillance focus almost exclusively on the negative implications of new surveillance

[28] Rose, N, *Powers of Freedom: Reframing Political Thought* (Cambridge, Cambridge University Press, 1999) 240–1.

[29] Gilliom, J, 'Struggling with Surveillance: Resistance, Consciousness and Identity' in K Haggerty and R Ericson (eds), *The New Politics of Surveillance and Visibility* (Toronto, University of Toronto Press, 2006) 111–40.

technologies.[30] Second, the intensification of surveillance has also transformed the way in which individuals are viewed and treated by the state and an increasing number of private organisations.

As surveillance has become more widespread (and information and communication technologies more efficient), the process of individual classification has become vastly more sophisticated. For example, whereas in the past government agencies may have been limited to using relatively simple categories when attempting to identify and distinguish between citizens, with the advent of computerised databases and automated data-matching techniques, they are now capable of cross-referencing large amounts of personal information and drawing extremely fine-grained individual distinctions. No longer are individuals sorted according to a handful of basic criteria such as gender, date and place of birth, income level and marital status. Instead, governments and private organisations are able to build profiles based on hundreds of separate pieces of information—such as how many cars someone owns or what periodicals he or she subscribes to—and instantly modify those profiles as new information becomes available. Equally, companies like Amazon.com that use software that relies on records of past purchases to make product recommendations to their regular customers can over time develop customer profiles that are extremely textured and eerily accurate in their ability to predict future preferences, a fact hailed with pride by the company's founder, Jeff Bezos:

> We not only help readers find books, we also help books find readers, with personalized recommendations based on the patterns we see. I remember one of the first times this struck me. The main book on the page was on Zen. There were other suggestions for Zen books, and in the middle of those was a book on how to have a clutter-free desk. That's not something that a human editor would have ever picked. But statistically, the people who were interested in the Zen books also wanted clutter-free desks. The computer is blind to the fact that these things are dissimilar in some way that's important to humans. It looks right through that and says yes, try this. And it works.[31]

The growing use and sophistication of surveillance-based methods of individual classification has important implications for the relationship between the individual and the state. More specifically, a tension has emerged between two fundamentally opposed conceptions of identity: the narrative and the categorical. According to Ricoeur, individuals typically seek to make sense of their own identities by constructing narratives about themselves and those around them, and it is through these narratives that an individual is able to develop a sense of self that

---

[30] For an example of such an account, see Davies, S, *Big Brother: Britain's Web of Surveillance and the New Technological Order* (London, Pan Books, 1996).

[31] Quote taken from a *Wired Magazine* interview with Jeff Bezos. See Anderson, C, 'The Zen of Jeff Bezos', *Wired Magazine*, January 2005, available at http://www.wired.com/wired/archive/13.01/bezos.html.

is fluid and that recognises the existence and autonomy of others.[32] Drawing on Ricoeur, Dauenhauer has observed:

> We make sense of our own personal identities in much the same way as we do of the identity of characters in stories. First, in the case of stories, we come to understand the characters by way of the plot that ties together what happens to them, the aims and projects they adopt, and what they actually do. Similarly I make sense of my own identity by telling a story about my own life. In neither case is the identity like that of a fixed structure or substance. These identities are mobile . . . Until the story is finished, the identity of each character or person remains open to revision.[33]

In contrast to such narrative identities, categorical identities stress the importance of particular personal characteristics with a view to determining whether an individual belongs to some pre-defined group. Personal information is viewed as static and capable of being distilled into data, which can in turn be combined and used as the basis for making statements about an individual's character and—even more crucially for states concerned about issues of security—predictions about his or her future behaviour. Whereas the notion of narrative identity focuses on the uniqueness of individuals and their innate capacity to evolve and develop relationships with other people, the notion of categorical identity is based on the belief that human beings are capable of being summarised and understood in terms of lists. As Franko Aas has written,

> [a categorical] identity is not marked by its unique biography and a certain internal development, but is rather adjusted to the 'computer's ontology': composed of items of information that like Lego bricks can be taken apart and clearly understood as well as fit with other items of information in new configurations.[34]

In part, the tension between these two notions of identity can be traced to the emergence of the modern bureaucratic state. Indeed, the categorical identity has its origins in the nineteenth-century paper file, which was a crucial tool in the first systematic attempts by governments to identify and collect information about individuals. During the first half of the twentieth century, for those concerned about the growth of state power and the dangers of totalitarianism, the file came to be seen as deeply symbolic of the dehumanising nature of bureaucracy and the struggle for individual freedom. Although it is now common to regard Orwell's novel *1984*, in which privacy is non-existent, as merely a dystopic vision, it can also be interpreted as an account of what happens when it is the state, rather than individuals, that makes even basic decisions about identity.

Regardless of how someone chooses to define himself or herself, or how individuals are seen by those who know them personally, in the modern state it is the

---

[32] See, inter alia, Ricoeur, P, 'Reflections on a New Ethos for Europe' (1995) 21(5) *Philosophy and Social Criticism* 6.

[33] Dauenhauer, B, 'Paul Ricoeur' in EN Zalta (ed), *The Stanford Encyclopedia of Philosophy*, Winter 2005 edn, available at http://plato.stanford.edu/?archives/?win2005/?entries/?ricoeur.

[34] Franko Aas, K, 'From Narrative to Database: Technological Change and Penal Culture' (2004) 6(4) *Punishment and Society* 386.

file that forms the basis of all administrative decision making. Furthermore, because it is necessary for the state to assume that the information contained in an individual's file is accurate, the categorical or administrative identity that emerges from that file must be preferred to any alternative narrative account. Someone may regard herself, for example, as a good mother who has made a new life for her children by moving to another country and earning money by cleaning other people's houses. For the state, however, if the information contained in a file says otherwise, then it is the categorical identity that will ultimately prevail: this same person is a single parent, unemployed and an illegal immigrant.

Although most people probably do not think of their relationship to the state (or private organisations) in terms of a competition between their own narrative accounts of themselves and some categorical identity that is constructed for them, this is largely because until very recently categorical identities and their real effects on everyday life have been relatively limited. These two conceptions of identity only come into competition when the categorical overlaps, contradicts and supplants the narrative, and so long as categorical identities are based on a narrow range of information, the possibility of such conflict remains limited. Yet as governments collect more and more personal information and as advances in information and communications technology make it easier to store, process and retrieve that information, the complexity and scope of the categorical identities they construct gradually increases, as does the potential for conflict with other conceptions of identity.

While personal narratives for most part remain the dominant means by which we understand identity in modern society, four related developments—all of which are taking place against a growing obsession with issues of security—have led to increased competition and conflict between narrative and categorical identities. First, advances in surveillance technology and techniques now make it possible for governments to collect many previously unavailable forms of information, such as digital recordings of activities in public (via CCTV), information about activities online (via surveillance programmes such as Carnivore) and records of communications between people (via mobile phone records, email, etc).

Second, developments in information technology have made it much easier for government agencies to share such information amongst themselves and with private institutions, and to draw additional information from the public domain. With the advent of sophisticated search engines, it is now possible for government officials and company employees to access large amounts of information about an individual from a vast array of sources. Furthermore, the ability to replicate and share digital information has meant that the idea of the single, comprehensive file has become largely redundant. Instead, categorical identities are increasingly based on the convergence of many separate bodies of information, all of which are brought together by a single identifier—such as a national insurance or social security number.

Third, advances in data matching and the development of so-called 'algorithmic surveillance' techniques have made it possible to automate many decision-making processes that rely on categorical identities.[35] Systems such as the US Computer Assisted Passenger Pre-screening System (CAPPS) programme are a good example of this, as are online application forms that compare the information submitted by an individual against multiple databases before making a decision on whether that individual is entitled to a particular welfare benefit or is required to pay more tax.

Finally, the failure of existing privacy and data protection frameworks to keep pace with these developments has meant that many individuals are unable to determine what exactly the state knows—or thinks it knows—about them. It is therefore difficult for individuals to contest with effectiveness the categorical identities that have been constructed for them.

Although not all of these developments are technologically determined, they can clearly be traced to recent advances in surveillance, information processing and digital communication. In the past such advances were largely driven by the desire of governments to streamline decision making and improve administrative efficiency. However, the extremely detailed, textured profiles of citizens that are now available to states hardly seem necessary merely to distinguish individuals from one another for the purposes of tax, benefits, voting, etc. Instead, since 9/11, it is security—defined in terms of the ability of the state to protect its citizens from internal and external threats—that is the primary rationale for increasing levels of state surveillance and improving data sharing. This has resulted in the rapid, simultaneous expansion and convergence of surveillance networks and databases in countries such as the United States and the United Kingdom.

Categorical identities have moreover become increasingly important, as they provide the basis for assessments of risk and pre-emptive measures aimed at increasing security. Perhaps the best example of this is the growing use of algorithmic surveillance in airports. Each time a passenger passes through airport security, various databases are drawn together, his or her categorical identity is reconstructed and automatically scrutinised, and then that identity is used to determine whether the passenger represents a threat to security. Passengers who are classified as such a threat can suddenly find themselves subjected to additional searches, questions and possible detention. Rarely, if ever, are individuals told why they are considered to be 'high risk', nor are they given opportunities to query the information or decision-making process that led to their 'high risk' classification. Once such a categorical identity has been established, it trumps all other competing accounts of the individual, at least insofar as matters of security are concerned.[36]

---

[35] See Norris, C, 'Algorithmic Surveillance' (1995) 20 *Criminal Justice Matters* 7–8; and Norris, C, Moran, J and Armstrong, G, 'Algorithmic Surveillance: The Future of Automated Visual Surveillance' in C Norris, J Moran and G Armstrong (eds), *Surveillance, Closed Circuit Television and Social Control* (Ashgate, Aldershot, 1998) 255–76.

[36] It is important to note that the distinction between narrative and categorical identities can never be an absolute one. Clearly, some markers of identity that are typically used as the basis for the construction of categorical identities, such as race, can be self-defined and, as such, are products of personal narratives. As a consequence, although acknowledging that the basic distinction between

The growing reliance on categorical identities has many serious implications.[37] As Calhoun has observed, the use of categorical identities has a tendency to produce repressive and discriminatory outcomes because the very notion of categorical identities favours sameness over difference and regards identity as a function of membership of a group:

> [The imposition of categorical identities] allows a kind of abstraction from the concrete interactions and social relationships within which identities are constantly renegotiated, in which individuals present one identity as more salient than another, and within which individuals achieve some personal sense of continuity and balance among their various sorts of identities ... The abstractness of categories encourages framing claims about them as though they offer a kind of trump card over the other identities of individuals addressed by them. This encourages an element of repression within the powerful categorical identities.[38]

As a case in point, a bank manager who must decide whether or not to grant a personal loan may not be willing (or allowed) to take into consideration the applicant's own account of his or her financial history; but the bank manager will almost certainly base the decision on a categorical identity made up of the applicant's credit rating, account history, employment status, etc. Even if the manager believes the applicant is sincere when he or she promises to repay the loan on time, and even if the manager believes the applicant has the means to do so, the categorical identity will almost certainly remain the primary determinant, and the loan may be refused.

Aside from having the effect of reducing the applicant to a handful of numerical indicators, this process of decision making is extremely hard to challenge.[39] Regardless of how implausible the categorisation, it typically is not the organisation that utilises the classification that must justify decisions but rather the individual in question who must prove that he or she been wrongly identified—as someone who is a credit risk, who requires regular tax audits, who should be on a no-fly list, etc. Furthermore, as the number of databases increases and the linkages

narrative and categorical identities is necessary if we are to fully understand the threat posed by various forms of surveillance and security measures, the line between the two is inevitably indistinct (particularly where a personal narrative is informed by official classification processes).

[37] One reason why categorical identities may have become more prominent in recent years—at least in terms of their use by the state and law enforcement agencies—is due to the declining use of 'human intelligence' since the end of the Cold War. Technological advances that have made electronic surveillance easier and cheaper have combined with a general 'technological ideology' to shift resources away from the use of human agents—such as informants and eavesdroppers—towards greater and greater financial and organisational investment in sophisticated surveillance devices and computer software. As a result, in many instances categorical identities become increasingly important simply because there are no available alternatives. I am indebted to Kevin Haggerty for this observation.

[38] Calhoun, CJ, *Critical Social Theory: Culture, History, and the Challenge of Difference* (Oxford, Blackwells, 1995) 220–1.

[39] Of course, it is important not to take the argument in favour of the narrative identity too far. The point here is not to suggest that we should rely only on narrative identities and ignore other information but rather to caution against the unquestioning reliance on categorical identities and the temptation of using them as trumps in decision-making. I am grateful to Simon Cole for alerting me to the danger of privileging personal narratives and thereby lapsing into 'wishy-washy humanism'.

between them become more complex and well established, it also becomes difficult for individuals to determine why they have been classified in a particular way in the first place. Credit records are, for example, now based on information drawn from a vast array of sources, making it extremely difficult for the average person to uncover where any 'black mark' may have come from.[40]

Taken to an extreme, the use of sophisticated categorical identities by the state and private companies has the potential to undermine the way in which ordinary individuals understand themselves. Confronted with a world in which identity is increasingly defined according to the information contained in databases, where routine decisions are made by algorithms rather than by people, it becomes progressively more difficult for individuals effectively to assert alternative visions of themselves.[41] If an 'intelligent' data-matching process that draws on a vast array of interconnected databases determines that I am a potential security risk, how do I deny this? Do I question the information on which the decision is based? The decision-making process itself? What if the information is correct and the decision is, on its face, reasonable, but wrong?[42] How do I explain, for example, that although I may have been interested in extremist politics as a student, I have now disavowed them? Or even more problematically, how do I argue that I still subscribe to radical political ideas but am not a terrorist risk because of a commitment to non-violence? Like a criminal record, the categorical identity has the potential to rob individuals of the right to define themselves beyond its confines and to develop as individuals.[43]

Although various social, political and technological changes have contributed to the growing importance of categorical identities over the past 40 years, developments since 9/11 threaten to tip the balance even more in favour of categorical identities. Looked at through a different lens, it is also possible to characterise

---

[40] Furthermore, as David Philips has usefully observed, although in many jurisdictions insurance companies and banks are obliged to reveal the information that they have used to reach decisions about offering insurance or providing loans, they are not required to disclose the algorithms that attribute relative weight and then categorise individuals according to that information. See? Phillips, D, 'Privacy, Surveillance, or Visibility: New Information Environments in the Light of Queer Theory', Paper presented at the annual meeting of the International Communication Association, New York City, available at http://www.allacademic.com/meta/p12412_index.html.

[41] This is a point that has also been made by Philip N Howard, who has suggested that, by its very nature, 'electronic technology may favour categorical identities more than dense social networks.' See Howard (2003) 219.

[42] One response to this question—and to many of the concerns raised about the use of categorical identities in this chapter—is to suggest that the problem lies not with the use of categories per se but rather with the fact that they are simply not detailed enough. If, for example, the state knew a great deal more about us than it does now and was therefore able to construct even more sophisticated categorical identities for each of us, would or should we object? I am grateful to Kevin Haggerty for raising this line of questioning. Although it is beyond the scope of this chapter to consider the argument in full, one response might be that the cost in terms of privacy that we would have to surrender in order for such a category to be constructed would simply outweigh the benefits of having more accurate, and only possibly less reductive, categorical identities.

[43] Taking this argument to its extreme, categorical identities can generate digital shadows of ourselves—or as Deleuze prefers to call them, 'dividuals'—that are stored within databases and can be created, altered and shared without our knowledge or consent. See Deleuze, G, 'Postscript on the Societies of Control' (1992) 59 *October* 3.

these changes in terms of the demise of administrative discretion and the emergence of a deep organisational reliance on automated decision making. Legislation such as the USA PATRIOT Act and the Anti-Terrorism, Crime and Security Act is significant not only because it seeks to remove barriers to information sharing and to promote co-operation between law enforcement agencies, but also because it helps to reinforce the view that categorical identities based on information obtained through surveillance and generated by data-matching techniques are the only appropriate basis of state–individual interaction. The pursuit of security along these lines is dangerous not simply because it undermines claims to individual privacy, but because it threatens to normalise and make ubiquitous a way of constructing identity that is inherently dehumanising and has the potential to institutionalise various forms of cultural and ethnic discrimination.

Faced with a growing emphasis on security and a steadily expanding network of state and commercial surveillance, what chance do we have for resisting the shift from narrative to categorical constructions of identity? The most obvious answer to this question is of course to bolster existing privacy protections with a view to making it more difficult for the state and private companies to acquire and share personal information. However, many of the agencies and institutions that represent a threat to privacy are powerful, well funded and closely integrated into larger state systems. Any attempt to limit them is therefore unlikely to be very effective. This is a point that is well-illustrated by the recent case of the Total Information Awareness (TIA) programme in the United States, which aimed at vastly improving the US government's data-mining capacities. Although the Defence Advanced Research Projects Agency (DARPA) was forced by Congress to suspend development of the TIA system following an outcry from civil libertarians and journalists, there can be little doubt that many of the activities planned for the TIA are now being performed by other government agencies.[44] As Galison and Minow have observed,

> Like a ball of mercury, the data-mining activities scatter and grow less visible once subjected to pressure. Public concerns about privacy have generated more secrecy about the government activities that jeopardise personal privacy.[45]

Given the difficulty of comprehensively protecting privacy interests through legislation and regulation, it is clear that a multi-pronged strategy is necessary to respond effectively to the growing obsession with security and surveillance. Legal and institutional reform must be accompanied by other measures that are designed to foster a general respect for privacy and to mitigate the dehumanising effects of categorical identities. With this larger aim in mind, the following section

---

[44] One of the major opponents of the TIA was the American Civil Liberties Union (ACLU), which argued that the sort of data-mining programme envisaged for the TIA would 'amount to a picture of your life so complete it's equivalent to somebody following you around all day with a video camera'. See Baer, S, 'Broader US Spy Initiative Debated; Poindexter leads Project to Assess Electronic Data, Detect Possible Terrorists; Civil Liberties Concerns Raised', *Baltimore Sun*, 5 January 2003, 1A (quoting Jay Stenley of the ACLU).

[45] Galison and Minow (2005) 266.

will consider several models of privacy and their implications for both security and personal identity.

III. PRIVACY, IDENTITY AND INFORMATIONAL SELF-DETERMINATION

1. The Value of Privacy

Privacy rights are notoriously difficult to define, in part because they often overlap with other substantive rights—such as the right to liberty—that are both well established and well defined, and also because there is often dispute over what it is that privacy seeks to protect.[46] According to Thomson, a leading proponent of the right to privacy, it is impossible to define privacy because the right to privacy is in fact composed of a cluster of other rights, typically property rights and the right to bodily integrity.[47] As such, when we claim that our privacy has been violated, what we really mean to say is that some other substantive right has been infringed upon. In this sense, privacy is a fundamentally derivative concept.[48]

One approach to the question of defining privacy is to regard privacy as the control of personal information.[49] In Westin's now famous book *Privacy and Freedom*, he argues that privacy is fundamentally concerned with the ability of 'individuals, groups or institutions to determine for themselves when, how and to what extent information about them is communicated to others'.[50] This view has recently been taken further by Parent, who suggests that one of the fundamental conditions of privacy is the ability to prevent others from acquiring or holding undocumented personal information about oneself.[51] For Parent, such personal information is necessarily factual and includes such things as details about one's health, marital and financial status, educational background and sexual orientation. While he does not go so far as to claim that there is a clear legal or moral right to privacy, Parent makes clear that the loss of control over such personal information can lead to far-reaching consequences and very real effects for the lives of individuals:

[46] Feldman, D, 'Secrecy, Dignity or Autonomy? Views of Privacy as a Civil Liberty' (1994) 47(2) *Current Legal Problems* 41; Feldman, D, 'Privacy-related Rights and their Social Value' in P Birks (ed), *Privacy and Loyalty* (Oxford, Clarendon Press, 1997) 15. See also arguments by Ronald Dworkin concerning the problems inherent in the relationship between privacy and liberty: Dworkin, R, *Taking Rights Seriously* (London, Duckworth, 1977) 266–78.

[47] Thomson, J, 'The Right to Privacy' (1975) 4 *Philosophy and Public Affairs* 295–314.

[48] *Ibid*. For a detailed critique of this position, see Scanlon, T, 'Thomson on Privacy' (1975) 4 *Philosophy and Public Affairs* 315–22; and Inness, J, *Privacy, Intimacy and Isolation* (Oxford, Oxford University Press, 1992).

[49] See, for example: Westin, A, *Privacy and Freedom* (New York, Atheneum, 1967); Fried (1970); and Parent, W, 'Privacy, Morality and the Law' (1983) 12(4) *Philosophy and Public Affairs* 269–88. For a brief synopsis of Westin's work on privacy, see DeCew, J, 'Privacy' in EN Zalta (ed), *The Stanford Encyclopedia of Philosophy*, Fall 2006 edn, available at http://plato.stanford.edu/archives/fall2006/entries/privacy.

[50] Westin (1967) 7.

[51] Parent (1983).

> [I]f others manage to obtain sensitive personal knowledge about us they will by that
> very fact acquire power over us. Their power could then be used to our disadvantage.
> The possibilities for exploitation become very real. The definite connection between
> harm and the invasion of privacy explains why we place a value on not having undoc-
> umented personal information about ourselves widely known.[52]

In contrast to this emphasis on the control of information, other writers have suggested that privacy is best understood in terms of its connection to ideas of personal autonomy, self-determination and human dignity. This approach, which
frequently leads to privacy being framed in terms of the right to a private or family life, has tended to dominate legal discussion of privacy in both the US Supreme
Court and the European Court of Human Rights. Privacy in this sense goes well
beyond control over information and looks to provide individuals with the means
to protect themselves against intrusions that might compromise their independence and represent an affront to their sense of human dignity.

According to Feldman, privacy rights are important because they enable individuals and groups to determine and, to some extent at least, control the boundaries between different interlocking social spheres.[53] In this regard, he argues, it is
important to recognise the communitarian aspects of the idea of privacy. If we
view society as a 'community of communities', made up of groups with different
memberships that may or may not overlap, then privacy provides the mechanism
by which these groups are able to preserve their independence while also interacting with one another. At the individual level as well, a notion of privacy is valuable
insofar as it enables us to limit the extent to which we are subjected to the demands
and judgements of others.

Within this framework, privacy rights deserve protection because they are essential for the maintenance of personal autonomy and enable individuals to maintain
a range of different and valuable social relationships.[54] If we are constantly required
to respond to the expectations of those around us, our choices are unlikely to be
free, nor are we likely to develop a capacity for self-determination or a degree of
self-fulfilment. Privacy is hence essential for the establishment and maintenance of
a unique sense of self. Indeed, as Galison and Minow have observed, privacy and
the construction of personal identity are intimately connected:

> Even though its meanings are multiple and complex, privacy in closely connected
> with the emergence of a modern sense of self. Its jeopardy signals serious risk to the
> very conditions people need to enjoy the kind of self that can experiment, relax, form
> and enjoy intimate connections, and practice the development of ideas and beliefs
> for valued expression.[55]

Of course, these two approaches—privacy as the control of information and privacy as the protection of individual autonomy—are not entirely incompatible

---

[52] *Ibid*, 276.
[53] See Feldman (1994) 41; and Feldman (1997) 15.
[54] Feldman (1994) 53–9.
[55] Galison and Minow (2005) 258.

with one another. If one views control over personal information not merely in terms of a narrow conception of ownership or of secrecy but rather as essential to the maintenance of individual autonomy and dignity, then it follows that spheres of privacy are as much about controlling how information about oneself is communicated to the outside world as they are about controlling who has access to us and our activities. After all, as Lustgarten and Leigh argue, the collection of personal information without an individual's consent can amount to a serious affront to human dignity and demonstrate an absence of respect for their need for personal autonomy:

> Imagine being unable to draw the curtain in your bedroom, so that others can see you naked at any time of their choosing. The fear and revulsion this image evokes has little to do with the beauty or otherwise of one's body, but everything to do with one's sense of *self*. If I have no control over what is known about me, I am seriously diminished as a person both in my own eyes and in those which are capable of intruding upon me.[56]

If we accept this view of privacy, then it follows that there is a clear relationship between privacy and the construction of personal identity. As we move from very private spheres (for example, the home) into increasingly less private ones (such as the workplace), each step requires us to surrender some amount of control over information about ourselves, information that can then be shared and its meaning potentially transformed. The more public my activities, the more susceptible they are to being known, interpreted and judged by others, with the result that my capacity to define myself—to construct my own narrative identity or to resist a categorical identity that might be imposed upon me by the state—diminishes. This is of course one of the reasons why we often feel most secure in the context of the home. It is not simply because we have considerable control over the space around us, but also because we can more or less be who we want to be.

Privacy rights are valuable then not simply because they are essential to the maintenance of personal autonomy or the defence of human dignity, or even because they endow us with some modicum of control over information about ourselves. Privacy is important because of its relationship to the construction of identity and because of the way in which it helps us to develop and defend particular visions of self. In making a demand for privacy, we reassert control over information about ourselves and make it more difficult for those who would seek to categorise us or reduce our identity to a list of particular traits or characteristics.

2. An Expanded Model of Privacy

The relatively broad conception of privacy outlined above may go some way in drawing a connection between privacy and human dignity—and hence human

---

[56] Lustgarten, L and Leigh, I, *In from the Cold: National Security and Parliamentary Democracy* (Oxford, Clarendon Press, 1994) 39–40.

rights—but it is unlikely on its own to provide an adequate basis for resisting the pressures of security and the attendant drive from narrative to categorical notions of identity. There are two reasons for this. First, central to even the broadest conception of privacy is the assumption that it is possible to agree on what constitutes personal information deserving of protection. Yet, as Nissenbaum has argued, the meaning of any piece of information is at least in part determined by its context and the manner in which it is disclosed. The fact that I choose to behave or present myself in a certain way in one context does not mean that I intend to be defined by that behaviour and identity in all other contexts. As Schoeman has rightly observed:

> A person can be active in the gay pride movement in San Francisco, but be private about her sexual preferences vis-à-vis her family and co-workers in Sacramento. A professor may be highly visible to other gays at the gay bar but discreet about sexual orientation at the university. Surely the streets and newspapers of San Francisco are public places as are the gay bars in the quiet university town. Does appearing in some public settings as a gay activist mean that the person concerned has waived her rights to civil inattention, to feeling violated if confronted in another setting?[57]

In a world in which surveillance is becoming ubiquitous and information can be transmitted almost instantaneously to a multitude of people at virtually zero cost, it is exceptionally easy for that information to be divorced from its context and for it to take on new and unexpected meanings. As a consequence, if we are to maintain any sense of privacy or control over how our identity is constructed, it is important to develop a concept of privacy that recognises that the meaning of information is heavily context-dependent and can easily be transformed, abused and/or misinterpreted.

Nissenbaum has suggested that the solution to this problem is to develop a model of privacy that is capable of maintaining 'contextual integrity', which is defined as 'compatibility with presiding norms of information appropriateness and distribution'.[58] According to this principle, we should move away from thinking about privacy in terms of dichotomies—such as sensitive and non-sensitive information, or distinctly private and distinctly public spaces—and instead recognise that all areas of life are subject to flows of information:

> Observing the texture of people's lives, we find them not only crossing dichotomies, but moving about, into, and out of a plurality of distinct realms. They are at home with families, they go to work, they seek medical care, visit friends, consult with psychiatrists, talk with lawyers, go to the bank, attend religious services, vote, shop, and more. Each of these spheres, realms, or contexts involves, indeed may even be defined by, a distinct set of norms, which governs its various aspects such as roles, expectations, actions, and practices. For certain contexts, such as the highly ritualized settings of many church services, these norms are explicit and quite specific. For

---

[57] Schoeman, F, 'Gossip and Privacy' in RF Goodman and A Ben-Ze'ev (eds), *Good Gossip* (Lawrence, University Press of Kansas, 1994) 73 (quoted in Nissenbaum, H, 'Privacy as Contextual Integrity' (2004) 79(1) *Washington Law Review* 101–39, 122).
[58] Nissenbaum (2004) 137.

others, the norms may be implicit, variable, and incomplete (or partial) . . . Contexts, or spheres, offer a platform for a normative account of privacy in terms of contextual integrity.[59]

The second, related reason why many existing models of privacy are unable to respond to the challenges of modern surveillance and the current overwhelming drive for security is that they—unlike many of the technologies that now threaten privacy—are rooted in an increasingly anachronistic view of the distinction between the public and the private. Modern information flows do not respect traditional physical boundaries: for example, when I surf publicly accessible internet sites in the privacy of my own home, am I moving in a private or a public domain? Moreover, many state institutions now draw on personal information that is collected by the private sector or has otherwise found its way into the public domain. As a consequence, privacy protections that can only be enforced against public bodies—such as the data protection provisions currently in operation in the United Kingdom—are severely limited in their application.[60]

In light of these difficulties, it is clear that if we are concerned about privacy and the effect that the current obsession with security is having on our ability to maintain control over our own identities, we must develop a new vision of privacy that recognises the importance of context and the increasing irrelevance of traditional notions of the public/private divide. The language and discourse of privacy must, as a basic starting point, acknowledge the deep connection between information and identity, while privacy protections must recognise that the meaning of information and informational norms—that is, the norms of appropriateness and distribution—vary according to context. Such a vision of privacy would represent a significant departure from the models that underpin the privacy and data protection laws of the United States and the United Kingdom. Furthermore, it almost certainly represents a departure from the way in which most people think about questions of privacy in their everyday lives. Yet just as we have come to accept that the nature and extent of surveillance has changed in recent years, so too must society begin to think more creatively and radically about the concept of privacy and the value of identity.

3. Informational Self-determination

Assuming that we are prepared to embrace a concept of privacy such as that outlined above, the question then arises as to how best to protect the privacy interests that arise from such a model. It is tempting to assume that all that is needed to achieve this are more expansive privacy laws. However, as Galison and Minow have argued, it may be possible to enact legislation that discourages the state from

---

[59] *Ibid*, 119–20.

[60] Furthermore, given the pressures associated with the pursuit of security, it makes little sense to entrust the state—via the courts or some external agency such as the Office of the Data Protection Commissioner—to both define and then police the boundary between the public and the private.

invading the privacy of individuals, but it is impossible to construct a system of laws that will provide for the complete protection of privacy or resolve the inevitable conflict between privacy and the demands of security.[61] Instead, what is needed is a multi-dimensional strategy that not only seeks to transform the way in which the law defines and protects privacy, but also generates a general demand for privacy within society:

> Without deliberate effort [to promote privacy] a downward spiral can become a vicious circle, eroding privacy through legal permission, technological access to unprecedented amounts of personal information, and diminishing public expectations of privacy. Deliberate initiatives in law, technology, and market and educational strategies designed to generate desire could, in contrast, promote an upward spiral, moving up while rotating back and forth between positive desires on the one side and legal/technological constraints on the other.[62]

Although it is well beyond the scope of this chapter to outline a comprehensive strategy for the promotion of individual privacy, one way in which privacy could be enhanced in the United States and the United Kingdom is the introduction of a free-standing right to informational self-determination. Insofar as such a right would increase the amount of control that individuals are able to exercise over personal information, its introduction would constitute an important step towards the development of a vision of privacy that properly recognises the fluid and contextual nature of information in modern society.

As has already been noted, in order to resist the unwanted imposition of a categorical identity, it is crucial that individuals are able to determine or at least have a say in what sorts of personal information are held by the state and, even more importantly, how that information is used. While data protection laws go some way to providing this, they typically focus only on regulating the manner in which information is acquired; the protection they offer to individuals is therefore limited. Once information has been shared and is in the public domain, individuals may be able to take action against the body that 'leaked' the information, but there is little they can do to prevent others from dealing in their personal information or passing it on. Consequently, what is needed in addition to data protection is some recognition that individuals 'own' information about themselves and should consequently have control about over what is ultimately done with that information.

For an example of how a right to informational self-determination might work in practice, one need only go so far as Germany, which legally recognised such a right over 20 years ago. In 1983, it was held by the Federal Constitutional Court that all German citizens have a right to what was referred to as 'informational self-determination'. Derived from Articles 1(1) and 2(1) of the Basic Law,[63] the right

---

[61] Galison and Minow (2005) 260.

[62] *Ibid*, 261.

[63] According to Art 1(1) of the Basic Law for the Federal Republic of Germany (Grundgesetz), 'Human dignity shall be inviolable. To respect and protect it shall be the duty of all state authority.' Further to this, Article 2(2) states: 'Every person shall have the right to free development of his personality insofar as he does not violate the rights of others or offend against the constitutional order or the moral law.'

is regarded as a personal right (*Persönlichkeitsrecht*) and is limited only by the 'predominant public interest'. In justifying the establishment of this new right, the court was clear in its desire to link issues of autonomy with control of information and the development of self:

> Who can not certainly overlook which information related to him or her is known to certain segments of his social environment, and who is not able to assess to a certain degree the knowledge of his potential communication partners, can be essentially hindered in his capability to plan and to decide. The right of informational self-determination stands against a societal order and its underlying legal order in which citizens could not know any longer who what and when in what situations knows about them.[64]

Clearly, this German conception of the right to informational self-determination goes a long way in addressing many of the concerns raised by Nissenbaum about the need to acknowledge the contextual dimension of personal information.[65] In addition, it avoids one of the great ironies of traditional privacy rights—that individuals are required to identify what they regard as private in order to protect themselves from unwanted intrusions, despite the fact that the mere act of claiming something is private tells the state that it is something the individual regards as valuable. The German formulation, however, reverses this burden by requiring the state—or any other user of personal information—to justify why the use does not infringe upon an individual's autonomy and his or her expectation to be able to control how that personal information is used. Finally, the right to informational self-determination has the advantage of not being contingent on transgressions of some imagined boundary between private and public space; it is therefore better equipped to protect individual interests in a world of information flows.

Given the existence of this right, it is perhaps unsurprising that despite similar calls for an expansion in state surveillance and the extension of existing security legislation, no equivalent of the USA PATRIOT Act or the Anti-terrorism, Crime and Security Act has as yet been enacted in Germany. In the face of a strong constitutional commitment to the idea that individuals have a right to determine how

---

[64] BVerfGE 65, 1.

[65] It is important to note, however, that concerns about the scope of the right to informational self-determination and the operation of the public interest exception have been raised by a number of German commentators. According to Wolf-Dieter Narr, for example, in recognising the right to informational self-determination the Federal Court has in effect helped to pave the way for what he refers to as 'Vorwärtsverrechtlichung' or 'forward legislation'. For Narr, regulation designed to ensure that police and security services are acting in the public interest have ironically led to a situation in which there has been an increase in police powers and what has been described by various commentators as an 'over-regulated absence of regulation'. On these points, see: Narr, W-D, 'Wir Bürger als Sicherheitsrisiko: Rückblick und Ausblick' (1998) 60 *Bürgerrechte & Polizei/CILIP* 30–40, available at http://www.cilip.de/ausgabe/60/narr60.htm; Pütter, N *et al*, 'Bekämpfungs-Recht und Rechtsstaat. Vorwärtsverrechtlichung in gebremsten Bahnen?' (2005) 82 *Bürgerrechte & Polizei/CILIP* 6–15; Kutscha, M, 'Auf dem Weg zu einem Polizeistaat neuen Typs?' (2001) *Blätter für deutsche und internationale Politik* 214–21, available at http://www.blaetter-online.de/archiv.php?jahr=2001&ausgabe=02; and Roggan, F, *Auf dem legalen Weg in einen Polizeistaat. Entwicklung des Rechts der Inneren Sicherheit* (Bonn, Pahl-Rugenstein, 2000).

information about themselves is used, it is difficult for the government, regardless of the public mood, to centralise the collection of personal details and remove institutional checks on the sharing of information in the way that has occurred in the United States and the United Kingdom since 9/11. Recognising such a right in the US or UK context may not provide an unassailable defence against the excessive surveillance demands of the state or the growing use of categorical identities, but it deserves serious consideration if only because it would add a new and substantial level of protection for privacy at a time when other protections are either failing or being fatally undermined.

In addition, thinking about privacy in terms of informational self-determination and attempting to shift current political and legal debates such that the onus is on the state better to justify the expansion of security-related surveillance powers may have other benefits that go beyond bolstering existing individual privacy protections. Closely related to the idea of informational self-determination is the notion that it is possible to own information about oneself, and as such one of the arguments in favour of the new right is that it may open the door to broader discussions about the possible economic value of privacy.

At present, we assume that once an individual (either willingly or unwillingly) reveals information about himself or herself, that individual's interest in and claim over that information is substantially weakened. He or she may attempt to prevent others from receiving that information or to stop it from being used by certain organisations, but there is no suggestion that such assertions of control are based on clear ownership or concepts of property. If, however, someone who possessed or used information about another individual were required to compensate that person financially—that is, required to pay for the privilege of using someone else's personal information and asserting a form of control over it—then it is possible that the use of categorical identities and certain types of surveillance and data matching would naturally be constrained.[66] Governments and organisations would, it seems reasonable to assume, think twice about acquiring information or sharing it if, in just the same way that copyright royalties are paid to artists, they may also have to pay the individuals to whom the information pertains.

Although such a market in personal information may be no more likely to come into being than Brin's 'transparent society', thinking about the applications and limits of the right to informational self-determination along these lines does provide the basis for the formulation/conception/conceptualisation of new ways of both resisting the imposition of categorical identities and reasserting the collective and individual interest in privacy.

---

[66] I am indebted to Kevin Haggerty first for raising the question of a potential market in personal information, and for providing various insights into the implications for privacy and surveillance of making users of that information pay for it. It is an intriguing and powerful idea that I hope he will take up in print.

CONCLUSION

In this chapter, an attempt has been made to show how the pursuit of security and the continued expansion in state surveillance affect privacy and identity. Although it is clear that legislation such as the Anti-terrorism, Crime and Security Act and the USA PATRIOT Act represents a threat to many well-established human rights—such as the right to silence and the right to a fair trial—there is a danger that because liberals and civil libertarians continue to focus much of their attention on the threat to these fundamental civil liberties, we risk losing sight of the fact that many other less well-defined but no less important rights—including privacy—are being gradually worn away. Furthermore, it is important to acknowledge that although the events of 9/11 were enormously significant in terms of shifting the balance in the security–rights debate, many of the threats to individual freedom and autonomy that now appear so clearly have in fact been present for a very long time.

Security, surveillance, identity and privacy are intimately connected. As states attempt to increase their ability to defend their citizens from external and internal threats, they also necessarily risk undermining the ability of the individuals within their borders to live free from scrutiny, suspicion, categorisation and discrimination. Many existing privacy protections are incapable of addressing the underlying challenges posed by the pursuit of security because they were developed during a time in which the distinction between the public and private was much clearer than it is today, and because the costs of acquiring, processing and sharing information were once much higher than they are today. If we are to maintain some degree of control about the way in which our identities are constructed and used, it is essential not only to begin to think about what identity and privacy mean, but also to take positive steps to develop legal and other means of resisting state demands to submit to categorisation and control. Unless we do so, regardless of whether we are more secure from physical threats, we may end up surrendering our identities—and in the process, surrender a part of ourselves.

REFERENCES

Alderman, E and Kennedy, C, *The Right to Privacy* (New York, Knopf, 1995).

Anderson, C, 'The Zen of Jeff Bezos', *Wired Magazine*, January 2005, available at http://www.wired.com/wired/archive/13.01/bezos.html.

Baer, S, 'Broader US Spy Initiative Debated; Poindexter leads Project to Assess Electronic Data, Detect Possible Terrorists; Civil Liberties Concerns Raised', *Baltimore Sun*, 5 January 2003.

Calhoun, CJ, *Critical Social Theory: Culture, History, and the Challenge of Difference* (Oxford, Blackwells, 1995).

Dauenhauer, B, 'Paul Ricoeur' in EN Zalta (ed), *The Stanford Encyclopedia of Philosophy*, Winter 2005 edn, available at http://plato.stanford.edu/archives/win2005/entries/ricoeur.

Davies, S, *Big Brother: Britain's Web of Surveillance and the New Technological Order* (London, Pan Books, 1996).

DeCew, J, *In Pursuit of Privacy: Law, Ethics, and the Rise of Technology* (Ithaca, Cornell University Press, 1997).

—— 'Privacy' in EN Zalta (ed), *The Stanford Encyclopedia of Philosophy*, Fall 2006 edn, available at http://plato.stanford.edu/archives/fall2006/entries/privacy.

Deleuze, G, 'Postscript on the Societies of Control' (1992) 59 *October* 3.

Doyle, C, 'USA Patriot Act: A Sketch', (Congressional Research Service report RS21203 for Congress, 2005).

—— 'USA Patriot Act Sunset: A Sketch' (Congressional Research Service report RS21704 for Congress, 2005).

Dworkin, R, *Taking Rights Seriously* (London, Duckworth, 1977).

Egger, SA, 'A Working Definition of Serial Murder and the Reduction of Linkage Blindness' (1984) 12 *Journal of Police Science and Administration* 348–57.

—— *Serial Murder: An Elusive Phenomenon* (Westport, CT, Praeger, 1990).

Feldman, D, 'Secrecy, Dignity or Autonomy? Views of Privacy as a Civil Liberty' (1994) 47(2) *Current Legal Problems* 41.

—— 'Privacy-related Rights and their Social Value' in P Birks (ed), *Privacy and Loyalty* (Oxford, Clarendon Press, 1997).

Franko Aas, K, 'From Narrative to Database: Technological Change and Penal Culture' (2004) 6(4) *Punishment and Society* 386.

Fried, C, *An Anatomy of Values* (Cambridge, Harvard University Press, 1970).

Galison, P and Minow, M, 'Our Privacy, Ourselves in the Age of Technological Intrusions' in R Ashby Wilson, *Human Rights in the 'War on Terror'* (Cambridge, Cambridge University Press, 2005).

Garland, D, *The Culture of Control* (Oxford, Oxford University Press, 2001).

GeneWatch UK, *The Police National DNA Database: Balancing Crime Detection, Human Rights and Privacy* (Buxton, GeneWatch UK, 2005).

Gilliom, J, 'Struggling with Surveillance: Resistance, Consciousness and Identity' in K Haggerty and R Ericson (eds), *The New Politics of Surveillance and Visibility* (Toronto, University of Toronto Press, 2006) 111–40.

Goold, B, 'Open to All? Regulating Open Street CCTV and the Case for "Symmetrical Surveillance"' (2006) 25(1) *Criminal Justice Ethics* 3–17.

Higgs, E, 'The Rise of the Information State: The Development of Central State Surveillance of the Citizen in England, 1500–2000' (2001) 14(2) *Journal of Historical Sociology* 175–97.

Inness, J, *Privacy, Intimacy and Isolation* (Oxford, Oxford University Press, 1992).

Kutscha, M, 'Auf dem Weg zu einem Polizeistaat neuen Typs?' (2001) *Blätter für deutsche und internationale Politik* 214–21, available at http://www.blaetter-online.de/archiv.php?jahr=2001&ausgabe=02.

Levi, M and Wall, DS, 'Technologies, Security, and Privacy in the Post-September 11 European Information Society' (2004) 31(2) *Journal of Law and Society* 203.

Lustgarten, L and Leigh, I, *In from the Cold: National Security and Parliamentary Democracy* (Oxford, Clarendon Press, 1994).

Lyon, D, *Surveillance Society: Monitoring Everyday Life* (Buckingham, Open University Press, 2001).

—— 'Surveillance Studies: Understanding Visibility, Mobility and the Phenetic Fix' (2003) 1(1) *Surveillance and Society* 3.

McCartney, C 'Forensic DNA Sampling and the England and Wales National DNA Database: A Sceptical Approach' (2004) 12 *Critical Criminology* 157–78.

Narr, W-D, 'Wir Bürger als Sicherheitsrisiko: Rückblick und Ausblick' (1998) 60 *Bürgerrechte & Polizei/CILIP* 30–40, available at http://www.cilip.de/ausgabe/60/narr60.htm.

Nissenbaum, H, 'Privacy as Contextual Integrity' (2004) 79(1) *Washington Law Review* 101–39.

Norris, C, 'Algorithmic Surveillance' (1995) 20 *Criminal Justice Matters* 7–8.

Norris, C, Moran, J and Armstrong, G, 'Algorithmic Surveillance: The Future of Automated Visual Surveillance' in C Norris, J Moran and G Armstrong (eds), *Surveillance, Closed Circuit Television and Social Control* (Ashgate, Aldershot, 1998) 255–76.

Parent, W, 'Privacy, Autonomy, and Self-Concept' (1983) 24 *American Philosophical Quarterly* 81–9.

—— 'Privacy, Morality and the Law' (1983) 12(4) *Philosophy and Public Affairs* 269–88.

Phillips, D, 'Privacy, Surveillance, or Visibility: New Information Environments in the Light of Queer Theory', Paper presented at the annual meeting of the International Communication Association, New York City, available at http://www.allacademic.com/meta/p12412_index.html.

Privacy International, 'Increased Abuse of Data and Disregard for Protections', press statement, 9 August 2004, available at http://www.privacyinternational.org.

—— 'Terrorism Profile: US' (3 October 2005), available at http://www.privacyinternational.org.

Pütter, N *et al*, 'Bekämpfungs-Recht und Rechtsstaat. Vorwärtsverrechtlichung in gebremsten Bahnen?' (2005) 82 *Bürgerrechte & Polizei/CILIP* 6–15.

Ricoeur, P, 'Reflections on a New Ethos for Europe' (1995) 21(5) *Philosophy and Social Criticism* 6.

Roggan, F, *Auf dem legalen Weg in einen Polizeistaat. Entwicklung des Rechts der Inneren Sicherheit* (Bonn, Pahl-Rugenstein, 2000).

Rose, N, *Powers of Freedom: Reframing Political Thought* (Cambridge, Cambridge University Press, 1999).

Scanlon, T, 'Thomson on Privacy' (1975) 4 *Philosophy and Public Affairs* 315–22.

Schoeman, F, 'Gossip and Privacy' in RF Goodman and A Ben-Ze'ev (eds), *Good Gossip* (Lawrence, University Press of Kansas, 1994).

Stanley, J and Steinhardt, B, 'Bigger Monster, Weaker Chains: The Growth of an American Surveillance Society' (ACLU Technology and Liberty Program, 2003).

Tempest, M, 'Britain Facing "Most Sustained Threat since WWII" says Reid', *The Guardian*, 9 August 2006, available at http://politics.guardian.co.uk/terrorism/story/0,,1840482,00.html.

Thomson, J, 'The Right to Privacy' (1975) 4 *Philosophy and Public Affairs* 295–314.

Torpey, JC, *The Invention of the Passport: Surveillance, Citizenship and the State* (Cambridge, Cambridge University Press, 2000).

Westin, A, *Privacy and Freedom* (New York, Atheneum, 1967).

Williams, R, Johnson, P and Martin, P, 'Genetic Information and Crime Investigation' (University of Durham School of Applied Social Sciences, report, 2004).

4

Muslim Profiles Post-9/11: Is Racial Profiling an Effective Counter-terrorist Measure and Does It Violate the Right to be Free from Discrimination?

BERNARD E HARCOURT

INTRODUCTION

IN THE AFTERMATH of the London bombings in July 2005, Paul Sperry of the Hoover Institution, a respected public policy institute at Stanford University, defended the police profiling of young Muslim men in New York City subways as a matter of simple common sense. Writing in the pages of the *New York Times*, Sperry argued that any future terrorist offender is likely to be young, male and Muslim:

> Young Muslim men bombed the London tube, and young Muslim men attacked New York with planes in 2001. From everything we know about the terrorists who may be taking aim at our transportation system, they are most likely to be young Muslim men.[1]

It makes no sense, Sperry contends, to search old ladies or children. Instead, the police should target the high-risk population. Profiling, Sperry writes, is 'based on statistics. Insurance companies profile policyholders based on probability of risk. That's just smart business. Likewise, profiling passengers based on proven security risk is just smart law enforcement.'[2] A similar column appeared in the *Washington Post* the next day, arguing that 'politically correct screenings won't catch Jihadists':

> It is a simple statistical fact. Yes, you have your shoe-bomber, a mixed-race Muslim convert, who would not fit the profile. But the overwhelming odds are that the guy

---

[1] Sperry, P, 'When the Profile Fits the Crime', *New York Times*, 28 July 2005, available at http://www.nytimes.com/2005/07/28/opinion/28sperry.html.
[2] *Ibid.*

bent on blowing up your train traces his origins to the Islamic belt stretching from Mauritania to Indonesia.[3]

Using random bag searches in the New York subways, the column concludes, is 'simply nuts'.

New York City Police Commissioner Raymond Kelly couldn't disagree more:

> Look at the 9/11 hijackers. They came here. They shaved. They went to topless bars. They wanted to blend in. They wanted to look like they were part of the American dream. These are not dumb people. Could a terrorist dress up as a Hasidic Jew and walk into the subway, and not be profiled? Yes. I think profiling is just nuts.[4]

Racial profiling is, in Kelly's words, 'ineffective' because it assumes that terrorists are not going to adapt to changing circumstances and, as a result, puts the police one step behind the enemy. Racial profiling focuses on an 'unstable' trait—a trait that can easily be switched—which, as Malcolm Gladwell explains, is precisely 'what the jihads seemed to have done in London, when they switched to East Africans because the scrutiny of young Arab and Pakistani men grew too intense'.[5] Plus, Kelly adds, in New York City, profiling is simply impracticable:

> If you look at the London bombings, you have three British citizens of Pakistani descent. You have Germaine Lindsay [the fourth London suicide bomber], who is Jamaican. You have the next crew [in London], on July 21st, who are East African. You have a Chechen woman in Moscow in early 2004 who blows herself up in the subway station. So whom do you profile? Look at New York City. Forty per cent of New Yorkers are born outside the country. Look at the diversity here. Who am I supposed to profile?[6]

So, is racial profiling post-9/11 'just smart law enforcement'? Or is it 'just nuts'? Moreover, does profiling young Muslim men violate the principle of non-discrimination embedded in international human rights and domestic civil rights jurisprudence? These two questions, I argue, are inextricably linked, and the answer to the first resolves the second: there is no reliable empirical evidence that racial profiling is an effective counter-terrorism measure and no solid theoretical reason why it would be. The possibility of recruiting outside the profiled group and of substituting different modes of attack renders racial profiling in the counter-terrorism context suspect.

The fact is that defensive counter-terrorism measures are notoriously tricky. The spotty empirical evidence tends to show a strong potential for substitution effects. The installation of metal detectors in airports in 1973, for instance, pro-

---

[3] Krauthammer, C, 'Give Grandma a Pass', *Washington Post*, 29 July 2005, available at http://www.washingtonpost.com/wp-dyn/content/article/2005/07/28/AR2005072801786.html.

[4] Quoted in Gladwell, M, 'Troublemakers: What Pit Bulls can Teach us about Profiling', *The New Yorker*, 6 February 2006, available at http://www.newyorker.com/fact/content/articles/060206fa_fact.

[5] *Ibid.*

[6] *Ibid.*

duced a dramatic reduction in the number and rate of airplane hijackings across the globe[7] but also resulted in a sharp and proportionally larger increase in bombings, assassinations and hostage-taking incidents.[8] Target hardening of US embassies and missions abroad produced a transitory reduction in attacks on those sites but an increase in assassinations.[9] Retaliatory strikes produce a spike in short-term terrorist attacks that later level off to the earlier mean.[10] In addition, anecdotal evidence suggests that suicide bombers in Israel tended to be young militant Muslim men at first but now include more secular Palestinians, women and teenage girls.[11] A recent and thorough review of the empirical literature, using an approved Campbell Collaboration protocol,[12] concludes that 'some evaluated [defensive counter-terrorism] interventions either didn't work or sometimes *increased* the likelihood of terrorism and terrorism-related harm'.[13] In sum, counter-terrorism measures are potentially double-edged swords.

There is no empirical evidence whatsoever, nor a solid theoretical reason why racial profiling would be an effective measure—rather than a counter-productive step resulting in detrimental substitutions and increased terrorist attacks. As a result, racial profiling is neither 'just' smart law enforcement, nor 'just' nuts. It is an unknown quantity. And precisely for that reason, there is no justification for making the human rights and civil rights trade-offs associated with racial profiling.

An important point to emphasise is that the issue turns on an empirical and theoretical analysis of the effectiveness of racial profiling, not on a legal or doctrinal review of human rights or civil rights law. Naturally, this raises the larger issue of the relationship between, on the one hand, international human rights, civil rights or, more generally, formal legal discourse and, on the other hand, the empirical effectiveness of disciplinary practices—what is often referred to as the 'effectiveness debate', a debate that is at the very heart of this volume of essays on security

---

[7] Landes, W, 'An Economic Study of US Aircraft Hijacking, 1961–1976' (1978) 21(1) *Journal of Law and Economics* 1–31.

[8] Cauley, J and Im, EI, 'Intervention Policy Analysis of Skyjackings and Other Terrorist Incidents' (1988) 78 *American Economic Review* 27–31; Enders, W and Sandler, T, 'The Effectiveness of Antiterrorism Policies: A Vector-Autoregression Intervention Analysis' (1993) 87(4) *American Political Science Review* 829–44.

[9] Enders and Sandler (1993) 842; see also Cauley and Im (1988) 30.

[10] Enders and Sandler (1993) 835.

[11] Tucker, JB, 'Strategies for Countering Terrorism: Lessons from the Israeli Experience' (2003) *Journal of Homeland Security*, available at http://www.homelandsecurity.org/journal/Articles/tucker-israel.html.

[12] The Campbell Collaboration is a non-profit organisation that promotes evidence-based policy making by supporting empirical evaluations of the existing empirical literature in different policy arenas, including crime and security through its Crime and Justice Coordinating Group. The study in question here (Lum, C, Kennedy, LW and Sherley, AJ, 'The Effectiveness of Counter-terrorism Strategies: A Campbell Systematic Review', Campbell Collaboration review paper, January 2006, available at http://www.campbellcollaboration.org/doc-pdf/Lum_Terrorism_Review.pdf, 5) had its review protocol approved by the Crime and Justice Coordinating Group. For information about the Campbell Collaboration, see http://www.campbellcollaboration.org.

[13] *Ibid*, 3.

and human rights. Many scholars—including many of the authors who have contributions in this book—eschew effectiveness arguments entirely, on the ground, primarily, that the evaluation of effectiveness undermines the validity and legitimacy of formal legal argument. 'What if racial profiling *were* an effective means of combating terrorism?' they may ask. Wouldn't we then be forced to engage in the kind of cost–benefit analyses that may potentially result in outcomes that violate human rights norms or the 'culture of justification'? Why go down the path of effectiveness?

The answer, very simply, is that the question of effectiveness is independent of the choice of law or of method of legal analysis. It does not bear, in any way, on the style of legal reasoning that we adopt to analyse security issues—whether consequentialist, deontological, critical or deconstructive—even assuming that the disciplinary practice in question promoted the government's law enforcement interests. The effectiveness issue is a *threshold* question: if the measures are not credibly effective, there is nothing further to discuss. Naturally, if the debate over racial profiling as a counter-terrorism measure takes place in the context of actual litigation, then legal arguments will be necessary; but again, the discussion of effectiveness does not control the form of legal argument. In this sense, the issue of effectiveness is a separate question that, outside the narrow confines of the courtroom, is a threshold matter for any further discussion.

1. Academic Matters

As a theoretical matter, the potential trade-offs associated with racial profiling do indeed raise a myriad of thorny issues. The first is whether the very use of race, colour, nationality or ethnic identity is a form of impermissible discrimination in a situation where there is solid evidence of disparate offending between racial or ethnic groups. A number of economists in the United States and Great Britain draw a distinction between what they term 'statistical discrimination' and racial bigotry: the first uses group traits to promote more efficient policing and extends only to the point where law enforcement has maximised the efficiency of their interventions—as evidenced, for instance, in the equalising of search success rates between members of different racial groups.[14] At that point, these economists suggest, law enforcement has achieved the best allocation of resources in a non-discriminatory manner. It is only when law enforcement uses group traits *beyond the point of efficiency* that their use of race or ethnicity becomes invidious. Economist Vani Borooah has suggested, for instance, that 'statistical discrimination, untainted by bigotry, is optimal from a policing perspective because it maximizes the number of

---

[14] For a detailed treatment of this, see Harcourt, BE, 'Rethinking Racial Profiling: A Critique of the Economics, Civil Liberties, and Constitutional Literature, and of Criminal Profiling More Generally' (2004) 71 *University of Chicago Law Review* 1275–381.

arrests consequent upon a given number of persons stopped'.[15] In this sense, the very definition of 'racial profiling' is hotly contested.[16]

A second definitional controversy involves the judicial distinction between, on the one hand, the use of race or ethnic origin *as part of* a multi-pronged profile and, on the other hand, the use of race *exclusively* as the sole factor in a profile. In the United States, for instance, the Supreme Court drew precisely this legal distinction in its notorious 1996 decision in *Whren v United States*[17]—as well as in several earlier decisions involving US Border Patrol searches at the Mexican–American border in the mid-1970s.[18] The Court in *Whren* expressly condoned the use of race as one factor among others, as long as there exist other independent justifications for police intervention. (In that case, youth, demeanour and gender were also important traits in the profile.) The result is that, in US jurisprudence today, there is an operative distinction between using race exclusively and using race as one among other factors: the first is unanimously condemned, the second practically always permitted.[19]

In international law as well there is ambiguity surrounding this distinction. The International Covenant on Civil and Political Rights, for instance, provides that, in times of public emergency, states may derogate from certain rights on condition that the measures 'do not involve discrimination *solely* on the ground of race, colour, sex, language, religion or social origin'.[20] Here too, the reference is to the *exclusive* use of race, not to the use of race as one among other factors.

Assuming that the use of race automatically violates the principle of non-discrimination, a third issue arises: is the non-discrimination principle absolute, or can it be limited in the case of counter-terrorism? This has both philosophical and legal doctrinal dimensions. At the philosophical level, the question is whether violations of rights in the present can be excused in order to prevent future rights

[15] Borooah, VK, 'Racial Bias in Police Stops and Searches: An Economic Analysis' (2001) 17 *European Journal of Political Economy* 17–37, 19. For a fruitful discussion of the difference between statistical discrimination and naked bigotry, compare Borooah, VK, 'Economic Analysis of Police Stops and Searches: A Reply' (2002) 18 *European Journal of Political Economy* 607–8 with Chakravarty, SP, 'Economic Analysis of Police Stops and Searches: A Critique' (2002) 18 *European Journal of Political Economy* 597–605. In the US, the leading works in the area include Knowles, J, Persico, N and Todd, P, 'Racial Bias in Motor Vehicle Searches: Theory and Evidence' (2001) 109 *Journal of Political Economy* 203–29; Hernández-Murillo, R and Knowles, J, 'Racial Profiling or Racist Policing? Bounds Tests in Aggregated Data' (2004) 45(3) *International Economic Review* 959–89; Persico, N, 'Racial Profiling, Fairness, and Effectiveness of Policing' (2002) 92 *American Economic Review* 1472–97; Manski, C, 'Search Profiling with Partial Knowledge of Deterrence', unpublished paper, 2005; Dominitz, J and Knowles, J, 'Crime Minimization and Racial Bias: What can We Learn from Police Search Data?' PIER Working Paper 05-019, 18 February 2005, available at http://ssrn.com/abstract=719981.

[16] See generally Harcourt (2004) 1276 n 2.

[17] 517 US 806 (1996).

[18] See Harcourt, BE, '*United States v Brignoni-Ponce* and *United States v Martinez-Fuerte*: The Road to Racial Profiling' in C Steiker (ed), *Criminal Procedure Stories* (New York, Foundations Press, 2006) [Harcourt (2006b)].

[19] See Banks, RR, 'Race-based Suspect Selection and Colorblind Equal Protection Doctrine and Discourse' (2001) 48 *UCLA Law Review* 1075, 1086–87, fn 47: 'The consensus view seems to be that race may be considered as one of many factors, but may not be the only factor in an officer's decision to stop an individual.' For a lengthy treatment of this, see Harcourt (2004) 1338–42.

[20] ICCPR, Art 4 (emphasis added).

violations—especially where those future rights violations are assumed to be more harmful in the aggregate. A significant body of literature explores the question of intergenerational rights transfers and would be applicable here: John Rawls' discussion of 'the problem of justice between generations'[21] and Joel Feinberg's discussion of the rights of unborn generations[22] chart out some avenues of analysis and offer guidance. Another body of literature addresses shorter-term trade-offs. The leading hypothetical here is whether torture may be permitted in the extreme case of a ticking time bomb[23]—but there are many others, some less hypothetical than others. The use of the atomic bomb at Hiroshima comes to mind. Many remarkable philosophical texts address these puzzles of moral reasoning under a variety of different rubrics, ranging from Jean-Paul Sartre's and Michael Walzer's discussion of 'dirty hands' to Martha Nussbaum's writings on 'tragic predicaments'.[24]

At the legal doctrinal level, there are human rights and domestic civil rights issues to contend with as well. In the international context, the main question is whether the right to be free from discrimination is derogable. In their thorough paper on counter-terrorism measures and human rights compliance, Alex Conte and Boaz Ganor set forth in detail the doctrinal structure for an analysis of this question,[25] marshalling the principal human rights texts that address racial discrimination and profiling—including recent reports on racial profiling and counter-terrorism from the United Nations Committee on the Elimination of Racial Discrimination (CERD) and the Inter-American Commission on Human Rights.[26] The CERD has repeatedly maintained that counter-terrorism measures may not discriminate on the grounds of race or national or ethnic origin. For their part, Conte and Ganor point to disagreement within the human rights community and conclude that the principle of non-discrimination is indeed a derogable right.

Finally, in the civil rights context, there are difficult questions. Under equal protection jurisprudence in the United States, for instance, the anti-discrimination principle is violated only if there is intentional discrimination with proven malice.

---

[21] Rawls, J, *A Theory of Justice* (Cambridge, MA, Harvard University Press, 1971) 284–93.

[22] Feinberg, J, 'The Rights of Animals and Unborn Generations' in W Blackstone (ed), *Philosophy and Environmental Crisis* (Athens, GA, University of Georgia Press, 1974).

[23] Eric Posner and Adrian Vermeule offer a useful review of the landscape here in discussing the moral limits on coercive interrogation: Posner, E and Vermeule, A, 'Should Coercive Interrogation Be Legal?' (2006) 104(4) *Michigan Law Review* 671, 676–82.

[24] See generally Sartre, J-P, *Les Mains sales* (Paris, Gallimard, 1948); Walzer, M, 'Political Action: The Problem of Dirty Hands' (1973) 2(2) *Philosophy and Public Affairs* 160–80; Nussbaum, M, The Fragility of Goodness: Luck and Ethics in Greek Tragedy and Philosophy (Cambridge, Cambridge University Press, 1986) especially chs 2 and 3.

[25] Conte, A and Ganor, B, 'Legal and Policy Issues in Establishing an International Framework for Human Rights Compliance when Countering Terrorism', Institute for Counter-terrorism (ICT) Paper, 2005, available at http://www.ictconference.org/var/119/20471-Ganor_Conte_Human%20 Rights.pdf.

[26] See Committee on the Elimination of Racial Discrimination, 'Statement on Racial Discrimination and Measures to Combat Terrorism', in *Report of the Committee on the Elimination of Racial Discrimination*, and Inter-American Commission on Human Rights, *Report on Terrorism and Human Rights*, both discussed in Conte and Ganor (2005) 37–8.

The Supreme Court's decisions in *McCleskey v Kemp*[27] and *United States v Armstrong*[28]—which extend the *Washington v Davis*[29] requirement of intent to the criminal justice sphere—provide that a successful equal protection challenge must rest on evidence of intentional discrimination, rather than on inference from unexplained disparate treatment. If the police are engaging in statistical discrimination to promote police efficiency, it is not clear whether invidious intent would be present.

Moreover, the intentional use of race may be permitted if there is a compelling governmental interest. Fighting terrorism—actually reducing the incidence of terrorist acts—would undoubtedly qualify as a compelling state interest.[30] Stephen Ellman at New York Law School argues that 'in times of terrorist emergency', strict scrutiny would allow profiling that 'is targeted carefully, and conducted with restraint'.[31] The key question for purposes of equal protection, however, is whether the use of race would be *narrowly tailored* to promote a compelling governmental interest.[32] The requirement of narrow tailoring precludes policing techniques that are ineffective or that have unacceptable collateral consequences on the profiled population. Although Ellman concedes that he does not know whether racial profiling would help combat terrorism, he nevertheless suggests that the constitutional balance favours the careful use of profiling. Other scholars, such as Philip Heymann and Juliette Kayyem in their book *Protecting Liberty in an Age of Terror*, disagree.[33] Naturally, the final determination would fall on the courts.

2. No Need for a Trade-off

These are all admittedly fascinating questions that deserve our attention. But they only arise *if* racial profiling is an effective defensive counter-terrorism measure. And on that score, there is no reliable evidence, nor a good theoretical reason to believe that profiling is effective. As an empirical matter, we do not know whether the profiling of young Muslim men in New York City, London, Paris or other

---

[27] 481 US 279 (1987). In *McClesky*, the Court rejected an equal protection claim for lack of a showing of actual discriminatory intent, where a petitioner produced evidence that murderers of white victims are 4.3 times more likely to be sentenced to death than murderers of African-American victims: *ibid*, 287, 291–9.

[28] 517 US 456 (1996). In *Armstrong*, the Court required evidence of discriminatory purpose in the context of a selective prosecution challenge: *ibid*, 465.

[29] 426 US 229 (1976). In *Davis*, the Court articulated the principle that the equal protection clause bars only intentional discrimination: *ibid*, 239–41.

[30] Although some question this conclusion, I have no doubt that post-*Grutter v Bollinger*, 539 US 306 (2003), which deemed promoting a diverse student body a compelling state interest (see *ibid*, 332–3), fighting crime most probably would as well. See generally Harcourt (2004) 1349–50.

[31] Ellman, S, 'Racial Profiling and Terrorism' (2002–03) 46 *New York Law School Law Review* 675.

[32] See, for example, *Gratz v Bollinger*, 539 US 244, 268–75 (2003) (applying strict scrutiny to a University of Michigan admissions policy favouring minority applicants).

[33] See Heymann, PB and Kayyem, JN, *Protecting Liberty in an Age of Terror* (Cambridge, MA, MIT Press, 2005) ch 9.

major cities would reduce the incidence of domestic acts of international terrorism or cause more and different attacks.

Profiling is a statistical method that draws, methodologically, on an actuarial approach first developed in the insurance industry. But unlike early insurance applications, which were relatively static,[34] profiling in the policing context involves a dynamic form of prediction: the profiling itself alters the behaviours of both those persons who are profiled and those not profiled. As a result, the success of profiling depends on several factors. First, in terms of detecting and preventing terrorist acts, it depends on identifying a stable group trait that correlates with higher offending—or at least a group trait that is stable enough to serve as a predictive factor during the next period of profiling. And second, in terms of deterring and preventing terrorist acts, it depends on how responsive different groups are to the targeted policing and whether they engage in forms of substitution. Taking a long-term view, profiling will only succeed if young, male Muslims are more or equally responsive to the increased risk of detection associated with police profiling than the non-profiled group members and, as a result, are not able to recruit non-profiled persons nor substitute with more harmful terrorist acts.

The effectiveness of profiling thus turns on the relative elasticity of the different groups—the profiled group of young, male Muslims on the one hand, and the non-profiled groups of other persons who might be recruited to commit the terrorist acts in the face of profiling on the other hand. But on this central question, we have absolutely no reliable data. As a result, as an empirical matter, we do not know whether profiling works in the counter-terrorism context or on the contrary causes more terrorist attacks.

In this chapter, I evaluate the empirical case for racial profiling. Surprisingly, although international terrorism is by no means a new phenomenon, there is extremely little reliable empirical research on the effectiveness of defensive counter-terrorist measures, and there is no reliable empirical research whatsoever on the use of racial profiling in this context. The little evidence there is on counter-terrorism measures more generally suggests that such defensive policing techniques may backfire, largely due to a phenomenon called 'substitution'. 'Substitution' encompasses two possible responses to profiling by terrorist organisations: (1) the recruitment of more individuals from non-profiled groups, which expands the overall pool of potential terrorists; and (2) the substitution of different types of terrorist attacks that are more immune to profiling and yet more devastating in terms of deaths and injuries. These potential responses raise a host of technical empirical questions that are at present entirely unresolved.

Before proceeding, it is important to identify precisely the type of measures in question. As most experts agree, there are two types of counter-terrorist initia-

---

[34] This is changing in the insurance area, and the field is becoming increasingly dynamic insofar as actuarial prediction is becoming more and more individualised, to the point that the determination of individual insurance premiums increasingly affects individual behaviour. This was not true of early insurance practices.

tives.[35] The first are called defensive or deterrence-based counter-terrorist policies. They aim to prevent or block the success of a terrorist attack and reduce the
likelihood that an attack will cause injuries. This type of defensive policy includes
the development and deployment of technology-based measures, such as metal or
explosives detectors at airports and the hardening of potential targets like
embassies and foreign missions. In contrast, proactive or pre-emptive policies aim
to dismantle terrorist organisations, for example, by means of infiltration, pre-
emptive strikes or invasion of supportive states.

Profiling can be used as part of both defensive and proactive counter-terrorist
measures. The profiling of young Muslim men in the New York City subways
exemplifies the former. But profiling can also be used in pre-emptive strategies, as
when, for example, the FBI engages in targeted interviews of Muslim and Arab
Americans in order to collect intelligence.[36] In this chapter, I address only racial
profiling by the police in defensive counter-terrorism operations.

EVALUATING THE EMPIRICAL CASE FOR RACIAL PROFILING

1. Profiling and Immediate Detection

As a theoretical matter, there is no doubt that the probability of detecting a terrorist attack increases in the *immediate* aftermath of the implementation of a criminal profiling method. This is simply an inexorable product of the laws of
probability: if the police dedicate more resources to investigating and searching
members of a higher-offending group, they will inevitably increase the detection
of terrorist activities within the profiled group and in society as a whole *in the
immediate aftermath.*

This reflects an iron law of probabilities—and it is precisely what gives rise to
the claim among proponents of profiling that it is 'based on statistics'[37] and is 'a
simple statistical fact'.[38] These claims are correct in the narrow time period
following the implementation of a profiling method. The basic intuition is that
policing is like sampling in the social sciences: when law enforcement agencies
profile members of a higher-offending group, they are essentially sampling *more*
from that higher-offending group. As such, they will detect more offenders with
the same resources because, by necessity, those searches are more likely to detect
offending.

Thus, profiling on a group trait that correlates with higher offending will necessarily increase the likelihood of detection *in the very first iteration.* This will have
significant benefits along at least two dimensions: first, in preventing the specific

---

[35] See generally, Enders and Sandler (1993) 829–44; Faria, JR, 'Terrorist Innovations and Anti-
terrorist Policies' (2006) 18 Terrorism and Political Violence 47–56; and Tucker (2003).

[36] Sheridan, MB, 'Interviews of Muslims to Broaden: FBI Hopes to Avert a Terrorist Attack',
Washington Post, 17 July 2004, p A1.

[37] Sperry (2005).

[38] Krauthammer (2005).

terrorist act that is detected, and second, in incapacitating apprehended terrorists from committing any future acts of terrorism.

As a practical matter—and still within the context of the *immediate* aftermath of implementing a profiling measure—the likelihood of realising any tangible benefits from racial profiling depends entirely on the frequency of the profiled event. The higher the frequency of the event, the more likely that profiling will immediately detect more of those events. A good illustration is mandatory screening at airports—an initiative that, to be sure, does not involve profiling but does involve increased sampling. Implemented in 1973, mandatory screening in the United States detected 4,783 firearms and 46,318 knives in 1975, and, according to the Federal Aviation Administration (FAA), prevented approximately 35 potential hijackers that year. To put that number in perspective, that same year there were 6 domestic hijackings in the United States.[39]

Low base-rate events, however, are far more difficult to predict[40] and as a result are much harder to detect for several reasons. First, it is extremely hard to predict where, when or how the low base-rate offence will occur. Second, low frequency affords more time to adjust to any counter-terrorism measure. A terrorist attack in the New York City subway qualifies as a low base-rate event—fortunately, there have not been any such attacks—but as a result, there is a lot of time between events and opportunity for terrorist organisations to adjust to the profiling. In the case of low frequency events, the central question is whether the increased likelihood of detection associated with the *immediate* implementation of a profiling measure will result in the *actual* detection of planned terrorist activity or instead in the rapid substitution of persons who do not meet the profile or alternative acts that are not as easily profiled.

2. Long-term Effects on the Frequency and Extent of Terrorist Attacks

Immediate detection is extremely important, especially to potential victims and their families, friends and communities who would suffer the greatest harm. Those potential benefits cannot be minimised. But they need to be considered in light of the long-term effects on terrorist attacks and the likelihood of future deaths, injuries and destruction. The central question here is whether racial profiling is likely to prevent future terrorist acts.

A. An Economic Model of Profiling

A number of able economists have turned their attention to racial profiling and argue that the use of profiling may amount to more efficient policing. They contend that profiling based on a group trait associated with higher offending rates—

---

[39] Landes (1978) 24, fn 41, and 3, Table 1.
[40] Rosen, A, 'Detection of Suicidal Patients: An Example of Some Limitations of the Prediction of Infrequent Events' (1954) 18 *Journal of Consulting Psychology* 397–403.

what they call 'statistical discrimination'—may in fact be the most effective way to allocate police resources. Drawing on Gary Becker's ground-breaking work on tastes for discrimination,[41] a group of US economists— notably John Knowles, Nicola Persico and Petra Todd at the University of Pennsylvania, and Jeff Dominitz at Carnegie Mellon University—have developed economic models of racial profiling. Similar analyses are taking place in Great Britain.[42] Although these economic models are being developed in the specific context of racial profiling on highways and city streets, the models apply equally to profiling as a defensive counter-terrorist measure.

The logic of the racial profiling models rests on the central assumption of the economic theory of crime, namely that any rational individual is less likely to engage in an activity if the cost of the activity increases. This is what is called, in more technical jargon, the 'elasticity of offending to policing' or simply 'elasticity'. The elasticity of offending to policing is the degree to which changes in policing affect changes in offending. Assuming that potential offenders respond rationally to the probability of detection and punishment, then targeting law enforcement on members of a higher-offending population will not only increase the amount of crime detected but more importantly decrease the offending rate among those members of the targeted group because of the increased cost. In its purest form, the economic model of crime suggests that law enforcement should target higher-offending populations until the point where their offending rates have fallen to the same level as the general population. At that point, the government has maximised the effectiveness of its law enforcement resources.

I have set forth elsewhere in great detail the logic of these economic models both in the broad context of criminal profiling[43] and in the specific context of racial profiling on the highways.[44] For present purposes, I offer a more streamlined description of the analysis and modify the models to address the specific context of counter-terrorism profiling.

The central assumption, of course, is that there are two different groups with different offending rates. The profiled group consists of young Muslim men, which, for purposes of the agent on the street, translates into young men of apparent Arab descent, young men who look Middle Eastern, Southeast Asian, North African or African—or, more generally, young men of colour (excluding young men from East Asia). The non-profiled group consists of all women, older men, and young men who are white or East Asian.

As a factual matter, this first assumption is probably correct, at least in the United States. Of the total US population, there are extremely few persons of European, American, African-American or East Asian descent who have engaged or are seemingly prepared to engage in suicide bombing or similar mass terrorist

---

[41] Becker, G, *Accounting for Tastes* (Cambridge, MA, Harvard University Press, 1996).

[42] See eg, Borooah (2001); Borooah (2002); Chakravarty (2002).

[43] Harcourt, BE, *Against Prediction: Profiling, Policing, and Punishing in an Actuarial Age* (Chicago, University of Chicago Press, 2006) [Harcourt (2006a)].

[44] Harcourt (2004).

acts against Americans. Richard Reid, known as the 'shoe bomber', who was travelling to the United States on a British passport, and Jose Padilla, a Hispanic-American who was arrested at Chicago's O'Hare airport and accused of plotting a terrorist attack, are the two people who immediately come to mind—out of a population of about 200 million (excluding children, the elderly and young men of colour). In contrast, the number of young men of Arab descent who have engaged in terrorist activities on US soil is larger and includes the 19 men who participated in the 9/11 terrorist attacks, as well as those who engaged in the earlier car bombing of the World Trade Center on 26 February 1993.

In addition, the denominator is much smaller: according to the 2000 US Census, there are 1,189,731 persons living in the United States who have one or more Arab ancestors, and approximately 10 per cent of those (or about 120,000) are young men between the ages of 15 and 30.[45] Naturally, the appearance of being of Arab descent encompasses many more young men of colour, so the denominator is probably higher. But even if we assume that it is one hundred or more times bigger, there is still an offending differential in the range of at least 1:100 for non-profiled versus profiled group members. It would be crucial to get a better handle on this first quantity of interest—but there is, in all likelihood, a significant offending differential.

In any event, assuming an offending differential, rational choice theory suggests that the use of statistical discrimination—here, racial profiling—improves the efficiency of policing. Figure 1 explains this by showing the relationship between the internal rate of searches conducted within each of the two groups—profiled and not profiled—and the offending rate of those different groups. At Time 1, counter-terrorism agents are not engaged in profiling of any sort: the police are searching both groups at the same internal search rate of 10 per cent. The graph reflects the basic assumption of non-spurious profiling, namely that young Muslim men are offending at a slightly higher rate than white men and all women—let's suppose 1.5 versus 1 per 100 million—resulting in higher successful search rates for the searches of young Muslim men.

Given the higher marginal success rate for searches of young Muslim men, the police may begin to search that group more than their share of the available population, and, as the proportion of searches targeting young Muslim men increases, the offending rate of that group decreases. This is the fundamental assumption of rational choice, namely that as the cost of offending increases, the rate decreases. The police continue to search marginally more young Muslim men until Time 2, when their offending rate is equal to that of white men and women—1.3 per 100 million. Now the police are using the profile in their decision to search: the police are searching about 18 per cent of the available young Muslim men and about 5 per cent of the available white men and women, resulting in a hypothetical total distribution of searches of, say, 60 per cent young males of colour and 40 per cent whites. At that dis-

[45] Brittingham, A and de la Cruz, GP, 'We the People of Arab Ancestry in the United States', US Department of Commerce, Economics, and Statistics Administration Census 2000 Special Reports, March 2005, available at http://www.census.gov/prod/2005pubs/censr-21.pdf.

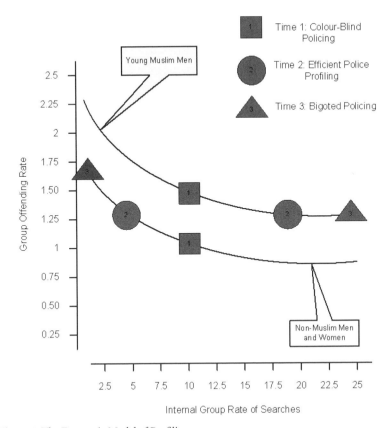

Figure 1. The Economic Model of Profiling

tribution of searches, the offending rates are similar—and, one can infer, so are the hit rates. At that distribution, an efficient police officer has no reason to change the distribution of searches: there is no incentive to search more young Muslim men than the 60/40 total distribution, which produces these different internal group search rates. At Time 2, even though the police are not allocating any more resources to the enterprise, the number of successful searches has increased, and the total societal level of offending has decreased from where it stood at Time 1.[46]

If the police are, in fact, searching more young Muslim men and getting to Time 3, where the offending rate of young Muslim men is lower than that of whites—1.3 versus 1.7 per 100 million—then the police must be bigoted: the only reason that a police officer would search more young Muslim men than at the Time 2 equilibrium—that is, would search, say, 80 per cent young Muslim men and 20 per cent whites, instead of the Time 2 distribution of 60/40—is if the officer had a *taste*

[46] This is a mathematical property of the model that I discuss in greater technical detail in Harcourt (2004) and (2006a).

for discrimination resulting in higher utility even though *fewer* young Muslim men are offending and thus *fewer* searches are successful.[47]

The three hypothetical distributions of searches between young Muslim men and all others—at Times 1, 2, and 3—correspond to three different sets of internal group search rates. These three scenarios also represent three different types of policing: colour-blind policing at Time 1 where the police take no account of race and therefore do not seek greater efficiency by targeting higher offenders; efficient police profiling at Time 2 where the police have sought to improve their hit rates by targeting higher offenders to the point of equilibrium; and excessive profiling or bigoted policing at Time 3 where the police are now searching more (beyond the point of efficiency) members of the lower-offending group. The three time points are represented in Figure 1.

The economic model represented by Figure 1 suggests that profiling increases the success rate of police investigations and reduces the overall societal level of offending with the same police resources. Naturally, additional judicial resources would be needed to process the increased detection of terrorist activities, although one expects that those costs would be offset by the harm that is prevented.

B. *Elasticity among the Non-profiled and Possible Substitution Effects*

Rational choice theory entails, however, that members of a profiled group are not the only ones who will respond to changes in policing. Members of the non-profiled group also change their behaviour as a result of the *decreased* cost of crime—but in their case, by *increasing* their offending. So, for instance, if the US taxing authorities target drywall contractors and car dealers for audits of their tax returns—as they did in the mid-1990s—we can expect that there will be less tax evasion by drywall contractors and car dealers because their cost of tax evasion has increased. But at the same time, we can expect that some, say, accountants and bankers will realise that they are less likely to be audited and may therefore cheat a bit more on their taxes. Similarly, if the highway patrol targets African-American motorists for stops and searches—again, there is evidence for this in several states in the United States—then we can expect African-American motorists to respond by offending less. But by the same token, white motorists may begin to offend more as they begin to feel increasingly immune from investigation and prosecution.

Similar substitution effects hold true in the terrorism context as well. It happened in Israel, for instance, when young girls and women started becoming suicide bombers. As Jonathan Tucker, a counter-terrorism expert has explained:

> At first, suicide terrorists [in Israel] were all religious, militant young men recruited from Palestinian universities or mosques. In early 2002, however, the profile began to change as secular Palestinians, women, and even teenage girls volunteered for suicide missions. On March 29 2002, Ayat Akhars, an 18-year-old Palestinian girl from Bethlehem who looked European and spoke Hebrew, blew herself up in a West

---

[47] As evidenced here, the model relies principally on Gary Becker's seminal work on tastes for discrimination. See generally Becker (1996).

Jerusalem supermarket, killing two Israelis. Suicide bombers have also sought to foil profiling efforts by shaving their beards, dyeing their hair blond, and wearing Israeli uniforms or even the traditional clothing of orthodox Jews.[48]

In this sense, the opponents of racial profiling are also correct—and, also, as a matter of 'statistical fact'. If we assume elasticity among rational actors, then profiling will *increase* offending among members of the non-profiled group. This has led many counter-terrorism experts to question or deny outright the effectiveness of profiling. As Bruce Hoffman has stated, 'profiling of suicide bombers is no longer effective. Suicide attacks can be young or old, male or female, religious or secular'.[49] It has led other counter-terrorism experts and practitioners, such as New York City Police Commissioner Raymond Kelly, to avoid profiling on traits that can substitute easily. As Malcolm Gladwell explains, 'It doesn't work to generalize about a relationship between a category and a trait when that relationship isn't stable—or when the act of generalizing may itself change the basis of the generalization.'[50] To avoid these 'unstable' traits, police chief Kelly does not rely on race but instead on traits like nervousness and inconsistency—traits that are more permanently associated with criminal offending and that do not lend themselves to substitution.

C. The Central Theoretical Puzzle

The fact that there may be elasticity and thus substitution among the non-profiled, however, does not end the debate about profiling. It does not mean that profiling is ineffective. Some substitution is inevitable. The real question is: how much substitution can we expect and will it outweigh the benefits of profiling? The central theoretical question is, in other words, *how do the elasticities of the two groups compare?* How does the elasticity of the profiled group compare to that of the non-profiled group?

The trouble with the economic model is that it assumes both groups are *equally* elastic to policing. This is reflected in the earlier graph by the parallel shape of the two offending curves. But this assumes away the central theoretical question. What matters most for the effectiveness of racial profiling is precisely the *comparative elasticity* of the two groups. If the targeted group members have *lower* elasticity of offending to policing—if their offending is *less* responsive to policing than other groups—then targeting them for enforcement efforts will increase the *overall* amount of crime in society because the increase in crime by members of the non-profiled group will exceed the decrease in crime by members of the profiled group. In raw numbers, the effect of the profiling will be greater on the more elastic non-profiled group and smaller on the less elastic profiled group.

---

[48] Tucker (2003).

[49] Hoffman, B, 'Defending America against Suicide Terrorism' in D Aaron (ed), *Three Years After: Next Steps in the War on Terror* (Santa Monica, RAND Corporation, 2005) 22.

[50] Gladwell (2006).

Again, this is true as well in the terrorism context. The central question here is how responsive young Muslim men are to police profiling practices and whether they are *less* elastic than non-Muslim men and women. If they are less responsive overall, then targeted policing may actually *increase* total incidents of terrorism by encouraging the non-profiled group members to engage in terrorist acts—since the price to them has *decreased*. This would enable and encourage terrorist organisations to recruit more heavily from outside the profiled group—women, white men and others who do not look like young Muslim men.

It is precisely the *comparative* elasticities of offending to policing that determine whether and to what extent there is substitution between members of the profiled and non-profiled groups. This is the central puzzle, but at this theoretical level, there is no good reason to assume that the higher-offending group is as responsive or more responsive to policing than members of the non-profiled groups. After all, we are assuming that the two groups have *different* offending rates. Whether it is due to different socio-economic backgrounds, to religious fanaticism, to education, culture, or upbringing, non-spurious profiling rests on the non-spurious assumption that one group of individuals offends *more* than the other, holding everything else constant. If their offending is different, then why would their elasticity be the same? If members of the profiled group are offending more because they are more religious, then might they also be *less* elastic to policing? There is no *a priori* reason why the group that offends more should be more or as elastic than the other.

The bottom line, then, is that if the profiled group has *lower* elasticity of offending to policing, profiling that group will probably increase the amount of terrorism in the long-term. I have demonstrated this elsewhere with mathematical equations,[51] but the proof is captured well and more simply by modifying the earlier graph to reflect different elasticities (see Figure 2). In essence, as long as the equilibrium point in offending at Time 2 is achieved *above* the average offending rate at Time 1, the profiling will produce increased crime in society.

In the terrorism context, the elasticity of offending represents only one form of possible substitution. There are other forms that can also result in an increased long-term rate of attacks, including, for instance, the use of different terrorist modes of attack that are less susceptible to detection by profiling. The central empirical issues, then, are: (1) whether and to what extent the group of profiled individuals (young, Arab-looking males) are elastic to policing; (2) whether and to what extent the group of non-profiled individuals (non-Arab-looking young men and all other men and women) are elastic to policing; (3) more importantly, *how those elasticities compare*; and (4) whether there are different forms of substitution that might also occur.

---

[51] See Harcourt (2006a).

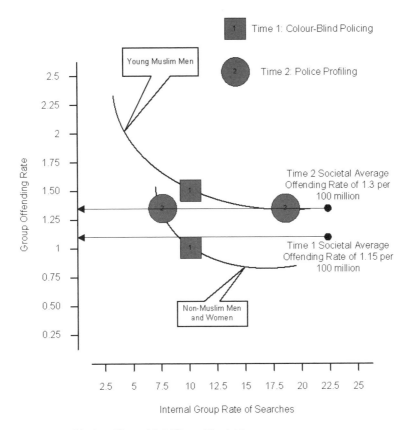

Figure 2. A Model of Profiling with Different Elasticities

E. Empirical Research on Counter-terrorism Measures

On these central questions, there is no reliable empirical evidence. There is no empirical research on elasticities, especially comparative elasticities, nor on substitution effects in the context of racial profiling.[52] The only forms of substitution that have been studied empirically in the counter-terrorism context involve substitution as between different methods of attack and different timing of attacks.

[52] The two closest empirical studies are both slightly off-point. The first is Paul Heaton's 2006 working paper on the effect of eliminating racial profiling policies in New Jersey on the offending of minorities: Heaton, P, 'Understanding the Effects of Anti-profiling Policies', working paper, March 2006, available at http://home.uchicago.edu/~psheaton/workingpapers/racialprofiling.pdf. However, Heaton's study does not address the issue of comparative elasticities. The other is Avner Bar-Ilan and Bruce Sacerdote's 2001 study, which explores the comparative responsiveness to an increase in the fine for running a red light among Jews and non-Jews: Bar-Ilan, A and Sacerdote, B, 'The Response to Fines and Probability of Detection in a Series of Experiments', National Bureau of Economic Research (Cambridge, MA) Working Paper No 8638, December 2001. However, their study does not address the issue of racial profiling.

Rigorous empirical research in the terrorism context traces its origins to a 1978 paper by William Landes that explores the effect of installing metal detectors in airports on the incidence of aircraft hijackings.[53] Extending the rational choice framework to terrorist activities, Landes developed an economic model to test whether mandatory screening reduced the likelihood of a terrorist hijacking. Using a dataset of US FAA records of aircraft hijackings from 1961 to 1976, Landes analysed the time intervals between hijackings to measure the frequency of these events. Landes found that 'increases in the probability of apprehension, the conditional probability of incarceration, and the sentence are associated with significant reductions in aircraft hijackings in the 1961-to-1976 time period'.[54] He estimated that between 41 and 67 fewer aircraft hijackings occurred on planes departing from the United States following mandatory screening and the installation of metal detectors in US airports.[55]

In his 1978 study, Landes used sophisticated quantitative analyses to regress the quarterly totals of aircraft hijackings, as well as time and flight intervals between successive hijackings, on the probability of apprehension. The effect, however, can be visualised here based on data from the RAND-MIPT Terrorism Incident Database Project.[56] Figure 3 charts both the number of aircraft hijackings between 1968 and 1980, as well as the proportion of terrorist acts that consisted of hijackings.

The graph clearly demonstrates that mandatory screening and the installation of metal detectors in 1973 coincided with a significant drop in both the absolute number and the proportion of international terrorist acts represented by hijackings. Landes' research suggests that terrorists' decisions about whether to engage in terrorist acts are a function of the probability and expected utility of different possible outcomes.

Subsequent research has built on Landes' framework to explore possible substitution effects. In a 1988 article, Jon Cauley and Eric Im used interrupted time series analysis to explore the impact of the installation of metal detectors on different types of terrorist attacks.[57] They found that, although the implementation resulted in a permanent decrease in the number of hijackings, it produced a proportionally larger increase in other types of terrorist attacks.[58] In 1993, Walter Enders and Todd Sandler also revisited mandatory screening, showing similarly

---

[53]   Landes (1978).

[54]   *Ibid*, 28.

[55]   *Ibid*, 28–29. Landes also found that the cost of mandatory screening of all passengers was 'enormous': 'The estimated net increase in security costs due to the screening program (which does not include the time and inconvenience costs to persons searched) . . . translates into a $3.24-to-$9.25 million expenditure to deter a single hijacking. Put differently, if the dollar equivalent to the loss to an individual hijacked passenger were in the range of $76,718 to $219,221, then the costs of screening would just offset the expected hijacking losses.' Landes (1978) 29.

[56]   The underlying data are also available in Anderton, CH and Carter, JR, 'Applying Intermediate Microeconomics to Terrorism', College of the Holy Cross, Department of Economics Faculty Research Series, Working Paper No 04-12, August 2004.

[57]   Cauley and Im (1988).

[58]   *Ibid*.

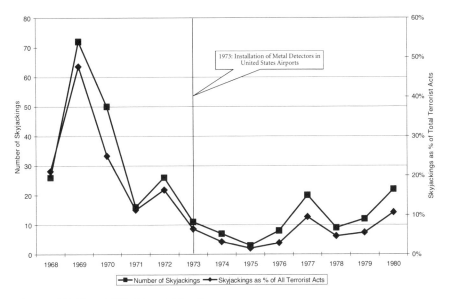

Figure 3. US Aircraft Hijackings, 1968–80

that, although mandatory screening coincided with a sharp decrease in hijackings, it also coincided with increased assassinations and other kinds of hostage attacks, including barricade missions and kidnappings.[59] The introduction of metal detectors, they showed, resulted in a steady increase in other kinds of hostage events— consistent with the idea that 'terrorist groups substituted away from skyjackings and complementary events involving protected persons and into other kinds of hostage incidents'.[60]

Still other researchers have found that the implementation of counter-terrorism measures has had no impact on the risk of terrorism-related hijacking attempts. Laura Dugan, Gary LaFree and Alex R Piquero, in their 2005 article, 'Testing A Rational Choice Model of Airline Hijackings', have analysed a dataset that included 1,101 attempted aerial hijackings around the world from 1931 to 2003 and explored the effectiveness of a range of counter-terrorism measures—from the installation or metal detectors and tighter baggage and customer screening to increased law enforcement presence and punitive sanctions.[61] When these researchers disaggregated their data into terrorist-related and non-terrorist related hijackings, they found that 'none of the three policies examined were significantly related to the attempts or success of terrorist-related hijackings'.[62] They concluded

---

[59] Enders and Sandler (1993).
[60] *Ibid*, 835.
[61] Dugan, L, LaFree, G and Piquero, AR, 'Testing a Rational Choice Model of Airline Hijackings' (2005) 43(4) *Criminology* 1031–65.
[62] *Ibid*, 1059.

that 'the counterhijacking policies examined had no impact on the hazard of terrorism-related hijacking attempts. By contrast, we found that metal detectors and increased police surveillance significantly reduced the hazard of nonterrorist-related hijackings.'[63]

Researchers have also looked at other forms of possible substitution. Retaliatory strikes, like the United States' strike on Libya on 15 April 1986, resulted in '*increased* bombings and related incidents';[64] but they tended to level off later. As Enders and Sandler explain, 'The evidence seems to be that retaliatory raids induce terrorists to *intertemporally* substitute attacks planned for the future into the present to protest the retaliation. Within a relatively few quarters, terrorist attacks resumed the same mean number of events.'[65] Enders and Sandler also found that the fortification of US embassies and missions in October 1976 resulted in a reduction of terrorist attacks against US interests but produced a substitution towards assassinations.[66] Cauley and Im also analysed the effect of target hardening of US embassies and found that they had an 'abrupt but transitory influence on the number of barricade and hostage taking events'.[67] Their conclusion was that 'the unintended consequences of an antiterrorism policy may be far more costly than intended consequences, and must be anticipated'.[68]

However, that is the extent of the solid empirical evidence. The most recent and thorough review of the empirical literature, based on a Campbell Collaborative protocol, identified only seven rigorous empirical studies:

> In the course of our review, we discovered that there is an almost complete absence of evaluation research on counter-terrorism strategies. From over 20,000 studies we located on terrorism, we found only seven which contained moderately rigorous evaluations of counter-terrorism programs. We conclude that there is little scientific knowledge about the effectiveness of most counter-terrorism interventions.[69]

[63] *Ibid*, 1056–7.
[64] Enders and Sandler (1993) 835.
[65] Enders, W and Sandler, T, 'What Do We Know about the Substitution Effect In Transnational Terrorism?' in A Silke and G Ilardi (eds), *Researching Terrorism: Trends, Achievements, Failures* (London, Frank Cass, 2004), available as an April 2002 working paper at http://www-rcf.usc.edu/~tsandler/substitution2ms.pdf, *16.
[66] Enders and Sandler (1993) 842.
[67] Cauley and Im (1988) 30.
[68] Enders and Sandler (1993) 843. These substitution effects can also be aggravated by innovation effects—which include new modes of attack and new techniques and weapons. Enders and Sandler explain: 'In the long term, terrorists will develop ingenious countermeasures to circumvent the technology. Immediately after airport vigilance was increased as a result of 9/11, Richard Reid (aka Tariq Rajah) was discovered on a flight from Paris to the United States with an explosive device in his shoes. Now that airport security routinely inspects shoes, plastic guns, electronic jamming equipment, bottles of flammable liquid or other explosive devices are predicted to be hidden on (or in) the terrorist or in carry-on luggage. Thus, there are dynamic strategic interactions; authorities must be vigilant to improve technology by anticipating ways of circumventing current technological barriers. This vigilance must lead to periodic upgrades in the technology prior to the terrorists exposing the technology's weakness through a successful attack': Enders and Sandler (2002/4) *18.
[69] Lum, Kennedy, and Sherley (2006) 3.

Moreover, there are no empirical studies on racial profiling in the terrorism context. I found only one article, and it is theoretical, not empirical.[70] Concerned that this may have been an artefact of a US bias, I contacted Dr Boaz Ganor (a leading researcher on terrorism in Israel) at the Institute for Counter-terrorism at the Interdisciplinary Center Herzliya (a leading research centre on terrorism in Israel) and asked him if there were any empirical studies on profiling in Israel. His response: 'no'. He is unaware of 'any empirical research that has been done in Israel on the efficiency of profiling'.[71] The reason, in large part, is that ethnic appearance is a poor indicator of terrorism in Israel. As Dr Ganor explained, 'There were many cases of public and security awareness that prevented or limited terrorist attacks in Israel based on the looks of the suspect, but it is sometimes difficult to define if this practice was based on national identity, ethnic profile or suspicious behaviour, or all of the above together.'[72]

F. Some Loose Ends

Naturally, there are a lot of other unanswered questions. Firstly, in all likelihood terrorist organisations are *already* recruiting outside the profiled group *regardless* of whether the New York City Police Department (NYPD) or other law enforcement agencies are engaged in racial profiling. What difference, then, would racial profiling make? Does the incremental cost of profiling in the subways really change the equation? And how sensitive are terrorists to such an incremental cost? Second, the decision to have police officers search bags and monitor subway entrances—*regardless* of whether they profile—already increases the cost of such an attack. What is the incremental difference achieved by racial profiling, and will it have any effect on behaviour?

Third, even if there is more substitution, might it lead to less harmful attacks? Enders and Sandler have written:

> Even some piecemeal policies that cause substitutions by focusing on only part of the overall terrorism problem may have some net positive impacts. To the extent that the National Defense Authorization Act leads to a reduction in the likelihood of biological terrorism, substitutions into other attack modes will occur. The desirability of such policies is that they may force terrorists to substitute into *less harmful* events. Anti-terrorist policies can be most effective when the government simultaneously targets a wide range of terrorist attack modes, so that the *overall* rise in the prices of terrorist attacks becomes analogous to a decrease in resources.[73]

Fourth, might racial profiling itself affect comparative elasticities? Is it possible that racial profiling might soften the elasticity of the non-profiled group, or harden that of the profiled group, by reinforcing a perception that the United

---

[70] Yetman, J, 'Suicidal Terrorism and Discriminatory Screening: An Efficiency–Equity Trade-off' (2004) 15(3) *Defence and Peace Economics* 221–30.
[71] Communication with Dr Boaz Ganor, 24 February 2006.
[72] *Ibid.*
[73] Enders and Sandler (2002/4) *18.

States and European countries are anti-Muslim? There is good reason to believe, for instance, that the torture at Abu Ghraib in 2004 may serve as a future recruitment tool for terrorist organisations. Anderton and Carter have suggested:

> It is likely that the degrading images of Iraqi prisoners hardened the preferences of terrorists against the United States. It may have also created terrorist preferences among some individuals who previously had flat indifference curves [as to terrorist activities]. Hence, the prisoner abuse scandal can be seen as a form of 'negative advertising' that may have reshaped terrorist preferences toward more terrorism.[74]

In the same way, might the profiling of young Muslim men in London, New York City or other Western cities serve as a form of 'negative advertising' that may undermine efforts to eradicate terrorism?

Finally, might racial profiling produce a loss of political legitimacy at home or abroad, possibly increasing the responsiveness of non-profiled group members to recruitment efforts? The perception that our counter-terrorism measures are illegitimate may affect obedience to the law. Psychologist Tom Tyler has demonstrated how perceptions of the legitimacy of criminal justice procedures affect the willingness of citizens to abide by the law.[75] Tyler's writings on procedural fairness and institutional legitimacy rest precisely on the idea that individuals derive a strong sense of identity from their relationship with legal authority. When the relationship is positive and respectful, a form of social trust—a concept closely linked to the idea of social capital made popular in Robert Putnam's book, *Bowling Alone*[76]—develops and promotes obedience to the law. '[S]ocial trust,' Tyler contends, 'is linked to creating a commitment and loyalty to the group and to group rules and institutions.'[77] This commitment and loyalty to the group translates into greater obedience to the law. When this loyalty is undermined, so too is obedience to the law. Will this affect the responsiveness of members of non-profiled groups?

These are all fascinating questions but all relatively minor compared to the central question: whether racial profiling such as that of young Muslim men in the New York subways will be likely to detect a terrorist attack or instead lead to the recruitment of non-profiled persons and the substitution of other acts for subway attacks—in other words, whether profiling will detect or increase terrorist attacks. The answer to this question is pure speculation. In the end, then, there is no need or reason to engage in a rights trade-off.

---

[74]   Anderton and Carter (2004) 10.

[75]   See Tyler, TR, *Why People Obey the Law* (New Haven, Yale University Press, 1990); and Tyler, T, 'Trust and Democratic Governance' in V Braithwaite and M Levi (eds), *Trust and Governance* (New York, Russell Sage Foundation, 1998).

[76]   Putnam, RD, *Bowling Alone: The Collapse and Revival of American Community* (New York, Simon & Schuster, 2000).

[77]   Tyler (1998) 289.

CONCLUSION

There is a lesson here. Defensive counter-terrorism measures need to be evaluated closely. As Enders and Sandler, Faria, Tucker and other counter-terrorist experts have emphasised, measures that raise the price of one and only one specific activity, such as airplane hijackings, are likely to produce troubling substitution effects; and measures that raise the price of *all* terrorist acts or conversely reduce the resources of terrorists are less problematic and less likely to produce unanticipated substitution.[78] The optimal strategy to combat terrorism is to reduce terrorist resources across the board. It is for this reason that intelligence and proactive counter-terrorism operations are generally viewed as a priority. As General Meir Dagan, former head of the Bureau for Counter-terrorism in the Israeli prime minister's office, has explained, 'Investments in intelligence are invisible, whereas increased security is visible but often wasteful. The first priority must be placed on intelligence, then on counter-terrorism operations, and finally on defence and protection.'[79]

Racial profiling as a defensive counter-terrorism measure is suspect for precisely this reason: it may well encourage the recruitment of terrorists from outside the core profile and the substitution of other terrorist acts. Does this mean that the NYPD should not harden targets like the subway system—targets that are attractive to terrorists because of the number of potential victims? No. It is probably better to divert terrorist attacks away from large groups of people, wherever and whenever possible. But it does mean that the police should harden those types of targets without deploying a racial profile. There is no point triggering the potential substitution effects associated with racial profiling.

REFERENCES

Anderton, CH and Carter, JR, 'Applying Intermediate Microeconomics to Terrorism', College of the Holy Cross, Department of Economics Faculty Research Series, Working Paper No 04-12, August 2004.

Banks, RR, 'Race-based Suspect Selection and Colorblind Equal Protection Doctrine and Discourse' (2001) 48 *UCLA Law Review* 1075.

Bar-Ilan, A and Sacerdote, B, 'The Response to Fines and Probability of Detection in a Series of Experiments', National Bureau of Economic Research (Cambridge, MA) Working Paper No 8638, December 2001.

Becker, G, *Accounting for Tastes* (Cambridge, MA, Harvard University Press, 1996).

---

[78] Enders and Sandler (2002/4) *10; Faria (2006); Tucker (2003).

[79] Quoted in Tucker (2003) *2. Walter Enders and Todd Sandler seem to agree: 'Governments must act to reduce the terrorists' resource endowments (ie, their finances, leadership, and membership) if an overall decrease in terrorism is to follow. Efforts to infiltrate and undermine terrorist groups and to freeze their assets have the consequence of reducing the overall amount of terrorism:' Enders and Sandler (2002/4) *17.

Borooah, VK, 'Racial Bias in Police Stops and Searches: An Economic Analysis' (2001) 17 *European Journal of Political Economy* 17–37.

—— 'Economic Analysis of Police Stops and Searches: A Reply' (2002) 18 *European Journal of Political Economy* 607–8.

Brittingham, A and de la Cruz, GP, 'We the People of Arab Ancestry in the United States', US Department of Commerce, Economics, and Statistics Administration Census 2000 Special Reports, March 2005, available at http://www.census.gov/prod/2005pubs/censr-21.pdf.

Cauley, J and Im, EI, 'Intervention Policy Analysis of Skyjackings and Other Terrorist Incidents' (1988) 78 *American Economic Review* 27–31.

Chakravarty, SP, 'Economic Analysis of Police Stops and Searches: A Critique' (2002) 18 *European Journal of Political Economy* 597–605.

Conte, A and Ganor, B, 'Legal and Policy Issues in Establishing an International Framework for Human Rights Compliance when Countering Terrorism', ICT Paper, 2005, available at http://www.ictconference.org/var/119/20471-Ganor_Conte_Human%20Rights.pdf.

Dominitz, J and Knowles, J, 'Crime Minimization and Racial Bias: What can We Learn from Police Search Data?', PIER Working Paper 05-019, 18 February 2005, available at http://ssrn.com/abstract=719981.

Dugan, L, LaFree, G and Piquero, AR, 'Testing a Rational Choice Model of Airline Hijackings' (2005) 43(4) *Criminology* 1031–65.

Ellman, S, 'Racial Profiling and Terrorism' (2002–03) 46 *New York Law School Law Review* 675.

Enders, W and Sandler, T, 'The Effectiveness of Antiterrorism Policies: A Vector-Autoregression Intervention Analysis' (1993) 87(4) *American Political Science Review* 829–44.

—— 'What Do We Know about the Substitution Effect In Transnational Terrorism?' in A Silke and G Ilardi (eds), *Researching Terrorism: Trends, Achievements, Failures* (London, Frank Cass, 2004), available as an April 2002 working paper at http://www-rcf.usc.edu/~tsandler/substitution2ms.pdf.

Faria, JR, 'Terrorist Innovations and Anti-terrorist Policies' (2006) 18 *Terrorism and Political Violence* 47–56.

Feinberg, J, 'The Rights of Animals and Unborn Generations' in W Blackstone (ed), *Philosophy and Environmental Crisis* (Athens, GA, University of Georgia Press, 1974).

Gladwell, M, 'Troublemakers: What Pit Bulls can Teach us about Profiling', *The New Yorker*, 6 February 2006, available at http://www.newyorker.com/fact/content/articles/060206fa_fact.

Harcourt, BE, 'Rethinking Racial Profiling: A Critique of the Economics, Civil Liberties, and Constitutional Literature, and of Criminal Profiling More Generally' (2004) 71 *University of Chicago Law Review* 1275–381.

—— *Against Prediction: Profiling, Policing, and Punishing in an Actuarial Age* (Chicago, University of Chicago Press, 2006) [Harcourt (2006a)].

—— '*United States v Brignoni-Ponce* and *United States v Martinez-Fuerte*: The Road to Racial Profiling' in C Steiker (ed), *Criminal Procedure Stories* (New York, Foundations Press, 2006b) [Harcourt (2006b)].

Heaton, P, 'Understanding the Effects of Anti-profiling Policies', working paper, March 2006, available at http://home.uchicago.edu/?~psheaton/?workingpapers/?racialprofiling.pdf.

Hernández-Murillo, R and Knowles, J, 'Racial Profiling or Racist Policing? Bounds Tests in Aggregated Data' (2004) 45(3) *International Economic Review* 959–89.

Heymann, PB and Kayyem, JN, *Protecting Liberty in an Age of Terror* (Cambridge, MA, MIT Press, 2005).

Hoffman, B, 'Defending America against Suicide Terrorism' in D Aaron (ed), *Three Years After: Next Steps in the War on Terror* (Santa Monica, RAND Corporation, 2005).

Knowles, J, Persico, N and Todd, P, 'Racial Bias in Motor Vehicle Searches: Theory and Evidence' (2001) 109 *Journal of Political Economy* 203–29.

Krauthammer, C, 'Give Grandma a Pass', *Washington Post*, 29 July 2005, available at http://www.washingtonpost.com/wp-dyn/content/article/2005/07/28/AR200507280 1786.html.

Landes, W, 'An Economic Study of US Aircraft Hijacking, 1961–1976' (1978) 21(1) *Journal of Law and Economics* 1–31.

Lum, C, Kennedy, LW and Sherley, AJ, 'The Effectiveness of Counter-terrorism Strategies: A Campbell Systematic Review', Campbell Collaboration review paper, January 2006, available at http://www.campbellcollaboration.org/doc-pdf/Lum_Terrorism_Review. pdf.

Lund, N, 'The Conservative Case against Racial Profiling' (2003) 66 *Albany Law Review* 329–42.

Manski, C, 'Search Profiling with Partial Knowledge of Deterrence', unpublished paper, 2005.

Nussbaum, M, *The Fragility of Goodness: Luck and Ethics in Greek Tragedy and Philosophy* (Cambridge, Cambridge University Press, 1986).

Pape, R, *Dying to Win: The Strategic Logic of Suicide Terrorism* (New York, Random House, 2005).

Persico, N, 'Racial Profiling, Fairness, and Effectiveness of Policing' (2002) 92 *American Economic Review* 1472–97.

Posner, E and Vermeule, A, 'Should Coercive Interrogation Be Legal?' (2006) 104(4) *Michigan Law Review* 671–707.

Putnam, RD, *Bowling Alone: The Collapse and Revival of American Community* (New York, Simon & Schuster, 2000).

Rawls, J, *A Theory of Justice* (Cambridge, MA, Harvard University Press, 1971).

Rosen, A, 'Detection of Suicidal Patients: An Example of Some Limitations of the Prediction of Infrequent Events' (1954) 18 *Journal of Consulting Psychology* 397–403.

Sartre, J-P, *Les Mains sales* (Paris, Gallimard, 1948).

Sheridan, MB, 'Interviews of Muslims to Broaden: FBI Hopes to Avert a Terrorist Attack', *Washington Post*, 17 July 2004.

Sperry, P, 'When the Profile Fits the Crime', *New York Times*, 28 July 2005, available at http://www.nytimes.com/2005/07/28/opinion/28sperry.html.

Stuntz, WJ, 'Local Policing after the Terror' (2002) 111 *Yale Law Journal* 2137.

Tucker, JB, 'Strategies for Countering Terrorism: Lessons from the Israeli Experience' (2003) *Journal of Homeland Security*, available at http://www.homelandsecurity.org/journal/Articlestucker-israel.html.

Tyler, TR, *Why People Obey the Law* (New Haven, Yale University Press, 1990).

—— 'Trust and Democratic Governance' in V Braithwaite and M Levi (eds), *Trust and Governance* (New York, Russell Sage Foundation, 1998).

Walzer, M, 'Political Action: The Problem of Dirty Hands' (1973) 2(2) *Philosophy and Public Affairs* 160–80.

Yetman, J, 'Suicidal Terrorism and Discriminatory Screening: An Efficiency–Equity Trade-off' (2004) 15(3) *Defence and Peace Economics* 221–30.

Zedner, L, 'Liquid Security: Managing the Market for Crime Control' (2006) 6(3) *Criminology and Criminal Justice* 267–88.

5

The Worst-case Scenario and the Man on the Clapham Omnibus

DIDIER BIGO and ELSPETH GUILD*

INTRODUCTION: THE PARAMETERS OF THE SECURITY AND HUMAN RIGHTS DEBATE

W HY DO WE have so many discussions about security and human rights nowadays? Are the reasons related to the intellectual debate about the status of human rights in the world? Do such discussions involve philosophical considerations of safety and security? Or, is it because practices of coercion and violence, carried out by liberal governments in the name of collective security, are considered by many lawyers and high courts as violating basic human rights? It may be all that, but certainly discussions have been inflamed by cases of torture, by laws justifying indefinite detention, by presidential acts justifying military-like rules for tribunals and by rejection of habeas corpus, the presumption of innocence and the right to legal counsel.[1]

Widespread discussion of the relationship between security and human rights has also been accompanied by the rapid development of technologies of surveillance and increasing control of large groups of people under the suspicion that they may in the future be of potential help to terrorists, even if the individuals and groups have no direct links with terrorists at present. Furthermore, the parameters of the debate changed with the proliferation of projects involving biometric identifiers in travel and identity documents, the increasingly easy exchange of data between 'competent' agencies at a transnational level and the existence of zones of detention that, in the name of the fight against terrorism and illegal migration, block the cross-border movements of persons in need of refuge, as well as others who are in search of work or attempting to visit family or relatives.[2]

---

* The authors are both members of the CHALLENGE programme of the EC Commission (6PCRD priority 7 security), http://www.libertysecurity.org. This chapter is grounded on the common research of the 23 European partners of this integrated programme.

[1] ELISE (European Liberty and Security), *Results of the Three-year Program*, final report, CD ROM (2004), http://www.libertysecurity.org/mot99.html.

[2] Anderson, M and Apap, J, *Striking a Balance between Freedom, Security and Justice in an Enlarged European Union* (Brussels, Centre for European Policy Studies, 2002) 95; Apap, J and Carrera, S,

The debate concerning security and human rights is then mainly political and not juridical—or, more precisely, it lies within the dynamic between the political and the legal. The question is political in the sense that the context within which it arises is characterised by widespread use of political violence by transnational political organisations and, in response, by coercive measures from some Western governments. It is also political in the sense that, unlike during previous periods such as the Cold War (when human rights were seen both as security tools and as objectives per se), liberal governments now consider human rights as a form of internal pressure coming from non-responsible groups, impeding the free will of states and their capacity for defence.

So, in the political realm, human rights are not considered as a useful weapon against the enemy but as a dangerous constraint against effective action. For example, some neo-conservative US commentators consider that even if the discourse of human rights as general values is distinctive of liberal regimes and is an advantage for mobilising populations against the enemy, the strict respect of them is not. Derogations are allowed when it is necessary to 'extract information' in order to win the war and to protect the people.

In such a case, the legal question and the role of judges become central: they must assess the practices of coercion and determine if they are compatible with human rights, and if a practice infringes human rights, decide if it is allowable and under what particular circumstances. If this role of judges as referees is rejected, then human rights are transformed by politicians into merely a 'brand' with no effect on their own practices. Here we assume, for the sake of the discussion, that human rights cannot be transformed into an ideology without destroying their meaning. These values cannot be framed in a liberal discourse and implemented in an illiberal way. Human rights suppose an ethical relation that is embedded into social and political practices and is applicable for all individuals, including foreigners, 'even the worst kind'.[3] When liberal governments ask for exceptions concerning derogation from their legal obligations to protect human rights, the relationship between the political, the ethical and the legal, which is at the heart of democracy, then comes to the fore.[4]

This chapter takes as its starting point the notion that security and freedom are not equals—that is, not two values that can be balanced for the sake of equilibrium; rather, security must be a goal only in order to achieve freedom and democracy, even in time of danger. This chapter seeks to assess the relation between the

'Maintaining Security within Borders: Towards a Permanent State of Emergency in the EU?', Policy Brief No 41, Centre for European Policy Studies, October 2003; Bigo, D, 'Global (In)security: The Field of the Professionals of Unease Management and the Ban-opticon' (2005) 4 *Traces* [Bigo (2005b)]; Bigo, D (ed), *Illiberal Practices in Liberal Regimes: The (In)security Games* (Paris, L'Harmattan, 2006) [Bigo (2006a)].

[3] See Frost, M, *Ethics in International Relations: A Constitutive Theory*, Cambridge Studies in International Relations, vol 45 (Cambridge, Cambridge University Press, 1996); and Frost, M, *Constituting Human Rights: Global Civil Society and the Society of Democratic States* (New York, Routledge, 2002).

[4] See the contribution by Ian Loader in this volume.

fears invoked by the way in which liberal political systems have reacted to the increasingly large scale of political violence by clandestine organisations (ie the fear of mass killings of civilians or what can be called the worst-case scenario), and the necessity and capacity to assess reasonably the limits of declarations about exceptional times.

How can third parties, often through judicial authorities, form their own judgments about the seriousness and extent of a threat, let alone the proportionality of the coercion and restrictions of freedom that are usually an inherent part of official strategies to combat that threat? In the UK legal tradition, 'a man on the Clapham omnibus' refers to an ordinary person, not an expert, whose opinion, because of his (or her) status as an ordinary person from an ordinary background, is conventionally used as a measure for determining whether one party or another should be legally liable in negligence.[5] References to this hypothetical figure therefore rely on the notion of 'a reasonable person'. In the context of the current debate, how can the man on the Clapham omnibus—that is, any average person—successfully navigate the overwhelming professional discourses surrounding the management of threats and not be under their 'charm'? Can references to human rights and the rule of law be mobilised to 'limit and enclose' the rising institutional claim of global insecurity, which appears to come from outside and inside, from nowhere and everywhere, from foreigners and citizens, and which is used to justify an 'unlimited' right of governments and professionals of security to securitise ever more sectors of everyday life? What forms of reasoning are necessary to mitigate worst-case scenario rationales and to halt the transformation of effective protection into a pre-crime climate of suspicion and exception?

To answer these questions, we will first set the scene and look at the actors involved in the debate over security and human rights and briefly discuss the conditions that allow the expression of a radically new situation concerning the threat of a global terrorism, justifying arguments for the exception in order to avoid the worst-case scenario. We will next move on to the substance of the debate over security and human rights by examining different conceptions about security and whom it is for.[6] The third section of this chapter will analyse who it is that determines the boundaries of both threats and their legitimate answers, looking at the technicalities that are at the heart of claims of exceptional times in liberal democratic regimes, where a plurality of voices is crucial to avoid a monopolisation of the definition of security by a restricted group of agents who call themselves 'intelligence'. We will conclude by analysing the rationality of the worst-case scenario with regard to the reasonable judgement of the man on the Clapham omnibus.

---

[5] It is suggested that the phrase was first used by Lord Bowen, QC in a court case in 1903.

[6] Wæver, O, 'Securitization and Desecuritization' in R Lipschutz (ed), *On Security* (New York, Columbia University Press, 1995) 46–86.

I. SETTING THE SCENE: PROFESSIONALS OF POLITICS, PROFESSIONALS OF (IN)SECURITY AND JUDGES

The relationship between security and human rights engages many actors: the victims of violations of human rights, their lawyers, the public and its diverse advocates, including journalists, non-governmental organisations (NGOs) and political parties.[7] It also involves more 'authoritative' actors, who compete for a final say on the definition of the terms of the debate and their limits: lawyers and academics, judges, professionals of (in)security management (and especially intelligence services); professionals of politics (and especially government sectors that are responsible for defence, justice and, from time to time, foreign affairs).[8] The relationship between security and human rights thus generates an inter-sectoral debate between these authoritative voices, which is accelerated by a sense of urgency and necessity. The debate involves 'fixing' the boundaries of the meaning of security, determining what level of priority to ascribe to human rights, and deciding whether and on what basis governments have the right to reformulate the juridical rules that embed these rights at both national and international levels. The debate also involves a range of technologies, which are often presented as 'solutions', as well as the ethical dimension of their use.[9]

If we roughly reconfigure the scene by positioning the actors along two sides, on one side we may say that some actors are more sensitive to the arguments of security than those of human rights. These actors are often professionals of security and especially intelligence services whose task is to 'prevent new threats' and to 'extract information' in order to have a better knowledge about risks and threats surrounding 'us'. They hope to have a complete picture of the risk, or at least the most accurate picture possible, and any means that can further this aim is useful,

---

[7] Lewis, A, 'Security and Liberty: Preserving the Values of Freedom' in RC Leone and G Anrig Jr (eds), *The War on Our Freedoms: Civil Liberties in an Age of Terrorism* (New York, Public Affairs, 2003) 47; Tsoukala, A, 'The Media Coverage of the Public Debate on Exceptionalism in Europe', paper presented at workshop on 'War, Sovereignty and Security Today', Université du Québec à Montréal, 15–16 March 2004.

[8] Brouwer, E, 'France: Focusing on Internal Security' in E Brouwer, P Catz and E Guild (eds), *Immigration, Asylum and Terrorism: A Changing Dynamic in European Law* (Nijmegen, Recht and Samenleving, 2003) 13; Guild, E, 'Exceptionalism and Transnationalism: UK Judicial Control of the Detention of Foreign "International Terrorists"' (2003) 28(4) *Alternatives* 491–515.; Catz, P, 'United Kingdom: Withdrawing from International Human Rights Standards' in E Brouwer, P Catz and E Guild (eds), *Immigration, Asylum and Terrorism: A Changing Dynamic in European Law* (Nijmegen, Recht and Samenleving, 2003) 71; Fekete, L, 'All in the Name of Security' in P Scraton (ed), *Beyond September 11: An Anthology of Dissent* (London, Pluto Press, 2002) 102; Tsoukala, A, 'Defining the Terrorist Threat in the Post-11 September Era' in D Bigo (ed), *Illiberal Practices in Liberal Regimes* (Paris, L'Harmattan, 2006).

[9] Bigo, D, *Polices En Réseaux: L'expérience Européenne* (Paris, Presses de Sciences Po, 1996); Bigo (2005b); Huysmans, J, 'Minding Exceptions: Politics of Insecurity and Liberal Democracy' (2004) 3(3) *Contemporary Political Theory* 321–41; Pastore, F, 'The Asymmetrical Fortress: The Problem of Relations between Internal and External Security Policies in the European Union' in M Anderson and J Apap (eds), *Police and Justice Co-operation and the New European Borders* (The Hague, Kluwer Law International, 2002) 59.

especially if the issue at hand is a catastrophe, a worst-case scenario. Anything preventing the obtaining of information is 'dangerous': 'ex post—following another terrorist attack that might have been prevented through the exercise of coercive interrogation—the price of my scruple might simply seem too high'.[10]

The key actors on this side of our security/human rights divide are supported not only by believers in the supremacy of national interests and sovereignty (so-called realists) but also by some human rights professors, who seek a balance between the two imperatives and who advocate a 'lesser evil' in order not to be 'naïve' and 'idealist'.[11] Such claims in favour of security may concede that coercive practices violate human rights but see them as justified in the prevention of the worst happening. Professionals of politics are also often ready, in the name of national or global security (of the West), to support this type of argument. They consider us to be at 'war', even if the war is not a declared one with specific rules and a recognised enemy. The 'war against terror' is rhetoric that encourages the use of language of exception and permits breaches of the corpus of human rights.

The novelty of this position in the debate is more and more its transnational character, as it is framed through a discourse of co-operation between states against terrorists, co-operation which can even go beyond liberal states to include any state that is willing to participate in a coalition against terror. The discourse includes 'trust' between the partners (that is, the states) but also a form of silence concerning how information has been 'extracted'. The most important consideration is the ability to prevent the worst-case scenario—a major attack by a clandestine organisation in the territory of one of the states that make up the coalition of the willing.

Another actor on this side of the security debate is more silent, but powerful nonetheless: the security industry, which provides technologies of surveillance, including biometric identifiers and software for profiling, for speedy access between databases and for encrypted communication and interception. These technologies are presented as the solution to the violence of clandestine organisations. Members of the security industry are often those most interested in the development of a 'risk approach' in terms of worst-case scenarios rather than approaches that involve probability and collective risk management.[12] They want

---

[10] Ignatieff, M, 'Moral Prohibition at a Price' in K Roth, M Worden and A Bernstein (eds), *Torture: A Human Rights Perspective* (New York, The New Press, 2005) 26. See also Ignatieff, M, *Human Rights as Politics and Idolatry* (Princeton, Princeton University Press, 2001); and Roth, K, 'Human Rights, the Bush Administration, and the Fight against Terrorism: The Need for a Positive Vision' in C Brown (ed), *Lost Liberties: Ashcroft and the Assault on Personal Freedom* (New York, The New Press, 2003) 237.

[11] See the critique of this notion of balance by Ian Loader in this volume. See also ELISE (2004); and ELISE, 'Suspicion et exception' (2005) 58 *Cultures et Conflits*.

[12] We have to differentiate between actuarial risk and worst-case scenarios, as they are two different forms of risk. In an actuarial risk approach (along insurance principles), the answer to the risk is proportionate with the probability of the event occurring. It is a collectivisation of individual risks that will happen for sure, even if we do not know to whom (eg, car accidents). In a worst-case scenario example of an atomic bomb possessed by fanatics, on the other hand, the probability of occurrence is near zero. After September 11, however, such scenarios have entered the realm of public imagination. 'The question is not if, but when' was a favourite phrase of US Secretary of Defense Donald Rumsfeld in

governments to invest in their technologies, even if the probability of the risk is very low, and use the nature of the consequences of the realisation of the risk as their major justification.

On the other side of our security/human rights divide are those who continue to think that human rights need to be implemented at all times, that they are a sign of civilisation and human progress, and that they are not subject to a reciprocity requirement. On the contrary, human rights are the distinctive feature differentiating the combatants, and their respect blocks the emergence of scapegoating and minimises rivalry.[13] Actors on this side of the debate believe that coercion on a large scale is not the solution for transnational political violence but rather the food that feeds the fire. Kenneth Roth, for example, clearly states:

> Torture and related abuses are antithetical to the entire concept of human rights. Rights define the limits beyond which no government should venture. To breach those limits in the name of some utilitarian calculus is to come dangerously close to the ends-justify-the-means rationale of terrorism.[14]

Most NGOs, civil rights activists, human rights lawyers and even some professionals of security, such as gendarmerie, traditional detectives and those involved in criminal justice, insist on the importance of the strict respect of human rights. This respect is manifested in limitations on the number of acceptable derogations for some rights and the impossibility of accepting any derogation for other rights. National and international judges (including many European institutions) are often inclined to support this view and to counter the discourse of the worst-case scenario by a discourse based on reasonable grounds for a reasonable person. The rule of law depends on the man on the Clapham omnibus as the reality check against exceptional legal decision making. He (or she) figuratively stands in every courtroom, determining whether the application of the law is just. And it is he (or she) who, as an allegorical figure of the public, is subject to and must evaluate the discourse of fear of the Apocalypse tomorrow, the rhetoric of the worst-case scenario, and the assertions of 'experts' about our future and about the justifications for extracting information from detainees.

But who is it that can make the claim to reasonableness? Who is the spokesperson for the man on the Clapham omnibus? Can we challenge the discourse of the

reference to bombings by Al Qaeda, supposedly with weapons of mass destruction (WMD). The consequences are so huge and so destructive, such reasoning goes, that we need to do something, even if the probability is low; and we need to put a lot of resources into it, against any actuarial risk strategy. If such reasoning is followed, the only limit is then the limitation of the political imagination.

The worst-case scenario is related more to the principle of precaution than with risk calculation. In environmental studies, however, the principle of precaution is framed through mathematic models assessing transformations of nature and the capacity of traceability and with the profiling of things that are happening. In the debate on security and terrorism, the assessment is based on supposition about the will and nature of the enemy, its size, scope, purpose in the future, etc. It depends on the 'prophecy' of the white notes of intelligence services. See the contribution by Bernard Harcourt in this volume.

[13] Girard, R and Williams, JG, *The Girard Reader* (New York, Crossroad, 1996).
[14] Roth, K, 'Justifying Torture' in K Roth, M Worden and A Bernstein (eds), *Torture: A Human Rights Perspective* (New York, The New Press, 2005) xxi.

'experts'? Can we discuss their assumptions about the future if they have more knowledge than 'we' on the Clapham bus have? Are we not obliged to trust them when they say they are acting to protect us, and that this protection supposes some individual sacrifices justified by the exceptional moment we live in and by the seriousness of the danger, about which they refuse even to speak openly in order not to make us panic? We cannot contest the 'expert' views on security and human rights if we do not first understand that they largely rely on the notions of threat and exception.

1. Threat, Security, Human Rights, Exception

The context in which the current discussion about security and human rights occurs reminds us more of the 1930s (the Weimar Republic) than the 1960s and 1970s (decolonisation and the first wave of political violence in Italy and Germany) and is central to an appreciation of what is at stake. The main strategy used to advocate the 'regaining' of freedom of action that is necessary to win the 'war on terror' involves redrawing the boundaries between the realm of politics and the realm of law.[15] Arguments along these lines are especially significant in the context of international humanitarian obligations and international human rights, as these forms of law are beyond the state in their scope but often depend on the state to be applied.[16] So, the formula of the state needs to be deconstructed in the discourse, in order to identify who it is who claims that they have 'state' authority—a form of symbolic capital that gives them the right to have the final say.[17] 'Security is always a contested concept',[18] and the term is of no use if we do not analyse the actors who have the capacity to define it, along with defining sovereignty and defining what is an exception to the rule.[19]

In other words, when issues about the relationship between security and human rights arise, it is not because of inconsistencies between bodies of domestic and international law defining the relationship; it is because the political actors involved want to redefine their sphere of competence, to re-negotiate their respective roles. As a case in point, some liberal governments not only use torture against their enemies but also seek to justify it as serious policy option by re-framing the limits of torture. Hence, concepts such as an 'adequate level of coercion necessary to extract information from enemy combatants' have emerged.[20] Such

---

[15] 'We cannot struggle against terrorists with a hand tied up behind the back, we need to regain our freedom [*sic*]' (French anti-terrorist magistrate Jean Louis Bruguière).

[16] Eberwein, WD, 'Le Paradoxe Humanitaire? Normes et Pratiques' (2006 *Cultures et Conflits* 60.

[17] Bourdieu, P, *Practical Reason: On the Theory of Action* (Stanford, Stanford University Press, 1998); Bourdieu, P, *Propos Sur Le Champ Politique* (Lyon, Presses Universitaires de Lyon, 2000).

[18] Buzan, B, *People, States and Fear: An Agenda for International Security in the Post-Cold War Era*, 2nd edn (New York, Harvester Wheatsheaf, 1991).

[19] Bigo (2005b).

[20] Ignatieff (2005). *Cf* Roth (2005).

notions betray a desire to develop illiberal practices while maintaining a liberal discourse.

Concepts such as 'adequate levels of coercion' arise when political actors attempt to enact a sort of permanent moment of exception, of emergency.[21] In 'normal' times, that is, in the routine, the role of judges as referees of boundaries is accepted, but with claims of specific new threats that lead to a moment of exception, the political actors open up the question of exceptions to the rule of law.

For such actors, in the name of emergency and threat to collective security, exceptions may infringe privacy, different forms of freedom (speech, movement) and human rights. The political actors remain somewhat constrained, however, by the written limits imposed by their more liberal predecessors. While at the national level new coercive laws can be passed to justify illiberal practices, international treaties and conventions are harder to amend or change. When accompanied by supra-national dispute-resolution mechanisms (that is, international courts), the interpretation of international human right standards escapes the control of national governments and becomes a frustrating obstacle to the achievement of the new framework. For judges who loyally uphold international human rights commitments, the respective principles of human rights and security have quite a clear hierarchy, and although some rights may allow for occasional derogation when the survival of a collectivity is in actual danger from an imminent threat, other rights may never be breached, even when an exceptional moment is declared.

The present discussion in the United States, Australia and the United Kingdom, and to a lesser degree in Russia, Spain and France, is related to attempts to change the boundaries of the common understanding of such fundamental concepts as 'universal declaration', 'constitution', 'rule of law', 'prisoner of war', 'criminal', 'detention', 'punishment', 'citizen' and 'foreigner', in order to justify what the governments have done. They consider that they can reframe the previous categories, by expanding or limiting them, and that they can insert new categories into the agenda, for example the invention of 'unlawful combatants' as neither prisoners of war nor criminals.[22]

The internal debate within the realm of law is thus subverted entirely by the very possibility that those in the political realm can stake out a sovereign right to change the rules and to suspend the law. To 'suspend the law' is used here in the sense given to the term by Hobbes, Carl Schmitt and, later on, Agamben—that is, to declare a state of exception outside rule of law prescriptions regarding object,

[21] Dillon, M, 'Network Society, Network-centric Warfare and the State of Emergency' (2002) 19(4) *Theory, Culture and Society* 71; Bonditti, P, 'From Territorial Space to Networks: A Foucaultian Approach to the Implementation of Biopolitics' (2004) 29(4) *Alternatives* 465–82.

[22] Cole, D and Dempsey, JX, *Terrorism and the Constitution: Sacrificing Civil Liberties in the Name of National Security* (New York, The New Press, 2002) 231; Cole, D, *Enemy Aliens: Double Standards and Constitutional Freedoms in the War on Terrorism* (New York, The New Press, 2003); Butler, J, 'Explanation and Exoneration, or What We can Hear' (2002) 20(3) *Social Text* 177–88; Jabri, V, 'Critical Thought and Political Agency in Time of War' (2005) 19(1) *International Relations* 70–9.

space and time,[23] and to redraw the boundaries of the language of law. The terminology of the present discussion is employed in the name of a 'radically new situation' that has never previously happened and is 'radically dangerous' as it touches on the issue of the very survival of a community.[24]

The exception or exceptional moment in this sense is then perceivably sensibly different from a state of exception or state of emergency that is already anticipated within the rule of law. In the latter case, the legal tradition involved and/or a written constitution gives freedom of action to the government, but powers of scrutiny are given to other sectors (parliament and/or courts), and there are therefore limits on the scope of exceptions. In the first case, however, the exception determines what is and what is not the law. The 'sovereign', that is, the government, decides the terms of the exception according to its own will, not along a 'codified legal order': 'It cannot be circumscribed factually and made to conform to preformed law.'[25]

Such exceptions are the product of contingency, of new situations, and are equivalent to moments of 'foundation'. And each person in charge considers himself or herself as a new Solon, creating new rules for a renewed community. This 'royal' position is so 'comfortable' that the temptation is strong to maintain the exceptional moment for as long as possible; and a permanent state of emergency is then instituted by encouraging a constant state of fear and unease among the population through 'alert codes' and a vocabulary of reassurance by professionals of politics that in fact reactivates and reinforces fears. The state of exception is moreover maintained by side-stepping the ability of parliament and the courts to decide about the object, space and time of the exception, in brief circumventing the processes that might judicialise a state of exception inside the law and limit the

---

[23] Boyle, K, Hadden, T and Hillyard, P, *Law and State: The Case of Northern Ireland*, Law in Society Series (London, Robertson, 1975) ix, 194; Campagna, N, 'Prerogative and Constitutional State: The Problem of State of Emergency Force in John Locke and Benjamin Constant' (2001) 40(4) *Der Staat* 553–79; Verdeja, E, 'Law, Terrorism, and the Plenary Power Doctrine: Limiting Alien Rights' (2002) 9(1) *Constellations* 89–97; Ferejohn, J and Pasquino, P, 'The Law of the Exception: A Typology of Emergency Powers' (2004) 2(2) *International Journal of Constitutional Law* 210–39; Walker, RJB, 'War, Terror and Judgement' in B Gökay and RJB Walker (eds), *11 September 2001: War, Terror and Judgement* (London, Frank Cass, 2003); Neal, WA, 'Cutting Off the King's Head: Foucault's *Society Must Be Defended* and the Problem of Sovereignty' (2004) 29(4) *Alternatives: Global, Local, Political* (special English language issue of *Cultures et Conflits*) 373–98; Aradau, C, 'Governing Populations and Ungovernable People: The Liberal State and the War on Terror' in V Jabri and RBJ Walker (eds), *Liberty, Security and the Limits of Modern Politics* (Brussels, CEPS, 2005).

[24] Agamben, G, *Etat d'Exception: Homo Saccer*, L'ordre Philosophique (Paris, Les Editions du Seuil, 2003) 152; Balke, F, 'Political Existence and "Bare Life": The Biopolitics of Carl Schmitt' (2001) 2 *Distinktion – skandinavisk tidsskrift for samfundsteori* 71–80; Walker (2003) 62–83; Turner, BS, 'Sovereignty and Emergency: Political Theology, Islam and American Conservatism' (2002) 19(4) *Theory, Culture and Society* 103; Arato, A, '*Minima Politica* after September 11' (2002) 9(1) *Constellations* 46–52; Hoff, B-I, 'The Displaced Financial State of Emergency: About the Financial-Political Accountability of Parliament and the Government and the Role of the Federation as Guardian of Economic Sovereignty' (2003) 44(3) *Politische Vierteljahresschrift* 417–19.

[25] Schmitt, C, *Political Theology: Four Chapters on the Concept of Sovereignty* (London, MIT Press, 1985 [1922]) 6.

will of the 'sovereign'.[26] Instead, post-September 11 security rhetoric produces an insecurisation of the world, which reinforces the so-called necessity in a sort of discursive political spiral that transforms the claims into 'evidence'.[27]

The dynamic between security and human rights is hence underpinned by these two parameters: first, the novelty and intensity of the threat; second, the limits of the exceptional moment—its necessity, legality, legitimacy. We will discuss these before analysing the relationship between security and human rights

II. THREAT OF POLITICAL VIOLENCE, MASS DESTRUCTION AND COLLECTIVE SECURITY AGAINST CLANDESTINE ORGANISATIONS

1. Fear of Armageddon: Justification for a State of Exception?

The question that has emerged after September 11 and is our major concern here is: have we entered a radically new world in which the monopoly of states over violence in their own territories is coming to an end? If the answer is 'yes', as the governments in the United States, Australia and the United Kingdom have tried to convince us—if we are facing a new kind of terrorism that, in its radicalism and its use of weapons of mass destruction without any warning or discussion because the ultimate goal is destruction and not negotiation of any kind, is different from the past—then the framing of new boundaries between law and politics, between executive and judicial powers, between military and civilian rules, between security and liberty, between surveillance and protection, is legitimate. The move to create new rules and to reframe others is right. What needs to be achieved is a new 'balance' between security and freedom, between the prevention of the worst-case scenario and privacy, between collective security and personal guarantees.

However, if the answer to our key question is 'no'—if the patterns of political violence of clandestine organisations have transformed but not in a radical way, if we can learn from past experiences, if political discussion, strategic actions and deterrence of rational actors are possible—then we have to look closely at existing solutions and legislation before establishing a (potentially permanent) exceptional moment.

The discussion between the United States and its allies, on one side, and France, Germany, Russia and a large majority of countries all over the world, on the other side, has been rooted in this difference of perspective concerning this key question. Beyond differing opinions about the war in Iraq and the threat of Al Qaeda, the fear of entering into a new period in which governments cannot confidently control the use of violence in their own territories seems shared by all Western liberal

---

[26] Armitage, J, 'State of Emergency: An Introduction' (2002) 19(4) *Theory, Culture and Society* 27; Dillon (2002); Steinmetz, G, The State of Emergency and the Revival of American Imperialism: Toward an Authoritarian Post-Fordism' (2003) 15(2) *Public Culture* 323–45; Braber, L, 'Korematsu's Ghost: A Post-September 11th Analysis of Race and National Security' (2002) 47(2) *Villanova Law Review* 451–90.

[27] Bigo (2002b); ELISE (2004).

countries. However, the reactions of governments and the methods chosen to deal with their own fear and unease toward the future differ across the affected states, depending on the scale of the violence, the ideology of the state and the political culture of the country, as well as the experience of previous bombing campaigns (or lack thereof).

In this respect, the attacks of September 11 were not the beginning of a new pattern of hyper-terrorism but merely an exception in terms of the scale of both the violence and the response of the authorities.[28] The idea that terrorism of that kind was radically new could only be sustained in a country that had not recently experienced political violence on its own soil, not to mention war or acts of aggression. The supposed novelty of the situation has been exaggerated by the radicalisation of the ideology and language of war, which essentialises the enemy as 'evil' in order to mobilise the population. The lack of structures at police and judicial levels for dealing with violence of this nature has also provided an opportunity for the development of military-like rules.

If we compare the post-September 11 situation in the United States with the post-bombing situations in Spain and the United Kingdom, however, we see first a decrease in the capacity of violence from Al Qaeda (and not an increase as expected after 9/11). Moreover, in the cases of Spain and the United Kingdom, there has been a more stoic response from both the governments and the populations, demonstrating that normalising can be part of the answer. The histories of the Basque Homeland and Freedom group (ETA) and the Provisional Irish Republican Army (Provisional IRA), as well as the way ordinary people have coped with these organisations by 'living with terrorism', certainly provide an alternative perspective on the US discourse about radical novelty.[29]

The US understanding of security is also central to this difference in attitude. In a country that has virtually never known invasion or war at home, security is seen as the outcome of power: if you are the most powerful, then you are safe; and after a terrorist attack, you need to show your strength by terrorising the terrorists. This (ir)realist assumption about security, especially in the face of an enemy with the capacity for stealth, differs greatly from the more European idea that achieving security requires dialogue and that generalised coercion reinforces the cycle of violence rather than stopping it. In this European view, the way to stop violence is a combination of firmness through criminal justice, which should be aimed against the perpetrators only, and dialogue with their potential supporters—not a 'war' against large groups of people based on the counter-insurgency strategies of

---

[28] ELISE (2004).

[29] Bigo, D, 'Reassuring and Protecting: Internal Security Implications of French Participation in the Coalition against Terrorism' in E Hershberg and KW Moore (eds), *Critical Views of September 11: Analysis from around the World* (New York, The New York Press, Social Science Research Council, 2002b); Glendening, PN, 'Governing after September 11th: A New Normalcy' (2002) 62 *Public Administration Review* 21–3; Brouwer, E, Catz, P and Guild, E (eds), *Immigration, Asylum and Terrorism: A Changing Dynamic in European Law* (Nijmegen, Recht and Samenleving, 2003); Guild, E and van Selm, J, *International Migration and Security: Immigrants as an Asset or Threat?* (London, Routledge, 2005).

military and intelligence services, and a pre-emptive criminal justice system based on the anticipation of risk.

It is not for us to judge immediately the argument of a radical novelty, of an unprecedented event, but it looks like the US government has tried to convince the world of its own right, by generalising its own specific fear. Solidarity across the Atlantic with the victims of September 11 is not necessarily a sign that Europeans share the same level of fear about the violence of clandestine organisations. The West is not at all homogeneous in that sense. Mobilising through fear to create two blocks and two blocks only (those who are with us and those who are against us) has been partly a success in the United States but a failure everywhere else. And in the United States, this mobilisation through fear reaches a quasi-religious tone when invoking the image of fanatics who are out of touch with reason and capable of suicide and mass killing for 'nothing' except hate. This strategy has nevertheless been very difficult to achieve, especially in academic circles and among the educated populations of big cities, although it may succeed more in other parts of the country.

The partial success of this strategy has necessitated a second argument for mobilisation. The 'radical novelty' of terrorism and the fear it generates are based on the notion of a planned Armageddon. In the face of such a potential disaster, so this second argument goes, any measure, even coercive measures specifically excluded by human rights obligations on an individual level, are acceptable in the name of protecting the freedom and human rights of the collectivity. A key promoter of this type of rhetoric was the UK government, even while the Prime Minister faced a population largely sceptical about the advent of a new age of terror.

2. The Right to Sacrifice Individual Rights in the Name of Collective Security?

The issue of a right to sacrifice individual rights in the name of collective security and freedom arises only if we agree that we are living in an exceptional moment. If we disagree, if we consider the world to be operating as 'usual', the answer is simple: utilitarian arguments cannot justify the sacrifice of lives and fundamental rights that are covered by the *jus cogens*.[30] If we accept the notion of the 'progress' of civilisation and some sort of universal conscience, it is necessary to refute the crude utilitarian argument and instead develop the idea of an international society of individuals. Moreover, as just discussed above, we have good reasons to doubt the radical novelty of the current situation and must be cautious when we hear rhetoric about an exception that would allow us to go beyond the otherwise

---

[30] The capacity of Michael Ignatieff to 'forget' about the difference between *jus cogens* and other rights in his discussion about 'lesser evil'—which is used to avoid issues of the limits of sovereignty and absolute limits on the state (ie, the government)—is astonishing at the academic level, and creates suspicion that the argument is framed more as justification for illiberal policy than to engage in an intellectual debate. See Ignatieff, M, *The Lesser Evil: Political Ethics in an Age of Terror* (Princeton, Princeton University Press, 2004).

generally accepted limits on coercion. In other words, to engage in a debate that assumes we are living in a new age of terror is already a problem as such. It already goes some way in justifying the idea of an exception, giving politicians the excuse to reframe laws. And any metaphor of balance between rights, or between freedom and security, implicitly accepts the premise of danger, obliging us to change in favour of more security, more collective protection and less robust individual rights.

Legislation at the national and European levels has already granted governments the possibility of derogating in specific cases, but in interpreting those laws and conventions, judges have continually refuted the idea that governments can use such occasions to reframe the boundaries of laws. The exceptions must occur inside the rule of law; they cannot frame the rule of law. In the liberal tradition, Neumann's argument that the rule defines the exception must always win against the anti-liberal argument of Carl Schmitt that the exception defines the rule.[31] So, to agree to certain cases in which exception may be used is not to give a blank cheque to the government.

3. The 'War on Words' and the 'Newspeak' of (In)security

The 'war on terror' is also a war on words and their established/customary/conventional meanings.[32] For the purpose of describing the current and supposedly new situation, a new vocabulary has emerged to justify the unjustifiable practices of liberal regimes. Torture has been disguised as 'the optimum conditions for the preparation of interrogation' in order to justify the systematic techniques of intelligence officers who want their prisoners to say what the officials suppose they know; the transfer of prisoners has been labelled 'rendition', mocking their human value; prisoners have been labelled 'unlawful combatants', 'terrorists of the worst kind' and 'pure evil' in order to negate their humanity; and 'exception' to the law in the sense of derogation has been used to suspend the law when it does not accord with government objectives.[33]

The military euphemisms for cruel, inhuman and degrading treatment have been carefully chosen in order to 'facilitate' the task of interrogators and so that they do not feel destabilised. 'Dietary manipulation' is easier to order than 'temporary starvation'; it is easier to write 'temperature adjustment' on a report than to describe dousing people with cold water and freezing them under sub-zero blasts from air conditioning; and the notion of 'taking advantage of individual phobias' is easier to accept than an explicit order to use dogs, strip off an individual's clothes, and so on.

---

[31] Huysmans (2004).

[32] Beck, U, 'The Terrorist Threat: World Risk Society Revisited' (2002) 19(4) *Theory, Culture and Society* 39–56.

[33] See Brody, R, 'The Road to Abu Ghraib' in K Roth, M Worden and A Bernstein (eds), *Torture: A Human Rights Perspective* (New York, The New Press, 2005).

The reports and written orders that use such language usually contain paragraphs about national security, the protection of citizens and the duty of the military to do their best in order to prevent terrorism. The term 'security' has in this way been used to justify coercion, torture, surveillance and control of large groups who 'might be' supporters of potential terrorists. Consequently, one of the first words whose meaning we need to 'restore' is 'security'.

III. BALANCING SECURITY AND HUMAN RIGHTS?

When we speak of security, we need always to ask the question, 'whose security?'. Are we speaking of the security of an individual? The security of the state? Are we speaking of a collective security? And, if so, 'collective' at what level? A community that has a majority inside a country, a national community unified behind its leader, a larger group sharing the same values, a humane community?

The critical security approach insists on what the authors call the 'referent object' of security and the possible contradiction between national, economic and environmental securitisation.[34] The security of one of the referent objects can generate insecurity for another one, so maximum security is an illusion.[35] When a situation has been 'securitised', the effect is often far from giving more protection to individuals. Securitising may also involve discriminating between a group that becomes more protected and a group that is even more at risk of violence (and/or coercion) after the securitisation than before. Furthermore, the move towards securitisation is not always the right thing to do, especially when it limits the options for peaceful or negotiated solutions. If securitisation means coercion without effective protection, then desecuritisation is a necessary step.[36]

The value of security is dependent on its effective practice and not on the wording that goes with it. Security as a shelter, as a form of individual protection, is different in its process than security as a form of surveillance and control.[37] When using the term 'security', we must be aware of what kind of social practices we are referring to. Security as individual safety, juridical guarantee, human security or social security can go hand in hand with human rights, but security as coercion, prevention, surveillance and marginalisation/exclusion of some groups infringes

---

[34] Buzan, B, 'Rethinking Security after the Cold War' (1997) 32(1) *Cooperation and Conflict* 5–28.

[35] Darcy, S, 'The Rights of Minorities in States of Emergency' (2002) 9(4) *International Journal on Minority and Group Rights* 345–69.

[36] Call, CT and Stanley, W, 'Protecting the People: Public Security Choices after Civil Wars' (2001) 7(2) *Global Governance* 151–72; Huysmans, J, Dobson, A and Prokhovnik, R (eds), *Politics of Protection: Sites of Insecurity and Political Agency* (London, Routledge, 2005); Wæver, O, *Concepts of Security* (Copenhagen, University of Copenhagen Institute for Political Science, 1997); Lipschutz, RD, *On Security: New Directions in World Politics* (New York, Columbia University Press, 1995) xiv, 233.

[37] See Bigo, D, 'Protection: Security, Territory and Population' in J Huysmans, A Dobson and R Prokhovnik (eds), *Politics of Protection: Sites of Insecurity and Political Agency* (London, Routledge, 2005) {Bigo (2005c)}; Guild, E, 'Judicialisation of Armed Conflict: Transforming the Twenty-first Century' in J Huysmans, A Dobson and R Prokhovnik (eds), *Politics of Protection: Sites of Insecurity and Political Agency* (London, Routledge, 2005).

human rights. In short, the notion of security, more so than human rights, is highly subject to variations of meaning. We need to analyse in each case what kind of social practice we are referring to when using the term 'security'. There is not necessarily a contradiction between the terms 'security' and 'human rights', but there are certainly contradictions between human rights and the practices that are referred to under some accepted usages of the term 'security'.[38]

The first conception of security as individual protection leads to understandings of the rights to life and security that view them as placing positive obligations on states to provide security from poverty, illness and degradation.[39] And as long as the concept of security is framed as individual security or the right to safety, the contradiction with human rights is not central.[40] However, the second form of 'security', surveillance and control, is on the contrary rooted in exceptionalism and the utilitarian right of a collectivity to sacrifice individual rights. It is only with this latter conception of security that a discourse of 'balance' can take place.[41]

This metaphor of balance between security and liberty (or between security and human rights) has been criticised as misleading:

> An important characteristic of contemporary debates about the relationship between claims about security and claims about liberty is the resort to the metaphor of striking a balance between liberty and security. It is a comforting metaphor. It suggests, not least, that someone is in a position to judge when a proper balance has been reached. Thus it is a metaphor that disables any understanding of how the relationship between these competing claims is, in practice, structurally one-sided. Some voices are in a much stronger position to be heard than others, just as some bank balances are considerably more impressive than others. Balance, in this case, suggests a situation of preponderance, not of equality. It is also a metaphor that discourages people from thinking about the way in which any possible judgement about when a balance has been reached will be made by agents who are very closely connected with security agencies—even though this is, after all, what is meant by a sovereign state having a monopoly over violence in a particular territory. Instead, the metaphor of balance encourages people to think about politics as a matter of simple choices, as if one can choose liberty or security, rather than conceiving of them as inseparable values that are always in potential conflict.[42]

The use of the cosy imagery of a balance in this context works precisely so as to deflect attention to what is at stake in the idea of the exception, in claims about the need for some sovereign decision to be made so as to suspend established norms, and freedoms, in the name of security in a state of emergency. The metaphor of a balance, in short, detracts attention from all the hard questions about responsibility, about judgement, about who gets to decide what warrants military and/or

---

[38] Jasson, C, 'The Need to Reaffirm Humanitarian Values' (2002) 21(3) *Refugee Survey Quarterly* 181–5; Nyers, P, *Rethinking Refugees: Beyond the Politics of Emergency* (London, Routledge, 2005).
[39] See the contribution by Sandra Fredman in this volume.
[40] See the contribution by Liora Lazarus in this volume.
[41] See the contribution by Ian Loader in this volume.
[42] ELISE (2004).

legal action, when derogations from the rule of law are appropriate, and whether suspects are to be treated as humans or as something else entirely.

Not the least reason to be sceptical of this metaphor under contemporary circumstances lies in the degree to which discourses about security are increasingly framed as a matter of co-operation and unification, while discourses about liberty are framed in relation to fragmented jurisdictions severely constrained by law and regulations. Security is now considered as a value without frontiers. Co-operation is seen as the key to efficient and centralised information, for anticipating events and profiling who is and who is not dangerous, who is and who is not suspect. European Union agreements have been pushed forward, especially by Spain, so as to structure an EU identity that views the various European countries as a single democracy struggling against the same terrorist enemies.[43] The United States wishes to have even more co-operation at the transatlantic level, albeit under its own strategic direction. Internal and external securities are being merged, in complex ways that certainly do not fit with conventional accounts of a 'security dilemma' between states but that have been examined in some detail.[44] On the other hand, the spaces for liberty have been carefully distinguished, especially in relation to freedom of movement and the crossing of borders.

The challenge before us does not lie in the mysterious task of identifying some acceptable balance between claims about security and claims about liberty. It lies in the need for much more rigorous scrutiny of the conditions under which claims about security warrant the suspension of liberties and freedoms. It requires much more sustained attention to the ways in which the restructuring of political life in response to many different forces is being shaped and distorted by agencies capable of converting serious threats that require democratically considered responses into extreme states of emergency that require military responses, new modalities of social control, intensified forms of surveillance and exclusion and unwarranted assaults on the most basic values of liberalism, democracy and the rule of law.[45]

Then, if difficult decisions are to be made, they need to be understood not in relation to a fuzzy and de-politicised metaphor of balance but in relation to hard questions about what it means to make an exception to the normal expectations of liberty, equality, democracy and the rule of law in modern political life.

IV. PROFESSIONALS OF SECURITY AND THE TECHNOLOGIES OF SURVEILLANCE: A DRIVING FORCE?

In the duel between professionals of politics and judges to determine what security is, the appropriateness of exception, and under what conditions human rights

---

[43] Guittet, E-P, 'European Political Identity and Democratic Solidarity after 9/11: The Spanish Case' (2004) 29(4) *Alternatives: Global, Local, Political* (special English language issue of *Cultures et Conflits*) 441–64.

[44] Bigo (2005b).

[45] ELISE (2004).

may be derogated from, professionals of security and members of (in)security management have a central role. The intelligence services of the police and of national defence agencies, which have both human and technical resources, tend to have different sources and differing views about the nature of threats, especially at the transnational level. However, once these differences are smoothed out in the name of collaboration, all doubts about the accuracy of the sources tend to disappear into a single, authoritative narrative about facts, secret facts and truth. Such narratives are then often the basis on which professionals of politics and judges make their decisions.

Because they are specialists and possess the technologies of surveillance, security professionals are invested by the public with a specific aura, and they are often the ones who most visibly give 'security' its meaning by labelling and prioritising the levels of threat and the nature of the threats and risks for a nation. And although they are far from playing a sovereign role, they are often nonetheless the ones who actuate a moment of exception by establishing the 'routines' that enable it to exist.[46] However, these same security professionals are often uneasy when the media insists on knowing the specifics of the information passed on to politicians and judges, and they are sometimes attacked by both the public and other government officials for being responsible for mistakes in the decision-making process. Their ability to affect public discourse is unquestionable, for in addition to providing the 'data' for decision-making, they also have the capacity to destabilise the 'truth' of political and judicial statements by leaking contradictory information—something that has occurred in the United States, Australia and, to a lesser extent, the United Kingdom.

The strength of intelligence services comes largely from their technologies of profiling, data mining and access to databases, rather than originating from their capacity to extract information from individuals. Human rights are therefore an issue not only when suspects are subject to questioning but also when more mundane tools than torture (including biometric identifiers, transnational databases, and the profiling of risks associated with certain individuals) are utilised. The rule of law is often less of a consideration for professionals in the security industry and their supporters than rumour, suspicion and the accumulation of information. We need to resist this will to control individuals via the link between databases and biometrics. In the same way, we must contest the desire to control time—both the present and the future—through techniques of prediction, which create a powerful mixture of fiction and reality and merge the boundaries of the virtual and the actual, thereby introducing fiction into reality.

[46] Bigo, D, 'Security, Exception, Ban and Surveillance' in D Lyon (ed), *Theorizing Surveillance* (Kingston, Willan, 2006) 240 [Bigo (2006b)].

V. THE PAST FUTURE, SIMULATION OF THE WORST-CASE SCENARIO AND THE REASONABLE PRESENT OF THE MAN ON THE CLAPHAM OMNIBUS

The notion of the imminence of an apocalypse provides a justification for 'proactive' policing, 'pre-emptive' military strikes and 'administrative and exceptional justice', all of which consider anticipated behaviour as sufficient reason for action. The judgement of those deciding is then based upon the 'belief' that there is a need for haste, and not upon carefully considered actions backed up by facts. Decisions are made on the basis of information possibly tainted by torture, on profiles rather than on past actions and on assumptions concerning the possible future—in other words, on the conviction that intelligence services operate with a grammar of *'futur antérieur'* ('past future'), that they can read the future as a form of past through their technologies of profiling.

The time criterion and capacity for prediction is created through the artefacts of statistics that identify those correlations that occur regularly and can be anticipated. The selection of data is framed by the 'morphing' of the different virtual paths from the point of departure to the point of arrival. This 'reversal' of time is supposed to prevent events from occurring, by identifying the causes of predictable events. However, such actuarial strategies are contradictory to the notions of duration and certainty that lie at the heart of the concept of justice.[47] Lucia Zedner explains:

> We are moving from a 'post-crime' society in which crime is thought about primarily as harm or wrong done and in which dominant ordering practices arise post-hoc, to a 'pre-crime' society in which the perspective is shifting to anticipate and forestall that which has yet to occur ... Although the impulse to pre-empt, particularly in the case of prospective grave harms, is hardly new, the urgency with which security is now pursued poses a considerable threat to individual liberties, not least because risk reduction targets sections of the population and licenses selective erosion of rights.[48]

Pre-crime, preventive and pre-emptive reasoning cannot be considered as progress with regard to the speed of justice and effective protection. This sort of reasoning perverts the act of justice by invoking arguments about the technology of the instantaneous and the 'past future' reasoning of the military apparatus.[49] This fantasy of total control by anticipation reveals in fact the 'astrological' dimen-

---

[47] See the contribution by Lucia Zedner in this volume; see also Zedner, L, 'In Pursuit of the Vernacular: Comparing Law and Order Discourse in Britain and Germany' (1995) 4 *Social and Legal Studies* 517–34; and Zedner, L, 'Pre-crime and Post-criminology?' (forthcoming, 2007) *Theoretical Criminology.*
[48] L Zedner in this volume.
[49] Virilio, P, *Vitesse Et Politique: Essai De Dromologie, L'espace Critique* (Paris, Galilée, 1977).

sion of scientific modernity and ultimately represents a false pretence that is fast becoming 'the' solution.[50]

Worst-case scenarios are never certain and are so often nearly zero in probability that to give them priority at the level of public policy is to be driven by nightmares and fears, not by rationality. As a counterpoint to the apocalyptic vision of the experts, we need the voice of the man on the Clapham omnibus, because he is not interested in what just might happen but is rather exclusively interested in what has happened and whether the penalty in respect of what has happened is appropriate in view of the immediate and future consequences. He has a reasonable approach to life in general and is not driven by nightmares coming from fears of the loss of power.

The man on the Clapham omnibus is not oblivious to possible futures. He or she must assess the likelihood of future suffering on the basis of past acts. But our hypothetical ordinary person turns his or her back on the extraordinary—the worst-case scenario—and incorporates a key component of the rule of law—foreseeability—in assessing what is reasonable and what is not. This is a mundane, common or garden foreseeability on the basis of which people and state actors can regulate their behaviour. It can never be the nightmare that masquerades as the foreseeable future in the worst-case scenarios of politicians and professionals of (in)security. Should the man on the Clapham omnibus adopt such a notion of what is foreseeable, believing the combination of experts and professionals of politics, the result would likely be a chaotic destabilisation of the rule of law. Nightmares concerning the future are best left in bed. A reasonable society does not need new priests clothed as actuarial 'scientists' and intelligence experts extracting information through suppression and surveillance, and pretending they know what will happen from their 'projections'. They cannot monitor the future and know the plans of would-be criminals. Prevention has to be rationally checked. Such visions of an apocalyptic future cannot be presented as a credible future, as an alternative reality in the waiting, in order to justify the suspension and destruction of individual security and freedom.

REFERENCES

Agamben, G, *Etat d'Exception: Homo Saccer*, L'ordre Philosophique (Paris, Les Editions du Seuil, 2003).
Anderson, M and Apap, J, *Striking a Balance between Freedom, Security and Justice in an Enlarged European Union* (Brussels, Centre for European Policy Studies, 2002).
Apap, J and Carrera, S, 'Maintaining Security within Borders: Towards a Permanent State of Emergency in the EU?', Policy Brief No 41, Centre for European Policy Studies, October 2003.

[50] Bigo, D, 'From Foreigners to "Abnormal Aliens": How the Faces of the Enemy have Changed following September 11th' in E Guild and J van Selm (eds), *International Migration and Security: Immigrants as an Asset or Threat?* (London, Routledge, 2005) [Bigo (2005a)]. See also the contribution by Lucia Zedner in this volume.

Aradau, C, 'Governing Populations and Ungovernable People: The Liberal State and the War on Terror' in V Jabri and RBJ Walker (eds), *Liberty, Security and the Limits of Modern Politics* (Brussels, CEPS, 2005).

Arato, A, '*Minima Politica* after September 11' (2002) 9(1) *Constellations* 46–52.

Armitage, J, 'State of Emergency: An Introduction' (2002) 19(4) *Theory, Culture and Society* 27.

Balke, F, 'Political Existence and "Bare Life": The Biopolitics of Carl Schmitt' (2001) 2 *Distinktion – skandinavisk tidsskrift for samfundsteori* 71–80.

Beck, U, 'The Terrorist Threat: World Risk Society Revisited' (2002) 19(4) *Theory, Culture and Society* 39–56.

Bendersky, JW, *Carl Schmitt: Theorist for the Reich* (Princeton, Princeton University Press, 1984).

Bigo, D, *Polices En Réseaux: L'expérience Européenne* (Paris, Presses de Sciences Po, 1996).

—— 'L'Impact des mesures anti-terroristes sur l'équilibre entre liberté et sécurité et sur la cohésion sociale en France' in E Bribosia and A Weyembergh (eds), *Lutte contre le Terrorisme et Droits Fondamentaux* (Bruylant, Nemesis, 2002) 219–47 [Bigo (2002a)].

—— 'Reassuring and Protecting: Internal Security Implications of French Participation in the Coalition against Terrorism' in E Hershberg and KW Moore (eds), *Critical Views of September 11: Analysis from around the World* (New York, The New York Press, Social Science Research Council, 2002) [Bigo (2002b)].

—— 'From Foreigners to "Abnormal Aliens": How the Faces of the Enemy have Changed following September 11th' in E Guild and J van Selm (eds), *International Migration and Security: Immigrants as an Asset or Threat?* (London, Routledge, 2005) [Bigo (2005a)].

—— 'Global (In)security: The Field of the Professionals of Unease Management and the Ban-opticon' (2005) 4 *Traces* [Bigo (2005b)].

—— 'Protection: Security, Territory and Population' in J Huysmans, A Dobson and R Prokhovnik (eds), *Politics of Protection: Sites of Insecurity and Political Agency* (London, Routledge, 2005) [Bigo (2005c)].

—— (ed), *Illiberal Practices in Liberal Regimes: The (In)security Games* (Paris, L'Harmattan, 2006) [Bigo (2006a)].

—— 'Security, Exception, Ban and Surveillance' in D Lyon (ed), *Theorizing Surveillance* (Kingston, Willan, 2006) [Bigo (2006b)].

Bonditti, P, 'From Territorial Space to Networks: A Foucaultian Approach to the Implementation of Biopolitics' (2004) 29(4) *Alternatives* 465–82.

Bourdieu, P, *Practical Reason: On the Theory of Action* (Stanford, Stanford University Press, 1998).

—— *Propos Sur Le Champ Politique* (Lyon, Presses Universitaires de Lyon, 2000).

Bovay, NML, 'The Russian Armed Intervention in Chechnya and its Human Rights Implications' (1997) 54 *Review International Commission of Jurists* 29–57.

Boyle, K, Hadden, T and Hillyard, P, *Law and State: The Case of Northern Ireland*, Law in Society Series (London, Robertson, 1975).

Braber, L, 'Korematsu's Ghost: A Post-September 11th Analysis of Race and National Security' (2002) 47(2) *Villanova Law Review* 451–90.

Brody, R, 'The Road to Abu Ghraib' in K Roth, M Worden and A Bernstein (eds), *Torture: A Human Rights Perspective* (New York, The New Press, 2005).

Brouwer, E, 'France: Focusing on Internal Security' in E Brouwer, P Catz and E Guild (eds), *Immigration, Asylum and Terrorism: A Changing Dynamic in European Law* (Nijmegen, Recht and Samenleving, 2003).

Brouwer, E, Catz, P and Guild, E (eds), *Immigration, Asylum and Terrorism: A Changing Dynamic in European Law* (Nijmegen, Recht and Samenleving, 2003).

Butler, J, 'Explanation and Exoneration, or What We can Hear' (2002) 20(3) *Social Text* 177–88.

Buzan, B, *People, States and Fear: An Agenda for International Security in the Post-Cold War Era*, 2nd edn (New York, Harvester Wheatsheaf, 1991).

Buzan, B, 'Rethinking Security after the Cold War' (1997) 32(1) *Cooperation and Conflict* 5–28.

Call, CT and Stanley, W, 'Protecting the People: Public Security Choices after Civil Wars' (2001) 7(2) *Global Governance* 151–72.

Campagna, N, 'Prerogative and Constitutional State: The Problem of State of Emergency Force in John Locke and Benjamin Constant' (2001) 40(4) *Der Staat* 553–79.

Carrera, S and Apap, J, 'Maintaining Security within Borders: Toward a Permanent State of Emergency in the EU?' (2004) 29(4) *Alternatives: Global, Local, Political* (Special English language issue of *Cultures et Conflits*) 399–416.

Catz, P, 'United Kingdom: Withdrawing from International Human Rights Standards' in E Brouwer, P Catz and E Guild (eds), *Immigration, Asylum and Terrorism: A Changing Dynamic in European Law* (Nijmegen, Recht and Samenleving, 2003).

Cole, D, *Enemy Aliens: Double Standards and Constitutional Freedoms in the War on Terrorism* (New York, The New Press, 2003).

Cole, D and Dempsey, JX, *Terrorism and the Constitution: Sacrificing Civil Liberties in the Name of National Security* (New York, The New Press, 2002).

Darcy, S, 'The Rights of Minorities in States of Emergency' (2002) 9(4) *International Journal on Minority and Group Rights* 345–69.

Diken, B and Laustsen, CB, '7-11, 9/11, and Postpolitics' (2004) 29(1) *Alternatives* 89–113.

Dillon, M, 'Network Society, Network-centric Warfare and the State of Emergency' (2002) 19(4) *Theory, Culture and Society* 71.

Eberwein, WD, 'Le Paradoxe Humanitaire? Normes et Pratiques' (2006) 60 *Cultures et Conflits.*

Edelman, MJ, *Constructing the Political Spectacle* (Chicago, University of Chicago Press, 1988).

ELISE (European Liberty and Security), *Results of the Three-year Program*, final report, CD ROM (2004), http://www.libertysecurity.org/mot99.html.

—— 'Suspicion et exception' (2005) 58 *Cultures et Conflits.*

Fekete, L, 'All in the Name of Security' in P Scraton (ed), *Beyond September 11: An Anthology of Dissent* (London, Pluto Press, 2002).

Ferejohn, J and Pasquino, P, 'The Law of the Exception: A Typology of Emergency Powers' (2004) 2(2) *International Journal of Constitutional Law* 210–39.

Frost, M, *Ethics in International Relations: A Constitutive Theory*, Cambridge Studies in International Relations, vol 45 (Cambridge, Cambridge University Press, 1996).

—— *Constituting Human Rights: Global Civil Society and the Society of Democratic States* (New York, Routledge, 2002).

Girard, R and Williams, JG, *The Girard Reader* (New York, Crossroad, 1996).

Giroux, HA, 'Democracy and the Politics of Terrorism: Community, Fear, and the Suppression of Dissent' (2002) 2(3) *Cultural Studies: Critical Methodologies* 334–42.

Glendening, PN, 'Governing after September 11th: A New Normalcy' (2002) 62 *Public Administration Review* 21–3.

Guild, E, 'Exceptionalism and Transnationalism: UK Judicial Control of the Detention of Foreign "International Terrorists"' (2003) 28(4) *Alternatives* 491–515.

Guild, E, 'Judicialisation of Armed Conflict: Transforming the Twenty-first Century' in J Huysmans, A Dobson and R Prokhovnik (eds), *Politics of Protection: Sites of Insecurity and Political Agency* (London, Routledge, 2005).

Guild, E and van Selm, J, *International Migration and Security: Immigrants as an Asset or Threat?* (London, Routledge, 2005).

Guittet, E-P, 'European Political Identity and Democratic Solidarity after 9/11: The Spanish Case' (2004) 29(4) *Alternatives: Global, Local, Political* (special English language issue of *Cultures et Conflits)* 441–64.

Harding, TW, 'Torture' (2002) 21(3) *Refugee Survey Quarterly* 135–8.

Hart, J, Kuhlau, F and Simon, J, 'Chemical and Biological Weapon Developments and Arms Control' (2003) *SIPRI Yearbook* 645–82.

Hoff, B-I, 'The Displaced Financial State of Emergency: About the Financial-Political Accountability of Parliament and the Government and the Role of the Federation as Guardian of Economic Sovereignty' (2003) 44(3) *Politische Vierteljahresschrift* 417–19.

Huysmans, J, 'Minding Exceptions: Politics of Insecurity and Liberal Democracy' (2004) 3(3) *Contemporary Political Theory* 321–41.

Huysmans, J, Dobson, A and Prokhovnik, R (eds), *Politics of Protection: Sites of Insecurity and Political Agency* (London, Routledge, 2005).

Ignatieff, M, *Human Rights as Politics and Idolatry* (Princeton, Princeton University Press, 2001).

—— *The Lesser Evil: Political Ethics in an Age of Terror* (Princeton, Princeton University Press, 2004).

—— 'Moral Prohibition at a Price' in K Roth, M Worden and A Bernstein (eds), *Torture: A Human Rights Perspective* (New York, The New Press, 2005).

Ielmini, C, *Le Léviathan et Le Terroriste* (Paris, L'esprit frappeur, 2005).

Jabri, V, 'Critical Thought and Political Agency in Time of War' (2005) 19(1) *International Relations* 70–9.

Jasson, C, 'The Need to Reaffirm Humanitarian Values' (2002) 21(3) *Refugee Survey Quarterly* 181–5.

Jenkins, R, *A Life at the Centre* (London, Macmillan, 1991).

Lewis, A, 'Security and Liberty: Preserving the Values of Freedom' in RC Leone and G Anrig Jr (eds), *The War on Our Freedoms: Civil Liberties in an Age of Terrorism* (New York, Public Affairs, 2003).

Lipschutz, RD, *On Security: New Directions in World Politics* (New York, Columbia University Press, 1995).

Loader, I, 'Fall of the "Platonic Guardians": Liberalism, Criminology and Political Responses to Crime in England and Wales' (2006) 46(4) *British Journal of Criminology* 561–86.

Monod, JC, 'Destins du paulinisme politique: K Barth, C Schmitt, J Taubes' (2003) 2 *Esprit* 113–24.

Neal, WA, 'Cutting Off the King's Head: Foucault's *Society Must Be Defended* and the Problem of Sovereignty' (2004) 29(4) *Alternatives: Global, Local, Political* (Special English language issue of *Cultures et Conflits*) 373–98.

Nyers, P, *Rethinking Refugees: Beyond State of Emergency* (London, Routledge, 2005).

Pastore, F, 'The Asymmetrical Fortress: The Problem of Relations between Internal and External Security Policies in the European Union' in M Anderson and J Apap (eds), *Police and Justice Co-operation and the New European Borders* (The Hague, Kluwer Law International, 2002).

Roth, K, 'Human Rights, the Bush Administration, and the Fight against Terrorism: The Need for a Positive Vision' in C Brown (ed), *Lost Liberties: Ashcroft and the Assault on Personal Freedom* (New York, The New Press, 2003).

Roth, K, 'Justifying Torture' in K Roth, M Worden and A Bernstein (eds), *Torture: A Human Rights Perspective* (New York, The New Press, 2005).

Roth, K, Worden, M and Bernstein, A (eds), *Torture: A Human Rights Perspective* (New York, The New Press, 2005).

Schmitt, C, *Political Theology: Four Chapters on the Concept of Sovereignty* (London, MIT Press, 1985 [1922]).

Schwab, G, *The Challenge of the Exception: An Introduction to the Political Ideas of Carl Schmitt between 1921 and 1936*, 2nd edn (New York, Greenwood Press, 1989) xv, 174.

Steinmetz, G, 'The State of Emergency and the Revival of American Imperialism: Toward an Authoritarian Post-Fordism' (2003) 15(2) *Public Culture* 323–45.

Tsoukala, A, 'The Media Coverage of the Public Debate on Exceptionalism in Europe', paper presented at workshop on 'War, Sovereignty and Security Today', Université du Québec à Montréal, 15–16 March 2004.

—— 'Defining the Terrorist Threat in the Post-11 September Era' in D Bigo (ed), *Illiberal Practices in Liberal Regimes* (Paris, L'Harmattan, 2006).

Turner, BS, 'Sovereignty and Emergency: Political Theology, Islam and American Conservatism' (2002) 19(4) *Theory, Culture and Society* 103.

United States Executive Office of the President, Office of Homeland Security, 'National Strategy for Homeland Security' (US White House, 2002).

Vander, F, 'Kant and Schmitt on Preemptive War' (2002) 125 *Telos* 152–66.

Verdeja, E, 'Law, Terrorism, and the Plenary Power Doctrine: Limiting Alien Rights' (2002) 9(1) *Constellations* 89–97.

Virilio, P, *Vitesse Et Politique: Essai De Dromologie, L'espace Critique* (Paris, Galilée, 1977).

Wæver, O, 'Securitization and Desecuritization' in R Lipschutz (ed), *On Security* (New York, Columbia University Press, 1995).

—— *Concepts of Security* (Copenhagen, University of Copenhagen Institute for Political Science, 1997).

Walker, RJB, 'War, Terror and Judgement' in B Gökay and RJB Walker (eds), *11 September 2001: War, Terror and Judgement* (London, Frank Cass, 2003).

Zedner, L, 'In Pursuit of the Vernacular: Comparing Law and Order Discourse in Britain and Germany' (1995) 4 *Social and Legal Studies* 517–34.

—— 'Pre-crime and Post-criminology?' (forthcoming, 2007) *Theoretical Criminology*.

Part II

Engaging Rights

6

Deference, Security and Human Rights

DAVID DYZENHAUS*

INTRODUCTION

T HIS CHAPTER EXPLORES the implications of a public commitment to
a 'culture of justification' for the roles of different constitutional actors in
relation to laws and decisions that both concern national security and affect
human rights. I take as my point of departure the central tension in the House of
Lords judgment in *A v Secretary of State for the Home Department*[1] between the
majority's approach to whether there existed a public emergency, which came
close to treating the question as non-justiciable, and its approach to whether
indefinite detention of foreign nationals without trial was a proportionate
response, which involved substantive review for justification.

As I will show, these approaches rely on different conceptions of deference. I
then ask whether the lack of a sufficiently theoretically grounded conception of
deference has been responsible for traditional judicial timidity in the area of
national security. I argue for a concept of due deference that is grounded in an
understanding of the constitutional order in terms of a culture of justification distinct from both liberal constitutionalism and democratic positivism. Finally, I
consider some of the practical and institutional implications of embracing such a
culture of justification: the need for more detailed information from the executive
about the nature and scale of the threat from terrorism, the need for greater parliamentary scrutiny of executive claims about national security, and the need for
courts to treat parliamentary materials as relevant to their own determinations of
compatibility.

* This chapter draws on the following work by the author: Dyzenhaus, D, 'The Politics of Deference:
Judicial Review and Democracy' in M Taggart (ed), *The Province of Administrative Law* (Oxford, Hart
Publishing, 1997); Dyzenhaus, D, *The Constitution of Law: Legality in a Time of Emergency* (Cambridge,
Cambridge University Press, 2006); it also draws on work by Murray Hunt: Hunt, M, *Using Human
Rights Law in English Courts* (Oxford, Hart Publishing, 1997); and Hunt, M, 'Sovereignty's Blight: Why
Contemporary Public Law Needs the Concept of "Due Deference"' in N Bamforth and P Leyland
(eds), *Public Law in a Multi-layered Constitution* (Oxford, Hart Publishing, 2003).
[1] [2005] 2 WLR 87 (hereafter *A*).

I. TWO CONCEPTIONS OF DEFERENCE

After 11 September 2001, the UK Parliament introduced in section 23 of the Anti-terrorism, Crime and Security Act 2001 (the 'Anti-terrorism Act') the power to detain indefinitely non-nationals who are determined by the Secretary of State for the Home Department to be a security risk but who cannot be deported because of some practical consideration or because deportation would subject them to a risk of torture. The power thus does not extend to British nationals, and the Government conceded throughout the litigation that ensued that this meant that nationals who were security risks escaped the indefinite detention visited on non-nationals.

Before the Bill was laid before Parliament, the Home Secretary notified the Secretary General of the Council of Europe that the Government intended to take measures derogating from Article 5 of the European Convention on Human Rights (ECHR),[2] which precluded such indefinite detention. Here the Government relied on Article 15(1) of the Convention:

> In time of war or public emergency threatening the life of the nation any High Contracting Party may take measures derogating from its obligations under this Convention, to the extent strictly required by the exigencies of the situation, provided that such measures are not inconsistent with its other obligations under international law.

And the Government made the Human Rights Act 1998 (Designated Derogation) Order 2001, which designated the detention powers under section 14(1) of the Human Rights Act 1998.

The Anti-terrorism Act did provide various safeguards: section 24 provided for the grant of bail by the Special Immigration Appeals Commission (SIAC); section 25 permitted a detainee to appeal to SIAC against his certification as a suspected international terrorist; section 26 provided for periodic reviews of certification to be conducted by SIAC; section 28 provided for periodic reviews of the operation of the detention scheme as a whole; section 29 provided for the expiry of the scheme subject to periodic renewal and the final expiry on 10 November 2006 unless renewed. Section 30 gave SIAC exclusive jurisdiction in derogation matters.

The detainees held under the Act claimed that there was no public emergency threatening the life of the nation and that indefinite detention was not strictly required by the exigencies of the situation. It followed, they argued, that there was no valid derogation under Article 15 of the ECHR. They also argued that the detention provisions were discriminatory in contravention of Article 14 of the ECHR, which had not been notified for derogation. That Article precludes discrimination on various grounds, including 'national . . . origin'.

---

[2] The Convention for the Protection of Human Rights and Fundamental Freedoms, also known as the European Convention on Human Rights (ECHR), Rome, 4 November 1950, in force 3 September 1953, 213 UNTS 221.

In *A*, the majority of the House of Lords found both that section 23 was not a proportional response to the emergency and that it was incompatible with the United Kingdom's commitment to the principle of non-discrimination. *A* is thus rightly regarded as a victory for the rule of law. But the victory is not unqualified.

According to Lord Bingham's summary of the Attorney General's argument in *A*, the Government submitted

> that as it was for Parliament and the executive to assess the threat facing the nation, so it was for those bodies and not the courts to judge the response necessary to protect the security of the public. These were matters of a political character calling for an exercise of political and not judicial judgment.[3]

In other words, the Government adopted the typical stance of governments that claim emergency powers by presenting an argument with two limbs: first, that the question whether there is an emergency is so quintessentially a matter for political judgement that courts must submit to the Government's and Parliament's assessment without examining the basis of that assessment; second, since the question of the most appropriate response to the emergency is no less quintessentially a matter for political judgement, courts must also submit to the Government and Parliament on that question, again without conducting any scrutiny of the justifications relied on. In effect, the Government was arguing that these are non-justiciable questions: questions not appropriate for or capable of judicial resolution. The House of Lords has a long tradition of accepting this argument, one that stretches from its decision in World War I in *Halliday*[4] through its decision in World War II in *Liversidge*[5] to its first post-11 September 2001 decision in *Rehman*.[6]

Lord Bingham's response to the Attorney General was that while Parliament, the executive and the judges have 'different functions', 'the function of independent judges charged to interpret and apply the law is universally recognised as a cardinal feature of the modern democratic state, a cornerstone of the rule of law itself'. It was thus wrong to 'stigmatise judicial decision-making as in some way undemocratic'.[7]

It is significant that Lord Bingham did not find his ultimate ground in the Human Rights Act but in the constitutional nature of the democratic state with its inherent commitment to the rule of law. Put differently, his understanding of the judicial role does not look to any particular statute, not even the Human Rights Act itself, as the basis for the judicial authority to review legislation and executive decisions for their compliance with human rights and the rule of law, since the

---

[3] See *A*, note 2 above, 110 (Lord Bingham) and 151 (Lord Scott).
[4] *R v Halliday, ex parte Zadig* [1917] AC 260.
[5] *Liversidge v Anderson* [1942] AC 206.
[6] [2002] 1 All ER 123.
[7] *A*, 113–14. Lord Bingham went on to state that it was 'particularly inappropriate' to stigmatise the judges when they could declare only that a statute was incompatible with human rights, a declaration that did not affect its validity.

legal order is assumed to be a constitutional one, and thus premised on judges having such authority.

Lord Rodger elaborated the implications of this point:

> If the provisions of section 30 of the 2001 Act are to have any real meaning, deference to the views of the Government and Parliament on the derogation cannot be taken too far. Due deference does not mean abasement before those views, even in matters relating to national security . . . The legitimacy of the courts' scrutiny role cannot be in doubt.[8]

However, these remarks of Lords Bingham and Rodger are confined to the issue of judicial scrutiny of the appropriateness of the legislative response to the emergency. When it came to the issue of whether there was an emergency, the majority held that if there is some reason to suppose that there is an emergency, the test established in *Rehman* should apply.[9] That is, as long as it not irrational to claim that there is an emergency, even if the judges doubt that there is, they still have to give the benefit of the doubt to the executive.

Thus the victory for the rule of law is qualified in that the majority of the House of Lords rejected outright only the second limb of the Government's argument, that the appropriateness of the response to the emergency was a political question not for judicial determination. In relation to the first question, the existence of a public emergency, the House of Lords did not accept the Government's non-justiciability argument but did accept that a more deferential stance was appropriate in light of the sorts of considerations relied on by the Government in support of its non-justiciability argument. The victory is, however, not merely qualified. It rests on an unarticulated tension and is thus unstable.

The remarks made by Lords Bingham and Rodger about the legitimacy of the judicial role are general in import. They apply equally to both limbs of the Government's argument, as the Government suggested, and as Lord Walker accepted in the lone dissent. The instability arises because in deciding the second question, the majority had to decide whether the Government's response was correctly calibrated to the emergency—whether it was a proportional response. Thus when they reviewed the appropriateness of the response, they had at least implicitly to review the judgement of the extent and kind of the emergency, indeed, whether there was an emergency at all in the sense that departures from the normal regime of law were justified.

The instability does not reside in the fact that the judges applied different standards of review to these two questions. Rather, it arises because the standard they applied to the question of whether there was an emergency did not seem to require the Government to make a proper justification for its claim. The risk here is that judges say that an issue is justiciable and so proceed to review, but their review is so unrigorous that it might have been better for them to assert non-justicability, that is, that the Government's decision was not controlled by the rule of law.

---

[8] *A*, 158.
[9] *Ibid*, 111.

I do not, however, underestimate the difficulty the majority faced in confronting the issue of reviewing the Government's claim that there was an emergency. There was no doubt that the United Kingdom faced a serious threat of terrorist attack, and the events of July 2005 confirmed the Government's claims in this regard. However, the issue of whether that threat, or indeed actual attacks, amounted to an emergency in accordance with the Article 15 ECHR definition was not so much debated but asserted, as one can gather from both the account in the judges' speeches of the Government's arguments and by Lord Hoffmann's cursory dismissal of those same arguments in the only speech that decided for the applicants on the basis that there was no emergency. Indeed, Lord Hoffmann's speech, which poured scorn on the claim that the situation was one in which there was a war or other public emergency threatening the life of the nation was a source of disquiet for the other judges. Three of the majority judges thus intimated or expressed their doubts about whether the Government had a serious case.[10] However, they found justification for their more deferential approach on this question in two claims.

First, SIAC, in coming to the decision that it should defer to the Government's claim that there was an emergency, had seen confidential material from the Government in closed session. The Attorney General, however, had declined to ask the House of Lords to read the same material. Still, the majority seemed to think that because SIAC had seen confidential material in closed session and come to a conclusion on its basis, the claim that there was an emergency must have been strengthened by that material.[11] And they thought this despite the fact that SIAC had expressly not relied on the confidential material in coming to its conclusion in its open judgment.[12]

But even if it were thought appropriate that the higher courts should be ready to defer to SIAC should SIAC adequately justify its decision, and, correspondingly, that both SIAC and the courts should be ready to defer to the Government when it provides such a justification, such deference cannot be blind. As Lord Rodger has put it, 'Due deference does not mean abasement'. To give the Government the 'benefit of the doubt', as one judge put it, at the same time as harbouring 'very grave doubt'[13] about the Government's case seems peculiar, especially when the court itself could have asked to see evidence that might have removed some of that doubt and when what debate had taken place in Parliament tended to undermine rather than support the Government's case.

Second, the majority relied on decisions of the European Court of Human Rights (ECtHR) that held that the Court should generally defer to a national Government's determination that there is such an emergency.[14] But such reliance

---

[10] *Ibid*, 104 (Lord Bingham), 151 (Lord Scott) and 155 (Lord Rodger).
[11] *Ibid*, 104–5.
[12] *Ibid*.
[13] *Ibid*, 151 (Lord Scott).
[14] *Ibid*, 105.

fails to give proper effect to the gap some of the judges acknowledged[15] between the situation on the one hand in which the European Court defers to a decision by a Government that has withstood challenges before that Government's national courts and the situation on the other hand in which the highest national court has to evaluate the Government's challenge. That is, a stricter standard is arguably appropriate in the latter situation, and the application of such a standard there would make more sense of the application of a more relaxed standard in the first situation.[16]

My argument in this chapter is not that the majority were necessarily wrong to defer on the first question, but that they failed to require that a proper case for deference be made by the Government and therefore failed to conduct anything approaching appropriate judicial scrutiny of the reasons underlying the Government's assertions about the existence of an emergency. That argument has to address two different though closely connected sets of problems: an institutional set and a theoretical set.

The institutional problems pertain to the dearth of resources facing judges who are prepared to acknowledge the inextricability of the two issues—the existence of the emergency and the appropriateness of the response. Such judges would need a better justificatory basis to scrutinise than the House of Lords had available to it in *A*. For there to be such a basis, the Government would have to be prepared to treat Parliament parliament as more than a rubber stamp for legislation when the Government thinks it needs more powers to confront an alleged crisis. The Government would not only have to forego its standard (and nearly always unjustified) line that there is no time to debate properly both the extent of the emergency and the appropriate responses to it. It would also have to be prepared to allow into the public domain more detailed information about the precise nature and scale of the threat; or, to the extent that it genuinely cannot do so, the Government or Parliament itself would have to devise some system within Parliament whereby that part of the Government's case that cannot be publicly debated can be heard. Thus more constitutional furniture would have to be put in place in order to ensure that the Government and Parliament could meet their justificatory responsibilities before the judges could carry out their duty properly to evaluate the Government's and Parliament's case. And for the judges to carry out that duty, they would of course have to be given by Parliament or devise themselves some means of testing the arguments made in any closed committee sessions, as well as those made in public.

While I will have more to say later about the institutional problems, my main task in this chapter is to confront the theoretical set of problems. Institutional reform requires a theoretical justification. If it is never appropriate for judges to defer to the executive or to parliamentary judgement about what the law requires,

---

[15] *A*, 112–13 (Lord Bingham) and 139 (Lord Hope).

[16] See Hickman, TR, 'Between Human Rights and the Rule of Law: Indefinite Detention and the Derogation Model of Constitutionalism' (2005) 68 *Modern Law Review* 655.

or if judges should always submit to such judgements, there is no need for these institutional resources.

It is important at this juncture to be clear about what I mean by deference to judgement. My conception of 'due deference' depends on a distinction between deference as respect and submissive deference, the equivalent of what Lord Rodger called deference as abasement.[17] Deference as respect requires judges to pay respectful attention to the reasons offered by a primary decision maker as justification for a particular decision. It requires not only that there are reasons but that the reasons are capable of justifying the decision. Such deference has therefore both a procedural and a substantive or qualitative aspect to it—going through the hoop of providing reasons does not suffice to earn respect since respect requires demonstration of the adequacy of the reasons offered to justify the conclusion reached. Deference is due to a decision maker when he has offered reasons to justify the result, and the reasons are moreover adequate to justify the result. Scrutiny of reasons for their 'adequacy' therefore involves a qualitative appraisal of the substantive reasons for a particular decision, but is not the same as scrutiny for correctness: it imposes a high threshold that the reasons must satisfy basic standards of rationality and not be inconsistent with the principles that underpin democracy; but it leaves space for a conclusion that the reasons are 'good enough' in a democratic society.

In contrast, submissive deference requires judges to submit to the intention of the legislature, on a positivist understanding of what constitutes that intention. If the legislature's intention is to delegate authority to an official to interpret and implement a statutory mandate, this conception of deference transfers the submissive stance it requires from the legislature to the official. Judges should defer to the primary decision maker's decision, as long as the decision maker does not stray beyond the limits of his statutory authority, positivistically construed. If a reviewing judge embarks on a process of evaluating the decision maker's reasons for decision, he or she is thus asking herself the wrong question. That question is likely to lead him or her to cross the line between the legitimate exercise of checking on legality or the limits of authority and the illegitimate exercise of substantive review, or review as to the merits. Since substantive review is to be avoided, there is no procedural requirement that the official give reasons. Indeed, the position that recommends submissive deference might go further than lack of support for a duty to give reasons. If the procedural duty invites substantive review, imposition of such a duty should be resisted.

I will come back to the distinction between deference as respect and submissive deference below. For the moment, I want to note two issues. First, one of the points of contention between these conceptions of deference is the idea of legal authority and legality. For deference as respect, legal authority is based on reasons, and legality is a matter of principles. A decision has authority when it is supported by reasons that show why all the relevant legal principles support the decision. For

---

[17] Dyzenhaus (1997) 286. And for refinement of the distinction, see Hunt (2003) 351–52.

submissive deference, authority attaches automatically to any decision that is made within the space delimited by the delegating power. That is, legality is spatially conceived, so that its limits are only those limits that are explicitly stipulated by the delegating power.[18]

Second, it is important to keep in mind that debate so far about deference has been largely shaped by the assumption that in issue is the kind of deference, if any, due to primary decision makers, who have been delegated authority by Parliament to make decisions. But my concern in this chapter is deference to both primary decision makers and Parliament itself. If, as deference as respect presupposes, authority is reason-based and legality a matter of principles, then statutes— Parliament's decisions—have authority only when they are supported by reasons that show why all the relevant legal principles support them.

In contrast, submissive deference presupposes that there are no limits on Parliament's authority, other than the requirements of manner and form that attend the proper enactment of statutes. These requirements are the equivalents of the limits on delegated authority—they are formally conceived, determinate boundaries of a space in which there are no substantive principles to which Parliament is answerable. It is that presupposition that underpins the idea that Parliament's intention is to be interpreted by positivistic tests as to what was in fact intended, so that the limits on the authority of primary decision makers are whatever and only the limits the omnipotent Parliament saw fit to stipulate. On this view, to conceive of Parliament as answerable to principles of legality is to conceive of its authority as substantively limited, which means that its delegates are similarly limited, thus providing the basis for judges to impose their understanding of those limits on the primary decision makers, an exercise in substantive review that amounts to a usurpation of the legislative role.

It is important to keep in mind that there is this connection between conceptions of deference to primary decision makers and some of the most fundamental issues in constitutional and legal theory about the nature of legal authority and legality. At stake in this debate is whether there is a conception of principle-based legality that does not collapse into either merits review (so that the conception of deference as respect turns out to be but a disguise for judicial supremacism, that is, for no deference at all) or judicial abdication (so that deference as respect turns out to be a non-justiciability doctrine, or submission by another name). As I will now try to show, developments in the last 10 years in the United Kingdom not only are more consistent with the idea of deference as respect than submissive deference, but also help to demonstrate that deference as respect is not a sham.

II. NATIONAL SECURITY: THE LAST PREROGATIVE?

At one time, decisions about national security, for example, who should be deported or detained as security risks, were regarded as matters so political and so

---

[18] See Hunt (2003) 339–40.

based on sensitive information that they were not justiciable or amenable to judicial review. In other words, such matters fell within the prerogative of the executive, an extra-legal space of political decision. In the twentieth century, however, the idea that certain decisions of the political branch of Government have authority despite their extra-legal status became increasingly difficult to sustain. The claim, articulated by Dicey, that political authority is constituted by law and that the executive must therefore demonstrate a legal warrant for any of its decisions that impinge on fundamental rights and values gained an ever-stronger grip on the public mind.

The extension of law's reach over the prerogative is good news for all those who regard it as a precondition of any Government's claim to legitimacy that it exercises power in accordance with the rule of law. But there are dangers to this extension because of the possibility of confusing the rule *of* law with rule *by* law, or rule *by* statute. If one assumes that as long as there is a warrant in a statute for what an official does, he or she is acting in accordance with the rule of law and therefore legitimately, it seems to follow that an official who is authorised by a statute to act arbitrarily is by definition acting in accordance with the rule of law and therefore also legitimately. In other words, if the extension of law's reach over the prerogative brings about the legal installation of the prerogative in all but name, it seems to legitimate arbitrary action by claiming that it is by definition legal. The rule of law is thus ultimately undermined.

I accept that this danger has to be taken seriously. In the context of an attempt to articulate a doctrine of due deference, it manifests itself in tests that amount to a stance of submissive deference. This stance allows the claim that certain acts of the executive are not justiciable to re-emerge as the claim that judges must defer to the executive unless the executive acts so irrationally that it is manifest that it has strayed beyond the limits of its legal authority, better known as '*Wednesbury* unreasonableness'. Unfortunately, Dicey's constitutional theory, taken as a whole, is not only an unhelpful basis for responding to this problem; it in large part helps to create it.

Dicey's advocacy of an ideology of legality, the content of which, he suggested, is to be found in common law presumptions about the liberty and equality of the individual, was undermined by his continuing support for the doctrine of legislative supremacy, which underpins submissive deference. While he thought that judges should maintain the rule of law by interpreting statutes in the light of common law presumptions, he also argued that judges must submit to clearly expressed legislative intentions, whatever their content. His theory of constitutionalism and the rule of law is thus radically unstable. It licenses judges to impose their views about what the rule of law requires on statutes, but only on condition that the statutes can bear these interpretations, a condition often stated as one to do with the 'ambiguity' of statutory language. However, if a statute unambiguously excludes such judicial presumptions, Dicey's theory requires judges to submit to parliament's will. Moreover, Dicey regarded the administrative state as in principle uncontrollable by the rule of law, since the statutes that set up that state granted to the frontline decision- makers an authority to act as they saw fit—to be a law unto themselves. Such statutes, in other words, create the equivalent of the prerogative within law.

It follows that, on the one hand, Dicey's theoretical legacy is one in which there is no doctrine of deference—judges simply interpret the law in accordance with their sense of its fundamental values. On the other hand, his legacy also requires judges to adopt the stance of submissive deference to clear legislative intent, including the intent to delegate virtually unfettered discretion to administrative officials. Judges who work with a Diceyan understanding of legality tend to shuttle between these two inconsistent parts of his legacy. If they are tempted to try to restrict delegations of authority by interpreting them as confined by common law presumptions, legislatures can react through privative clauses that oust judicial review, by framing delegations so as to make it clear that officials' decisions depends on their subjective judgment, or by a combination of both devices.

Despite these concerns, the extension of law's reach over the prerogative must be seen as a potentially helpful first step in establishing the control of the rule of law over political decisions about national security. Moreover, during World War I and World War II, not only did the indefinite detention of individuals who were perceived to be risks to national security have to follow a procedure set out in statute and regulations, but each decision was in principle subject to appeal to an executive committee.

However, as Brian Simpson has shown, the committee lacked teeth.[19] Not only did it fail to require the real reasons for detentions from the intelligence branch, but in any case the committee could advise the Home Secretary only if someone had been wrongly detained. One can view these facts from two very different perspectives: either the kind of legality contemplated by these detention regimes was a cynical façade designed to legitimate the illegitimate; or it represented genuine, though ineffective, attempts to ensure that the executive did not act arbitrarily.

There is an advantage to adopting the latter perspective—it permits judges to try to work up the regime of legality into something with more rule of law teeth, on the basis that the very attempt to design a regime of legality is evidence of Parliament's intention to rule not only by law, but also in accordance with the rule of law. There are risks, namely that judges might end up giving the imprimatur of the rule of law to an administrative regime that does not provide those subject to it with any real protection. However, the more cynical perspective is not really available to judges. They have to try to make sense of the regime as a legal one, which means that they have only limited options. First, as suggested, they can try to make sense of the regime by attempting to give it rule of law teeth. Second, they

---

[19] Simpson, AWB, *In the Highest Degree Odious: Detention Without Trial in Wartime Britain* (Oxford, Oxford University Press, 1992). Simpson, especially in ch 3, points out that the Government effectively pulled the wool over the judges' eyes. While the statutory scheme required the Secretary of State to have reasonable grounds and to communicate those grounds to the chairman of the advisory committee, not only were the grounds not communicated to the appealing detainee, but the chair was also not given the reasons. To find out the true grounds, the public officials would have had to be subpoenaed and questioned in court

can say that the regime is legal without making the attempt, in which case they give the regime the imprimatur of the rule of law by equating that rule with rule by law. Finally, they might find that the regime is illegal because it is incompatible with fundamental principles of legality.

The majority of the House of Lords in *Halliday* and in *Liversidge* adopted the second option. They said that the demands of legality were satisfied by the detention regimes under consideration and that such regimes were appropriate given the contexts, that is, periods of national emergency. In contrast, Lord Shaw in his dissent in *Halliday* started with the assumption that Parliament must be taken to intend that its delegates act in accordance with the rule of law, which means that it must explicitly authorise any departures from the rule of law. Since the Defence of the Realm Consolidation Act 1914 did not authorise a detention regulation, the regulation that brought the detention regime into play was invalid.

When civil servants subsequently put together the detention regime for World War II, they took note of Shaw's dissent and so ensured that the authorising statute explicitly permitted the establishment of a detention regime by regulation. Again, one can view this step either as a progress towards the realisation of the rule of law or as yet another embellishment to the façade. But, in addition to this response to a dissenting judge, the Government responded to concerns raised in Parliament about the wording of the initial version of the detention regulation. It substituted 'reasonable cause to believe' when it came to the grounds for detention for the original 'if satisfied that'. And it was on the basis of this substitution that Lord Atkin held in his famous dissent in *Liversidge* that a court was entitled to more than the Government's say-so that an individual is a security risk, although the majority disagreed on the basis that it was inappropriate in wartime for judges to go beyond the mechanism explicitly put in place (that is, the toothless review committee).

Lord Atkin's dissent was held up after the war as the correct stance for judges faced with executive decisions on national security grounds. However, an inspection of other judicial decisions in this area reveals a consistent pattern of executive-minded decisions by courts. In addition, when developments in 'normal' administrative law—where the issue was not national security—made it inevitable that judges asserted a comprehensive authority to control public power in general, including the prerogative, they also said eventually that the prerogative to deal with national security is subject to the rule of law and thus to judicial review. But in the same breath they said that the executive say-so as to what is required in the interests of national security must prevail. In other words, they reinvented the prerogative under the guise of a doctrine of judicial deference.[20]

The legal landscape changed in this regard when the ECtHR rejected the United Kingdom's argument in *Chahal v UK*[21] that national security grounds are

---

[20] *Council of Civil Service Unions v Minister for the Civil Service* [1985] AC 374. For discussion, see Dyzenhaus, D, *Hard Cases in Wicked Legal Systems: South African Law in the Perspective of Legal Philosophy* (Oxford, Oxford University Press, 1991) ch 8.

[21] (1996) 23 EHRR 413.

inherently incapable of being tested in a court of law, holding that the advisory panel for those subject to deportation on national security grounds did not constitute the 'effective remedy' as required by Article 13 of the ECHR.

The UK Government responded through Parliament in 1997 with a statute that established SIAC. Of the three members on the SIAC panel, one member had to have held high judicial office, the second to have been the chief adjudicator or a legally qualified member of the Immigration Appeals Tribunal, while the third would ordinarily be someone with experience of national security matters. The 1997 statute gave individuals who would have had the right to appeal against a deportation order but for the fact that national security was involved a right to appeal to SIAC and granted SIAC the authority to review the Secretary of State's decision on the law and the facts as well as the question whether the discretion should have been exercised differently. There was a further appeal to the Court of Appeal on 'any question of law material to' SIAC's determination. In addition, the statute provided for the appointment of a special advocate who could represent appellants if parts of the proceedings before SIAC took place in closed session. SIAC decisions can be based on both closed and open sessions. It gives both open judgments, which do not disclose information from the closed sessions, and closed judgments, which are given to only the Government.

SIAC thus seemed to be, at least to some extent, an answer to concerns that the rule of law cannot control decisions on national security grounds. However, in *Rehman* the House of Lords held, on separation of powers grounds that, whilst the issue of what constitutes national security is a question of law, and hence for SIAC and the courts to interpret, it is for the executive to decide what is 'in the interests of national security'.[22] The result is little different from the majority's claim in *Liversidge* that detention orders were not arbitrary since the courts could still check that they were made in good faith.

The question why this court did not give full effect to the legislative machinery contemplated by the establishment of SIAC becomes even more pressing when one notes that two of the judges on the bench—Lords Steyn and Hoffmann—are responsible for articulating a principle of legality in ordinary administrative law that requires all executive acts to be demonstrated as justifiable in law, where law is assumed to include fundamental values.[23] It is puzzling that these two judges find that in some cases that they are driven to constitutional bedrock, which they find to be full of values and principles, whilst in other cases they treat the constitution as only a very rigid and formalistic doctrine of the separation of powers.

One response to this puzzle is to point out that in the cases in which this principle of legality was articulated, the people affected by the decisions were citizens of the United Kingdom whose fundamental rights—liberty, freedom of expression and access to the courts—were threatened by the executive decisions. This

---

[22] [2002] 1 All ER 123.
[23] See *R v Secretary of State for the Home Department, ex parte Pierson* [1998] AC 539 at 587; and *R v Secretary of State, ex parte Simms* [2000] 2 AC 115 at 131.

response is reinforced by Lord Woolf's judgment in the Court of Appeal's decision in *A*,[24] which denies the rule of law value of equality before the law in accepting that non-citizens may be legitimately treated as not being full bearers of human rights.[25]

However, a better explanation for this puzzle is that, as I suggested in my account of Dicey, without an adequate account of deference, judges are condemned to shuttle back and forth between a position that exhibits no deference at all and a stance of submissive deference.[26] This only can explain how in *Rehman* Lord Hoffmann could on separation of power grounds require submissive deference to the executive when it comes to national security, while in *A* he cursorily dismissed the executive's argument that there was a state of emergency sufficient to justify a derogation and did not even mention SIAC's position on this point.

My illustration of the extension of the law's reach over the prerogative is not meant to point out merely that an effective principle of legality in which there is the rule of law as well as rule by law requires an adequate account of deference. An effective principle of legality requires the institutions and legal culture that make deference possible. Those institutions cannot all be put in place by judges, although judges may play a considerable role in prompting government and the legislature to design them. And such a legal culture can only come into being and thrive if all the institutions of legal order are committed to what I will call, following the late South African lawyer Etienne Mureinik, a 'culture of justification'. In such a culture, the political order accepts that all official acts, all exercises of state power, are legal only on condition that they are justified by law, where law is understood in an expansive sense, that is, as including fundamental commitments such as those entailed by the principle of legality and respect for human rights.[27] And I take the majority of the House of Lords in *A* to have expressed, albeit imperfectly, its commitment to the main elements of that culture.

In the next section, I will explore the theoretical implications of a commitment to a culture of justification and its doctrine of deference in order to prepare the way for a sketch of the process of both institutional and cultural reform that is necessary to take the rule of law project further.

III. DEFERENCE AND CONSTITUTIONAL THEORY

The idea that the principle of legality requires a doctrine of due deference raises deep puzzles for legal and constitutional theory. Indeed, it is anathema to many who argue for the existence and importance of a common law principle of legality. In their view, judges must have the last word when it comes to the content of

---

[24] [2002] EWCA Civ 1502.
[25] For a similar stance, see the Australian decision *Al-Kateb v Godwin* (2004) 208 ALR 124.
[26] See Hunt (2003) 339–40.
[27] For an account of the late Etienne Mureinik's position, see Dyzenhaus, D, 'Law as Justification: Etienne Mureinik's Conception of Legal Culture' (1998) 14 *South African Journal on Human Rights* 11.

fundamental law, because only an independent judiciary can be trusted to come up with the answer about what the law requires, especially when fundamental principles of legality are at stake. This position might appear all the more attractive in an era when the Government seems intent on loosening to the greatest extent possible the control of legality on its response to threats to national security and when Parliament itself offers very little effective resistance to that determined intent. At a time when it is most important for the judiciary to assert its guardianship of the rule of law, as the majority of the House of Lords did in *A*, it might seem worse than foolhardy to articulate a doctrine that contemplates the possibility of judges deferring to other institutional actors on questions about the content of legality.

Indeed, of the three main positions in the debate about the idea and place of deference in public law generally and in the area of human rights and security in particular, only two suppose that public law requires any doctrine of deference. For, as already suggested, the idea of deference is anathema to the position of many who argue for a common law principle of legality. On their 'liberal' position, law is a matter of moral principles, the content of which judges are the exclusive guardians. When judges have to review an official's interpretation of the law, there is no need for a doctrine of deference, because the question for the judge is whether the official's interpretation of the law matches the judge's sense of what the law requires. Hence, a doctrine of deference is more than not required; it is outright prohibited. Judges who adopt it abdicate their constitutional responsibility to determine what the law requires.[28]

I will refer to the second position as 'democratic positivism'. It is democratic in that it argues that the legislature is the only institution of legal order with the legitimacy to make law. It is positivist in that it imposes on those who have to interpret the law a duty to interpret it in accordance with the actual intentions of those who made it, avoiding above all imposing their own moral views on the content of the law. And it thus requires the stance of submissive deference on the part of judges.

I do not have a convenient label for my own position, as it is both liberal and democratic in inspiration, seeking to reconcile the democratic urge to place the development of the law in the hands of the representatives of the people with the liberal urge to ensure that such development does not interfere with the rights of individuals more than can be justified in even a democratic society. Its distinctiveness is best captured by the idea just mentioned of legality as a culture of justification.

Now the idea of a culture of justification may seem trite, as just about everyone seems to recognise its main components. Hardly anyone today denies that every

---

[28] The best know articulation of this position is by Ronald Dworkin, and it has been developed in a complex and sophisticated form in the United Kingdom by Allan, T, 'Common Law Reason and the Limits of Judicial Deference' in D Dyzenhaus (ed), *The Unity of Public Law* (Oxford, Hart Publishing, 2004) 289; and Allan, T, *Constitutional Justice: A Liberal Theory of the Rule of Law* (Oxford, Oxford University Press, 2001).

official act must have a warrant in law.[29] The claim is hardly novel that there is, or should be, a duty to give reasons when officials make decisions that affect important interests of the individual and that judges must advert to those reasons on review. It is very difficult to find any prominent legal or constitutional theorist who does not seek to reconcile elements of both the liberal and the democratic positivist position. Finally, everyone recognises that often the only intention that can be determined in statutes that delegate authority to officials is that the officials have authority to interpret their legislative mandate within the broad outlines of the statute. It follows that there is general acceptance of the claim that judges who review these interpretations must preserve a distinction between inappropriate merits or correctness review and appropriate review of legality.

However, the liberal and democratic positivist positions still exercise an unproductive grip on both practice and legal and constitutional theory. While both liberals and democratic positivists find themselves compelled to respond to the elements of a culture of justification, their traditional commitments do more than truncate their responses. They are unproductive in maintaining and taking forward the rule of law project entailed in that culture. Indeed, both liberals and democratic positivists must reject the idea of due deference.

Democratic positivists must reject due deference because it is too substantive: deference as respect is likely to lead to merits review by judges, disguised as review for legality. Liberals must reject it because it is not substantive enough: it is likely to result in an empty kind of proceduralism, whereby as long as officials go through the motions of producing reasons, judges will have to defer. And both liberals and democratic positivists are driven to this rejection because they cannot take into account the way in which the reasons for judges to consider deferring to the decisions of other institutions in legal order (the structural or second-order reasons for deference) interacts with their scrutiny of the actual reasons offered (the first-order reasons) for the decision.

The sorts of second-order reasons for deference that I have in mind include a range of considerations such as: the nature of the right in question; the relative expertise of the court and the decision maker in the subject matter in question; the relative institutional competence of the original decision maker to determine the type of issue in question; the degree of democratic accountability of the original decision maker; how well democratic mechanisms are working in practice; the extent to which the decision or measure was preceded by a thorough compatibility inquiry; and the opportunities afforded in that process, or through other accountability mechanisms, to the interests affected.[30]

---

[29] For an exception, see Loughlin, M, 'Constitutional Law: The Third Order of the Political' in N Bamforth and P Leyland (eds), *Law in a Multi-layered Constitution* (Oxford, Hart Publishing, 2003) 27.

[30] See Hunt (2003) 353–54, where it is emphasised that no single factor is ever likely to be determinative of the inquiry into the degree of deference due, which is likely to turn on the interaction of a number of different factors.

On the democratic positivist position, judges should not take these second-order reasons into account because there is, strictly speaking, only one second-order reason for deference, supplied by majoritarian democratic theory—the fact that the legislature has issued a command. That fact requires submissive deference either to the legislature or to the delegate to whom the legislature has given authority to interpret its mandate. The way that democratic positivists understand the second-order reason for deference—as focusing the interpreter on the question of the content of the legislative command, positivistically understood—means that questions about what first-order reasons were given to justify that command and whether they in fact justified it are inappropriate for the interpreter. Put differently, on the democratic positivists' approach, the second-order reason for deference excludes consideration by a reviewing judge of first-order reasons.

Given this, there is a legitimate question about why judges should be involved in review at all, on the democratic positivist position. Some democratic positivists have bitten the bullet on this question and argued that judicial review should be excluded altogether. But most regard review by independent judges as necessary to ensure that legality, in the sense of limits on authority, is respected, although they want the idea of limits to be understood in as formal a fashion as possible.

Consistent democratic positivists should therefore reject a duty to give reasons. They are drawn to the idea that the very fact that the legislature, as they understand it, has delegated a relatively open-ended authority to an official should be taken by judges as a signal not to review, unless the official does something so absurd that it is manifestly beyond the limits of delegated authority. In other words, the fact of the matter to which judges should submissively defer is the fact of the delegation of authority to decide to the official. Any attempt by judges to impose a stricter form of scrutiny than a test for absurdity will put them on to a slippery slope to second-guessing the official on the merits. Since an official strays outside the limits of delegated authority only when he or she does something absurd, to impose a duty to give reasons so that judges may evaluate whether the reasons justify the result is to step onto the slippery slope to correctness review. Thus, not only is there no self-sufficient reason for democratic positivists to want a duty to give reasons, they should in fact be opposed to it.

On the liberal position, the only relevant question for a judge is whether an official's judgement about what the law requires is correct. Hence, what I have called second-order reasons for deference are not 'legal' but pragmatic considerations that are extraneous to the interpretative exercise. That the legislature delegated authority to an official might be politically justified by the official's expertise, but the official's expertise is not a factor that can figure in the judge's review of the official's reasons. All that matters within the internal, legal perspective of the judge is the quality of the official's reasons. Indeed, while liberals might argue that officials have a duty to give reasons on various bases, they should rule out the basis that, in the absence of such a duty, judges are not able to decide whether a case for deference exists. As I have suggested, for liberals that basis is constitutionally prohibited—there are no second-order reasons for deference—because judges have a monopoly when it comes to interpretation of the law, especially of the most fundamental or constitutional law.

In contrast, within a culture of justification, the duty to give reasons is constitutional, based as it is in the principle of legality or the rule of law. As such, it has two dimensions. First, the duty to give reasons makes sense only if the reasons do in fact support the decision. When the decision is one that requires an official to come to a view of what the law requires—to interpret the law—those reasons must be advanced as justifying that interpretation. That is, the duty to give reasons presupposes that the judgement as to the law depends on the reasons—not on any old set of reasons, but on reasons that in fact justify that judgement. Hence, the duty entails that the reasons are subject to review in order to ensure that they have the requisite quality of justifying the decision.

The second dimension of a duty to give reasons that is based in the principle of legality entails officials having a legitimate role in determining what the law requires. Put more strongly, that duty presupposes that the officials have a legitimate role in the constitutional order, the order created by the common law principle of legality, in interpreting the law and so are entitled to deference as long as they carry out their role effectively. In sum, a constitutionally based duty to give reasons presupposes a doctrine of due deference, a stance whereby the judiciary concedes that other institutional actors in the legal order have a legitimate role in interpreting the law but at the same time stands ready to review these actors' decisions to ensure that the decisions are properly justified.

In a culture of justification, 'law' must be taken to include more than the law of the statute that is the basis for an official's authority. The common law principle of legality requires that the authority of officials is understood as constituted not only by their enabling statutes but also by the fundamental law of the land. It is that requirement that leads to the interpretative obligation of judges to interpret the positive law of a statute in accordance with common law presumptions about the liberty and equality of the legal subject and in accordance with other fundamental law, for example, an entrenched bill of rights, a Human Rights Act like that of the United Kingdom or international human rights regimes.[31] But if the authority of officials is constituted by law in this expansive sense, it follows from the doctrine of due deference that judges should be prepared to defer to appropriate official interpretations of all the law that constitutes their authority, where such interpretations are good enough in a democratic society.

Hence, in a culture of justification, second-order reasons for deference have a legal relevance because they make it incumbent on decision makers to provide the first-order reasons that make deference as respect possible. The second-order reasons are not about some threshold, so that judges should consider them in order to decide whether an issue is justiciable or amenable to review. If, for example, the authority to make decisions about where best to place motorways is delegated to an expert body that has to balance a complex array of policy considerations, judges

[31] See Hunt (1997).

should not be content with the fact that the body is expert and has in fact deliberated on the basis of appropriate considerations. The quality of that process of deliberation matters because the body must not only be capable of demonstrating, but in fact have demonstrated that its reasons for decision are adequate to justify that decision.

Within the internal, legal perspective of the judge reviewing the decision, the two levels of second-order and first-order reasons must merge in one inquiry. To take the procedural dimension of the decision seriously is to take seriously the idea that procedure is important because of its effects on substance, which means that substance cannot be ignored.[32] The second-order reasons for deference, far from excluding consideration of the quality of the first-order reasons, invite the court's evaluation of that quality. But at the same time they focus the court on the correct question—whether the decision maker has justified the decision and not whether the decision is one that the court would have reached had it itself been the primary decision maker. In other words, in a culture of justification, the very possibility of deferring is what makes evaluation of the quality of reasoning necessary, but that evaluation is of whether the decision maker's reasons are good enough in a democratic society.

Not only does procedure necessarily merge with substance in the judicial inquiry, but it is not the case that the distinction between second-order and first-order reasons can be mapped onto a distinction between process and substance. Recall that on my list of second-order reasons was the nature of the right in question. Thus, for example, if the right in question is a right that is agreed to be absolute in nature, say, the right not to be tortured, any decision that potentially undermines that right should be subject to the most rigorous form of scrutiny possible. Judges should still take seriously reasons offered by decision makers seeking to show why the right is not in fact undermined, but there is no issue of balance and so little or no leeway for a conclusion that the reasons are good enough in a democratic society.[33] In contrast, where the metaphor of balancing is appropriate, for example, where a measure seeks to decide the competing claims of the right to privacy and the right to freedom of expression, good-enough reasons will suffice, although, given that competing fundamental rights are in play, scrutiny will be more rigorous than of the decision about the placement of motorways.

It follows that the weaker the second-order reasons for deference, the stronger the justification for evaluating the reasons with a rigour approaching a correctness standard. Conversely, the stronger the second-order reasons for deference, the weaker the justification for such a rigorous evaluation of the quality of first-order reasons. In particular, even very strong second-order reasons for deference cannot compensate for very poor first-order reasons, while strong first-order reasons will

---

[32] See Fredman, S, 'From Deference to Democracy: The Role of Equality under the Human Rights Act 1998' (2006) 122 *Law Quarterly Review* 53, especially 68. At 77, Fredman criticises my approach, or at least the version of it articulated in Dyzenhaus (1997), for being wholly procedural.

[33] For an excellent discussion of balance, see Zedner, L, 'Securing Liberty in the Face of Terror: Reflections from Criminal Justice' (2005) 32 *Journal of Law & Society* 507.

be required when the second-order reasons are weak. The conclusion that the official has earned respect thus requires the judge to consider the structural or second-order reasons for deference together with the question of the quality of the first-order reasoning. But the analytical distinction between the two orders still does some work, in that the second-order reasons can be individuated prior to the exercise of evaluating the first-order reasons.[34]

This view of deference has been developed as an account of the deference due to primary decision-makers. I now have to confront the question whether deference to the legislature raises different considerations. On my account, it does not in principle: when courts review the constitutionality of legislation, or in the United Kingdom, its compatibility with the ECHR, the same types of questions arise as when they review the legality of executive or administrative action. However, for precisely this reason, my account does require not only a rather different understanding of the legislature, but reform in both the practice and the institutional make-up of the legislature in order to bring its operation into line with that understanding.

On both the democratic positivist and liberal positions, parliamentary debates as resources for the reasons that justify statutes are not only irrelevant but prohibited. Members of a legislature are the political agents of the people they represent, and the content of the decisions of the legislature is to be found, according to democratic positivists, within the four corners of the statute, and, according to the liberals, within the statute interpreted in the context of legal commitments to individual rights and freedoms.

In contrast, within a culture of justification the members of a legislature are not merely representatives of political parties but also legal officials who have, like all other legal officials, an obligation of fidelity to law in the expansive sense. To use Hobbesian language, they are not simply natural persons, representing their own conception of self-interest or the interest of their faction. In taking up office as parliamentarians, they step into an artificial role with special responsibilities, including the responsibility to ensure that parliament is an institution in which reasons are properly debated, in order that legislation might take forward the rule of law project. They are not quite in the position of the executive or public officials, who are under a duty to give reasons for their decisions. But the government is under such a duty, and so their role is to ensure that parliament is a reason-demanding institution.

---

[34] I do not, however, support the Canadian approach in which it is alleged that one of three different standards of review can be determined purely on the basis of the second-order reasons prior to the evaluation of the quality of the reasoning. That approach substitutes one threshold for another—a threshold of standards for a justiciability threshold. And it introduces a false sense of precision into the work done when judges get to the stage of evaluating the reasoning, which opens judges to the charge that they are smuggling in judgements about correctness under the guise of the other two standards—reasonableness or patent unreasonableness review. Rather, one should see that all there is, is evaluation of quality, but that evaluation will be different from context to context. In this respect Lord Steyn is right that, in law, context is everything.

Before the enactment of the Human Rights Act 1998 (HRA), the institutional make-up of the United Kingdom was explicable both by the democratic positivist position, if one left out of the picture the institution of judicial review on the basis of a substantive principle of legality, and by the liberal position, as long as Parliament did not explicitly override the courts' understanding of the content of legality. However, democratic positivists must find that the HRA section 3 interpretative obligation is in tension with their understanding of how to determine legislative intention and that a section 4 declaration of incompatibility looks like an event with no legal significance. And while the liberal position is comfortable with the section 3 interpretive obligation, it is uncomfortable with the possibility of a statute that cannot be so interpreted, indeed even more uncomfortable than it was in the context prior to the Human Rights Act. For before 1998, the liberal position could hold out the possibility with Sir Edward Coke that 'the common law will controul Acts of Parliament, and sometimes adjudge them to be utterly void: for when an Act of Parliament is against common right and reason, or repugnant, or impossible to be performed, the common law will controul it, and adjudge such act to be void'.[35] However, a finding of incompatibility entails that the statute that is found incompatible remains valid.

But, as the idea of a culture of justification can explain, a declaration of incompatibility is an event with legal significance because it anticipates responses from the government that maintain its commitment to the rule of law project. It anticipates a response from the government that the court is wrong, that the statute is in fact compatible, which then requires the government to appeal against the finding to the next judicial level, or to leave it to the ECtHR to decide the compatibility question by not amending the law and waiting for the case to be taken to Strasbourg. Or it anticipates that the legislation will be amended, either to get rid of the offensive provision or to find a way of achieving the objective of that provision in a fashion compatible with a section 3 interpretation. Indeed, in the absence of a government declaration of incompatibility when the statute is enacted, the legislature commits itself to the proposition that the statute is compatible, which then provides an explicit basis for judges so to interpret the statute.

In all of these scenarios the culture of justification assumes the possibility of a justification by either the Government or Parliament of the compatibility of the statute with the Human Rights Act. Naturally, the more work that has been done to ensure compatibility, the more judges may be prepared to find that the statute is compatible, at least if the work done is reflected in good quality reasons. Indeed, the point is better put by saying that the more work that is done to ensure compatibility prior to enactment, the smaller the chance that the statute will end up in court, challenged because of its incompatibility. But if that work has been done, then it should be taken at least as seriously by the court as the court would take work done after a declaration of incompatibility, work which either attempts to show that the court was wrong or which seeks to respond positively to that declaration.

---

[35] *Dr Bonham's Case* (1610) 8 Co Rep 114.

This understanding of the legal order of the United Kingdom after 1998 in terms of a culture of justification does not suppose that that culture began once the Human Rights Act came into force. When I suggested that the liberal and democratic positivist positions could explain the legal order prior to that event, I did not mean to indicate that their explanations were good, only that they were less inconsistent with the order of legality than they are today. As Murray Hunt has argued,[36] prior to the enactment of the Human Rights Act, the best way to make sense of the common law principle of legality was in terms of an interpretative obligation on judges to determine the meaning of statutes in accordance with common law presumptions and international human rights commitments. At the same time, we have both argued that the constitutional place of the administrative state in the legal order had to be recognised, which in turn required the development of a doctrine of due deference.

The Human Rights Act is perhaps best interpreted as giving concrete institutional expression to a culture that was already developing, at least for those who were committed to what I have called the rule of law project. Neither the democratic positivist nor the liberal position could adequately explain those elements of the project that they were willing to concede existed prior to the Human Rights Act—for democratic positivists, the common law principle of legality; for both democratic positivists and liberals, the development of reason-giving as a constitutionally required aspect of the administrative process.

To the extent that the democratic positivist and liberal positions seek to account for elements of the rule of law project, they depart from their commitments in ways that introduce inconsistency and tension into their positions. But much more important than such theoretical problems are the practical problems that ensue when institutional actors do not fulfil their roles in the rule of law project. When courts defer submissively to either the legislature or the executive, or fail to defer at all, there is an institutional failure, as there is when the executive or the legislature do not make the effort to participate as, respectively, reason-giving or reason-demanding institutions in the rule of law project. As I have indicated, it is likely that these failures will be disguised; for example, the Government will not admit that it is departing from a commitment to an absolute prohibition on torture but will try instead to tinker with the legal controls that have been developed to give force to that prohibition in order to secure its ends.

Judges should respond to all such failures by using the remedies available to them to declare executive action invalid or to find legislation incompatible with human rights commitments. But sometimes the problems that arise for the rule of law project are not problems that can be dealt with on a case-by-case basis, as they indicate a systematic institutional failure that judges cannot effectively deal with, although they can in their judgments prompt the kind of reform that is necessary. Indeed, the point of the tale from *Halliday* to *A* was to show that at times institutions of Government have to be reformed in order to maintain the rule of law

[36] Hunt (1997).

project. And I will now turn to a discussion of some of the reforms that might be necessary to take such a project forward.

IV. PRACTICAL AND INSTITUTIONAL IMPLICATIONS

What are the practical and institutional implications, in the context of national security, of this theoretical understanding of the United Kingdom's constitutional order in terms of a culture of justification? I want to explore three in particular. The first concerns the need for more detailed information to be made available about the nature and level of the threat from terrorism in order properly to assess the proportionality of measures proposed or adopted in response to that threat. The second concerns the need for greater independent scrutiny of executive assertions about threats to national security and what measures are necessary to avert them and, to the extent necessary, to devise the means for conducting such independent scrutiny without compromising legitimate security concerns or the minimum requirements of procedural justice. The third concerns the need for courts to refine their approach to the legal relevance of parliamentary material to their own determination of legal issues of human rights compatibility.

1. The Availability of Information to Facilitate Scrutiny for Proportionality

The first important practical implication, which flows from reconceiving the nature of scrutiny for legality as a principled exercise in evaluating justifications, is that it requires more detailed information to be made available by the executive in order for there to be meaningful independent scrutiny of its assertions about what is required in the interests of national security. As I suggested at the outset, meaningful assessments of the proportionality of measures taken in order to protect national security can be made only if sufficient information is available about the precise nature of the threat, including, for example, the type of attack that is plausibly possible, the scale of the threat in terms of the numbers of people who may be plotting such attacks, the likelihood of such attacks taking place and the likely frequency of such attacks in the future. Courts in the United Kingdom have traditionally been very reluctant to call for such information or evidence in the context of national security claims by the executive. As I pointed out above, for example, the House of Lords majority in *A* held for the Government on the issue of whether there was a 'public emergency threatening the life of the nation' within the meaning of Article 15 ECHR, without even asking to see the 'closed material' about the nature of the threat which had been before SIAC.

The structure of Article 15 ECHR, which entitles states to derogate from their Convention obligations if certain conditions are satisfied, encourages this judicial submissiveness to some extent, by appearing to require, as separate conditions, first, that there be a public emergency threatening the life of the nation and, second, that the derogating measures be only such as are strictly required by the exigencies of the situation. This has led courts considering the lawfulness of derogations under Article 15 to isolate the first question of the existence of a public emergency from the second question of proportionality, which they regard as more of a 'legal' question. But on any view, determination of the latter question necessarily involves consideration of the former: it is the fact of the emergency that justifies the derogating measures, and assessing their proportionality in meeting the emergency must necessarily involve consideration of the nature and level of the threat.[37] The nature of the exercise is no different in principle from reviewing the lawfulness of non-derogating measures that engage those human rights which are in principle capable of being interfered with if there is a sufficiently strong justification. Evidence of the precise nature and level of the threat is central to determining the proportionality of the measures adopted in response. In a culture of justification, consideration of such evidence is therefore unavoidable if genuine scrutiny for proportionality is to be carried out.

The main sources of information about the nature and scale of threats are ministerial speeches, government documents,[38] court judgments summarising the Government's case[39] and information now provided by MI5 on its website.[40] The kind of information to be found in these places gives a general indication of the nature of the threat, mainly by reference to the facts of terrorist incidents that are already public knowledge, but contains virtually nothing to enable any meaningful assessment of the likelihood of such threatened attacks materialising, the number of people thought to be actively plotting them or the probability of terrorists gaining access to and having the technical ability to deploy weapons of mass destruction such as nuclear weapons. The MI5 website, for example, features a 'current threat picture', comprising a summary prepared by the Joint Terrorism Analysis Centre (JTAC) of the current threat from international terrorism to the United Kingdom and to UK interests overseas. It states that the threat to the United Kingdom from international terrorism remains 'real and serious'. It states that both British and foreign nationals linked to or sympathetic with Al Qaeda are known to be present within the United Kingdom, and that 'a significant number of terrorist attacks have been thwarted in the UK since 11 September 2001'. However, it does not given any further details and indeed states its policy that the Security Service does not comment publicly on the general level of threat. Such limited information hardly enables proper scrutiny of the proportionality of proposed responses.[41]

[37] See Joint Committee on Human Rights (JCHR), *Eighteenth Report of 2003–04, Review of Counter-terrorism Powers* paras 18 and 19; and Zedner (2005) 511–12.
[38] Eg, 'Counter-terrorism Powers: Reconciling Security and Liberty in an Open Society: A Discussion Paper' (Home Office Consultation Paper, February 2004.
[39] Eg, *A* itself, but in particular the generic part of the open decision of SIAC in the individual appeals against certification under Part IV of the Anti-terrorism Crime and Security Act (2001), available on the SIAC website.
[40] http://www.mi5.gov.uk.
[41] The webpage summarising the threat picture states that it will be regularly reviewed and updated. On 8 March 2006 the information there had not been reviewed since 8 August 2005, a period of seven

Ministers frequently refer to the more serious nature of the threat from international terrorism, compared to that posed by Irish republican terrorism, and often invoke the possibility of terrorists using chemical, biological or nuclear weapons in indiscriminate attacks on the civilian population. The information that is made available by ministers or the police is sometimes inconsistent, such as when, on the day the House of Commons was being asked to pass the Prevention of Terrorism Bill providing for control orders, the Prime Minister said in a radio broadcast that there were 'several hundred' people in the United Kingdom who the Government believe are engaged in plotting or trying to commit terrorist acts,[42] while the Home Secretary a few weeks earlier had told Parliament, defending the proportionality of the proposed control orders regime, that the new powers in the Bill were required to deal with 'an absolute handful of people'.[43] Other information that has been provided about terrorist threats has subsequently turned out to be wrong, such as when the London Metropolitan Police announced that a substance found at premises raided by Anti-terrorist Branch officers had tested positive for the poison ricin.[44] In fact, it subsequently transpired that no ricin had been found at the premises.

The unsatisfactory nature of the information that has been made publicly available about the nature and scale of the terrorist threat has exposed the Government to charges from across the political spectrum that it has manipulated the information about the nature of the threat in the same way as it was accused of manipulating the intelligence about weapons of mass destruction in Iraq.[45]

In the wake of both the Hutton and Butler inquiries, there is now widespread acknowledgement that the reliance placed by the Government on the existence of weapons of mass destruction in Iraq as its justification for invasion has done enormous damage to public confidence not only in the reliability of intelligence information but also in the use to which such information is put by politicians.[46] The House of Lords itself, in *A*, commented on the damage done to the public's confidence in the reliability of intelligence material. The Home Secretary, in evidence to parliamentary committees, has also expressly accepted that the issue of the security assessment of weapons of mass destruction has weakened confidence in the Security Service.[47] Lord Carlile, the government-appointed reviewer of the operation of counter-terrorism laws, recently said in his evidence to the Home Affairs Committee that he would like the Government to say more about the

months, notwithstanding that on 14 February 2006 Parliament had been asked by the Government to renew the control orders regime contained in the Prevention of Terrorism Act (2005).

[42] Interview on BBC Radio 4's Woman's Hour, 28 February 2005.

[43] Oral evidence to JCHR on 9 February 2005, JCHR Tenth Report of Session 2004–05, *Prevention of Terrorism Bill*, HL Paper 68, HC 334, Ev3, Q6.

[44] Metropolitan Police press statement, 6 January 2003.

[45] See eg, Oborne, P, *The Use and Abuse of Terror: The Construction of a False Narrative on the Domestic Terror Threat* (London, Centre for Policy Studies, 2006).

[46] See eg, Blick, A, Byrne, I and Weir, S, 'Democratic Audit: Good Governance, Human Rights, War against Terror' (2005) 58 *Parliamentary Affairs* 408.

[47] Oral evidence to the JCHR on 9 February 2005, note 43 above, Ev2, Q5; and, to similar effect, oral evidence to the Home Affairs Committee on 8 February 2005.

nature of the terrorist threat, and that he considered that there was scope for the Government to put more into the public domain about the nature and scale of the threat from terrorism.[48] The Home Secretary recently accepted in the House of Commons, when announcing his intention to exercise his power to renew the control orders regime in the Prevention of Terrorism Act 2005 by order, that the Government needs to 'share information as much as we can, with Parliament and with society more widely.'[49]

The case for making more detailed information available than has hitherto been usual therefore seems largely to have been accepted, including, now, by the Government.[50] The more difficult question is exactly how this should be done.

2. Parliamentary Scrutiny of National Security Claims

The fact that this point has been reached gives rise to the second institutional implication of reconceiving legality in terms of a culture of justification: that Parliament itself ought to require more from the executive by way of information about the nature and scale of the threat as part of the justification for laws which Parliament is asked to pass in response to the threat from terrorism. This has been a recurrent theme in reports of the Joint Committee on Human Rights (JCHR). In *A*, Lord Bingham referred to the 'continuing anxiety' of the Joint Committee as to whether there existed a 'public emergency threatening the life of the nation'.[51] In a series of reports, the JCHR has consistently pointed out that neither it nor Parliament has ever been presented with the evidence that would enable it to be satisfied of the existence of such a public emergency,[52] finally observing that if the

---

[48] Uncorrected transcript of oral evidence to the Home Affairs Committee, 14 February 2006, to be published as HC 910-ii, Qs 75–7.

[49] HC Deb, 2 February 2006, col 485. The comment was in response to a request by Brian Jenkins MP that the Home Secretary ask the Intelligence and Security Committee and the Director General of the Security Service to prepare a report for Members of Parliament that could be placed in the library. He went on: 'In addition, will he ask them to push the envelope in respect of the information that any such report can contain? In these circumstances, the more information that hon. Members have the better, especially when it comes from an independent and neutral source, although I recognise the difficulties that our security services encounter in making such information available.'

[50] Although it is notable that both the Home Secretary and Lord Carlile assume that the availability of more information will inevitably persuade the public of the justification for the measures, rather than provide material for testing that justification. The Home Secretary, for example, said: 'I accept without qualification . . . that our security will be stronger if the information is more widely shared and understood.' Lord Carlile similarly said that he would like to see the Government simplifying the kind of information which is available in the SIAC generic judgment and putting it into the public domain so that people understand the nature of the threat better: oral evidence to the Home Affairs Committee on 8 February 2005, note 47 above,Q76.

[51] *A v Secretary of State for the Home Department*, at para 26.

[52] See eg, Second Report of 2001–02 (HL Paper 37, HC 372) para 30 (recognising that there may be evidence of the existence of a public emergency threatening the life of the nation but that 'none was shown by [the Home Secretary] to this Committee'); Fifth Report of 2002–03 (HL Paper 59, HC 462) at para 20 (noting that SIAC, which had upheld the existence of a public emergency, had had sight of closed as well as open material, and suggesting that each House might wish to seek further information from the Government on the public emergency issue); Sixth Report of 2003–04 (HL Paper 38, HC

threat is likely to remain indefinitely, as the Director General of the Security Service has indicated, 'democratic legitimacy demands some independent confirmation that the emergency remains at the level which justified unusual measures'.[53]

Given the importance of being able to appraise the nature and level of the threat from international terrorism in order properly to assess the proportionality of counter-terrorism measures, the JCHR thought it necessary to explore ways in which the Government could present for public and/or parliamentary scrutiny more of the material on which its assessment of the threat from international terrorism is based, without prejudicing legitimate concerns about revealing intelligence sources or methodologies.[54] Indeed, in light of public concerns about the reliability of intelligence material and the use to which it is put, it considered this to be an issue of the democratic legitimacy of counter-terrorism laws. The JCHR therefore invited the Government to give careful consideration to ways in which it could increase the independent democratic scrutiny of its claims about the level of the threat from international terrorism. It asked the Government to consider two questions.

First, it asked whether more could not be done to provide both Parliament and the public with more of at least the gist of the intelligence on which the Government's assessment of the threat is based, without prejudicing what the JCHR recognised were legitimate security interests. It suspected that 'protective anxiety' pervades the culture of the intelligence services and prevents the disclosure of information that does not in reality pose any threat of harm to intelligence sources or working methods. Second, it encouraged the Government to give careful consideration to whether the Intelligence and Security Committee (ISC) has a role in scrutinising the material on which the Government's assertions about the level of the threat are based. It considered that, if Parliament had the benefit of the view of that Committee when deciding whether particular measures are a proportionate response to the emergency in question, this would introduce, for the first time, an important element of independent democratic scrutiny.

One of the problems is the very limited extent to which the security services are currently accountable to Parliament, and the limited extent to which Parliament itself has asserted such a claim to scrutinise. According to a 1985 written answer from the Prime Minister concerning the attendance of members of the security services before select committees:

> There is a long-standing convention under which the Government do not provide information or answer questions in Parliament on matters of security or intelligence, and the Government would regard themselves as bound by that convention in relation to departmental Select Committees, no less than in relation to Parliament itself.

---

381) at para 34 (noting that insufficient evidence had been presented to Parliament to make it possible for the Committee to accept that derogation under ECHR Art 15 is strictly required by the exigencies of the situation to deal with a public emergency threatening the life of the nation).

[53]   Eighteenth Report of 2003–04 (HL Paper 158, HC 713) para 19.

[54]   *Ibid*, para 20.

In the light of that policy the Government would not consider it appropriate for the Director General or other members of the Security Service to appear before a Select Committee.[55]

The reference to a 'long-standing convention' according to which the Government does not provide information or answer questions in Parliament on matters of security or intelligence is somewhat surprising. If such a convention ever existed (as opposed to being merely asserted by the Government when convenient), it would have been entirely at odds with the existence of the type of culture of justification that is the subject of this chapter. In keeping with the greater transparency surrounding the security services since 1985, however, the Government appears no longer to hold to this convention: the Director General of the Security Service has given evidence to select committees, including the Home Affairs Committee, about the threat situation on a number of occasions in recent years.

Again there appears now to be widespread acceptance of the need for better parliamentary scrutiny, including by the Government itself. Chancellor Gordon Brown, in his recent speech on terrorism to the Royal United Services Institute, for example, referred to the need to build public trust in the United Kingdom's security regime through accountability to Parliament.[56] Both Lord Newton and Baroness Hayman, members of the Committee of Privy Counsellors, which produced the remarkable Newton Report on the powers in Part IV of the Anti-terrorism Act, told the JCHR in evidence that it would be helpful for Parliament to have the benefit of the view of the ISC when deciding on whether particular counter-terrorism measures are proportionate responses to the emergency. The question, therefore, would appear to be not whether but by what means there could be greater parliamentary scrutiny of the information that forms the basis of the Government's assessment of the threat.

The Home Secretary, asked whether he accepted that, in order to command public confidence, there should be some element of independent scrutiny of the Government's assessment of the nature and level of the overall threat to the life of the nation, has said that he is not in favour of any constitutional structure beyond the ISC to second-guess those assessments.[57] In his view, that committee plays an important role in assessing the existence and role of threats, and it is, he claimed, 'independent, containing, as it does, Members from both Houses and right across the political spectrum of opinion'.

It is certainly correct that the ISC has a well-established role in relation to sensitive intelligence material and well-developed procedures for dealing with the protection of such information. Its annual reports also include sections on 'The Threat'. The ISC is not, however, independent in the sense of a parliamentary committee accountable to Parliament: it is a statutory committee appointed by and reporting to the Prime Minister. It is questionable therefore, whether

---

[55] HC Deb, 25 March 1985, col 13W.

[56] 'Securing Our Future', speech by Chancellor Gordon Brown MP to the Royal United Services Institute, 13 February 2006.

[57] Oral evidence to JCHR on 9 February 2005, note 43 above, Ev1, Q1.

conferring this role on the ISC would provide sufficiently independent scrutiny within Parliament to satisfy the demands of a culture of justification. In his more recent statement, the Home Secretary appears to envisage a role for the JCHR and the Home Affairs Committee in making this information available, but it is not clear what that role would be.[58] Indeed, if it were proposed that those committees develop procedures for dealing with such material in closed session and without being able to refer to such material in published reports, this would cause a considerable dilemma of role for those committees, which generally pride themselves on the transparency of their procedures and the public availability of the evidence given to them.

3. Parliamentary Materials and Judicial Scrutiny

The third institutional implication concerns the relationship between judicial and legislative scrutiny of the human rights compatibility of legislation in a culture of justification. Should a court that is considering the human rights compatibility of legislation regard reports of scrutiny committees and subsequent parliamentary debates about compatibility as being of any legal relevance to the issues it has to determine? In particular, are such debates and reports relevant to the question of whether the court should defer to the judgment of the legislature, and if so, how? I suggest that it follows from the above that parliamentary materials such as committee reports and parliamentary debates about compatibility must be relevant to courts when they are assessing the human rights compatibility of legislative measures.

The issue was considered by the House of Lords in *Wilson*.[59] It held that when determining the ECHR compatibility of legislation it is permissible for a court to have regard to matters stated in Parliament, as recorded in *Hansard*, as a source of background information to enable the court, for example, to understand the nature and extent of the social problem at which the legislation is aimed. However, such legitimate reference to parliamentary materials was to be distinguished from reference to such debates in order to ascertain the reasons that led Parliament to enact a particular statutory provision. Lord Nicholls said:

> Beyond this use of Hansard as a source of background information, the content of parliamentary debates has no direct relevance to the issues the court is called upon to decide in compatibility cases and, hence, these debates are not a proper matter for investigation or consideration by the courts. In particular, it is a cardinal constitutional principle that the will of Parliament is expressed in the language used by it in its enactments. The proportionality of legislation is to be judged on that basis. The courts are to have due regard to the legislation as an expression of the will of

[58] Statement to the House of Commons, op cit, 2 February 2006: 'There are various procedures that we can follow to make that information available—through the Intelligence and Security Committee, the Joint Committee on Human Rights and the Home Affairs and other Select Committees.'

[59] *Wilson v First County Trust Ltd (No 2)* [2003] UKHL 40; [2004] 1 AC 816.

Parliament. The proportionality of a statutory measure is not to be judged by the quality of the reasons advanced in support of it in the course of parliamentary debate, or by the subjective state of mind of individual ministers or other members. Different members may well have different reasons, not expressed in debates, for approving particular statutory provisions. They may have different perceptions of the desirability or likely effect of the legislation. Ministerial statements, especially if made ex tempore in response to questions, may sometimes lack clarity or be misdirected. Lack of cogent justification in the course of parliamentary debate is not a matter which 'counts against' the legislation on issues of proportionality. The court is called upon to evaluate the proportionality of the legislation, not the adequacy of the minister's exploration of the policy options or of his explanations to Parliament. The latter would contravene article 9 of the Bill of Rights. The court would then be presuming to evaluate the sufficiency of the legislative process leading up to the enactment of the statute.[60]

To a human rights lawyer, this has an air of unreality about it. Much human rights adjudication is about evaluating in a principled way the cogency of the justifications offered for interfering with rights. The ECtHR frequently considers the quality of the reasoning relied on in support of a legislative measure when deciding compatibility questions. In *Hirst v UK*, for example, the ECtHR considered the compatibility of the UK's blanket disenfranchisement of convicted prisoners with the right to vote guaranteed by Article 3 of Protocol 1 ECHR.[61] The UK Government argued that a wide margin of appreciation was to be allowed to contracting states in determining the conditions under which the right to vote was exercised, and that the policy of a blanket ban on convicted prisoners had been adhered to over many years with the explicit approval of Parliament. The Court rejected this argument:

As to the weight to be attached to the position adopted by the legislature . . . in the United Kingdom, there is no evidence that Parliament has ever sought to weigh the competing interests or to assess the proportionality of a blanket ban on the right of a convicted prisoner to vote . . . It may perhaps be said that, by voting the way they did to exempt unconvicted prisoners from the restriction on voting, Parliament implicitly affirmed the need for continued restrictions on the voting rights of convicted prisoners. Nonetheless it cannot be said that there was any substantive debate by members of the legislature on the continued justification in light of modern day penal policy and of current human rights standards for maintaining such a general restriction on the right of prisoners to vote.[62]

In my view the approach of the Court in *Hirst* is to be preferred to the approach of the House of Lords in *Wilson*. In a culture of justification, Parliament should be required to earn judicial deference from the courts on human rights questions, by demonstrating the quality of its reasoned judgments on compatibility, not entitled to expect it by virtue of its sovereign position in the constitution. But courts, for

---

[60] [2004] 1 AC 816 at 843–4, para 67.
[61] App no 74025/01 (judgment of 6 October 2005).
[62] Para 79.

their part, must entertain the possibility of giving due deference to Parliament's legislative decision because of the quality of those reasons, evaluated in light of the sort of second-order reasons for deference that I sought to articulate above.

CONCLUSION

What does all this mean for what I described at the outset as the unarticulated tension in the *A* decision? On the approach that I say is necessary in a true culture of justification, the Government would have recognised the need to make more detailed information available to Parliament. Parliament, in its role as a reason-demanding institution, would itself have secured more information in order to subject it to rigorous parliamentary scrutiny in determining, not whether an emergency existed, but whether it was satisfied that the scale and nature of the threat was sufficiently great to justify the extreme measures being taken. This in turn would have provided both the public and the courts with a record of the reasons for Parliament's determination that its derogation from Article 5 was compatible with Article 15 ECHR, which in turn would provide courts with a basis for their own determination of the compatibility question.

In the absence of the first two stages being properly performed (that is, by the executive supply of information and parliamentary scrutiny of it), it is impossible for anyone to say whether the judgment of the House of Lords in the *A* case might have been different in any respect. It is possible (although I think unlikely in view of the seriousness of the interference with liberty and due process rights) that, had the court required a case for deference to be made out, it would have been persuaded that Parliament's reasons for enacting the derogating measures were good enough in a democracy to earn judicial deference. It is also possible that it would have reached exactly the same decision. Without the more detailed information it is impossible to say. But whatever decision the court would have reached, it would at least have articulated a substantive vision of the rule of law which does not contain within it the seeds of its own undoing.

To be precise, a culture of justification requires both vigilance and effort to maintain. *A* should be seen as a fruitful step in the rule of law project. It continued the work of the dissents in *Halliday* and *Liversidge*, and of Parliament both in its enactment of the Human Rights Act and the positive legislative response to *Chahal*. And in so doing, the majority of the House of Lords can rightly be regarded as having reset the course of English public law from its earlier attempt in *Rehman* to return to the jurisprudence of the majorities in *Halliday* and *Liversidge*. But one should not regard *A* as an unqualified victory for the rule of law:[63] *Rehman* remains an explicit and disturbing influence in its reasoning. And as the Government experiments with ways to undermine *Chahal* and to hollow out commitments to legality in its response to *A*, the presence of *Rehman*'s influ-

---

[63] See Fredman (2006) and Zedner (2005).

ence provides a foothold for a return to an era in which all that the extension of law's reach over the prerogative has brought about is the installation of the prerogative in all but name in the law.[64] And that, as I have indicated, is worse from the perspective of the rule of law since it seems to legitimate arbitrary action by claiming that it is by definition legal.

REFERENCES

Allan, T, 'Common Law Reason and the Limits of Judicial Deference' in D Dyzenhaus (ed), *The Unity of Public Law* (Oxford, Hart Publishing, 2004).
—— *Constitutional Justice: A Liberal Theory of the Rule of Law* (Oxford, Oxford University Press, 2001).
Blick, A, Byrne, I and Weir, S, 'Democratic Audit: Good Governance, Human Rights, War against Terror' (2005) 58 *Parliamentary Affairs* 408.
Dyzenhaus, D, *Hard Cases in Wicked Legal Systems: South African Law in the Perspective of Legal Philosophy* (Oxford, Oxford University Press, 1991).
—— 'The Politics of Deference: Judicial Review and Democracy' in M Taggart (ed), *The Province of Administrative Law* (Oxford, Hart Publishing, 1997).
—— 'Law as Justification: Etienne Mureinik's Conception of Legal Culture' (1998) 14 *South African Journal on Human Rights* 11.
—— *The Constitution of Law: Legality in a Time of Emergency* (Cambridge, Cambridge University Press, 2006).
Fredman, S, 'From Deference to Democracy: The Role of Equality under the Human Rights Act 1998' (2006) 122 *Law Quarterly Review* 53.
Hickman, TR, 'Between Human Rights and the Rule of Law: Indefinite Detention and the Derogation Model of Constitutionalism' (2005) 68 *Modern Law Review* 655.
Hunt, M, *Using Human Rights Law in English Courts* (Oxford, Hart Publishing, 1997).
—— 'Sovereignty's Blight: Why Contemporary Public Law Needs the Concept of "Due Deference"' in N Bamforth and P Leyland (eds), *Public Law in a Multi-layered Constitution* (Oxford, Hart Publishing, 2003).
Loughlin, M, 'Constitutional Law: The Third Order of the Political' in N Bamforth and P Leyland (eds), *Law in a Multi-layered Constitution* (Oxford, Hart Publishing, 2003).

[64] Consider, for example, *Re MB* [2006] EWHC 1000 (Admin), where Sullivan J found that aspects of the control order regime imposed by Parliament (Prevention of Terrorism Act 2005) in response to the House of Lords decision in *A* are incompatible with the Article 6.1 guarantee of a right to 'a fair and public hearing within a reasonable time by an independent tribunal established by law'. In particular, Sullivan J found that a judge could review the executive decision to impose a control order only on the basis of the information as tested by a special advocate at the time that the order was made, so that subsequent information was irrelevant for the purpose of deciding whether that decision was flawed (para 29). He thus found (para 80) that the court had to review the 'lawfulness . . . of earlier decisions that will necessarily have been taken on a completely one-sided view of the case'. In his opinion, the Act created a 'thin veneer of legality' that could not 'disguise the reality' (para 103). Sullivan J's judgment is not a direct attack on the role of the special advocate per se in detention decisions, or in control order decisions where the level of control is such that the courts find that these are tantamount to deprivations of liberty. However, he clearly regarded the fact that the special advocate procedure operates without the person subject to the order being able to give his or her input as contributing to the overall unfairness of the particular control order issue he faced.

Oborne, P, *The Use and Abuse of Terror: The Construction of a False Narrative on the Domestic Terror Threat* (London, Centre for Policy Studies, 2006).

Simpson, AWB, *In the Highest Degree Odious: Detention Without Trial in Wartime Britain* (Oxford, Oxford University Press, 1992).

Zedner, L, 'Securing Liberty in the Face of Terror: Reflections from Criminal Justice' (2005) 32 *Journal of Law & Society* 507.

7

The Legal Authority of the United Nations Security Council

CH POWELL*

INTRODUCTION

A S SOUTH AFRICA held her first democratic elections, a constitutional lawyer, Etienne Mureinik, depicted South Africa's shift from parliamentary supremacy to a constitutional democracy as a shift from a 'culture of authority' to a 'culture of justification'. In the former, government is obeyed without question; in a culture of justification, 'every exercise of power is expected to be justified', and 'the leadership given by government rests on the cogency of the case offered in defence of its decisions, not the fear inspired by the force at its command'.[1]

Mureinik saw the constitutional Bill of Rights as the 'chief strut' of a culture of justification,[2] and because he focused on the Bill of Rights, the courts were regarded as the chief guardians of the culture of justification. However, Mureinik's description of the role of the Bill of Rights makes clear that the court is considered merely a conduit for the people to whom the government owe account:

> A Bill of Rights is a compendium of values empowering citizens affected by laws or decisions to demand justification. If it is ineffective in requiring governors to account to people governed by their decisions, the remainder of the Constitution is unlikely to be very successful.[3]

In his contribution to this volume, Dyzenhaus draws on the concept of a culture of justification to consider questions of institutional design, proposing a 'due deference' model for the relationship between the judiciary and government in cases involving national security. Their analysis grapples with the specific case-law and

* A number of friends and colleagues gave me ideas for this chapter and comments on earlier drafts. I am particularly grateful to Christina Murray, Tom Bennett and Salim Nakhjavani. Thank you, too, to Vaughan Lowe for his comments at the Oxford Colloquium on Security and Human Rights (March 2006).
[1] Mureinik, E, 'A Bridge to Where?' (1994) 10 *South African Journal on Human Rights* 10, 31–32.
[2] *Ibid*, 32.
[3] *Ibid.*

institutional design of the United Kingdom, but their proposed model can be applied in any domestic legal system because it is, in their analysis, an incident of the rule of law. Indeed, to the extent that current institutions and practice do not reflect a culture of justification in the United Kingdom, Dyzenhaus suggests that changes in the institutional design may be necessary.

This chapter looks to the institutional design of the international legal order. The first section examines whether the international order reflects a culture of justification, focusing in particular on the anti-terrorism programme of the United Nations Security Council (SC). It sets out the powers of the SC and the measures the SC has taken in its anti-terrorism programme, then considers a range of criticisms of Council practice. The second section of this chapter engages with a particular capacity that the SC has claimed in its anti-terrorism programme: namely, the capacity to make laws for the international community. Drawing on the concept of a culture of justification, the next section argues that the SC's law-making capacity is limited. The fourth section examines how a culture of justification might be realised in the international arena, looking in particular at the SC's role in the creation of customary law.

I. CRITIQUES OF SECURITY COUNCIL PRACTICE

This section reviews the recent practice of the Security Council and the critiques of this practice. Because the UN Charter provides very few express limitations on the SC's power, criticism of its actions often draws on implied Charter limitations to the Council powers or on general principles of law. Sections I.2 to I.4 describe the three main bases of criticism of the SC, namely human rights law, (global) administrative law and fundamental principles of law.

1. Security Council Practice on Terrorism

The end of the Cold War ushered in a period of heightened activity for the Security Council. Freed from the frustration of the veto, it began to use its Chapter VII powers in a manner unlikely to have been anticipated by the framers of the Charter. It has intervened in states where there was no apparent threat to international peace and security,[4] set up international criminal tribunals,[5] promoted regime change in Iraq[6] and determined national borders.[7] But it is probably in its

---

[4] See, for example, Security Council Resolution (SCR) 1529 of 2004 on Haiti, available at http://www.un.org/Docs/sc/unsc_resolutions.html.
[5] SCR 827 of 1993 and SCR 955 of 1994, both available at http://www.un.org/Docs/sc/unsc_resolutions.html.
[6] See Reisman, WM, 'The Constitutional Crisis in the United Nations' (1993) 97 *American Journal of International Law* 83, 85.
[7] See UN Doc S/22412 (1991) and SCR 687 of 1991, available at http://www.un.org/Docs/sc/unsc_resolutions.html and reprinted in (1991) 30 *International Legal Materials* 847. See also Reisman, note 6 above, 85.

counter-terrorism measures that the Council's influence has been most pervasive and enduring.

Concerted Security Council action against terrorism has resulted in more than 40 resolutions (SCRs) on terrorism and a huge bureaucracy that monitors and administers state compliance with the obligations stipulated under the resolutions. Through this anti-terrorism programme, the Council has created mechanisms to designate certain persons and organisations 'terrorist', and it mandates and co-ordinates a range of sanctions against these 'terrorists' and other targets on an ongoing basis. These two categories of measures are discussed below.[8] Particularly significant for the purposes of this chapter are the general obligations imposed by the resolutions on states to implement a broad, international anti-terrorism programme. The Council's committees monitor and support the implementation of the anti-terrorism programme at the domestic level.

SCR 1373 (2001) contains the most significant general anti-terrorism measures. These include an obligation not to provide any kind of support to terrorist groups and to prevent terrorist acts through early warning systems and mutual assistance in investigation and prosecution.[9] States also have to establish and prosecute a range of terrorist offences within their domestic criminal justice systems and must suppress recruitment to terrorist groups.[10] In addition, SCR 1373 attempts to fast-track the crystallisation of international norms against terrorism. It calls on states to sign all international conventions and protocols relating to terrorism,[11] including, specifically, the International Convention for the Suppression of the Financing of Terrorism (1999).[12]

There are currently four Security Council committees on terrorism: the '1267 Committee',[13] the Counter-terrorism Committee (CTC),[14] the '1540 Committee'[15] and the '1566 Working Group'.[16] The '1267 Committee', initially established to monitor the compliance of states with a range of sanctions imposed against Al Qaeda and the Taliban, has had its mandate extended by later resolutions.[17] It administers one of the most controversial of the SC's anti-terrorism mechanisms: the so-called 'listing' system.

---

[8] See the discussion of SCR 1267.

[9] Arts 1(a) and 2(a)(b) of SCR 1373 of 2001, available at http://www.un.org/Docs/sc/unsc_resolutions.html.

[10] Art 2 of SCR 1373.

[11] Art 3(d) of SCR 1373. See also Art 2(a) of SCR 1456, available at http://www.un.org/Docs/sc/unsc_resolutions.html.

[12] Hereafter 'the Financing Convention'. See http://untreaty.un.org/English/Terrorism.asp.

[13] Set up by SCR 1267 of 1999. See the committee's website at http://www.un.org/Docs/sc/committees/1267Template.htm.

[14] Set up by SCR 1373. See the committee's website at http://www.un.org/Docs/sc/committees/1373/.

[15] Set up by SCR 1540. See the committee's website at http://disarmament2.un.org/Committee1540/.

[16] Set up by SCR 1566. See the committee's website at http://www.un.org/Docs/sc/committees/1566Template.htm.

[17] See for example, SCR 1363 of 2001, SCR 1390 of 2002 and SCR 1526 of 2004, all available at http://www.un.org/documents/scres.htm.

Under this mechanism, the committee designates a person or organisation as linked to Al Qaeda once one or more states have submitted the name of this person or organisation, the name has been circulated to other states, and no objection has been received within 48 hours. The delisting procedure is far more onerous, requiring negotiation between the government that wants to remove the name and the original, 'designating' government.[18] Once a person or organisation has been listed, a range of sanctions follow, to which states are obliged, under Chapter VII of the Charter, to give effect. States therefore have to freeze the financial assets of individuals and entities appearing on the list, deny them entry into and transit through their territories and prevent them from selling and supplying military equipment, whether such sales and supplies are carried out from their territories or even by their nationals outside their territories.[19]

The Counter-terrorism Committee was set up by SCR 1373 of 2001 to monitor compliance with a range of general obligations set out in the resolutions. Since September 2005, it has also monitored compliance with SCR 1624, which 'calls on' states to criminalise the incitement to terrorism.[20] Apart from requiring, evaluating and publicising reports from member states of the UN on their compliance with the SCRs, the Counter-terrorism Committee presents itself as an advisor to states, facilitating the drafting and passing of legislation that is required by the resolutions.[21] Among other measures, it provides a list of best practices,[22] which includes models for domestic anti-terrorism legislation.[23]

The '1540 Committee' monitors the implementation of a resolution against weapons of mass destruction. This resolution prohibits states from providing any form of support to non-state actors who attempt to develop weapons of mass destruction and implements a range of measures, including legislative measures, to prevent non-state actors from acquiring the materials for such weapons or trading in the materials or technology.[24] The committee is mandated to report regularly to the SC, as well as to recommend to the Council measures to improve the execution of the resolution.[25] Like the Counter-terrorism Committee, it has a hand in the development of domestic legal systems, through the co-ordination of a system that assists states in setting up legal and regulatory infrastructures that

---

[18]   The delisting procedure was added only after Sweden challenged the listing of three of its nationals. See Kingsbury, B, Krisch, N and Stewart, R, 'The Emergence of Global Administrative Law', IILJ Working Paper 2004/1, Global Administrative Law Series, available at www.iilj.org, also published in (2005) 68 *Law and Contemporary Problems* 15, 19 fn 21, and the authorities listed there; Gutherie, P, 'Security Council Sanctions and the Protection of Individual Rights' (2004) 60 *NYU Annual Survey of American Law* 491, 511–13.

[19]   Paragraphs 2(a)–(c) of SCR 1390, reaffirmed by SCR 1455 and SCR 1456 of 2003, all available at http://www.un.org/Docs/sc/unsc_resolutions.html.

[20]   See SCR 1624 of 2005, available at http://www.un.org/terrorism/sc.htm.

[21]   See Rosand, E, 'The Security Council as "Global Legislator": Ultra Vires or Ultra Innovative?' (2005) 28 *Fordham International Law Journal* 542, 582.

[22]   See http://www.un.org/sc/ctc/bestpractices.shtml.

[23]   Available at http://www.unodc.org/pdf/crime/terrorism/explanatory_english2.pdf.

[24]   SCR 1540, available at http://www.state.gov/t/np/rls/other/31990.htm.

[25]   http://disarmament2.un.org/Committee1540/work.html at para 2(e).

will enable them to carry out their obligations under the resolutions and relevant treaty law.[26]

Finally, the '1566 Working Group' is meant to deal with terrorist groups not falling within the purview of the 1267 Committee, and is therefore tasked with examining 'practical measures to be imposed upon individuals, groups or entities involved in or associated with terrorist activities, other than those designated by the Al-Qaeda/Taliban Sanctions Committee' and 'the possibility of establishing an international fund to compensate victims of terrorist acts and their families'.[27]

2. Human Rights Law

Those who argue that the SC is bound by the international human rights regime point out that the SC, like the UN as a body, is bound by the Charter, which includes the protection of human rights as one of its fundamental principles.[28] The SC's anti-terrorism programme threatens a range of internationally recognised human rights, including the right to property[29] and the right to due process.[30] Using international and comparative human rights law, the literature in this area considers the extent to which these rights may legally be limited or derogated from in the cause of security.[31]

Because Article 103 of the United Nations Charter gives SC decisions primacy over competing treaty obligations, it has been suggested that the SC is not bound by general norms of customary international law, and some commentators have suggested that it is not even bound by norms of *jus cogens*.[32] However, most authors agree that the SC's powers are limited by norms of *jus cogens*,[33] a view

---

[26] See guidelines for the Committee's work, available at http://disarmament2.un.org/Committee1540/work.html.

[27] See the website of the 1566 Working Group at http://www.un.org/Docs/sc/committees/1566Template.htm.

[28] *Case concerning Questions of Interpretation and Application of the Montreal Convention arising out of the Aerial Incident at Lockerbie (Provisional Measures)*, ICJ Reports 1992, dissenting opinion of Judge Weeramantry; De Wet, E and Nollkaemper, A, 'Review of Security Council Decisions by National Courts' (2002) 45 *German Yearbook of International Law* 166, 171–6.

[29] Protected by Art 17 of the Universal Declaration of Human Rights (UDHR), available at http://www.un.org/Overview/rights.html.

[30] Protected by Art 14(2) of the International Covenant on Civil and Political Rights (ICCPR) and Art 11(1) of the UDHR. In the case of civil proceedings, international human rights law protects the right to a fair and public hearing before an independent and impartial tribunal. If the measures are criminal in nature, then some of the measures taken against persons designated by the relevant committees offend against the presumption of innocence.

[31] Gutherie, P, 'Security Council Sanctions and the Protection of Individual Rights' (2004) 60 *NYU Annual Survey of American Law* 491; De Wet, E, *The Chapter VII Powers of the United Nations Security Council* (Oxford, Hart Publishing, 2004); de Wet and Nollkaemper (2002).

[32] Kelsen has maintained that the Council was not bound by any international law. See the discussion of this view in Reisman (1993) and Rosand (2005) 557–58.

[33] De Wet (2004) 187 and the authors cited there.

recently confirmed by the EC Court of First Instance in the case of *Kadi v EU*.[34] In this case, the Court accepted *jus cogens* as the 'one limit to the principle that resolutions of the SC have binding effect: namely, that they must observe the fundamental peremptory provisions of *jus cogens*'.[35]

The primacy of *jus cogens* norms can be argued at a number of levels.[36] A literal interpretation of the UN Charter would maintain the primacy of not only *jus cogens* but all customary international law, because Article 103 of the Charter subjugates conflicting treaty obligations only. At a deeper level, some commentators seem to find it self-evident that *jus cogens* limits the SC's powers because of the nature of the values that this category of norms protects. Thus, Judge Lauterpacht stated in the *Case concerning the Application of the Genocide Convention*:

> [T]he prohibition of genocide . . . has generally been accepted as having the status not of an ordinary rule of international law but of jus cogens . . . The relief which Article 103 of the Charter may give the Security Council in case of conflict between one of its decisions and an operative treaty obligation cannot—as a matter of simple hierarchy of norms—extend to a conflict between a Security Council resolution and jus cogens. Indeed, one only has to state the opposite proposition thus—that a Security Council resolution may even require participation in genocide—for its unacceptability to be apparent.[37]

3. Administrative Law

The procedures adopted by the SC in reaching its decisions raise concern for several reasons, one of which is that individuals who are affected by the Council's decisions are powerless to influence them. For example, Gutherie describes the listing procedure of the 1267 Committee in the following terms:

> The requirements for adding names are . . . vague and relatively standardless . . ..
> Furthermore, the de-listing procedures are inadequate. There is no opportunity for sanctioned individuals to directly contest their inclusion on the list. They must first get the support of the state of their nationality or residence. If cooperation is not forthcoming from those countries, then the Committee has provided no avenue for an individual to come before the Committee directly. In addition, consensus decisions mean that any one state can prevent de-listing, and the state is not required to provide any reasoning or justification.[38]

---

[34] *Kadi v European Union* Judgment of the Court of First Instance (Second Chamber, extended composition) of 21 September 2005, case number Case T-315/01, available at http://curia.europa.eu/jurisp/cgi-bin/form.pl?lang=?en&Submit=?Submit&docj=?docj&numaff=?&datefs=?&datefe=?&nomusuel=?kadi&domaine=?&mots=?&resmax=100.

[35] *Ibid*, para 230.

[36] De Wet (2004) 187–90.

[37] *Case concerning Application of the Convention on the Prevention and Punishment of the Crime of Genocide* (1993) *ICJ Reports* 325, 440. See also Koskenniemi, M, 'The Pull of the Mainstream' (1990) 88 *Michigan Law Review* 1946, 1952 for a discussion of the source of fundamental humanitarian and human rights norms.

[38] Gutherie (2004) 513–14.

If the SC is an administrative body, and its action an administrative action, then an argument can be made that it is constrained by administrative law. The *Global Administrative Law Project* suggests that the Council fulfils the function of 'international administration' and identifies a range of administrative law principles that constrain international and supranational bodies, including the SC.[39] This critique of SC action is linked to the human rights-based approach but can result in more stringent standards of review. It examines both the procedural and substantive elements of SC decisions. Its procedural principles include procedural participation (the right of affected individuals to have their views and information considered before a decision is taken), reasoned decisions and review.[40] Criteria for review of the substance of a SC decision include proportionality, avoidance of unnecessarily restrictive means and legitimate expectations.[41]

Benedict Kingsbury, Nico Krisch and Richard Stewart identify a range of sources for these criteria and for the emerging discipline of global administrative law.[42] Although these sources include the usual treaties, custom and general principles, the authors argue that the normative practice in the field goes beyond the principles contained in these sources, and that a better source for the existing normative practice could be seen as a revived *ius gentium*, which 'could encompass norms emerging among a wide variety of actors and in very diverse settings, rather than any kind of *ius inter gentes* built upon agreements among states'.[43]

4. Critiques based on Fundamental Principles of Law

The third basis of criticism of SC practice is related to and informs the other two bases, but reaches more deeply into law as a normative system. This argues that particular decisions or actions of the SC are inconsistent with fundamental principles of law and must therefore be null and void.

Dyzenhaus criticises the listing mechanism of the 1267 Committee on this basis. He argues that law entails the rule of law, which is itself informed by the principle of legality. Upholding such principles maintains the integrity of international law and its claim to be law at all.[44] Dyzenhaus emphasises that his argument moves beyond institutional design and therefore applies whether the legal system in question maintains a formal separation of powers. In his analysis, the rule of law is not about the maintenance of a formal separation of powers but about the service of all the institutions of legal order, whether international or domestic, to its underlying values:

[39] Kingsbury, Krisch and Stewart (2005) 19.
[40] *Ibid*, 37–9.
[41] *Ibid*, 40.
[42] *Ibid*, 29–30.
[43] *Ibid*, 29.
[44] Austin's claim that international law is not law has been the basis of a major debate in international legal theory. See Koskenniemi, M, *The Gentle Civilizer of Nations* (Cambridge, Cambridge University Press, 2001) 34–5 and 48ff.

> [V]iolations of the rule of law are to be determined by looking to the substantive values which the separation of powers is supposed to protect rather than to whether the particular arrangement of powers in a legal order has been disturbed.[45]

Because the underlying basis of the rule of law is the doctrine of legality—to which the legislature, judiciary and executive are equally subject—Dyzenhaus criticises the SC listing procedure on the basis that the principle of legality has been contravened. Discussing the analogy between listing and legislative bills of attainder, he points out:

> The repugnance of such statutes to the common-law tradition is born of the idea that while a legislature can enact into law its understandings of subversion and other offences, the rule of law requires both that the offence be framed generally and that anyone accused of such an offence be tried in a court of law. In other words, the argument is a deeply normative one, which is not as much about the separation of powers as it is about the reasons for the separation of powers. The constitutional role of the judges is to guard the civil rights of the individual, here both the right to a fair trial and the right to be treated as equal before the law.[46]

Dyzenhaus claims that his argument is independent of the institutional design of any particular governmental system, but it does maintain a special place for the judiciary, because this is the institution through which other organs of government are kept within the rule of law. Under this argument, the substance of the law determines the judges' duties as upholders of the rule of law.

In 1995, the International Criminal Tribunal for the Former Yugoslavia (ICTY) employed arguments based on the rule of law to find that it had certain judicial capacities that no other governmental body, including the SC, could remove. In the *Tadić* decision, the ICTY emphasised that it had an inherent power to determine its own jurisdiction, noting in an *obiter dictum* that that the SC might not be able to limit this power should such a limitation threaten the independence of the Tribunal. It claimed as part of its incidental jurisdiction the power to scrutinise the legality of its own creation,[49] thereby refusing to place its creator—the Security Council—above the law. In holding the SC to the international human rights law requirement that a court must be 'established by law', the Tribunal interpreted this phrase to mean 'in accordance with the rule of law'.[50] To flesh out the implications of the rule of law for its own procedure, the Tribunal relied on international human rights law and found that the SC was bound to respect certain trial rights.[51]

---

[45] Dyzenhaus, D, 'The Rule of (Administrative) Law in International Law' (2005) 68 *Law and Contemporary Problems* 127, 152.

[46] *Ibid*, 150–1.

[47] *Prosecutor v Tadić*, Case No IT-94-1-AR72, Decision on the Defence Motion for Interlocutory Appeal on Jurisdiction, 2 October 1995, reprinted in (1996) 35 *International Legal Materials* 32, paras 14–19.

[48] *Ibid*, para 19.

[49] *Ibid*, paras 20–2.

[50] *Ibid*, paras 41–2.

[51] *Ibid*, paras 42, 46. Faiza Patel King criticises this interpretation for conflating two separate requirements of Art 14 of the ICCPR, namely, that the Tribunal be 'established by law' and that the

5. The Focus of the Criticism

All three critiques set out above have as their target a particular type of decision of the SC—one that is directed at a particular person, state or entity and has a direct effect on individual rights. In this way, the criticism is generally levelled at SC actions that we would in a municipal system classify as administrative.

This is demonstrated most clearly by the *Global Administrative Law Project*, which describes the SC as an international administrative body and defines administrative action as 'all rule-making and adjudications or other decisions of particular matters that are neither treaty-making nor simple dispute settlement between disputing parties'.[52] Kingsbury, Krisch and Stewart see this definition as an elaboration of the more intuitive sense of administrative action as state acts that are neither legislative nor judicial.[53] By adopting such a definition in the designation of the SC as an international administrative body, they are clearly steering the discipline away from the legislative function of the SC. Furthermore, the range of principles proposed by the *Global Administrative Law Project* to restrain global administrative action focuses on the content of decisions and the process by which they are made, not on the powers of the decision maker.

Human rights-based criticisms and those based on fundamental principles of law have a wider application than those based on administrative law, and they can and do critique legislation as well as administrative acts. Human rights critics thus take issue with the general mandates issued by the SC as well as their legislative enactment in national systems, on the basis that they are too vague and over-inclusive and that they exclude necessary human rights guarantees.[54] However, they do not take issue with the SC for legislating per se. Dyzenhaus's rejection of legislative bills of attainder, cited above, focuses expressly on their content, and not on the organ that issues them. Indeed, it would seem to be implicit in Dyzenhaus's reasoning that the listing mechanism could be brought into compliance with the rule of law if the SC first produced a resolution that framed the offence of terrorism in general terms. Under the definition of legislation suggested below, such a resolution would constitute legislative action by the SC.

---

hearing be fair and public. See King, FP, 'Sensible Scrutiny: The Yugoslavia Tribunal's Development of Limits on the Security Council's Powers under Chapter VII of the Charter' (1996) 10 *Emory International Law Review* 509, 572–3.

[52] Kingsbury, Krisch and Stewart (2005) 17.

[53] *Ibid.*

[54] See Gutherie (2004); De Wet and Nollkaemper (2002); de Wet (2004) especially 195–200 and 219–26; Jagwanth, S and Soltau, F, 'Terrorism and Human Rights in Africa' in J Cilliers and K Sturman (eds), *Africa and Terrorism: Joining the Global Campaign* (Pretoria, Institute for Security Studies, 2002) 27–8.

II. THE LEGISLATIVE CAPACITY OF THE SECURITY COUNCIL

1. The Legislative Practice of the Security Council

For some commentators,[55] legislation is one of the new powers that the SC has arrogated to itself in recent years, particularly in response to the 'war on terrorism'. The decisive step seems to have been taken with Resolution 1373, in which the SC used its Chapter VII powers to order all states to take particular steps against international terrorism and to refrain from others.

Szasz explains that SCR 1373 constituted a break with past practice because the SC had previously used its Chapter VII powers only with reference to particular conflicts or situations, such as when it imposed sanctions against states[56] or non-state entities[57] in order to force compliance with international law. This use of the mandatory power was not legislative because the resolutions were limited to specific subject matters and specific time periods.[58] When the SC did decide on measures with respect to an open-ended problem, such as the position of children and civilians in armed conflict, these measures were not phrased in compulsory terms but as recommendations. They too did not produce the sense of binding legislation.[59]

What is different about SCR 1373 is that it is a mandatory order with no time limit, and it is not confined to a particular conflict but rather aimed at an undefined threat: 'global terrorism'. For Szasz, this resolution can therefore be said to 'establish new binding rules of international law—rather than mere commands relating to a particular situation'.[60]

Szasz sees the defining feature of this new activity by the SC as the general nature of the obligations it imposes on states. Talmon adds two main elements: that the legislation applies to an indefinite number of cases and is not limited in time,[61] which also implies that the legislation is forward-looking. Together, these aspects

---

[55] Szasz, P, 'The Security Council Starts Legislating' (2002) 96 *American Journal of International Law* 901, 901–2; Talmon, S, 'The Security Council as World Legislature' (2005) 99 *American Journal of International Law* 175; Lavalle, R, 'A Novel, if Awkward, Exercise in International Law-making: Security Council Resolution 1540 (2004)' (2004) *Netherlands International Law Review* 411; Marschik, A, 'The Security Council as World Legislator? Theory, Practice and Consequences of an Expanding World Power', IILJ Working Paper 2005/18, available at http://www.iilj.org/papers/documents/2005.18Marschik.pdf; and Rosand (2005).
[56] See, for example, SCR 418 of 1977, which imposed an arms embargo against South Africa; and SCR 421 of 1977, which set up a sanctions committee on South Africa. Both resolutions are available at http://www.un.org/documents/scres.htm.
[57] See, for example, SCR 864 of 1993, SCR1127 of 1997 and SCR 1173 and SCR 1176 of 1998, which imposed sanctions against the Angolan rebel movement Unita and its leaders. The resolutions are available at http://www.un.org/documents/scres.htm.
[58] Dyzenhaus (2005) 141.
[59] Szasz (2002) 901–2.
[60] *Ibid*, 902. The binding nature of the new rules is underscored by the mechanism that SCR 1373 creates to monitor compliance. See Art 6 of SCR 1373 at http://www.un.org/Docs/scres/2001/sc2001.htm.
[61] Talmon (2005) 176.

suggest an understanding of SC legislation that is best described in the following terms:

> '[L]egislative powers' [are] the powers of the Security Council to enact general, abstract norms that are directly binding on all Member States of the UN. The ensuing norms do not enforce the peace in a specific political crisis, but regulate rights and obligations of States on a wider issue with long-term or indefinite effect.[62]

Only a small number of the SC practices described above can be classified as legislation. The controversial listing procedure affects named individuals only and imposes only specific obligations on states. Similarly, any other procedure that results in specific recommendations or measures against named persons or organisations—such as the recommendations likely to proceed from the 1566 Working Group—would count as administrative action and not as legislation. By contrast, the SC legislates in two main ways. First, and most importantly, it issues resolutions imposing general obligations, such as those contained in SCR 1373. But there is a second source of legislation which should not be overlooked: the SC imposes an obligation on states to co-operate with its committees. To the extent that the committees oversee and influence the adaptation of states' domestic legal systems to comply with SC measures—a role that the Counter-terrorism Committee in particular has assumed with fervour—the SC is creating new legislation at the domestic level.[63]

2. Responses to the Council's Legislative Practice

Critics have condemned at some length what we can call the executive and administrative acts of the SC. By contrast, its legislative acts have often been met with acquiescence[64] or even approval.[65] Talmon suggests (and discounts) four main objections to the legislative role of the SC: that a body as patently undemocratic and unrepresentative as the SC is not suited to lawmaking; that SC resolutions are not recognised as a source of international law; that Council practice violates the basic structure of the international legal order in that it is not based on the consent of states; and that a body that carries out the general role of a 'policeman' is ill suited to adopt the role of 'a legislature or jury'.[66] Only this last objection argues directly that the constitutional role of the SC is to be an executive rather than a legislative body. All of the objections, however, raise questions about the legitimacy

---

[62] Marschik (2005) 5.

[63] See the country reports submitted to the CTC and the CTC's programme for analysing and evaluating them at http://www.un.org/Docs/sc/committees/1373/submitted_reports.html and http://www.un.org/sc/ctc/workprogramme.shtml.

[64] Talmon cites the example of Mexico, which had objected to the creation of ad hoc criminal tribunals but raised no objections to SCR 1373. See Talmon (2005) 177.

[65] Talmon (2005); Rosand (2005); Lavalle (2004). See also, generally, the review of state responses to SCR 1373 and SCR 1540 in Marschik (2005) 14–21.

[66] Talmon (2005) 179.

of the SC and echo Alvarez's view that the SC was not intended to act as a 'global legislator'.[67]

An analysis of the arguments both for and against the SC's legislative function reveals their circular nature. This is particularly the case when commentators attempt to rely on as open-ended a document as the UN Charter, because their interpretations of the Charter provisions are deeply influenced by the specific case they are trying to prove. The circular reasoning results from an unfortunate lacuna in the scholarship on governance. Theories of representation that support the internal constitutional arrangement of states do not transfer easily to the international arena, with the result that we have no way of ascertaining when the assumption of international governance by any one body is legitimate.[68] Without a tool to determine the legitimacy of the SC's claim of acting for the global community, we are left to fall back on some unspoken assumptions when we interpret its powers.[69]

This chapter proceeds on the assumption that we are dealing with a situation of global governance when the SC exercises its Chapter VII powers. The opposing assumption—what may be called a 'private law' approach—treats the international legal order as a community of equals and views the relationship between its members through a contractual rather than constitutional lens. This approach is perhaps most clearly demonstrated by the arguments with which Talmon dismisses the objections to the SC's legislative function.

Talmon supports the idea that the Council works within a legal framework and aligns himself to the view of the ICTY that the Council is not unbound by law.[70] However, the legal framework that he chooses for the Council appears to be restricted to the UN Charter. Thus he meets the objection that the SC is a policeman, not a legislature, with the remark that the SC's powers should be determined not by reference to that body's general role but 'on the basis of the provisions of the UN Charter'.[71]

Despite some references to past UN practice,[72] Talmon also tends to treat the Charter as a complete document, the meaning of which does not need to be ascertained with reference to factors outside of the document. Thus, as the UN Charter does not in its wording distinguish between legislative and executive functions, Talmon is able to work from the assumption that there is no difference between these two functions. Conflating these two functions at the outset in itself answers many of the criticisms that Talmon identifies against SC legislation. Thus, for example, he disposes of the objection that the SC is unrepresentative by pointing

---

[67] Alvarez, J, 'Hegemonic International Law Revisited' (2003) 97 *American Journal of International Law* 874, 875 fn 9. See also Lavalle (2004).

[68] Allot discusses the need for a theory of representation to legitimate international law and governance: Allot, P, *Eunomia* (Oxford, OUP, 1990) para 16.16.

[69] See also Reisman (1993) 93 for a related criticism of scholarship that attempts to find in the UN Charter implied limitations to the SC's powers.

[70] Talmon (2005) 178.

[71] *Ibid*, 179.

[72] *Ibid*, 180.

out that the Charter allows this unrepresentative body *some* powers. He ignores the executive nature of these already accepted powers and claims that there is no difference between them and the power of legislation:

> It can hardly be maintained that authorizing the use of force requires less democratic legitimacy than imposing an obligation to prevent and suppress the financing of terrorist acts.[73]

Similarly, another argument merges quasi-judicial and legislative acts:

> [I]f the Council can require states to freeze the funds of every single person who commits a specific terrorist act, it must—a fortiori—also be able to order states to freeze the funds of all persons who commit such acts. In this sense, the imposition of general obligations is nothing but the generalization of individual obligations.[74]

Talmon's reliance on the International Court of Justice (ICJ) 'application' of resolutions of the SC—which, he argues, renders the SC resolutions a source of law[75]—also ignores the difference between legislative and executive acts. In a municipal system, a court can quite easily recognise the validity of an executive act—and give effect to it—without elevating that executive act into a legal principle.[76] I would argue that this is what the Court has done in Talmon's example of the 'application' of an SC resolution by the ICJ.[77] The resolution in this example is the one by which the SC directed Libya to surrender the Lockerbie bombing suspects to the United Kingdom.[78] It was directed at a specific situation and specific addressee and, as such, does not meet Talmon's own criteria for 'legislation' by the SC. By giving effect to this resolution, the ICJ recognised its validity, but it did not turn the Council's decision into law.

Ironically, a different starting point—namely, an understanding of the SC as an executive and not a legislative organ—can make some of Talmon's arguments easier to accept. For example, one of his assertions relies on the delegated power of the SC, which Talmon uses to discount two main objections to the SC's legislative function. To the objection that the SC overrides the consent of states, he suggests that under Article 25 of the UN Charter, states have given what amounts to almost blanket consent to abide by any decision that the SC finds necessary to make, and that the 'consent' element of the international legal order is thereby being maintained.[79] He also uses the delegated power in Article 25 to link SC action to a

---

[73] *Ibid,* 179.
[74] *Ibid,* 182.
[75] *Ibid,* 179.
[76] If, for example, a domestic court imposes a fine on a taxi driver for operating her business outside the terms of her taxi licence, the court is implicitly recognising the validity of the administrative decision to grant the taxi driver a licence on certain terms. It is not, however, turning the terms of the taxi licence into law.
[77] Talmon (2005) 179 fn 44.
[78] SCR 748 of 1992, available at http://www.un.org/Docs/sc/unsc_resolutions.html.
[79] Talmon (2005) 179.

treaty—the UN Charter—thereby bringing SC resolutions under the auspices of a source of law recognised by the ICJ statute.[80]

This argument is not tenable if the UN Charter is seen simply as a contract between sovereign states. States do not sign a blank cheque on joining the UN. Certainly, there is no corresponding concept of consent in comparative private law. Relationships that arise from agency, contracts, *negotiorum gestio* all vest some form of control in the consent giver, either by including terms in the initial contract or by imposing strict fiduciary duties on the person controlling another's assets. In public law, however, there is the concept of delegated legislation, which, in a Westminster-type constitutional system, allows the executive broad discretion because the executive is answerable to the legislature.[81] Because the executive's discretion is linked to its accountability to the legislature, however, its powers are more restrictively interpreted where there are fewer mechanisms for legislative oversight.[82] For a public lawyer in the Westminster mould, the absence of express limitations on the SC's powers would therefore be a reason to limit, not to extend, the executive's powers.

The circular nature of the responses to the legislative practice of the SC points to the need to examine the interpretive framework of the applicable legal principles, and our discussion will remain inconclusive as long as we treat the Charter as the sole source of these principles. The following section argues for a public law framework and proposes that constitutional principles can and should be applied to the international system of governance. In particular, it argues that the doctrine of separation of powers is applicable in the international sphere.

III. A PUBLIC LAW PARADIGM

1. A General Framework

Although they concern themselves with the executive rather than legislative function of the SC, the objections to SC practice described in section I above provide a precedent for a public law paradigm. Apart from reinforcing a general 'public law'

---

[80]   Talmon (2005) 179.

[81]   It is beyond the scope of this chapter to compare parliamentary and presidential systems of government. As an (over-)generalisation, however, presidential systems require less accountability from the executive to the legislature even though the executive may on occasions exercise wide, and even legislative powers (see Sargentich, T, 'The Delegation of Lawmaking Power to the Executive Branch' in K Harriger (ed), *Separation of Powers: Documents and Commentary* (Washington DC, CQ Press, 2003) 116–31; and Braveman, D, Banks, W and Smolla, R, *Constitutional Law: Structure and Rights in our Federal System*, 4th edn (Newark, Matthew Bender/Nexis Lexis, 2000) 75–106. This need not, however, be seen as a rejection of the requirement of accountability. Instead, through providing for direct election of the president, presidential systems are replacing accountability to the legislature with accountability to an electorate.

[82]   See the review of national approaches to this issue in *Executive Council of the Western Cape Legislature v President of the Republic of South Africa* 1995 (4) SA 877 (CC) (South Africa), especially para 55.

discourse, they all suggest that the need to constrain the SC arises from the fact that the Council is exercising public power.

In a 1963 article that argued for the application of comparative public law to international institutions, Karl Zemanek suggested that many international institutions had acquired a 'constitutional' character, and that their constitutive acts could be seen as constitutions and their activities as administration in the public law sense, subject to the controls of administrative law.[83] In his analysis, Zemanek acknowledged that international law had, until recently, borrowed exclusively from private law concepts, particularly those of Roman law. Public law had generally been ignored. He related this lacuna to the relatively late development of public law, the wide variety of domestic manifestations of public law concepts, and the fact that international law had, until the time of writing, been seen as a legal system governing equals and therefore was better suited to the private law paradigm.[84]

The point at which public law becomes relevant, in Zemanek's view, is the point at which states integrate into an international system. While Zemanek focused expressly on the notion of integration before 'relations of a public law character'[85] emerge, it is clear from his analysis that this integration accompanies an uneven distribution of power between the organs and the subjects of the legal community. The central role of a power imbalance is implicit in the contrast Zemanek drew between the public law regime and its opposite, the relationship of equals, as well as from the example he chose of a well-integrated system—the European Union. The less 'integrated' character of the UN, which Zemanek considered less suited to public law concepts, must therefore have resulted from its fairly egalitarian structure.

Recent years have seen the notion of international constitutional law gain momentum.[86] Once again, authors point to the increasing integration of the international community,[87] a term which seems to encapsulate both a normative unity and a political hierarchy. Thus some of the arguments for international constitutional law claim that the international community is based on a universal value

---

[83]   Zemanek, K, 'Was kann die Vergleichung staatlichen öffentlichen Rechts für das Recht der internationalen Organisationen leisten?' (1964) 24 *Zeitschrift für ausländisches öffentliches Recht und Völkerrecht* 453, 454–5 and 462ff.

[84]   *Ibid*, 454, 470.

[85]   Zemanek uses the term 'Beziehungen . . ., die öffentlich-rechtlichen Charakter haben'. See Zemanek (1964) 455.

[86]   Proponents include De Wet, E, 'The International Constitutional Order' (2006) 55 *International and Comparative Law Quarterly* 51; de Wet (2004) ch 3; Tomuschat, C, 'International Law: Ensuring the Survival of Mankind on the Eve of a New Century. General Course on Public International Law' (1999) 281 *Recueil des Cours* 10; and Helfer, L, 'Constitutional Analogies in the International Legal System' (2003) 37 *Loyola of Los Angeles Law Review* 193. Criticism of the notion of international constitutional law can be found in Herdegen, M, 'The "Constitutionalization" of the UN Security System' (1994) 27 *Vanderbilt Journal of Transnational Law* 135; Reisman (1993). See also von Bogdandy, A, 'Constitutionalism in International Law: Comment on a Proposal from Germany' (2006) 47 *Harvard International Law Journal* 223, 240 and the authorities cited in fn 77.

[87]   De Wet (2006) 57–63; Tomuschat (1999) 237, discussed with approval by von Bogdandy (2006) 228–9.

system[88] with commonly held norms,[89] which include obligations that are owed to the international community as a whole.[90] On the other hand, the term 'integrated' is also juxtaposed with the increasing power of supra-national and international organisations. So, for example, Erika De Wet notes that 'public decision-making' is no longer located within the state,[91] and Christian Tomuschat calls for common institutions at regional levels or a universal level to compensate for the extent to which 'the State forgoes or is compelled to relinquish its role as guarantor of the common interest of its citizens'.[92]

To the extent that these arguments relate the international constitutional order to a shared normative system, they face criticism that the international legal order lacks legitimacy, particularly as it has no democratic basis. However, if it can be established that some principles of constitutional law are applicable outside democratic systems (as is argued below), the argument for a public law paradigm does not depend on a shared normative system. Instead, the central factor is the imbalance of power in the society under review.

If we examine the international sphere, we therefore find a strong argument for the application of constitutional principles. An 'integrated' system has developed not only regionally but also internationally, and in that system, a strong hierarchy characterises two central sets of relationships: that between the SC and nation states; and that between the SC and individual human beings. The SC's power over states is also growing as it extends its understanding of the terms that trigger Chapter VII and allow it to impose binding measures on states; and these measures have on occasions severely restricted the rights of individual human beings. The individuals, on the other hand, have no right of access to the Council before or even after the Council takes its decisions, and there exists no procedure for individuals to appeal against Council decisions.

The bottom line within both relationships is that the SC exercises power over the other entity—power that is supported by and expressed through a range of integrated, institutional mechanisms. It is this use of power that has attracted the public law paradigms of human rights and administrative law, and the notion of the rule of law, as states and commentators attempt to find a suitable theoretical framework for an analysis of an international governmental system.

2. The Doctrine of Separation of Powers

In his discussion of the limits that the rule of law places on the power of government, Dyzenhaus remarks:

---

[88] De Wet (2006) 53; von Bogdandy (2006) 226.
[89] De Wet (2006) 74.
[90] *Ibid*, 54–55.
[91] *Ibid*, 53.
[92] Tomuschat (1999) 226.

If judges cannot carry out their constitutional duty, it does not follow that they have no such duty. What does follow is that legal reform is required in order for the legal order to maintain its claim to be such, to be an order governed by the rule of law.[93]

Dyzenhaus proposes that the rule of law necessarily vests certain powers in the judiciary. In one way, it is possible to downplay the aspect of institutional design that this argument introduces and to see the judiciary's protected position merely as a guarantor of specific substantive rights. But his argument goes beyond the protection of specific rights; it uses the judiciary to protect an ongoing process by which those who exercise power are called continually to account for and justify its use. This chapter suggests further institutional implications for the rule of law: namely, that it also delineates, in broad outline, the powers and capacities of the executive and legislature.

This argument rests squarely on the notion that the structure of government is a fundamental aspect of the rule of law. It is, however, a somewhat neglected aspect:

> Together with representative government, [rights] have defined constitutionalism, providing the chief means for combining the rule of law with government by fallible and occasionally sinful men . . .
>
> In recent years, however, [rights have] come to predominate. Rights, upheld by judicial review, are said to comprise the prime component of constitutionalism, providing a normative framework within which politics operates.[94]

Bellamy criticises this emphasis, pointing out the central role of the organisation of government in promoting the substantive values of a legal community:

> The organization of government serves not simply to control and limit the power of those who exercise it. As sovereignty has passed from monarchs to the people, the aim increasingly becomes to channel that power so that the values and interests represented by rights are promoted and identified with as well as safeguarded.[95]

This view emphasises the role of constitutional design, but it also draws attention to a possible obstacle to a redesign of the international arena by suggesting that design becomes important only once democracy is realised in a society. An argument for the doctrine of separation of powers at the international level must therefore establish the relationship between this doctrine and democracy.

The history of the doctrine of separation of powers demonstrates that one of its first functions was to provide for a form of mixed government in which all social estates or groups could be adequately represented.[96] The earliest forms of the

---

[93] Dyzenhaus (2005) 150–1.

[94] Bellamy, R, 'The Political Form of the Constitution: The Separation of Powers, Rights and Representative Democracy' (1996) 44 *Political Studies* 436.

[95] *Ibid*, 436–7.

[96] *Ibid*, 440–4; Vile, M, *Constitutionalism and the Separation of Powers* (Oxford, Clarendon Press, 1967) chs 1 and 3; Heun, W, 'Gewaltenteilung in inhrer verfassungsgeschichtlichen Entwicklung' in C Starck (ed), *Staat und Individuum im Kultur- und Rechtsvergleich* (Baden Baden, Nomos Verlagsgesellschaft, 2000) 95, 96ff.

doctrine were therefore concerned with some form of representative government, not to promote individual freedom or empowerment but simply to attain stability through the balance of social power.[97] Theorists of the seventeenth and eighteenth centuries developed and transformed the doctrine by emphasising that governmental power needs to be divided and separated to prevent the abuse of power by any one branch and so preserve the liberty of the individual.[98] Common to these discussions is the notion that legislative and executive powers should not be combined.[99] Large assemblies were considered too cumbersome and inefficient to implement laws and policy, which meant a separate executive was needed. On the other hand, this executive should not be able to make the law that it is enforcing. If it were, laws would not be made in the common interest, and officials could not be held to account.[100]

Throughout its history, the doctrine of separation of powers has not required a democratic foundation and indeed has often sat uneasily with democracy. Democracy is a system in which the state, and the legislature in particular, is seen to represent the interests of the entire *demos* as a unit. Historically, however, the doctrine of separation of powers has often assumed that the different branches of government represent different interest groups.[101] The resulting tension was resolved partially by focusing on the different functions of the three branches of government, rather than on the social estate that the branch represented.[102] Even in its present forms, however, the doctrine of separation of powers can obstruct the realisation of popular will, either by frustrating it or by diluting it. Thus, in Westminster-type systems in which only the legislature is directly elected, the doctrine of separation of powers insulates the executive and judiciary from the will of the *demos* by giving these bodies some independence from the legislature—and, indeed, by giving them a check over the legislature.[103] On the other hand, in

---

[97] The doctrine can be traced back to Greek antiquity. See Vile (1967) ch 2; Heun (2000) 96 ff; and Bellamy (1996) 442–4. Vile describes these earliest forms of the doctrine as 'mixed government', in which government represents different interest groups, and distinguishes it from pure separation of powers, in which government is divided into functions rather then interest groups (fn 98 33ff). Acknowledging the close connection between the two concepts, he describes mixed government as the 'parent' of separation of powers (fn 98 47).

[98] In particular, Locke and Montesquieu. See Vile (1967) chs 3 and 4; Bellamy (1996) 444; and Heun (2000) 98–101.

[99] See Vile (1967) chs 6 and 7; Bellamy (1996) 443–5 and 447ff; Heun (2000) 98–105. Note, however, that seventh-century writers included many judicial functions under the executive. See Vile (1967) 29ff.

[100] Bellamy (1996) 443. Heun (2000) 101 points out that even Rousseau, who rejected the notion of separation of powers as a violation of the sovereignty of the people, advocated a strict separation between legislature and executive. Separation of executive and legislature is also integral to Kant's republican ideal (see Dyzenhaus (2005) 152).

[101] See nn 96–7 above. Bellamy further notes that Montesquieu criticised the merely formal separation of powers in the Venetian governmental system for allowing all three branches to be staffed by magistrates from the same social estate. See Montesquieu, C-L, *De l'Esprit de Lois* (Paris, Garnier-Flammarion, 1979) Book XI, ch 6, 295, cited by Bellamy (1996) 444.

[102] Bellamy (1996) 446.

[103] The so-called 'counter-majoritarian dilemma' refers to the tension created by constitutional democracies when they subject decisions of elected representatives to judicial control—particularly when the judiciary has no democratic mandate of its own. A number of theorists have addressed this

systems in which the executive and the judiciary have their own democratic mandates, the doctrine of separation of powers has been described as a 'filtering mechanism' that divides power and makes it 'difficult for majorities to aggregate'.[104]

Viewed from another angle, this development means that, in its current form, the doctrine of separation of powers responds to a fundamentally different problem from that which democracy is meant to address. Democracy is about representation; separation of powers is about limited government. The latter therefore has a role to play in every society. The thesis underlying the doctrine of separation of powers—that government, whether representative or unrepresentative, needs to be limited to avoid the concentration and abuse of power—is therefore equally applicable to the international sphere.

Indeed, there may be a fairly close correlation between the political environments in which the doctrine has been proposed in the past and the environment presented by the international community today. Perhaps we could even speak of a cycle, an historical pattern repeating itself at a different level. The focus of the international community at the founding of the UN was stability. Both the size and the elevated powers of the Security Council were justified by the need for security and efficient action against threats to that security. These arguments, which echoed the calls for strengthened and streamlined executives at the national level, are still brought today by commentators who emphasise the dangers posed by international terrorism.[105]

At the same time, two further developments in international law and international relations emphasise that a strong executive is no longer sufficient. Instead, the international community should now import other aspects of domestic constitutional systems subject to the rule of law. Thus, while the need for stability has remained, the international community has acknowledged the importance of rights—echoing the emphasis on liberty in the literature of the seventeenth and eighteenth centuries. As set out above, a rights-based conception of the rule of law might seem to protect human rights without affecting the institutional design. But even so conceived, the rule of law requires a particular position for the judiciary.

---

tension, including: Dworkin, R, 'Constitutionalism and Democracy' (1995) 3 *European Journal of Philosophy* 2; Habermas, J, *Between Facts and Norms: Contributions to a Discourse Theory of Law and Democracy*, W Rehg (trans) (Cambridge, MA, MIT Press, 1996) 321; Davis, D, 'Integrity and Ideology: Towards a Critical Theory of the Judicial Function' (1995) 112 *South African Law Journal* 104; and Osborne, M and Sprigman, C, 'Behold: Angry Native becomes Postmodernist Prophet of Judicial Messiah' (2001) 118 *South African Law Journal* 693, 700.

[104] Zasloff, J, 'Taking Politics Seriously: A Theory of California's Separation of Powers' (2004) 51 *UCLA Law Review* 1079, 1124–5. See also the sources cited by Zasloff, 1125, fn 213.

[105] See, eg, Rosand's argument for extending the powers of the SC to include legislation: '[T]o continue to read . . . [the exclusion of legislative capacity] into the Charter at a time when the most urgent threats to international peace and security are limited by neither time nor geography would prevent the Council from fulfilling its responsibility under the Charter to maintain international peace and security through "prompt and effective action" ': Rosand (2005) 559.

ver, the judiciary is not the only guardian of rights. For seventeenth- and ath-century proponents of the separation of powers, the protection of the ary was not sufficient or, for some theorists, even necessary. What was essen- /as that the body applying the law (the executive) is not applying law that it ha₃ itself made—and thereby usurping the role of the legislature. It was this mixture of powers that would defeat liberty because it would render the executive unaccountable.

It is therefore the doctrine of separation of powers that provides an institutional framework for the accountability required by a culture of justification. In Mureinik's analysis, the culture of justification entails a substantive normative system that requires those wielding power to give account to those affected by that power. The normative system must be effective, a point developed by Dyzenhaus in this volume when he argues that a culture of justification also entails institutional mechanisms that can ensure that account is given. Accountability therefore links the culture of justification to the doctrine of separation of powers, as it is the latter that provides the minimum institutional requirements essential for an ongoing process of accountability.

IV. ACCOUNTABILITY AND LAW-MAKING IN THE INTERNATIONAL SPHERE

The above has suggested that a culture of justification requires a particular relationship between power and accountability:[106] to the extent that a body governs, it must be accountable to those who are governed; conversely, the amount of power that a constitutional arrangement confers on a body is commensurate with the extent of that body's accountability to the community it affects. Section I of this chapter demonstrated that the Security Council wields considerable power in the global community and, furthermore, that it has been incrementally increasing its power since the end of the Cold War. While a full study is beyond the scope of this chapter, a brief examination of UN mechanisms is necessary to establish whether the SC's power is coupled with a similar measure of accountability. This section then returns to the question of law-making, examining the role that the current process of international law-making can have both in empowering and in constraining the SC.

1. Accountability

Because the international community has evolved into a global community of states, individuals and non-state bodies,[107] the first task in examining the account-

---

[106] See the critique of Talmon in section II, and the general discussion in section III.
[107] Kingsbury, Krisch and Stewart (2005) 16.

ability of the SC is to establish to whom it should be held accountable. Should it be accountable to states? To individuals? To non-state bodies?

Grant and Keohane suggest two models for accountability: the power-wielder can be held accountable either to the persons affected by the exercise of power (the participation model) or to those who delegate power to the body that wields it (the delegation model).[108] They reject the participation model for most international governance because the global community lacks a *demos*.[109] However, a delegation model is still possible in the international sphere—that is, a model in which the SC would be accountable to the General Assembly (GA). This is because the state parties to the UN Charter, who together make the GA, have delegated power to the SC to make certain decisions on their behalf.

In Mureinik's terms, a culture of justification requires governors to be accountable to those 'governed by their decisions', in other words, those affected by them. This suggests that the SC would be accountable to the entire global community, including individual human beings, as all the members of this community are affected by SC decisions. However, Mureinik distinguishes between those affected by the exercise of power and the mechanisms through which the power-wielders are held to account. In his analysis, the courts would play a pivotal institutional role in holding the governors to the substantive normative system of current international institutions. In the international sphere, the UN might be expected to provide a mechanism for holding the SC to account, particularly the GA and the ICJ.

At first blush, the GA appears to be a good candidate for oversight and constraint of the SC, for several reasons. It is the most representative body in the international community;[110] it has the right to discuss any matter within its jurisdiction; and it may address recommendations on these matters to organs of the UN.[111] Its recommendations are legally binding on members if they relate to the internal affairs of the UN, which include the organisation's budget.[112] The SC has to deliver annual reports to the GA,[113] and finally, the GA appoints two thirds of the SC's members.[114] Nonetheless, it is almost powerless to hold the SC to account.[115] Its legal control is negligible because it may not make recommendations on any matter of which the SC is seized, and its recommendations are not legally binding if they relate to matters other than the internal affairs of the UN. Its

---

[108] Grant, R and Keohane, R, 'Accountability and Abuses of Power in World Politics', IILJ Working Paper 2004/7, Global Administrative Law Series, available at http://www.iilj.org/papers/2004/2004.7%20Grant%20Keohane.pdf,) 5ff.

[109] *Ibid*, 12–14.

[110] Every member state of the UN (currently 191 states in total) has one vote in the GA. States can, however, lose their votes through non-payment of their financial contributions to the UN (Arts 18–19 of the UN Charter).

[111] Art 10 of the UN Charter.

[112] *Ibid*, Art 17.

[113] *Ibid*, Art 15.

[114] *Ibid*, Art 23.

[115] De Wet (2006) 64; Bedjaoui, M, *The New World Order and the Security Council* (The Hague, Kluwer Academic Publishers, 1994) 122–6.

power to approve or limit the budget has also been restricted in an advisory opinion of the ICJ.[116] Its political control is 'very weak, or perhaps even non-existent'.[117]

As discussed above, the ICJ has indicated that it may refuse to enforce decisions of the SC that are contrary to fundamental principles of law. However, the ICJ has a limited ability to call the SC to account. Because it lacks an express power of review and because its jurisdiction is based on the consent of states, it will hear relatively few cases involving challenges to SC decisions.[118]

The SC's lack of accountability points to the need for reform of the UN as a constitutional arrangement, but it also suggests that the SC's existing powers should be interpreted as restrictively as possible. Because the SC itself seems to view one of its powers as the power to make laws, the next section returns to the question of international law-making.

2. Law-making in the International Sphere

This chapter has argued that the powers of the Security Council should be restricted as much as possible. The doctrine of separation of powers suggests one way to do this—that is, by restricting the SC to a purely executive function and denying it any legislative capacity. However, in one area in particular—the law on the use of force by states—the Security Council has been part of the process of creating international law almost since the inception of the UN.

It is worth noting that the traditional sources of international law do not accord a role to the SC. As set out by Article 38 of the Charter of the International Court of Justice, these consist of treaties, custom (a consistent practice accompanied by a sense of legal obligation) and general principles.[119] A fourth source, the judgments of international and domestic courts and the writings of publicists, functions as a subsidiary source providing evidence of the primary sources.

Not only is the SC conspicuous by its absence in Article 38 of the ICJ Statute, but nothing in the UN Charter expressly accords the SC the right to determine the legality of the use of force by states. On the text, there is no connection between the task the SC has to perform, even when it authorises the use of force, and the specific rule that binds states in their interactions with one another. Article 2(4) of the UN Charter prohibits states from using 'force' against one another, while Article 51 protects their 'inherent right of . . . self-defence'. Article 39, by contrast, allows the SC to decide on mandatory and other measures if it finds a 'threat to the peace, breach of the peace, or act of aggression'. As commentators have noted,

---

[116] *Effects of Awards of the United Nations Administrative Tribunal*, ICJ Reports 1954, 47. See the discussion by Bedjaoui (1994) 123–4, who also notes that the GA's refusal of the budget to the ICTY for the first year of its functioning had no legal or practical consequences.

[117] Bedjaoui (1994) 126.

[118] See generally De Wet (2004) chs 1–3.

[119] As treaties are binding only on signatory states, the term 'general international law' is used here to refer only to custom and general principles.

there is therefore 'no necessary identity between what is legally prohibited by Article 2(4) and what the Council seeks to control in the discharge of its responsibilities'.[120]

In apparent disregard for this distinction, however, states and commentators place considerable emphasis on the SC's response to the use of force by individual states. They use the SC's response not primarily to give meaning to the terms in Article 39, terms that trigger SC action under Chapter VII of the UN Charter, but instead to inform their understanding of Articles 2(4) and 51. In so doing, they factor the SC's view into the formation and interpretation of rules governing the use of force by states.

Thus, for example, Murphy equates SC resolutions with international 'case law'.[121] Harris explains the lack of clarity on the meaning of Article 2(4) by reference to the lack of debate on this Article in both the SC and the GA and focuses specifically on the SC in his discussion of individual cases, noting SC approval, condemnation and even mere silence in his discussions.[122] Similarly, leading authors on the use of force in international law stress the SC's rejection of, or silence about, particular defences for the use of force.[123] Byers bases part of his argument that states have attained the right to use force against state-sponsored terrorism on the SC's changing reaction to this defence over the years,[124] a development that has brought some states and commentators to suggest that use of force against state-sponsored terrorism is permissible only if the SC affirms the right in advance.[125]

This history of reference—or deference—to the SC in the area of use of force may be one of the factors that facilitated SCR 1373. The resolution is extremely significant, not because it was the first time the SC took part in the process of law creation, but because of the manner in which it did so. Previously, the Council had been one of the factors influencing the creation of new legal norms. However, in SCR 1373, it purported to establish general and binding norms by its fiat alone. Its move from the pre-existing mode of law-making to that of SCR 1373 is a move

---

[120] Goodrich, L, Hambro, E and Simons, A, *Charter of the United Nations* (New York, Columbia University Press, 1969) 46, cited by Murphy, J, 'Force and Arms' in C Joyner (ed), *The United Nations and International Law* (Cambridge, ASIL and CUP, 1999) 101.

[121] Murphy (1999) 99.

[122] Harris, DJ, *Cases and Materials on International Law*, 6th edn (London, Sweet and Maxwell, 2004) 889. Harris notes reaction and lack of reaction by the SC to armed force at pp 913, 925, 938, 930, 932 and 940 fnn 71–2 and note 1 on p 940 (India's invasion of Goa; Argentina's invasion of the Falkland Islands; the 'cumulation of events' approach to an armed attack; Israel's raid on Beirut in December 1968; Israel's raid on Lebanon 1982; Israel's bombing of PLO headquarters in Tunisia 1985; and the Harib Fort Incident 1964).

[123] Bowett, D, 'Reprisals Involving Recourse to Armed Force' (1972) 66 *American Journal of International Law* 1.

[124] Byers, M, *War Law* (London, Atlantic Books, 2005).

[125] Gray notes: 'Another possible restriction on this apparently very wide and, for many States, new doctrine of self-defence is that the right of self-defence against terrorism may exist only in cases where the right has been asserted by the Security Council . . . Several States regarded this Security Council backing as crucial to the US claim to self-defence': (Gray, C, 'Self-defence against Terrorism Post 9/11', quoted in Harris (2004) 942.

from a co-operative, consensus-building process to the relatively autonomous act of a municipal legislature.

The pre-existing law-making power of the SC is both an obstacle and a support to the thesis that the SC lacks legislative capacity. It is an obstacle because it demonstrates that that the Council can never be stripped of all law-making power. The Council's authority in the area of the use of force is entrenched by well-established practice and may also be implicit in the Charter, if not explicit. There is a connection between Articles 2(4), 51 and 39—after all, acts that threaten peace tend to involve force, and acts of aggression must entitle a state to act in self-defence. Furthermore, the fact that Article 51 recognises a right of self-defence 'until the SC has taken measures necessary to maintain international peace and security' suggests that the Council's actions form part of the boundary of the concept of self-defence.

But the pre-existing legislative practice of the SC also suggests an institutional control which the international community has hitherto exercised, and can continue to exercise. The significance of the co-operative nature of the established process of law creation should not be under-estimated. When the Council helps to create norms on the use of force, its legal authority is tempered by the presence of other factors that establish the new rule. These include the practice and legal opinions of states[126] and even secondary sources such as case-law and jurisprudence.[127]

There is a tendency to see limitations on an institution's powers as meaningless unless there is another institution with the power to enforce those limitations.[128] Writers who suggest limits to the Council's powers therefore often devote substantial effort to establishing that there is an institution that can enforce these limits, focusing particularly on the International Court of Justice.[129] But the fact that law-making is a co-operative process in which states, international organisations and even individuals play a part, in itself constitutes a limit on the Council's powers. Given the co-operative nature of the formation of customary international law, a sea change in the other parties who form it—a change of culture—can have a significant influence at the international level.

CONCLUSION

This chapter has investigated the place of a culture of justification in the international sphere, asking both whether this sphere reflects a culture of justification, and whether a culture of justification forms part of international law. The answer

---

[126] Art 38(1)(b) of the Charter of the ICJ provides two elements for custom: state practice; and the conviction of states that this practice is accepted as law.

[127] Art 28(1)(d) lists the decisions of courts and the writings of publicists as subsidiary sources of law.

[128] See, for example, Reisman (1993) 92.

[129] De Wet (2003) ch 3; de Wet and Nollkaemper (2002); Schweigman, D, *The Authority of the Security Council under Chapter VII of the UN Charter* (The Hague, Kluwer Law International, 2001) ch 5; Bedjaoui (1994).

to the first question seems to be 'no'. While some areas of international law—particularly international human rights law[130]—suggest that the international community reflects a culture of justification, the increasing power of the SC and the relative acquiescence of many states and commentators to this power suggests we find ourselves in a culture of authority.

This chapter has, however, also argued that the answer to the second question is 'yes'. Because all law, including international law, entails the rule of law, it requires that the law constrain those who wield power and hold them to account. The international community is therefore required to create and sustain a culture of justification, and this in turn requires an ongoing process of accountability. The process needs to be secured by the institutions of governance. This entails not just that a particular role is assumed by the judiciary, but also that the two other bodies involved in the process of international governance are separated from the judiciary and each other and constrained from acting outside their powers. In particular, the executive body, with the power to enforce law and its own executive decisions, must be prevented from making law as far as possible and required to account for its use of its powers. In the international sphere, a culture of justification requires that, while there may be justifications for the SC's influence on the development of the law, those justifications must be brought, and the legislative function of the Council never treated as a given.

The opposing cultures suggested by established international law and developing international practice point to a conflict between law and power in the international arena. The rule of law resolves this conflict in favour of law because it views law as that which constrains power. But it is faced with a particular challenge by the growing legislative practice of the Council. If the SC manages to extend its legal function beyond the established, co-operative law-making process to claim autonomous legislative capacity, then there is the danger that law itself can become a legitimating mechanism—a mechanism whereby the Council can claim primacy for its own decisions in the event of conflict with other norms of the international legal order. If accepted as a source of law, the SC can set up an anti-terrorism regime as a legal system in its own right.

The established norm-creation process of international law both enables the Council to assume something of a legislative role and allows the other participants in the law-making process to limit that role. In this way, there is some institutional protection within the international system. If the Security Council acts beyond its powers, it is the other actors in the law-making process who can and must make a choice for a culture of justification.

---

[130] International human rights law permits states to limit or even derogate from the rights that it guarantees, but there are strict requirements for such limitations and derogations. When states have to defend themselves against complaints of rights violations before international human rights bodies, they are drawn into a process of justifying the limitations and derogations that they have made. See Art 4 ICCPR and General Comment 29 of the Human Rights Committee, UN Doc GAOR A/56/40.

REFERENCES

Allot, P, *Eunomia* (Oxford, OUP, 1990).

Alvarez, J, 'Hegemonic International Law Revisited' (2003) 97 *American Journal of International Law* 874.

Bedjaoui, M, *The New World Order and the Security Council* (The Hague, Kluwer Academic Publishers, 1994).

Bellamy, R, 'The Political Form of the Constitution: The Separation of Powers, Rights and Representative Democracy' (1996) 44 *Political Studies* 436.

Bowett, D, 'Reprisals Involving Recourse to Armed Force' (1972) 66 *American Journal of International Law* 1.

Braveman, D, Banks, W and Smolla, R, *Constitutional Law: Structure and Rights in our Federal System*, 4th edn (Newark, Matthew Bender/Nexis Lexis, 2000).

Byers, M, *War Law* (London, Atlantic Books, 2005).

Davis, D, 'Integrity and Ideology: Towards a Critical Theory of the Judicial Function' (1995) 112 *South African Law Journal* 104.

de Wet, E, *The Chapter VII Powers of the United Nations Security Council* (Oxford, Hart Publishing, 2004).

—— 'The International Constitutional Order' (2006) 55 *International and Comparative Law Quarterly* 51.

de Wet, E and Nollkaemper, A, 'Review of Security Council Decisions by National Courts' (2002) 45 *German Yearbook of International Law* 166.

Dworkin, R, 'Constitutionalism and Democracy' (1995) 3 *European Journal of Philosophy* 2.

Dyzenhaus, D, 'The Rule of (Administrative) Law in International Law' (2005) 68 *Law and Contemporary Problems* 127.

Goodrich, L, Hambro, E and Simons, A, *Charter of the United Nations* (New York, Columbia University Press, 1969).

Grant, R and Keohane, R, 'Accountability and Abuses of Power in World Politics', IILJ Working Paper 2004/7, Global Administrative Law Series, available at http://www.iilj.org/papers/2004/2004.7%20Grant%20Keohane.pdf.

Gutherie, P, 'Security Council Sanctions and the Protection of Individual Rights' (2004) 60 *NYU Annual Survey of American Law* 491.

Habermas, J, *Between Facts and Norms: Contributions to a Discourse Theory of Law and Democracy*, W Rehg (trans) (Cambridge, MA, MIT Press, 1996).

Harris, DJ, *Cases and Materials on International Law*, 6th edn (London, Sweet and Maxwell, 2004).

Helfer, L, 'Constitutional Analogies in the International Legal System' (2003) 37 *Loyola of Los Angeles Law Review* 193.

Herdegen, M, 'The "Constitutionalization" of the UN Security System' (1994) 27 *Vanderbilt Journal of Transnational Law* 135.

Heun, W, 'Gewaltenteilung in inhrer verfassungsgeschichtlichen Entwicklung' in C Starck (ed), *Staat und Individuum im Kultur- und Rechtsvergleich* (Baden Baden, Nomos Verlagsgesellschaft, 2000).

Jagwanth, S and Soltau, F, 'Terrorism and Human Rights in Africa' in J Cilliers and K Sturman (eds), *Africa and Terrorism: Joining the Global Campaign* (Pretoria, Institute for Security Studies, 2002).

King, FP, 'Sensible Scrutiny: The Yugoslavia Tribunal's Development of Limits on the Security Council's Powers under Chapter VII of the Charter' (1996) 10 *Emory International Law Review* 509.

Kingsbury, B, Krisch, N and Stewart, R, 'The Emergence of Global Administrative Law', IILJ Working Paper 2004/1, Global Administrative Law Series, available at www.iilj.org, also published in (2005) 68 *Law and Contemporary Problems* 15.

Koskenniemi, M, 'The Pull of the Mainstream' (1990) 88 *Michigan Law Review* 1946.

—— *The Gentle Civilizer of Nations* (Cambridge, Cambridge University Press, 2001).

Lavalle, R, 'A Novel, if Awkward, Exercise in International Law-making: Security Council Resolution 1540 (2004)' (2004) *Netherlands International Law Review* 411.

Marschik, A, 'The Security Council as World Legislator? Theory, Practice and Consequences of an Expanding World Power', IILJ Working Paper 2005/18, available at http://www.iilj.org/papers/documents/2005.18Marschik.pdf.

Montesquieu, C-L, *De l'Esprit de Lois* (Paris, Garnier-Flammarion, 1979).

Mureinik, E, 'A Bridge to Where?' (1994) 10 *South African Journal on Human Rights* 10.

Murphy, J, 'Force and Arms' in C Joyner (ed), *The United Nations and International Law* (Cambridge, ASIL and CUP, 1999).

Osborne, M and Sprigman, C, 'Behold: Angry Native becomes Postmodernist Prophet of Judicial Messiah' (2001) 118 *South African Law Journal* 693.

Reisman, WM, 'The Constitutional Crisis in the United Nations' (1993) 97 *American Journal of International Law* 83.

Rosand, E, 'The Security Council as "Global Legislator": Ultra Vires or Ultra Innovative?' (2005) 28 *Fordham International Law Journal* 542.

Sargentich, T, 'The Delegation of Lawmaking Power to the Executive Branch' in K Harriger (ed), *Separation of Powers: Documents and Commentary* (Washington DC, CQ Press, 2003).

Schweigman, D, *The Authority of the Security Council under Chapter VII of the UN Charter* (The Hague, Kluwer Law International, 2001).

Szasz, P, 'The Security Council Starts Legislating' (2002) 96 *American Journal of International Law* 901.

Talmon, S, 'The Security Council as World Legislature' (2005) 99 *American Journal of International Law* 175.

Tomuschat, C, 'International Law: Ensuring the Survival of Mankind on the Eve of a New Century. General Course on Public International Law' (1999) 281 *Recueil des Cours* 10.

Vile, M, *Constitutionalism and the Separation of Powers* (Oxford, Clarendon Press, 1967).

von Bogdandy, A, 'Constitutionalism in International Law: Comment on a Proposal from Germany' (2006) 47 *Harvard International Law Journal* 223.

Zasloff, J, 'Taking Politics Seriously: A Theory of California's Separation of Powers' (2004) 51 *UCLA Law Review* 1079.

Zemanek, K, 'Was kann die Vergleichung staatlichen öffentlichen Rechts für das Recht der internationalen Organisationen leisten?' (1964) 24 *Zeitschrift für ausländisches öffentliches Recht und Völkerrecht* 453.

8

Between Idealism and Pragmatism: Legal and Political Constraints on State Power in Times of Crisis

VICTOR V RAMRAJ*

INTRODUCTION

T HERE IS A profound tension in law and legal theory between idealism and
pragmatism, between faith in the ability of law and legal institutions to
address social problems and scepticism about whether law can ever be the
answer. This tension is perhaps most apparent in the context of violent conflict
and its aftermath. There is, for instance, a serious tension in public international
law between the idealistic view that the use of force can never be justified (except
perhaps in self-defence) and the pragmatic view that war is inevitable and the
means of warfare must therefore be regulated to minimise harm.[1] Similarly, there
is a clear tension between aspirations for retributive justice for victims of oppression after the fall of authoritarian regimes and the practical need for amnesties as
a step toward peace and reconciliation.[2] In this chapter, I focus on another such
tension—the tension, in times of crisis,[3] between an idealistic desire for legality
and a pragmatic demand for extra-legal powers.

Contemporary theoretical responses to international terrorism can be placed
on a spectrum between idealism and pragmatism. At the idealistic end of the spectrum, we find attempts to restrain state abuses of power in the counter-terrorism
context by appealing to the importance of human rights and legality, and thus to

* I am particularly grateful to David Dyzenhaus, Oren Gross, Tom Hadden and the participants of
the Oxford Colloquium on Security and Human Rights for their incisive comments on drafts of this
chapter. Some of the arguments in this chapter were previously presented in seminars and benefited
from discussions at the Human Rights Centre, Queen's University Belfast and the Transitional Justice
Institute, University of Ulster.

[1] Roberts, A and Guelff, R (eds), *Documents on the Laws of War*, 3rd edn (Oxford, OUP, 2000)
28–30.

[2] Hadden, T, 'Punishment, Amnesty and Truth: Legal and Political Approaches' in A Guelke (ed),
Advancing Peace in Deeply Divided Societies (Houndmills, Palgrave Macmillan, 2004) 196–217.

[3] Although times of crises can arise either out of natural disasters or through war or political violence, this paper focuses on the latter sort.

a substantive conception of the rule of law.[4] This approach seeks to prevent the abuse of state power by maintaining, as far as possible, substantive legal norms and otherwise insisting on judicial supervision of any deviation from those norms. At the pragmatic end of the spectrum, we find acceptance of the inevitability of abuses of power and the inability of the law to contain them; we also find efforts to restrain state power by non-judicial means, namely political checks.

Neither approach is wholly satisfactory. The idealistic approach, while laudable in its normative aspirations, is often unable fully to constrain state power in practice. And the pragmatic approach is similarly problematic in the faith it places in political controls on state power, which may well perpetuate the underlying crisis by fuelling feelings of alienation in some communities. This chapter takes a critical look at two recent theoretical responses to emergencies that stake out a sophisticated middle ground between idealism and pragmatism—David Dyzenhaus's defence of legality and the rule of law[5] and Oren Gross's argument that in times of crisis, to preserve the rule of law in the long term we must sometimes be prepared to go outside it and to use extra-legal measures.[6] While both theories attempt to reconcile the insights of an idealistic approach to the rule of law with a pragmatic recognition of the limits of judicial review, they nevertheless fail to provide a comprehensive theory that combines the virtues of legality with the pragmatism of a political response to emergencies.

This essay maps out such a theory by acknowledging the importance of aspirations of legality, while recognising the strain they come under in times of crisis and accepting the need for a complementary, political approach. Specifically, it advances two propositions. First, from an internal perspective and as a general

---

[4] Following Craig, P, 'Formal and Substantive Conceptions of the Rule of Law: An Analytic Framework' (1997) *Public Law* 467, I understand a substantive conception of the rule of law to encompass a rights-based conception of law and adjudication, in contrast to a formal conception that does not 'seek to pass judgment upon the actual content of the law itself' and is unconcerned 'with whether the law was in that sense a good law or a bad law, provided that the formal precepts of the rule of law were themselves met' (at 467).

[5] See, for example, Dyzenhaus, D, 'The State of Emergency in Legal Theory' in VV Ramraj, M Hor and K Roach (eds), *Global Anti-terrorism Law and Policy* (Cambridge, CUP, 2005) 65–89. The contribution by Dyzenhaus in this volume, in which they argue for 'defence as respect' within a culture of justification, may be seen as an extension of Dyzenhaus's earlier articulation and defence of the model of legality. I have defended the importance of judicial review on the basis that the judiciary can be in a better position institutionally than either the legislative or the executive branches to make a dispassionate assessment of the risk of terrorism; courts can be a forum in which the effectiveness of anti-terrorism policies can be assessed against the impact of those policies on fundamental freedoms: see Ramraj, VV, 'Terrorism, Risk Perception, and Judicial Review' in VV Ramraj, M Hor and K Roach (eds), *Global Anti-terrorism Law and Policy* (Cambridge, CUP, 2005) 107–20.

[6] Gross, O, 'Chaos and Rules: Should Responses to Violent Crises Always be Constitutional?' (2003) 112 *Yale Law Journal* 1011, 1023–4: '[T]here may be circumstances where the appropriate method of tackling grave dangers and threats entails going outside the constitutional order, at times even violating otherwise accepted constitutional principles, rules, and norms. Such a response, if pursued in appropriate circumstances and properly applied, may strengthen rather than weaken, and result in more rather than less, long-term fidelity and commitment to the rule of law.' Later, he explains: 'While going outside the legal order may be a "little wrong," it is advocated here in order to facilitate the attainment of a "great right," namely the preservation not only of the constitutional order, but also of its most fundamental principles and tenets.'

aspiration, principles of legality must not be compromised in times of crisis; they must be maintained to the greatest extent possible, under the general purview of the courts. Second, while every effort should be made to deal with official abuses within the legal system, the courts on their own may not be capable of preserving the rule of law in times of crisis. And so, political measures that might at times strain legal principles are also necessary. But these measures need not conflict with, and may well reinforce, an aspirational approach to legality and facilitate the long-term preservation of the rule of law.

I. CONTEMPORARY THEORETICAL APPROACHES TO EMERGENCIES

Theoretical approaches to the prevention of abuses of power in times of crisis vary in emphasis and complexity. Some emphasise the role of the courts and principles of legality; others stress the importance of advance legislative directives or *ex post* political checks on power. Nevertheless, it is important conceptually to distinguish between those approaches that take seriously substantive legal principles that limit the powers of government, relying on the courts as the guardians of these principles, and those approaches that question the effectiveness of the courts, relying principally on political checks. This section examines these two approaches, focusing on Dyzenhaus's defence of legality[7] and Gross's extra-legal measures model.[8] I provide an overview of each approach, examining how each deals with the major criticisms levelled against it.

1. The Rule of Law and the Model of Legality

In times of crisis, ordinary legal principles stressing the importance of fundamental rights, due process and judicial supervision of legislative and executive power come under strain. There is a tendency among governments to press for new powers or to claim latent executive powers to deal with emergencies. There is equally a tendency to see ordinary legal principles as a hindrance to effective suppression of violence, together with an attempt, which can be traced to John Locke's defence of prerogative power,[9] to justify state responses outside the normal legal constraints on power.[10]

One response to these tendencies to extraordinary power is simply to insist on the supremacy of ordinary legal principles and the rule of law, even in times of emergency. Ordinary criminal law and the substantive and procedural safeguards

---

[7] Note 5 above.

[8] Note 6 above.

[9] See Locke, J, *Second Treatise on Government* in P Laslett (ed), *Two Treatises of Government* (Cambridge, CUP, 1988) §159.

[10] As the US government attempted to do in respect of its detention of 'unlawful combatants' at the US naval base in Guantanamo Bay—an argument rejected by the Supreme Court in *Rasul v Bush* 124 SCt 2686 (2004).

associated with it provide most of the tools required to deal with even exceptional violence, making departures largely unnecessary. And it is precisely when faced with a crisis that the law is crucial and the need for legal constraints on power is the greatest. Yet this response may be seen as unrealistic. It is commonly observed, for instance, that the courts 'have performed badly, and will necessarily continue to perform badly'[11] in the regulation of emergency situations and consistently 'disappoint the expectations of those who hope that they might uphold the rights of citizens in times of tension'.[12] And to the extent that courts become involved in the assessment of emergency measures, they tend to allow the executive considerable leeway, thus creating a 'veneer of legality'[13] to departures from rule of law principles.

For Dyzenhaus, the problem arises in part because of an inflexible conception of the separation of legislative, executive and judicial powers. If the legitimate interests of the executive, say, in the protection of informants or confidential intelligence sources during an emergency, cannot be accommodated within the ordinary legal system, the system breaks down in the face of the emergency. But acknowledging the need for legal adjustments to be made during emergencies does not necessarily undermine the rule of law. Within the common law tradition, Dyzenhaus points to 'a highly developed rule of law system for administrative officials, including controls of reasonableness, independence, impartiality, and often a requirement to give reasons' with an ultimate 'check of judicial review, accompanied by the understanding that administrative officials have an expertise in their area of decision-making which generalist judges lack'.[14] The development of administrative law in this way allows judges to allow administrative officials greater latitude in areas where they hold a particular expertise, interfering with their decisions only on the more deferential basis of unreasonableness, rather than the more exacting standard of correctness.

So Dyzenhaus regards the creation in the United Kingdom of a specialised administrative tribunal, the Special Immigration Appeals Commission (SIAC), to deal with deportation orders in national security cases positively, as a 'remarkable exercise in imaginative institutional design' and a 'workable answer to concerns about the sensitivity of security issues and the need to hold public officials accountable to the rule of law'.[15] As an administrative tribunal with technical and legal expertise in national security matters and special procedures for dealing with sensitive intelligence information, SIAC is able, at least in theory, to address security issues while preserving the rule of law under the general supervision of the courts.

[11] Alexander, GJ, 'The Illusory Protection of Human Rights by National Courts during Periods of Emergency' (1984) 5 *Human Rights Law Journal* 1, 1.
[12] Livingstone, S, 'The House of Lords and the Northern Ireland Conflict' (1994) 57 *Modern Law Review* 333, 355.
[13] See Dyzenhaus, D, 'States of Emergency' in *Blackwell's Companion to Political Philosophy* (forthcoming 2007, manuscript on file) at 9.
[14] Dyzenhaus (2005) 79.
[15] *Ibid*, 82.

Dyzenhaus is critical of the unwillingness of the House of Lords to 'concede to SIAC the capacity to be a more effective enforcer of the rule of law than a generalist court'.[16] Yet he remains optimistic that governments that 'have the luxury of time to craft a response to emergency situations should do so in a way that complies with the rule of law' by finding imaginative institutional ways to address concerns of security, while preserving the assumption that legal responses to emergencies must be constitutional, and so act without compromising the values of the rule of law.[17]

Dyzenhaus attempts to respond to emergencies not by modifying substantive legal norms (an approach that, as we shall see, Gross criticises) but by adapting our institutions to allow for national security concerns to be taken into account. Indeed, recent examples in the United Kingdom of the judiciary standing up to the executive in times of crisis, such as the declarations of incompatibility by the House of Lords in respect of the detention of non-citizens, and the use of evidence obtained under torture in the Belmarsh cases,[18] suggest that the sort of institutional adaptations recommended by Dyzenhaus need not prevent the courts from playing a limited role in checking abuses of state power.

However, institutional adaptations within a system of ultimate judicial supervision may not be enough to prevent the rise of the security state. In the UK context, declarations of incompatibility are not formally binding on the government. Moreover, the case-law suggests that in times of crisis, the courts still tend to back down when faced with a determined government, which raises questions about their ultimate effectiveness in upholding the rule of law.[19] This practical concern about the ultimate effectiveness of the courts exposes a residual weakness in the legality model, and in turn suggests a different approach to preserving the rule of law—one that relies on political rather than legal checks on power.

2. Political Checks on Power and the Extra-legal Measures Model

What unifies political approaches is their scepticism about the ability of the courts to prevent abuses of power in times of crisis.[20] For instance, George Alexander, in

---

[16] *Ibid*, referring to *Secretary of State for the Home Department v Rehman* [2002] 1 All ER 123.

[17] *Ibid*, 83.

[18] See the two *A v Secretary of State for the Home Department* cases, respectively at [2004] UKHL 56 and [2005] UKHL 71.

[19] For example, see, in the United States, *Hamdi v Rumsfeld* 124 SCt 2633 (2004) (which acknowledges the need for judicial oversight but does not insist on express Congressional authority for the detention of citizens); and, in the United Kingdom, *A v Secretary of State for the Home Department* [2005] UKHL 71 (where despite holding that evidence obtained by torture is inadmissible, the majority nevertheless held, on the question of the burden of proof, that it had to be 'established, by means of such diligent inquiries into the sources that it is practicable to carry out and on the balance of probabilities, that the information relied on by the Secretary of State was obtained under torture' (at para 121)—a burden of proof that, the minority observed, a detainee 'for reasons beyond his control . . . can seldom discharge' (at para 80)).

[20] See, for instance, Alexander (1984).

his 1984 study of the performance of national courts in times of emergency, despaired of the 'demonstrably unreliable' record of the courts in times of grave emergency and concluded that 'the best one can hope for is a political alternative'.[21]

More recently, Oren Gross has rejected the view that 'ordinary legal rules and norms continue to be followed strictly with no substantive change even in times of emergency and crisis'.[22] He rejects this 'business-as-usual' model on the basis that it is 'either naïve or hypocritical in the sense that it disregards the reality of governmental exercise of extraordinary measures and powers in responding to emergencies'.[23] Similarly, attempts to accommodate security considerations within the existing normative structure either legislatively (through the enactment of emergency measures and powers) or judicially (when the courts reinterpret ordinary rules and principles contextually) prove unable to contain the spread of extraordinary measures into the ordinary legal system.[24] In short, either courts refuse to enter the fray, or when they do, they tend to dilute the substantive legal principles they purport to apply.

In light of these shortcomings, Gross proposes the extra-legal measures model, which holds that 'there may be circumstances where the appropriate method of tackling grave dangers and threats may entail going outside the constitutional order, at times even violating otherwise accepted constitutional principles, rules and norms'.[25] Specifically, the model 'calls upon public officials having to deal with catastrophic cases to consider the possibility of acting outside the legal order while openly acknowledging their actions and the extra-legal nature of such actions'.[26] If an official determines that it is necessary to act outside the law, then he or she may do so, although the 'basic rule continues to apply to other situations (that is, it is not cancelled or terminated), it is not even overridden in the concrete case at hand'.[27] The official must then publicly acknowledge the extra-legal act, and it is for the public, the 'society as a whole', to decide after the fact whether 'to hold the actor accountable for the wrongfulness of her actions, or [to] approve them retrospectively . . . [which means that] the official does not know what the personal consequences of violating the rule are going to be'.[28]

Gross's model implies that judicially authorised torture warrants, as an instance of accommodation, should not be permitted as they would confer legitimacy on the government's actions and establish a pattern of legal precedents that would

---

[21] Alexander (1984) 65.

[22] Gross (2003) 1021.

[23] *Ibid.*

[24] The shortcoming of these models, Gross argues, is 'found in their innate susceptibility to manipulation and the danger that accommodating counter-emergency responses within the existing legal system starts us down a slippery slope toward excessive governmental infringement on individual rights and liberties while undermining constitutional structures and institutions in the process' (*ibid*, 1022).

[25] Gross, O, 'Stability and Flexibility: A Dicey Business' in VV Ramraj, M Hor and K Roach (eds), *Global Anti-terrorism Law and Policy* (Cambridge, CUP, 2005) 92.

[26] *Ibid.*

[27] *Ibid.*

[28] Gross (2003) 1023.

normalise the practice.[29] But while he insists on an absolute ban on torture, he allows that 'in truly catastrophic cases the appropriate method of tackling extremely grave national dangers and threats may call for going outside the legal order, at times even violating the otherwise entrenched absolute prohibition on torture'.[30] Such an approach, he argues, would add 'another layer of insulation against the normalization [of torture] and its transformation into part of the ordinary legal system'.[31]

What Gross seeks to do, above all, is to confine the inevitable use of extra-legal measures to truly exceptional situations while preserving and insulating the rule of law in the long term through what he regards as a more realistic, political approach.[32] His model relies not on the courts (which might set bad precedents) but on the political process, which must provide the ultimate check on official disobedience. But even if we accept that Gross's approach here is more realistic in its assessment of what the courts would do in an emergency, he is rather idealistic on three counts: first, in his assumption that officials will be deterred from engaging unnecessarily in extra-legal acts by the uncertainty that their acts would be ratified;[33] second, in his assumption that officials will be motivated to disclose their illegal conduct; and third, in the picture he paints of the process by which the issue of ratification would be publicly addressed.

Consider first the assumption that officials would be deterred from resorting to extra-legal measures in all but the most exceptional of circumstances, because of the uncertainty of ratification. Why should the uncertainty of public ratification be any more of a deterrent than the legal prohibition would be in the first place? Gross seems to think that legal threat of a criminal conviction coupled with an uncertainty about ratification and exoneration is a greater deterrent than the legal threat of a criminal conviction alone. But an official who believes it is necessary to perform preventive interrogational torture on a terrorist suspect to learn the location of a ticking time-bomb would already know that the conduct is illegal. So why would the additional possibility of public ratification create a greater deterrent? Wouldn't the prospect of exoneration rather make the official *less reluctant* to engage in torture? Perhaps the courts would be more inclined to convict officials for torture because they know that in appropriate cases, the public would

---

[29] Gross, O, 'Are Torture Warrants Warranted? Pragmatic Absolutism and Official Disobedience' (2004) 88 *Minnesota Law Review* 1481, 1543.

[30] *Ibid*, 1486–7.

[31] *Ibid*, 1544.

[32] See Gross (2003) 1135, referring to *Korematsu v United States* 323 US 214, 248 (1944) where Jackson J, in dissent, suggests that the 'chief restraint upon those who command the physical forces of the country . . . must be their responsibility to the political judgments of their contemporaries and to the moral judgments of history'.

[33] Gross (2003) 1024: 'By separating . . . action and ratification . . . the model adds an element of uncertainty hanging over the head of the public official . . . [and] serves the important function of slowing down any possible rush to use extralegal powers by governmental agents. Although the model may seem open to the challenge that its application would result in a downward spiral toward authoritarian rule and totalitarianism, as it seemingly dispenses with existing constitutional norms and structures, there are other, perhaps more important, checks against governmental abuse of extralegal powers.'

exonerate officials faced with these sorts of tragic choices, and that the official, knowing this, would be deterred by the uncertainty.[34] But even if the courts were influenced in this way (which is contestable), we now have a rather idealistic view of the motivation-structure of an official faced with an urgent decision about whether to engage in torture.

There is a second concern. As we have seen, Gross seeks to contain the use of extra-legal measures by relying on the uncertainty of public ratification. But before public ratification is considered, officials who resort to extra-legal measures must first 'go public' with their disobedience: The extra-legal measures model 'informs public officials that they may act extralegally when they believe that such action is necessary for protecting the nation and the public in the face of a calamity, *provided that they openly and publicly acknowledge the nature of their actions*'.[35] Unfortunately, Gross provides no mechanism for ensuring that public officials would publicly acknowledge their actions, nor is it clear what such a mechanism would look like. Since Gross's model does not purport to be a *legal* one, it could not be a legal prerequisite to ratification. Nor is it clear that disobedient officials would have any pragmatic incentive to disclose their conduct, particularly if they made a miscalculation and the preventive interrogational torture did not yield the expected results, or the ticking time-bomb turned out to be based on mistaken intelligence reports. Nor is there any mechanism for preventing ratification of an act of official disobedience that is not voluntarily disclosed but subsequently comes to light.

This brings us to a third problem—concerning the process of ratification. The extra-legal measures model supposedly 'promotes, and is promoted by, ethical concepts of political and popular responsibility, political morality, and candor [which] . . . promotes deliberation after the fact, as well as establishes the individual responsibility of each member of the community for the actions taken on behalf of the public during the emergency'.[36] Here, Gross paints a picture of a deliberative democracy free from the politics of fear and the 'othering' of minorities, which he describes elsewhere.[37] Yet we have good reason to be sceptical as to whether these political conditions would obtain in reality. Gross's pragmatism about the role of the courts in an emergency, it seems, does not extend to the idealistic picture of deliberative democracy.

There are serious problems with Gross's extra-legal measures model on its own terms. But whatever the specific problems of this approach, its Lockean conception of prerogative power, coupled with a political check on that power, has a pragmatic appeal and so remains an attractive model for governments in times of crisis. As we shall see, however, the limits of both this and the legality model endorsed by Dyzenhaus point us in the direction of a more nuanced approach to the preservation of the rule of law in times of crisis—one that acknowledges the

[34] Gross (2004).
[35] Gross (2003) 1023, emphasis added.
[36] *Ibid*, 1024.
[37] *Ibid*, 1037.

importance of legality while recognising the limits of the law, and welcomes both legal and political means of addressing the underlying conflict.

II. LEGALITY AND THE LIMITS OF THE LAW

Common to both approaches described above is an assumption that in extraordinary circumstances, the courts will face considerable pressure not to uphold the rule of law. Dyzenhaus, however, retains some faith in the ability of the courts (or specialised administrative tribunals under judicial supervision) to uphold the rule of law even in the face of emergencies of indefinite duration. The central insight of his theory is its attempt to minimise the strain on the rule of law by modifying institutions to take into account new pressures to deal with the emergency, subject to the supervisory jurisdiction of the courts, while preserving legal substantive norms. This, I argue, is basically the right approach,[38] although it is important to be realistic about how much the courts and other administrative bodies can do, even on Dyzenhaus's theory, to prevent abuses of power.

For Gross, the solution lies outside the courts, which cannot be relied on to uphold fundamental legal principles in times of crisis. His solution involves a political check on abuses of power, one that acknowledges both that extra-legal activities do take place and that, in 'truly extraordinary circumstances'—involving, for instance, a ticking time-bomb—they should do so.[39] While Gross is right to question the ability of the courts to preserve the rule of law in times of crisis, and thus to expose the limits of the law, his attempt to replace a judicial check on power with a political one risks prolonging the underlying conflict, compounding and perpetuating state abuses of power. But Gross's reminder to us of the limits of the law suggests another extra-legal but complementary approach to preserving the rule of law, an approach that stresses the importance of *resolving* the underlying social, political and economic causes of conflicts as part of an overall strategy for preserving the rule of law in the long term.

1. Narrowing the Disagreement: Legality and its Limits

For Dyzenhaus and Gross, the objective is the same—to preserve as best we can the rule of law during emergencies. Both are concerned that left to their own devices, the courts might do no more than to lend legitimacy—a 'veneer of

---

[38] Provided that, as I have argued elsewhere, specialised administrative tribunals and other supervisory bodies are both independent and effective and that the courts continue to provide a public forum for contesting broader policy decisions that purport to weigh rights against security concerns: see Ramraj (2005) 122–3.

[39] Gross argues that his model 'does not seek to do away with the traditional discourse over emergency powers. It does not claim to exclude the constitutional models of emergency powers. It is a model for truly extraordinary occasions'. See Gross (2004) 92–93, citing a passage from his article 'Chaos and Rules': Gross (2003) 1134.

legality'[40]—to deviations from the rule of law, which is more dangerous than complete judicial deference because it prevents a public airing of the issues through an open debate between the government and the courts.[41] Yet both Gross and Dyzenhaus recognise the ultimate importance of legality. For Dyzenhaus, the model of legality is an ideal to which the law should aspire. It 'holds that to the extent that political power can be successfully subjected to the discipline of the rule of law, it should'.[42] And it:

> functions not as an assumption but as an ideal; at most it is a regulative assumption, an assumption one adopts for political reasons because it will regulate practice in the best possible way. One assumes its truth to bring the legal order closer to the ideals which underpin it.[43]

For Gross, the judiciary plays a more important role than would first appear. Gross wants to avoid dangerous precedents[44] that tend to normalise emergency powers by limiting the jurisdiction of the courts; and yet the possibility of public ratification of official disobedience depends on the willingness of the courts to hold officials responsible, and hence on a wide scope of justiciability. That the extra-legal measures model depends on the willingness of the courts to engage in judicial review of acts of official disobedience becomes apparent in Gross's approach to torture, in which he defends 'an absolute ban on torture' with the possibility of 'going outside the legal order, at times even violating the otherwise entrenched absolute prohibition on torture' in 'truly catastrophic cases'.[45]

Here it becomes apparent that the ability of the extra-legal measures model to effectively limit abuses of power depends precisely on the willingness of the courts to take seriously every act of torture, including one that might later be subject to ratification. This suggests that the extra-legal measures model is *dependent upon* the courts taking seriously their role in upholding the rule of law. For the extra-legal measures model to be effective then, as far as the courts are concerned, it really *ought* to be 'business as usual' during an emergency, at least with regard to torture.

Where Dyzenhaus and Gross differ, however, is on where the ultimate check on extra-legal measures ought to be. For Dyzenhaus, it remains within a body of institutions entrusted to preserve the rule of law, under the general supervisory gaze of

---

[40] Dyzenhaus (2007 forthcoming).
[41] *Ibid.*
[42] Dyzenhaus (2005) 84.
[43] *Ibid.*
[44] Gross (2004) 1544–5: 'The official disobedience model, however, minimizes the problem of precedent. The extralegal nature of the governmental action adds another layer of insulation against the normalization of such a "dangerous precedent," and its transformation into part of the ordinary legal system. "A breach of the law, even a necessary one, that ought to be justified, can never destroy the law . . . But an act legally done can always be drawn into precedent." Although certain *ex post* ratifications may work to change existing legal rules, norms, and structures, transforming an extralegal, political precedent into a legal one, such a shift cannot happen under my proposed model without informed public participation and accountability in the process.'
[45] *Ibid,* 1486–7.

the courts: 'All a court should say is that if officials are going to torture they should expect to be criminally charged and may try a defence of necessity.'[46] For Gross, the threat of prosecution plays an important role in deterring the conduct, but the ultimate decision in such cases (whether to ratify or condemn the conduct) rests with the public. Yet ultimately, for both Dyzenhaus and Gross, the courts should play a central role in regulating extra-legal conduct.

Dyzenhaus recognises that legality need not be preserved solely by the courts. This strategy of redesigning our institutions to cope with entrenched emergencies while preserving the rule of law finds some support in the case-law. For instance, in *Brannigan and McBride v The United Kingdom*,[47] the European Court of Human Rights (ECtHR) held that although Article 15 of the European Convention on Human Rights limits the period in which preventive detention is unsupervised by the courts, even in an emergency, the detention could be acceptable if accompanied by effective safeguards against arbitrary behaviour and incommunicado detention.[48] Similarly, recent security legislation in the United Kingdom (in addition to SIAC) has included novel ways of checking abuses of power, such as regular reviews of security legislation by an independent reviewer.[49] Dyzenhaus's approach reminds us that institutions other than the courts may well be able to contribute to a broader institutional attempt to limit the abuse of discretionary emergency powers and uphold principles of legality, provided that the courts retain the ability to check abuses of power.

Not all such innovations will be effective in practice, however, and potential for abuse remains. For instance, the need for some form of independent judicial oversight[50] may be diluted through institutional design, as can be seen in the system of ministerial authorisation, subject to review by a Commissioner who 'holds or has held high judicial office', for warrants issued under the Security Service Act 1989.[51] Nor does innovative institutional design necessarily avoid the problem of seepage (the tendency for security measures to spread into the ordinary justice system); institutions can be redesigned and judicial review curtailed for reasons that have

---

[46] Dyzenhaus (2005) 84.

[47] (1993) 17 EHRR 539.

[48] Specifically, the Court mentioned the availability of *habeas corpus* to test the lawfulness of the arrest and detention; the right to consult a lawyer after 48 hours from the time of arrest; the right to inform a relative or friend of the detention and the right of access to a doctor; and provisions for the regular, independent review of the law's operation (*ibid*, paras 63–5); but see *Aksoy v Turkey* (1996) 23 EHRR 553 where the Court held that the safeguards against the abuse of the power of detention were insufficient to justify holding a terrorist suspect in incommunicado detention without access to a judge; in particular, the Court held that 'the denial of access to a lawyer, doctor, relative or friend and the absence of any realistic possibility of being brought before a court to test the legality of the detention meant that [Aksoy] was left completely to the mercy of those holding him' (paras 83, 84).

[49] See Anti-terrorism, Crime and Security Act 2001, s 28, as well as the reports on this Act and other security legislation prepared by Lord Carlile of Berriew, available at http://security.homeoffice.gov.uk/news-and-publications1/publication-search/independent-reviews/. This mechanism for checking abuses of power was approved in principle in *Brannigan* (note 47 above) at 65.

[50] See note 38 above.

[51] Sections 3 and 4.

little to do with security.[52] But even if institutional adjustments, aimed at preserving the rule of law, can be limited to security cases, the 'submissive deference'[53] often shown by the courts leaves considerable latitude to the executive; and internationally, the ECtHR's margin of appreciation doctrine allows considerable leeway to national governments in crafting responses to public emergencies.[54] And where the courts *are* prepared to scrutinise the use of emergency powers, their decisions are retrospective, the damage to the individual and society caused by the abuse of power already having taken place.[55]

The courts and other legal institutions continue to play an important role in checking abuses of power and preserving the rule of law. But the danger remains that legal strategies to contain abuses of power will have only limited effectiveness and, in some cases, might even facilitate those abuses. So, notwithstanding aspirations to be ruled by principles of legality in times of crisis, complementary political strategies will continue to play an important role in preserving the rule of law in the long term.

2. Moving Beyond Law: Resolving the Underlying Conflict

Gross, as we have seen, recognises as much. His central insight is that in times of crisis, legal institutions on their own are incapable of preserving the rule of law and might, in some cases, serve to undermine it. In this respect, Gross is right; we should not be too sanguine about the ability of the courts to preserve the rule of law, even perhaps on Dyzenhaus's more nuanced understanding of the role that both judicial and administrative institutions play in this regard. We must, therefore, be conscious of the limits of the law. But Gross's proposed solution is

---

[52] See note 24 above. I am grateful to David Dyzenhaus for pointing out this potential difficulty with his theory.

[53] See Dyzenhaus, note 5 above.

[54] As some have argued, international judicial systems play a crucial role, removed as they are from the immediate political pressures arising from the emergency. See for example, Livingstone (1994) 357–8 (the European Court of Human Rights, 'shielded to some extent (by both law and geography) from the national governments whose exceptional measure they condemn', might be a 'more fruitful avenue for pursuing human rights challenges to exceptional measures in Northern Ireland'); and yet the ultimate effectiveness of even these courts remains in doubt, given their use of the margin of appreciation doctrine where emergency measures are challenged. See Gross, O and Ní Aoláin, F, 'From Discretion to Scrutiny: Revisiting the Application of the Margin of Appreciation Doctrine in the Context of Article 15 of the European Convention on Human Rights' (2001) 23 *Human Rights Quarterly* 625 (arguing, at 648, that the jurisprudence on Art 15 demonstrates 'the willingness of this supranational body . . . to accord a wide margin of discretion to . . . national governments'). See the influential passage in *Ireland v The United Kingdom* (1979–80) 2 EHRR 25, in which the ECtHR observed that by 'reason of their direct and continuous contact with the pressing needs to the moment, the national authorities are in a better position than the international judge to decide both on the presence of such an emergency and on the nature and scope of derogations necessary to avert it' and that in this matter, 'Article 15(1) leaves those authorities with a wide margin of appreciation' (para 207).

[55] One clear example is the 1978 decision of the ECtHR in *Ireland v The United Kingdom* (1979–80) 2 EHRR 25, which dealt with interrogation techniques and internment that took place in 1971 and had long been discontinued by the time the judgment was rendered.

problematic since, in the long term, it is likely to prolong the underlying conflict, compounding and perpetuating state abuses of power.

While Gross's model is commendable in its attempt to encourage officials to come clean with their extra-legal conduct (although I have concerns as to whether it provides a workable mechanism for doing this[56]), by allowing the public to pass ultimate judgment on official misconduct, including torture, it may well exacerbate the problem. Consider the problem of the alienation of minorities in times of crisis, which is exacerbated by abuses of emergency powers and recognised as a serious impediment to the process of conflict resolution. In Northern Ireland, for instance, it has been said that the anti-terrorism strategies involving mass 'screening' and regular house searches by the military in the early 1970s 'so alienated the Catholic community in the areas of insensitive army activity that *a continuing flow of new [rebel] recruits was ensured*'.[57] The 'fact that the principal impact of these military security techniques was in Catholic areas, while the RUC continued to operate the "reformed" criminal justice system in most Protestant areas, exacerbated the feeling of discrimination and alienation among most Nationalists'.[58]

Similar feelings of alienation are evident in Muslim communities today, which in the United Kingdom, as elsewhere, are bearing the brunt of contemporary anti-terrorism policies and experiencing a social backlash.[59] The danger is that broad, discretionary emergency powers intended to respond to political violence have an unfortunate tendency to exacerbate the problem, leading to an escalation of the crisis and creating sympathy and even outright support for those engaging in the violence in the first place.[60]

[56] See paragraph accompanying note 35 above.

[57] Hadden, T, Boyle, K and Campbell, C, 'Emergency Law in Northern Ireland: The Context' in A Jennings (ed), *Justice Under Fire* (London, Pluto Press, 1990) 1–26, 8 (emphasis added).

[58] *Ibid.*

[59] Before the London bombings, the Home Affairs Committee in April 2005 announced that community relations had deteriorated post-9/11, and that that international terrorism '*and the response to it* have contributed to this deterioration, particularly in relations between the majority community and the Muslim community' (para 88, emphasis added): see 'Terrorism and Community Relations', Sixth Report of Session 2004–05, available at http://www.publications.parliament.uk/pa/cm200405/cmselect/cmhaff/165/165.pdf.

Three weeks after the bombings, religious hate crimes in London had increased six-fold ('Hate Crimes Soar after Bombings', *BBC News*, 4 August 2005, available at http://news.bbc.co.uk/1/hi/england/london/4740015.stm), and 20% of Muslim Britons indicated that they or their family members 'had experienced hostility or abuse' from non-Muslims because of their religion since the bombings took place ('Two-thirds of Muslims Consider Leaving the UK', *Guardian Unlimited*, 26 July 2005, available at http://politics.guardian.co.uk/polls/story/0,11030,1536259,00.html. For the full poll, see http://www.icmresearch.co.uk/reviews/2005/Guardian%20-%20muslims%20july05/Guardian%20Muslims%20jul05.asp.

As Tariq Modood observes, Muslims in Europe 'have found themselves bearing the brunt of a new wave of suspicion and hostility, and strongly voiced if imprecise doubts being cast on their loyalty as citizens'. See Modood, T, 'Muslims and the Politics of Difference' (2003) 74 *Political Quarterly* 100, 101.

[60] See Campbell, C and Connolly, I, 'A Model for the "War on Terrorism"? Military Intervention in Northern Ireland and the 1970 Falls Curfew' (2003) 30 *Journal of Law and Society* 341, 373 (indiscriminate 'policing' methods, amplified by military involvement in the Northern Ireland conflict created 'an environment within the communities most affected by the initiatives, in which political violence and terrorism were either tolerated or supported').

Gross's extra-legal measures model legitimises much more than the wide, discretionary powers that typically give rise to official abuse; rather, it officially and publicly sanctions the use of extra-legal measures that, however *effective* they might be in suppressing political violence in the short term (eg, by enabling public officials to defuse ticking time-bombs), are likely to be morally, politically and emotionally charged[61]—and a symbolic rallying point for further acts of political violence. The subsequent ratification of such official misconduct by an intimidated public may well be resented by an already vulnerable minority community, doing even greater damage to the prospects for a peaceful resolution to the crisis. And the damage would be even greater if by further alienating minority communities and perpetuating the cycle of political violence, more political pressure were brought to bear by the majority for greater emergency powers that further undermine the rule of law. So, however effective the extra-legal measures model might be in dealing with an immediate and serious threat to security with minimal short-term damage to the rule of law, it is not clear that in the long term, the model can address the legal and political damage such measures and their possible ratification are likely to cause.[62]

So while Gross is correct in recognising that legal institutions cannot alone sustain the rule of law in times of crisis, the political check on official abuse of power is likely to do more harm than good in addressing the underlying conflict. Gross's insight into the limits of the law, however, suggests another approach. Tom Hadden observes that there is:

> ample evidence from political and ethnic conflicts throughout the world that the resolution of the underlying political or ethnic problems has been a necessary precondition for the elimination of the abuses associated with states of emergency or repression.[63]

This suggests in turn that a key long-term strategy for ending abuses of state power is ending the underlying political or ethnic causes of the conflict.[64] A wider range of strategies for preserving the rule of law is therefore required. Here, the peace process in Northern Ireland illustrates very well the interplay between the legal and political dimensions of preserving the rule of law.

The alternative political strategy that emerges from that peace process[65] is to address the problem of minority alienation squarely both by entrenching rule of

---

[61] As Gross recognises: see Gross (2004) 1489, 1553–5.

[62] Compare Donohue, LK, *Counter-terrorist Law and Emergency Powers in the United Kingdom 1922–2000* (Dublin, Irish Academic Press, 2001) at 354 (while emergency powers 'in the short term . . . may well impact the immediate level of violence, in the long term they do unimaginable damage to the social and political dynamics of the conflict').

[63] Hadden, T, 'Human Rights Abuses and the Protection of Democracy during States of Emergency' in E Cotran and Sherif, AO (eds), *Democracy, the Rule of Law and Islam* (London, Kluwer Law International, 1999) 111–31, 124.

[64] *Ibid*, 124–5.

[65] For an overview, see Harvey, CJ, 'The New Beginning: Reconstructing Constitutional Law and Democracy in Northern Ireland' in CJ Harvey (ed), *Human Rights, Equality and Democratic Renewal in Northern Ireland* (Oxford, Hart, 2001) 9–51.

law protections (for instance, human rights and equality guarantees) and by reforming key institutions to build confidence. At the same time, however, these legal and institutional measures might not be enough. For instance, the deeper the underlying crisis and the more entrenched the cycle of political violence, the more important it is to consider political options that go beyond and perhaps sit uneasily with a strict rule of law approach.[66] For instance, in order to address underlying social and political concerns, it may be necessary to grant political amnesties as a way of facilitating the peace process[67] or to consider institutional reforms (eg, to communal representation in the police service[68]) that extend beyond a rights-centred approach. In a more complex conflict (or set of conflicts), such as the current 'war on terror', it may be necessary to resort to multiple strategies, legal and political.

In this contemporary context, legal measures for controlling abuses of power remain important. Recent decisions of the House of Lords suggest that the courts still have an important role to play in vindicating rule of law values.[69] And entrenching a human rights culture in other public institutions and institutionalising a 'culture of justification' would go some distance in reducing the scope of abuse.[70] But while Gross is correct to question whether legal checks are sufficient, the sorts of political measure that are called for are not the ones he has in mind. More effective, perhaps, would be complementary political measures to address the underlying social and political causes of the conflict, including efforts to confront the alienation of and backlash against vulnerable minority communities, to deal with discriminatory policing practices and to reconsider foreign policy initiatives (such as the invasion and occupation of Iraq) that perpetuate minority alienation both at home and abroad.[71]

3. Pragmatism Revisited: The Inevitability of Extra-legal Measures?

These arguments are unlikely to satisfy Gross. Any attempt to contain the use of extra-legal measures through the legal system, he might respond, is likely to drive the practice underground. We certainly need to be realistic about the ability of the

---

[66] As Steven C Greer observes in Greer, SC, 'Military Intervention in Civil Disturbances: The Legal Basis Reconsidered' (1983) *Public Law* 573, 590 (the deployment of the military 'would. . .mark the profound failure of civil policing methods . . . [and] would indicate the surfacing of a deep social crisis requiring a political solution').

[67] Hadden (2004).

[68] McCrudden, C, 'Northern Ireland, the Belfast Agreement, and the British Constitution' in J Jowell and D Oliver (eds), *The Changing Constitution*, 5th edn (Oxford, OUP, 2004) 221–3.

[69] Note 20 above.

[70] See Dyzenhaus, D, 'Recrafting the Rule of Law' in D Dyzenhaus (ed), *Recrafting the Rule of Law: The Limits of Legal Order* (Oxford, Hart, 1999) 1–12, 9.

[71] According to one poll in December 2002, more than three-quarters of British Muslims opposed Western military intervention in Iraq; a quarter said 'they would regard any Western attack on Iraq not as a war against a dangerous dictator but as a war against Islam itself': see King, A, 'Most UK Muslims Oppose War', *news.telegraph* (7 December 2002), available at http://www.telegraph.co.uk/news/main. jhtml?xml=/news/2002/12/07/nmus07.xml.

law to prevent the worst atrocities. Liberty, Gross reminds us, citing Learned Hand, 'lies in the hearts of men and women; when it dies there, no constitution, no law, no court can even do much to help it. While it lies there it needs no constitution, no law, no court to save it'.[72] There is a kernel of truth to this, but Gross nevertheless overstates his case. We can acknowledge the limits of the law, while recognising that the structure of our legal institutions and, crucially, their underlying institutional culture, make a difference to the impact that the law will have. For instance, the Home Office recognised the importance of institutional culture when, prior to the coming into force of the Human Rights Act 1998, it set up a Human Rights Task Force 'to help create a culture of rights and increase public awareness about rights and responsibilities inherent in the Convention'.[73] The Home Office was keenly aware that the success or failure of the Human Rights Act as a quasi-constitutional instrument would depend not only on its text but on the institutional culture that underpinned it.

So too with counter-terrorism measures that threaten rule of law values. A multifaceted and nuanced approach to protecting those values embedded in a pre-emergency institutional culture that takes seriously rule of law values is much more likely to be able to contain official abuses of power, making it more difficult for them to shift underground. Of course, some of them will inevitably do so, which is precisely why we must not rely only on law to prevent abuses of power and must equally invest in political strategies to resolve or at least mitigate the underlying causes of the conflict. It is not clear that the possibility (perhaps even likelihood) of some extra-legal practices moving underground necessarily undermines the approach advocated in this chapter. But in any event, as I have argued, it is not obvious that Gross's alternative is any more likely to encourage public officials to come clean with their illegal conduct.[74]

CONCLUSION

The Gross–Dyzenhaus debate focuses our attention on the tension in times of crisis between idealism and pragmatism, and between legal and political means of preserving the rule of law in the long term. Efforts to preserve the rule of law through the courts, even on Dyzenhaus's nuanced understanding of the broad institutional framework for vindicating principles of legality, might not be enough to prevent abuses of power. But dispensing with rule of law ideals entirely, in favour of more pragmatic political checks, may well have the perverse effect of undermining prospects of peaceful long-term resolutions of crises, particularly in an already fragile social and political context. What is needed is a broad, multifac-

---

[72] Gross (2003) 1014, citing Hand, L, *The Spirit of Liberty: Papers and Addresses of Learned Hand*, Irving Dilliard (ed), 3rd edn (New York, Knopf, 1960) 189–90.

[73] McGoldrick, D, 'The United Kingdom's Human Rights Act 1998 in Theory and Practice' (2001) 50 *International and Comparative Law Quarterly* 901, 911.

[74] See paragraph accompanying note 36 above.

eted approach, one that acknowledges the rule of law in times of crisis as an important institutional aspiration, but at the same time recognises the limits of the law and the need for political measures to address the underlying causes of the violence and to help preserve legality and the rule of law in the long term.

REFERENCES

Alexander, GJ, 'The Illusory Protection of Human Rights by National Courts during Periods of Emergency' (1984) 5 *Human Rights Law Journal* 1.

Campbell, C and Connolly, I, 'A Model for the "War on Terrorism"? Military Intervention in Northern Ireland and the 1970 Falls Curfew' (2003) 30 *Journal of Law and Society* 341.

Craig, P, 'Formal and Substantive Conceptions of the Rule of Law: An Analytic Framework' (1997) *Public Law* 467.

Donohue, LK, *Counter-terrorist Law and Emergency Powers in the United Kingdom 1922–2000* (Dublin, Irish Academic Press, 2001).

Dyzenhaus, D, 'Recrafting the Rule of Law' in D Dyzenhaus (ed), *Recrafting the Rule of Law: The Limits of Legal Order* (Oxford, Hart, 1999).

—— 'The State of Emergency in Legal Theory' in VV Ramraj, M Hor and K Roach (eds), *Global Anti-terrorism Law and Policy* (Cambridge, CUP, 2005).

—— 'States of Emergency' in *Blackwell's Companion to Political Philosophy* (forthcoming 2007, manuscript on file with the author).

Greer, SC, 'Military Intervention in Civil Disturbances: The Legal Basis Reconsidered' (1983) *Public Law* 573.

Gross, O, 'Chaos and Rules: Should Responses to Violent Crises Always be Constitutional?' (2003) 112 *Yale Law Journal* 1011.

—— 'Are Torture Warrants Warranted? Pragmatic Absolutism and Official Disobedience' (2004) 88 *Minnesota Law Review* 1481.

Gross, O and Ní Aoláin, F, 'From Discretion to Scrutiny: Revisiting the Application of the Margin of Appreciation Doctrine in the Context of Article 15 of the European Convention on Human Rights' (2001) 23 *Human Rights Quarterly* 625.

Hadden, T, 'Human Rights Abuses and the Protection of Democracy during States of Emergency' in E Cotran and Sherif, AO (eds), *Democracy, the Rule of Law and Islam* (London, Kluwer Law International, 1999).

—— 'Punishment, Amnesty and Truth: Legal and Political Approaches' in A Guelke (ed), *Advancing Peace in Deeply Divided Societies* (Houndmills, Palgrave Macmillan, 2004).

Hadden, T, Boyle, K and Campbell, C, 'Emergency Law in Northern Ireland: The Context' in A Jennings (ed), *Justice Under Fire* (London, Pluto Press, 1990).

Hand, L, *The Spirit of Liberty: Papers and Addresses of Learned Hand*, Irving Dilliard (ed), 3rd edn (New York, Knopf, 1960).

Harvey, CJ, 'The New Beginning: Reconstructing Constitutional Law and Democracy in Northern Ireland' in CJ Harvey (ed), *Human Rights, Equality and Democratic Renewal in Northern Ireland* (Oxford, Hart, 2001).

House of Commons Home Affairs Committee (UK), 'Terrorism and Community Relations', Sixth Report of Session 2004–05, available at http://www.publications.parliament.uk/pa/cm200405/cmselect/cmhaff/165/165.pdf.

King, A, 'Most UK Muslims Oppose War', *news.telegraph* (7 December 2002), available at http://www.telegraph.co.uk/news/main.jhtml?xml=/news/2002/12/07/nmus07.xml.

Livingstone, S, 'The House of Lords and the Northern Ireland Conflict' (1994) 57 *Modern Law Review* 333.

Locke, J, *Second Treatise on Government* in P Laslett (ed), *Two Treatises of Government* (Cambridge, CUP, 1988).

McCrudden, C, 'Northern Ireland, the Belfast Agreement, and the British Constitution' in J Jowell and D Oliver (eds), *The Changing Constitution*, 5th edn (Oxford, OUP, 2004) 221–3.

McGoldrick, D, 'The United Kingdom's Human Rights Act 1998 in Theory and Practice' (2001) 50 *International and Comparative Law Quarterly* 901.

Modood, T, 'Muslims and the Politics of Difference' (2003) 74 *Political Quarterly* 100.

Ramraj, VV, 'Terrorism, Risk Perception, and Judicial Review' in VV Ramraj, M Hor and K Roach (eds), *Global Anti-terrorism Law and Policy* (Cambridge, CUP, 2005).

Roberts, A and Guelff, R (eds), *Documents on the Laws of War*, 3rd edn (Oxford, OUP, 2000).

9

Security, Terrorism and the Value of Human Rights

ANDREW ASHWORTH

MANY PUBLIC STATEMENTS, whether by politicians or by judges, assume that we are living amidst a conflict between human rights and the demands of security and public safety, and that the most fair and appropriate way of dealing with this conflict is to seek to achieve a balance between the two sets of interests. Thus in 2005 the British Prime Minister stated that the 'rules of the game' must change; the Lord Chancellor said that legislation might be introduced to overrule the way in which Article 3 of the European Convention on Human Rights (ECHR) (the right not to be subjected to torture or to inhuman or degrading treatment) has been applied in the British courts, following the Strasbourg jurisprudence; and the then Home Secretary told the Council of Europe that the Convention was 'established over 50 years ago in a quite different international climate'[1] and was now being used in an 'outdated and unbalanced' way.[2] The Prime Minister has subsequently argued that repeal of the Human Rights Act 1998 would be a false solution, but that 'there are issues to do with the way the Act is interpreted and its case law, which we are examining'.[3] The senior British judiciary, although not shrinking from robust decisions on human rights issues, tends to adopt the position that the essence of human rights reasoning lies in proportionality and balance.[4]

The purpose of this chapter is to challenge that analysis, and to reject both the diagnosis and the remedy. In order to do this, section I inquires about the nature of human rights, chiefly in the European context; section II examines two

---

[1] Some might wish to dispute the substance of the distinction, inasmuch as they draw parallels between the threat from fascism in the 1930s and 1940s (against which the Convention was a reaction) and the threat from Muslim extremism in the present decade: *cf* the views discussed by Wilson, RA, 'Human Rights in the "War on Terror"' in RA Wilson (ed), *Human Rights in the 'War on Terror'* (Cambridge, Cambridge University Press, 2005) 12.

[2] These quotations are set out on the first page of Lester, A and Beattie, K, 'Risking Torture' (2005) *European Human Rights Law Review* 565.

[3] Speech of the Prime Minister, the Rt Hon Tony Blair, in Bristol on 23 June 2006, available at http://news.bbc.co.uk/1/hi/uk_politics/5108158.stm.

[4] For examples, see notes 50–1 below and accompanying text.

particular positions, the 'fundamental contradiction' thesis and the 'balanced response' thesis; section III asks whether some human rights are more fundamental than others; and section IV discusses examples of what a 'security model' of the criminal process might look like, and how it might relate to European human rights law.

I. CAN HUMAN RIGHTS BE BOTH FUNDAMENTAL AND CONTESTABLE?

Without going into the justifications for applying the epithet 'human' to the term 'rights', we can take it that such rights are intended to be treated as fundamental: their official designation as human or fundamental rights in international and national constitutional documents identifies them as a kind of higher law, with a correspondingly greater claim to respect by citizens and governments alike. In the overleaping prose typical of international instruments, the Vienna Declaration of 1993 asserted that:

> All human rights are universal, indivisible and interdependent and interrelated. The international community must treat human rights globally in a fair and equal manner, on the same footing, and with the same emphasis.[5]

This appears to adopt a kind of absolutist standpoint on human rights. Does it deny that there is room for argument in the human rights sphere? We may identify three levels of contestability of human rights.

First, the list of fundamental rights is open to debate—not only is there controversy over the inclusion of social and economic rights as well as civil and political rights,[6] but also within particular spheres such as criminal justice, the question is whether human rights instruments capture the most fundamental of rights. In relation to the rights enshrined in the European Convention on Human Rights, one may argue that the right to trial by one's peers, or the right not to receive a sentence disproportionate to the gravity of the offence,[7] or various victims' rights should qualify as fundamental. The European Convention has been enlarged by various Protocols since 1950, but the differences in the rights declared by the various international instruments indicate some contestability at this basic level.

Second, even if there were agreement on the list of fundamental rights, there is the further question of defining the rights: human rights tend to be drafted in a broad manner that leaves much to interpretation and development during adjudications. What is an inevitable feature of all legal instruments becomes a particularly prominent element in human rights. Thus self-defence is a recognised exception to the right to life, but what are the parameters of that exception, and

---

[5] UN World Conference on Human Rights, Vienna Declaration and Programme of Action (1993), para 5.

[6] The European Union's Charter of Fundamental Rights (2000), in force since 2003, is one of the few instruments to include all four forms of rights. *Cf* the further argument that social rights can be derived from civil and political rights: see the contribution by Sandra Fredman in this volume.

[7] This is included, for example, in the EU's Charter, *ibid*, at Art 49.

should there be different rules for state officials and ordinary citizens? The privilege against self-incrimination is also a familiar component of declarations of fundamental rights,[8] but there are serious issues about whether it is absolute, whether exceptions ought to be made, and, if so, what they should be. It may seem paradoxical that in human rights law the widespread agreement that certain rights are fundamental exists alongside disagreements about their proper definition.[9]

Third, the contestability of adjudicative determinations and of the interpretations on which they are based reaches still further. In some instances it is not simply a question of deciding the ambit of a particular right, but rather a matter of deciding whether a particular interference with a right can be justified as 'necessary in a democratic society' (which requires a court to weigh countervailing public interests) or whether one person's right should give way to another person's conflicting right (eg, a defendant's right to confront witnesses versus a particular witness's right to security of person and/or to respect for private life).[10] Major decisions of this kind form an inevitable part of human rights in action, and yet there is typically no 'meta-principle to guide rational choice,'[11] no indication in human rights documents that conflicts should be resolved in a particular way. Indeed, even where a document does contain such a meta-principle—such as the concept of human dignity in the German Basic Law—a significant element of open texture remains.[12]

In the result, human rights may be described as at once fundamental and, in three different ways, contestable. However purple the prose used by human rights advocates, the element of contestability is undeniable. Moreover, in Europe and in most states with constitutional bills of rights, recognition of fundamental rights seems to go hand in hand with judicial power to interpret and develop those rights. Thus, right-sceptics argue not only that rights discourse is inherently individualistic and therefore undervalues collective and public interests, but also that it is accompanied by a tendency to locate the power of interpretation in the judiciary rather than bestowing a prominent role on other constitutional bodies (such as an ombudsman or a human rights commission).[13] Many of these sceptics are not

---

[8] Although it does not appear in the ECHR and was left to the Strasbourg Court to abstract the privilege from the right to a fair trial: see *Murray v United Kingdom* (1996) 22 EHRR 29 and *Saunders v United Kingdom* (1997) 23 EHRR 313.

[9] An analogy here may be the widespread agreement in the UK that there should be a crime of murder, distinct from other forms of homicide, which exists alongside disagreement about the killings that should be included within the category of murder.

[10] For the Strasbourg Court's attempt to negotiate the latter conflict, see *Doorson v Netherlands* (1996) 22 EHRR 330, discussed below: see text at notes 55–6.

[11] A criticism developed by Douzinas, C, 'Justice and Human Rights in Postmodernity' in C Gearty and A Tomkins (eds), *Understanding Human Rights* (New York, Mansell, 1996) 129–30, where he refers to the 'necessary in a democratic society' qualification in the ECHR as an example of 'squatting parasitical counter-principles.'

[12] For discussion of the German law, see Lazarus, L, *Contrasting Prisoners' Rights: A Comparative Examination of England and Germany* (Oxford, Oxford University Press, 2004) 23–37.

[13] These and other criticisms are elaborated in Campbell, T, Ewing, KD and Tomkins, A (eds), *Sceptical Essays on Human Rights* (Oxford, Oxford University Press, 2001); see particularly the 'Introduction' by A Tomkins.

opponents of human rights, but rather advocates of 'human rights as a vital part of a culture of controversy',[14] recognising their special weight but promoting them as a part of political debate and decision making rather than as peremptory or conclusive in their application.

Leading members of the British government now seem to be moving towards the sceptics' camp. We saw at the beginning of this chapter that senior members of the British government, having initially vaunted the protection for individuals introduced by the Human Rights Act 1998,[15] are now arguing that ECHR rights are insufficiently flexible and need reconsideration and readjustment in the light of terrorist attacks. Often they call for a 'better balance' between human rights and the 'needs of security', and this argument about balance is examined below.

II. RECONCILING RESPECT FOR HUMAN RIGHTS WITH SECURITY

The debate between the advocates of human rights and those who emphasise security and public protection is sometimes conducted rather crudely, but it can be rich and intricate.[16] I wish to select two positions for closer examination here—the fundamental contradiction thesis and the balanced response thesis.

The fundamental contradiction thesis is a pro-human rights argument: in essence, terrorists have forsaken the democratic path and are by their methods attacking democratic values, constitutionalism and human rights; and therefore if governments respond to such attacks by abandoning constitutionalism and human rights protections, they are behaving in the same way as the terrorists and undermining the same values. This reasoning underlies the leading judgments in the two US Supreme Court cases on judicial review for detained suspected terrorists.[17] At its most emotive and rhetorical the argument is that governments who abandon human rights protections in this context are colluding with the terrorists. A more sober characterisation is that there is a fundamental contradiction between condemning the methods used by terrorists and then resorting to exceptional measures that trample on human rights. The terrorists depart from normal, acceptable means of political protest, and so the state responds by departing from normal human rights protections and giving exceptional powers to its agents.

Many of those who propound the fundamental contradiction thesis contend that, if there is to be a 'fight against terror', it should be a fight for human rights and for the rule of law.[18] Any special measures taken against terrorism should be

---

[14] Campbell, T, 'Human Rights: A Culture of Controversy' (1999) 26 *Journal of Law and Society* 6, 26.

[15] Eg, Jack Straw, then Home Secretary and promoter of the Bill in the House of Commons, asserted that it 'will guarantee to everyone the means to enforce a set of basic civil and political rights, establishing a floor below which standards will not be allowed to fall': HC Deb 1998, vol 307, col 769.

[16] For wider analysis, see particularly Zedner, L, 'Securing Liberty in the Face of Terror: Reflections from Criminal Justice' (2005) 32 *Journal of Law and Society* 507.

[17] *Hamdi v Rumsfeld* (2004) 124 SCt 2633; *Rumsfeld v Padilla* (2004) 124 SCt 2711.

[18] Thus the Vienna Declaration (note 5 above), para 17, denounces terrorism as destructive of human rights but does not support the abandonment of those rights as part of the strategy for combating terrorism.

taken within the framework of human rights law, so as to ensure that there is no vitiating contradiction in the approach of states.[19] This position has been taken consistently by the Council of Europe in its declarations on counter-terrorist measures.[20] If, *per contra*, states argue that the ends (preserving freedom and democratic institutions) justify the means (curtailing human rights), then their reasoning is no more acceptable than that of terrorists who maintain that the means (causing death, injury, fear, disruption) are justified by the ends that they are pursuing.

Among the issues raised by this position are two that are noteworthy in the context of this chapter. First, the fundamental contradiction thesis accepts the starting point that those who resort to terrorism are abusers of democracy and human rights inasmuch as they abuse the liberty assured by the values of a consti-tutional democracy. The thesis responds by reiterating the need to uphold those values, rather than by proposing their curtailment.

Second, the essence of many of the rights in the ECHR, and particularly those in Articles 5 and 6, is that they insist on particular procedures rather than pre-scribing or proscribing particular legal regimes. Thus human rights safeguards do not constrain states from enacting far-reaching offences with high maximum penalties, so long as the laws are clear and the penalties not so disproportionate as to breach Articles 3 or 5.[21] Moreover, states can respond to terrorism by increas-ing the style and volume of policing or by adopting more creative means of reduc-ing risk, without having to curtail fundamental rights.[22] Thus, for example, the surveillance powers taken under the Regulations of Investigatory Powers Act 2000 (UK) are extensive. In many respects they share the Convention's emphasis on fair procedures,[23] and if greater resources were available they could be deployed to good effect against suspected terrorists without the need for additional powers.[24]

We turn now to the balanced response thesis, much favoured by the UK gov-ernment. The starting point is that terrorist threats present an unavoidable dilemma between striving to protect the basic freedoms of citizens from attack by terrorists on the one hand, and upholding the human rights values enshrined in the Convention on the other hand. That proposition is, of course, rejected by

---

[19] See the various strains of this view advanced in debates in the European Parliament in the early years of this decade: Tsoukala, A, 'Democracy against Security: The Debates about Counter-terrorism in the European Parliament, September 2001–June 2003' (2004) 29 *Alternatives* 417.

[20] Eg, Council of Europe, *Crime Policy in Europe in a Time of Change*, Recommendation R (96) 8; Council of Europe, Strasbourg.

[21] The parameters are broad but not infinitely elastic: see note 79 below.

[22] See, eg, Valverde, M, 'Governing Security, Governing through Security' in RJ Daniels, P Macklem and K Roach (eds), *The Security of Freedom: Essays on Canada's Anti-terrorism Bill* (Toronto, University of Toronto Press, 2002).

[23] Not in all respects, however—eg, the absence of direct judicial involvement in the grant of per-missions (*cf Kopp v Switzerland* (1999) 27 EHRR 91). Despite the possibility of challenge to some aspects of the legislation, its general spirit is more orientated towards human rights compliance than much subsequent legislation.

[24] For discussion of the argument that more resources would be more effective than more powers, see House of Commons Home Affairs Committee, *Terrorism Detention Powers*, Fourth Report, 2005–06 (HC 910-1, 2006), paras 97–100 and Appendix, which details police manpower problems.

proponents of the fundamental contradiction thesis—and in this volume, by Sandra Fredman, Liora Lazarus, Ian Loader and Lucia Zedner—who see no such incompatibility. Supporters of the balanced response thesis go on to argue that governments must strike a balance between the two horns of the dilemma, the two conflicting sets of values. There are well-known problems with positions of this kind: they tend to assume, for example, that the 'public interest' does not include protecting people's fundamental rights;[25] and they also overlook the threat to people's rights from the actions of government officials.[26] Beyond those two problems, however, there are major questions about the meaning and implications of 'balance'.

For one thing, the very conceptualisation of this approach, in particular the use of the imagery of 'balance', is dubious. By adopting this imagery the thesis trades on a cluster of associated terms—such as proportionality, reasonableness and fairness—that appear almost incontrovertible. Thus the term 'balance' tends to disarm opponents because it has no tenable antithesis: nobody, that is, would stand up and argue for imbalance, or indeed for disproportionality, unreasonableness or unfairness. More will be said about this below.

But there is also an empirical component in the reasoning. The essence of the balanced response thesis is that in order to fight terrorism adequately it is necessary to take measures that curtail human rights: this is a complex empirical proposition, and unless it can be substantiated, the alleged dilemma that underlies the 'balanced response' thesis does not exist. Moreover, as we have seen, the concept of security has both its subjective and its objective aspects: no curtailing of human rights simply to alleviate insecurity in the subjective sense should be contemplated, because human rights are much too serious for that. The strongest case for any curtailment of human rights must be predicated on a reduction of security in the objective sense. Much of the evidence necessary to substantiate or disprove the proposition is not in the public domain, which in itself calls for an institutional remedy.[27] Attention will be given here to three aspects of this use of 'balance'.

First, the balanced response thesis appears to assume a hydraulic relationship between human rights safeguards and the promotion of security, that is that as one goes up the other must go down, and vice versa. This is essentially an empirical

[25] On this, see the United Nations, *Siracusa Principles on the Limitation and Derogation of Provisions in the International Covenant on Civil and Political Rights* ('the Siracusa Principles'), UN Doc E/CN.4/1984.4 (1984), para 22: 'Respect for human rights is part of public order (*ordre public*).'
[26] On which see the contribution by Lucia Zedner in this volume.
[27] On which see the contribution by David Dyzenhaus in this volume. It is easy for politicians to claim that such curtailment is necessary for greater security (eg, the Rt Hon Gordon Brown, reported in *The Guardian*, 13 February 2006), but there are many in high places—such as Dame Stella Rimington, former Director of MI5, and Lord Carlile of Berriew, independent reviewer of the Anti-terrorism, Crime and Security Act 2001—whose experiences lead them to doubt that simple view. See now the report of the Home Affairs Committee (note 24 above), recognising the problem of lack of evidence in the public domain and also the lack of public trust in official assertions of necessity. In its report the Committee criticises the Prime Minister and the Home Secretary for failing to scrutinise the evidential basis of the claim by the police that the upper limit on detention of terrorists for questioning should be raised to 90 days.

proposition, on which it is difficult to obtain conclusive evidence: governments make great play of the extra security allegedly provided by new measures,[28] without providing the necessary evidence. This kind of hydraulic explanation is familiar to those who work in criminal justice, since it is often drawn upon explicitly or implicitly by governments when announcing tougher measures or higher sentence levels. The assumption is that a more punitive system will lead to less crime in society, and vice versa, and this assumption may be adopted uncritically in the mass media. However, the findings of research on general deterrence and on incapacitation cast serious doubt on this.[29] Therefore, reliance on the hydraulic explanation in relation to human rights heightens the need for supporting evidence rather than mere assertions or 'worst-case scenarios'.

Second, the concept of 'balance' itself requires close scrutiny.[30] It is not just that it is a concept without a tenable antithesis. Jeremy Waldron has pointed out several difficulties with the use of the metaphor of balancing in this context. One is that its practical impact often drifts towards a 'balance' that involves restricting the rights of a small minority in the hope of enhancing the security of the majority,[31] so that the liberty of a few is curtailed and the liberties of the majority are in practice unlikely to be affected. This discriminatory effect often goes unacknowledged, and yet it may be a form of oppression and almost certainly runs counter to the notion of human rights as protecting the liberty of individuals against the claims (or suspicions) of the authorities and others.

Another difficulty of the 'balance' metaphor is that the resulting curtailment of liberties may have unintended effects, notably that of expanding the powers of the state so as to augment another threat to security (ie from state officials).[32] Indeed, Waldron emphasises the point made above, that so many of the arguments have both principled and empirical components that it is essential to have robust estimates of the actual consequences (intended and unintended) of adopting particular strategies. Too frequently the vital evidence is not in the public domain, which again introduces a lack of public accountability.

Third, there are further difficulties with two concepts that have different but related meanings. The term 'balancing' implies some process of quantification and

---

[28] See eg, *The Times* and other British newspapers for 16 February 2006, reporting assertions by the Prime Minister and others that the introduction of a new offence of glorifying terrorism (which many regard as insufficiently certain, and therefore in breach of ECHR Art 7) is a major step in protecting the public from terrorists.

[29] For a neutral summary of the evidence on these points, see the Home Office report: Halliday, J, 'Making Punishments Work: Report of a Review of the Sentencing Framework for England and Wales' (London, Home Office Communications Directorate, 2001) Appendix 6.

[30] See particularly Zedner (2005).

[31] What David Luban ridicules as the 'OPR theory', that other people's rights count for less, and the white middle classes may happily contemplate the curtailment of these rights on the basis that they are never likely to trouble them: see Luban, D, 'Eight Fallacies about Liberty and Security' in RA Wilson (ed), *Human Rights in the 'War on Terror'* (Cambridge, Cambridge University Press, 2005) 243–4. A similar point is made by Dworkin, R, 'Terror and the Attack on Civil Liberties' (2003) 50(17) *The New York Review of Books* 37.

[32] Waldron, J, 'Security and Liberty: The Image of Balance' (2003) 11 *Journal of Political Philosophy* 191. See also the contribution by Lucia Zedner in this volume.

a fairly accurate methodology, both of which are problematic, but the relevant vocabulary gives rise to a further ambiguity. As commonly used, it may be the process that is being described (balancing various values and/or consequences) or the outcome (the balance that is thereby achieved).

The process of balancing or 'trading off' various alternatives is difficult enough to conceive: not only does it involve assigning weights to different rights as well as ascertaining the levels of confidence in predictions of consequences—both likely to be highly contestable—but it also requires a comparison of the weight of certain rights against the weight of certain consequences. After that, one has to decide how the 'balance' should be struck. The metaphor assumes a set of scales, and it cannot be sufficient to say that there should be some weight on each side. The question is: how much weight on each side? Must they necessarily be equally weighted in order to justify the application of the term 'balance'? These are all metaphorical terms unless some firm common ground can be located. The danger is that there may be an illegitimate transfer of approval from one meaning of the term to another.

The process of balancing is difficult enough, but it is to be found in most corners of human decision making. The outcome—achieving a balance—is much more contestable, because there is the extra element of determining exactly where the desired equilibrium is to be found. But, if achieved, the outcome—the balance—may be represented as an all-things-considered, fair and reasonable compromise. The danger is that the core of fairness in the notion of 'balance' as balanced outcome may wash back over the process of balancing, illegitimately investing the various weighting and balancing operations with a degree of objectivity they manifestly do not possess.

Enough has surely been said to establish that the concepts of 'balance' and 'balancing' need careful handling. It has not been suggested that they should never be used, or that they cannot form part of a helpful process of decision making. The argument thus far is that they may be used improperly, and that anyone who makes an assertion that uses either term should be required to specify exactly what is meant. Beyond that, we must recognise that there may be accommodations to be reached, and that one first step in that direction must be to reassess the priority and weight of different human rights.

III. ARE SOME HUMAN RIGHTS MORE FUNDAMENTAL THAN OTHERS?

Growing public and political concern about security in general, and specifically about what is described as the 'terrorist threat', has brought calls for more intrusive investigative powers, for revisions of criminal procedure, for new and wider criminal laws and for harsher penalties.[33] One reason why members of the British

---

[33] The Terrorism Act 2006 (UK) contains further examples of the trend already evident in the Terrorism Act 2000; the Anti-terrorism, Crime and Security Act 2001; and the Prevention of Terrorism Act 2005. For a summary and critique, see Amnesty International, 'Human Rights: A Broken Promise', available at www.amnesty.org.uk (23 February 2006). See also the criticisms of the Canadian Bill C-36,

government are calling for some ECHR rights to be revisited, as we saw at the beginning of this chapter, is frustration with decisions of the Strasbourg Court that hold that a state is in breach of Article 3 (the right to be free from torture) if it returns a person to his or her country of origin when there is a real risk of that person being subjected to torture there.[34] Yet the terms of the *Chahal* decision make the European Court's stance perfectly clear:

> Article 3 enshrines one of the most fundamental values of democratic society. The Court is well aware of the immense difficulties faced by States in modern times in protecting their communities from terrorist violence. However, even in these circumstances, the Convention prohibits in absolute terms torture or inhuman or degrading treatment or punishment, irrespective of the victim's conduct . . . The prohibition provided by Article 3 against ill-treatment is equally absolute in expulsion cases . . .[35]

This passage embodies a recognition of the force of security considerations but declines to give way to them.

Before we examine the relationship of the *Chahal* decision to the structure of the ECHR, we should note that the Supreme Court of Canada has indicated a willingness to introduce notions of balancing and proportionality into a right that, internationally speaking, has always been recognised as absolute. Thus in *Suresh v Canada* (2002) the Supreme Court stated:

> We do not exclude the possibility that in exceptional circumstances, deportation to face torture may be justified . . . Insofar as Canada is unable to deport a person where there are substantial grounds to believe he or she would be tortured on return, this is not because article 3 of the Convention Against Torture directly constrains the actions of the Canadian Government, but because the fundamental justice balance under Section 7 of the Charter generally precludes deportation to torture when applied on a case by case basis. We may predict that [the balance] will rarely be struck in favour of expulsion where there is a serious risk of torture. However, as the matter is one of balance, precise prediction is elusive. The ambit of an exceptional discretion to deport to torture, if any, must await future cases.[36]

This decision strikes an intermediate note, recognising the strength of the prohibition on torture but leaving open the possibility that exceptional circumstances might justify deportation. The concept of 'balance' is employed in this reasoning, largely because of the particular structure of the Canadian Charter (notably section 1, which has no counterpart in the ECHR).[37] The British government is keen

---

the Anti-terrorism Act 2001, in Roach, K, 'The New Terrorism Offences and the Criminal Law' in RJ Daniels, P Macklem and K Roach (eds), *The Security of Freedom: Essays on Canada's Anti-terrorism Bill* (Toronto, Toronto University Press, 2002).

[34] The leading decisions are *Soering v United Kingdom* (1989) 11 EHRR 439 and *Chahal v United Kingdom* (1996) 23 EHRR 413.

[35] *Chahal v United Kingdom* (1996) 23 EHRR 413, paras 79–80.

[36] [2002] 1 SCR 3, para [78].

[37] Section 1 of the Canadian Charter states that rights are guaranteed 'subject only to such reasonable limits prescribed by law as can be demonstrably justified in a free and democratic society', a proviso that has been developed through the jurisprudence of the Supreme Court. No such general proviso is to be found in the ECHRs.

for a similar approach to be adopted in respect of Article 3 of the ECHR.[38] What are the obstacles to this?

The main obstacle lies in the structure of the Convention itself: this can be taken to establish an internal hierarchy in which four rights are regarded as deserving greater protection than any of the others, in the sense that they are non-derogable. The necessary first step is to contend that designating a right as non-derogable is to regard it as deserving greater protection, and therefore as more fundamental, than the others. This is not an uncontroversial proposition. As we have seen, the Vienna Declaration asserts that human rights are indivisible and should be treated on an equal footing.[39]

The principle of indivisibility is maintained by many passionate advocates of human rights, some of whom also argue pragmatically that any notion of a hierarchy of rights is the beginning of a slippery slope, leading soon to the discarding of certain 'weaker' rights in the face of political imperatives.[40] While that may be a danger, it is one that should be guarded against rather than used to defeat the idea of a hierarchy of rights. Within European human rights law, however, non-derogability is a practical test of priority. When states agree that certain rights cannot be derogated from, even in extreme circumstances, this must imply that they are regarded as the most basic to human dignity. Thus Article 15 of the Convention declares:

1. In time of war or other public emergency threatening the life of the nation, any High Contracting Party may take measures derogating from its obligations under this Convention to the extent strictly required by the exigencies of the situation, provided that such measures are not inconsistent with its other obligations under international law.

2. No derogation from Article 2, except in respect of deaths resulting from lawful acts of war, or from Article 3, 4 (paragraph 1) and 7 shall be made under this provision.

The first paragraph of Article 15 sets the conditions for derogation, chiefly the existence of a war or other public emergency, and the confinement of the special measures to the minimum necessary interference with rights.[41] Our present interest lies in the second paragraph, which singles out four Convention rights as non-derogable: the right to life (Article 2); the right not to be subjected to torture or

---

[38] See a recent survey commissioned by the Foreign Office: Foreign and Commonwealth Office (UK), 'Counter-terrorism Legislation and Practice: A Survey of Selected Countries', October 2005, available at www.fco.gov.uk, para 23.

[39] Note 5 above and accompanying text. Indeed, much of the Vienna Declaration is concerned with rights to food and the means of survival, and with the right not to be discriminated against.

[40] See Sieghart, P, *The International Law of Human Rights* (Oxford, Oxford University Press, 1983) 12; and the broader discussion in Koji, T, 'Emerging Hierarchy of International Human Rights and Beyond: From the Perspective of Non-derogable Rights' (2001) 2 *European Journal of International Law* 917.

[41] These were the conditions interpreted and applied by the House of Lords in the landmark decision of *A and Others v Secretary of State for the Home Department* [2004] UKHL 56, when the power to detain 'suspected international terrorists' indefinitely without trial was held incompatible with the Convention.

inhuman or degrading treatment (Article 3); the right not to be held in slavery (Article 4, paragraph 1); and the right not to be subjected to retrospective criminal laws or penalties (Article 7).[42]

Should these four rights be singled out for greater protection?[43] The right to life surely has a claim to be among the most fundamental rights, since without life there is nothing to which to attach any human right. The right not to be subjected to torture may be thought to embody freedom from the greatest assault on an individual's dignity, autonomy and self-determination. Torture is defined fairly narrowly, so as to include only deliberate inhuman treatment inflicted by agents of the state (or knowingly tolerated by them) that causes very serious and cruel suffering.[44] However, Article 3 also prohibits inhuman or degrading treatment, which is a lower level of deliberately inflicted suffering and the classification of which depends on the effect of the conduct on the victim, taking account of his or her age, sex and health.[45] This means that Article 3 includes not only torture but also assaults in the middle range of seriousness, and some might question whether freedom from assaults in the middle range of seriousness justifies the same high ranking as that accorded to torture.[46]

This is not to argue that protecting young children from physical abuse at the hands of their parents or carers is unimportant, or that moderate violence by the police against suspects is excusable. The Strasbourg Court has taken the view, in its *Chahal* judgment and elsewhere, that there is no question of the Article 3 right being subjected to any process of 'balancing'. It would reject the former Home Secretary's contention that 'the right to be protected from torture or ill-treatment [should be] considered side by side with the right to be protected from the death and destruction caused by indiscriminate terrorism'[47] and instead insist that the state should find other ways of protecting its citizens.

[42] These four rights are also listed as non-derogable in the Siracusa Principles (see note 25 above), para 69. The same is true of Article 4 of the International Covenant on Civil and Political Rights and Article 27 of the American Convention on Human Rights (1978), although those two instruments add further non-derogable rights, such as the right to freedom of thought and religion and the right to recognition as a person. See further Shelton, D, 'Hierarchy of Norms and Human Rights: Of Trumps and Winners' (2002) 65 *Saskatchewan Law Review* 301, 313–15.

[43] It should be noted that several Protocols have been added to the Convention, and that Protocol 6 (abolition of the death penalty) and Protocol 7, Art 4 (the right not to be tried or punished twice) are both declared non-derogable under Art 15. There are also those who argue that different rights are fundamental, such as the principle of non-discrimination: Shelton (2002), 308–13; *cf* the earlier arguments of Meron, T, 'On a Hierarchy of International Human Rights' (1986) 80 *American Journal of International Law* 1. [I am grateful to Dr Patricia Londono for these references.]

[44] See *Ireland v United Kingdom* (1978) 2 EHRR 25, and the other authorities set out in Mowbray, A, *Cases and Materials on the European Convention on Human Rights* (London, Butterworths, 2001) ch 3. Note that in the US there have been calls for an even narrower definition of torture, both by government and by advocates of modified liberalism such as M Ignatieff, *The Lesser Evil: Political Ethics in an Age of Terrorism* (Princeton, Princeton University Press, 2004) 136–43.

[45] A violation was found in *A. v United Kingdom* (1998) 27 EHRR 611, because English law on the lawful chastisement of children failed to protect them adequately from beatings that would amount to degrading treatment.

[46] *Cf* the recent decision of the Grand Chamber in *Jalloh v Germany*, App No 54810/00.

[47] The Rt Hon Charles Clark, speech to the Parliamentary Assembly of the Council of Europe, 7 September 2005.

Little discussion about slavery (Article 4, paragraph 1) is required here, since it is relatively unusual and is clearly the most far-reaching deprivation of liberty. But what about the Article 7 prohibition on retrospective criminal laws and penalties? It seems that this must be connected with a basic element of individual autonomy, in the sense that people cannot be expected to organise their conduct so as to conform to the law if states are allowed to create criminal laws that have retrospective effect. To treat individuals as rational, responsible and autonomous subjects, it is necessary to have criminal laws that specify in advance, and with sufficient certainty, what conduct amounts to an offence. If states criminalise conduct that has already taken place, this is an abuse of their power and a denial of a necessary condition of individual autonomy. In that sense, the principle of legality embodied in Article 7 is properly regarded as fundamental. But this is not to conceal the judgments of degree that are necessary in order to determine how certain the definition of an offence must be to satisfy Article 7, just as there are questions of degree involved in the definitions of both torture and inhuman and degrading treatment in Article 3. Once again, we find that rights can be both fundamental and, at least to some extent, contestable.

The structure of the Convention yields more about the relative strength of its rights. Articles 8, 9, 10 and 11 are phrased in a different style, with the right declared in the first paragraph and the grounds on which interference with that right may be justified in the second paragraph. These four rights—the right to respect for private life (Article 8); the right to freedom of thought and religion (Article 9); the right to freedom of expression (Article 10); and the right to freedom of assembly and association (Article 11)—are therefore examples of qualified rights, in the sense that on the face of the Convention there are grounds on which each of these rights may be curtailed by a state, if it is 'necessary in a democratic society' for one of the reasons articulated.

There is a considerable Strasbourg jurisprudence on the limits of interference with each of these four Articles,[48] and the upshot is that, for example, a person's right to respect for private life may be significantly curtailed by the use of electronic surveillance techniques by state officials, so long as those techniques are authorised as part of a legal regime that satisfies the requirements of necessity, proportionality and openness to challenge entailed by paragraph 2 of Article 8. In these qualified rights, therefore, the conflict between rights and utility is 'resolved' by allowing consequentialist calculations to be taken into account, but only within the particular framework set out in each Article.

What then is the place of Articles 5 and 6 in the Convention's structure? The right to liberty and security of person, and the right to a fair trial, are particularly likely to be curtailed in the name of enhancing security. How fundamental are they? Clearly they are not among the four core Articles from which derogation is not allowed. On the other hand, the Convention does not declare them to be qualified rights, which member states may interfere with if that is held to be 'necessary

---

[48] See further Mowbray (2001), chs 8–11.

in a democratic society' for one of a list of reasons. No such paragraph appears in Articles 5 and 6. This means that the concept of proportionality, which plays such a significant role in setting the boundaries for interferences with the rights declared by Articles 8, 9, 10 and 11, is not relevant in the same sense to Articles 5 and 6. Neither the Convention nor the Strasbourg jurisprudence suggests that the rights enumerated in those Articles can simply be pushed aside for public policy or other consequentialist reasons, on the ground that such curtailments are proportionate.[49]

Unfortunately, the seeds of heresy were planted in British law at an early stage of human rights adjudications by Lord Bingham, in his tone-setting speech in the first major Human Rights Act case of *Brown v Stott* (2001),[50] when he held that a particular curtailment of the privilege against self-incrimination implied into Article 6 (right to a fair trial) was 'not a disproportionate response to the problem of maintaining road safety'. Lord Bingham thus held that, in order to decide whether this Article 6 right could be interfered with, it is necessary to balance the 'general interests of the community against the interests of the individual'. That is wrong on two counts: Article 6 provides for no such balancing; and if *per contra* some proportionality judgment were permissible, one would expect the conditions to be tougher than those set out in paragraph 2 of Article 8, rather than more relaxed and open-ended.[51]

Lord Bingham's approach to proportionality is inconsistent with major decisions in Strasbourg. When the Irish government claimed that the privilege against self-incrimination should be curtailed in order to bolster anti-terrorist measures, the European Court said it could not.[52] The same response was forthcoming when the French government sought to rely on statements from anonymous witnesses in the 'fight against drug-trafficking'[53] and when the British government claimed that the privilege against self-incrimination should be curtailed in order to combat serious fraud.[54] Lord Bingham's idea that interference with an Article 6 right is permissible if it can be cast as a proportionate response to a legitimate public interest, repeated by other senior judges and members of the government, is a heresy and does not represent European human rights law.

This is not to argue that rights guaranteed by Articles 5 and 6 of the ECHR can never be curtailed. The submission is that they cannot simply be balanced away on

---

[49]   Some of the authorities are reviewed in Ashworth, A, *Human Rights, Serious Crime and Criminal Procedure* (London, Sweet & Maxwell, 2002) 52–62.

[50]   [2001] 2 WLR 817.

[51]   Lord Bingham made a further error when analysing Art 15 in *A and Others v Secretary of State for the Home Department* [2004] UKHL 56, where he stated at [30]: 'Article 15 requires that any member state in derogation of its obligations under the Convention should not go beyond what is "strictly required by the exigencies of the situation". Thus the Convention imposes a test of strict necessity or, in Convention terminology, proportionality.' The last five words are wrong. The Art 15 test is stronger than the test of proportionality used in other Articles such as Arts 8–11, and the two should be kept apart.

[52]   *Heaney and McGuinness v Ireland* (2000) 33 EHRR 264.

[53]   *Saidi v France* (1993) 17 EHRR 251; see also the rejection of this argument in the entrapment case of *Teixeira de Castro v Portugal* (1999) 28 EHRR 101.

[54]   *Saunders v United Kingdom* (1997) 23 EHRR 313.

some vague notion of proportionality, as Lord Bingham and others have done. Two examples of curtailment of Article 6 rights can be given, so as to demonstrate alternative patterns of reasoning. In the landmark decision in *Doorson v Netherlands*,[55] the Strasbourg Court held that the defendant's right to examine witnesses against him or her has to be balanced against the rights of the witnesses themselves, notably where a witness has cause to fear violent reprisals if his or her identity becomes known. However, the reasoning of this judgment must be scrutinised with care. In the first place, the interests 'balanced' were both rights of individuals: the case does not involve the 'public interest' or some future and contingent interest of unspecified individuals. Second, the Court maintained that each individual's interest must be protected to the maximum. In particular, defence rights should be curtailed as little as possible. Thus, 'the handicaps under which the defence laboured [must be] sufficiently counterbalanced by the procedures followed by the judicial authorities', such as appropriate directions from the judge; and any conviction should not be based 'solely or mainly' on the evidence of the witnesses who give their evidence anonymously.[56] This use of extra safeguards shows that the right being curtailed is nevertheless being taken seriously—a way of keeping faith with human rights that is quite different from Lord Bingham's approach of balancing rights away.

Another example of a structured approach may be found in Strasbourg judgments on the prosecution's duty to disclose documents to the defence, and on the doctrine of 'public interest immunity', which prevents the disclosure of documents in certain circumstances. In the leading decision of *Rowe and Davis v United Kingdom*[57] the Court held that the principle of equality of arms is a requirement of fairness under Article 6, but that:

> the entitlement to disclosure of relevant evidence is not an absolute right. In any criminal proceedings there may be competing interests, such as national security or the need to protect witnesses at risk of reprisals or keep secret police methods of investigating crime. In some cases it may be necessary to withhold certain evidence from the defence so as to preserve the fundamental rights of another individual or to safeguard an important public interest. However, only such measures restricting the rights of the defence which are strictly necessary are permissible under Article 6(1). Moreover, in order to ensure that the accused receives a fair trial, any difficulties caused to the defence by a limitation on its rights must be sufficiently counterbalanced by the procedures followed by the judicial authorities.[58]

There may be room for debate about whether the Court has insisted on sufficient 'counterbalancing' procedures in these cases of public interest immunity,[59] but it

---

[55] (1996) 22 EHRR 330.

[56] *Ibid*, para 72; *cf van Mechelen v Netherlands* (1997) 25 EHRR 547.

[57] (2000) 30 EHRR 1.

[58] *Ibid*, para 61.

[59] There appears to be some disagreement on the need to adopt the safeguard of employing special counsel: compare *Edwards and Lewis v United Kingdom* (2005) 40 EHRR 593 with *R v H and C* [2004] 2 WLR 335.

is evident that no straightforward 'balancing' process is envisaged. The Court thus insists on the strict necessity of any curtailment, on preserving the essence of the defendant's right, and on adopting counterbalancing procedures.

A structured approach, of the kind demonstrated in these two examples, is distinctly preferable to a broad 'balancing' approach as a method of accommodating conflicting interests, by retaining respect for human rights while allowing some scope for other interests to be protected.[60] A structured approach might, for example, take the form of adopting a 'necessary in a democratic society' test (as developed by the Strasbourg Court for Articles 8–11 of the ECHR); or adopting a rule and circumscribed exception (as developed in *Rowe and Davis* on disclosure of evidence); or adopting compensating procedures (as in *Doorson* on witness anonymity). Simple balancing, of the kind propounded by Lord Bingham, should be rejected as both unfaithful to human rights and inappropriately lacking in sophistication.

IV. THE VALUE AND RESILIENCE OF ARTICLE 6

The UK government has twice invoked Article 15 in order to enter derogations from Article 5 of the Convention. A derogation in respect of Article 5(3) extending the number of days for which a suspect may be held before being brought to court from four to seven, was upheld during the worst of the Northern Ireland troubles,[61] while a derogation from Article 5 enabling the indefinite detention of 'suspected international terrorists', was entered when the Anti-terrorism, Crime and Security Act 2001 was enacted, and lasted until December 2004, when it was held by the House of Lords not to fall within Article 15 because it was both too extensive and discriminatory.[62] The Terrorism Act 2006 now increases the length of time a suspected terrorist can be held before charge from 14 to 28 days; this increase in police power, which represents a departure from Article 5 and its jurisprudence, is granted in the belief that it will improve the effectiveness of police investigations.[63] However, the focus here will be on Article 6 and how curtailments of the right to a fair trial should be viewed.

I now propose a thought experiment, in which we should imagine the fate of the right to a fair trial if a government were to move from what we might term the 'justice model' required by human rights to a 'security model' of the criminal process.[64] What curtailments or derogations might be contemplated by such a

---

[60] See Greer, S, ' "Balancing" and the European Court of Human Rights: A Contribution to the Habermas-Alexy Debate' [2004] *Cambridge Law Journal* 412.

[61] *Brannigan and McBride v United Kingdom* (1993) 17 EHRR 539.

[62] In *A and Others v Secretary of State for the Home Department* (note 51 above). see Tomkins, A, 'Readings of *A v Secretary of State for the Home Department*' (2005) *Public Law* 259.

[63] For a relatively critical assessment of the new power and the evidential basis on which it was introduced, see the report of the Home Affairs Committee (note 24 above).

[64] These terms are taken from an Oxford Amnesty lecture delivered by Conor Gearty on 23 February 2006: see Gearty, C, *Can Human Rights Survive?* (Cambridge, Cambridge University Press, 2006).

'security model', and what values would they threaten? How would a structured approach to balancing, as outlined in section III above, assist in dealing with such challenges? Let us imagine some eight changes that might be made:

1. The burden of proof would be reversed in significant ways, so that offences would be drafted in a minimalist, strict liability manner, and defences provided on the basis that the defendant must prove them.
2. Those reasonably suspected of terrorist offences would be required to answer questions about their activities at a certain time and place, with a penalty of imprisonment for non-compliance.
3. Speedy trials would be mandated for those charged with terrorist offences (although it is often the police and prosecution that need more time).
4. Legal aid and assistance would be more strictly controlled, requiring those charged with terrorist offences to fund their own defence unless they proved that they could not, and the same would apply to the use of interpreters.
5. Hearsay evidence would be more widely admissible and special measures more widely available, so that witnesses would not have to be literally confronted by defendants or defence lawyers.
6. Evidence obtained by entrapment or by other breaches of the Convention would be admissible for the prosecution.
7. There would be a presumption in favour of long indeterminate sentences for terrorist offences, based on the prevention of dangerous conduct.
8. The release of such offenders from prison would be a decision of the Home Secretary, taken in the interest of public safety and security.

Would anything of great value be sacrificed if changes of these kinds were made? Would each of them require a derogation, or could the relevant right be curtailed without derogation?

1. Reversing the Burden of Proof

The first change required by our thought experiment, reversing the burden of proof, is a fine test case. When a terrorist offence is charged and the accused wishes to raise a defence, is it not right that he or she should bear the burden of establishing that defence on a balance of probabilities? Proponents of this view will cite the difficulty of investigating terrorist crimes, the seriousness of the threat to public safety and security, and the fact that the accused is likely to be the person in possession of most of the facts about what happened. Plausible as these arguments may sound, none of them makes a strong case.

Before engaging with the detail of the proponents' arguments, it is important to look more deeply into the justifications for enshrining the presumption of innocence in a declaration of human rights. Criminal conviction is a serious matter in itself, the more so when it may lead to a sentence of loss of liberty, and wrongful conviction would be a major affront to personal autonomy. Tribunals are fallible, and therefore it is right to presume an accused person innocent until proven guilty. Moreover, reversing the onus of proof leads to a presumption of guilt, whereby the accused would be required to marshal evidence so as to establish innocence and would be liable to be convicted even though significant doubt about guilt remained. Given the state's greater resources, it is doubly wrong to impose this burden on an accused. The prosecution should be required to establish guilt (and to negative defences credibly raised by the accused), and the accused should not be at peril of conviction for failure to establish innocence.

The three arguments raised by proponents of reversing the burden of proof fail. First, the difficulty of investigating crimes must be overcome through better surveillance and greater police resources, not by risking the conviction of the innocent. (If that risk materialised, not only would it be a gross injustice to the innocent person, but the real perpetrator would remain free). Second, the seriousness of the offence fares no better, because just as terrorist offences pose a serious threat to society, so conviction of a terrorist offence is an extremely serious matter for any individual, and all proper safeguards must be observed. And finally, the fact that the accused has personal knowledge is not a good reason for overturning the burden of proof, since subjective requirements such as intention or recklessness are to be found throughout the criminal law; to accede to the 'personal knowledge' argument would be to undercut the whole presumption of innocence. Thus the presumption emerges as a protector of the standing and the liberty of accused persons, and the power of states should not be allowed to overwhelm it. Arguments from public safety and security should therefore not succeed in this quarter.[65]

However, the Strasbourg jurisprudence reveals a weaker presumption of innocence than that now established in the United Kingdom and in many Commonwealth jurisdictions.[66] The leading decision of *Salabiaku v France* makes it clear that the presumption may be displaced by contrary presumptions, so long as states 'confine them within reasonable limits which take into account the importance of what is at stake and maintain the rights of the defence'.[67] The vagueness of this endorsement of the presumption has never been remedied, and the facts of *Salabiaku* demonstrate that the presumption may be displaced even when imprisonment is a penalty, reducing the meaning of 'what is at stake' to an empty gesture. This, then, is an example of the right's contestability being so extensive as to undermine its claim to being fundamental, although curiously that applies at the European but not at the domestic British level, where the right is taken more seriously.[68]

---

[65] For a fuller development of all these arguments, see Ashworth, A, 'Four Threats to the Presumption of Innocence' (2006) 123 *South African Law Journal* 62–96.

[66] The leading British decision of *R v Lambert* [2002] 2 AC 545 relies heavily on Commonwealth cases from Canada, South Africa and elsewhere.

[67] (1988) 13 EHRR 379, at para 27.

[68] See the review by Dennis, I, 'Reverse Onuses and the Presumption of Innocence: In Search of Principle' (2005) *Criminal Law Review* 901.

2. Self-incrimination

The opposite is true of the privilege against self-incrimination, which would be violated if suspects were required to answer questions on pain of conviction and imprisonment for non-compliance. The Strasbourg Court has recognised the privilege as an implied right in Article 6, arguing that it is a necessary component of the right to a fair trial that statements from the defendant should be obtained without compulsion. In the leading decision of *Saunders v United Kingdom*[69] the Court rejected the government's argument that the privilege should give way to the exigencies of investigating serious fraud, and indeed in *Heaney and McGuinness v Ireland*[70] the Court rejected the Irish government's argument that this power was essential in the 'fight against terrorism'.

The likely response of the British courts to such arguments remains uncertain: the leading British decision stands at the opposite end of the spectrum, and, as described earlier, Lord Bingham took a minimising and critical view of the *Saunders* judgment, arguing that because the privilege against self-incrimination is merely an implied right, it can be balanced against the public interest in improving road safety.[71] However, it could be said that the approach to non-disclosure by a car owner ought to be different from that to failure to answer questions by a suspected terrorist. In principle, any proposal to force suspected terrorists to speak on pain of conviction and punishment, especially deprivation of liberty, should be rejected as inconsistent with respect for individual autonomy and for the presumption of innocence. It would violate Article 6 rights and would require a formal derogation.

3. Speedy Trial

Speedy trials are an excellent goal in principle, but defendants must be allowed adequate time and facilities for the preparation of the defence. This right is guaranteed by Article 6, paragraph 3(b) of the Convention, and it surely rules out trials held a week or two after a terrorist incident. That may happen in some parts of the world, but it should not be allowed (even if, unusually, the prosecution were in a position to proceed so soon). There are some older Strasbourg authorities holding that rapid trials may breach Article 6,[72] but the more likely problem is lengthy delay in bringing the matter to trial—which would breach the defendant's right to trial within a reasonable time, guaranteed by Article 6, paragraph 1 of the Convention.

---

[69] (1997) 27 EHRR 313, followed in *Shannon v United Kingdom* (2006) 42 EHRR 660.
[70] (2000) 33 EHRR 264.
[71] *Brown v Stott* (note 50 above and accompanying text); *cf* now *Jalloh v Germany* (note 46 above).
[72] Notably two early cases against Austria, discussed in van Dijk, P and van Hoof, GJH, *Theory and Practice of the European Convention on Human Rights*, 3rd edn (The Hague, Kluwer, 1999) 466.

4. Legal Aid and Assistance

Moving on to the argument that those defending terrorist charges should be made to pay for themselves, this should be rejected as likely to produce injustice and unfairness. The normal rules ought to be applied: there is no reason to suppose that terrorist suspects are more likely to have funds than others, and the whole point of legal aid and advice is to ensure that the prosecution is put to proof and that any credible defences are properly put to the court. The rationale for this right, guaranteed by Article 6, paragraph 3(c) of the Convention, derives from similar arguments to those supporting the presumption of innocence. The Strasbourg Court's principle of equality of arms, developed in Article 6 cases, also points in the same direction.[73] Thus any change such as this would amount to a violation of Article 6 and would therefore require a derogation consistent with the terms of Article 15.

5. Hearsay Evidence

English law in the past has been technical and somewhat inconsistent. The Criminal Justice Act 2003 has introduced a new set of rules and wider admissibility of hearsay. Moreover, greater efforts are now made to ensure witness protection through special measures in court and protection schemes out of court. Both these developments are to be broadly welcomed, but there are limits. Article 6, paragraph 3(d) declares a defendant's right to examine or have examined witnesses against him or her, and it is arguable whether the English hearsay reforms have gone too far in whittling down this right.[74] Moreover, live video links, screens and other special measures of witness protection in court may rightly be permitted, but the Strasbourg Court has made it clear that 'the handicaps under which the defence laboured [should be] sufficiently counter-balanced by the procedures followed by the judicial authorities.'[75] It is notable that in ministerial statements about defendants' rights in terrorist cases, no such qualification is usually to be found. While the Strasbourg case-law on this right is generally deferential to domestic legal systems, it insists on maximal protection of the respective rights of defendants and of witnesses, and plainly does not regard this as a 'zero-sum game' in which increasing the rights of one (the witness) should necessarily be allowed to decrease the rights of another (the defendant).

[73] See eg, *Pham Hoang v France* (1992) 16 EHRR 53, and Emmerson, B and Ashworth, A and Macdonald A, *Human Rights and Criminal Justice* 2nd edn (London, Sweet & Maxwell, 2007) ch14A.
[74] *Cf* Choo, A, *Evidence* (Oxford, Oxford University Press, 2006) 244–8.
[75] *Doorson v Netherlands* (1996) 22 EHRR 330, para. 72.

6. The Admissibility of Evidence

On the admissibility of evidence obtained through violation of a Convention right, there are at least two deep splits. There are those who adhere doggedly to the separation thesis, whereby the violation of a Convention right is a serious matter but should be pursued under the Article that has been breached. To admit evidence obtained by that breach does not affect the fairness of the trial, so the separation thesis goes, because trials are properly concerned only with the reliability of the evidence and not with the means whereby it was obtained. This view has been confirmed in the House of Lords[76] and in the Strasbourg Court[77] in a case where Article 8 was breached (by planting listening devices without proper authority) in order to secure the evidence on which the accused was convicted, both courts holding that the fairness of the trial was unaffected even though this was the most telling evidence for the prosecution.

Recently, however, the House of Lords has distanced itself from the separation thesis where torture is concerned: it appears that a fair trial under Article 6 would not be possible if key evidence was probably obtained by the use of torture contrary to Article 3 of the Convention.[78] In that context, there is no reluctance to hold that the trial would be tainted if a court received evidence obtained through torture, and the integrity of the criminal process would be undermined. Thus the House of Lords believes that the admission of evidence obtained by violating Article 3 renders the trial unfair but that the admission of evidence obtained by violating Article 8 does not. Can this be defended as a reflection of the hierarchy of rights described in section III above? Or should we say that the integrity of the system is undermined in all cases where some of the evidence against the defendant was obtained by breaching another Convention right?

The legal system would surely engage in hypocrisy if it allowed any such evidence to feature in a criminal trial: this is a question not of trying to discipline the police for their unlawfulness but rather of ensuring that the defendant is not disadvantaged by the breach of Convention right and ensuring that the court does not equivocate about the fundamental nature of human rights.[79] However, the prevailing view at present appears to be that there is no right not to be convicted on evidence obtained by breach of the Convention, unless the breach amounts to torture.

---

[76] *Khan (Sultan)* [1997] AC 558.

[77] *Khan v United Kingdom* (2000) 31 EHRR 1016.

[78] *A v Secretary of State for the Home Department* [2005] UKHL 71. Note, however, that Lord Bingham (at para 53) would not necessarily hold a trial unfair if it admitted evidence obtained by inhuman or degrading treatment contrary to Article 3 rather than torture contrary to Article 3, the latter being a more serious invasion of rights. To the same effect, see *Jalloh v Germany* (note 46 above).

[79] This view, contrary to the separation thesis, is argued in Ashworth, A, 'Exploring the Integrity Principle in Evidence and Procedure' in P Mirfield and R Smith (eds), *Essays for Colin Tapper* (Oxford, Oxford University Press, 2003).

7. Dangerousness

The final two proposals associated with the thought experiment should fail for different reasons. Dangerous offender legislation is controversial enough on its own, but any presumption of dangerousness based on the category of the offence of conviction is likely to breach the Convention, either Article 3 or (more likely) Article 5.[80] The Convention requires courts to satisfy themselves as to the risk of further serious offences in each case before imposing such a sentence, and in that respect terrorism should be no different. However, there is little to prevent the legislature from prescribing very high penalties for terrorist offences, without any presumption of dangerousness, since the proportionality constraints of human rights law are relatively elastic.[81]

8. Fair Procedures for Detention and Release

As for the notion that the British Home Secretary should determine the release of convicted terrorists, because only such a senior politician could make an informed judgment of the risk to public safety of releasing such a person, that argument has been put and rejected in both the Strasbourg Court[82] and the House of Lords.[83] Article 5, paragraph 4 of the ECHR requires reviews of detention to be carried out by a court, and Article 6, paragraph 1 regards a fair trial as requiring an 'independent and impartial tribunal'. For a government minister to have the power of release would therefore fail to have due regard to the basic elements of fair procedure. European human rights law could not be stretched to accommodate either this proposal or that in 7., unless a derogation under Article 15 were made.

* * *

One of the purposes of this thought experiment was to explore the values that would be compromised if such moves towards a 'security model' of criminal process were introduced. The presumption of innocence emerges as a foundational value, from which several of the other principled arguments flow. So far as European human rights law is concerned, it is apparent that five of the Article 6 rights could only be modified if a derogation were entered under Article 15 (duty to answer questions, very speedy trials, withdrawal of legal aid, presumption of dangerousness, release authorised only by Home Secretary), whereas the other three could be modified more easily because their boundaries appear to be more flexible. Thus the legislature has modified the Article 6, paragraph 3(d) right to

---

[80] See Lord Woolf CJ in *Offen (No 2)* [2001] 1 Cr App R 37 and, more generally, van Zyl Smit, D and Ashworth, A, 'Disproportionate Sentences as Human Rights Violations' (2004) 67 *Modern Law Review* 541.

[81] The decisions, especially *Weeks v United Kingdom* (1988) 10 EHRR 293, are discussed by van Zyl Smit and Ashworth (2004).

[82] *Stafford v United Kingdom* (2002) 35 EHRR 1121.

[83] *Anderson v Secretary of State for the Home Department* [2002] 4 All ER 1089.

examine witnesses by introducing new provisions in the Criminal Justice Act 2003; the Strasbourg jurisprudence might be read as permitting the legislature to reverse the burden of proof in terrorist cases, although the House of Lords has ruled against this in domestic law;[84] and there is no need to legislate for the admissibility of evidence obtained by a breach of a Convention right because the courts already allow this, save in the case of evidence obtained by torture. This survey further demonstrates the contestability of human rights, although the margin of contestability is small in five of the rights and much wider in the other three.

V. THE VALUE OF HUMAN RIGHTS

Although a major reason for recognising human rights is to defend the interests of individuals or minorities against those of the majority or the collectivity, it has been argued here, specifically by reference to European human rights law, that a more nuanced analysis is required to capture the true value of human rights. In considering the alleged challenge to human rights from the growing emphasis on security, particularly in the context of 'anti-terrorist' measures, we have noted a number of approaches to human rights—the absolutism of some human rights advocates, who regard human rights as indivisible and of equal weight; the relativism of some human rights sceptics, who regard human rights as part of a 'culture of controversy' in public affairs but not as conclusory or even as trumps; and a middle way adopted by some judges and politicians, which claims to recognise the value of human rights but argues that they must always be balanced against the public interest.

All three approaches to human rights are rejected here. The absolutist argument goes too far in denying that there can be different levels and strengths of human rights, and also tends to overlook the elements of indeterminacy and negotiation that would be an inevitable part even of an absolutist system. The sceptical approach appears to deny that there is any point to ranking and weighting human rights: scepticism may be healthy in confronting the absolutists, and in confronting those, typically governments, who make empirically based assertions (about the impact on security of curtailing a particular right) without providing the evidence to any scrutineer, but one of the purposes of this chapter has been to argue that progress can be made in structuring arguments about human rights. As for those who claim that it is all a question of balance and/or proportionality, their standpoint is far too crude to do justice to the subject matter.

It has been argued here that human rights are both fundamental and contestable. There is also considerable indeterminacy in the scope of some human rights. But what has emerged most clearly from this study is that, just as it is right to maintain (as do the Siracusa Principles) that 'respect for human rights is part of

---

[84] Specifically, in relation to terrorist offences, in *Attorney-General's Reference No 4 of 2002* [2004] UKHL 43.

ordre public,[85] so it is also right to recognise that the structure of human rights can allow weight to be given to security considerations. This should not be through some unanalysed and heavily rhetorical notion of balance or proportionality: a more appropriate and probably more fruitful approach lies through (a) the establishment of a hierarchy of human rights, and then (b) the development of patterns of reasoning that allow security considerations to play a different role in respect of rights of different weights. Examples of such a strategy, drawing on European human rights law without implying that it is beyond improvement, were given in section III above. It remains true, however, that much will still depend on the disposition of the decision-making body, be it judicial or otherwise, and on the quality and quantity of the evidence adduced on crucial issues of security.

REFERENCES

Amnesty International, 'Human Rights: A Broken Promise', available at www.amnesty.org.uk (23 February 2006).

Ashworth, A, *Human Rights, Serious Crime and Criminal Procedure* (London, Sweet & Maxwell, 2002).

—— 'Exploring the Integrity Principle in Evidence and Procedure' in P Mirfield and R Smith (eds), *Essays for Colin Tapper* (Oxford, Oxford University Press, 2003).

—— 'Four Threats to the Presumption of Innocence' (2006) 123 *South African Law Journal* 62–96.

Campbell, T, 'Human Rights: A Culture of Controversy' (1999) 26 *Journal of Law and Society* 6.

Campbell, T, Ewing, KD and Tomkins, A (eds), *Sceptical Essays on Human Rights* (Oxford, Oxford University Press, 2001).

Choo, A, *Evidence* (Oxford, Oxford University Press, 2006).

Dennis, I, 'Reverse Onuses and the Presumption of Innocence: In Search of Principle' (2005) *Criminal Law Review* 901.

Douzinas, C, 'Justice and Human Rights in Postmodernity' in C Gearty and A Tomkins (eds), *Understanding Human Rights* (New York, Mansell, 1996).

Dworkin, R, 'Terror and the Attack on Civil Liberties' (2003) 50(17) *The New York Review of Books* 37.

Emmerson, B and Ashworth, A and Macdonald A, *Human Rights and Criminal Justice* 2nd edn (London, Sweet & Maxwell, 2007).

Foreign and Commonwealth Office (UK), 'Counter-terrorism Legislation and Practice: A Survey of Selected Countries', October 2005, available at www.fco.gov.uk.

Gearty, C, *Can Human Rights Survive?* (Cambridge, Cambridge University Press, 2006).

Halliday, J, 'Making Punishments Work: Report of a Review of the Sentencing Framework for England and Wales' (London, Home Office Communications Directorate, 2001).

House of Commons Home Affairs Committee, *Terrorism Detention Powers*, Fourth Report, 2005–06 (HC 910-1, 2006).

Ignatieff, M, *The Lesser Evil: Political Ethics in an Age of Terrorism* (Princeton, Princeton University Press, 2004).

---

[85] United Nations Siracusa Principles, note 25 above, para 22.

Koji, T, 'Emerging Hierarchy of International Human Rights and Beyond: From the Perspective of Non-derogable Rights' (2001) 2 *European Journal of International Law* 917.

Lazarus, L, *Contrasting Prisoners' Rights: A Comparative Examination of England and Germany* (Oxford, Oxford University Press, 2004).

Lester, A and Beattie, K, 'Risking Torture' (2005) *European Human Rights Law Review* 565.

Luban, D, 'Eight Fallacies about Liberty and Security' in RA Wilson (ed), *Human Rights in the 'War on Terror'* (Cambridge, Cambridge University Press, 2005).

Meron, T, 'On a Hierarchy of International Human Rights' (1986) 80 *American Journal of International Law* 1.

Mowbray, A, *Cases and Materials on the European Convention on Human Rights* (London, Butterworths, 2001).

Roach, K, 'The New Terrorism Offences and the Criminal Law' in RJ Daniels, P Macklem and K Roach (eds), *The Security of Freedom: Essays on Canada's Anti-terrorism Bill* (Toronto, University of Toronto Press, 2002).

Shelton, D, 'Hierarchy of Norms and Human Rights: Of Trumps and Winners' (2002) 65 *Saskatechewan Law Review* 301.

Sieghart, P, *The International Law of Human Rights* (Oxford, Oxford University Press, 1983).

Tomkins, A, 'Introduction' in T Campbell, KD Ewing and A Tomkins (eds), *Sceptical Essays on Human Rights* (Oxford, Oxford University Press, 2001).

—— 'Readings of *A v Secretary of State for the Home Department*' (2005) *Public Law* 259.

Tsoukala, A, 'Democracy against Security: The Debates about Counter-terrorism in the European Parliament, September 2001–June 2003' (2004) 29 *Alternatives* 417.

United Nations, *Siracusa Principles on the Limitation and Derogation of Provisions in the International Covenant on Civil and Political Rights,* UN Doc E/CN.4/1984.4 (1984).

Valverde, M, 'Governing Security, Governing through Security' in RJ Daniels, P Macklem and K Roach (eds), *The Security of Freedom: Essays on Canada's Anti-terrorism Bill* (Toronto, University of Toronto Press, 2002).

van Dijk, P and van Hoof, GJH, *Theory and Practice of the European Convention on Human Rights,* 3rd edn (The Hague, Kluwer, 1999).

van Zyl Smit, D and Ashworth, A, 'Disproportionate Sentences as Human Rights Violations' (2004) 67(4) *Modern Law Review* 541.

Waldron, J, 'Security and Liberty: The Image of Balance' (2003) 11 *Journal of Political Philosophy* 191.

Wilson, RA, 'Human Rights in the "War on Terror"' in RA Wilson (ed), *Human Rights in the 'War on Terror'* (Cambridge, Cambridge University Press, 2005).

Zedner, L, 'Securing Liberty in the Face of Terror: Reflections from Criminal Justice' (2005) 32 *Journal of Law and Society* 507.

10

Sources and Trends in Post-9/11 Anti-terrorism Laws

KENT ROACH*

INTRODUCTION

IN THE FIVE years since the terrorist attacks on the United States, a stagger-ing array of new anti-terrorism laws have been enacted throughout the world.[1] A genealogical examination of the sources of anti-terrorism law may seem to be a premature attempt at history at a time when many countries are still making history with new anti-terrorism initiatives. Nevertheless, excavating the sources of recent anti-terrorism laws may contribute to 'a history of the present'[2] that can reveal how international and domestic organisations often draft anti-terrorism initiatives on the fly. These organisations engage in bricolage with what is at hand,[3] but with limited information about the effects of various measures on security and human rights. In short, the sources used to make anti-terrorism laws can reveal much about their substance. In particular, they can expose the contingent, ques-tionable but not easily reversed choices that have been made with respect to both security and human rights.

In this chapter, I will focus on three influential sources for the anti-terrorism laws found in a number of jurisdictions including Australia, Canada, South Africa, the United Kingdom and the United States. It is possible to focus on only a few sources, in part because there has been a faddish aspect to post-9/11 anti-terrorism laws, with a number of countries following trends established by a small

footnote* The financial assistance of Canada's Social Sciences and Humanities Research Council is gratefully acknowledged, as are helpful comments from the editors and other participants at the Oxford Colloquium on Security and Human Rights and helpful sources and comments provided by EJ Flynn and CH Powell.

[1] See, eg, the country reports submitted to the United Nations Counter-terrorism Committee, avail-able at http://www.un.org/Docs/sc/committees/1373/submitted_reports.html. See also Ramraj, V, Hor, M and Roach, K (eds), *Global Anti-terrorism Law and Policy* (Cambridge, Cambridge University Press, 2005).

[2] Garland, D, *The Culture of Control: Crime and Social Order in Contemporary Society* (Chicago, University of Chicago Press, 2001) ch 1.

[3] Tushnet, M, 'The Possibilities of Comparative Constitutional Law' (1999) 108 *Yale Law Journal* 1225.

number of influential international and domestic instruments. In some instances, the directions set by influential sources of anti-terrorism law already seem dated even though it has been only five years since the new wave of anti-terrorism laws was launched.

The first source to be examined, and the most influential, is Security Council Resolution (SCR) 1373, adopted by the United Nations Security Council on 28 September 2001. This Resolution stipulates that all states shall prevent and suppress the financing of terrorist acts and called upon them to become parties to the International Convention for the Suppression of the Financing of Terrorism (1999). Resolution 1373 was also influential in drawing a link between immigration and anti-terrorism law by calling on all states to ensure that refugee status was not abused by terrorists.

When the Security Council decided with SCR 1373 to focus on the financing of terrorism and the danger that refugee law would be abused by terrorists, it was acting with limited information about the causes of 9/11 and the terrorist threat. The US 9/11 Commission Report, released in 2004, revealed significant limits on the ability of financing laws to prevent even massive acts of terrorism like 9/11, let alone the smaller and less expensive bombings in Bali, Madrid and London. It also revealed that the 9/11 hijackers entered the United States in a variety of ways, none of which included claims of asylum.[4] The UK House of Lords in its first Belmarsh case[5] has also subsequently revealed the dangers for both human rights and security of relying on immigration law as anti-terrorism law.

Resolution 1373 has been extremely influential but does not provide any guidance about the proper definition of terrorism. For such guidance many states have turned to the definition of terrorism in the UK Terrorism Act 2000.[6] The UK definition was taken as a starting point despite the fact that it is much broader than previous definitions of terrorism in UK or international law and that it goes well beyond what is required to respond to Al Qaeda's murder and maiming of civilians. This use of the UK law has attracted widespread concern in many democracies that dissenters could be caught in the broad definition of terrorism. The influence of UK anti-terrorism law, especially in its former colonies, is an important factor to consider as UK anti-terrorism law continues to grow.

The third influential source of anti-terrorism law is SCR 1624, adopted by the UN Security Council on 14 September 2005. It calls upon all states 'to counter incitement of terrorist acts motivated by extremism and intolerance and to prevent the subversion of educational, cultural, and religious institutions by terrorists and supporters'. This recent resolution has already borne fruit in terms of new laws enacted in Australia in 2005 targeting speech that praises terrorism [7] and new offences in the UK Terrorism Act 2006[8] against speech and publications that

---

[4] National Commission on Terrorist Attacks upon the United States, *The 9/11 Report* (New York, St Martins Press, 2004).

[5] *A and Others v Secretary of State for the Home Department* [2004] UKHL 56.

[6] Chapter 11.

[7] Anti-terrorism Act (No 2) 2005, No 144, 2005, Parts 5.1 and 5.3.

[8] Chapter 11, ss 1–3.

directly or indirectly encourage terrorism. The trend to criminalise speech associated with terrorism has obvious human rights implications, but it is also possible that in a few years, the effectiveness of laws targeting speech in promoting security will begin to be questioned in much the same manner as laws against the financing of terrorism, the use of immigration law as anti-terrorism law or broad definitions of terrorism. All of these previous trends have been revealed to have limited effectiveness in preventing terrorism while having adverse impacts on human rights .

Trends in anti-terrorism laws, unlike trends in fashion, do not fade away. They build and feed on each other. The new emphasis in SCR 1624 on speech and extremism reflects the failure of past initiatives, including the focus on the financing of terrorism and the use of immigration law as anti-terrorism law in SCR 1373. In other words, laws against the financing of terrorism and the use of immigration law as anti-terrorism law were unable to stop low-cost acts of terrorism such as the 2005 London bombings. The new response seems to be to focus on terrorist speech, while not rethinking the previous strategies that failed to prevent terrorism. New offences of incitement or encouragement of terrorism will aggravate the danger of overbroad definitions of terrorism taken from the Terrorism Act 2000, which include politically motivated property damage or disruptions of essential services. New incitement offences will also be applied in a context in which many Western states have, through the use of immigration laws and other measures, focused on Arab and Muslim communities as likely sources of terrorism.

The limited sources and trends of post-9/11 anti-terrorism law raise the issue of what corrective measures can be taken to prevent additional misguided trends in anti-terrorism laws and to re-evaluate old trends. One response would be to ensure pre-enactment scrutiny of Security Council Resolutions and other instruments that are likely to become influential sources for anti-terrorism laws throughout the world. In this respect, some pre-enactment scrutiny with a focus on compliance with human rights is carried out before the enactment of UK anti-terrorism legislation, but little pre-enactment scrutiny seems to take place before the United Nations Security Council enacts influential resolutions that require or encourage the enactment of anti-terrorism laws. In addition, compliance with these resolutions is monitored by a Counter-terrorism Committee (CTC) that has not seen human rights as within its mandate. The CTC should pay greater attention to the impact that the anti-terrorism laws it encourages has on human rights. Another corrective measure to the trendy nature of post-9/11 anti-terrorism laws may be to include 'sunset provisions' that would require anti-terrorism strategies to be re-evaluated in light of their effectiveness and their effects on human rights. Finally and most importantly, independent adjudicative bodies have a special role in evaluating and invalidating anti-terrorism trends that violate human rights and are not effective in preventing terrorism.

I. SECURITY COUNCIL RESOLUTION 1373
AND THE FINANCING OF TERRORISM

Resolution 1373 was adopted by the United Nations Security Council on 28 September 2001. Although longer informal negotiations had undoubtedly already taken place, it took only five minutes during a formal meeting for the momentous Resolution to be unanimously approved by all 15 members of the Security Council.[9] Given its influence as an important source for post-9/11 anti-terrorism laws, its operative provisions will be quoted at some length:

Acting under Chapter VII of the Charter of the United Nations, [the Security Council]

1. Decides that all States shall:

(a) Prevent and suppress the financing of terrorist acts;
(b) Criminalize the wilful provision or collection, by any means, directly or indirectly, of funds by their nationals or in their territories with the intention that the funds should be used, or in the knowledge that they are to be used, in order to carry out terrorist acts;
(c) Freeze without delay funds and other financial assets or economic resources of persons who commit, or attempt to commit, terrorist acts or participate in or facilitate the commission of terrorist acts; of entities owned or controlled directly or indirectly by such persons; and of persons and entities acting on behalf of, or at the direction of such persons and entities, including funds derived or generated from property owned or controlled directly or indirectly by such persons and associated persons and entities;
(d) Prohibit their nationals or any persons and entities within their territories from making any funds, financial assets or economic resources or financial or other related services available, directly or indirectly, for the benefit of persons who commit or attempt to commit or facilitate or participate in the commission of terrorist acts, of entities owned or controlled, directly or indirectly, by such persons and of persons and entities acting on behalf of or at the direction of such persons;

2. Decides also that all States shall:

(a) Refrain from providing any form of support, active or passive, to entities or persons involved in terrorist acts, including by suppressing recruitment of members of terrorist groups and eliminating the supply of weapons to terrorists;
(b) Take the necessary steps to prevent the commission of terrorist acts, including by provision of early warning to other States by exchange of information;
(c) Deny safe haven to those who finance, plan, support, or commit terrorist acts, or provide safe havens;
(d) Prevent those who finance, plan, facilitate or commit terrorist acts from using their respective territories for those purposes against other States or their citizens;

---

[9] United Nations Security Council Minutes, 28 September 2001, S/PV/4385.

(e) Ensure that any person who participates in the financing, planning, preparation or perpetration of terrorist acts or in supporting terrorist acts is brought to justice and ensure that, in addition to any other measures against them, such terrorist acts are established as serious criminal offences in domestic laws and regulations and that the punishment duly reflects the seriousness of such terrorist acts;

(f) Afford one another the greatest measure of assistance in connection with criminal investigations or criminal proceedings relating to the financing or support of terrorist acts, including assistance in obtaining evidence in their possession necessary for the proceedings;

(g) Prevent the movement of terrorists or terrorist groups by effective border controls and controls on issuance of identity papers and travel documents, and through measures for preventing counterfeiting, forgery or fraudulent use of identity papers and travel documents. . .;

The Resolution also created a Counter-terrorism Committee (CTC) to monitor its implementation and called upon all states to report to the new Committee no later than 90 days after the Resolution. In a number of countries, including Canada and the United Kingdom, this short reporting deadline was taken as a virtual deadline for the enactment of new anti-terrorism laws.[10] Although many countries have at various times enacted anti-terrorism laws in a hurry in response to acts of terrorism, the effects of the SCR 1373 reporting requirement in encouraging rushed enactment of anti-terrorism laws in jurisdictions that did not experience acts of terrorism should not be ignored. Neither should the continued influence of the CTC, which has frequently asked formal questions about each state's compliance with the Resolution; most states have submitted multiple reports to the Committee.[11]

There are repeated references to the financing of terrorism in SCR 1373. Indeed the first paragraph is devoted entirely to preventing the financing and funding of terrorist acts. It creates the impression that terrorism is not so much the weapon of the weak but the weapon of those who receive extensive financing. The second paragraph focuses more on the prevention and criminalisation of terrorist acts, but even in that paragraph, there are repeated references to the financing of terrorism.

Why did the United Nations place such great emphasis on the prevention of the financing of terrorism in the immediate aftermath of 9/11? One factor may have been suspicions that the mastermind of the 9/11 attacks was Osama bin Laden, a reputed financier of terrorism.[12] In 1999, the Security Council had issued SCR

---

[10] Anti-terrorism Act SC 2001 (c 41); Anti-terrorism, Crime and Security Act 2001 (c 24). On the legislative history of these laws see Roach, K, *September 11: Consequences for Canada* (Montreal, McGill Queens Press, 2003); Walker, C, *Blackstone's Guide to the Anti-terrorism Legislation* (Oxford, Oxford University Press, 2002).

[11] For example, Australia has filed six reports with the Committee; Canada, South Africa and the United Kingdom have each filed five reports. See http://www.un.org/Docs/sc/ ommittees/1373/c.htm.

[12] The 9/11 Commission found that Osama bin Laden's fortune had been seriously overestimated. See National Commission on Terrorist Attacks (2004) 5.4.

1267, which among other matters called for the Taliban to hand over bin Laden, who had been indicted in connection with the 1998 bombings of US embassies in Kenya and Tanzania, and to freeze various assets associated with the Taliban. Like SCR 1373, SCR 1267 created its own committee to consider reports from states on compliance with the Resolution. In 2000, the Security Council issued SCR 1333, which attempted to freeze bin Laden's funds and assets and those of associated individuals and entities.[13] Efforts both to list terrorists and to prohibit financial dealings with them were an established part of UN procedures before the 9/11 terrorist attacks.[14] These Resolutions, however, were not mentioned in SCR 1373, perhaps in recognition of their failure to prevent 9/11.

Another reason why SCR 1373 focused on the financing of terrorism is found in paragraph 3(d), which calls upon states to 'become parties as soon as possible to the relevant international conventions and protocols relating to terrorism, including the International Convention for the Suppression of the Financing of Terrorism of 9 December 1999'.[15] This Convention was at the time the most recent convention on terrorism. Although it had been signed by a number of countries before 9/11, including Canada, the United States and the United Kingdom, it had been ratified by only a few states, including the United Kingdom. The Security Council had an interest in promoting the financing convention and did so despite evidence that attempts to starve Al Qaeda of funds had not worked in the past.

The quickest responses to SCR 1373 in Australia, Canada and the United Kingdom were the promulgation of regulations under existing United Nations Acts that incorporated or built on the listing process started by the 1267 Committee.[16] The use of subordinate legislation facilitated quick compliance with SCR 1373 while avoiding the controversies that accompanied the enactment of new anti-terrorism laws in all these countries—even though the regulations that were enacted often mirrored the new anti-terrorism laws in prohibiting financial dealings with listed persons and placing obligations on various individuals to report any such dealings.

Laws against the financing of terrorism can only be enforced by placing positive duties on institutions and individuals to report suspected financial dealings with terrorists to the appropriate authorities. In this sense, laws against the financing of terrorism fit well into modern security and policing strategies in which there are often more private than public police, and the state governs indirectly by requiring individuals and organisations to monitor and report on risky activities. At the same time, however, anti-terrorism financing strategies are generally not adopted voluntarily or willingly by individuals, who instead often comply on pain of a

---

[13] SCR 1333 at para 8(c).

[14] For a list of various SCRs relating to the work of the 1267 Committee see http://www.un.org/Docs/sc/committees/1267/1267ResEng.htm.

[15] Available at http://untreaty.un.org/English/Terrorism/Conv12.pdf.

[16] United Nations Suppression of Terrorism Regulations, SOR/2001-360 (2 October 2001); Terrorism (United Nations Measures) Order 2001, SI 2001 No 3365 (10 October 2001); Charter of the United Nations (Anti-terrorism Measures) Statutory Rule No 297 of 2001 (8 October 2001).

conviction of a serious criminal terrorist offence. For example, section 19 of the Terrorism Act 2000 places duties on those engaged in a trade, profession, business or employment to report both beliefs and suspicions relating to terrorist fund-raising and money laundering to the police or a designated person in their company. Breach of those duties is an offence under the Terrorism Act subject to five years' imprisonment. Although there are provisions for lawyer–client privilege, section 20(2) of the Act permits disclosure notwithstanding any other law restricting disclosure.

Although the United Kingdom was one of the few countries to have ratified the 1999 Convention on the Financing of Terrorism before 9/11, this did not stop the United Kingdom from enacting its own legislative response to 9/11 within the 90-day reporting timeline set by SCR 1373. The Anti-terrorism, Crime and Security Act 2001[17] expanded the reporting requirements of the Terrorism Act 2000 with respect to various regulated sectors.[18] Moreover, it created a general duty to report information that a person knows or believes will prevent an act of terrorism or assist in its apprehension, prosecution or conviction.[19] The latter amendment revived and extended a controversial provision in section 18 of the Prevention of Terrorism (Temporary Provisions) Act 1989 that applied to all acts of terrorism. The already controversial strategy of requiring the co-operation of private authorities with respect to the financing of terrorism extended to a more general and even more divisive provision for the reporting of all information about terrorism.[20]

Canada's Anti-terrorism Act, enacted within 90 days of SCR 1373, featured several broad offences against the financing of terrorism and amended money-laundering legislation to include the financing of terrorism. The latter legislation places special reporting obligations on various financial institutions, and the former places a specific duty on all Canadians to report knowledge about terrorist-owned property to the heads of the national police force and the civilian security intelligence agency.[21] Concerns have been raised that the Canadian provisions may be in tension with human rights because they make no exceptions for access to legal or other necessary services.[22] There are also fears that terrorist-financing laws may have a disproportionate effect on Muslim charities in Canada and elsewhere.

In its 2004 report, the 9/11 Commission reached some significant conclusions that suggest that the United Nations and countries following SCR 1373 may have placed too much faith in measures aimed at the financing of terrorism as a means of preventing terrorism. The 9/11 Commission found that the 9/11 plotters spent US$400,000–$500,000 on the plot and that they 'moved, stored, and spent their money in ordinary ways, easily defeating the detection mechanisms at the time.

---

[17] Chapter 24.

[18] *Ibid*, Sch 2.

[19] *Ibid*, s 117, adding s 38B to the Terrorism Act 2000.

[20] Walker (2002) 108–16.

[21] Criminal Code of Canada, s 83.1 as amended by the Anti-terrorism Act SC 2001 (c 41).

[22] Davis, K, 'The Financial War Against Terrorism' in V Ramraj, M Hor and K Roach (eds), *Global Anti-terrorism Law and Policy* (Cambridge, Cambridge University Press, 2005) 185.

The origins of the funds remain unknown'.[23] It expressed considerable scepticism about the ability of financing laws and practices of the type contemplated by SCR 1373 to prevent future acts of terrorism like 9/11. It concluded that 'if a particular funding source had dried up, Al Qaeda could have easily tapped a different source or diverted funds from another project'[24] and that 'trying to starve the terrorists of money is like trying to catch one kind of fish by draining the ocean'.[25] The pessimism of the 9/11 Commission regarding the possibility of preventing terrorism through the blocking of terrorist financing is only increased by estimates that the post-9/11 Bali bombings cost US$15,000–$35,000, the Madrid bombings cost about US$15,000 and the London bombings were even less expensive to carry out.[26]

In addition to concerns about the effectiveness of laws aimed at the financing of terrorism, there are also concerns about their effects on human rights. Many countries, including Australia, Canada, South Africa and the United Kingdom, followed the United Nations in creating various mechanisms that allow the executive to produce lists of terrorist groups and associated individuals and entities as a means of facilitating the enforcement of laws against the financing of terrorism. Such lists have been criticised as bills of attainder because they allow individuals to be declared outlaws by legislative or executive as opposed to judicial acts.[27] In some cases, individuals have been wrongly added to lists, a fact that is unsurprising given the absence of adversarial hearings or challenges of evidence before a person is listed either domestically or internationally as a terrorist.[28] The effects of an error in listing (including problems caused by common names) can be devastating because it is unlawful for almost anyone to associate with or have dealings with a listed person.

The emphasis placed on preventing the financing of terrorism in SCR 1373 was not the result of informed analysis of either the causes of 9/11 or the effectiveness of laws prohibiting the financing of terrorism. Indeed, the Security Council enacted SCR 1373 with a blinding speed that eclipsed the enactment of post-9/11 anti-terrorism laws in the United States, the United Kingdom and Canada. The United Nations had its own institutional reasons for promoting measures against the financing of terrorism. The Security Council, like domestic bodies struggling

---

[23] National Commission on Terrorist Attacks (2004) 5.4.

[24] *Ibid.*

[25] *Ibid,* 12.3.

[26] 'Looking in the Wrong Places' *The Economist,* 20 October 2005, available at http://www.economist.com/displaystory.cfm?story_id=5053373.

[27] Dyzenhaus, D, 'The Rule of (Administrative) Law in International Law' (2005) 68 *Law and Contemporary Problems* 127, 141–53. See also Powell, CH, 'Terrorism and the Separation of Powers in the National and International Spheres' (2005) 18 *South African Journal of Criminal Justice* 151, who also makes the point that the listing process augments executive power in both domestic and international politics.

[28] For an account of how a Canadian man, Liban Hussein, was wrongly placed on both the United Nations and Canadian lists, see Dosman, EA, 'For the Record: Designating "Listed Entities" for the Purposes of Terrorist Financing Offences at Canadian Law' (2004) 62 *University of Toronto Faculty of Law Review* 1.

to do something to reassure the public,[29] engaged in a form of bricolage, relying on the 1999 Convention and the SCR 1267 process as starting points, despite the fact that the latter process did not and probably could not have prevented 9/11.

Reliance on what is at hand may result in measures that are not optimal nor even effective for the prevention of acts of terrorism. The consequences of error are particularly great when the Security Council acts under Chapter VII because all 192 UN member states will be under pressure to follow its lead down what may be the wrong path. Having started down such a path, both the Security Council and member states may be reluctant to retreat. The CTC continues to question member states about their efforts to comply with SCR 1373's financing provisions, and many states have established laws and institutions in order to satisfy the Resolution.

II. SECURITY COUNCIL RESOLUTION 1373 AND THE USE OF IMMIGRATION LAW AS ANTI-TERRORISM LAW

In addition to its focus on the financing of terrorism, SCR 1373 also makes specific mention of immigration law. Paragraph 2(g) makes reference to the need for 'effective border controls' to 'prevent the movement of terrorists or terrorist groups', and paragraph 3 provides that all states should:

(f) Take appropriate measures in conformity with the relevant provisions of national and international law, including international standards of human rights, before granting refugee status, for the purpose of ensuring that the asylum seeker has not planned, facilitated or participated in the commission of terrorist acts;

(g) Ensure, in conformity with international law, that refugee status is not abused by the perpetrators, organizers or facilitators of terrorist acts, and that claims of political motivation are not recognized as grounds for refusing requests for the extradition of alleged terrorists . . .

The reference to border controls and identity papers in the Resolution is understandable given that the 9/11 hijackers entered the United States with a variety of visas. On the other hand, the singling out of refugee status for special attention is more troubling. None of the 9/11 hijackers had applied for refugee status, which normally attracts increased scrutiny of the applicant's history, including any involvement in political or terrorist organisations. Although there are some examples of Al Qaeda terrorists applying for refugee status,[30] it is far from clear why SCR 1373 singled out refugee applicants as possible security threats.

---

[29] On the need to reassure the public in the aftermath of acts of terrorism see Ackerman, B, 'The Emergency Constitution' (2004) 113 *Yale Law Journal* 1029.

[30] An oft-cited case is that of Ahmed Ressam, who applied but was denied asylum in Canada before being apprehended at the Canadian–US border with a Canadian passport obtained with a stolen baptismal certificate and with plans and materials to bomb the Los Angeles Airport at the Millennium. See National Commission on Terrorist Attacks (2004) 6.1

Immigration law was also featured in one of the ten parts of the USA PATRIOT Act. The amendments provided for increased vigilance in 'protecting the Northern Border', something that responded to widespread but false claims that the 9/11 plotters had entered the United States from Canada.[31] This again illustrates the dangers of making security policy on the fly. In the immediate aftermath of 9/11 the United States also made widespread use of immigration law to detain suspects of terrorism, who were subject to closed hearings, denied access to counsel, and detained and removed on the basis of expressive and associational activities. However, few, if any, genuine terrorism charges emerged from the immigration law detentions.[32] Expedited removal proceedings under US immigration law were used in 2002 to detain and remove Maher Arar to Syria on the basis of a conclusion that he was a member of Al Qaeda. A recent Canadian inquiry determined that Mr Arar was subsequently tortured in Syria before eventually being released. The inquiry also found that the US process relied on inaccurate information provided by Canadian officials and that there was no evidence that Mr Arar was guilty of any terrorism-related offence or was a threat to national security.[33]

Until the June 2006 arrest of 17 persons on criminal charges under the Anti-terrorism Act 2001, Canada relied almost exclusively on immigration law as anti-terrorism law in a manner that threatened both human rights and security. For example, five non-citizens, all Muslim men from Arab countries, have been subject to indeterminate detention under security certificates under allegations that they are associated with Al Qaeda.[34] It is much easier for Canadian authorities to detain a person under immigration law than under the criminal law. For example, non-citizens can be rendered inadmissible on the basis not only that they have engaged in terrorism, but also that they are a danger to the security of Canada or are 'member[s] of an organization that there are reasonable grounds to believe engages, has engaged or will engage' in terrorism.[35] Under Canada's Anti-terrorism Act, the liability rules are more restrained in part because a deliberate choice was made not to follow the UK example of criminalising membership in a terrorist group and because various intent requirements were added to terrorism offences to ensure their constitutionality under Canada's Charter of Rights and Freedoms.

Canadian immigration law has not only broader liability rules but a much lower standard of proof than the criminal law. Under immigration law, all that is

[31] Roach (2003) 5–6.
[32] The Department of Homeland Security claimed that the Special Registration Program had identified eight suspected terrorists, but none of these were charged: Cole, D, *Enemy Aliens* (New York, New Press, 2003) 26.
[33] Commission of Inquiry into the Actions of Canadian Officials in Relation to Maher Arar, *Report Relating to the Events Relating to Maher Arar Factual Background*, vol 1 (Ottawa, Public Works and Government Services, 2006) 204ff.
[34] Roach, K, 'Canada's Response to Terrorism' in V Ramraj, M Hor and K Roach (eds), *Global Anti-terrorism Law and Policy* (Cambridge, Cambridge University Press, 2005).
[35] Immigration and Refugee Protection Act SC 2001 (c 27), s 34(1).

required to be proven is that 'there are reasonable grounds to believe' that the facts that give rise to inadmissibility 'have occurred, are occurring or may occur'.[36] This standard has been interpreted by the courts to be less than the civil standard of balance of probabilities, requiring only a serious possibility that the facts exist based on reliable, credible evidence.[37] In contrast, a Canadian criminal trial judge affirmed the high standard of proof beyond a reasonable doubt as 'the essence of the Rule of Law', which 'cannot be applied any less vigorously in cases of horrific crimes'[38] when in 2005 he acquitted two men charged with the murder of 329 people in the 1985 terrorist bombing of an Air India plane.

Canadian state officials also have an enhanced ability to protect the confidentiality of intelligence in immigration as opposed to criminal proceedings. The Canadian immigration security certificate process allows the state to present evidence to the reviewing judge without the presence of detainees or their lawyers. A judge can use information that if disclosed would injure national security or the safety of any person to determine the reasonableness of a security certificate but is prohibited from including any such information in a summary of the information that is provided to the detainee.[39]

In 1992, the Supreme Court upheld a predecessor provision under the Canadian Charter of Rights and Freedoms on the basis that the detainee can learn through the edited summary the substance of the charges and that the state had a legitimate interest in protecting intelligence methods and sources from disclosure.[40] In late 2004, the Federal Court of Appeal also upheld the security certificate process from Charter challenge, stating that while the judge's use of evidence that was not disclosed to the detainee 'derogates in a significant way from the adversarial process normally adhered to in criminal and civil matters', it was justified by the judge's 'pro-active role in the interest of ensuring fairness' and the security interests of society as a whole.[41] The Canadian Supreme Court recently reversed this decision, holding that the security certificate process did not allow the affected persons to know the case against them or adversarial challenge of the secret intelligence that the government presented to the judge.[42] The Court has given Parliament a year to reform the process by for example allowing security-cleared special advocates but it did not nullify existing or new security certificates.

The broad liability rules, low standards of proof and low disclosure standards used in Canadian immigration law raise the question of whether innocence can survive as a meaningful concept when immigration law is used as anti-terrorism

[36] *Ibid,* s 33.
[37] *Charkaoui v Canada* [2004] FCA 421 at para 73; *Chiau v Canada* [2001] 2 FC 207, 209 (FCA).
[38] *R v Malik and Bagri* [2005] BCSC 350 at paras 662, 1254.
[39] Immigration and Refugee Protection Act SC 2001 (c 27), s 78(g), (h).
[40] *Canada (Minister of Employment and Immigration) v Chiarelli* [1992] 1 SCR 711.
[41] *Charkaoui v Canada* 2004 FCA 421 at paras 75, 80, 84.
[42] *Charkaoui v Canada* 2007 SCC 9. In *Hamdan v Rumsfeld* 548 US (2006), the United States Supreme Court stressed that military commissions used at Guantanamo Bay violated domestic and international law because they allowed the government to introduce evidence in the absence of the detainee and his lawyer in order to protect intelligence sources and methods and other national security interests.

law. The UK experience of wrongful convictions of suspected IRA terrorists in the 1970s serves as an important reminder of the dangers of misidentification of people as terrorists. Not only was the reputation of UK administration of justice and anti-terrorism efforts tarnished, but such miscarriages caused grievous harms to the innocent and allowed the guilty to go free.

A number of these wrongful convictions were eventually overturned in the 1990s on the basis of new evidence,[43] but it is doubtful whether immigration detentions and removals can be identified as miscarriages of justice in the same way as criminal convictions can be identified as wrongful. The allegation in immigration cases will often not be that a person has planned or participated in a specific act of terrorism but rather that he or she is a member or supporter of a terrorist group. It is far more difficult to disprove the latter allegation than the former,[44] and any standard of review will incorporate deference to the executive as well as the lower standard of proof. Indeed, it is even possible that a court could conclude that, although an immigration law detainee is not in fact a member or supporter of a terrorist group, the initial decision-maker nevertheless had a reasonable basis for such a conclusion.[45]

Maher Arar's expedited immigration removal from the United States to Syria on the mistaken and inaccurate basis that he was member of Al Qaeda is an example of a post-9/11 miscarriage of justice. This miscarriage of justice was revealed only after a multi-year and multi-million-dollar judicial inquiry in Canada, which was hindered by the refusal of US and Syrian officials to participate in the inquiry. It is likely that many other post-9/11 miscarriages of justice will never come to light because of the broad nature of allegations concerning support for and membership of terrorist groups, and the secrecy of many national security proceedings.

Attempts to question the reliability of information used in immigration detention cases by questioning the sources and methods used may be stymied by claims that such information cannot be disclosed because of national security concerns. Innocent errors such as mistaken eyewitness identification and culpable errors such as unreliable information obtained through torture or extreme interrogation techniques may go undetected, in part because the state is allowed to protect its sources and methods for reasons of national security.[46] Even under the UK system of security-cleared special advocates, there is a danger that special advocates will not appreciate problems with the credibility and motivation of sources because of restrictions on their ability to convey classified information to detainees.

Part IV of the UK's Anti-terrorism, Crime and Security Act 2001 derogated from fair trial rights in order to provide for the indeterminate detention of non-

---

[43] *R v McIlkenny* (1991) 93 Crim App R 287; *R v Maguire* (1992) 94 Crim App R 133; *R v Ward* (1993) 96 Crim App R 51.

[44] As Lord Hoffmann has observed, 'suspicion of being a supporter is one thing and proof of wrongdoing is another': *A and Others v Secretary of State for the Home Department* [2004] UKHL 56, para 87.

[45] Stewart, H, 'Is Indefinite Detention of Terrorist Suspects Really Constitutional?' (2005) 54 *University of New Brunswick Law Journal* 235.

[46] Roach, K and Trotter, G, 'Miscarriages of Justice in the War Against Terror' (2005) 109 *Penn State Law Review* 967, 988ff.

citizen terrorist suspects who could not be deported because of concerns that they would be tortured. This provision and the derogation from the European Convention on Human Rights (ECHR) received criticism in part because the United Kingdom was the only nation in Europe to derogate from the ECHR.[47] The derogation was held by the House of Lords in late 2004 to be disproportionate and discriminatory. Many of the Law Lords stressed that some terrorist suspects are citizens,[48] a fact that was tragically affirmed by the London bombings in July 2005. A report on the London bombings has revealed that the intelligence community was slow to recognise that the terrorist threat was not confined to non-citizens.[49]

The use of immigration law as anti-terrorism law may in fact provide terrorist groups with incentives to recruit citizens to commit acts of terrorism. The immigration law shortcut may prevent investigators and prosecutors from developing the procedures that are needed to withstand the rigours of criminal prosecutions with their demands for full disclosure and proof beyond a reasonable doubt. Conversely, reliance on immigration law may prevent the criminal trial process from adjusting to the demands of terrorism by modifying rules of disclosure to protect national security confidentiality.[50]

The ultimate aim of immigration law is removal, not punishment, and this is not an optimal disposition given the international nature of much modern terrorism. This flaw was underlined in *A* by the fact that two of the eight appellants had agreed to leave the United Kingdom for Morocco and France respectively. Lord Bingham therefore concluded:

> The choice of an immigration measure to address a security problem had the inevitable result of failing adequately to address the problem (by allowing non-United Kingdom suspected terrorists to leave the country with impunity and leaving British suspected terrorists at large) while imposing the severe penalty of indefinite detention on persons who, even if reasonably suspected of having links with al Qaeda, may harbour no hostile intentions towards the United Kingdom.[51]

The immigration law remedies of removal or deflection may often displace terrorism rather than stop it, and for this reason it is especially strange that the UN in SCR 1373 placed such an emphasis on using the limited tools of immigration law as a response to international terrorism.

The references to immigration law in SCR 1373 are also notable because they include the only mention in the entire Resolution of international human rights

---

[47] Tomkins, A, 'Legislating against Terror Law' (2002) *Public Law* 205; Fenwick, H, 'The Anti-terrorism, Crime and Security Act' (2002) 65 *Modern Law Review* 724.

[48] *A and Others v Secretary of State for the Home Department* [2004] UKHL 56 at para 32.

[49] Intelligence and Security Committee, *Report into the London Terrorist Attacks on 7 July 2005*, Cm 6785, May 2006, paras 92 and 108.

[50] Lord Newton, Chair, *Anti-terrorism, Crime and Security Act 2001 Review Report*, 18 December 2003, at para 241, suggesting the need for 'a more structured disclosure process that is better designed to allow the reconciliation of the needs of national security with the rights of the accused to a fair trial'. In Canada, there are complex provisions to protect national security confidentiality that can fracture and prolong criminal trials. See Roach, K, 'Did September 11 Change Everything?' (2002) 47 *McGill Law Journal* 893, 931–2.

[51] *A and Others v Secretary of State for the Home Department* [2004] UKHL 56, para 43.

law. Paragraph 3(f) directs states to act 'in conformity with the relevant provisions of national and international law, including international standards of human rights, before granting refugee status'. This raises the important question of whether respect for international human rights can be an effective restraint on a state's anti-terrorism activities. As discussed above, the United Kingdom accepted that it could not deport a non-citizen to face torture but responded by derogating from fair trial rights to authorise the indefinite detention of non-citizens who could not be deported. Although Parliament repealed this provision in light of the House of Lords decision in *A*, it immediately followed up by enacting the Prevention of Terrorism Act 2005,[52] which allows strict control orders—including those that derogate from rights to liberty under Article 5 of the ECHR—to be placed on citizens and non-citizens alike who are reasonably suspected of terrorism.[53] The government is also trying to obtain assurances that will allow it to deport terrorist suspects to countries with dubious human rights records.

Although control orders and assurances are less drastic measures than indeterminate detention or candid deportation to torture, the end result of this dialogue about rights suggests that respect for international human rights has not proven to be inconsistent with robust crime control activities. The willingness to question basic rights such as the rights against torture or rights against indeterminate detention has some undesirable effects, including making alternative measures seem better than they are simply because they are less restrictive or less rights-invasive. For example, reliance on assurances that countries with poor human rights records will not engage in torture is better than candid deportation to torture, but it is still a very dangerous measure that could result in torture or harsh treatment. Similarly, control orders restrict liberty less than indeterminate detention, but they still can constitute severe and long-term restrictions on liberty.

In Canada, the right against torture has played out differently than in the United Kingdom. The 2002 Supreme Court case *Suresh v Canada* addressed the question of whether the deportation of someone considered a security threat to another state where there would be a substantial risk of torture violates the Canadian Charter. The Court examined international law including international human rights law in detail and found that the prohibition of torture was a peremptory norm of international law that should prevail over Article 33(2) of the Refugee Convention, which had been read by lower courts in Canada as depriving those found to be security threats of the benefits of non-refoulement.[54]

Although the Court resolved ambiguities in international law in favour of the right against torture, it also went out of its way to leave open the possibility that deportation to torture might be constitutional in Canada under undefined 'excep-

---

[52] Chapter 2.

[53] The independent reviewer has reported that 17 of the first 18 persons subject to control orders are non-citizens: Lord Carlile, *First Report of the Independent Reviewer Pursuant to Section 14(3) of the Prevention of Terrorism Act 2005*, 2 February 2006, para 18. The Court of Appeal has subsequently held that six of the control orders derogate from Art 5 of the ECHR and are invalid because no formal derogation has been entered: see *Secretary of State v JJ et al* [2006] EWCA Civ 1141.

[54] *Suresh v Canada* [2002] 1 SCR 3 at paras 59–75.

tional circumstances'.[55] It also indicated that courts should only reverse the minister's decision that a person would not face a substantial risk of torture if it was patently unreasonable, and other Canadian courts have refused to stay deportations to countries such as Iran to allow the person to bring proceedings before the United Nations Human Rights Committee.[56] The Canadian experience suggests that even a country that prides itself on being a good international citizen[57] may not respect international human rights norms, while the UK experience suggests that respect for the right against torture may inspire questionable detention and deportation practices.

In summary, SCR 1373 has been influential in singling out immigration and especially refugee law as anti-terrorism law. Post-9/11 legislation in both the United States and the United Kingdom amended immigration laws to facilitate the detention of suspected terrorists. Other countries such as Canada and New Zealand[58] used existing immigration laws to detain terrorist suspects. The UK House of Lords decision in *A*, however, has raised serious questions about the use of immigration law as anti-terrorism law, with respect to both security and human rights. With respect to security, the House of Lords has questioned whether the deportation of suspected terrorists to other countries is an effective remedy against international terrorism, and it presciently pointed out that the terrorist threat is not limited to non-citizens. With respect to human rights, the House of Lords rightly affirmed the grave dangers of indeterminate detention without trial and will soon have to consider whether restrictive control orders require a derogation from the right to liberty.

There are some parallels between the House of Lords' pessimism about attempts to stop international terrorism through immigration law and the 9/11 Commission's pessimism about attempts to prevent terrorism through laws against the financing of terrorism. Both anti-terrorism strategies were promoted by SCR 1373, and both trends are questionable with respect to both protecting human rights and security. The two main pillars of SCR 1373—the focus on terrorism financing and immigration law—already appear outdated and ineffective, despite the fact that this momentous Resolution was only enacted five short years ago.

---

[55] *Ibid*, para 78.

[56] *Ahani v Canada* [2002] 1 SCR 78 (upholding decision to deport to Iran); *Ahani v Canada* (2002) 58 OR (3d) 107 (CA) (refusing to grant stay); *Ahani v Canada* UN Doc CCPR/C/80/D/105/2002 (UN Human Rights Committee) (2004) (criticising Canada's decision not to respect the Committee's interim measures). See generally Roach, K, 'Constitutional, Remedial and International Dialogues about Rights: The Canadian Experience' (2005) 40 *Texas International Law Journal* 537.

[57] Welsh, J, *At Home in the World: Canada's Global Vision for the 21st Century* (Toronto, Harper Collins, 2004).

[58] *Zaoui v New Zealand* [2005] NZSC 38.

III. THE INFLUENCE OF THE BROAD DEFINITION OF TERRORISM IN THE UK TERRORISM ACT 2000

Resolution 1373 did not address the fundamental question of what constitutes terrorism, and a special rapporteur on human rights and terrorism has recently criticised the CTC, which was established by SCR 1373, for demonstrating little interest in how countries define terrorism, despite the danger that over-broad definitions pose for human rights.[59] In the absence of any guidance about how to define terrorism in SCR 1373 or from the CTC, many countries have looked to the broad definition of terrorism contained in the United Kingdom's Terrorism Act 2000[60] as the starting point for their post-9/11 anti-terrorism laws.

Section 1 of the Terrorism Act 2000 defines terrorism as actions or threats of actions involving serious violence, danger to a person, serious risk to public health or safety, serious damage to property or serious disruption of an electronic system if they are 'designed to influence the government or to intimidate the public or a section of a public; and the use or threat is made for the purpose of advancing a political, religious or ideological cause'. The prohibited acts are broadly defined in an attempt to include modern forms of biological, chemical and cyber-terrorism.[61] The idea that politically motivated property destruction constitutes terrorism, however, is questionable from a human rights perspective, especially because there is no exemption for protests or strikes.[62] The definition of terrorism in the Terrorism Act 2000 is significantly broader than prior definitions of terrorism in UK[63] or international law and has been criticised as an overly 'elastic' definition that blurs the distinction between organised crime and terrorism.[64]

The definition of terrorist activities in Canada's Anti-terrorism Act is quite similar to the UK definition. It follows the UK government in requiring proof of political, religious or ideological objectives, but with an amendment that the expression of such beliefs or opinions will not constitute acts of terrorism unless they satisfy other parts of the definition of terrorism. The reference to 'influencing govern-

---

[59] Report of the Special Rapporteur on Human Rights and Terrorism, December 2005, E/CN.4/2006/98, paras 60–2.

[60] Chapter 11. The USA PATRIOT Act also defines terrorism but does so in a more complex fashion that depends on predicate offences. In many countries there is more resistance to American influenced anti-terrorism legislation than British influenced anti-terrorism, but many Arab and Muslim countries have also avoided the British definition with its focus on political and religious motives as an essential element of terrorism. Welchman, L, 'Rocks, Hard Places and Human Rights: Anti-terrorism Law and Policy in Arab States' in V Ramraj, M Hor and K Roach (eds), *Global Anti-terrorism Law and Policy* (Cambridge, Cambridge University Press, 2005) 587–88.

[61] Walker (2002) 20–30.

[62] Golder, B and Williams, G, 'What is Terrorism? Problems of Legal Definition' (2004) 27 *University of New South Wales Law Journal* 270, 289.

[63] Before 2000, the UK defined terrorism as 'the use of violence for political ends and includes any violence for the purpose of putting the public or any section of the public in fear'. See the Prevention of Terrorism (Temporary Provisions) Act 1989, s 20(1).

[64] Ashworth, A, *Human Rights, Serious Crime and Criminal Procedure* (London, Sweet and Maxwell, 2002) 30.

ments' was changed to 'compelling governments', and the compulsion can be directed at domestic and international organisations as well as at governments. This latter feature is more consistent with international definitions of terrorism. The UK Terrorism Act 2006[65] has subsequently added international governmental organisations to the UK definition of terrorism while maintaining the broader idea of 'influencing' those organisations and governments.

Although some of the adaptations made by Canada have narrowed the UK definition of terrorism, others have expanded it by including the compulsion of persons and disruptions of any essential public and private services (rather than merely electronic systems). Canada also broadened the concept of intimidation of the public with respect to its 'security' to include the intimidation of the public with respect to 'economic security'.[66] The Canadian definition treats terrorism as not only crimes designed to destabilise the state, but also crimes that can be committed through causing economic damage and attempting to compel corporations and private persons to act in particular ways.

In some important respects, the Canadian definition is more restrained than the UK definition. For example, property damage is included only when it is likely to cause death or serious bodily injury, endangers a person's life or causes a serious risk to public health or safety. The Canadian definition also includes an exemption for protests and strikes so long as they are not intended to endanger life, health or safety. The Canadian exemption was originally limited to lawful protests and strikes, but the lawful requirement was deleted after unions, Aboriginal groups and others expressed concerns that illegal strikes and blockades might fall under the broad definition of terrorism. These features of the Canadian law undoubtedly advance the freedom to protest. At the same time, they may also help prevent limited enforcement and intelligence resources being devoted to radical wings of the animal rights, anti-globalisation or Aboriginal movements, which do not present threats of the same magnitude as Al Qaeda or those inspired by Al Qaeda.

The original definition of terrorism proposed in post-9/11 Australian anti-terrorism law was almost a carbon copy of the UK definition. The UK reference to disruptions of electronic systems was more broadly defined to include information, telecommunication, financial, utility, transport and governmental systems.[67] The Australian law also includes a Canadian-style exemption for lawful protests and strikes, and as in Canada, the government eventually agreed to delete the requirement that the protests and strikes be lawful.[68] It is likely there would have been much less civil society resistance to both the Canadian and Australian laws

---

[65] Chapter 11, s 34.

[66] Criminal Code of Canada RSC 1985, c C-34, s 83.01.

[67] Security Legislation Amendment (Terrorism) Act 2002 No 65, s 100.1(2).

[68] A Senate Committee in Australia received 431 public submissions on the Bill and concluded that 'there is no compelling reason why Australian legislation should reach further than legislation enacted in the United Kingdom, United States or Canada . . .': Senate Legal and Constitutional Legislation Committee (Australia), *Consideration of Legislation Referred to the Committee: Security Legislation Amendment (Terrorism) Bill 2002 [No 2]* (2002) 39. On opposition to the Canadian Bill from a variety of groups see Roach (2003) ch 3.

had the drafters not started with the broad UK definition of terrorism or limited exemptions to lawful protests and strikes.

In response to apartheid-era abuses, South Africa commenced a process of revising its security laws long before SCR 1373 and only enacted a new anti-terrorism law in 2004. Nevertheless, South Africa followed the UK law by including substantial damage to property in its list of proscribed harms. It also followed the Canadian and Australian expansions of the definition to include harms to a broad range of essential public and private services including essential infrastructure facilities and emergency services.[69] South Africa also added the causing of 'any major economic loss' to the proscribed harms and followed Canadian law in providing that intimidation of the public includes threats to 'economic security'—with the added gloss that the causing of 'feelings of insecurity' was one of the elements of terrorism.[70]

The evolution of security to include economic security and subjective feelings of insecurity underlines the expansive and potentially limitless nature of the term.[71] In both Canada and South Africa, the inclusion of compulsion of persons, combined with references to economic security and property damage, allows some illegal acts against corporations to be treated as acts of terrorism.[72] Although illegal acts against corporations should be prosecuted, it is far from clear that subjecting such crimes to the special treatment accorded terrorism crimes is justifiable given the present threat environment.

The broad definition of terrorism in the UK Terrorism Act 2000 has had a huge influence in establishing the foundation for many countries' post-9/11 definitions of terrorism, but it is questionable with respect to both security and human rights. Both before and after 9/11, alternative definitions of terrorism were available that focused more directly on the type of terrorism committed on 9/11 and presented far fewer risks of dissenters being characterised as terrorists. Although the Security Council featured the 1999 Convention for the Suppression of the Financing of Terrorism in many other parts of SCR 1373, it did not encourage states to adopt the 1999 Convention's general definition of terrorism as acts that:

> intended to cause death or serious bodily injury to a civilian, or to any other person not taking an active part in hostilities in a situation of armed conflict, when the purpose of such act, by its nature or context, is to intimidate a population or to compel a government or an international organization to do or abstain from doing any act.[73]

This definition is quite close to best efforts at a universal definition of terrorism as well as the definition of terrorism used in subsequent Security Council

---

[69] Protection of Constitutional Democracy and Related Activities Act (2004), Act 33 of 2004, s 1(xxv)(a)(vi).

[70] *Ibid.*

[71] Zedner, L, 'Securing Liberty in the Face of Terror: Reflections from Criminal Justice' (2006) 32 *Journal of Law and Society* 507, 516ff.

[72] Roach, K, 'A Comparison of South African and Canadian Anti-terrorism Legislation' (2005) 18 *South African Journal of Criminal Justice* 127.

[73] International Convention for the Suppression of the Financing of Terrorism, Art 2(1)(b).

Resolutions.[74] In 2002, the Supreme Court of Canada praised the 1999 Convention definition as one that 'catches the essence of what the world understands as "terrorism"' and one that should be read into otherwise undefined references to terrorism in Canadian immigration law.[75] Unlike the UK Terrorism Act 2000, the general definition of terrorism in the 1999 Convention does not include any form of property damage or disruptions of electronic or essential services, and it does not require proof of political or religious motive. It is regrettable that the Security Council did not promote this restrained definition of terrorism in SCR 1373 even though it promoted many other parts of the 1999 Convention in that Resolution. After having adopted and defended a broad definition of terrorism, it will now be difficult for the United Kingdom, Canada, Australia or South Africa to adopt a narrower definition of terrorism even if such a definition would better respect human rights while catching the most serious threats to security.

IV. SECURITY COUNCIL RESOLUTION 1624 AND THE REGULATION OF TERRORIST SPEECH

Security Council Resolution 1624 was adopted on 14 September 2005 and calls upon all states to take steps to prevent incitement to commit terrorist acts. The resolution declares that states have 'obligations under international law to counter incitement of terrorist acts motivated by extremism and intolerance and to prevent the subversion of educational, cultural and religious institutions by terrorists and their supporters'. Enacted two months after the London bombings, the Resolution was sponsored by the United Kingdom and defended by Prime Minister Tony Blair on the basis that 'the root cause of terrorism was not a decision on foreign policy, however contentious, but was a doctrine of fanaticism'. Blair declared that terrorism had to be combated 'by fighting not just their methods, but their motivation, their twisted reasoning, wretched excuses for terror'.[76]

In its focus on speech and extremism, SCR 1624 seems to be motivated by Karl Lowenstein's theory of militant democracy, which suggests that democracies need to be more aggressive towards those who do not believe in democracy.[77] Resolution 1624 received more debate and deliberation within the Security Council than SCR 1373, but it was also paired or log-rolled with another resolution on humanitarian intervention in Africa in a successful attempt to gain unanimous approval by the 15 states on the Security Council.[78]

---

[74] SCR 1566 (2005) para 3.

[75] *Suresh v Canada* [2002] 1 SCR 3 at para 98.

[76] United Nations Security Council Press Release, 14 September 2005, available at http://www.un.org/News/Press/docs/2005/sc8496.doc.htm.

[77] Lowenstein, K, 'Militant Democracy and Fundamental Rights' (1937) 31 *American Political Science Review* 417, 638. See generally Sajo, A (ed), *Militant Democracy* (Amsterdam, Eleven Publishing, 2004).

[78] SCR 1625.

The role of the United Kingdom in sponsoring SCR 1624 was related to the failure of previous anti-terrorism strategies—including the focus on the financing of terrorism and the targeting of non-citizens in SCR 1373 and the broad definition of terrorism in the UK Terrorism Act 2000—to stop the London bombings in the summer of 2005. The UK's decision to single out speech associated with terrorism may also have been related to its longstanding willingness to sanction expression and organisations associated with terrorism: broadcast bans have been used by the UK government against the IRA; section 59 of the Terrorism Act 2000 makes it an offence to incite terrorism overseas; and section 11 makes it an offence to be a member or to profess membership in a terrorist group. The House of Lords has held this latter offence to be a proportionate restriction on freedom of expression simply by concluding that 'the necessity of attacking terrorist organizations is . . . clear', without any sustained analysis of how such crimes will prevent terrorism or whether there are effective alternatives that constitute a less drastic infringement of freedom of association and freedom of speech.[79]

Existing UK laws against incitement of murder and racial hatred were used in February 2006 to convict and sentence Abu Hamza al-Masri to seven years' imprisonment for various speeches at the Finsbury Park Mosque. Much attention was drawn to the fact that a number of terrorists including Richard Reid and two of the 7 July London bombers listened to some of Hamza's hate-filled speeches.[80] Nevertheless, as the judge acknowledged at sentencing, it is impossible to conclude that Hamza's speeches played a causal role in any acts of terrorism. The Hamza prosecution, however, fits into the trend encouraged by SCR 1624 of prosecuting people for speech associated with terrorism even though it is far from clear that such prosecutions will help prevent future acts of terrorism. The prosecution and imprisonment of Hamza in the United Kingdom continues to delay attempts to extradite him to the United States, where he faces charges for involvement in various acts of terrorism including murder, kidnapping and training of terrorists.[81] Indeed, the UK's willingness to prosecute people for terrorist speech and associations can be contrasted with a more libertarian US tradition on such issues.[82]

Despite existing laws against incitement of crimes and racial hatred, the Blair government in the wake of the London bombings initially proposed an extremely aggressive approach towards speech associated with terrorism. One early proposal would have criminally prohibited any statement that 'glorifies, exalts or celebrates the commission, preparation or instigation (whether in the past, in the future or

---

[79] *Sheldrake v DPP; Attorney General's Reference (No 4 of 2002)* [2005] 1 AC 264 at para 54.

[80] 'Abu Hamza and the 7/7 bombers', *The Times*, 8 February 2006.

[81] 'US Eager to Start Extradition Process', *The Times*, 8 February 2006.

[82] A news article in the *New York Times* commented: 'The charges against Mr Masri made no reference to specific acts of violence committed by specific people. By contrast, in the United States, only speech that directly calls for imminent violence can be punished. In practice, that standard protects essentially everything said from a pulpit, at a rally, on the radio and in a newspaper, no matter how ugly': 'Cleric Convicted of Stirring Hate', *New York Times*, 8 February 2006. On the distinctiveness of the libertarian US approach to speech and association see Roach, K, 'Anti-terrorism and Militant Democracy: Some Eastern and Western Responses' in A Sajo (ed), *Militant Democracy* (Amsterdam, Eleven Publishing, 2004).

generally) of acts of terrorism'.[83] Not surprisingly given the breadth of the proposed offence, the government retreated from this proposal. It also abandoned another proposal for control and eventual closure orders with respect to religious institutions that foster extremism defined as support for proscribed organisations and encouragement of terrorism.[84]

Although the UK government backed off from its most draconian proposals, it secured new offences against speech associated with terrorism in sections 1–3 of the Terrorism Act 2006.[85] The previously proposed offence of glorifying terrorism was merged into an offence of directly or indirectly encouraging terrorism subject to the maximum penalty of seven years' imprisonment. The offence applies if the person who publishes statements is reckless or actually intends for people to be directly or indirectly encouraged or otherwise induced by the statement to commit, prepare or instigate acts of terrorism.[86]

The new offence incorporates existing broad definitions of terrorism, confirming the ability of a new trend in anti-terrorism law (here, the prohibition of speech) to build on an older trend (broad definitions of terrorism). Indirect encouragement of terrorism under the new offence is defined broadly as including every statement that 'glorifies the commission or preparation (whether in the past, in the future or generally)' of terrorist acts or offences when 'members of the public could reasonably be expected to infer that what is being glorified is being glorified as conduct that should be emulated in existing circumstances'.[87] The new offence clearly targets speech, and it is deemed irrelevant to guilt 'whether any person is in fact encouraged or induced by the statement to commit, prepare or instigate' any act of terrorism.[88] It also targets speech that advocates terrorism short of violence and speech that advocates terrorism against repressive regimes in foreign lands. Related offences apply to 'terrorist publications', which include both publications that provide information about how to commit a terrorist act and those that directly or indirectly encourage terrorism.[89]

In light of SCR 1624 and the UK Terrorism Act 2006, many countries may now consider enacting laws that target speech that is thought to incite or encourage terrorism. Sedition laws in Australia were already amended at the end of 2005 to criminalise as a form of sedition subject to seven years' imprisonment the act of

---

[83] Draft terrorism bill dated 13 September 2005, originally posted at http://security.homeoffice.gov.uk/news-and-publications1/publication-search/legislation-publications/proposed-terrorism-bill.

[84] Home Office, *Preventing Extremism Together: Places of Worship*, 6 October 2005. The proposal was withdrawn after many religious groups argued it was a disproportionate restriction on freedom of religion. See Roach, K, 'National Security, Multiculturalism and Muslim Minorities' (2006) *Singapore Journal of Legal Studies* 405.

[85] Chapter 11.

[86] *Ibid*, s 1(2).

[87] *Ibid*, s 1(3).

[88] *Ibid*, s 1(5)(b).

[89] *Ibid*, ss 2–3. For a useful distinction between knowledge-based speech about vulnerabilities and weapons that can be used for terrorism and political or religious speech that advocates or praises terrorism, see Donohue, L, 'Terrorist Speech and the Future of Free Expression' (2005) 27 *Cardozo Law Review* 233, 326ff.

urging a group distinguished by race, religion, nationality or political opinion to use force or violence against another group so distinguished, or to assist the enemy in a war, whether or not it has been declared. To be sure, such prosecutions allow some defences relating to good faith reports on matters of interest,[90] but the expansion of sedition law can place an obvious burden on extreme and unpopular forms of political and religious expression. The 2005 Australian law also expanded the definition of terrorist groups that could be proscribed to include groups that praise the doing of a terrorist act, if there is a risk that such praise may have the effect of leading any person to engage in a terrorist act.

Resolution 1624 puts pressure on other states to consider the adequacy of their existing laws against incitement of terrorism. It could, for example, be used to support a revival of the withdrawn Hong Kong security Bill, which featured offences against sedition and subversion.[91] Time will tell whether SCR 1624, which, unlike SCR 1373, was not enacted under Chapter VII of the UN Charter, will be as influential a source of anti-terrorism law as SCR 1373.

Resolution 1624 stresses the need to respect international human rights law, including the right to freedom of expression, and this could enable the CTC to demonstrate greater concern than it has in the past about human rights. Even if the CTC takes a greater interest in human rights, it will focus largely on the legitimacy of the limits on freedom of expression that are encouraged in SCR 1624. A recent report by the CTC outlines how 69 nations, including many that do not have a tradition of respecting freedom of expression, have already reported back to the CTC on their implementation of SCR 1624.[92] The report outlines these responses in a factual and general manner, mentioning no country by name. It notes that some states have raised concerns about respecting freedom of expression and that countries differ with respect to whether there should be a crime of incitement in the absence of some probability that incitement will lead to the commission of an act of terrorism. The CTC report fails to conclude that any state has engaged in unreasonable or disproportionate restrictions of freedom of expression. This suggests that the CTC is not yet comfortable with criticising states for violating human rights in their anti-terrorism efforts or in taking a position on which anti-terrorism measures are or are not consistent with human rights.

Resolution 1624 may help to legitimate laws that will restrict freedom of expression at a time when it is unclear what effects prosecutions of extremist speech will have on security. The possibility that terrorist speech prosecutions could counter-

---

[90] Anti-terrorism Act (No 2) 2005, No 144, 2005, Part 5.1.

[91] See generally Fu, H, Petersen, C and Young, S (eds), *National Security and Fundamental Freedoms: Hong Kong's Article 23 under Scrutiny* (Hong Kong, Hong Kong University Press, 2005). On the eagerness of China to use the new focus on terrorism against secessionist movements and various political and religious dissenters see Fu, H, 'Counter-revolutionaries, Subversives, and Terrorists: China's Evolving National Security Law' in Fu Hualing, C Petersen and S Young (eds), *National Security and Fundamental Freedoms: Hong Kong's Article 23 under Scrutiny* (Hong Kong, Hong Kong University Press, 2005) 83–9.

[92] 'Report of the Counter-terrorism Committee on the Implementation of Resolution 1624', 15 September 2006, S/2006/737 at para 9.

productively result in greater attention and sympathy for those who glorify and incite terrorism should not be dismissed, nor should the possibility that driving extremism underground may make it more difficult to identify and monitor terrorist suspects. Although the Security Council seems confident that there is a causal relationship between extremist speech and terrorism, not enough is known about why people commit terrorism. Moreover, the Security Council was equally as confident at the time that SCR 1373 was drafted about the effectiveness of laws against the financing of terrorism and the use of immigration law as anti-terrorism law. Given this track record, states should think twice before following yet another new trend in anti-terrorism law.

V. POSSIBLE CORRECTIVES TO THE TRENDY NATURE OF POST-9/11 ANTI-TERRORISM LAWS

What are the practical implications of the fact that post-9/11 anti-terrorism laws have been heavily influenced and shaped by a small number of dubious sources and distinct trends? First, the Security Council should take greater care and engage in greater deliberation before calling on states to enact specific types of anti-terrorism laws. The effects of Security Council resolutions on both security and human rights in various nations should be carefully and independently monitored by those not invested in the resolutions. The CTC in particular should pay greater attention to the effects of anti-terrorism laws on human rights.

Although successive UN Human Rights Commissioners have urged the CTC to pay more attention to human rights, until recently the CTC has not considered the issue of compliance with human rights as within its mandate. A 2003 briefing of the UN Human Rights Committee by the CTC clearly demonstrates this bureau-cratic, not-my-jurisdiction mindset:

> While United Nations Secretary-General Kofi Annan had stressed that there could be 'no trade-off between effective action against terrorism and the protection of human rights', the Chairman of the CTC stated that the CTC would 'not trespass onto the areas of competence of other parts of the United Nations system'.[93]

More recently, the CTC has included a senior human rights officer as part of its executive directorate, but the extent to which the CTC will pay serious attention to human rights issues remain very much in doubt.[94]

The CTC should not simply monitor compliance with the Security Council's various anti-terrorism resolutions but should also evaluate their effectiveness and

[93] 'Human Rights Committee Briefed on Work of the Counter-terrorism Committee', UN Press Release, 27 March 2003, available at http://www.unhchr.ch/huricane/huricane.nsf/view01/FFB9934C2667CC3FC1256CF7003D5B36??opendocument.
[94] A December 2005 report by the CTC to the Security Council made a brief mention of the need for compliance with international human rights laws, but its focus remains on compliance with SCR 1373 including matters of technical assistance. See Report of the CTC to the Security Council S/2005/800.

their impact on human rights. Some small steps have recently been taken in this direction,[95] but much work remains to be done to ensure that the CTC includes human rights as a central part of its work. The UN cannot afford to maintain a bureaucratic and segmented approach whereby the human rights implications of anti-terrorism measures are left to human rights bodies, and the Security Council and the CTC act as if human rights were outside of their mandate.

The United Kingdom should also recognise that its anti-terrorism measures are very influential throughout the Commonwealth and beyond. UK innovations such as broad definitions of terrorism, offences against terrorist speech, control orders and extended periods of preventive arrest can quickly spread to other countries. Indeed, the Blair government's role in sponsoring SCR 1624 and then enacting offences against the encouragement of terrorist and terrorist publications in the Terrorism Act 2006 underlines the considerable influence that the United Kingdom exerts on global anti-terrorism agendas. It is interesting to note, however, that the Blair government had much more difficulty in imposing its views about the dangers of speech associated with terrorism on Parliament as opposed to the Security Council. This sort of increased deliberation before the enactment of anti-terrorism measures needs to be encouraged.

One approach that may increase deliberation and serve to break dubious trends in anti-terrorism law is independent review and criticism. Within the UN, it might be helpful to ask the Human Rights Commissioner or some other body with expertise in human rights to prepare reports on the implications of proposed Security Council anti-terrorism resolutions. In addition, there should be independent human rights reviews and audits of the work of the CTC as well as of the reports submitted by countries to this committee. In some European countries and even in Canada, proposed anti-terrorism Bills could be referred to the judiciary for an assessment of constitutionality before enactment. In the UK, pre-enactment scrutiny can be provided by committees and officers of Parliament.

These processes have been used with respect to recent UK anti-terrorism legislation but with limited effectiveness. Lord Carlile, the independent reviewer appointed by the government to review anti-terrorism law, concluded that the speech-based offences in the Terrorism Act 2006 are a proportionate response to terrorism and are compatible with the Human Rights Act 1998; but he elided the difficult questions concerning both rights and security that were rightly the focus of the House of Lord's analysis in *A*.[96] For example, he assumed that the criminalisation of speech that glorifies terrorism is rationally connected with preventing terrorism, whereas the House of Lords in *A* seriously questioned whether using

---

[95] In May 2006, an agreement was reached within the CTC to incorporate human rights analysis and advice in its work monitoring compliance with Resolutions 1373 and 1624 and also to liaise with the Office of the High Commissioner for Human Rights and, as appropriate, with other human rights organisations in matters related to counter-terrorism.

[96] Lord Carlile, Interim Report, 'Proposals by Her Majesty's Government for Changes in the Terrorism Laws', 10 October 2005, originally posted at http://security.homeoffice.gov.uk/news-and-publications1/publication-search/independent-reviews/carlile-review-121005?view=Standard&pubID=241429, para 23.

immigration law as anti-terrorism law was rationally connected to the objectives of combating international terrorism. Lord Carlile also assumed that criminalising speech will prevent 'young radically minded people being persuaded towards terrorism'.[97]

The causal determinants of terrorism, particularly suicide terrorism, are complex, and it is simplistic to assume that prosecuting some speech will prevent terrorism. Lord Carlile's analogy between speech that glorifies terrorism and a manual about how to commit a crime is also inapt given that the encouragement offence will catch impassioned political and religious speech that may praise terrorism but not explain how it can be committed. He also did not address whether there are alternative methods of addressing extremism, either through existing incitement laws such as those used against Abu Hamza or through interventions that do not employ criminal sanctions. Finally, he also did not consider the limited effectiveness of the proposed offence given the sheer amount of information that is distributed in the modern age. This sort of insufficiently robust pre-enactment scrutiny may be worse than no pre-enactment scrutiny at all because it may be used as a means to legitimate dubious anti-terrorism proposals.[98]

Another, marginally more effective, form of independent review in the United Kingdom is pre-enactment scrutiny by the Joint House of Commons and House of Lords Committee on Human Rights. This Committee has been critical of some previous terrorism Bills and has been able to obtain some changes to them.[99] With respect to the Terrorism Act 2006, for example, the Joint Committee on Human Rights took a more critical approach than Lord Carlile, concluding that the proposed offence was incompatible with the ECHR because of the vagueness of the term 'glorification' and because 'glorification' could refer to property damage.[100] In this way, the committee reminded Parliament that its proposed new offence would build on the already broad definition of terrorism found in the Terrorism Act 2000.

At the same time, however, the Joint Committee's analysis did not closely examine whether new offences against directly or indirectly encouraging terrorism and against publications that encourage terrorism were rationally connected to the legitimate and important objective of preventing terrorism and whether they are necessary and proportionate to such an objective. The Joint Committee's criticisms were important and valid, but they nibbled on the edges of the proposed Bill and did not criticise them in a root and branch manner. It appears that rigorous proportionality analysis of the fundamentals of the new encouraging terrorism

---

[97] *Ibid.*

[98] In Canada, the government went to great lengths to argue that its post-9/11 anti-terrorism law was carefully vetted by government lawyers as consistent with the Charter. See Roach (2003) ch 3.

[99] Hiebert, J, 'Parliament and the Human Rights Act: Can the JCHR Help Facilitate a Culture of Rights?' (2006) 4 *International Journal of Constitutional Law* 1, 27–31.

[100] House of Lords, House of Commons Joint Committee on Human Rights, *Counter-terrorism Policy and Human Rights, the Terrorism Bill and Related Matters* 2005–2006, HC 561-1, HL 75-1 at para 36.

offences and whether they constitute a proportionate violation of freedom of expression may have to await judicial review.[101]

The record on pre-enactment scrutiny is at best mixed, and there may not always be adequate time for pre-enactment scrutiny of new anti-terrorism measures. For these reasons, it is important to build in after-the-fact mechanisms to evaluate both the effectiveness of anti-terrorism measures and their effects on human rights. UK anti-terrorism legislation, including the Terrorism Act 2006, provides for periodical independent reviews of operation. Such reviews have the potential to point out problems in trends with anti-terrorism laws, including unanticipated effects on human rights or security, but they must be conducted with rigour and with independence. As a case in point, the 9/11 Commission made an important contribution in evaluating the limited effectiveness of laws against terrorist financing, in part because it had no particular stake in the policy being evaluated and in part because it had considerable resources and powers.

One way to help make review more meaningful is to provide 'sunset provisions' that require renewal of provisions. Such sunset clauses were used with respect to parts of US, UK and Canadian anti-terrorism legislation. Legislatures may, however, wait until the last minute to deliberate about sunset provisions and Canada allowed preventive arrests and investigative hearings to expire after a rushed and unsophisticated public debate in 2007.

A final corrective for the recent tendency of governments to follow poorly thought-out trends in anti-terrorism law is to recognise that independent judiciaries have a particularly important role to play in questioning the effects of such laws on both rights and security. The House of Lords' first decision in *A v Secretary of State*[102] demonstrates how independent judges may be able to achieve critical distance on the state's anti-terrorism efforts. The decision not only affirmed the importance of human rights but provided valuable criticisms of the limited efficacy of immigration law when used as an anti-terrorism strategy—criticisms that seemed to have escaped the attention of the Security Council and the UK government.

Courts should not be criticised for judging the effectiveness of anti-terrorism laws when those laws violate rights because the question of whether a measure is rationally connected to preventing terrorism and whether there are less rights-invasive alternatives are central components of the proportionality analysis that is the foundation for modern rights protection. Courts can enrich the sources of anti-terrorism laws by imagining and describing less restrictive alternatives to current anti-terrorism measures. They can also challenge the idea that the Security Council and governments have a monopoly on security expertise. Courts should approach the emerging trend in anti-terrorism laws—the prohibition of incitement of terrorism, typified by SCR 1624—with the same critical and rational detachment that the House of Lords brought to bear on the use of immigration law as anti-terrorism law.

---

[101] Roach, K, 'Must We Trade Rights for Security? The Choice Between Smart, Harsh, or Proportionate Security Strategies in Canada and Britain' (2006) 27 Cardozo Law Review 2157, 2182ff.
[102] [2004] UKHL 56.

CONCLUSION

Greater attention to the limited sources and trends of post-9/11 anti-terrorism laws tells us much about their substance, in terms of both their contribution to the prevention of terrorism and their effects on human rights. Resolution 1373 has been the most influential source, despite the fact that it was formulated under time pressures and with imperfect information about the causes of 9/11. Institutional interests within the United Nations, including the desire to promote the 1999 Convention on the Suppression of the Financing of Terrorism and the SCR 1267 process, may explain the emphasis that SCR 1373 places on the financing of terrorism. Laws against the financing of terrorism have certainly been the flavour of the day, but more critical attention needs to be paid to their effects on human rights and their efficacy in preventing terrorism. Terrorist-financing laws and institutions are increasingly entrenched in many countries, and it may be difficult if not impossible to roll back such laws, at least in the absence of sunset provisions or robust judicial review.

Resolution 1373 also singled out immigration law, especially refugee law, as a focus for anti-terrorism efforts, despite the fact that not one of the 9/11 plotters had applied for asylum. Many countries have subsequently followed the lead of the Security Council and used immigration law as anti-terrorism law. This has had adverse effects on human rights because immigration proceedings typically offer fewer procedural protections for detainees than criminal proceedings and because a number of countries are re-evaluating the right not to be deported to torture. The focus on immigration law can also have adverse effects on security because, as the London bombings tragically confirm, citizens can also commit acts of terrorism.

Resolution 1373 makes no attempt to define terrorism, but many countries have taken the broad definition of terrorism in the UK Terrorism Act 2000 as their starting point when drafting their own anti-terrorism laws. There is a need for continued critical evaluation of the effects of such broad definitions of terrorism on both human rights and security, due in part to the danger that they could facilitate the targeting of extremists in domestic protest movements. Broad definitions of terrorism could have adverse effects on security, as well as on human rights, if they result in a misallocation of limited law enforcement and security intelligence resources.

Finally, attention should be paid to the cumulative effects of successive trends in anti-terrorism laws. The ineffectiveness of the financing and immigration trends at preventing acts such as the London bombings has fuelled the demand for more interventions and new trends such as SCR 1624 and new laws against speech associated with terrorism. The trendy nature of anti-terrorism law may result in the exponential growth of anti-terrorism law, as each new trend is discredited without hard decisions being made to discard or revise prior ineffective policies. The new incitement laws called for by SCR 1624 will very likely build on existing broad definitions of terrorism, as well as incorporate the focus on newcomer communities that is encouraged by the use of immigration law as anti-terrorism law.

Pre-enactment scrutiny has failed to stop either SCR 1624 or the UK Terrorism Act 2006, and there are no sunset provisions for the new offences against terrorist speech. The task now will fall on independent judiciaries to consider whether such new offences are rationally connected to the prevention of terrorism and whether they constitute a proportionate restriction on freedom of expression.

REFERENCES

Ackerman, B, 'The Emergency Constitution' (2004) 113 *Yale Law Journal* 1029.

Ashworth, A, *Human Rights, Serious Crime and Criminal Procedure* (London, Sweet and Maxwell, 2002).

Cole, D, *Enemy Aliens* (New York, New Press, 2003).

Commission of Inquiry into the Actions of Canadian Officials in Relation to Maher Arar, *Report Relating to the Events Relating to Maher Arar Factual Background*, vol 1 (Ottawa, Public Works and Government Services, 2006)

Davis, K, 'The Financial War Against Terrorism' in V Ramraj, M Hor and K Roach (eds), *Global Anti-terrorism Law and Policy* (Cambridge, Cambridge University Press, 2005).

Donohue, L, 'Terrorist Speech and the Future of Free Expression' (2005) 27 *Cardozo Law Review* 233.

Dosman, EA, 'For the Record: Designating "Listed Entities" for the Purposes of Terrorist Financing Offences at Canadian Law' (2004) 62 *University of Toronto Faculty of Law Review* 1.

Dyzenhaus, D, 'The Rule of (Administrative) Law in International Law' (2005) 68 *Law and Contemporary Problems* 127.

Fenwick, H, 'The Anti-terrorism, Crime and Security Act' (2002) 65 *Modern Law Review* 724.

Fu, H, 'Counter-revolutionaries, Subversives, and Terrorists: China's Evolving National Security Law' in Fu Hualing, C Petersen and S Young (eds), *National Security and Fundamental Freedoms: Hong Kong's Article 23 under Scrutiny* (Hong Kong, Hong Kong University Press, 2005).

Fu, H, Petersen, C and Young, S (eds), *National Security and Fundamental Freedoms: Hong Kong's Article 23 under Scrutiny* (Hong Kong, Hong Kong University Press, 2005).

Garland, D, *The Culture of Control: Crime and Social Order in Contemporary Society* (Chicago, University of Chicago Press, 2001).

Golder, B and Williams, G, 'What is Terrorism? Problems of Legal Definition' (2004) 27 *University of New South Wales Law Journal* 270.

Hiebert, J, 'Parliament and the Human Rights Act: Can the JCHR Help Facilitate a Culture of Rights?' (2006) 4 *International Journal of Constitutional Law* 1.

Home Office, *Preventing Extremism Together: Places of Worship*, 6 October 2005.

House of Lords, House of Commons Joint Committee on Human Rights, *Counter-terrorism Policy and Human Rights, the Terrorism Bill and Related Matters* 2005–2006, HC 561-1, HL 75-1.

Intelligence and Security Committee, *Report into the London Terrorist Attacks on 7 July 2005*, Cm 6785, May 2006.

Lord Carlile, 'First Report of the Independent Reviewer Pursuant to Section 14(3) of the Prevention of Terrorism Act 2005', 2 February 2006.

Lord Carlile, Interim Report, 'Proposals by Her Majesty's Government for Changes in the Terrorism Laws', 6 October 2005, available at http://security.homeoffice.gov.uk/news-and-publications1/publication-search/independent-reviews/carlile-review-121005?view=Standard&pubID=241429.

Lord Newton, Chair, *Anti-terrorism, Crime and Security Act 2001 Review Report*, 18 December 2003.

Lowenstein, K, 'Militant Democracy and Fundamental Rights' (1937) 31 *American Political Science Review* 417.

National Commission on Terrorist Attacks upon the United States, *The 9/11 Report* (New York, St Martins Press, 2004).

Powell, CH, 'Terrorism and the Separation of Powers in the National and International Spheres' (2005) 18 *South African Journal of Criminal Justice* 151.

Ramraj, V, Hor, M and Roach, K (eds), *Global Anti-terrorism Law and Policy* (Cambridge, Cambridge University Press, 2005).

Roach, K, 'Did September 11 Change Everything?' (2002) 47 *McGill Law Journal* 893.

—— *September 11: Consequences for Canada* (Montreal, McGill Queens Press, 2003).

—— 'The Worldwide Expansion of Anti-terrorism Laws after 11 September 2001' (2004) CXVI (III Serie, LIII) 2004-Fasc 3 *Studi Senesi (University of Siena Law Review)* 487.

—— 'Anti-terrorism and Militant Democracy: Some Eastern and Western Responses' in A Sajo (ed), *Militant Democracy* (Amsterdam, Eleven Publishing, 2004).

—— 'Canada's Response to Terrorism' in V Ramraj, M Hor and K Roach (eds), *Global Anti-terrorism Law and Policy* (Cambridge, Cambridge University Press, 2005).

—— 'A Comparison of South African and Canadian Anti-terrorism Legislation' (2005) 18 *South African Journal of Criminal Justice* 127.

—— 'Constitutional, Remedial and International Dialogues about Rights: The Canadian Experience' (2005) 40 *Texas International Law Journal* 537.

—— 'Must We Trade Rights for Security? The Choice Between Smart, Harsh, or Proportionate Security Strategies in Canada and Britain' (2006) 27 *Cardozo Law Review* 2157.

—— 'National Security, Multiculturalism and Muslim Minorities' (2006) *Singapore Journal of Legal Studies* 405.

Roach, K and Trotter, G, 'Miscarriages of Justice in the War Against Terror' (2005) 109 *Penn State Law Review* 967.

Sajo, A (ed), *Militant Democracy* (Amsterdam, Eleven Publishing, 2004).

Senate Legal and Constitutional Legislation Committee (Australia), *Consideration of Legislation Referred to the Committee: Security Legislation Amendment (Terrorism) Bill 2002 [No 2]* (2002).

Stewart, H, 'Is Indefinite Detention of Terrorist Suspects Really Constitutional?' (2005) 54 *University of New Brunswick Law Journal* 235.

Tomkins, A, 'Legislating against Terror' (2002) *Public Law* 205.

Tushnet, M, 'The Possibilities of Comparative Constitutional Law' (1999) 108 *Yale Law Journal* 1225.

Walker, C, *Blackstone's Guide to the Anti-terrorism Legislation* (Oxford, Oxford University Press, 2002).

Welchman, L, 'Rocks, Hard Places and Human Rights: Anti-terrorism Law and Policy in Arab States' in V Ramraj, M Hor and K Roach (eds), *Global Anti-terrorism Law and Policy* (Cambridge, Cambridge University Press, 2005).

Welsh, J, *At Home in the World: Canada's Global Vision for the 21st Century* (Toronto, Harper Collins, 2004).

Zedner, L, 'Securing Liberty in the Face of Terror: Reflections from Criminal Justice' (2006) 32 *Journal of Law and Society* 507.

11

Seeking Security by Eroding Rights: The Side-stepping of Due Process

LUCIA ZEDNER[*]

INTRODUCTION

S ECURITY IS SO powerful an aspiration that it tends to trump all other
considerations and silence countervailing concerns. Its capacity to license
draconian measures is fuelled both by the impossibility of knowing precisely
against which threats security measures must protect and by sheer weight of numbers—not least when mass public protection is juxtaposed against loss of individual rights for the few.[1] This chapter examines recent security measures, broadly
defined, that have particular implications for individual liberties because they
circumvent the procedural requirements of the criminal law to impose prospective constraints in respect of remote harms.

Let us first set out a few preliminary challenges to prevailing presumptions
about the provision of security. First, it is commonly presumed that security is a
good in its own right. Understood this way, security denotes objective protection
or guarantee or perhaps a subjective sense of personal safety. The difficulty with
these definitions, however, is that they seem to license forms of defensive cocoon-
ing that are potentially burdensome and, ultimately, without point. I can wrap
myself and my family in cotton wool, bolt the doors and bar the windows in order
that we be safe, but to what end? We may feel and even be safe but at no small cost
to quality of life.[2] Conceiving of security in this way invites the question: what is

* With thanks to participants at the Workshop on Law, Probability and Risk in Penal Justice,
University of Edinburgh; the Oxford Colloquium on Security and Human Rights; the GERN Interlabo,
Oxford; and the British Criminology Conference, Glasgow, at which earlier versions of this chapter
were delivered. Thanks also to Lisa Gourd, Emily Coates and Ravinder Thukral for their assistance.
Much of the research for this chapter was conducted during a British Academy-funded Research
Readership, the support of which I gratefully acknowledge. An earlier version of this chapter appeared
as 'Security for Whom? Reducing Risk by Eroding Rights' in a Festschrift for Professor Heike Jung,
G Britz et al (eds) (Baden-Baden, Nomos Verlag, 2007).
¹ Dworkin, R, 'Terror and the Attack on Civil Liberties' (2003) 50(17) *The New York Review of Books*
37.
² Davis observes that Los Angeles millionaires 'are hardening their palaces like missile silos' (248).
His observation of conditions in LA housing projects is even bleaker: 'Visitors are stopped and frisked,

security for? Trying to articulate exactly what is at stake might lead us to think of security less as a good in its own right than as the means to or pre-condition of other goods such as justice, equality, trust, social inclusion, and, not least, liberty.[3] If these ulterior goods justify its very pursuit, logically security should not trample upon them.

A second key question is: whose security do we pursue? Posing this question tackles head-on the assumption implicit in much rhetorical recourse to security that just as there are threats, so too are there those who threaten and that *we*—an ill-defined larger public—need protection against *them*—an ill-defined predatory minority. One way to contest this assumption is to acknowledge that in large measure our own security depends upon the security of others.[4] Understood this way, effective security must be security for all. The difficulty is to ensure a realm of security in which each of us is able to exercise the widest possible freedom compatible with the same realm of security for others. Maximising security therefore necessarily has distributive implications.[5]

Our third question is: how should we pursue security? Acknowledging that security is best conceived as serving other goods and that our own security is dependent upon that of others has important implications for the channels and instruments by which we pursue it. Duff and Marshall have persuasively argued that the means by which security is pursued must be rendered consistent with its ends.[6] It follows that the ends or goals of security measures need to be specified in such a way as to ensure that the means are appropriate to them. Searching your colleagues as they leave your office might secure your book collection but would hardly be conducive to fostering a healthy and trusting academic community. Similarly, acknowledging that my security depends upon your security requires that the means I employ in pursuit of my own safety do not unduly encroach upon your interests and that yours do not trespass upon mine. New forms of moral reasoning are needed to capture these dual aspects of security.

This chapter tackles these questions by examining how they are played out in one particular domain. Recent years have seen the introduction in Britain of a slew of diverse measures that have in common only the shared aspect of seeking to pre-empt future risks. Many of these measures do not operate squarely within the domain of the criminal law, as they would once have done. Rather they are distinct orders ancillary to criminal sanctions or operating in parallel systems of question-

while the police routinely order residents back into their apartments at night. Such is the loss of freedom that public housing tenants must now endure as the price of "security"': Davis, M, *City of Quartz: Excavating the Future in Los Angeles* (London, Pimlico, 1990) 244.

[3] Dinwiddy, J, 'The Classical Economists and the Utilitarians' in EK Bramsted and KJ Melhuish (eds), *Western Liberalism: A History in Documents from Locke to Croce* (London, Longman, 1978) 21.

[4] Loader, I and Walker, N, 'Locating the Public Interest in Transnational Policing' in A Goldsmith and J Sheptycki (eds), *Crafting Global Policing* (Oxford, Hart Publishing, 2006).

[5] Nozick, R, *Anarchy, State and Utopia* (Oxford, Blackwell, 1974) ch 7; Rawls, J, *A Theory of Justice* (Oxford, Oxford University Press, 1973) ch 1.

[6] Duff, RA and Marshall, S, 'Benefits, Burdens and Responsibilities: Some Ethical Dimensions of Situational Crime Prevention' in A von Hirsch, D Garland and A Wakefield (eds), *Ethical and Social Perspectives on Situational Crime Prevention* (Oxford, Hart Publishing, 2000).

able justice: according to the less exacting requirements of the civil process or enforced via hybrid systems in which breach of civil orders results in criminal sanctions. Whilst this paper focuses on legislative innovation in Britain, parallels can and will be drawn with developments elsewhere, not least the deployment of civil containment against sexual offenders in the United States—a development that has spawned a large and critical law review literature of its own.[7] These developments furnish a timely and fertile basis for asking for whom we provide security and at what cost.

I. FROM PUNISHMENT TO PRE-EMPTION

The measures with which this chapter is concerned have their origins in a larger temporal shift. We are moving from a 'post-crime' society in which crime is thought about primarily as harm or wrong done and in which dominant ordering practices arise *post-hoc*, to a 'pre-crime' society in which the perspective is shifting to anticipate and forestall that which has yet to occur.[8] Under the post-crime model, the dominant mechanisms of crime control are the police, the criminal process, trial and punishment. Dedicated to detecting offences, ascribing responsibility, determining guilt, they impose penal burdens either proportionate to the wrong done or consistent with consequentialist aims of punishment. The pre-crime model has a different, prospective orientation, concerned rather with the calculation of risk and the prevention of future harms in the name of security.

Prevention is hardly new: the preventive possibilities of policing were recognised even in its origins.[9] It is also an established pillar of the criminal law, manifest most clearly in the articulation of inchoate offences whose perpetrators may be punished for inciting, conspiring and attempting to do harm. What has changed is that the point of intervention has been brought forward. The licence to intervene earlier against as yet remote harms is perhaps best captured by the notion of pre-emption. We borrow the term from international relations, where resort to pre-emption or what international lawyers call 'anticipatory self-defence' is justified by reference to the need to avert the gravest threats.[10]

Pre-emption stands temporally prior to prevention of proximate harms: it seeks to intervene when the risk of harm is no more than an unspecified threat or propensity as yet uncertain and beyond view. Whereas the preventive turn of the

[7] Slobogin, C, 'A Jurisprudence of Dangerousness' (2003) 98 *Northwestern University Law Review* 1–62; Slobogin, C, 'The Civilization of the Criminal Law' (2005) 58 *Vanderbilt Law Review* 121–68; Janus, E, 'Civil Commitment as Social Control' in M Brown and J Pratt (eds), *Dangerous Offenders: Punishment and Social Order* (London, Routledge, 2000); Janus, E, 'Hendricks and the Moral Terrain of Police Power Civil Commitment' (1998) 4 *Psychology, Public Policy, and Law* 297–322; Morse, SJ, 'Fear of Danger, Flight from Culpability' (1998) 4 *Psychology, Public Policy, and Law* 250–67.
[8] Dick, PK, *Minority Report* (London, Gollancz, 2002) 2–3; Zedner, L, 'Pre-crime and Post-criminology?' (2007, forthcoming) *Theoretical Criminology*.
[9] Chadwick, E, 'Preventive Police' (1829) 1 *London Review* 252–308.
[10] Freedman, L, *Deterrence* (Cambridge, Polity Press, 2004) ch 6, 'From Deterrence to Pre-emption'.

criminal law is triggered in the main by acts 'more than merely preparatory' to a specified offence, pre-emption legitimates substantial curtailments of individual liberty at earlier points in time—often without the requirement of *mens rea*, still less *actus reus*. This temporal shift is hardly peculiar to Britain; US commentators have also noted it.[11] Janus, for example, observes:

> what might be called radical prevention . . . differs from routine prevention in two ways. First, radical prevention seeks to intervene where there is some sort of 'propensity' or risk of future harm, whereas routine prevention responds to actual or attempted harm. Second, radical prevention operates by substantially curtailing people's liberty before harm results, whereas in routine prevention individuals suffer deprivations of liberty only after actual harm is done or attempted.[12]

The impulse towards pre-emption or 'radical prevention', particularly in the case of prospective grave harms, is at some level understandable. Those charged with public protection must continually seek to avert grave harm before it occurs or risk being called to account for the failure of their security measures.[13] Yet the urgency and licence with which pre-emptive intrusions are now contemplated and condoned are of a different order of magnitude. The impact of 9/11 and the Bali, Madrid and London bombings has accelerated an existing trend toward pre-emptive endeavours, particularly in respect of serious crime and political violence. But there are other causal factors at work. In what follows we sketch three such factors that appear to drive current trends: namely the rise of 'actuarial justice'; the influence of the 'precautionary principle'; and the decline of 'social prevention'.

The concepts of actuarial justice,[14] the 'new penology',[15] and the 'pursuit of security',[16] capture in differing ways significant shifts in the focus and means of crime control. Actuarial justice is the means by which high-risk populations are identified, classified, and contained. It is debatable whether it is driven principally by the demand for security or rather by the very possibility of calculation. Arguably too little attention has been paid to the degree to which the growing

---

[11] Dershowitz's recent work appeared too late for me to consider here: Dershowitz, AM, *Preemption: A Knife that Cuts Both Ways* (New York, WW Norton, 2006).

[12] Janus, E, 'The Preventive State, Terrorists and Sexual Predators: Countering the Threat of a New Outsider Jurisprudence', William Mitchell Legal Research Studies Paper No 11, May 2005, available at http://ssrn.com/abstract=687165 (accessed 12 December 2006) 2.

[13] Just as this chapter was in its final draft, a leading article in *The Independent* called for a public inquiry into the failure of the intelligence and security services to foresee and prevent the London bombings of 7 July 2005: see 'The Irresistible Case for a Public Enquiry' *The Independent*, 12 May 2006.

[14] Feeley, M and Simon, J, 'Actuarial Justice: The Emerging New Criminal Law' in D Nelken (ed), *The Futures of Criminology* (London, Sage, 1994); Feeley, M, 'Actuarial Justice and the Modern State' in G Bruinsma, H Elffers and JW de Keijser (eds), *Punishment, Places, and Perpetrators: Developments in Criminology and Criminal Justice Research* (Cullompton, Willan Publishing, 2004).

[15] Feeley, M and Simon, J, 'The New Penology: Notes on the Emerging Strategy of Corrections and its Implications' (1992) 30 *Criminology* 449–74; Simon, J and Feeley, M, 'The Form and Limits of the New Penology' in TG Blomberg and S Cohen (eds), *Punishment and Social Control* (New York, Aldine de Gruyter, 2003).

[16] Zedner, L, 'The Pursuit of Security' in T Hope and R Sparks (eds), *Crime, Risk and Insecurity: Law and Order in Everyday Life and Political Discourse* (London, Routledge, 2000); Shearing, C, 'Punishment and the Changing Face of Governance' (2001) 3 *Punishment and Society* 203–20.

sophistication of actuarial tools and huge advances in computational power both enable and legitimate pre-emptive intervention. Quantitative risk assessment tools are not only commonplace in the insurance industry but play an increasingly important role in the criminal process. It is claimed that these tools have superior reliability and should therefore rightfully displace the subjective clinical judgement of psy-professionals that have historically been relied upon in criminal trials.[17] The widespread application of these tools generates statistical artefacts of 'good' and 'bad' risks that are then used pre-emptively to manage conduct yet to occur. For example, in 1996, Virginia became the first US state to incorporate a specified risk assessment instrument into its legislative framework for sentencing guidelines.[18]

Although this reliance upon actuarial tools suggests a high level of confidence in their statistical validity, it is debatable whether risk assessment is truly a scientific endeavour separate from the political and policy choices of risk management. Much of the power of predictive and risk assessment tools derives from the fact that they can be presented as independent, objective, and scientific. Yet, as we will consider below, their claim to objectivity is questionable. A larger issue still is that although actuarial justice purports to be about identifying suspect populations and assessing the risk they pose, the focus and impact of actuarialism falls no less heavily upon the individual than conventional retributive penal regimes. Thus although leading commentators on actuarial justice aver that it 'focuses not on individuals but on the population itself as a target of power' and that 'actuarial crime policy is not designed for individuals but is designed to respond to the problem of dangerousness',[19] in application its ramifications for individual liberty are just as serious as those of the so-called 'old penology'.

The precautionary principle is a second driving force behind pre-emption. As a guiding framework for public decision-making, the precautionary principle is only now beginning to influence thinking about the risks of crime and terrorism. In the fields of natural science, engineering and environmental law, the precautionary principle has long licensed early intervention by imposing strict demands upon public authorities in the face of scientific uncertainty.[20] The precautionary principle requires that where there is a threat of serious harm, 'lack of full scientific certainty' should not be used as a reason for inaction.[21] Indeed, the principle requires policy makers to take precautionary steps even in the absence of clear scientific evidence where the potential harm is life threatening, or gravely damaging to human safety, health or the environment. The precautionary principle is thus a

---

[17] Janus, E and Prentky, R, 'Forensic Use of Actuarial Risk Assessment: How a Developing Science can Enhance Accuracy and Accountability' (2004) 16 *Federal Sentencing Reporter* 176–81.

[18] Feeley (2004) 74.

[19] *Ibid*, 63.

[20] Haggerty, K, 'From Risk to Precaution: The Rationalities of Personal Crime Prevention' in R Ericson and A Doyle (eds), *Risk and Morality* (Toronto, University of Toronto Press, 2003).

[21] Fisher, E, 'Precaution, Precaution Everywhere: Developing a "Common Understanding" of the Precautionary Principle in the European Community' (2002) 9 *Maastricht Journal of European and Comparative Law* 7–28.

powerful driver of government regulation over risky industries, farming practices and scientific decision-making. The danger is that applied to the management of threat by human individuals, rather than companies or nation-states, the precautionary principle poses no small threat to civil liberties. Enforcing precautionary measures against the directors of a petro-chemical factory or a nuclear plant does not inflict the same deprivation of liberty that is entailed, for example, by pre-emptively containing individuals who are thought to pose a particular risk.

The decline of social prevention is a third factor in driving the pre-emptive turn. Social prevention was devoted to identifying the fundamental causes of social disorder and sexual and political violence. It has been displaced by a move towards secondary prevention, namely a focus on forestalling the risk posed by known or suspected offenders.[22] Social prevention sought to identify and address the deeper roots of crime and security threats—in poverty, social inequality, poor education, unemployment and health care.[23] Secondary prevention, on the other hand, is the product of a neo-liberal polity in which concern for collective, social and structural dimensions is displaced by a focus on the governance of risky individuals and risky situations. Intervention is based upon technologies of crime control such as 'target hardening', 'opportunity reduction' and 'situational controls'.[24] As such, social and moral considerations are displaced by an economic rationality that is concerned less with the constitutive mechanisms of civil society than with the narrower goal of loss management. Responding to crime as a moral wrong becomes secondary to estimating, calculating, preventing, and minimising losses and insuring against harm.[25]

II. PRE-EMPTIVE MEASURES

Together the diverse driving forces of actuarial justice, the precautionary principle and the decline of social prevention stand behind a series of equally diverse measures that, each in different ways, may be said to signify the shift to what Janus has called the 'preventive state'.[26] These measures span the spectrum of security risks and in Britain include at the lower end of the tariff: 'disqualification from driving'; 'disqualification from acting as a company director'; 'disqualification from

---

[22] Reiner, R, 'Beyond Risk: A Lament for Social Democratic Criminology' in T Newburn and P Rock (eds), *The Politics of Crime Control* (Oxford, Oxford University Press, 2006); Rose, N, 'The Death of the Social? Reconfiguring the Territory of Government' (1996) 25 *Economy and Society* 327–56.

[23] Downes, D, 'What the Next Government Should Do about Crime' (1997) 36 *The Howard Journal* 1–13, 1.

[24] Felson, M and Clarke, RV, *Opportunity Makes the Thief: Practical Theory for Crime Prevention,* Police Research Series No 98 (London, Home Office, 1998); Zedner, L, 'Opportunity Makes the Thieftaker: The Influence of Economic Analysis on Crime Control' in T Newburn and P Rock (eds), *The Politics of Crime Control* (Oxford, Oxford University Press, 2006).

[25] O'Malley, P, 'Risk, Power, and Crime Prevention' (1992) 21 *Economy and Society* 252–75; O'Malley, P, *Risk, Uncertainty and Government* (London, Glasshouse Press, 2004).

[26] Janus (2004).

working with children'; 'travel restriction orders'; and 'exclusion from licensed premises orders'.[27]

One of the more important and controversial such provisions in Britain is the 'anti-social behaviour order' (ASBO), introduced under the Crime and Disorder Act 1998. The ASBO is a civil order designed to tackle behaviour that causes offence or harassment or intimidates neighbours, or a community in general.[28] Further up the tariff, the sexual offences prevention order and the risk of sexual harm order (RSHO), both created under the Sexual Offences Act 2003, are likewise civil preventive orders aimed specifically at protecting the public from serious sexual harm.[29] Both ASBOs and RSHOs require no criminal conviction; impose wide-ranging constraints for a minimum of two years; and, if breached, may result in imprisonment for up to five years.[30]

At the very top of the tariff lies the introduction of control orders against terrorist suspects under the Prevention of Terrorism Act 2005. In the words of the Home Office, 'control orders are preventative orders which impose one or more obligations upon an individual which are designed to prevent, restrict or disrupt his or her involvement in terrorism-related activity'.[31] They can impose wide-ranging conditions including curfews; tagging; restrictions on access, for example, to computers or communications equipment; reporting requirements; and limits upon personal associates for a period of up to 12 months at a time (renewable on application to the court). Breach of a condition imposed by a control order is a criminal offence punishable by imprisonment. In order to avoid criminal sanction a 'controlled' individual must engage in continual self-surveillance and self-imposed restrictions that impact adversely not only on his or her own quality of life but also that of family and friends. The Act also foresees special 'derogating control orders', including house arrests, that would require derogation from Article 5 of the European Convention of Human Rights (ECHR), although none has yet been imposed.

There is a large academic and policy literature that takes issue with the very necessity of such measures (not least since no such measures were thought necessary in the years immediately following 9/11).[32] As Shami Chakrabarti, Director of Liberty, has observed:

[27] For a fuller list and details of the statutory framework of these preventive orders see Ashworth, A, *Sentencing and Criminal Justice* (Cambridge, Cambridge University Press, 2005) 335–40.

[28] On ASBOs in particular, see Ashworth, A, 'Social Control and Anti-social Behaviour Order: The Subversion of Human Rights?' (2004) 120 *Law Quarterly Review* 263–91; Ashworth, A, Gardner, J, Morgan, R, Smith, ATH, von Hirsch, A and Wasik, M, 'Neighbouring on the Oppressive: The Government's "Anti-social Behaviour Order" Proposals' (1998) 16 *Criminal Justice* 7–14.

[29] Shute, S, 'New Civil Preventative Orders: Sexual Offences Prevention Orders, Foreign Travel Orders and Risk of Sexual Harm Orders' (2004) *Criminal Law Review* 417–40, 425.

[30] Ashworth (2004).

[31] See the Home Office website: http://www.homeoffice.gov.uk/security (accessed 12 December 2006).

[32] Fenwick, H, 'The Anti-terrorism, Crime and Security Act 2001: A Proportionate Response to 11 September?' (2002) 65 *Modern Law Review* 724–62; Lowe, V, ' "Clear and Present Danger": Responses to Terrorism' (2005) 54 *International and Comparative Law Quarterly* 185–96; Walker, C, 'Terrorism and Criminal Justice: Past, Present and Future' (2004) *Criminal Law Review* 311–27; Zedner, L,

> The control order regime is descending still further into cruel and futile farce. Confused individuals who have never been charged with a recognisable criminal offence are running around on plastic tags. They fear imprisonment at any moment for breaches of the broadest and vaguest of restrictions—all decided, and then variable, by a politician.[33]

Together these various preventive measures can be seen as contributing to the larger 'security architecture' presently being developed as a defensive barrier against the spectrum of risks and that includes the work of intelligence agencies as well as military operations against security threats.[34] Although, as we have indicated, it is the need to avert grave harms that provides the theoretical justification for pre-emption, many of these measures are aimed at harms at the lower end of the tariff. As is the case in so many areas of present public policy, the gravest security risks furnish the underlying rationale and licence for measures that tackle much lesser risks but pose no small threat to basic liberties.

III. EVADING THE PROTECTIONS OF DUE PROCESS

One of the most damaging aspects of the move to pre-emption is that the demands of security are deemed to warrant departure from the ordinary strictures of the criminal process. A common means by which this is achieved is, as in the measures just described, by the ruse of placing pre-emptive powers within the civil rather than the criminal process or by asserting that measures are preventive not punitive. Whereas the prosecution, trial and punishment of offenders is directed at proving guilt for past actions, holding offenders to account, and sentencing in proportion to the blameworthiness and gravity of past action, the deployment of civil measures legitimates decisions based largely upon legal determinations about future conduct. With minimal flourish and less debate, the core criminal law requirement of culpability and sanction-justifying condition of blameworthiness is dispatched in favour of a prospective concern for future risk that licenses earlier, more expansive, and enduring intervention.

Whereas resorting to penal measures requires special justification and intervention is constrained by the principles of the criminal process and the requirements of proof, culpability and proportionality to offence seriousness, by contrast, pre-emptive endeavour in the civil sphere is said to be 'jurisprudentially unconstrained'.[35] According to John Monahan, a leading US proponent of preventive

'Securing Liberty in the Face of Terror: Reflections from Criminal Justice' (2005) 32 *Journal of Law and Society* 507–33.

[33] See the Liberty website: http://www.liberty-human-rights.org.uk/press/2005/control-orders-cruel-and-futile-farce.shtml (accessed 12 December 2006).

[34] Günther, K, 'World Citizens between Freedom and Security' (2005) 12 *Constellations* 379–91, 380.

[35] Or so Monahan argues in respect of the civil commitment of sexual offenders. The significant exception of race and ethnicity to this blanket permission arises from the provisions of US equal protection scrutiny.

intervention, 'any risk factor that validly forecasts violence—with the exception of race or ethnicity—is a legitimate candidate for inclusion'.[36] In short, promotion of civil measures, even up to and including indefinite commitment, is justified by reference not to past wrongs but to future risks.

This claim assumes a deceptively unproblematic distinction between civil and criminal procedure that permits the courts free rein in determining the appropriate legal context in which decisions are to be made. Once that is decided, it is argued, the courts need only 'apply accepted jurisprudential principles that govern decision making in that context'.[37] However, the danger is that to permit such jurisprudential context-shopping allows too great a discretion to resort to civil measures and, in so doing, risks riding roughshod over the procedural requirements of the criminal law. Even if it were possible to say with absolute accuracy which categorical risk groups threaten and which do not, this would do little to assuage the larger moral, legal, and utilitarian objections that arise as civil measures—and with them civil proceedings—come to encroach ever more upon the territory of the criminal law.

Different legal contexts legitimately require different procedural standards and operate according to different principles and values. The requirement of proof 'beyond all reasonable doubt' in the criminal trial, for example, is an appropriate and proper reflection of the fact that conviction upon proof of guilt attaches profound stigma and may result in substantial loss of liberty. This and the larger array of due process protections that surround the criminal trial have evolved over time in explicit recognition that the consequences for the individual of breaching the criminal law are very serious indeed. It follows that moves to pursue matters properly belonging to the criminal process in a different legal context (be it civil, administrative or contractual) are liable to result in the application of inappropriate or improper standards, principles and values. Placing a measure in a particular legal context or procedural channel should not determine jurisprudential principle without reference to the normatively prior question of whether the choice of context is itself defensible.[38]

Let us be clear, this is not to argue that all matters of future risk or threat to security are better dispatched in the criminal process. Criminalisation commonly entails stigma; conviction may have long-term consequences for life and career chances; and many forms of punishment are painful and burdensome. To this extent it might be thought that avoiding recourse to the criminal process is generally to be welcomed. Indeed, criminal lawyers have argued for the shifting of lesser harms into alternate categories of civil wrong or regulatory offence.[39] On the other hand, the very fact that the consequences of conviction are serious is one reason why the criminal process is wrought with strictures and safeguards designed to

---

[36] Monahan (2006) ms p 7.

[37] *Ibid*, ms p 56.

[38] Steiker, C, 'Civil and Criminal Divide' in J Dressler (ed), *Encyclopedia of Crime and Justice* (New York, Macmillan Reference, 2002) 165.

[39] Ashworth (2004) 63.

uphold the rights of those subject to it.[40] Where measures impose burdens equal to or, more especially, greater than those characteristic of criminal sanctions, then the argument against criminalisation begins to look less convincing. In such circumstances, shifting measures out of the criminal process by labelling them civil (or inventing new or hybrid legal forms) only undermines the protections of due process, and it is disingenuous to claim, simply because they are so labelled, that principles of civil procedure suffice.[41]

Furthermore, punishment under criminal sanction is justified by reference to the conduct of individual offenders. As Goodman makes clear: 'It is a fundamental orthodoxy of our criminal justice system that the punishment should fit the crime and the individual, not the statistical history of the class of persons to which the defendant belongs.'[42] It follows therefore that the only valid risk factor for violence admissible in criminal sentencing is past criminal behaviour. But when one shifts the decision as to disposal to the civil context, this stricture simply vanishes. The jurisprudential considerations that bind the criminal law have no force in the legal context of civil procedure. The effect of labelling measures as civil rather than criminal appears therefore to permit unconstrained use of predictive or risk factors.[43]

Yet if resort to civil procedure is no more than a pretext by which to circumvent the strictures of the criminal law, then mere reliance upon the fact of the legal context ought not to suffice. We need to interrogate the motives lying behind such categorisation, to challenge the formal ascription of the criminal and civil labels, and to develop criteria by which to judge which context is appropriate. Only then is it safe to invoke the accepted jurisprudential principles that pertain in that context and not before. At a time when more and more formerly criminal matters are being recast as civil and when breaches of civil orders are followed by severe penal sanctions,[44] then the very categorisation of a security measure as civil must be regarded as inherently suspect. If the immediate or likely subsequent effect of a civil order is inherently punitive, then all the labels in the world will not render it justifiably civil, and the question of appropriate jurisprudential considerations must remain open to challenge.

[40] Zedner (2005); Steiker, C, 'Punishment and Procedure: Punishment Theory and the Criminal–Civil Procedural Divide' (1997) 85 *Georgetown Law Journal* 775–819, 806ff.

[41] Steiker, C, 'The Limits of the Preventive State' (1998) 81 *Journal of Criminal Law and Criminology* 771–808.

[42] Goodman, D, 'Demographic Evidence in Capital Sentencing' (1987) 39 *Stanford Law Review* 499–543, 521.

[43] With the significant exception of Fourteenth Amendment limitations on the admissibility of race or ethnicity as 'constitutionally suspect classifications', US courts have robustly defended risk as the basis for civil confinement, *viz*: 'There can be little doubt that in the exercise of its police power a State may confine individuals solely to protect society from the dangers of significant antisocial acts': Berger, CJ, concurring in *United States v Salerno* 481 US 739 (1987). See also the leading case of *Kansas v Hendricks* 521 US 346 (1997): 'It . . . cannot be said that the involuntary civil confinement of a limited subclass of dangerous persons is contrary to our understanding of ordered liberty.'

[44] As is the case in respect of anti-social behaviour orders, breach of which is punishable by up to five years' imprisonment. See the UK Crime and Disorder Act 1998, s 1.

In what follows we will suggest that attempts to circumvent the procedurally burdensome requirements of the criminal process have resulted in a range of dubious measures designed to operate in parallel systems of questionable justice; to operate according to the less exacting procedural requirements of the civil process; or to be enforced via hybrid systems that pursue the breach of civil orders with criminal sanctions. Side-stepping the criminal process or 'changing lanes', as Günther calls it,[45] into less demanding procedural avenues ought properly to be regarded as in itself a threat to security. As Nickel rightly insists, 'due process rights are security rights'.[46]

It cannot be by chance that these moves to circumvent the strictures of the criminal process coincide with the British government's avowed commitment to the incorporation of the ECHR into domestic law through the Human Rights Act 1998. Janus-faced, the government simultaneously declares itself publicly committed to the human rights agenda and, in the name of security, good order and public safety, shows itself only too willing to undermine, evade and even formally derogate from the provisions of ECHR.

It is a moot point how one should interpret these apparently contradictory impulses. A sympathetic, though hardly benign, interpretation is that the British government has found itself bound to uphold human rights at precisely the historic moment when world events and public opinion seemed to call for a sacrificing of individual freedoms in the name of collective security.[47] The result is a game of cat and mouse between activist lawyers, judges and the government, as each side seeks to defend what it deems an appropriate balance between security and liberty. A more cynical interpretation is that what the government has given in respect of human rights with one hand, it takes away with the other. This second reading might appear implausible were it not for the fact that whilst the larger public basks in the warm glow of rights received, it is only a small and unpopular minority that bears the brunt of simultaneous deprivation.[48]

IV. THE PERILS OF RESORTING TO CIVIL PROCEEDINGS

Several objections might be raised to the resort to civil procedure and, in particular, civil containment measures in the name of public protection and security. Given the relatively long history of the resort to civil commitment of those deemed to be at risk of sexual violence,[49] it is not surprising that it is in this domain that consideration of the issues at stake is most developed and sophisticated. Building upon objections developed in respect of the civil containment of sexual offenders,

---

[45] Günther (2005) 381.

[46] Nickell, J, 'Terrorism, Emergencies, and Due Process Rights' (forthcoming) ms p 10.

[47] On the US see Glassner, B, *The Culture of Fear: The Assault on Optimism in America* (New York, Basic Books, 2003).

[48] The most obvious example of which is the raft of preventive civil measures introduced against sexual offenders discussed above. See Shute (2004).

[49] Janus (2000) 72ff.

what follows is an endeavour to elaborate the perils inherent in resorting to civil measures in respect of lesser security threats. By way of analytic convenience these perils are set under three headings: procedural, empirical and moral.

We have already observed that the widespread resort to civil procedure has developed rapidly at the same time as the incorporation of human rights instruments into domestic law and an avowed commitment to engender a larger human rights culture. Given that the most stringent strictures of human rights instruments rightly apply to the protection of liberties within the criminal process, any attempt to switch operations to the less taxing forum of the civil process might be thought inherently suspect.[50]

There is an important academic literature and ECHR jurisprudence attending to the claim that insofar as these measures are preventive, they are not punitive.[51] The distinction is important not least because human rights protections that apply to criminal punishment are not available in respect of merely preventive measures. To the extent that the procedures, outcomes and likely consequences of civil means are punitive in intent, character or impact, the absence of principled protections by which the criminal process is bound is unsafe. And insofar as civil measures permit enduring or indefinite deprivation of freedoms or detention, the protections for individual liberties should be higher, not lower, than those of the criminal process. Such civil preventive measures and civil commitment schemes as are permitted to exist should be limited, principled exceptions to the presumptive dominance of the criminal process and punishment.

To allow the expansive application of civil measures against large swathes of the criminal population risks sweeping away the criminal justice system and instituting civil procedure in its stead.[52] The extensive provisions of ASBOs, the civil preventive sexual offender orders, and control orders against terrorist suspects substantially extend the scope of state power to act in the name of security. Yet not only are they perilous to those whom we deem to threaten our security, they are perilous also to our own security. In sum, to permit the state to evade the prescriptions and strictures of the criminal process by unfettered resort to the altogether less burdensome procedures of civil law is to license an alternate system of social control whose justification in the name of security belies the threat such measures pose to security properly conceived. In this, as in other domains where security is at stake, we appear to have lost sight of the classical liberal conception of security as the security of the individual against an overbearing state.

A further set of objections focuses upon the empirical foundations of resorting to what has been called the 'civilization' of security.[53] A central justification for the pre-emptive endeavour is that actuarial risk assessment schedules are now sufficiently sound to form a reliable basis for prediction. Whether and to what extent

---

[50] Ashworth, A, 'Four Threats to the Presumption of Innocence' (2006) 123 *South African Law Journal* 62–96.

[51] See, eg, *Welch v UK* (1995) 20 EHRR 247; *Ibbotson v UK* (1999) 27 EHRR CD 332.

[52] On the erosion of this division more generally see Steiker (1997).

[53] Slobogin (2005).

these tools can be safely relied upon is likely to be a matter of some scientific controversy. It does not take a high level of statistical sophistication, however, to consider the implications of the outcomes of such tools. As a case in point, one of the leading US actuarial prediction tools, devised by the MacArthur study, found that 76 per cent of those classified in the highest risk category committed further acts of violence in the 20 weeks following discharge.[54] Read simply as a forecast of future threat, the tool clearly has a rather impressive predictive power. Read, however, as a basis for the continuing incarceration of individuals, the figure of 76 per cent is worryingly low and well below that formally required by the 'beyond all reasonable doubt' strictures of the criminal law.

The MacArthur study and its like may have bettered the success rate of clinical predictions, yet even that does not meet the demands of criminal standards of proof.[55] Given the inescapably punitive quality of many civil orders, it is arguable that even where that order is formally civil rather than penal, court proceedings ought to abide by principles and standards close to those that pertain in the criminal process.[56]

The origins of statistical computation of risk in the natural sciences and the sophistication of the actuarial techniques now employed combine to give risk assessment an appurtenance of accuracy that may simply be misleading when applied to the messier context of human behaviour. A particular difficulty is that actuarial techniques require human frailties to be reduced to quantitative indicia such that only those characteristics amenable to being reproduced numerically will count. It follows that non-quantifiable indicia of risk may be excluded or overlooked because they cannot readily be incorporated into the calculative machine. This is hardly surprising. Risk assessment tools developed in areas like engineering, drug production, environmental harm and the nuclear energy industry can hardly be expected to be applied to individual human behaviour without difficulty.

Too little attention has yet been given to the degree to which risk assessment, far from its claims to scientific objectivity, is context based. Categories of suspicion are liable to be informed quite as much by institutional, social and, above all, political considerations as by objective indicia of the risk posed. Indeed, one unsung merit of actuarialism is that, in setting out formally the categorical bases of suspicion, it exposes the underlying prejudices that inform them. A critical rereading of the scientific data might well reveal less than objective predictive variables. Moreover, there is the related danger of circularity. Context-based considerations

---

[54] Monahan (2006).

[55] At least of formal criminal standards of proof. Legal realists might argue that proof 'beyond reasonable doubt' posits an artificially high standard that is in fact rarely met by the criminal courts. The courts commonly rely upon the professional, and possibly subjective, opinions of experts and less than reliable witness testimony. Realists might argue, therefore, that in practice criminal convictions may only rarely be based upon evidence of guilt proven beyond all reasonable doubt.

[56] In the case of ASBOs, the English courts have insisted that the standard of proof be in effect that required in the criminal trial of 'beyond all reasonable doubt': *Clingham and McCann* [2003] 1 AC 787 at para 83; Ashworth (2006).

feed back into the manner in which categories are applied by agents of policing such that they become self-fulfilling. Put crudely, if control efforts are targeted according to pre-determined categorical assumptions, then they will pull into the system those who fit those categories. The categories will prove themselves.

Recourse to civil measures based upon actuarial categorisation justifies intervention and containment less on the grounds of what people have done, than on the grounds of the particular suspect sub-population or risk category to which they belong. In so doing it moves intervention away from classical criminal ascription of personal responsibility, instead casting individuals into predetermined categorical risks. The effect is to undermine offenders' sense of responsibility for past actions and deny them volition over future deeds.[57] Quite apart from the moral objections (to which we will turn in a moment), the effect is counterproductive to any effort to hold offenders to account, to convey blame—and still less to engage their moral reasoning in potentially penitent or reformative directions.[58]

It may also be that when 'risky' individuals are aware of the ways personal information may be used, they will be reluctant to divulge it or to co-operate with the system. For example, sexual offenders may refuse to give personal information during treatment programmes for fear it may later be used against them as grounds for indefinite civil commitment. In such a case it is arguable that the very fact of civil commitment acts as an inhibition on effective therapeutic intervention.

As Janus points out, the cost of civil commitment schemes is very high: 'the annual cost to civilly commit and confine a sexual offender is about 100 times the per capita amount spent on sex offender treatment in prisons'.[59] This striking figure inevitably raises the question as to whether the sums allocated to civil commitment might not better be spent on alternative forms of correction, therapeutic intervention in prison or the community, and intensive supervision designed to minimise risk by less invasive means.

Finally, in addition to procedural and empirical problems, there are serious moral objections to resorting to civil procedure insofar as it usurps the traditional role of the criminal process as the dominant means of social control. The resort to civil measures has a legitimate and established place in respect of those who so lack capacity that they cannot fairly be held to account during the ordinary course of a criminal trial.[60] It might be argued that lack of capacity entails a diminished moral status such that the individual concerned is not owed the panoply of rights ordinarily due to those of full capacity. If this line of reasoning provides a limited basis

---

[57] However, there are those who claim that risk management has a reflexive quality that can effect change in those subject to it. See Hacking, I, 'Making up People' in T Heller (ed), *Reconstructing Individualism* (Stanford, Stanford University Press, 1986) 222–36.

[58] Duff, RA, *Punishment, Communication and Community* (Oxford, Oxford University Press, 2001) chs 4 and 6.

[59] Janus (2000) 81.

[60] Richards, EP, 'The Jurisprudence of Prevention: The Right of Societal Self-defense against Dangerous Individuals' (1989) 16 *Hastings Constitutional Law Quarterly* 329–92.

upon which to deny individuals their rights, it also imposes tight restrictions on the class of person against whom such measures can justifiably be applied. Whereas, for example, civil commitment may be defended under mental health law in respect of those who cannot control their behaviour, those who can be held to account or, in the case of convicted offenders, have already been held to account properly deserve the censure and sanction of punishment.

It follows that when the behaviour concerned is criminal and the offenders can be held responsible for their behaviour (as opposed to those of such unsound mind that they cannot be held liable), then the criminal process, not the civil process, is the appropriate context in which to hold them to account for their wrongdoing. When the resort to civil measures extends beyond that population of individuals who lack capacity then it must be justified by reference to different criteria. Increasingly, as we have seen, it is the actuarial categorisation of risk that furnishes the ostensible moral basis for designating 'dangerous' populations whose rights to due process are overridden solely because they belong to a particular group. The requirement of culpability for past acts upon the basis of which punishment is said to be deserved is forgone in favour of mere categorical belonging.

Although not without its critics, the German device of *Sicherungsverwahrung* permits confinement based on security concerns for select offenders who are found to constitute a high risk of recidivism whilst maintaining a much more direct connection between the criminal offence and the confinement. As such, at least according to one commentator, the *Sicherungsverwahrung* 'may provide a more satisfying blueprint for accommodating goals of punishment and risk considerations.'[61] Although legal transplant across jurisdictions is problematic, observing how other jurisdictions tackle similar problems of security whilst maintaining regard for due process and proportionality is potentially illuminating.

To the extent that civil measures are punitive in their effect, the question arises: is it justifiable to punish for offences yet to be committed? There has been sophisticated debate amongst philosophers as to whether pre-punishment is justifiable. New and Statman argue that when there is a strong reason to believe someone is about to commit an offence as is sufficient to merit post-punishment, then that person is 'predeserving' of punishment.[62] Yet even if it appears almost certain that the person will commit an offence, as Smilansky powerfully argues, respect for the individual as a moral agent must acknowledge a categorical 'window of moral opportunity' or chance to remain innocent.[63] To close this window pre-emptively fails to respect the moral autonomy of the individual to choose to do right. If security is a precondition of freedom, in the absence of imminent grave harm, it cannot make sense casually to license measures that are liberty-denying.

---

[61] Demleitner, N, 'Abusing State Power or Controlling Risk? Sex Offender Commitment and *Sicherungverwarhrung*' (2003) 30 *Fordham Urban Law Journal* 1621–69.

[62] New, C, 'Time and Punishment' (1992) 52 *Analysis* 35–40; Statman, D, 'The Time to Punish and the Problem of Moral Luck' (1997) 14 *Journal of Applied Philosophy* 129–35.

[63] Smilansky, S, 'The Time to Punish' (1994) 54 *Analysis* 50–3, 52.

CONCLUSION

The use of civil orders as mechanisms of control in respect of behaviours ordinarily deemed to lie within the purview of the criminal justice system is increasingly widespread. Civil measures have been used at both ends of the spectrum of seriousness from the introduction of ASBOs to combat offensive but not criminal behaviour, to the use of civil containment against sexually violent offenders, and wide-ranging restrictions imposed upon those suspected of involvement in terrorism. Despite the fact that they evidently span very different levels of threat, these civil measures share certain common features: they are pre-emptive, they are categorical and, in differing ways, they are incapacitative.

In *The Culture of Control*,[64] Garland claims to identify two simultaneous trajectories of contemporary crime control. One is the hysterical, expressive 'criminology of the other', which manifests itself in punitive rhetoric and draconian penalties. The other is the 'criminology of everyday life', an adaptive response that seeks to 'define deviance down' and set an altogether cooler tone. The analysis in this chapter suggests that the resort to civil measures and civil containment in pursuit of security transgresses the divide identified by Garland between hysterical and adaptive responses. The resort to civil procedure succeeds in being simultaneously non-inflammatory and non-stigmatising, yet in its licensing of indefinite containment upon the basis of purportedly scientific instruments of statistical calculation, it surrenders no less to popular punitivist demands to lock up the 'monstrous' and throw away the key.[65]

A central feature of civil restriction and containment measures is that they rely upon targeting those who can be said to pose the highest risk. This selectivity is a common characteristic of legislative and policy measures aimed at increasing security. At one level, it makes perfect sense to target security measures at those deemed most to threaten. Yet an inherent danger of selectivity is that precisely because it imposes restrictions only on targeted sections of the population, it is less likely to invoke the natural political resistance generated by burdens that affect us all.[66] It is all too obvious that the larger the population likely to benefit from security-driven restrictions and the smaller the population liable to bear the burden of them, the less likely is there to be effective opposition. Sunstein points out:

> People are likely to ask, with some seriousness, whether their fear is in fact justified *if* the steps that follow from it impose burdensome consequences on them. But if indulging in fear is costless, because other people face the relevant burdens, then the mere fact of 'risk', and the mere presence of fear, will seem to provide a justification.[67]

[64] Garland, D, *The Culture of Control* (Oxford, Oxford University Press, 2001).
[65] Simon, J, 'Managing the Monstrous: Sex Offenders and the New Penology' (1998) 3 *Psychology, Public Policy and Law* 452–67.
[66] Sunstein, C, *Laws of Fear: Beyond the Precautionary Principle* (Cambridge, Cambridge University Press, 2005) 204–5.
[67] *Ibid*, 208.

It follows that when security-driven restrictions are directed at pre-identified minorities or otherwise selective groups, others must bear a particular responsibility to protect their interests against unwarranted intrusion. Absent the natural political resistance that arises where infringements upon civil liberties are widely shared, it falls to academics, to lobby organisations and, above all, to the courts to exercise presumptive mistrust of the legitimacy of burdens that fall only on minority groups or sub-populations. Or as Sunstein puts it, 'if the government imposes a burden on an identifiable subclass of citizens, a warning flag should go up. The courts should give careful scrutiny to that burden'.[68] The purpose of this chapter has been, in similar spirit, to wave such a warning flag and to suggest that we should not permit demands for collective security against distant and ill-defined threats to obliterate the security of the individual to make correct moral choices today.

REFERENCES

Ashworth, A, 'Social Control and Anti-social Behaviour Order: the Subversion of Human Rights?' (2004) 120 *Law Quarterly Review* 263–91.

—— *Sentencing and Criminal Justice* (Cambridge, Cambridge University Press, 2005).

—— 'Four Threats to the Presumption of Innocence' (2006) 123 *South African Law Journal* 62–96.

Ashworth, A, *et al*, 'Neighbouring on the Oppressive: The Government's "Anti-social Behaviour Order" Proposals' (1998) 16 *Criminal Justice* 7–14.

Chadwick, E, 'Preventive Police' (1829) 1 *London Review* 252–308.

Davis, M, *City of Quartz: Excavating the Future in Los Angeles* (London, Pimlico, 1990).

Demleitner, N, 'Abusing State Power or Controlling Risk? Sex Offender Commitment and Sicherungverwahrung' (2003) 30 *Fordham Urban Law Journal* 1621–69.

Dershowitz, AM, *Preemption: A Knife that Cuts Both Ways* (New York, WW Norton, 2006).

Dick, PK, *Minority Report* (London, Gollancz, 2002).

Dinwiddy, J, 'The Classical Economists and the Utilitarians' in EK Bramsted and KJ Melhuish (eds), *Western Liberalism: A History in Documents from Locke to Croce* (London, Longman, 1978).

Downes, D, 'What the Next Government Should Do about Crime' (1997) 36 *The Howard Journal* 1–13.

Duff, RA, *Punishment, Communication and Community* (Oxford, Oxford University Press, 2001).

Duff, RA and Marshall, S, 'Benefits, Burdens and Responsibilities: Some Ethical Dimensions of Situational Crime Prevention' in A von Hirsch, D Garland and A Wakefield (eds), *Ethical and Social Perspectives on Situational Crime Prevention* (Oxford, Hart Publishing, 2000).

Dworkin, R, 'Terror and the Attack on Civil Liberties' (2003) 50(17) *The New York Review of Books* 37.

---

[68] *Ibid*, 216.

Feeley, M, 'Actuarial Justice and the Modern State' in G Bruinsma, H Ellfers and J de Keijser (eds), *Punishment, Places, and Perpetrators: Developments in Criminology and Criminal Justice Research* (Cullompton, Willan Publishing, 2004).

Feeley, M and Simon, J, 'The New Penology: Notes on the Emerging Strategy of Corrections and its Implications' (1992) 30 *Criminology* 449–74.

—— 'Actuarial Justice: The Emerging New Criminal Law' in D Nelken (ed), *The Futures of Criminology* (London, Sage, 1994).

Felson, M and Clarke, RV, *Opportunity Makes the Thief: Practical Theory for Crime Prevention*, Police Research Series No 98 (London, Home Office, 1998).

Fenwick, H, 'The Anti-terrorism, Crime and Security Act 2001: A Proportionate Response to 11 September?' (2002) 65 *The Modern Law Review* 724–62.

Fisher, E, 'Precaution, Precaution Everywhere: Developing a "Common Understanding" of the Precautionary Principle in the European Community' (2002) 9 *Maastricht Journal of European and Comparative Law* 7–28.

Freedman, L, *Deterrence* (Cambridge, Polity Press, 2004).

Garland, D, *The Culture of Control* (Oxford, Oxford University Press, 2001).

Glassner, B, *The Culture of Fear: The Assault on Optimism in America* (New York, Basic Books, 2003).

Goodman, D, 'Demographic Evidence in Capital Sentencing' (1987) 39 *Stanford Law Review* 499–543.

Günther, K, 'World Citizens between Freedom and Security' (2005) 12 *Constellations* 379–91.

Hacking, I, 'Making up People' in T Heller (ed), *Reconstructing Individualism* (Stanford, Stanford University Press, 1986).

Haggerty, K, 'From Risk to Precaution: The Rationalities of Personal Crime Prevention' in R Ericson and A Doyle (eds), *Risk and Morality* (Toronto, University of Toronto Press, 2003).

Janus, E, 'Hendricks and the Moral Terrain of Police Power Civil Commitment' (1998) 4 *Psychology, Public Policy, and Law* 297–322.

——'Civil Commitment as Social Control' in M Brown and J Pratt (eds), *Dangerous Offenders: Punishment and Social Order* (London, Routledge, 2000).

—— 'The Preventive State, Terrorists and Sexual Predators: Countering the Threat of a New Outsider Jurisprudence', William Mitchell Legal Research Studies Paper No 11, May 2005 (available at http://ssrn.com/abstract=687165).

Janus, E and Prentky, R, 'Forensic Use of Actuarial Risk Assessment: How a Developing Science can Enhance Accuracy and Accountability' (2004) 16 *Federal Sentencing Reporter* 176–81.

Loader, I and Walker, N, 'Locating the Public Interest in Transnational Policing' in A Goldsmith and J Sheptycki (eds), *Crafting Global Policing* (Oxford, Hart Publishing, 2006).

Lowe, V, '"Clear and Present Danger": Responses to Terrorism' (2005) 54 *International and Comparative Law Quarterly* 185–96.

Monahan, J, 'A Jurisprudence of Risk Assessment: Forecasting Harm among Prisoners, Predators, and Patients' (2006) 92 *Virginia Law Review* 391.

Morse, SJ, 'Fear of Danger, Flight from Culpability' (1998) 4 *Psychology, Public Policy, and Law* 250–67.

New, C, 'Time and Punishment' (1992) 52 *Analysis* 35–40.

Nickell, J, 'Terrorism, Emergencies, and Due Process Rights' (forthcoming).

Nozick, R, *Anarchy, State and Utopia* (Oxford, Blackwell, 1974).

O'Malley, P, 'Risk, Power, and Crime Prevention' (1992) 21 *Economy and Society* 252–75.

—— *Risk, Uncertainty and Government* (London, Glasshouse Press, 2004).

Rawls, J, *A Theory of Justice* (Oxford, Oxford University Press, 1973).

Reiner, R, 'Beyond Risk: A Lament for Social Democratic Criminology' in T Newburn and P Rock (eds), *The Politics of Crime Control* (Oxford, University Press, 2006).

Richards, EP, 'The Jurisprudence of Prevention: The Right of Societal Self-defense against Dangerous Individuals' (1989) 16 *Hastings Constitutional Law Quarterly* 329–92.

Rose, N, 'The Death of the Social? Reconfiguring the Territory of Government' (1996) 25 *Economy and Society* 327–56.

Shearing, C, 'Punishment and the Changing Face of Governance' (2001) 3 *Punishment and Society* 203–20.

Shute, S, 'New Civil Preventative Orders: Sexual Offences Prevention Orders, Foreign Travel Orders and Risk of Sexual Harm Orders' (2004) *Criminal Law Review* 417–40.

Simon, J, 'Managing the Monstrous. Sex Offenders and the New Penology' (1998) 3 *Psychology, Public Policy and Law* 452–67.

Simon, J and Feeley, M, 'The Form and Limits of the New Penology' in TG Blomberg and S Cohen (eds), *Punishment and Social Control* (New York, Aldine de Gruyter, 2003).

Slobogin, C, 'A Jurisprudence of Dangerousness' (2003) 98 *Northwestern University Law Review* 1–62.

—— 'The Civilization of the Criminal Law' (2005) 58 *Vanderbilt Law Review* 121–68.

Smilansky, S, 'The Time to Punish' (1994) 54 *Analysis* 50–3.

Statman, D, 'The Time to Punish and the Problem of Moral Luck' (1997) 14 *Journal of Applied Philosophy* 129–35.

Steiker, C, 'Punishment and Procedure: Punishment Theory and the Criminal–Civil Procedural Divide' (1997) 85 *Georgetown Law Journal* 775–819.

—— 'The Limits of the Preventive State' (1998) 81 *Journal of Criminal Law and Criminology* 771–808.

—— 'Civil and Criminal Divide' in J Dressler (ed), *Encyclopedia of Crime and Justice* (New York, Macmillan Reference, 2002).

Sunstein, C, *Laws of Fear: Beyond the Precautionary Principle* (Cambridge, Cambridge University Press, 2005).

Walker, C, 'Terrorism and Criminal Justice: Past, Present and Future' (2004) *Criminal Law Review* 311–27.

Zedner, L, 'The Pursuit of Security' in T Hope and R Sparks (eds), *Crime, Risk and Insecurity: Law and Order in Everyday Life and Political Discourse* (London, Routledge, 2000).

—— 'Securing Liberty in the Face of Terror: Reflections from Criminal Justice' (2005) 32 *Journal of Law and Society* 507–33.

—— 'Opportunity Makes the Thief-taker: The Influence of Economic Analysis on Crime Control' in T Newburn and P Rock (eds), *The Politics of Crime Control* (Oxford, Oxford University Press, 2006).

—— 'Pre-crime and Post-criminology?' (2007, forthcoming) *Theoretical Criminology*.

12

The State's Duty of Self-defence: Justifying the Expansion of Criminal Law

SHLOMIT WALLERSTEIN*

I N RESPONSE TO the rise of terrorism in recent years, many governments have reviewed the criminal measures they employ against those involved in terrorist activities within their borders. New laws have been put into place granting more powers to the various authorities involved in the fight against terrorism, both in terms of loosening the strict rules governing criminal procedures and in terms of developing new and far-reaching criminal offences. The creation of new criminal offences has been accompanied by two types of debate: the first questions the necessity and efficacy of these offences, and the second focuses on their moral permissibility and their tendency to expand the criminal law beyond its previously recognised boundaries. The underlying fear that has triggered both types of debate is that these new state powers will have negative implications for individual liberties.[1] At the same time, it is essential to explore the possibility that in some situations, the creation of new offences may be justified in order to enhance security. In light of the political rhetoric surrounding the extension of the criminal law[2] and the fear of misuse of the 'security' reasoning, it is vital to develop clear philosophical frameworks that can be used as benchmarks against which to assess these assertions.

This chapter concentrates on the second of these debates—the moral permissibility of new criminal offences—by developing a moral justification for certain expansions of the substantive criminal law. It should be stressed that this chapter

* With thanks to participants at the Oxford Colloquium on Security and Human Rights (March 2006); to participants at the conference 'The Philosophical Justifications of Political Violence', Oxford Centre for Ethics and Philosophy of Law (June 2006); and to Andrew Ashworth, Nick Barber, John Gardner, Andrew Von Hirsch, Jeremy Horder and Micah Schwartzman for their valuable comments. Any mistakes are of course mine alone.

[1] See, eg, the contributions by Lucia Zedner and Kent Roach in this volume, although they focus on new *procedural* measures, whereas the focus of this chapter is *substantive* criminal law.

[2] See, for example, Home Secretary David Blunkett's remark in the House of Commons during debates about the UK Anti-terrorism, Crime and Security Act 2001, '. . . no one would understand a position whereby we failed to take the necessary action and, having so failed, were later proved to have failed to provide the necessary protections. That is the spirit in which I intend to proceed': *Hansard*, HC Deb, vol 1909 (10–13 December 2001) p 896.

is concerned with the use of criminal law in 'ordinary' conditions, as opposed to its use in 'states of emergency'. The declaration of 'a state of emergency' may put on hold many of the general principles that govern and subsequently limit criminal law in a democracy. Yet, some Western countries such as the United States and the United Kingdom have not declared states of emergency following terrorist attacks within their borders,[3] with the result that general principles ought to continue to govern and restrict state coercion, including the use of criminal law.[4]

Ordinarily, criminal law is governed by the harm principle together with its two supporting principles: the minimalist principle and the principle of fair imputation.[5] These principles limit the reach of criminal law to prohibitions of conduct that causes direct (and serious) harm. At times, however, criminal law extends its reach beyond these limitations. Such extensions are usually regarded as exceptions to the general rule, based on the seriousness and the gravity of the potential harm. With increased attention on fighting terrorism, however, some have argued for the need to extend the criminal law based on 'the state's right to defend itself against terrorism'. The question, of course, is whether a state's right to defend itself is a sound basis on which to ground further exceptional extensions to criminal law. Do democratic states have a right to self-defence against their own citizens? And assuming they do, what justifies that right? What are the implications of that right? And what are its limits? This chapter explores what is entailed by the concept of 'self-defence' and suggests one way in which it is capable of grounding or justifying a limited extension of criminal law. In answering the above questions it argues for a justification of self-defence that is not a straightforward claim of a state's *right* of self-defence. Instead, it is based on a *duty* of the state that derives from the citizens' right of self-defence, where such a right exists. The advantage of such a justification is that it reconciles at least some of the exceptions to the general rule that only conduct causing direct harm may be criminalised, while providing clear moral boundaries to the creation of new exceptional offences.

The first section of this chapter reviews the existing law concerning the treatment of exceptions to the general rules limiting criminalisation. It begins by describing the criminalisation of remote harm and examining two ways of understanding claims of self-defence. It is then suggested that the state's claim of self-defence derives from the individual's right of self-defence. Section II presents an overview of the individual's right of self-defence and its internal limitations: the

---

[3] At least there have not been formal declarations. Indeed, it might be argued that the abrogation from the European Convention on Human Rights at present indicates the possibility of some type of exceptional state. However, given the lack of formal declaration, the regular rules that limit democracy still apply. These are the exact situations with which the current chapter is concerned.

[4] As long as there is no declaration of emergency or a state of war, a time limitation—such as the one included in the sunset provisions of the USA PATRIOT Act 2001—cannot, in itself, justify ignoring the restrictions required by general principles. Note that of over 150 provisions in the Act, only 16 could be classed as sunset provisions. See USA PATRIOT Act 2001, Pub L No 107-56, 115 Stat 2172, §§ 201, 202, 203(b)(d), 204, 206, 207, 209, 212, 214, 215, 217, 218, 220, 223, 224, 225. Setting aside such restrictions may be justified on other grounds.

[5] Other principles such as proportionality also have a role in criminal law, but those principles are not relevant to the current discussion.

conditions of unjust threat, necessity, imminence and proportionality. Section III suggests one explanation for the connection between the individual's *right* of self-defence and the state's *duty* of self-defence. This explanation is rejected as unsatisfactory, and in section IV, a second explanation is developed, arguing that the individual's right to self-defence is triggered not only by a threat to one's life but also by a threat to one's liberty. In addition, an attempt is made to justify the state's duty by appealing to the individual's core right and liberty-extended right of self-defence. Three possibilities are considered: (a) a state's duty of self-defence that corresponds to the individual's right (similar to the duty of unspecified third persons); (b) a duty that is part of the general duty of care (similar to the duty of third parties who owe special duties of care, such as parents to their children); and (c) a duty that derives from the individual right that is also a *just* course of action in these circumstances, which is transformed into a duty in the shift from the individual to the state. The first two possibilities are rejected in favour of the third explanation that is defended as the most accurate description of the state's duty. Section V explains how the duty of self-defence justifies extending the scope of criminal law, even though the individual's right of self-defence has a very limited scope. The concluding section presents some general observations about possible implications of the state's duty of self-defence and about the types of threats that might trigger it.

I. CRIMINALISING REMOTE HARM

The harm principle, together with its accompanying minimalist principle, is commonly understood to stipulate that only conduct causing direct harm to others should be criminalised. Most Western legal systems nevertheless contain criminal prohibitions on some conduct that does not cause direct harm. Offences that criminalise conduct resulting in remote harm are usually justified by the overriding consideration of the dangerousness of a potential remote harmful result. Such offences do not comply with the minimalist principle. The exception is justified because the primary concern of criminal law is the prevention of harm rather than its occurrence.[6] The guiding rationale is that the more important the interest, the more protection it should receive. Hence, the proscribed conduct can be further away from the direct harmful results.

Instead of the grounds for such offences being based on overriding considerations of dangerousness (hereafter: the dangerousness consideration), it is submitted that at least some of these exceptions can be justified by reference to the concept of self-defence. Claims of national self-defence, as frequently invoked by executive officials and legislators, can be understood in two ways. One way is to view the reference to the idea of self-defence loosely, as pointing to the need to

---

[6] In other words, it is concerned more with the prevention of harm than with the punishment of those who have caused harm to society.

respond to a serious threat. The concept of self-defence is used only to stress the gravity of the threat and does not refer to the 'narrow' concept of self-defence recognised in criminal law, that is, a defender's right to use violence against an offender under strict conditions. Understood this way, such claims of self-defence have nothing new to add. They are merely rephrasing the overriding consideration of prevention in response to the dangerousness of a potential harm.

A second way of understanding these claims takes them more seriously, as referring to the right of self-defence and to its moral justification as a source of moral permission to use force. Such claims are both wider and narrower than the dangerousness consideration. They are wider because, if sustainable, they may allow the criminalisation of some acts even beyond the currently recognised boundaries of criminal law, which extend to some forms of remote harm subject to the principle of fair imputation and the minimalist principle.[7] Indeed, the essence of bringing up this claim is to allow for further extension of criminal law. At the same time, it is narrower than the dangerousness consideration because only some of the threatening conduct currently proscribed on the basis of the dangerousness consideration would fall into the category of threats that may trigger some right of self-defence. The question then is: can claims of self-defence set a basis for an extension of criminal law?

II. THE INDIVIDUAL RIGHT OF SELF-DEFENCE

Can the right of self-defence, advanced by the state, justify the extension of criminal law? The state might have a *right* to defend itself, but the argument is that a more stringent claim can be made—one that entails a prima facie *duty*. This duty, however, is not a simple one. The state's claim of self-defence can be understood as a *duty* owed by the state to its citizens to defend them. The claim for a prima facie *duty* of self-defence, or more accurately, a *duty* to defend its citizens, is stronger as it may *require* the state to act whereas a mere *right* of self-defence only *permits* state action. This chapter will concentrates on this second claim of self-defence as a *duty*, leaving for another time the discussion of possible claims for a *right* of self-defence.[8] This position, which grounds the state's claim of self-defence in the individual citizens' right of self-defence, is far from trivial.

---

[7] For the imputation principle, see Von Hirsch, A, 'Extending the Harm Principle: "Remote" Harms and Fair Imputation' in AP Simester and ATH Smith (eds), *Harm and Culpability* (Oxford, Clarendon Press, 1996) 259. For a general discussion of the limitations imposed by the general principles see Wallerstein's, 'Criminalising Remote Harm and The Case of Anti-democratic Activity' (2007) 28 (6) Cardozo Law Review 101 (forthcoming). In this paper I argue that it should be given a wider interpretation and consequently should have a more significant role in guiding the criminalisation of remote harm.

[8] The decision to concentrate on the latter claim is based on the fact that it is a stronger claim and also because any justification of a state's *right* of self-defence is inevitably connected to a specific political theory of the democratic state, whereas the justification offered is consistent with the whole range of democratic theories.

The starting point is the understanding of the individual right of self-defence. Legal systems are based on the idea of monopolisation of coercion. Only the state is permitted to use force against its people, to prevent them from harming and violating the interests of others and to punish those who have violated the law. Nevertheless, it is accepted that there may be situations in which the infliction of harm on an individual is imminent, and the only way to avoid it is by using force against those who threaten to inflict the harm. In such situations, legal systems may recognise a right of individuals to use force to defend themselves. Note that the law of self-defence is found in criminal law only because it provides an exemption from the general rule that prohibits the killing (or injuring) of another. This exemption gives a defender *permission* to resist, repel or ward off an oncoming attack. It does not permit a defender to engage in 'private punishment' or other forms of retribution.[9]

The limited purpose of the right to self-defence is reflected in the internal conditions that govern its legitimate use. By general consensus, self-defence is triggered only under the following four conditions: (a) 1. unjust threat; (b) 2. necessity; (c) 3. imminence; and (d) 4. proportionality. One has a right to self-defence only when presented with an *unjust threat* that is *imminent* and that *necessitates* the use of force in response, and such force must be *proportional* to the potential harm that would have been inflicted. The details of these conditions are somewhat controversial. Compliance with all four, however, is essential for a defensive act to be regarded as an act of self-defence.

1. Unjust Threat

The notion of unjust threat is the root of various justifications of self-defence, and for that reason, it has attracted a great deal of controversy, most notably in the debate among theorists who justify the right of self-defence on the basis of 'the rights theory'.[10] The central question in that debate is what actions give rise to the right of self-defence. The commonly accepted view is that the unjust threat triggers the right. According to this view, the scope of the right to self-defence includes the use of force in response to non-culpable and non-agent aggressors.[11]

---

[9] For a more in-depth analysis of the different goals of self-defence and punishment, see, eg, Fletcher, GP, 'Punishment and Self-defense' (1989) 8 *Law & Philosophy* 201; Fletcher, GP, *A Crime of Self-Defense: Bernhard Goetz and the Law on Trial* (Chicago, University of Chicago Press, 1988) 18–38; Nozick, R, *Anarchy State and Utopia* (New York, Basic Books, 1974) 62–3.

[10] See, eg, Uniacke, S, *Permissible Killing* (Cambridge, CUP, 1994); Thomson, JJ, 'Self-defense and Rights' in W Parent (ed), *Rights Restitution and Risk: Essays in Moral Theory* (Cambridge, MA, Harvard University Press, 1986) 33; JJ Thomson, 'Self-Defense' (1991) 20 *Philosophy & Public Affairs* 283, 362; Rodin, D, *War and Self-defence* (Oxford, OUP, 2002) 70–90.

[11] Non-culpable aggressors are those aggressors who pose an unjust threat through an unintentional aggressive act; they are unaware of the threat or the nature of the threat that they pose, eg, a five-year-old child who points a loaded gun at a person who is entering the room. Non-agent aggressors include people who pose an unjust threat but not through an act of aggression; rather, non-agents are used as objects to threaten. Consider Nozick's example of a person thrown down a narrow well towards another person who is unable to move to avoid the impact. See Nozick (1974) 34.

The right of self-defence is triggered by the *unjust act of aggression* aimed at the defender. Thus the right cannot be asserted against an innocent bystander, who does not pose such a threat.[12]

At the other end of the spectrum, David Rodin advances the view that it is the *unjust aggressor* that triggers the right to self-defence; the key is the moral-fault component of the aggressor's conduct.[13] This approach establishes a narrow right of self-defence that covers only the use of force against culpable aggressors. One of the problems with this position is that it might be interpreted to mean that self-defence has some role in punishment (even if only a minor one). However, punishment is founded on different principles and is aimed at achieving distinct ends, none of which are consistent with the reasons on which the defender may act.[14]

2. Necessity

The requirement of necessity is often viewed as the most important requirement for a claim of self-defence. It addresses two questions. The first is: when may force be used? To which the answer is: only when it is necessary, that is, only as a last resort. The second question is; how much force may be used? The answer to that question is: only that amount necessary to resist the attack.

The necessity requirement raises two related issues: the first concerns the need to retreat, and the second involves the defender's right to go about his or her own business. In some states, the law does not demand that the defender retreat in the face of an imminent threat. Two types of reasons have been given to justify the lack of mandatory retreat. The first is 'right reasoning', or the view that right should never yield to wrong, and the second is 'honour reasoning', which holds that it would be disgraceful for a person to run away from danger.[15] The response to 'right reasoning' is that the freedom of movement and action enjoyed by law-abiding citizens ought to give way when the life of a human being is at stake.[16] As for 'honour reasoning', it is worth pointing out that sparing a person's life cannot be compared with maintaining a person's honour.

The only exception to the rule of retreat is when the attack is taking place in one's home. Here, contrary to the general rule, the common law follows psychological feelings that 'a person's home is their castle' and thus deserves greater protection.[17] Unlike the demand to withdraw in the face of an imminent attack, a

---

[12] Innocent bystanders are those who do not pose a threat to the life of a defender but can be used by the defender in order for him or her to avoid the harm at the cost of harming the innocent bystander. The killing of an innocent bystander might still be justified or excused on grounds of necessity, also known in the US as 'a lesser evil'. See, for example, the American Model Penal Code §3.04 (1985).

[13] Rodin (2002) 77–83.

[14] See note 9 above.

[15] See Beale, JH, 'Retreat from a Murderous Assault' (1903) 16 *Harvard Law Review* 567; Mischke, PE, 'Criminal Law, Homicide, Self-defense, Duty to Retreat' (1981) 48 *Tennessee Law Review* 1000.

[16] Beale (1903) 581.

[17] Ashworth, A, 'Self-defence and the Right to Life' (1975) 34 *Cambridge Law Journal* 282, 284–85, 293–94.

person is not required to refrain from going about his or her own business in anticipation of possible danger. The freedom of law-abiding citizens has a favoured status so as to allow them to continue acting lawfully and move around freely instead of limiting their movement in early attempts to avoid danger.

3. Imminence

A condition of the legitimate exercise of self-defence is that the danger triggering it must be imminent. If the threat is not imminent the defender has to pursue an alternative line of action (eg, turning to the authorities for help). Although this requirement stands on its own, its underlying reasoning suggests that it is derived from the requirement of necessity. Only when a threat is *imminent* is the use of force *necessary* (and hence permitted).[18]

The imminence requirement raises the question of pre-emptive defensive action. Most natural law theorists hold that (within civil society) a pre-emptive attack is permitted as an act of self-defence when the anticipated attack is immediate—for example, when the aggressor has already taken up a weapon. Pre-emptive attack is not permitted when based on mere suspicion and fear.[19] Although this condition is commonly accepted, in recent years the understanding of the condition as requiring an *immediate* or close connection in time between any pre-emptive defensive response and a potential attack (hereafter: immediacy) has attracted much criticism, especially in connection with battered women who kill their abusive partners while the partners are sleeping.

To understand this criticism, consider a hostage held by kidnappers. The hostage is told that she will probably be executed within a week. The history of the kidnappers, as known to the hostage, demonstrates that there is a good chance they will kill her. The hostage finds herself alone with only one guard who has fallen asleep. Her only chance of escape is to kill the guard, who will otherwise call for help when he awakes.[20] The threat posed to the hostage cannot be deemed immediate because she still has an entire week before she will be killed. However, the threat is *imminent* considering that this is probably her last chance to escape. Can it be said, then, that killing the guard is not an act of self-defence merely

---

[18] *Cf* Grotius, H, *The Right of War and Peace*, W Whewell (ed) (Cambridge, CUP, 1853); Rodin (2002) 41; Robinson, PH, *Criminal Law Defenses*, vol 2 (St Paul, MN, West, 1984) §§ 131(b)(3), (c)(1), at 76, 78–9; Lafave, WR and Scott, AW, *Criminal Law*, 3rd edn (St Paul, MN, West, 2000) § 5.7(d), at 495; Rosen, RA, 'On Self-defense Imminence and Women who Kill their Batterers' (1993) 71 *North Carolina Law Review* 371.

[19] Grotius (1853); Locke, J, *Two Treatises of Government*, P Laslett (ed) (Cambridge, CUP, 1988) 279; Pufendorf, S, *On the Duty of Man and Citizen according to Natural Law*, J Tully (ed) (Cambridge, CUP, 1991) 49. Pufendorf even adds that the aggressor has to be in close range of the defender.

[20] This is the example used by McColgan, A, 'In Defence of Battered Women who Kill' (1993) 13 *Oxford Journal of Legal Studies* 508, 517–19, 525; Horder, J, 'Killing the Passive Abuser: A Theoretical Defence' in S Shute and AP Simester (eds), *Criminal Law: Doctrines of The General Part* (Oxford, OUP, 2002) 283; Horder, J, 'Redrawing the Boundaries of Self-defence' (1995) 58 *Modern Law Review* 431, 436; *R v Lavallee* [1990] 1 SCR 852, 889.

because the threat to the hostage's life was not an *immediate* one? In such situations where the threat is 'all over' the defender, there is a 'second-order threat', that is, the threat that, when the aggressor initiates an anticipated and highly probable attack, the danger will be inescapable and the defender will not be able to resist, repel or ward off the attack. This second-order threat makes the first-order threat *imminent*, and it is this characteristic of the first-order threat that justifies the use of force even though the threat is not *immediate*.[21]

This modified imminence requirement is founded on the principle underlying the requirement of *immediacy*, namely, that human life is valuable and should be maintained as long as possible. Joshua Dressler has observed that in recognising the problems faced by battered women while keeping faithful to the value of human life, the American Model Penal Code expanded the right to self-defence to include attempts to avoid harm, even when that harm is not immediately forth-coming. It did so by changing the requirement of 'imminence' to 'immediate necessity'.[22] Yet this definition still falls short of the definition offered by Aileen McColgan, who claims that recognising self-defence in the situations discussed above conforms with the 'lesser harmful results' theory: if a defender has to wait for the anticipated attack in order to use force, then society gains nothing, and the risk of being killed unjustly falls solely on the defender.[23]

Jeremy Horder suggests yet another definition of imminence, which would bal-ance the risk of being killed unjustly by requiring 'a fair and reasonable opportu-nity to do otherwise'. Whereas the requirement of *immediacy* shifts the burden of risk from the aggressor to the defender, and only a subjective requirement of fair opportunity (ie, in cases of putative self-defence) would shift the risk to the aggres-sor, Horder's requirement gives equal treatment to both.[24] In so doing it follows the need to preserve human life.[25] This interpretation is more flexible and is con-sistent with the position that the requirement of imminence is merely one element

---

[21] This term has been suggested by McColgan (1993).

[22] Model Penal Code § 3.04 (1985); Dressler, J, 'Battered Women who Kill their Sleeping Tormentors: Reflections on Maintaining Respect for Human Life while Killing Moral Monsters' in S Shute and AP Simester (eds), *Criminal Law: Doctrines of the General Part* (Oxford, OUP, 2002) 259; Finkelstein, CO, 'Self-defense as a Rational Excuse' (1995–96) 57 *University of Pittsburgh Law Review* 621, 628. The new definition is supposed to include cases in which violence against the defender is about to occur, such as when the abuser is going to his room to fetch a rifle and the woman kills him with a kitchen knife; but it does not include cases of killing sleeping abusers, since there is no 'imme-diate necessity'.

[23] McColgan (1993) 527–8.

[24] Horder (2002) 292–3.

[25] Other suggestions that have been introduced in the US literature include reading the require-ments of 'reasonableness' and 'imminence' as 'inevitable' by referring to the concepts of fairness and equality, which are the grounds for these requirements. (The important element is not the immediacy of the threat but the immediacy of the response necessary in defence.) See Ripstein, A, 'Self-defense and Equal Protection' (1995–96) 57 *University of Pittsburgh Law Review* 685, 702–4. Rosen criticises Ripstein by saying that there are different meanings to the words 'imminence' and 'inevitable', and the interpretation is thus impossible. He proposes cancelling the requirement of imminence and staying with the notion of necessity, which expresses the underlying concept of inevitability or unavoidability. See Rosen (1993), note 17 above. For more criticism and other suggestions, see the symposium articles published in (1995–96) 57 *University of Pittsburgh Law Review*.

of necessity. Ultimately, the defender has to prove that the use of defensive force was necessary, and no other less harmful alternative was available to her. This interpretation is appealing and, as will be explained below, has an important implication when applied to the state's duty of self-defence.

4. Proportionality

The final requirement of claims of self-defence is that of proportionality. The condition is that in the worst situations any harm inflicted on the aggressor must not exceed the potential harm that the aggressor would have inflicted on the defender. Thus a defender may not break an attacker's legs even if this is the only way to avoid getting a 'black eye'.

The proportionality requirement raises the question of what interests fall within the scope of self-defence. Natural law theorists have differentiated between the state of nature and civil society. In a state of nature the right to self-defence extends to acts taken to protect one's life, physical integrity, personal freedom and property. Hobbes justified this expansive view of self-defence by appealing to the liberty each individual has to do everything within his or her power.[26] For Locke, the fact that the aggressor does not respect the defender's right to property means the defender cannot be sure that his or her right to life and freedom will be respected.[27]

In civil society, however, the right is much more limited. It is generally agreed that the right of self-defence extends to resisting aggressors who threaten one's life or who threaten the infliction of severe physical injury. (This right shall be called hereafter the *core-right* to self-defence or *core-right*.) But that agreement does not reach the protection of freedom and property. Pufendorf argues that there is no right to use force in the defence of property itself, unless the thief threatens the life of the defender. In other words, Pufendorf holds that there is no right to self-defence to protect property, only to protect life, and he accepts that life may be threatened in the course of a robbery.

Locke took this position one step further. He claimed that although self-defence cannot be used against a thief who has stolen 'all that I am worth', defensive force may be used against the thief because of the implicit threat the thief poses to the life of the defender. That is, even if the thief does not threaten the life of the defender directly, the force used by the thief to steal the defender's property may still constitute an indirect threat to the life of the defender. The thief might still turn his or her force against the defender, and it is this threat to the defender's life that justifies the defender's response. Yet not all instances of theft, or even all instances of robbery, entail a real or serious threat to the defender's life.[28] This is a

[26] Hobbes, T, *Leviathan*, R Tuck (ed) (Cambridge, CUP, 1991) 91.
[27] Locke (1988). See also Pufendorf (1991).
[28] At least according to current English law, which holds that robbery includes cases in which force was used to seize property but not to threaten the life of the victim (*R v Clouden* [1987] Crim LR 56, CA). Obviously, in cases of theft (ie which do not involve the use of force) the threat to the defender's life is reduced even further.

matter of case-by-case evaluation. Thus, given that Locke's justification for the use of force is the threat to life and limb and not the threat to property, it cannot constitute a general rule for the use of force in defence of property. Grotius holds that force may be used in defence of property only when the life of the defender is endangered either by the thief or by the loss of property. However, this right extends to those situations in which the defender comes into danger trying to defend or recover his or her goods. That is because the defender has a right to try and recover his or her property.

Most contemporary scholars ignore the possibility of self-defence to protect property, probably because they concentrate on the use of lethal force, which would be prohibited as disproportionate to the potential harm to property. Rodin finds the use of force in defence of property upon which one's life directly depends permitted, such as when a thief steals all the water from a person travelling in the desert. That is, in such cases, killing the thief in self-defence is proportionate and thus permissible. Following Grotius, Rodin bases the permission to kill in such cases on the threat to life rather than to property. In all other instances, where there is no threat to life, Rodin argues, the defender is prohibited from using lethal force in defence of property. The reason is that there are established and effective *post facto* means of redress following attacks on property, whereas such means are obviously not available after an attack on a person's life.[29] However, as already mentioned, Rodin's discussion is limited to the use of lethal force and does not address the prospect of self-defence of property.

However, in my view, self-defence ought to be permitted in defence of property, provided it fulfils the standard requirements of necessity, imminence and proportionality.[30] This would mean, among other things, that: (a) proportionate power may be used only to stop an imminent threat to property and not in an attempt to stop a retreating empty-handed thief; and (b) force may be used only if there is no other way *ex ante* to protect the property. It should be stressed that, on this view, under no circumstances would killing be a proportionate use of force in defence of property, unless the loss of property generates a direct threat to life. It is noted that the practical application of this principle raises some difficulties, but the discussion of these must be postponed to another time. Here, it is enough to note that this position is accepted today in England and other jurisdictions, and there are jurisdictions that permit even killing in defence of property.[31] Similarly, jurisdictions in which self-defence is justified by the theory of a vindication of autonomy (eg, Germany) hold that the right of self-defence extends to protect

---

[29] Rodin (2002) 44–5.

[30] For a similar view, see Getzler, J, 'Use of Force in Protecting Property' (2006) 7 *Theoretical Inquiries in Law* 131.

[31] See the wide definition of s 3 of the Criminal Law Act 1967, which covers the use of force in the prevention of crime against property, and the explanation in Smith, J and Hogan, B, *Criminal Law*, 10th edn (London, Butterworths, 2002) 283, 712. See also the law in Israel: Criminal Code 1977, s 34J. But see Fletcher (1988) 35 for the position of some states in the United States that permit killing in defence of property.

against the unjustified violation of a defender's rights, including his or her right to property.[32]

III. FROM THE INDIVIDUAL'S RIGHT TO THE STATE'S DUTY: AN ANALOGY-BASED EXTENSION

The following discussion of the connection between the individual right of self-defence and the state's duty to defend its citizens will involve reference to the individual right of self-defence against threats to life, property and liberty, and to a state's duty to defend its citizens against threats to life and liberty. The distinction between the various types of threats that trigger the individual right and the state's duty are of great importance. The individual right of self-defence against threats to life will be called the *core-right* of self defence, and possible extensions of the individual's right of self-defence to protect against threats to property or to liberty will be called *property-extended* and *liberty-extended* rights respectively, or generally, the *extended* right of self-defence. Subsequently, the state duty to defend its citizens against threats to life will be called *core-duty*, and possible extensions of the duty to include defence against threats to liberty will be called *liberty-extended* duty or *extended* duty.

The best way to explain the connection between the individual right of self-defence and the state's special duty to defend its citizens is either (a) as the duty corresponding to the individual core-right against threats to life, or (b) as derivative from the individual's core-right to self-defence. Both explanations limit the state's duty to the conditions established for the proper exercise of the individual's core-right. A right cannot generate a corresponding duty that requires another person to act beyond the boundaries set by the conditions under which exercise of the right is permissible. If A has a right to X and not to Y, it means that others have a duty to act either in a way that at the very least does not interfere with A's actions with regard to X, or in a way that actively helps A to obtain X. But A's right to X cannot generate a duty in others to act in a way that does not interfere with or promotes Y. Similarly, a derivative right or duty cannot extend beyond the scope of the right from which it derives.

Nevertheless, I propose that the state has a special *extended* duty to respond not only to threats to life but also to severe threats to liberty. One way to establish this connection is to argue that the individual core-right of self-defence generates a special core-duty of self-defence against threats to life or serious physical injury, which is owed by the state to its citizens. The extension of the state's duty to respond also to threats to *liberty* would then be justified by analogy to the state's duty against threats to *life*. The need for an *analogy-based* justification rests on the fact that the core-right of self-defence cannot directly create a wider derivative

---

[32] Fletcher, G, *Rethinking Criminal Law* (Boston, Little Brown, 1978) 864. This is coupled with the absence of a requirement of proportionality—although Fletcher goes on to explain the way in which the German law can limit the scope of self-defence to only physical attacks.

duty. However, as shall be seen, this analogy-based justification is bound to fail. The failure is nevertheless illuminating and aids understanding of the connection between the individual right of self-defence and the state's extended duty to defend its citizens.

This account of the state's liberty-extended duty involves two stages: first, it is necessary to establish that the individual core-right to self-defence generates the corresponding state duty of self-defence against threats to the *life* of its citizens; and subsequently, it is necessary to justify by analogy the extension of the state's core duty of self-defence to include the duty to respond to threats to the *liberty* of its citizens. The argument is that in the realm of the individual, the right to self-defence has been extended by analogy to protect threats to property; and, similarly, we ought to be able to draw on some characteristics of the state's core duty of self-defence against threats to life in order to extend, by analogy, to the state's duty to protect against threats to liberty.

This account, however, suffers from a major weakness, namely, that the two stages of the argument for the state's liberty-extended duty cannot be reconciled. The argument advanced in the second stage is that the individual has only a core-right to self-defence against threats to life, whereas the duty of the state that this right generates extends, by analogy to the core-duty, to include threats to liberty. Yet this argument is unsustainable. According to the analogy-based argument, once we have established that the state has a core duty of self-defence against threats to the lives of its citizens, it is possible to justify the state's extended duty to defend itself from severe threats to liberty as an analogous duty. This is similar to the claim that the right to self-defence should extend to include defence of property. In the discussion of self-defence of property, the claim that defence of property might be justified by appealing to the right not to be killed was expressly rejected. Instead, it was argued that defence of property per se, even when no threat to life is involved, ought to be recognised provided it is subject to the same conditions of necessity, imminence and proportionality that characterise the core-right to self-defence.

Along these lines, it might seem possible to argue for an extension of the state's duty of self-defence to include threats to liberty. The problem with this line of reasoning is that there are important differences between the justifications that ground the individual core-right to self-defence and those that ground the state's core-duty of self-defence. In the individual realm, the core-right to self-defence against threats to life is justified by appealing to a basic right not to be killed, or the right to life. Therefore, it seems legitimate to appeal to a second basic right, that is, the right to property, to ground an analogous derivative right to protect against threats to property.

To draw a similar analogy in the realm of the state, the justification both of the core-duty of self-defence against threats to life and of the extended duty of self-defence against threats to liberty must be of the same kind. However, the core-duty of the state is justified by appealing to the individual core-right to self-defence. Theoretically, this means that the liberty-extended duty of self-defence ought to be justified by reference to an individual's liberty-extended right to self-defence. But the point of this account is to overcome the problem that individual citizens do not have a right to self-defence against threats to liberty. If individual citizens do have such a right, then the most straightforward way to justify the state's core and liberty-extended duties would be to appeal to the individual's liberty-extended right. Indeed, as will be argued in the following sections, individual citizens have an extended right to self-defence against threats to liberty, and consequently, the state's extended duty derives from this right.

IV. THE STATE'S DERIVATIVE DUTY OF SELF-DEFENCE

A second account of the relationship between the individual's right to self-defence and the state's duty of self-defence against threats to life and liberty claims that the individual right to self-defence extends to include a right of self-defence against threats to liberty. This liberty-extended right generates a liberty-extended duty that is owed by the state to its citizens, to defend them against severe threats to liberty. This account requires a two-stage analysis. The first stage establishes an extension of the individual's right to self-defence to include responses to threats to liberty. In the second stage of the analysis, the state's extended duty is derived from the individual's extended right of self-defence.

1. A Right to Self-defence against Threats to Liberty

Do threats to liberty trigger the individual's right to self-defence? Locke was the first to argue that self-defence entails the right to use force, including lethal force, in defence of liberty. He feared that if an aggressor were permitted to take away a defender's freedom, nothing would prevent the aggressor from also depriving the defender of his or her life.[33] Giving a further, intrinsic justification, Rodin argues:

> Life and liberty are often listed together as basic human goods of central importance, and it is sometimes claimed that it is justifiable to kill in defence of liberty. These assertions derive their plausibility from the observation that liberty is a necessary condition for the shaping of any meaningful life. Liberty is both a component of, and a precondition for, many of the substantive goods that we value; in part we value life because of the liberty that it enables us to exercise. For this reason, it is conceived that it may sometimes be proportionate to defend one's liberty with lethal force, for to deprive a person of liberty in certain contexts is to deprive them of meaningful life.[34]

---

[33] This reasoning tallies with the flexible interpretation of the requirement of imminence: defensive force to protect freedom is permitted because that is the last reasonable opportunity for the defender to protect his or her life (even though at the time the defendant is deprived only of freedom, and it is not certain that he or she will be killed later on).

[34] Rodin (2002) 47.

However, on Rodin's view, lethal force may be used only in very extreme situations such as enslavement, lifetime incarceration or other very grave violations of liberty. Even the deprivation of one's political freedoms does not permit the use of lethal force, for only in extreme situations can the loss of liberty compare to the loss of life. Yet although Rodin is willing to permit the use of lethal force in extreme situations, he adds that, under such circumstances, it will usually be difficult to fulfil the requirement of necessity, because of the problem of determining whether and when it is necessary to kill to escape the harm.

Although the justification Rodin gives for the use of lethal force in defence of liberty is sound, the limits he places on that permission are incorrect. Obviously, not every violation of liberty generates permission to use lethal force. In many cases, such force would be disproportionate to the loss of liberty, and in many cases *post facto* redress is possible. However, the loss of political freedom, by which it is meant the loss of the possibility to maintain self-government, is a grave loss of liberty. A loss of this kind triggers a right to self-defence and would justify even the use of lethal force. As Locke argued, once political freedom is lost, individuals have no way to ensure control over future decisions regarding their preferred way of life or the preservation of the way of life they have already chosen. When controls over past and future choices are directly impeded, and when individual freedoms are severely violated, citizens are probably not in a position where they can effectively oppose or stop potential harms, including the possible loss of life. Thus, at the time they are faced with the loss of their political freedom, the threat to their individual freedoms may be imminent, even if some time passes before the threat is realised.

This Lockean argument draws on the basic right not to be killed and on other fundamental rights to our various basic interests. It draws on the basic right not to be killed because life is closely connected with the idea of liberty, and is at least partly justified by it. As Rodin explained, liberty is a necessary condition for a meaningful life. It is both a component of and a precondition for many substantive goods we value. It is an indispensable means to the advancement of personal projects and interests. Therefore, a threat to one's liberty is also a potential threat to one's life. The argument is also supported by other fundamental rights, for a threat to liberty is a threat to an entire range of basic interests. The combined basic rights on which this extension draws, and the importance of the right not to be killed in the justification of this extension, make the extension an inseparable part of the right to self-defence rather than a mere analogy to the right to self-defence against threats to life.[35]

The practical implications of the interest in liberty do not cause special difficulties, as Rodin claims. This conclusion holds even if we adopt the more stringent approach of determining whether the necessary conditions for self-defence have been satisfied by using an objective test with subjective elements. A two-stage test can be constructed in the following manner: (a) did the defender honestly believe

---

[35] It is interesting that Art 2, para 2(c)) of the European Convention of Human Rights allows for the use of lethal force in response to 'insurrection', a term that includes non-violent revolution—and thus captures threats to liberty per se.

that his or her actions were a necessary and proportionate response to an imminent attack? If so, (b) was the defender's response reasonable, that is, would a *reasonable* person (or a more subjective test of a reasonable person with the characteristics of the defender) respond in a similar way, given the information that was *reasonably* available in the circumstances?[36] The practical implication of this test means that future knowledge as to the accuracy of the judgement is not relevant. It is a question of common sense. Similarly, as argued above, the imminence condition should be interpreted broadly to include 'the last reasonable opportunity', even if the attack is not immediate in time.

2. Arguments for the State's Derivative Duty of Self-defence

A. The Argument from Third-party Duties

The first stage of the argument for the state's duty of self-defence showed that the individual right to self-defence can be extended to include a right to protect against threats to liberty. Having completed that part of the argument, we now address the second stage, which requires showing that the state's duty can be derived from the individual's liberty-extended right. Two arguments for this derivation will be examined and rejected, before developing what is the most promising line in favour of it.

The first attempt to justify the state's duty is based on a comparison between the state and unspecified third parties who come to the help of a defender. Although this argument is ultimately flawed, it is important to review it so as to understand the alternative justification offered below.

A defender's right to self-defence gives permission (*liberty*) to unspecified third parties[37] to come to the aid of the defender. The aim of this corresponding permission is to help save the life and protect the physical integrity of the defender, and nothing here prevents the state from acting as the relevant third party. If the state through its agents can provide the requisite aid, it is, at the very least, *permitted* to do so. The comparison between the state and other possible third-party defenders must obviously be sensitive to the distinct characteristics of the state— its powers and the restrictions placed on their use for various reasons. But the justification for granting third-party permission to engage in self-defence does not distinguish directly between different types of third-party defenders. As such, it applies equally to the state.

Still, this line of reasoning can take us only so far. All it can do is establish *permission* for the state to intervene, whereas it purports to justify the claim that the

---

[36] Obviously, if we adopt the more lenient approach, which demands only that the defender honestly believe in the imminence of the attack and in the necessity of the response, we would not encounter any special difficulties.

[37] The reference is to 'unspecified' third parties, to distinguish them from third parties who owe a special duty of care to the defender. The latter are discussed below under '2. The Argument from a Special Duty of Care'.

state has a *duty* to intervene—one that is not dependent on the state's goodwill but on an *obligation* that the state is expected to satisfy. The answer to this objection lies in this correct understanding of the nature of the permission to intervene. Permission, it must be remembered, is a weak form of a duty that corresponds to the individual's right.[38]

However, many jurisdictions do not recognise the conceptual structure of the relationship between the right of self-defence and the corresponding duty, which would not only *permit* but would also *require* third-party intervention. Two arguments are commonly given for refusing to recognise an *obligation* to intervene, although, as shall be seen, neither applies in the case of the state.[39] The first argument is that intervention will often entail danger to the life of the third-party intervener or rescuer.[40] Coming to the aid of a defender may mean putting your own life at risk. But this reasoning only justifies limiting the duty to cases in which third parties will not be putting their lives in danger. It cannot explain the refusal to recognise a limited duty to intervene where no significant risk is required.[41]

The second argument says that a duty (ie, an obligation) to intervene would involve a substantial intrusion into the freedom of the third-party intervener. The

[38] Raz holds that 'to have a right means that an aspect of one's well-being formulates a sufficient reason for holding some other person(s) to be under duty with regards to X'; Raz, J, *Morality of Freedom* (Oxford, Clarendon Press, 1986) 166. Thus, if the right of self-defence is to be understood as a right, it must generate a corresponding duty. The aggressor's duty not to attack the defender derives from the defender's fundamental right not to be killed, which is, in turn, the basis for the defender's right of self-defence. Therefore, the right of self-defence does not impose any meaningful additional duty on the aggressor. At most, we can talk about a duty not to thwart a defensive response. Hence, it must be regarded as imposing a duty on third parties to come to the help of the defender.

[39] A third-party obligation to intervene on behalf of a defender is a sub-category of the general duty to rescue. The obligation to aid a defender is only one instance in which a third party may be required to rescue a person in physical distress. These are often among the more problematic situations, because in helping, the third party may put his or her own life at risk. Thus, the various reasons given to explain why a general duty to rescue is not recognised bear extra weight in these cases—so much so that even in jurisdictions that do recognise the 'good Samaritan law', the obligation to intervene is limited to only those situations in which such intervention does not endanger the helper's life. On the other hand, an obligation to intervene in the case of self-defence differs from other instances covered by the general duty to rescue. This is because in instances of self-defence, the intervention, practically, means giving permission to third parties to use force against other people (aggressors), whereas in other situations of distress, a duty to rescue does not necessarily entail such permission (eg, intervention in situations that fall under the heading of necessity). For a more detailed discussion of the general duty to rescue, see Malm, HM, 'Bad Samaritan Laws: Harm, Help or Hype?' (2000) 19 *Law and Philosophy* 684; Woozley, AD, 'A Duty to Rescue: Some Thoughts on Criminal Liability' (1983) 69(2) *Virginia Law Review* 1273; Silver, J, 'The Duty to Rescue: A Re-examination and Proposal' (1985) 26 *William & Mary Law Review* 423. *Cf* Ashworth, A, 'The Scope of Criminal Liability for Omissions' (1989) 105 *Law Quarterly Review* 424.

[40] Hereafter, the terms 'third-party intervener' and 'rescuer' will be used interchangeably.

[41] One answer to this objection is that if we were to create a legal duty to rescue only with respect to situations not involving risk to the rescuer, especially in situations that give rise to a right to self-defence, the duty recognised would be so marginal as to make it worthless. See Woozley (1983) 1276. However, in those jurisdictions that do recognise a general duty to rescue, it is indeed limited to situations in which helping a person in distress does not involve putting at risk the rescuer's life. For example, see the law in Israel: Thou Shalt Not Stand Idly by The Blood of Thy Neighbour Act (1998), which states in s 1(a): 'Any person faced with another person who is in serious and immediate danger to her life, physical integrity or health must provide help unless doing so puts the helper and/or other persons in danger' (author's translation).

aim of the law is to maximise individual liberty so as to allow each individual to pursue his or her own conception of good. Therefore, the only legitimate constraints to one's freedom are those necessary to restrain someone from causing injury or loss to another person. An obligation to rescue requires a person to act in a specific way and at a specific time. By its nature, this demand may be inconvenient to the rescuer, may conflict with his or her interests and may prevent him or her from doing anything else at that particular time.[42] A related argument is that even if it is appropriate to require some positive action, rescue is not one of them. The decision to rescue a person in distress should be left to the conscience of each individual. The imposition of a legal duty would be a form of illegitimate paternalism on the part of the state.

Even if we accept the above reasons for rejecting a general duty to rescue, they do not apply in the case of the state. Unlike individual citizens, the state has a prima facie duty to rescue its citizens. It cannot argue that because the life of its agents may be put at risk (which is the only sensible way to interpret the idea of 'putting the state's life at risk'), there can be no obligation to rescue its citizens.[43] Similarly, the concept of individual freedom is not applicable in the case of the state. The state itself has no interest in 'freedom'. Hence, it seems possible to argue that with respect to the state, the right to self-defence generates a duty—an obligation—and not mere permission.

B. The Argument from a Special Duty of Care

Although it may be possible to ground the state's obligation on a general duty owed to defenders by unspecified third parties, our demands on the state are more basic than that argument allows. It is not merely that the reasons given above do not apply to the state, but rather that the state is created *for the very purpose of providing defensive aid*. At least one of the major roles of the state is to secure the lives and liberty of its citizens and protect them from internal and external threats.[44] One of the state's core functions, and perhaps even the central reason for its existence, is to guarantee security. Thus, the state has a prior duty of care based on its

---

[42] This would be true whether failure to fulfil such an obligation were dealt with in criminal law or civil law.

[43] It should be stressed that the argument is only for a prima facie duty. Obviously, it does not necessarily mean that the state ought to rescue its citizens whatever the risk to its agents. State agents are, of course, also citizens, and their well-being should also be taken into account. All that is argued for is that the state ought to rescue its citizens even if some risk is involved. The balancing point between the lives of the rescuers and the lives of the persons in distress differs depending on whether the rescuer is a private citizen or a state agent. Arguments by the state that maintain, for example, that the lives of many firefighters should not be risked to save a few trapped miners, or that police officers should not be stationed on airplanes to meet terrorists when they board because it would constitute a suicide mission, do not undermine the existence of a duty to rescue. Such arguments only show that the level of risk to the lives of state agents is also a relevant consideration, and when the level of risk is very high it might tilt the balance against the rescue mission.

[44] This role of the state is commonly accepted by the various traditions of democracy, whether as the sole role in the libertarian tradition, or as one of many of the roles of the state in communitarian traditions.

underlying protective purpose. For that reason, rather than a comparison between the state and unspecified third parties, the better comparison is to third parties who have a special duty of care.

As we have seen, the right to self-defence is commonly understood to give unspecified third parties mere *permission* to intervene; yet it is also agreed that those third parties who owe a special duty of care to the defender *must* intervene. They are under an obligation to assist the defender even at great risk to their own lives, although the level of risk they are required to undertake may vary according to the specific duty of care. Thus, a mother must aid her son when the latter is being attacked; a doctor must try to stop a nurse who is about to inject a patient with a lethal amount of morphine; a lifeguard must attempt to rescue a person who is drowning, and so on. Similarly, a police officer has a duty to intervene on behalf of someone trying to fend off wrongful aggression. It would be an unnecessary complication to explain the police officer's duty of care as arising from his or her contract with the state, and the state's duty as arising from a comparison to the general duties of unspecified third parties. The more direct explanation of the police officer's duty is based on the state's special duty of care to protect its citizens.

What is the source of the obligation to intervene owed by third parties with special duties of care? Does it derive from the defender's right to self-defence, or is it rooted in some other explanation? The answer is found in the common characteristics that define this category of third parties. The duty originates in the special duty of care, rather than in the defender's right to self-defence. More accurately, the obligation to act is embodied in the special moral relationship between the third party and the defender, although, again, this moral relationship may differ from one case to another depending on the circumstances of its formation (eg, by promise, contract, familial conduct, etc).

Although special moral relationships may establish a duty to protect defenders, the content of this special duty, in the case of self-defence, does in a sense derive from or correspond to the defender's right to self-defence, at least in the core case of intentional attack by a culpable person. Third parties are permitted and required to intervene only when a defender is permitted to defend himself or herself. Moreover, their permission extends only to actions that are permitted to the defender, ie, they are restricted by the requirements that there be an unjust threat, necessity, imminence and proportionality, Thus, third parties draw on a distinct and independent duty of care to explain why they are not only at liberty to assist the defender but are obligated to do so. They appeal to the defender's justification to explain why they are permitted to harm another person.

Unlike other situations in which third-party assistance does not involve hurting others, cases of self-defence often require the defender to inflict harm and perhaps even to take the life of an aggressor. Thus a third party must provide a justification for preferring the life of the defender to that of the aggressor. The justification is that of the defender himself or herself. The third-party claim is as follows: I have a duty to protect the life of the defender; therefore, in any situation in which the defender is permitted to protect himself or herself, I must assist him or her. Situations of self-defence are no exception to this duty—whatever right of self-defence the defender has, his or her permission extends to include third-party help.[45] So, although the duty to aid the defender is based on a special duty of care, it is nevertheless correct to refer to this duty as being derived from the defender's right to self-defence.

C. The Argument from Transference of the Individual Right

Despite its plausibility, the argument about a special duty of care ultimately falls short of giving a proper description of the relationship between citizens and the state. The 'special duty of care' is the basis for the state's *existing* duty to use the criminal law in its current scope. However, if the individual's right of self-defence is to ground a special duty that, in turn, makes the state duty-bound in certain situations to expand the scope of criminal law beyond its commonly recognised boundaries, then the relationship between citizens and the state must be even stronger than a special duty of care. For the state to have a special duty of self-defence, not only must citizens have a right of self-defence that generates a corresponding special duty, but that corresponding duty must be *transferred* to the state.

Not every threat that triggers the individual's right of self-defence entails this type of transference. Threats that trigger the state's duty of self-defence are distinct in that they pose a danger to all, or at least to a large majority of citizens. This requirement—that at least a very large majority will be threatened—is justified as an institutional limitation. Ordinarily, criminal law can be used only when the public interest is threatened, and that principle ought to be maintained even when the law undergoes expansion. Furthermore, unlike typical situations of self-defence, an individual citizen whose liberty is threatened in this type of situation does not appear face-to-face with one or a small number of aggressors. The number of aggressors is unknown, and the threat, although not physically present, may nevertheless be a real and imminent one.

These types of threats to the life or liberty of individuals cannot be answered by individual citizens. In these circumstances, not only do individual citizens appeal to the state for help, but they transfer their extended right of self-defence to the state as the only institution that can effectively resist the threat against them. This, so it seems, is the reason for referring to the state's duty to defend itself in terms of a right—because it is the result of individuals transferring their rights of self-defence to the state. In this transfer, the rights of citizens are transformed into a duty, in the same way that other rights are transformed when they are transferred

---

[45] In other words, whether this right is based on a theory of forced consequences, forced choice, lesser harmful results or rights theory, it would extend to allow the use of defensive force by third parties who owe a general duty of care to the defender. See Wallerstein, S, 'Justifying Self-defense: A Theory of Forced Consequences' (2005) 91 *Virginia Law Review* 999 (discussing possible justifications for the right to self-defence).

to third parties. When the rights of a landowner are transferred to a guardian, the guardian is obligated (and not merely permitted) to take all necessary steps to act on behalf of and to preserve the rights of the owner.

D. The Just Cause of Action Requirement

Up to this point, the focus has been on the existence of a right to self-defence in the criminal law, which prevents ascription of blame to a defender, or to third parties who intervene to provide assistance. But having a right means that one 'has a right to do wrong' without the interference of others.[46] Acting upon one's right is not necessarily the *just* course of action, or to use Suzanne Uniacke's terminology, it may not be the right thing to do, 'all things considered'.[47] Indeed, at times, justice might require that a person *not* exercise his or her right. For example, when someone has a right to freedom of expression, he or she is entitled to express sympathy for Nazism if he or she wishes. But that does not make his or her act of expression the right thing to do. We can say coherently that this person has exercised his or her legitimate right and, at the same time, acted wrongly.

Similarly, there is an important distinction between having a right to self-defence and acting justly in self-defence. The state is a special entity and is expected to act on principles of justice. Thus, unless it can be established not only that the individual has a right to self-defence against threats to liberty but also that exercising that right is a *just* course of action, the right to self-defence cannot form the basis of the state's liberty-extended duty of self-defence. This is especially true if the duty is meant to justify the state's power to use coercive measures via the criminal law.

The question, then, is whether acting in self-defence against intentional (and politically motivated) threats to the life and liberty of citizens is also a just cause of action. In this context, acting in self-defence against a culpable aggressor does indeed seem to be a just response. Intentional (and politically motivated) actors are aware of the harmful consequences involved and choose to carry out harmful, criminal enterprises. According to the forced consequences theory by which, as argued elsewhere, the right of self-defence is justified,[48] a defensive response to intentional threats to life and liberty of the types discussed here is supported by the guilt-based justification of the causer pays. According to this theory, an aggressor forces the victim to choose either to use force against the aggressor or else to be injured by the aggressor. By contrast, the aggressor faces no such forced choice. *Ex hypothesi*, he has the option of refraining from attacking the victim and has acted culpably in refusing to exercise restraint. Thus, if some harm must befall either the

---

[46] Raz, J, *The Authority of Law: Essays on Law and Morality* (Oxford, Clarendon Press, 1979) 266–7; Dworkin, R, *Taking Rights Seriously* (Cambridge, MA, Harvard University Press, 1977) 188; Waldron, J, 'A Right to Do Wrong' (1981) 92 *Ethics* 21; Waldron, J, 'Galston on Rights' (1983) 93 *Ethics* 325; Galston, W, 'On The Alleged Rights to Do Wrong: A Response to Waldron' (1983) 93 *Ethics* 320; but see Mackie, J, 'Can There Be a Right-based Moral Theory?' (1978) 3 *Midwest Studies in Philosophy* 350.

[47] Uniacke (2004).

[48] Wallerstein (2005) 1027.

aggressor or the victim in an attempt to prevent the threat from materialising, it is the aggressor who deliberately created the situation and who deserves to suffer the harm.[49] That is, in such instances, the moral guilt of the aggressor plays a role in justifying the exercise of the right to self-defence.[50] Thus, the argument is that the individual is justified (ie, for reasons of justice) in acting in self-defence against intentional threats to liberty and life, and consequently, the state has a duty, based on principles of justice, to act in self-defence.[51]

V. THE SPECIAL DUTY OF SELF-DEFENCE AND CRIMINAL LAW

So far, we have established that a special duty originates from the individual's right of self-defence, which, when exercised to protect against intentional threats to life and liberty of the type discussed here, is not merely a *right* but also a just cause of action. It is still necessary, however, to explain how this special duty creates an obligation for the state to expand the scope of the criminal law, in certain situations.

The structure of the right to self-defence incorporates two levels of protection. At the first level, the state is required to respond to any 'real threat' by enforcing the criminal law. This duty will be called the state's protection-duty. This is the ordinary duty of the state to protect its citizens. Only when this first level of protection fails and threats become 'real and imminent' are individuals permitted to

[49] Note that the term 'desert' does not refer to penal desert generally but specifically to the guilt-based theory for self-defence. Desert, it is argued, is the reason, for example, why the state is allowed to kill a person who is holding hostages in a bank robbery. The police may be permitted to kill the robber (assuming there is not another, less extreme way to neutralise him or her while ensuring the well-being of the hostages), because the robber intentionally created a threat to the lives of the hostages and hence deserves the consequence of whatever (proportional) force is necessary to resolve the situation.

[50] In contrast, according to the forced consequences justification, the right to self-defence against non-culpable and non-agent aggressors is based on the causal connection per se. Consequently, in these instances, acting on the right to self-defence is not necessarily consistent with acting justly. Thus, although a right to self-defence may be recognised, it might be the case that the defender will be required to compensate the aggressor in the aftermath of the attack. Other situations can also be imagined in which, notwithstanding the defender's right to defend himself or herself, the just thing to do would be to refrain from any response. Consider, for example, a single defender who is faced with a large number of innocent aggressors, or a defender who is facing a young child who is playing with a loaded gun. Scholars have had conflicting intuitions regarding this type of situation. The defender theoretically has a right to kill the child in self-defence and would not be ascribed criminal liability for doing so, even if this is the wrong course of action and the defender should refrain from acting on his or her right. (This is the meaning of having a right—a right to do wrong. See note 46 above.) Some of those who believe that the defender should refrain from responding to the oncoming attack mistakenly conclude that there should be no right to self-defence in these situations; the correct analysis, however, distinguishes between having a right and doing the right thing in the specific circumstances.

[51] It should be noted that the fact that an aggressor deserves whatever harm follows from an act of self-defence does not mean that the defender may act for reasons of desert. First, the desert referred to here is *not* the type of desert concerning punishment—what might be called *penal desert*—generally associated with the concept of 'desert' within criminal law. Second, the defender, when responding to an imminent threat, cannot be motivated by or act for reasons of penal desert, ie, because the aggressor deserves to be *punished* for his or her actions. Instead, the defender may act only to resist the attack because he or she is faced with a forced choice between his or her life and the life of the aggressor.

use force. That is to say, in enforcing the criminal law, the state is supposed to stop threats at an earlier stage, before they become imminent.

Things change, however, when we turn to examine the state's duty of self-defence. The reason for recognising this special duty is to expand the power of the state in order to enable the state to thwart at early stages criminal enterprises that would otherwise not be prohibited by the criminal law. In other words, an appeal to the duty of self-defence is based on the understanding that in certain areas all the threats that may be restricted in accordance with the principles that govern the state's protecting duty are threats that are 'last-resort-to-the-state'. However, the category of acts that are the last reasonable opportunity for the state to effectively intervene includes more than just those acts that can be restricted by 'ordinary' criminal law (the principles that govern the state's protecting duty); the restriction of these additional acts can be justified only by the duty of self-defence.

To understand how the scope of the duty of self-defence can be so far-reaching, we need to turn to the requirement of imminence, which is an aspect of necessity. Earlier it has been argued that this requirement ought to be understood as 'the last reasonable opportunity to respond'. This interpretation recognises that there might be situations in which the last reasonable opportunity to act is some time before the danger becomes immediate, such as in the hostage example discussed above. Threats that trigger the individual's right to self-defence may in many instances pose a type of danger similar to the type that kidnappers impose on their hostages. The only way to resist the danger effectively is to act some time before it becomes immediate. When the danger becomes immediate, it may be too late to eliminate it. Hence, the last reasonable opportunity to respond effectively to the threat is to intervene at a much earlier stage in its formation.

This idea is not foreign to criminal law and is evident, for example, in the offence of conspiracy, which stems from the recognition of the additional threat posed by the group element and the need to stop criminal enterprises at earlier stages in order to prevent eventual harm. Yet we have to be very careful that the last reasonable opportunity does not become *any* reasonable opportunity. The importance of personal liberties, including the freedoms of speech and association, cannot be overemphasised. If the last reasonable opportunity is defined incorrectly, enormous harm could be done to these freedoms in the name of the state's duty of self-defence.

Despite the notion of 'the last reasonable opportunity to respond', the individual right to self-defence applies only to narrowly defined emergency situations in which the threat is too immediate to resort to normal legal processes. Such restrictions on the right help to ensure that the principle of self-defence cannot be employed to undermine the normal safeguards of criminal law. How, then, can we expand the scope of self-defence to allow the criminalisation of conduct that is temporally remote from its harmful consequences and that is not otherwise prohibited by 'ordinary' criminal law? The answer is found in the relationship between the two levels of protection described above, namely between the individual's right to self-defence and the state's 'ordinary' use of criminal law.

Every person has a basic right to protect his or her life and liberty from inevitable unjust harm by another, a right that originally extended to allow all actions necessary to resist or repel the unjust threat. However, because the state is significantly more effective in preventing such harms, and because leaving the issue of personal safety to individuals may lead to anarchy and the collapse of organised society, the state has taken over the main responsibility of preventing harm to others. Under this arrangement, individuals retain the right of self-defence only for those emergency situations in which unjust harm is inevitable and the state cannot respond. The underlying assumption is that, apart from such emergencies, the state can provide a sufficient and comprehensive defence to its citizens through the use of 'ordinary' criminal law. Thus, in non-emergencies, individuals are no longer forced to choose between their lives and the lives of aggressors,[52] since they can turn to state authorities to prevent non-immediate harms. Consequently, the individual right to self-defence is defined through its internal requirements as a complimentary right that does not overlap with criminal law.

The threats that trigger the state's duty of self-defence, however, present us with a different picture, which diverges from the underlying assumption described above in two respects. First, 'ordinary' criminal law does not provide a sufficient response even to situations that trigger the individual right of self-defence; that is, the threats of the type discussed here can often be stopped only if the state may intervene at a very early stage, which is not permitted under 'ordinary' criminal law. The intervention at this early stage is, nevertheless, *necessary* and is 'the last reasonable opportunity to respond' to stop the threat from materialising (ie, the threat is *imminent*).

Second, in these emergency situations (be it at the early stages of the criminal enterprise or at a later stage), individuals cannot effectively resist, repel or ward off such threats. Their inability to resist the threat generates the state's derivative extended duty to protect its citizens (ie, duty of self-defence), as explained in the previous section. Furthermore, because the 'ordinary' criminal law fails to provide sufficient comprehensive defence to situations that trigger the right of self-defence, the state is permitted to go beyond the 'ordinary' criminal law in carrying out its duty of self-defence. This extension is justified by the objective of self-defence: to resist, repel or ward off an imminent unjust threat. The narrow definition of the individual right to self-defence, which ensures that the right will not undermine the safeguards of criminal law, is based on the assumption that criminal law provides a comprehensive defence. Hence, when 'ordinary' criminal law may be applied, there is no need for the individual to resort to the use of force. However, when regular legal procedures cannot be used to defend the individual and when there is no way to avoid the threat, the individual is permitted to respond as necessary. When the individual cannot, the state must.

---

[52] This explanation is based on 'forced choice' as the preferred justification in the case of culpable aggressors. See also notes 50–1 above and accompanying text.

CONCLUSION

It has been argued that, in carrying out its duty of self-defence, the state has two special features that distinguish it from individual actors. First, the state does not defend itself, but rather its citizens. Second, the state is an artificial entity created for the purpose of securing its citizens. This means that the state has a unique role in identifying and punishing those who wrong others. The state is responsible for maintaining a secure sphere for its citizens and is granted permission to use coercive measures to accomplish its purpose. The criminal law is a primary means to achieve that end, and it is also one of the main tools used by the state in carrying out its duty of self-defence. In practice, this means that two main responsibilities of the state—to punish and to defend its citizens—may coincide, and this convergence raises some interesting questions.[53]

As an artificial entity, the state also has far more power than any particular individual in relation to aggressors. However, the number and strength of the aggressors are not necessarily important factors. In some instances, small groups of aggressors whose members are placed in strategic positions may generate more severe dangers than groups with larger memberships. This difference does not affect the nature of the internal restrictions placed on the state's duty of self-defence. Rather, it changes what counts as an imminent threat triggering the state's duty of self-defence and what amounts to a necessary and proportionate response.

The idea of the state as uniquely situated as an agent of self-defence raises obvious concerns. It is necessary to ensure that the duty of self-defence will not be abused by granting the state more powers than the duty requires. The state's acquisition of power inevitably comes at the expense of civil liberties, and we must take care not to give away too much of our freedom. When we extend the state's permission to criminalise activity that would otherwise go unpunished, we inevitably reduce our freedom of expression and action. The balance is a delicate one: on the one hand, it is necessary to grant the state sufficient powers to secure our liberty, and, on the other hand, any power given to the state reduces the very liberty it aims to protect. The fear of violating citizens' rights refers both to the rights of law-abiding citizens and to the rights of aggressors. For, although aggressors may have no standing to argue for their rights, justice demands that the violation of their rights be minimal and limited.[54]

---

[53] These questions must be left for a later discussion.

[54] See Rawls, J, *A Theory of Justice*, 2nd edn (Cambridge, MA, Harvard University Press, 1999) 190–1. Rawls explains that '[a] person's right to complain is limited to violations of principles he acknowledges himself. A complaint is a protest addressed to another in good faith. It claims a violation of a principle that both parties accept'. Nevertheless, not giving the aggressor a stand does not entail automatically having a right to suppress and restrict her activities: 'Others may have a right to complain. They may have this right not as a rustice to uphold it] whenever others are disposed to act unjustly.'

There is, of course, an additional practical concern that the powers granted may be abused by the state. This practical concern, which focuses on how state authorities implement the moral duty to use their powers, is distinct from the theoretical concern about the need to restrict moral permission (and duty) to use force only to those instances in which it is found necessary. There has been no attempt to address the practical concern here, in part because it bears on the current discussion only if one believes that without a way to ensure that authorities will not abuse their powers, we ought not to grant those powers in the first place. To accept that view, one must also believe that the threat posed by the likelihood that state authorities will abuse the special powers accorded to them is more real, and thus more serious, than the one posed by the potential threats to liberty and life discussed here. However, current legal arrangements, such as the separation of powers and the role of the courts and the legislature, are capable of ensuring that the duty to use special powers will not be abused, or at least of minimising the likelihood of this concern materialising to the point that there is a substantially higher risk from a threat of the kind that triggers the special duty of self-defence.

This chapter has shown that a duty of self-defence can form the basis for an extension of criminal law beyond the restrictions of direct harm and even beyond its currently recognised boundaries. However, this special duty is triggered only when the threat is of the kind discussed above, that is, a threat of direct harm to the whole society and of a kind that cannot be responded to by individual citizens. Yet even when such a duty is triggered, and it is further shown that the 'ordinary' criminal law does not provide sufficient protection, the state's powers are limited by the application of the internal requirements of the individual right of self-defence: necessity, imminence and proportionality. It must be clear that the state's duty of self-defence developed here is not really a duty to defend *itself* but rather to defend its citizens. Furthermore, those who invoke the state's duty must be sensitive to the unique features of the state as a defender.

The state has a positive duty to defend its citizens against certain threats. This duty exists regardless of the internal conditions within the democratic state. Of course, it does *not* follow that there is one set of laws and regulations that must be implemented in all states, or at all costs. The failure of a state to introduce particular laws does not necessarily entail the state's failure to uphold its obligations. On the contrary, the internal requirements of the duty of self-defence are flexible and sensitive to, among other things, issues such as the stability of the state and its society. A case-by-case assessment of threats to the citizens and the state is required to uphold the conditions of necessity and imminence. Hence, the duty to put in place new far-fetching criminal restrictions may differ from one state to another.

It should also be stressed that the need to comply with various limitations has its price—one that we must recognise and accept. If we want to keep our basic freedoms and maintain our democratic systems while protecting ourselves from these types of threats, we must accept that there is no hermetic protection. We will, sometimes, have to compromise on the quality of that protection and take some risks.

One final comment: this chapter has argued that a right of self-defence may justify some of the currently recognised exceptions that proscribe remote harm and may allow for even further restrictions to be placed in certain situations, and under strict conditions. Although the discussion has proceeded here in general terms, it is clear that there are only a very limited number of threats that can comply with the threshold conditions necessary to trigger the state's special duty of self-defence and that are further left unanswered by the ordinary criminal law. One that comes to mind is the threat posed by anti-democratic groups aiming to overthrow democratic regimes. This type of threat has unique characteristics that appear to require very early intervention to be effective. More in-depth analysis of this type of threat, however, will have to be left to another time. As for the threat posed by terrorism as such, terrorism, it must be remembered, is only a tool to achieve further goals. It is unclear if terrorism itself is a threat that triggers the state's duty of self-defence. Some of the ends to which terrorism aims, however, may be threats of this type. Yet any particular case will require careful analysis.

REFERENCES

Ashworth, A, 'Self-defence and the Right to Life' (1975) 34 *Cambridge Law Journal* 282, 284–85, 293–94.

—— 'The Scope of Criminal Liability for Omissions' (1989) 105 *Law Quarterly Review* 424.

Beale, JH, 'Retreat from a Murderous Assault' (1903) 16 *Harvard Law Review* 567.

Dressler, J, 'Battered Women who Kill their Sleeping Tormentors: Reflections on Maintaining Respect for Human Life while Killing Moral Monsters' in S Shute and AP Simester (eds), *Criminal Law: Doctrines of the General Part* (Oxford, OUP, 2002).

Dworkin, R, *Taking Rights Seriously* (Cambridge, MA, Harvard University Press, 1977).

Finkelstein, CO, 'Self-defense as a Rational Excuse' (1995–96) 57 *University of Pittsburgh Law Review* 621.

Fletcher, GP, *Rethinking Criminal Law* (Boston, Little Brown, 1978).

—— *A Crime of Self-Defense: Bernhard Goetz and the Law on Trial* (Chicago, University of Chicago Press, 1988).

—— 'Punishment and Self-defense' (1989) 8 *Law & Philosophy* 201.

Galston, W, 'On the Alleged Rights to Do Wrong: A Response to Waldron' (1983) 93 *Ethics* 320.

Getzler, J, 'Use of Force in Protecting Property' (2006) 7 *Theoretical Inquiries in Law* 131.

Grotius, H, *The Right of War and Peace*, W Whewell (ed) (Cambridge, CUP, 1853).

Hobbes, T, *Leviathan*, R Tuck (ed) (Cambridge, CUP, 1991).

Horder, J, 'Redrawing the Boundaries of Self-defence' (1995) 58 *Modern Law Review* 431.

—— 'Killing the Passive Abuser: A Theoretical Defence' in S Shute and AP Simester (eds), *Criminal Law: Doctrines of The General Part* (Oxford, OUP, 2002).

Lafave, WR and Scott, AW, *Criminal Law*, 3rd edn (St Paul, MN, West, 2000).

Locke, J, *Two Treatises of Government*, P Laslett (ed) (Cambridge, CUP, 1988).

Mackie, J, 'Can There Be a Right-based Moral Theory?' (1978) 3 *Midwest Studies in Philosophy* 350.

Malm, HM, 'Bad Samaritan Laws: Harm, Help or Hype?' (2000) 19 *Law and Philosophy* 684.

McColgan, A, 'In Defence of Battered Women who Kill' (1993) 13 *Oxford Journal of Legal Studies* 508.

Mischke, PE, 'Criminal Law, Homicide, Self-defense, Duty to Retreat' (1981) 48 *Tennessee Law Review* 1000.

Nozick, R, *Anarchy State and Utopia* (New York, Basic Books, 1974).

Pufendorf, S, *On the Duty of Man and Citizen according to Natural Law*, J Tully (ed) (Cambridge, CUP, 1991).

Rawls, J, *A Theory of Justice*, 2nd edn (Cambridge, MA, Harvard University Press, 1999).

Raz, J, *The Authority of Law: Essays on Law and Morality* (Oxford, Clarendon Press, 1979).

—— *Morality of Freedom* (Oxford, Clarendon Press, 1986).

Ripstein, A, 'Self-defense and Equal Protection' (1995–96) 57 *Universirt of Pittsburgh Law Review* 685.

Robinson, PH, *Criminal Law Defenses*, vol 2 (St Paul, MN, West, 1984).

Rodin, D, *War and Self-defence* (Oxford, OUP, 2002).

Rosen, RA, 'On Self-defense Imminence and Women who Kill their Batterers' (1993) 71 *North Carolina Law Review* 371.

Silver, J, 'The Duty to Rescue: A Re-examination and Proposal' (1985) 26 *William & Mary Law Review* 423.

Smith, J and Hogan, B, *Criminal Law*, 10th edn (London, Butterworths, 2002).

Thomson, JJ, 'Self-defense and Rights' in W Parent (ed), *Rights Restitution and Risk: Essays in Moral Theory* (Cambridge, MA, Harvard University Press, 1986).

—— 'Self-Defense' (1991) 20 *Philosophy & Public Affairs* 283.

Uniacke, S, *Permissible Killing* (Cambridge, CUP, 1994).

Von Hirsch, A, 'Extending the Harm Principle: "Remote" Harms and Fair Imputation' in AP Simester and ATH Smith (eds), *Harm and Culpability* (Oxford, Clarendon Press, 1996).

Waldron, J, 'A Right to Do Wrong' (1981) 92 *Ethics* 21.

—— 'Galston on Rights' (1983) 93 *Ethics* 325.

Wallerstein, S, 'Justifying Self-defense: A Theory of Forced Consequences' (2005) 91 *Virginia Law Review* 999.

Woozley, AD, 'A Duty to Rescue: Some Thoughts on Criminal Liability' (1983) 69(2) *Virginia Law Review* 1273.

Part III

Security as a Right: the Resolution?

13

The Positive Right to Security

SANDRA FREDMAN

INTRODUCTION

CURRENT CONCERNS ABOUT the need for security from terrorists have had a perverse effect on human rights discourse. Instead of reaffirming the commitment to human rights in the face of threats to democracy, 'rights talk' has been used to undermine rights. Powerful rhetoric about the right to security and the right to life has been marshalled in support of removing rights to a fair trial, to freedom of speech and to freedom from torture. Even more conspicuous are the ways in which positive duties, usually associated with egalitarian principles and the welfare state, have been harnessed to this corrosive purpose. Thus, it is said that detention without trial is a necessary part of the positive obligation on states to protect the rights of citizens to security from others who might be intent on causing injury. This contrasts with alternative understandings of the right to security, which view the state's positive duty to provide security from poverty, illness and degradation as at least as fundamental as its duty to protect individuals from harm by others.

In this essay, I aim to explore the notion of a positive right to security. The first part looks at ways of understanding the positive dimension. I argue that the right arises from a deeper understanding of human freedom, one which does not simply prevent interference in free choices but instead seeks actively to remove constraints on choice and facilitate agency. The right to security is not simply a right to non-interference but a right to positive state action—state action that aims to protect the individual from risks to the person, whether they are caused by fellow citizens, poverty or the state itself.

On this understanding, the right to security is a platform for the exercise of real freedom and agency. However, because a positive approach makes demands on the community and the state, it is necessary to incorporate too an analysis of responsibility. In the second part of this essay, I address the potential conflict between a positive notion of the right to security and other rights, such as the right to freedom, and argue for a notion of responsibility that moves beyond competitive rights and questions the primacy of an individual's right to choose only in self interest. The third part aims to anchor this discussion in legal possibilities, examining the role of legal and constitutional provisions in elaborating such a right. I contrast the approach of the Canadian Supreme Court to the right to security with that of the South African Constitutional Court and a recent British House of Lords judgment to show the extent to which background understandings of choice and responsibility influence outcomes. Finally, I briefly consider possible principles of adjudication of the positive right to security.

I. THE POSITIVE RIGHT TO SECURITY: A CAPABILITIES APPROACH

As traditionally understood, positive and negative rights differ according to the nature of the duty imposed on the state. Negative rights are said to impose a duty of restraint on the state, whereas positive rights require action by the state. At first glance, the right to security is quintessentially a negative right. Its core is defensive: the right not to have one's person or personal space invaded. However, on closer inspection, it is clear that the right to security cannot be limited to a duty of restraint on the state. At the very least, it must extend to protection of the individual against the acts of other individuals, whether fellow citizens or enemy forces. Indeed, the duty of the state to protect individuals from each other is fundamental to the social contract envisaged by early liberal political theorists. But this requires far more than a duty of restraint: it necessitates a raft of positive measures, ranging from a criminal justice system to laws of property. This in turn demonstrates, as Shue has argued, that rights cannot sensibly be divided into positive and negative rights.[1] Instead, all rights give rise to a range of both positive and negative duties. Shue classified these duties into three groups: duties of restraint, duties to protect individuals against other individuals and duties to provide.[2]

The right to security clearly includes both the duty of restraint and the duty to protect. It is argued here that it also includes the duty to provide for basic needs of individuals. This is based on an understanding of security that is not so much about freedom from invasion but instead entails the right to be free from threats to one's bodily survival, to the extent that such threats can be deflected by human agency. Protection against hunger, want and other material deprivations that threaten a person's existence are then as much part of the right to personal security as protection against assaults by the state or others. Correspondingly, the duty of the state includes both the duty to protect rights holders against those who obstruct or invade their means of survival and the duty to make positive provision of such means of survival, where necessary.

Thus the core of the right to security is not simply a defensive right to be free from interference. If it were, the right to security would be co-extensive with the right to liberty. The relationship between liberty and security is more complex than this. As a start, major human rights instruments refer to a right to liberty *and*

[1] Shue, H, *Basic Rights* (Princeton, Princeton University Press, 1980).
[2] *Ibid*, 51–64.

security.[3] This suggests that the right to security is more than a rhetorical flourish. Second, and more substantively, the right to security can just as well conflict with liberty as reinforce it. Indeed, political theorists have repeatedly portrayed the state in terms of a trade-off of liberty for security. Thus Hobbes depicted the formation of society in terms of a decision by individuals to surrender their liberty in return for guarantees of security.[4] In the more liberal, Lockean portrayal, individuals achieve the right to security by agreeing to curtail their own freedom as a quid pro quo for others being required to do the same.[5] Third, whereas the individual liberty right is formulated as pre-dating society, the right to security is an essentially social right arising directly from the need to co-operate. Security from assault can only be achieved through social co-operation. Similarly, security from want cannot in practice be achieved in isolation but requires co-operation from others.

Thus at one level, security provides the social constraint on the liberty right. At another level, however, security is an essential prerequisite for the exercise of freedom. Without basic security, individuals cannot exercise their liberty. This is as true for protection against want as it is for protection against assault. In this sense, the positive understanding of the right to security feeds into a richer concept of the right to liberty, which focuses on autonomy and genuine freedom of choice, rather than freedom from interference. This shifts the focus to constraints on autonomy arising from socio-economic conditions and power structures in society. A positive approach stresses the need, not just to protect individuals from interference with choice, but to address the constraints on such choice. The right to security from want is an essential means to facilitate such choice.

The theories of Amartya Sen and Martha Nussbaum provide the framework for such an approach. For Sen, substantive freedom of choice is about agency and the actual ability to achieve valued functionings if one chooses to do so.[6] These substantive freedoms he calls capabilities, which he distinguishes from functionings. Functionings are the things a person may value doing or being, while capabilities refer to the alternative combinations of functionings that are feasible for a particular individual to achieve.[7] This distinction is important because, as a result of social or economic or physical constraints, it may not be feasible for people to achieve the valued functionings they would otherwise have chosen. This in turn generates the need to address the constraints on such functioning. 'What people can achieve is influenced by economic opportunities, political liberties, social powers and the enabling conditions of good health, basic education, and the encouragement and cultivation of initiatives.'[8] Thus development requires the 'removal of major sources of un-freedom: poverty as well as tyranny, poor

---

[3] See eg, European Convention on Human Rights (ECHR), Art 5; International Covenant on Civil and Political Rights (ICCPR), Art 9; Canadian Charter, s 7.

[4] Hobbes, T, *Leviathan* (London, Penguin Classics, 1985) Part I, ch 14, 190–1.

[5] Locke, J, 'Second Treatise of Government' in P Laslett (ed), *Two Treatises of Government: A Critical Edition* (Cambridge, Cambridge University Press, 1967) paras 123–4.

[6] Sen, A, *Development as Freedom* (Oxford, Oxford University Press, 1999).

[7] *Ibid*, 75.

[8] *Ibid*, 5.

economic opportunities as well as systematic social deprivation, neglect of public facilities as well as intolerance or over-activity of repressive states'.[9] It can be seen from this that the right to security from want is just as essential as the right to security from state repression to the achievement of freedom as agency.

Sen's argument also demonstrates the converse relationship—that liberty as agency contributes to ensuring the right to security from want and deprivation. Thus, Sen argues, free agency of people is a major engine of expanding the real freedoms that all individuals can enjoy. The enabling conditions of good health and basic education are essential to the extent to which people can exercise political freedoms. But, conversely, the 'liberty to participate in social choice and the making of public decisions' are necessary to determine the meaning and nature of social needs and influence the institutional arrangements for achieving these enabling conditions.[10] Moreover, choosing is a valued functioning in itself: fasting and starving might look like the same outcome, but in terms of substantive freedom, they are entirely different. Thus the freedom to choose is valuable both for itself and for the outcome it leads to.[11]

Sen's approach does not specify whether achieving these developmental aims should take place within the political arena or whether they should be entrenched as human rights. Nussbaum takes Sen's conceptual apparatus of capability into the heartland of human rights law. Her aim is ambitious: to provide the philosophical underpinning for an account of basic constitutional principles that should be respected and implemented by governments of all nations, as a bare minimum of what respect for human dignity requires. Basic constitutional principles, she argues, should provide for a threshold level of each capability below which truly human functioning is not available. The social goal, therefore, is to get citizens above this capability threshold.[12] Notably, she sees the threshold as more important than equality of capability, allowing her to defer questions about what needs doing after all citizens are above the threshold. She therefore maintains that her approach is compatible with several different accounts of distribution above threshold.[13]

Nussbaum gives more concrete form to these abstract principles by attempting to enumerate those threshold capabilities that she believes can be universally accepted. These are generated from the core idea that human beings, as distinct from animals, are dignified free beings who shape their own lives in co-operation and reciprocity with others.[14] The Kantian ideal that each person is a bearer of value and an end in himself or herself is supplemented with the Marxist perception that the major powers of a human being need material resources to support them. Nussbaum then enumerates ten basic capabilities that are necessary for fully

---

[9] Sen, A, *Development as Freedom* (Oxford, Oxford University Press, 1999), 3.

[10] *Ibid*, 5.

[11] *Ibid*, 18.

[12] Nussbaum, M, *Women and Human Development* (Cambridge, Cambridge University Press, 2000) 5–6.

[13] *Ibid*, 12.

[14] *Ibid*, 72.

human functions; these include both the positive and negative dimensions of the right to security. On the negative side are bodily integrity and the right to move freely and to be secure against assault. On the positive side are life—in the sense of being able to live to the end of a human life of normal health—and health, which includes reproductive health, and adequate nourishment and shelter. Similarly they include both expression and education.[15] These, with the remaining principles, she argues, constitute the underpinning of principles that can be embodied in constitutional guarantees.

II. WHO PAYS? RECONCEPTUALISING RESPONSIBILITIES

Central to the perspective outlined thus far is the recognition not just that human beings should be free to pursue their own versions of the good life, but that the major powers of a human being need material resources to support them.[16] The reason why this causes difficulties within an individualist human rights framework is because it immediately raises the question of where the resources will come from. Will some have to sacrifice their right to pursue and achieve the fulfilment of their own capabilities in order to ensure that others achieve the minimum? In other words, is the right to security won at the expense of rights to non-interference? So long as individuals are simply restrained from interfering with each other, and so long as states are similarly constrained, rights to freedom and security can be reconciled. But because the capabilities approach insists on the duty to provide material resources to support individual freedom, it requires a different conceptualisation of the structure of freedom and responsibility.

From an individualistic perspective, three problems arise in respect of the positive right to security as framed above. First, it seems to rest on a distinction between 'costless' rights and 'costly' rights. Rights such as freedom of speech, association, religion and assembly and freedom from interference in family and private life are portrayed as costless, while rights to the minimum resources to fulfil our capabilities seem costly. This is particularly relevant for theories of adjudication, since judges are said to be reluctant to adjudicate on resource allocation issues.

Second, the approach outlined above requires us to create a distinction between rights that apply to all and those that apply only to the needy or disadvantaged. Thus everyone has a right to freedom of speech, but, although everyone has a right to the minimum material resources, many people are in a position to provide for themselves. If we follow this argument, the right to minimum resources places a duty on the state only in some cases. Even more problematically, it seems that those who can provide for themselves should give up some of what they provide

[15] *Ibid*, 78–80.
[16] *Ibid*, 73. Major powers of a human being refer to those functions which are particularly central to human life, both in their substance and in the fact they are preformed in a truly human, not merely animal way. In particular, the phrase refers to the powers of practical reason and sociability: 'a life that is really human is one that is shaped through by these human powers of practical reason and sociability'. See Nussbaum (2000) 72.

for others in society. Indeed, the capabilities approach could be said specifically to require this result: Sen argues that since social, economic and physical constraints do not operate evenly throughout the community, some individuals might require more or different resources in order to achieve valued functionings.[17]

Third, and as a logical implication of the first two points, negative freedom arguably conflicts with positive freedom. Thus in order to provide basic resources to some, the state must step over the boundaries of non-interference and require some to contribute so that others' rights can be protected.

These problems can be addressed by adopting a more sophisticated analysis, beginning with the distinction between costless and costly rights. The recognition that all rights give rise to a threefold set of duties immediately demonstrates that civil and political rights are far from costless. It has been demonstrated above that the right to security is more than a right of restraint: it requires the state to put in place systems to defend the security rights of citizens, in the form at the very least of a defence force and a criminal justice system. These are far from costless. An even more far-reaching answer can be found in the capabilities approach itself. Speech, religion, assembly, and association appear costless, but they too might need resources if our capability set cannot support them on their own. Thus if I own a large hall, or a newspaper, I can exercise my freedom of assembly or speech without input from the state; but if I do not, I might need access to a venue or to print media to achieve this functioning. On closer inspection, even if I already own a hall, I am not exercising a costless right. Although background private law is taken for granted, property ownership itself requires state provision of a panoply of property laws.[18]

The second problem—that positive rights apply only to some while negative rights apply to all—can also be addressed by a more sophisticated analysis. On closer inspection, it can be seen that it is not true to say that rights available to those who need them are not universal. Instead, anyone for whom the need arises can claim them. This is true, for example, in relation to rights to security in unemployment, illness and old age. In addition, the positive right to security need not be targeted only at the needy. Rights to security can be set up in a wide variety of ways, as is evidenced by different models of the welfare state.[19] It is true that, using Esping Anderson's terms, a 'liberal' regime targets only the poor, merely providing a safety net when the market fails.[20] However, an alternative, 'social democratic' regime takes a different view. Instead of targeted, means-tested assistance, rights are attached to individuals and based on citizenship, therefore avoiding the stigmatic 'we–they' divide of the liberal welfare regime.[21] On this model, rather than simply transferring income to the poorest in society, the right to security has

---

[17] Sen (1999) 90–1.
[18] Alexy, R, *A Theory of Constitutional Rights* (Oxford, Oxford University Press, 2004) ch 9.
[19] See Esping-Anderson, G, *Social Foundations of Post-industrial Economics* (Oxford, Oxford University Press, 1998).
[20] *Ibid.*
[21] *Ibid*, 78–80.

a public and universal dimension. Access to public services, such as vocational training, health care, transport, education and child care, are considered collective benefits, giving individuals real rather then formal opportunities.[22] Such public facilities build up social capital as well as take the pressure off income as the chief means of fulfilling individual needs. In this way, social progress is seen as the best path to achieve individual well-being. Crucial too is the community solidarity that comes from giving everyone a stake in the welfare state.

The third problem, the supposed conflict between the negative and the positive, opens up a more fundamental debate as to the understanding of the right to positive security. The assumption so far is that rights are individualised, in that they benefit only the individual rights holder. Correspondingly, a right is portrayed as a package of commodities. The implication of this is that the benefit to one could be a cost to another, therefore requiring a further theory that justifies imposing positive duties to make provision for others.

An alternative view, however, would see the benefit of rights as diffused through the community. On this view, state responsibility for ensuring all reach a minimum capability threshold is a contribution to the community as a whole,[23] not simply to particular individuals. Thus Ritchie argued at the end of the nineteenth century that fundamental or natural rights were:

> mutual claims which cannot be ignored without detriment to the well-being and in the last resort to the very being of a community . . . They represent a minimum of security and advantage which a community must guarantee to its members.[24]

In a more modern version of this approach,[25] Third Way thinkers portray social rights not as a burdensome cost to society but as a 'productive factor', an essential contribution to the economy and therefore to the benefit of the community as a whole.[26]

This movement beyond the isolated rights-bearing individual to one embedded in the community generates a richer sense of the meaning and objectives of choice and human agency. Individual self-development is not defined wholly in terms of the freedom of individuals to pursue their own self-interest or their own versions of the good life. It also entails a contribution to the community. For Sen,

> [I]ndividual freedom is quintessentially a social product, and there is a two-way relation between (1) social arrangements to expand individual freedoms and (2) the use

---

[22] Supiot, A, *Beyond Employment* (Oxford, Oxford University Press, 2001) 144.

[23] Freeden, M, 'Rights, Needs and Community: The Emergence of British Welfare Thought' in A Ware and R Goodin (eds), *Needs and Welfare* (London, Sage, 1990) 55.

[24] Ritchie, D, *Natural Rights* (London, Allen & Unwin, 1894) 87.

[25] Blair, T, *The Courage of Our Convictions* (London, Fabian Society, 2002); Giddens, A, *The Third Way and Its Critics* (London, Polity Press, 2000); White, S, 'The Ambiguities of the Third Way' in S White (ed), *New Labour: The Progressive Future?* (New York, Palgrave, 2001). For a critique, see Fredman, S, 'The Ideology of New Labour Law' in G Morris (ed), *Essays in Honour of Bob Hepple* (Oxford, Hart Publishing, 2004).

[26] Commission of the European Communities, 'Social Policy Agenda', COM (2000) 379 final, para 1.2.

of individual freedoms not only to improve the respective lives but also to make the social arrangements more appropriate and effective.[27]

This in turn generates a more vivid conception of mutual obligation, transcending the divisive notion of redistributive justice as a transfer of wealth from rich to poor.

Drawing on the Aristotelian view of the individual as achieving perfection through social and political participation,[28] this approach views social participation as an end in itself—and an essential part of the development of the self.[29] On this view, participation is both a right and a duty, so that it is not only the state but also the individual that has responsibilities. This makes it possible to move away from the spectre that positive freedom for some encroaches on the freedom of others. The contribution of wealthier individuals to social welfare is not merely a burdensome distribution from rich to poor but a part of their civic virtue. Those who have access to power, particularly in the form of material wealth, have specific responsibilities to the community to contribute proportionately to their ability.[30] More radically, given the role of the state in setting up private property law regimes, it could be argued that the transfer of wealth is not from the rich to the poor, but from those on whom the state has already endowed property to the community as a whole.

III. ADJUDICATING A POSITIVE RIGHT TO SECURITY

1. Constitutional Provisions

The right to security, as it appears in major human rights instruments,[31] is generally coupled with the right to liberty and framed in a way that emphasises the negative duty, the duty of restraint. In major international documents, this is sometimes twinned with the right to social security, with its more positive connotations, but notably the latter is expressed in more aspirational or programmatic terms than the negative right to security. Thus Article 5 of the European Convention on Human Rights (ECHR) makes clear that the right to security primarily focuses on immediately realisable duties of restraint, stating as it does, 'Everyone has the right to liberty and security of person. No one shall be deprived of his liberty save in the following cases and in accordance with a procedure prescribed by law.'

Correspondingly, the European Social Charter (ESC) contains a right to positive security, which is expressed in more programmatic terms. Parties are required to 'pursue policies to attain the conditions in which specified rights may be

---

[27] Sen (1999) 31.
[28] Aristotle, *Politics* (New York, Random House, 1943) Book I, ch 3, 19–41.
[29] Lister, R, *Citizenship: Feminist Perspectives* (Basingstoke, Palgrave Macmillan, 2003) 13, 15–16.
[30] Hutton, W, *The World We're In* (London, Abacus, 2002).
[31] ECHR, Art 5; ICCPR, Art 9; Canadian Charter, s 7.

realised'. These include the right 'to benefit from any measures enabling [them] to enjoy the highest possible standard of health attainable'; and to 'benefit from social welfare services'.[32] Similarly, Article 9 of the ICCPR states: 'Everyone has the right to liberty and security of the person.' Correspondingly, the International Covenant for Economic, Social and Cultural Rights (ICESCR) uses a more programmatic form, stating in Article 9 that the states parties 'recognise the right of everyone to social security, including social insurance'.

A similar pattern is found in the Charter of Fundamental Rights of the European Union: Article 6 gives the right to liberty and security, whereas Article 34 states merely that the 'Union recognises and respects the entitlement to social security benefits and social services'. The rest of the Article is similarly programmatic, stating that 'in order to combat social exclusion and poverty, the Union recognises and respects the right to social and housing assistance so as to ensure a decent existence for all those who lack sufficient resources, in accordance with the rules laid down by Community law and national laws and practices'.

There is one potentially important exception to this pattern which seems to give an express right rather than a more opaque 'recognition': Article 35 of the Charter gives everyone the 'right of access to preventive health care and the right to benefit from medical treatment under the conditions established by national laws and practices'. It goes on to state that 'a high level of human health protection shall be ensured in the definition and implementation of all Union policies and activities'.

The twinning of a negative with a positive aspect of the right is, however, absent from both the Canadian Charter and the UK Human Rights Act 1998. Section 7 of the Canadian Charter states: 'Everyone has the right to life, liberty and security of the person and the right not to be deprived thereof except in accordance with the principles of fundamental justice'. Likewise, the UK Human Rights Act 1998 provides for the right to liberty and security of the person in Article 5 of the ECHR. The European Social Charter, together with the corresponding provision, has not been incorporated. In both these instruments, therefore, the existence of a positive dimension is left to judicial interpretation.

Only the South African (SA) Constitution expressly confronts the role and status of positive duties. The overriding rubric of the SA Constitution is that the state has a threefold duty in respect of all the relevant rights: the duty to respect, protect and fulfil. The duty to respect corresponds to the negative duty not to interfere. The duty to protect places a positive obligation on the state to protect individuals from interference by other individuals, while the duty to fulfil requires the state to take positive measures either to facilitate the exercise of a right or directly to provide resources to do so. At the same time, the Constitution does not envisage that the positive duties should be immediately realisable in the way in which negative duties are. In respect of the key socio-economic rights, the duty of the state is to take 'reasonable legislative and other measures, within its available resources, to achieve the progressive realisation' of each of the rights.

---

[32] ESC, Part I, paras 11 and 14.

The result is that the South African Constitution has a similar division between the negative and positive right to security. Thus there is an immediately realisable right to life and security, which is expressly focused on the duties of non-interference, namely, the rights not to be deprived of freedom arbitrarily or without just cause; not to be detained without trial; to be free from all forms of violence from both public and private sources; not to be tortured in any way; and not to be treated or punished in a cruel, inhuman or degrading way.[33] Correspondingly, there are positive rights to security, including the right to have access to health care services, including reproductive health care; sufficient food and water; and social security and appropriate social assistance. However, the latter are not immediately realisable but rather cast a duty on the state to take reasonable legislative and other measures within its available resources, to achieve the progressive realisation of each of these rights. Only the right not to be refused emergency medical treatment is an immediate claim on the state.

2. Courts and Conceptual Frameworks

To what extent have courts been able or willing to shape a positive right to security in the sense described above, namely, that the state provide a threshold level of each capability below which truly human functioning is not available? The contrasting case-law in Canada, South Africa and the United Kingdom reveals the extent to which judicial approaches to the right to security are influenced by background ideology: the emphasis on freedom of choice as freedom from interference by the state, as evidenced in the Canadian cases, contrasts with a notion of state responsibility to remove constraints on freedom and to provide essential resources for human agency in the South African and UK cases. Each will be examined in turn.

In the Canadian case-law, the Supreme Court of Canada was asked to apply the right to security in Article 7 of the Canadian Charter in the novel arenas of health care and basic subsistence provision. At first glance, the case-law seems to accept that a right to security can include a right to health care. However, on closer examination it becomes clear that the real issue is not whether the state is under a positive duty to provide for security in the form of health care but whether the state should be restrained from interfering in individuals' right to take steps to protect their own security or health. This is because the challenge is to state regulation of access to health care. The alleged interference is therefore more with freedom of contract than with substantive freedom as discussed above.

This line of argument emerges from the development of the case-law from *Morgentaler*[34] to *Chaouilli*.[35] In both cases, the right to security is interpreted as including a right of access to health care in circumstances in which denial of health

---

[33] Section 12.
[34] *R v Morgentaler* [1988] 1 SCR 30, Supreme Ct of Canada.
[35] *Chaouilli v Quebec (Attorney General)* (2005) SCC 35, Supreme Ct of Canada.

care would present a serious threat to an individual's health and quality of life. The two cases, however, represent radically different approaches to the meaning of individual freedom. In the *Morgentaler* case, the interference to access came from criminal sanctions attached to procedures for obtaining an abortion. Thus, according to Beetz J, security of the person within the meaning of section 7 of the Charter

> must include a right of access to medical treatment for a condition representing a danger to life or health, without fear of criminal sanction. If an Act of Parliament forces a pregnant woman whose life or health is in danger to choose between, on the one hand, the commission of a crime to obtain effective and timely medical treatment and, on the other hand, inadequate treatment or no treatment at all, her right to security of the person has been violated.[36]

The case therefore positively addresses constraints on individual agency, furthering substantive equality by giving women better access to abortion services.

Morgentaler did not represent a choice between public and private provision but rather a choice between a criminal sanction and no provision. It was in the later case of *Chaouilli* that this challenge arose. A doctor and a patient claimed that the prohibition on private health insurance in Quebec infringed their right to security, because it denied them access to health care by subjecting them to long waiting lists for publicly funded health care. This propelled the courts into the centre of a political controversy over the best way to provide health care services. The Quebec government argued in its defence that the reason for the prohibition was that private insurance would lead to a two-tier health care system, which in turn would seriously undermine the coverage, effectiveness and quality of the publicly funded health system. Again, the majority of the court appears to uphold a positive understanding of the right to security, drawing on the *Morgentaler* principle that the right to security includes the right to health care. However, the emphasis is on access. By prohibiting private insurance, the majority held, the state was preventing individuals from having access to potentially life-saving health care. Although the Court stated that this was based on a right to security, the result was to endorse the right to freedom of contract rather than the right to the provision of health care resources.

Underlying this approach is a depiction of individual freedom as consisting primarily of the right to pursue one's own self-interest, a right which state redistributive measures appear to restrict. While *Morgentaler* addressed the prohibition on any lawful health care in respect of abortion, *Chaouilli* was concerned with the difference between some health care for all, and better health care for some. Absent here is any notion of the individual as part of a community, where individual benefit is bound up with benefit to the others within the community. Also missing from this analysis is any conception of substantive freedom and equality, in Sen's terms. Such an approach would factor into the analysis not just the opportunity to gain access to health care or other basic resources, but the actual capability of

---

[36] *Morgentaler*, note 34 above, para 78.

individuals to do so. By ignoring substantive freedom and equality, the court made it appear as if it was endorsing the right of access to health care, while in fact it was replicating the very structure of wealth and power that had led to a highly uneven ability to access health care in the first place.

Chaouilli establishes that the state should be restrained from interfering in individuals' rights to take steps to protect their own security. The converse is established in *Gosselin*:[37] if an individual is formally able to protect his or her own security, then he or she has no right to demand assistance from the state to obtain the basic necessities. In *Gosselin*, the Supreme Court of Canada was asked to define the right to security as including the right to a level of social security sufficient to meet basic needs. The majority rejected the claim. McLachlan CJ, writing for the majority, stressed that section 7 had never been construed either as covering issues unconnected with the administration of justice, or as imposing positive duties on the state:

> Section 7 speaks of the right *not to be deprived* of life, liberty and security of the person, except in accordance with the principles of fundamental justice. Nothing in the jurisprudence thus far suggests that section 7 places a positive obligation on the state to ensure that each person enjoys life, liberty or security of the person. Rather, section 7 has been interpreted as restricting the state's ability to *deprive* people of these. Such a deprivation does not exist in the case at bar.[38]

While she left open the possibility that 'a positive obligation to sustain life, liberty, or security of person may be made out in special circumstances', McLachlan CJ found that the 'frail platform provided by the facts of this case cannot support the weight of a positive state obligation of citizen support'.[39]

Operating from a particularly clear basis in individual freedom from interference rather than individual freedom to act is the judgment of Bastarache J, who saw the right to security as limited to protection against coercive state action.[40] 'In order for section 7 to be engaged, the threat to the person's right itself must emanate from the state.' He accepted that legislation could make it impossible for a person to exercise his or her right. In this case, however, the exclusion of the claimant and others under the age of 30 from the full, unconditional benefit package did not render them substantially incapable of exercising their right to security of the person without government intervention:

> My concern here is with the ability of the appellant's group to access the right itself, not to benefit better from the statutory scheme. The appellant has failed to show a substantial incapability of protecting her right to security. She has not demonstrated that the legislation, by excluding her, has reduced her security any more than it would have already been, given market conditions.[41]

[37] *Gosselin v Quebec* (2002) SCR 84.
[38] *Ibid*, [81].
[39] *Ibid*, [83].
[40] *Ibid*, [215].
[41] *Ibid*, [222].

Instead, the threat to the appellant's security was a result of the vagaries of the economy. Thus the same freedom to operate in the market in order to achieve one's own security, which was protected against state intervention in *Chaouilli*, meant that the state was not responsible for the destitution brought on the applicant apparently by market conditions. In both cases, the actual capability to exercise rights was left out of consideration.

This view of rights can be contrasted with an alternative vision, which draws on the analysis in the first sections of this essay. There are two elements to this vision. The first focuses as much on individual capability as formal freedom. Thus Arbour J, dissenting in *Gosselin,* reflected the capabilities approach when she held that the state has a duty to intervene, not only when it is directly responsible for a breach of a right, but whenever government intervention is needed to secure the effective exercise of a claimant's fundamental rights.[42]

The second element moves away from a conflict between freedom and distributive justice, towards a vision of the individual as embedded in a community where benefits to some are beneficial to all. At the forefront of this approach is the South African Constitutional Court, where the right to substantive security is expressed in terms that resonate with communitarian values. In a recent case in which the desperate housing needs of squatters on private land were pitted against property ownership, Sachs J emphasised that responsibility extended to the community as a whole:

> It is not only the dignity of the poor that is assailed when homeless people are driven from pillar to post . . . Our society as a whole is demeaned when State action intensifies, rather than mitigates, their marginalisation.[43]

Similarly, in holding that the constitutional right to social security extended beyond citizens to permanent residents, Mokgoro J emphasised that

> sharing responsibility for the problems and consequences of poverty equally as a community represents the extent to which wealthier members of the community view the minimal well-being of the poor as connected with their personal well-being and the well-being of the community as a whole.[44]

Liebenberg argues that the courts have an important rhetorical role in framing a dispute within the context of transformative vocabulary even if they are constrained in making remedial orders that might have an extensive effect on budgetary allocations. By locating the discourse in the vocabulary of community rather than individualism, courts can destabilise existing preconceptions about the role of publicly funded benefits in society.[45]

---

[42] *Ibid*, [381].

[43] *Port Elizabeth Municipality v Various Occupiers* (2005) (1) SA 217, SA Constitutional Ct, [18].

[44] *Khosa and Mahlaule v Minister for Social Development* 2004 (6) BCLR 569, South African Constitutional Court, [48].

[45] Liebenberg, S, 'Needs, Rights and Transformation: Adjudicating Social Rights', Centre for Human Rights and Global Justice Working Paper, Economic and Social Rights Series, 2005, 31.

The UK House of Lords approach in the recent case of *Limbuela*[46] forms an interesting middle ground. In this case, the court held that the government had breached the right not to be subjected to inhuman treatment or punishment when it failed to provide the basic necessities of life to asylum seekers who had not claimed asylum at the moment they entered the United Kingdom. The case is similar to *Chaouilli* in its focus on the fact that the state had blocked access to the means by which individuals might provide for their own security. Here, the state was held responsible for the destitution of late asylum seekers because it was the statutory regime that removed any source of social support while prohibiting them from supporting themselves through paid work. The response in *Limbuela* is, however, different: rather than insisting that individuals be allowed to provide for themselves, it held that the state should provide the basic necessities.

This points to an alternative way in which the Supreme Court of Canada could have approached *Chaouilli*. Instead of insisting on a privatised remedy, which benefits those who can afford it and ignores those who cannot, it could have brought the equality value into play and held that the right to security, including the right of access to health care, should be provided to all. Thus the real solution is a right to demand, not the freedom to contract out of the public health system, but the right to proper health care through the public health system. Delays that prejudice the right to security through damage to physical and emotional well-being surely prejudice all Canadians and not just those who can take out private insurance. The real right is to demand a better delivery of health services. However, courts see this as a resource allocation decision better suited to the political arena. In what way, then, can a legitimate role for courts be carved out in this context?

3. Principles of Adjudication

A representative of the Charter Committee on Poverty Issues and the Canadian Health Coalition, which intervened in the *Chaouilli* case to advocate for the recognition of an inclusive right to health, commented wryly:

> [C]ritics of the idea of using courts to promote social and economic justice will see the *Chaouilli* decision as our 'just deserts' for being foolish enough to encourage an increasingly neo-liberal Supreme Court, with little sympathy evidenced for the plight of the poor, to adjudicate rights in the field of complex issues such as health care delivery.[47]

However, he continued, 'the judgment of the majority in *Chaoulli* was not the result of a court stepping into the field of social rights, but rather, of a court refusing to do so.'[48] Indeed, it is highly problematic to argue that courts, already

---

[46] *R v Secretary of State for the Home Department, ex parte Limbuela* [2005] UKHL 66.

[47] Porter, B, 'A Right to Health Care in Canada: Only if You can Pay for It' (2005) 6 *Economic and Social Rights Review* page?.

[48] *Ibid.*

apprised of the jurisdiction of duties of restraint, should defer on rights that give rise to positive duties to protect or provide. Protection of negative duties without positive duties skews the judicial approach in favour of the former whenever there is a clash. Since rights giving rise to duties of restraint are already enforceable, they will inevitably be capable of trumping state policy in the area of positive provision.[49] To frame a response in terms of deference is simply to agree to support one side or the other without saying so. This is illustrated by contrasting *Gosselin* (where the deferent approach was used to reject a claim by a disadvantaged litigant that the right to security entailed a right to the minimum amount of social security necessary for subsistence) with *Chaouilli* (where an interventionist approach was used to uphold the claim of an advantaged applicant).

What principles then could courts use to adjudicate in these areas? One source is the values and principles enshrined in constitutions. Thus the directive principles in the Indian constitution, although expressly non-justiciable, provide an important source of values for interpreting justiciable rights. The Indian approach is relevant to the UK domestic scene because there are clear signs that the principles in the EU Charter of Fundamental Rights will be used as interpretive aids by the European Court of Justice (ECJ)[50]—and thereby have a direct influence on domestic law in the United Kingdom.

More importantly, it is submitted that the United Kingdom's unwritten constitution also contains unwritten principles, which the court in *Limbuela* partly articulated. This is boldly signalled in the unequivocal acceptance that it is a fundamental value of our society that the degradation of destitution must be prevented, whether it arises from direct state violence, or is a result of circumstances for which the state can be said to be responsible. Thus Lord Brown in *Limbuela* emphatically stated:

> It seems to me one thing to say . . . that within the contracting states there are unfortunately many homeless people and whether to provide funds for them is a political, not judicial, issue; quite another for a comparatively rich . . . country like the UK to single out a particular group to be left utterly destitute on the streets as a matter of policy.[51]

In support he cites Prime Minister Tony Blair's own statement that 'people sleeping rough on our streets . . . is not a situation that we can continue to tolerate in a modern and civilised society'. It is against this bedrock principle that positive duties need to be considered.

A second criterion for courts to use in adjudicating is reasonableness. The South African Constitution, with its expressly justiciable socio-economic rights, uses reasonableness as the touchstone of judicial supervision. Reasonableness, however, is more than the bare rationality of US Supreme Court jurisprudence or UK

---

[49] Fredman, S, 'Substantive Equality and the Positive Duty to Provide' (2005) 21 *South African Journal of Human Rights* 163–90, 167–8.

[50] *R v Secretary of State for Trade and Industry, ex parte BECTU* [2001] ECR I-4881, ECR opinion, para 28; cf *Bowden v Tuffnells Parcels* [2001] ECR I-7031, ECJ.

[51] *Limbuela*, note 46 above, [99].

Wednesbury reasonableness, incorporating substantive values of dignity and fairness. Instead, it has a substantive content. According to Sachs J, 'The starting and ending point of the analysis must be to affirm the values of human dignity, equality and freedom.'[52] However, it would be risky to transplant reasonableness review into the UK context, where principles of review have only just emerged from the formless standard of *Wednesbury* unreasonableness. Even in the South African context, the ease with which reasonableness can descend into a highly deferent standard of review has frequently been noted.[53]

Third, courts in several jurisdictions have been impelled towards equality as a standard of review of the duty to provide. This is because it permits the court to adjudicate on the ways in which the state has chosen to provide benefits, rather than insisting on provision in the first place. However, if equality merely means consistent treatment, it would easily be fulfilled by providing benefits for no one, leaving destitute people to their fate. This result can be avoided only if equality is tied closely to a substantive right such as the positive right to security. Thus in *Gosselin*, Arbour J stressed that the claim of under-inclusion was more than just an equality claim: the exclusion from the statutory right to welfare sufficient to meet their needs violated the self-standing rights to life and security of the person of those excluded.

In the context of the positive right to security, it seems clear that what is at issue is the basic minimum for security. Equality is engaged to the extent of recognising that different capabilities yield different levels of functioning, and therefore allocative decisions must be made to ensure that all can achieve the minimum basic. However, as Nussbaum argues, distributive decisions above the minimum are open to wider debate. It is therefore at the level of basic needs that the positive right should operate. Thus, Yacoob J declared in the famous *Grootboom* case: 'A society must seek to ensure that the *basic necessities of life* are provided to all if it is to be a society based on human dignity, freedom and equality.'[54] This is echoed by Mokgoro J in *Khosa*: 'A society must seek to ensure that the basic necessities of life are accessible to all if it is to be a society in which human dignity, freedom and equality are foundational.'[55] Thus, as Liebenberg persuasively argues, where basic needs are at issue, courts should adopt a rigorous proportionality standard to scrutinise state inaction to achieve the basic threshold. This can be seen too in the application in *Limbuela* of the absolute standard demanded by the Article 3 right not to be subject to inhuman or degrading treatment or punishment.

Equally important is Liebenberg's insight, drawn from the work of Nancy Fraser, that in assessing claims courts should move beyond the immediate focus of the claims before them, to investigate

---

[52] *Port Elizabeth Municipality v Various Occupiers*, note 43 above, [15].

[53] Liebenberg (2005).

[54] *Government of the Republic of South Africa v Grootboom* 2000 (11) BCLR 1169 (CC), South African Constitutional Court, [44].

[55] *Khosa*, note 44 above, [52]. See also Sachs J in *Port Elizabeth Municipality v Various Occupiers*, note 43 above, [18].

more intensively on the position of the claimant in society, the nature and causes of the deprivation experienced and its impact on her and others in a similar situation. Close attention should be paid to the . . . lack of access to economic and social resources, the social stigma and stereotypes associated with poverty and their interaction with other forms of recognition injustice, such as race, gender and sexual orientation.

It is at this level that the Canadian Supreme Court lost its way.

CONCLUSION

Although it is often argued that positive duties to provide security are political rather than legal issues, it has become increasingly clear that whether they like it or not, courts are required to make decisions as to whether rights generate positive duties. At present, armed only with the narrow liberal understanding of choice, courts tend to see such positive duties as conflicting with individuals' right to freedom. To give proper shape to the positive duty to security, courts will need to deepen their understanding of the ways in which positive rights and obligations interact. In this essay, I have attempted to sketch out the contours of a positive right to security as the right to demand from the state the minimum resources necessary to fulfil one's capabilities. This in turn requires us to locate the right within a community with reciprocal benefits and responsibilities, rather than in the competitive arena of individualised rights-bearers. The UK House of Lords and the SA Constitutional Court have already started down this road, but there remain many unanswered questions.

REFERENCES

Alexy, R, *A Theory of Constitutional Rights* (Oxford, Oxford University Press, 2004).

Aristotle, *Politics* (New York, Random House, 1943).

Blair, T, *The Courage of Our Convictions* (London, Fabian Society, 2002).

Esping-Anderson, G, *Social Foundations of Post-Industrial Economics* (Oxford, Oxford University Press, 1998).

Fredman, S, 'The Ideology of New Labour Law' in G Morris (ed), *Essays in Honour of Bob Hepple* (Oxford, Hart Publishing, 2004).

—— 'Substantive Equality and the Positive Duty to Provide' (2005) 21 *South African Journal of Human Rights* 163–90.

Freeden, M, 'Rights, Needs and Community: The Emergence of British Welfare Thought' in A Ware and R Goodin (eds), *Needs and Welfare* (London, Sage, 1990).

Giddens, A, *The Third Way and Its Critics* (London, Polity Press, 2000).

Hobbes, T, *Leviathan* (London, Penguin Classics, 1985).

Hutton, W, *The World We're In* (London, Abacus, 2002).

Liebenberg, S, 'Needs, Rights and Transformation: Adjudicating Social Rights', Centre for Human Rights and Global Justice Working Paper, Economic and Social Rights Series, 2005.

Lister, R, *Citizenship: Feminist Perspectives* (Basingstoke, Palgrave Macmillan, 2003).

Locke, J, *Second Treatise of Government* in P Laslett (ed), *Two Treatises of Government: A Critical Edition* (Cambridge, Cambridge University Press, 1967).

Morris, G (ed), *Essays in Honour of Bob Hepple* (Oxford, Hart Publishing, 2004).

Nussbaum, M, *Women and Human Development* (Cambridge, Cambridge University Press, 2000).

Porter, B, 'A Right to Health Care in Canada: Only if You can Pay for It' (2005) 6 *Economic and Social Rights Review* page.

Ritchie, D, *Natural Rights* (London, Allen and Unwin, 1894).

Sen, A, *Development as Freedom* (Oxford, Oxford University Press, 1999).

Shue, H, *Basic Rights* (Princeton, Princeton University Press, 1980).

Supiot, A, *Beyond Employment* (Oxford, Oxford University Press, 2001).

Ware, A and Goodin, R (eds), *Needs and Welfare* (London, Sage, 1990).

White, S, 'The Ambiguities of the Third Way' in S White (ed), *New Labour: The Progressive Future?* (New York, Palgrave, 2001).

14

Mapping the Right to Security

LIORA LAZARUS

Everyone has the right to liberty and security of person.

Article 5, European Convention on Human Rights

PUBLIC DEBATE SPARKED by national security policy since 9/11 has overwhelmingly focused on the balance between 'security' on the one hand and 'liberty' on the other. The debate ranges far beyond the confines of academia.[1] Judges, politicians and journalists are all exercised by the attempt to find and shape this elusive balance.[2] Given that liberty and security are articulated as part of the same right in most human rights documents, this binary opposition, so pervasive in public rhetoric, is curious. It would be easy to blame this oversight on the tendency of politicians, journalists and intellectuals to ignore the precise language of and jurisprudence about human rights law. But the fact is that very little attention has been paid by lawyers and legal academics to the notion of a 'right to security'. Perhaps this is because we commonly do not think of 'security' as a legal right but as a political aspiration. Certainly this would make sense of Attorney-General Lord Goldsmith's peculiar statement: 'I do not believe this can

---

[1] Waldron, J, 'Security and Liberty: The Image of Balance' (2003) 11(2) *Journal of Political Philosophy* 191; Zedner, L, 'Securing Liberty in the Face of Terror: Reflections from Criminal Justice' (2005) 32(4) *Journal of Law and Society* 507; Cole, D, *Enemy Aliens: Double Standards and Constitutional Freedoms in the War on Terrorism* (New York, New York Press, 2003); Heymann, P, *Terrorism, Freedom, and Security: Winning without War* (Cambridge, MA, MIT Press, 2004); Taylor, SJ, 'Rights, Liberties and Security: Recalibrating the Balance after September 11' (2003) 21(1) *The Brookings Review* 25; Daniels, R, Macklem, P and Roach, K (eds), *The Security of Freedom: Essays on Canada's Anti-terrorism Bill* (Toronto, University of Toronto Press, 2001); Ignatieff, M, *The Lesser Evil: Political Ethics in an Age of Terror* (Princeton, Princeton University Press, 2004).

[2] *A and X v Secretary of State for the Home Department* [2005] 2 WLR 87; *Sheldrake v DPP, AG's Reference (No 4 of 2002)* [2003] 2 All ER 497; *Hamdi v Rumsfeld*, 524 US 507 (2004); *American Civil Liberties Union v National Security Agency*, 438 F Supp 2d 754 (2006); Prime Minister Tony Blair, Monthly Downing Street Press Conference, 5 August 2005, available at http://www.pm.gov.uk/out put/Page6825.asp; Foreign and Commonwealth Office of the UK, 'Liberty and Security: Striking the Right Balance', paper by the UK Presidency of the EU, 2005, available at www.fco.gov.uk/ Files/kfile/LibertySecurity.pdf; (now former) Home Secretary David Blunkett, 'Balancing Human Rights and Security', address to Harvard Law School, 8 March 2004, available at www.hno.harvard. edu/gazette/2004/03.11/27-rights.html; Stephens, P, 'If the Balance Tilts towards Security, Liberty Will Pay', *The Guardian*, 11 March 2005, 17; Blitz, R and Burns, J, 'Civil Liberties and National Security Prove a Difficult Balance to Strike', *Financial Times*, 9 September 2005, 4; Rosen, J, 'Liberty Wins—So Far', *The Washington Post*, 15 September 2002, B01.

be a simple utilitarian calculation of balancing the right to security of the many against the legal rights of the few'.[3]

Whatever the reasons for this state of affairs, it is fair to say that amidst the extensive public debate on the appropriate balance between the maintenance of national, public and individual security on the one hand, and the protection of individual liberty on the other, and despite the incipient international tendency to talk about 'human security' in the rhetoric of rights,[4] remarkably little attention has been paid to the question of what precisely is meant by the 'right to security' in the legal sense. The purpose of this chapter is to provide some clarity on this question. It starts with the premise that the 'right to security' needs to be meaningful and specific. Just as we are wary of undifferentiated and uncritical references to the public pursuit of 'security' in the pervasive attempts to limit individual rights,[5] we need also to be careful about vague allusions to a 'right to security'. The words 'security' (with its allure of comfort or its narrower promise of the absence of danger and hardship) and 'rights' (with its call on the legitimacy of both morality and law) are heavily loaded terms in today's political climate. We must be careful that the 'right to security' does not become the overarching legitimating principle and rhetorical tool upon which we ground arguments for all other desirable human goods.

Seeking clarity in this context is not just an analytical pursuit. It is grounded also in broader human rights principles, and is part of what I refer to elsewhere as 'the onus of justification'.[6] In systems committed to the statutory or constitutional protection of human rights, it is incumbent on all public authorities, including the judiciary, to justify any limitation of human rights and any failure to secure them. This onus of justification requires that judicial reasoning around human rights is transparent, consistent and clear. If citizens are to engage fully and critically with rights reasoning—be it legislative, executive or judicial—they must at the very least know why rights are asserted or limited.

In much the same way as Dyzenhaus has spoken about the notion of 'deference' in a 'culture of justification',[7] I will argue here that positive rights assertions, as well as those concerning the ambit and limitation of negative rights, must be clear and precise. The onus of justification, given the constitutional context in which it arises, places more stringent requirements of clarity on legal assertions of human rights than it does on rhetorical assertions of human rights. Consequently, the requirements of specificity are not merely analytical requirements: in a democratic society, they are central to the notion of citizenship, the attribution of responsibility to the state as well as to private parties, and the limitation of both state and private power. In this regard, more must be discharged if we are to say that some-

[3] Lord Goldsmith QC, 'How Should Britain Protect its Citizens?' *The Times*, 11 May 2004.
[4] See for example, Art 143 of United Nations General Assembly, '2005 Summit Outcome', A/60/L.1, 15 September 2005; see also United Nations Development Programme (UNDP), *Human Development Report 1994* (New York, Oxford University Press, 1994) ch 2.
[5] See the contribution by Lucia Zedner in this volume.
[6] Lazarus, L, 'Conceptions of Liberty Deprivation' (2006) 69(5) *Modern Law Review* 738, 740–4.
[7] See their contribution in this volume.

thing is a legally enforceable human or constitutional right than if we are to make rhetorical or policy assertions as to the pursuit of security. To assert a policy objective for state actors, or international bodies, to pursue human security is one thing; to say that we are all bearers of a 'right to security' is another.

This chapter argues for the narrowest possible conception of the notion of security in the context of a legally enforceable 'right to security'. Such a right should only protect that which other self-standing and established rights cannot, on their face, protect. Consequently, the 'right to security' should not encompass long-established and self-standing rights such as the rights to life, dignity, liberty, health, freedom from torture and so on. If the 'right to security' means anything at all, it must protect against something not already and explicitly captured by these fundamental and self-standing rights. That is not to say that it is not possible for courts to imply or develop from these self-standing fundamental rights specific rights to aspects of security. But, for reasons examined below, it is less problematic to derive specific rights to security as grounded in existing fundamental rights than to talk of these as being derived from an overarching and self-standing *meta-right* to security.

Given contemporary political antipathy to human rights, rights advocates are understandably tempted to harness the language of security as a novel and contemporary legitimation *for* human rights. What better way, in the face of popular anxiety about security, to turn the supposed dichotomy between security and human rights in on itself and, by arguing from an overarching right to security, to protect against the loss of our traditional rights or even to develop new ones? This temptation is also strong for those seeking to develop and promote previously neglected social and economic rights as positive obligations on the state. By getting states to acknowledge their duty to ensure the security of their citizens, rights activists can argue that the battle for positive rights has been won in principle. Moreover, exploiting the connection between the security of a society and its overall material well-being fits neatly with the quest to extend citizens' social and economic rights against poverty, homelessness, degradation and sickness.[8]

However, the gains to be made by using security as an instrumental platform for human rights campaigns need to be weighed against the danger of simultaneously eroding the non-instrumental foundations of human rights. A minimum threshold of security might well constitute a material condition for a citizen's enjoyment of his or her liberty, dignity or equality, but it is quite another thing to argue metaphysically that these fundamental, and arguably *meta-*, rights are grounded in security. While many argue, for example, that life provides the precondition to liberty, they do not claim that life grounds liberty. Security in a similar sense is best seen 'as the means to or pre-condition of other goods'.[9] Alternatively, if security is

---

[8] A clear example of this can be found in the work of the Commission on Human Security, eg, *Human Security Now* (New York, Commission on Human Security, 2003). See also Alkire, S, 'A Conceptual Framework for Human Security', CRISE Working Paper #2, 2003, available at http://www.crise.ox.ac.uk/pubs/workingpaper2.pdf, 33–5.

a right, then it is best seen as a consequence of established and pre-existing fundamental rights. A state's failure to criminalise, police or punish domestic violence,
for example, is easily framed as a violation of a citizen's fundamental rights to
liberty, dignity and equality, which in turn might ground a citizen's specific right
to security in this context. So security can be seen as both a material pre-condition
of the exercise of foundational rights as well as a specific right consequent upon
their realisation.

Holding the right to security clearly in this place, however, becomes very difficult when we start to view it as the legitimating principle upon which all fundamental rights are grounded. In a political climate where security has been shown
so often to trump fundamental rights, the practical outcomes of toying with the
fragile consensus around the foundations of human rights are particularly concerning. There is a danger that when the right to security slips into becoming the
meta-principle grounding other rights, it can also displace the non-instrumental
values upon which it properly ought to rest. In this way the right to security can
inadvertently legitimise security measures that encroach upon those values it has
now displaced. There is therefore a difference between securing rights and 'securitising' rights:

> With an increasing convergence of human rights and human security . . . one will
> have to be careful that human security is not served as a more palatable dish instead
> of human rights. If the 'entrenched opposition' came from a government wishing to
> defy its obligations under international human rights law, then turning 'rights-talk'
> into 'policy-talk' and obligations into aspirations under the pretext of protecting
> human security instead of human rights would present a tempting policy option. It
> is such concerns that have led observers to warn that 'the precision and legality of the
> human rights framework could suffer if too closely allied with the ambiguity and
> mere rhetorical appeal to human security'.[10]

Understandably, many argue that the consequence of the risks associated with
securitising rights is necessarily an outright rejection of the possibility of a 'right to
security'[11] and, moreover, that vesting individuals with enforceable legal rights to
security is at odds with the inherently collective and polycentric pursuit of safeguarding security in society.[12] By enforcing an individual's immediate right to
security, are we at risk of undermining the security of others—and hence the
longer-term security of us all? This all-or-nothing approach also has its shortcomings, for it fails to engage adequately with what is a widely expressed right in
human rights treaties, domestic bills of rights and judicial case-law.

---

[9]   See the contribution by Lucia Zedner in this volume.

[10]   Oberleitner, G, 'Porcupines in Love: The Intricate Convergence of Human Rights and Human
Security' (2005) 6 *European Human Rights Law Review* 588, 596, quoting David Petrasek, 'Human
Rights "Lite" Thoughts on Human Security' (2004) 35 *Security Dialogue* 59–62, 59.

[11]   This was the response of a number of participants at the Oxford Colloquium on Security and
Human Rights, 17–18 March 2006.

[12]   For a compelling account of security as a public and collective good, see Loader, I and Walker, N,
Civilizing Security (Cambridge, Cambridge University Press, 2007).

The notion of security is dangerously opaque. While concepts such as human dignity are also vague, security's close relationship with inscrutable perceptions of future risk particularly undermines jurisprudential constraints on the potential range of associated rights claims. Consequently, if the 'right to security' is on the table, we need to engage with what it ought to express in law. There is also merit, given the dangerous opacity and rhetorical power of security, to injecting a more sober and legalistic approach into the political discourse surrounding the 'right to security'.

Hence, this chapter argues that if the 'right to security' is to exist at all, it must be rigorously and narrowly construed. In the context of a justiciable right, it conforms with only the first half of Alkire's stipulation that 'human security' should safeguard 'the vital core of all human lives from critical and pervasive threats, in a way that is consistent with long-term human fulfilment'.[13] Thus, the corollary of a 'right to security' is a state duty to develop structures and institutions that are capable of responding to and minimising 'critical and pervasive threats' to human security (by which I mean an absence of harm in the most core physical sense of harm to person). In short, the right to security cannot equate to a right to be secure.

I. THE BASIC QUESTIONS

The essential question that this mapping exercise seeks to answer is whether we can talk about the right to security as a *self-standing legal right*, and, if so, what kind of right is it? In other words, is it a distinctive right, or is it merely a right that consists of or is derived from other self-standing rights? What do we mean when we say it is a legal right? Is it simply a question of justiciability? Is the existence of a legal right a necessary correlative of the existence of a traditional legal remedy? Or can we speak of a legal right in a broader context of institutional enforcement? Is the right to security a negative right, prohibiting states from infringing upon it, or is it a positive right, enjoining states to protect individual security? If it is a positive right, what is the scope of the legal duty imposed? Where does the correlative duty of a legal right to security lie? Finally, is it a duty on states alone, or does it bind non-state actors?

II. WHAT IS MEANT BY A LEGAL RIGHT?

In strictly formal terms, an individual asserts a legal 'right' when he or she makes a claim to performance, either action or forbearance, on the part of another that is

---

[13] Alkire (2003) 29.

asserted and enforceable in law.[14] In the municipal context, this might involve a right being enshrined in a constitution, code or statute, or it might be held to be part of the common law. The legal claim may be *justiciable* in the sense that it gives rise to a formal legal remedy or may guide the actions of other enforcement bodies such as regulatory bodies, human rights commissions, or parliamentary agencies.[15] The remedy or relief people may obtain when their right has been breached will vary depending on whether the right is justiciable, regulatory or otherwise. Similarly, in international law the strength of a right depends on the extent to which it can be enforced by international bodies. Mostly, it makes more sense to say that an international human right is only justiciable when it can be invoked in a judicial forum such as the European Court of Human Rights (ECtHR). Of course there are many other possible forms of enforcement of an international human right beyond the judicial forum, but it would not make sense to call such a right a *justiciable* right.

A legal right can be distinguished from a moral or political right, which we may assert in principle by reference to a variety of political or moral frameworks, but which does not necessarily have the force of law. Legal rights need also to be dissociated from 'rights rhetoric'. Rights rhetoric arises when rights assertions are 'used to frame, discuss and debate issues relevant to social policy' within public or political rhetoric.[16] Commonly, rhetorical assertions of rights are vague with regard to their political, legal and moral foundations. They are generally used to promote particular social or political ends.

For the purposes of clarity, therefore, it makes sense to distinguish at the outset between a justiciable right to security; a non-justiciable right to security that is supported by non-judicial compliance mechanisms; the expression of a human rights standard or aspiration within an institutional context; and the expression of a human rights aspiration within political rhetoric or philosophical discourse. The '*right to security*' is expressed in all of these contexts.

III. NON-JUSTICIABLE RIGHTS TO SECURITY

Assertions of 'the right to security' that are non-justiciable are increasingly gaining institutional foundations, as demonstrated by the international development of the right to 'human security' and the correlative acknowledgment of the 'responsibility to protect' (R2P).[17] This area has been more comprehensively

---

[14] This definition encompasses the Hohfeldian notion of a 'claim right' and a 'liberty right'. See Hohfeld, W, *Fundamental Legal Conceptions as Applied in Judicial Reasoning* (New Haven, Yale University Press, 1919).

[15] Campbell, T, Goldsworthy, J and Stone, A (eds), *Protecting Human Rights: Instruments and Institutions* (New York, Oxford University Press, 2003) chs 10–16.

[16] Feldman, E, 'Patient's Rights, Citizen's Movements and Japanese Legal Culture' in Nelken, D (ed.), *Comparing Legal Cultures* (Dartmouth, Aldershot, 1997) 215, 216.

[17] United Nations General Assembly, '2005 World Summit Outcome', A/60/L.1, 15 September 2005.

addressed in other chapters in this volume by Neil McFarlane and Jennifer Welsh. Suffice it to say here that assertions regarding human security and the responsibility to protect range from declarations sufficient to form the basis of institutional action in pursuit of its realisation, to statements of mere aspiration by international institutions. A good example of the former rests in the cumulative resolutions of the Security Council that have led to the development of the principle of protection of civilians in armed conflict.[18] An example of an aspirational statement can be found in Article 143 of the United Nations '2005 World Summit Outcome' document, which draws heavily on rights language to underpin the undertaking on the part of the General Assembly to further 'discuss and define' the notion of human security:

> We stress the right of people to live in freedom and dignity, free from poverty and despair. We recognize that all individuals, in particular vulnerable people, are entitled to freedom from fear and freedom from want, with an equal opportunity to enjoy all their rights and fully develop their human potential. To this end, we commit ourselves to discussing and defining the notion of human security in the General Assembly.

It is striking, when we look at the language of Article 143, just how broad and all-encompassing the rhetorical notion of human security has become. The UN conception now encompasses what many of us consider long-established, fundamental and self-standing rights: under Article 143, human security expressly encompasses a right to 'dignity', 'equality' in the broadest sense of having an 'equal opportunity to enjoy all their rights and fully develop their human potential', and 'liberty' in the broadest positive sense of being 'free from fear and want' and 'poverty and despair'. Is the United Nations suggesting that the notion of human security should now displace 'dignity', 'liberty' and 'equality' as the 'rights of rights', to become the underlying foundation of all other human rights? In light of the risks of securitising rights, we need to ask serious questions about this formulation. Not only does such vagueness and expansiveness here have problematic implications for policy development and implementation and raise strong analytical concerns,[19] but the securitisation of human rights has serious implications for their protection more generally.

Surely, if a right to 'human security' is to exist, it must exist distinctly, and not as a catch-all for other significant and self-standing rights, which hardly need deriving from a prior notion of human security. Like the right to life, the right to 'human security' should have an essential element that we can specify and differentiate from the moral rights that we might consider integrally linked with it. As it stands, Article 143 is unclear on what human security might mean in the absence of all its constituent rights. This suggests a dangerous conceptual vacuum that

---

[18] Security Council Resolution 1265 (1999) para 10; Security Council Resolution 1296 (2000); Statement of the President of the Security Council (15 March 2002). See the contribution by Neil McFarlane in this volume.

[19] Paris, R, 'Human Security: Paradigm Shift or Hot Air?' (2002) 26(2) *International Security* 87–102; Oberleitner (2005) 588.

cannot be dismissed simply by the essentially rhetorical nature of its inclusion in the 2005 World Summit Outcome document.

IV. JUSTICIABLE RIGHTS TO SECURITY

While the UN 2005 World Summit Outcome document might be considered a series of merely aspirational statements, the trend to subsume self-standing fundamental rights into the concept of a justiciable right to security can also be seen in a number of jurisdictions. Before exploring these examples, it is important to be clear about what it is we are referring to when we speak about a justiciable right.

Any examination of what is in legal terms actually contained in a justiciable right to security must start by distinguishing between the negative right to security (namely against the state) and the positive right to security enjoining the state or third parties to protect it. It also has to distinguish between express rights to security, which articulate the word 'security' within the language of the right, and implied rights to security, which consist of values that we commonly associate with personal security as part of, or as a subset of, another right.

1. Express Rights to Security

A *justiciable* express right to security would consist in any one of the following provisions:

Article 5 European Convention on Human Rights:

'Everyone has the right to liberty and security of person. No one shall be deprived of his liberty save in the following cases and in accordance with a procedure prescribed by law: . . .'

Article 7(1) American Convention on Human Rights:

'Every person has the right to personal liberty and security.'

The Constitution of South Africa 1996:

'*Freedom and security of the person*
12. (1) Everyone has the right to freedom and security of the person, which includes the right

    (a) not to be deprived of freedom arbitrarily or without just cause;
    (b) not to be detained without trial;
    (c) to be free from all forms of violence from either public or private sources;
    (d) not to be tortured in any way; and
    (e) not to be treated or punished in a cruel, inhuman or degrading way.

(2) Everyone has the right to bodily and psychological integrity, which includes the right

(a) to make decisions concerning reproduction;
(b) to security in and control over their body; and
(c) not to be subjected to medical or scientific experiments without their informed consent.'

The Canadian Charter of Rights and Freedoms 1985, section 7:

'Everyone has the right to life, liberty, and security of the person, and the right not to be deprived thereof except in accordance with the principles of fundamental justice.'

Constitution of Hungary (1949, as amended in 1997), Article 55 [Liberty, Security, Arrest]:

'(1) In the Republic of Hungary everyone has the right to freedom and personal security; no one shall be deprived of his freedom except on the grounds and in accordance with the procedures specified by law.'

While much more can be said about how these rights have been shaped in courts and about the duties and obligations arising from them, their inclusion in constitutional documents and international treaties makes their classification here as justiciable rights uncontroversial. This is also not an exhaustive list of provisions around the world that include references to a 'right to security', but the number and variety of examples should leave us in no doubt as to the existence for many years now of posited rights to security, in both national and international law.

Finally, I want to exclude the assumption at this stage that there is anything necessarily better in terms of the practical effects of the protection of individual security in having an expressly posited justiciable right. Clearly there is much in favour of alternative enforcement mechanisms in this context, particularly in the framework of armed conflict. Nonetheless, in light of the increasing rhetorical tendency to invoke the 'right to security', distinguishing the justiciable express right to security is an important part of our mapping exercise here.

A. The Express Negative Right to Security

The classical expression of the right to security, like most traditional civil and political liberties, consists of restrictions on the state from infringing upon personal individual security. Article 5 of the European Convention on Human Rights (ECHR) is an archetypical example of this right, marking out security alongside liberty as a right that the state must desist from infringing without justification. As the above table shows, all justiciable provisions align liberty and security, while many also include bodily integrity. So what is meant by security in these provisions? How is security per se to be distinguished from liberty in the legal sense? The answers from courts internationally demonstrate a curious schizophrenia between a view of security as indistinct from and submerged within liberty, and a clearly autonomous notion of security as inclusive of liberty and many other rights.

At one end of the spectrum, the jurisprudence arising from Article 5 ECHR demonstrates an almost complete elision of the express rights of security and liberty. This is already evident in the language of Article 5, the first sentence of which—'everyone has the right to liberty and security of person'—slips suddenly into the next—'no one shall be deprived of his liberty save in the following cases . . .'. So we shift from the opening normative commitment to 'security and liberty' to the question of how 'liberty', and only 'liberty', is to be lawfully restricted. As a consequence, although the Commission on Human Rights has made reference to an autonomous right to security,[20] very few decisions of the ECtHR refer to a separate notion of 'security' under Article 5 ECHR.

One passing mention of an autonomous right to security can be located in *Kurt v Turkey*[21] and was later reiterated in *Orhan v Turkey*.[22] The cases concerned the disappearance of Turkish citizens after their arrest by Turkish authorities. The ECtHR in assessing the application of Article 5 ECHR stated:

> What is at stake is both the protection of the physical liberty of individuals as well as their personal security in a context which, in the absence of safeguards, could result in a subversion of the rule of law and place detainees beyond the reach of the most rudimentary forms of legal protection.[23]

In another case, *Cyprus v Turkey*, a challenge based on an autonomous right to security was not upheld on the evidence, but the Court did not dispute, nor particularly acknowledge, the existence of such a right.[24]

Other than these examples, however, the Strasbourg Court normally treats the rights to liberty and security as one. Hence, in *Adler and Bivas v Federal Republic of Germany*, the Court argued that the terms 'liberty' and 'security' must be read as a whole.[25] Similarly, textbooks on the ECHR, with some notable exceptions,[26] discuss Article 5 solely as a protection of liberty.[27] In a particularly well-known edition, a chapter, despite bearing the title 'Personal Liberty and Security', begins by saying that 'the object of Article 5 is to guarantee liberty of the person' and omits any discussion of what the inclusion of the word 'security' in Article 5 might mean from a legal perspective.[28]

The jurisprudence of the ECtHR contrasts strongly with that of the Canadian Supreme Court on section 7 of the Canadian Charter of Rights and Freedoms,

---

[20] Report of 14 July 1974, *Kamma*, Yearbook XVIII (1075), p 300 (316); *East African Asians v United Kingdom* [1981] EHRR 76 (1973).

[21] *Kurt v Turkey* (1999) 27 EHRR 373, 417, para 212.

[22] *Orhan v Turkey* [2002] ECHR 25656/94, para 368. See also *Khudoyorov v Russia* [2005] ECHR 6847/02, para 142.

[23] *Kurt v Turkey* (1999) 27 EHRR 373, 378, para 6(b).

[24] *Cyprus v Turkey* (2001) 11 BHRC 45, paras 223–27.

[25] Appls 5573/72 and 5670/72, Yearbook XX (1977) p 102 (146).

[26] See Van Dijk, P and van Hoof, GJH, *Theory and Practice of the European Convention on Human Rights* (The Hague, Kluwer, 1998) 344; Harris, DJ, O'Boyle, M and Warbrick, C, *Law of the European Convention on Human Rights* (London, Butterworths, 1995) 103.

[27] Janis, M, Kay, R and Bradley, A, *European Human Rights Law*, 2nd edn (Oxford, OUP, 2000); Jacobs, F and White, R, *The European Convention on Human Rights*, 2nd edn (Oxford, Clarendon, 1996); Ovey, C and White, RCA, *Jacobs & White: The European Convention on Human Rights*, 4th edn (Oxford, OUP, 2006).

[28] Ovey and White (2006) ch. 7.

which has developed an autonomous notion of 'security of the person'. In many ways the right to personal security has been a platform for the creation of a number of rights not expressly included in the Canadian Charter. For example, in *Morgentaler (No 2)*, the right to security—the protection of the health of a woman—was the platform upon which restrictions on the right to abortion, previously contained in section 251 of the Criminal Code, were declared unconstitutional.[29] The case contained a variety of judicial rationales for linking restrictions on abortion to the 'right to security'. Some suggested that 'state interference with bodily integrity and serious state-imposed psychological stress, at least in the criminal context, constitute a breach of security of the person'.[30] But the majority agreed at the very least that the risk to the health of the woman caused by various restrictions on access to abortion constituted a breach of the right to security of the person.[31]

In *Rodriguez*, the ambit of the right to personal security was extended to protect the right to euthanasia. The majority declared:

> there is no question that personal autonomy, at least with respect to the right to make choices concerning one's own body, control over one's physical and psychological integrity, and basic human dignity are encompassed within security of the person, at least to the extent of freedom from criminal prohibitions which interfere with these.[32]

Finally, in *Chaouilli*, delays in the delivery of public health care, accompanied by a legislative prohibition on access to private health care, were held to be in violation of the right to security under section 7 because they gave rise to psychological or physical distress on the part of the claimants.[33]

It is clear that the Canadian constitutional jurisprudence takes a very broad view of the 'right to security of the person' as encompassing health, personal and psychological integrity, as well as basic human dignity. To the extent that it reflects the definition outlined at the outset of this chapter (absence from pervasive and critical threats of personal harm), the relationship between a risk to health and personal security is a plausible one. It would nevertheless be preferable if the right to health existed as a self-standing right within the Canadian Charter, as it does under the South African Constitution, or at least had grounding in a broader principle, such as such as human dignity, than the right to personal security.

Particularly dubious, however, is the suggestion by the Canadian Supreme Court that the right to security encompasses human dignity, which is a long-standing, foundational human right, internationally and in a number of other

---

[29] *R v Morgentaler (No 2)* [1988] 1 SCR 30.

[30] Wilson J and Dickson CJ.

[31] See further: Hogg, PW, *Constitutional Law of Canada*, 4th edn (Toronto, Carswell, 1997) 1072; Weinrib, L, 'The *Morgentaler* Judgment: Constitutional Rights, Legislative Intention and Institutional Design' (1992) 42 *University of Toronto Law Journal* 207.

[32] *Rodriguez v British Columbia (Attorney General)* [1993] 3 SCR 519 (author's own emphasis). See also Weinrib, L, 'The Body and the Body Politic: Assisted Suicide under the Canadian Charter of Rights and Freedoms' (1994) 39 *McGill Law Journal* 618.

[33] *Chaoiulli v Quebec (Attorney General)* 2005 SCC 35.

jurisdictions.[34] The problematic implication here, as with Article 143 of the UN 2005 World Summit Outcome document, is that the right to personal security provides a higher-order constitutional norm than human dignity, that somehow human dignity can be derived from personal security. This cannot be excused by the absence of an express right to human dignity within the Canadian Charter, for it would have been possible for the Supreme Court to argue that personal security is founded on the value of human dignity, central to human rights thinking internationally since 1948, rather than human dignity being a consequence of personal security.

Canada's development of an autonomous concept of security under section 7 of the Charter has been followed by express constitutional provisions elsewhere. In South Africa, section 12 of the 1996 Constitution ('Freedom and Security of the Person') expressly delineates a notion of security as distinct from liberty in a number of ways. First it specifies the 'right to security of the person' as the right 'to be free from all forms of violence from either public or private sources'.[35] Second, it specifies that the right to security includes the right not to be tortured and the right 'not to be treated or punished in a cruel, inhuman or degrading way'.[36] Finally, it specifies that the 'right to bodily and psychological integrity' under section 12(2) includes the right to 'security in and control over their body'.[37] This is probably the most extensively defined autonomous, express and justiciable right to security in any constitutional document around the world.[38]

Nonetheless, it is questionable whether it was necessary to include the negative rights to freedom from torture and inhuman and degrading treatment within the concept of liberty and security. Few rights are as well established and long-standing as the right to freedom from torture and degrading treatment, and few can claim such a close connection to human dignity, which itself is enshrined elsewhere in the South African Constitution.[39] It is also unclear why the notion of freedom and security of person is enhanced by the inclusion of the right against

---

[34] See Art 1 of the Universal Declaration of Human Rights (1948); Art 1(1) of the German Basic Law; s 10 of the Constitution of South Africa (1996). One need only look at the extensive protection of the right to human dignity under the German constitution and the jurisprudence of the Federal Constitutional Court, and its effect on the jurisprudence of the newer South African Constitutional Court, to see just how established the right to human dignity has become: Feldman, D, 'Human Dignity as a Legal Value: Part I' (1999) *Public Law* 682.

[35] Section 12(1)(c).

[36] Section 12(1)(d) and (e) respectively.

[37] Section 12(2)(b).

[38] Interestingly, it is far broader than the wording of section 11 of the South African Interim Constitution:

Section 11: Freedom and Security of the Person

1. Every person shall have the right to freedom and security of the person, which shall include the right not to be detained without trial.
2. No person shall be subject to torture of any kind, whether physical, mental or emotional, nor shall any person be subject to cruel, inhuman or degrading treatment or punishment.

[39] The Constitution of South Africa, 1996, s 1.

torture. While there is clearly a relationship between personal security and the prohibition on torture and inhuman and degrading treatment, there seems little need for the former to ground the latter. This is not to underrate the jurisprudence of the South African Constitutional Court in its application of the right to freedom from torture and inhuman and degrading treatment, in particular its use of it in abolishing the death penalty (*Makyanwane*) and indeterminate sentences (*Niemand*).[40] However, just as we should be wary of subsuming all other human values under the woolly notion of 'human security' within international relations discourse, we should resist the growing tendency to subsume traditionally estab-lished rights within an umbrella right to personal security.

Can we nevertheless distil within the stipulations of section 12 a distinct right to security? The parts of section 12 that we might think of as distinctive rights to secu-rity are sections 12(1)(c) (the right to freedom from public or private violence), section 12(2)(b) (the right to security in and control over your own body) and sec-tion 12(2)(c) (the right not to be subjected to medical or scientific experiments without informed consent). These provisions express something specific and cen-tral to the notion of personal security, in the sense of absence from personal harm, which is not expressly captured by other self-standing posited rights within the South African Constitution. In some senses the right to freedom from violence and the right to security in and control over one's own body are mirror images of one another: capturing a distinct notion of security in both a positive and negative sense.

The case-law on section 12(1)(c) will be examined in the next section, but it is worth noting that the South African Constitutional Court has not yet had an opportunity to elaborate extensively on section 12(2)(b) and (c). In the South African Supreme Court, however, the right to abortion was explicitly underpinned by both the right to control of reproduction (section 12(2)(a)) and the right to security in and control over your own body (section 12(2)(b)), with no strong ref-erence made to the right to health, which is also enshrined under the South African Constitution.[41] So unlike the Canadian case, where 'personal security' contributed to the protection of abortion rights only via the 'risk to health', in the South African case, the notion of 'security in and control over your body' was a direct constituent of the foundations of the right to abortion.

B. The Express Positive Right to Security: The Central Case?

Section 12(1)(c) of the 1996 Constitution of South Africa, the right 'to be free from all forms of violence from either public or private sources', expresses most dis-tinctly the positive aspect of the 'right to personal security'. A similar right is proposed in the Draft Bill of Rights by the Northern Ireland Human Rights

---

[40]   *S v Makwanyane* 1995 (6) BCLR 665 (CC); *S v Niemand* 2002 (3) BCLR 219 (CC).

[41]   *Christian Lawyers Association of South Africa and Others v Minister of Health and Others* 1998 (4) SA 1113 (T); *Christian Lawyers Association of South Africa and Others v Minister of Health and Other (Reproductive Health Alliance as Amicus Curiae)* 2005 (1) SA 509 (T).

Commission, which enshrines 'the right to be protected from violence', including threats of violence from private sources.[42] The Draft Bill articulates this right in two ways. In the Preamble, it is expressed as a self-standing principle: 'everyone has the right to live free from violence, fear, oppression and intimidation, with differences to be resolved through exclusively democratic means without the use of threat or force'. The right to be protected against violence is also grounded in the 'right to dignity and physical integrity' under section 6 of the Draft Bill, which is a marked divergence from the South African alignment of the protection against violence with 'freedom and personal security'.

There is much to be recommended in the Northern Irish approach, which makes no reference to the opaque notion of 'security' in its wording and which, correctly in my view, grounds the right against violence in the 'right to dignity and physical integrity'. Nevertheless, it is worth examining in some detail how the South African case-law has framed the positive right to security and, importantly, how it has delimited its potential reach through the careful construction of its correlative duty.

Justice Albie Sachs gave an early clarification of the positive duty arising under section 12(1)(c) of the 1996 Constitution in *Baloyi*.[43] The case concerned the burden of evidence required for establishing the guilt of persons accused of breaching interdicts regarding domestic violence. It had to confront the balance between fair trial protections and the constitutional duty of the state to protect citizens from criminal harm. Justice Sachs read section 12(1)(c) in conjunction with section 7(2), which states: 'the State must respect, protect, promote and fulfil the rights in the Bill of Rights'. He argued that, together, these sections oblige 'the state directly to protect the right of everyone to be free from private or domestic violence'.[44]

The process of developing the duty on the state to protect citizens from criminal and violent behaviour began in earnest, however, with *Carmichele*[45] and culminated more recently with *Metrorail*.[46] In *Carmichele*, a defendant accused of rape was released on bail and subsequently viciously assaulted the applicant. Carmichele argued that the police and prosecutor's decision to allow the defendant's release on bail constituted a breach of their constitutional duty to protect citizens from crime. The court, influenced by the approach of the ECtHR in *Osman*,[47] acknowledged that such a positive duty existed as a consequence of the rights to human dignity, life, liberty and security of the person, and the principle that the state must be held accountable for the discharge of its constitutional duties:

---

[42] Northern Ireland Human Rights Commission, 'Progressing a Bill of Rights for Northern Ireland: An Update', April 2004.

[43] *State v Baloyi (Minister of Justice Intervening)* 2000 (1) BCLR 86 (CC).

[44] *Ibid*, p 11.

[45] *Carmichele v Minister of Safety and Security and Another* 2001 (4) BCLR 938 (CC).

[46] *Rail Commuters Action Group and Others v Transnet Ltd t/a Metrorail and Others* 2005 (4) BCLR 301 (CC).

[47] *Osman v UK* (1998) 29 EHRR 245. See further discussion of this case in the section below entitled 'Implied Positive Rights to Aspects of Security'.

It follows that there is a duty imposed on the State and all of its organs not to perform any act that infringes these rights. In some circumstances there would also be a positive component which obliges the State and its organs to provide appropriate protection to everyone through laws and structures designed to afford such protection.[48]

The case established that the state could be held liable for the failure to perform its constitutional duties, unless it could be shown that there was a compelling reason to deviate from them. Such a deviation might be warranted where it would not be in the public interest to inhibit the police or prosecution in the proper performance of their duty.

After *Carmichele*, a number of cases decided in the South African Supreme Court developed principles relating to the state's liability arising as a consequence of its constitutional obligations under the rights to dignity, life, liberty and security.[49] These cases established that the constitutional principle of accountability was relevant to the type of duty (public law or private law) and, by implication, the remedy arising from the breach of any recognised duty. In *Van Duivenboden*, for example, it was argued that 'the norm of accountability must necessarily assume an important role in determining whether a legal duty ought to be recognised in any particular case'.[50]

This was the line of reasoning exploited by the Rail Commuters Action Group (RCAG) in *Metrorail*.[51] Formed in the Western Cape when a final-year engineering student was stabbed and killed on his way home on the train, the RCAG sought to respond to the pervasive violence occurring on the South African railways. The group brought an action against the public companies providing the rail service (Transnet and Metrorail), the South African Rail Commuters Corporation, the Minister of Transport and the Minister of Safety and Security. They sought, inter alia, mandatory relief to enjoin all the respondents

> to take steps (including interim steps) as are reasonably necessary to put in place proper and adequate safety and security services on rail commuter facilities used by rail commuters in the Western Cape, in order to protect those rights of rail commuters as are enshrined in the Constitution, to life, to freedom from all forms of violence from private sources and to human dignity.[52]

The Court, led by the judgment of Justice Kate O'Regan, asserted that the first two respondents, due to their specific statutory obligations under South African rail legislation and their monopoly over rail provision, bore a constitutional duty to rail commuters. Their duty was articulated in the socio-economic context of South Africa's apartheid legacy:

---

[48] *Carmichele*, note 45 above, para. 44.

[49] *Minister of Safety and Security v Hamilton* 2001 (3) SA 50 (SCA); *Minister of Safety and Security v Van Duivenboden* 2002 (6) SA 431 (SCA); *Van Eeden v Minister of Safety and Security* 2003 (1) SA 389 (SCA); *Minister of Safety and Security v Carmichele* 2004 (2) BCLR 133 (SCA).

[50] *Van Duivenboden*, note 48 above, para 21.

[51] Note 46 above.

[52] *Ibid*, para 48.

[T]he spatial planning of our cities means that those most in need of subsidized public transport services are those who often have the greatest distances to travel. Those people are also often the poorest members of our communities who have little choice in deciding whether to use rail services or not. The rail commuter services operated by the first and second respondent are used by hundreds and thousands of commuters on a daily basis. Another relevant consideration is the fact that once a commuter enters a train, he or she cannot easily leave it while it is in motion. Boarding a train renders commuters intensely vulnerable to violent criminals who target them. The applicants emphasized in argument the double bind in which commuters find themselves: they generally have little choice about using the train, and once on the train they are unable to protect against attack by criminals.[53]

In formulating the public law duty in question, Justice O'Regan emphasised the principle of accountability in enjoining the respondents to 'provide rail commuter services in a way that is consistent with the constitutional rights of commuters'.[54] The duty was formulated within certain bounds, namely 'to ensure that reasonable measures are in place'.[55] Factors relevant to 'reasonableness' in this context were:

the nature of the duty, the social and economic context in which it arises, the range of factors that are relevant to the performance of the duty, the extent to which the duty is closely related to the core activities of the duty-bearer—the closer they are, the greater the obligation on the duty-bearer, and the extent of any threat to fundamental rights should the duty not be met as well as the intensity of the harm that may result. The more grave is the threat to fundamental rights, the greater is the responsibility on the duty bearer. Thus, an obligation to take measures to discourage pickpocketing may not be as intense as an obligation to take measures to provide protection against serious threats to life and limb.[56]

In addition, Justice O'Regan argued that resource considerations would have a bearing on the Court's perception of reasonableness. But the principle of accountability made it impossible for the state to avoid its constitutional obligations by making bald assertions as to resource constraints. Rather,

details of the precise character of the resource constraints, whether human or financial, in the context of the overall resourcing of the organ of State will need to be provided. The standard of reasonableness so understood conforms to the constitutional principles of accountability, on the one hand, in that it requires decision-makers to disclose their reasons for their conduct, and the principle of effectiveness on the other, for it does not unduly hamper the decision-maker's authority to determine what are reasonable and appropriate measures in the overall context of their activities.[57]

Metrorail is a 'central case' examination of a justiciable positive right to security. By carefully examining the extent of the obligation correlative on the right to

---

[53] Note 46 above, para 82.
[54] *Ibid*, para 83.
[55] *Ibid*, para 84.
[56] *Ibid*, para 88.
[57] *Ibid*.

security, it establishes a human rights framework in which to test justifications for state action or inaction. In defining the duty, it is careful to set out the social and economic environment in which security might be pursued and, importantly, highlights that the duty on the state in pursuing security is delimited by notions of proximity and reasonableness. This framework is sensitive to the separation of powers between courts and political branches of government by avoiding the specification of 'how' the duty might be fulfilled, but it nevertheless places an onus on the state to justify failures to protect its citizens from violence. But while the *Metrorail* case is an exemplar, it is not unique. Like *Carmichele*, it rests on a preexisting line of cases in various jurisdictions implying aspects of the right to security from other rights. It is to these cases that this chapter will now briefly turn.

2. Implied Positive Rights to (Aspects of) Security

While the South African Constitution contains the most explicitly delineated express and justiciable right to security, the process of implying a duty on the state to protect citizens has been evident in international law and in a number of domestic jurisdictions for some time now. The express provisions under section 12 of the South African Constitution and the jurisprudence pursuant to it thus embody a growing acknowledgement of protective duties on states to safeguard individual human rights such as the right to life; freedom from torture and inhuman and degrading treatment; and the right to physical integrity.

In both treaty and customary international law, the general principle that states are required to protect and ensure human rights is well established.[58] More specifically, states are enjoined in various ways under international law to establish institutions and procedures that are effective in the criminalisation and investigation of violations of rights such as the rights to life and to physical integrity.[59] A concrete example of this exists in the jurisprudence surrounding Article 2 of the ECHR, as confirmed in the English common law.[60] In *Osman*, the duty on the state regarding the protection of the right to life under Article 2 required the state 'not only to refrain from the intentional and unlawful taking of life, but also to take

---

[58] Henkin, L, 'Human Rights' in Max Planck Institute for Comparative Public Law and International Law, *Encyclopedia of Public International Law*, vol 2 (Amsterdam, North-Holland/ Elsevier, 1995) 886, 890–1.

[59] See for example Human Rights Committee (United Nations), 'General Comment No 6 on the Right to Life (CCPR)', 1982, available at http://www.unhchr.ch/tbs/doc.nsf/(Symbol)/84ab9690ccd 81fc7c12563ed0046fae3?Opendocument; and the Torture Committee ('*Rodriguez v Uruguay*', Communication 322/1988, available at http://www.unhchr.ch/tbs/doc.nsf/385c2add1632f4a8c12565a 9004dc311/c6100f530629eae48025672300553422?OpenDocument?&Highlight=0,322%2F1988; '*Bautista v Colombia*', Communication 563/1993), available at http://www.unhchr.ch/tbs/doc.nsf/ 385c2add1632f4a8c12565a9004dc311/3a9eb3fc49aea4d68025670b003e78d1?OpenDocument&Highli ght=0,563%2F1993.

[60] *Osman* note 47 above; *Keenan v UK* (2001) EHRR 38R; *Amin v Secretary of State for the Home Department* [2003] UKHL 51; *Edwards v UK* (2002) 35 EHRR 19; *Oneryildiz v Turkey* [2004] ECHR 48939/99.

appropriate steps to safeguard the lives of those within its jurisdiction'.[61] This includes:

> putting in place effective criminal law provisions to deter the commission of offences against the person backed up by law-enforcement machinery for the prevention, suppression and sanctioning of breaches of such provisions. Article 2 may also imply in certain well-defined circumstances a positive obligation on the authorities to take preventive operational measures to protect an individual whose life is at risk from the criminal acts of another individual.[62]

The duties identified by the ECtHR are subject to specified limitations such as proximity, reasonableness and, importantly, the protection of other rights limitations, such as the right to liberty and fair trial. Normally, for a breach of a specific operational obligation to arise there must have been a real and immediate risk to life that the authorities were reasonably capable of avoiding. Clearly, the Court acknowledges that:

> bearing in mind the difficulties involved in policing modern societies, the unpredictability of human conduct and the operational choices which must be made in terms of priorities and resources, such an obligation must be interpreted in a way which does not impose an impossible or disproportionate burden on the authorities.[63]

This trend in the ECtHR is echoed in India, where a series of cases has established that the state could be held liable for negligent acts resulting in the violation of the right to life (what many now refer to as a 'constitutional tort').[64] As the Indian Supreme Court argued in *National Human Rights Commission*:

> the State is bound to protect the life and liberty of every human being, be he a citizen or otherwise . . . No State Government worth the name can tolerate . . . threats by one group of persons to another group of persons; it is duty bound to protect the threatened group from such assaults and if it fails to do so, it will fail to perform its Constitutional as well as statutory obligations. Those giving such threats would be liable to be dealt with in accordance with law. The State Government must act impartially and carry out its legal obligations to safeguard the life, health and well being of Chakmas residing in the State.[65]

In Germany, a similar outcome was arrived at far earlier than this, without recourse to private law reasoning. The Federal Constitutional Court (FCC) has

---

[61] *Osman v UK* note 47 above, para 115.

[62] *Ibid.*

[63] *Ibid*, para 116.

[64] *M Hongray v Union of India AIR* (1984) SC 1026; *Challa Ramkonda Reddy v State of Andhra Pradesh* (1990) ACJ 668; *R Gandhi v Union of India AIR* (1989) Mad 205; *M/s Inderpuri General Stores v Union of India AIR* (1992) J&K 11; *Manjit Singh Sawhney v Union of India* (2005) Indlaw DEL 379; Cooper-Stephenson, K, 'The Emergence of Constitutional Torts Worldwide', paper presented at the Conference on Comparative Constitutionalism, University of Kwazulu, Natal, South Africa, 12 December 2005.

[65] *National Human Rights Commission v State of Arunachal Pradesh and another AIR* (1996) SC 1234.

consistently held that a positive duty to protect life (*Schutzpflicht*) arises from the basic rights to life and physical integrity, which are enshrined in Article 2(2) of the German Basic Law.[66] The jurisprudence of protective duties in the German context is extensive and cannot be entered into lightly here.[67] Suffice it to say that the criminal law in Germany is conceived by the FCC as in part a consequence of the state's protective duties. Protective duties, combined with the notion of fundamental rights as objective norms that radiate throughout the system and bind private parties,[68] also underpin the FCC's development of duties on the state to develop organisations and procedures to protect against violations of certain fundamental rights such as life and physical integrity.[69] The Court has repeatedly acknowledged that the state has evaluative leeway in the extent to which it fulfils its constitutional protective duties.[70] However, the more fundamental the constitutional right, and the graver the violation, the less likely it is that the state can assert such evaluative leeway to avoid its constitutional obligations.[71]

Despite the unquestionable existence of the state's protective duties, these duties are clearly limited. This was manifest in a recent decision of the FCC, which struck down powers under the Aviation Security Act to shoot down an aircraft that is hijacked with the intention of using the aircraft 'as weapons in crimes against human lives'. The Court argued that these measures violated the essence of the right to life and the right to human dignity of the innocent passengers on the plane, who had been made into the mere objects of state action directed at the security of others. This 'objectification'—the use of individuals as a means to an end in the pursuit of security—was of particular concern to the FCC, which argued that this resulted in a violation of not only their right to life, but also of their inviolable dignity.[72]

This decision of the German FCC provides a compelling example of the sobering role that courts can play in heated political debate about appropriate pursuits of security. It is certainly a clear example of why the right to security cannot become the right of rights, trumping or even grounding the non-instrumental values, such as human dignity, that properly ought to ground and guide the realisation of other human rights.

---

[66] Jarrass, HD and Pieroth, B, *Grundgesetz für die Bundesrepublik Deutschland*, 6th edn (Munich, CH Beck, 2002) 87–8.

[67] See Lazarus, L, *Contrasting Prisoners Rights: A Comparative Examination of England and Germany* (Oxford, OUP, 2004) 28ff; Alexy, R, *A Theory of Constitutional Rights* (Oxford, OUP, 2002) ch 9; Isensee, J, 'Das Grundrecht als Abwehrrecht und als staatliche Schutzpflicht' in J Isensee and P Kirchhoff (eds), *Handbuch des Staatsrechts der Bundesrepublik Deutschland, Band IV: Allgemeine Grundrechtslehren* (Heidelberg, Müller, 1992). As the FCC is equivocal on this matter, I will not here enter the ongoing debate over whether *Schutzpflichten* should be seen as objective state duties or as correlative duties derived from subjective individual rights to state protection. See Alexy (2002) 301ff.

[68] See the Lüth Judgement, *BVerfGE* 7, 198.

[69] Most controversially, however, protective duties have been used to protect the unborn foetus: *BVerfGE* 39, 1

[70] *BVerfGE* 46, 160/164; 56, 54/80ff; 79, 174/202; 85, 191/212.

[71] Jarrass and Pieroth (2002) 87–8.

[72] *BVerfGE* (2006) 1 BvR 357/05, 15 February 2006, paras 120–1.

CONCLUSION

There is real danger that, without consistent analytical rigour, the rhetoric of a 'right to security' will undermine the hard won, carefully reasoned, yet fragile consensus around fundamental rights. The rhetorical and political appeal of security and rights has within it a potentially explosive combination, not only to erode the protections of competing rights such as liberty, but also to undermine accepted understandings of the foundations of fundamental rights reasoning. Once we start to shift, however implicitly, to the idea of 'security' as the grounding for human dignity, alarm bells need to ring. Throw into that rhetorical cocktail the legitimacy of a legal claim of a broad justiciable right to security, and we are in even more trouble. There is therefore a serious imperative on constitutional courts and international human rights tribunals, which are in a very particular position to guard the integrity of human rights reasoning, to be specific about what is meant by the legal 'right to security'. Their objective must be to ensure that the right to security does not become the catch-all justificatory foundation for a range of self-standing fundamental rights, just as they should not allow broad and undifferentiated assertions of the social pursuit of security to erode fundamental rights.

As the final section on implied rights to security shows, it is possible to arrive at specific rights protections that are highly relevant to the safeguarding of security with reference to only pre-existing fundamental rights such as the rights to life and physical integrity. The implied nature of these protections is to be preferred to a process of usurpation by which the 'right to security' becomes a meta-right. If the express right to security is to exist at all—and the Northern Ireland Draft Bill of Rights suggests it need not—then it is best viewed restrictively. Courts are under a duty to clarify how these rights apply and, importantly, to develop a coherent framework for the delineation of state duties correlative to them. The careful reasoning regarding state duties in *Metrorail* is instructive for this reason, particularly if read with the explicit stipulation in *Osman* and by the German Federal Constitutional Court that a state's fulfillment of its protective duties are restricted by its respect for existing negative rights such as life, dignity, fair trial and the prohibition against arbitrary detention.

So the development of a 'right to security' can go two ways: towards the usurpation and erosion of existing fundamental rights, or towards a delineated, transparent and narrower notion of the 'right to security' that respects and is grounded in other fundamental rights. Given the world we now live in and given the claim to legitimacy that law so often makes, courts have a very important role to play in urging the second route over the first. Theirs is the task of stemming the rhetoric of security in a global environment of insecurity, and of resisting the temptation to found rights to dignity, health and the many human goals we value on the basis of a right to security.

REFERENCES

Alexy, R, *A Theory of Constitutional Rights* (Oxford, OUP, 2002).

Alkire, S, 'A Conceptual Framework for Human Security', Centre for Research on Inequality, Human Security and Ethnicity (CRISE) Working Paper 2, available at http://www.crise.ox.ac.uk/pubs/workingpaper2.pdf.

Blair, T, 'Monthly Downing Street Press Conference', 5 August 2005, available at http://www.pm.gov.uk/output/Page6825.asp.

Blitz, R and Burns, J, 'Civil Liberties and National Security Prove a Difficult Balance to Strike', *Financial Times*, 9 September 2005, 4.

Blunkett, D, 'Balancing Human Rights and Security', address to Harvard Law School, 8 March 2004, available at www.hno.harvard.edu/gazette/2004/03.11/27-rights.html.

Campbell, T, Goldsworthy, J and Stone, A (eds), *Protecting Human Rights: Instruments and Institutions* (New York, Oxford University Press, 2003).

Cole, D, *Enemy Aliens: Double Standards and Constitutional Freedoms in the War on Terrorism* (New York, New York Press, 2003).

Commission on Human Security, *Human Security Now* (New York, Commission on Human Security, 2003).

Cooper-Stephenson, K, 'The Emergence of Constitutional Torts Worldwide', paper presented at the Conference on Comparative Constitutionalism, University of Kwazulu, Natal, South Africa, 12 December 2005.

Daniels, R, Macklem, P and Roach, K (eds), *The Security of Freedom: Essays on Canada's Anti-terrorism Bill* (Toronto, University of Toronto Press, 2001).

Feldman, D, 'Human Dignity as a Legal Value: Part I' (1999) *Public Law* 682.

Feldman, E, 'Patient's Rights, Citizen's Movements and Japanese Legal Culture' in D Nelken, (ed), *Comparing Legal Cultures* (Dartmouth, Aldershot, 1997) 215.

Foreign and Commonwealth Office of the United Kingdom, 'Liberty and Security: Striking the Right Balance', paper by the UK Presidency of the EU, 2005, available at www.fco.gov.uk/Files/kfile/LibertySecurity.pdf.

Lord Goldsmith QC, 'How Should Britain Protect its Citizens?' *The Times*, 11 May 2004.

Harris, DJ, O'Boyle, M and Warbrick, C, *Law of the European Convention on Human Rights* (London, Butterworths, 1995).

Henkin, L, 'Human Rights' in Max Planck Institute for Comparative Public Law and International Law, *Encyclopedia of Public International Law*, vol 2 (Amsterdam, North-Holland/Elsevier, 1995) 886.

Heymann, P, *Terrorism, Freedom, and Security: Winning without War* (Cambridge, MA, MIT Press, 2004).

Hogg, PW, *Constitutional Law of Canada*, 4th edn (Toronto, Carswell, 1997).

Hohfeld, W, *Fundamental Legal Conceptions as Applied in Judicial Reasoning* (New Haven, Yale University Press, 1919).

Human Rights Committee (United Nations), 'General Comment No 6 on the Right to Life (CCPR)', 1982, available at http://www.unhchr.ch/tbs/doc.nsf/(Symbol)/84ab9690ccd81fc7c12563ed0046fae3?Opendocument.

Ignatieff, M, *The Lesser Evil: Political Ethics in an Age of Terror* (Princeton, Princeton University Press, 2004).

Isensee, J, 'Das Grundrecht als Abwehrrecht und als staatliche Schutzpflicht' in J Isensee and P Kirchhoff (eds), *Handbuch des Staatsrechts der Bundesrepublik Deutschland, Band IV: Allgemeine Grundrechtslehren* (Heidelberg, Müller, 1992).

Jacobs, F and White, R, *The European Convention on Human Rights*, 2nd edn (Oxford, Clarendon, 1996).

Janis, M, Kay, R and Bradley, A, *European Human Rights Law*, 2nd edn (Oxford, OUP, 2000).

Jarrass, HD and Pieroth, B, *Grundgesetz für die Bundesrepublik Deutschland*, 6th edn (Munich, CH Beck, 2002).

Lazarus, L, *Contrasting Prisoners Rights: A Comparative Examination of England and Germany* (Oxford, OUP, 2004).

—— 'Conceptions of Liberty Deprivation' (2006) 69(5) *Modern Law Review* 738.

Loader, I and Walker, N, *Civilizing Security* (Cambridge, Cambridge University Press, 2007).

Northern Ireland Human Rights Commission, 'Progressing a Bill of Rights for Northern Ireland: An Update', April 2004.

Oberleitner, G, 'Porcupines in Love: The Intricate Convergence of Human Rights and Human Security' (2005) 6 *European Human Rights Law Review* 588.

Ovey, C and White, RCA, *Jacobs & White: European Convention on Human Rights*, 4th edn (Oxford, OUP, 2006).

Paris, R., 'Human Security: Paradigm Shift or Hot Air? (2002) 26(2) *International Security* 87–102.

Rosen, J, 'Liberty Wins—So Far', *The Washington Post*, 15 September 2002, B01.

Stephens, P, 'If the Balance Tilts towards Security, Liberty Will Pay', *The Guardian*, 11 March 2005, 17.

Taylor, SJ, 'Rights, Liberties and Security: Recalibrating the Balance after September 11' (2003) 21(1) *The Brookings Review* 25.

United Nations Development Programme (UNDP), *Human Development Report 1994* (New York, Oxford University Press, 1994).

United Nations General Assembly, '2005 World Summit Outcome', A/60/L.1, 15 September 2005.

Van Dijk, P and van Hoof, GJH, *Theory and Practice of the European Convention on Human Rights* (The Hague, Kluwer, 1998).

Waldron, J, 'Security and Liberty: The Image of Balance' (2003) 11(2) *Journal of Political Philosophy* 191.

Weinrib, L, 'The *Morgentaler* Judgment: Constitutional Rights, Legislative Intention and Institutional Design' (1992) 42 *University of Toronto Law Journal* 207.

—— 'The Body and the Body Politic: Assisted Suicide under the Canadian Charter of Rights and Freedoms' (1994) 39 *McGill Law Journal* 618.

Zedner, L, 'Securing Liberty in the Face of Terror: Reflections from Criminal Justice' (2005) 32(4) *Journal of Law and Society* 507.

15

Human Security and the Law of States

S NEIL MACFARLANE

INTRODUCTION

A NOVEMBER 2005 issue of the *International Herald Tribune* carried an op-ed piece by former Speaker of the US House of Representatives Newt Gingrich and former Senator George Mitchell, the chairmen of a US task force on American interests and United Nations reform.[1] The piece contained a set of observations that are worth quoting at length:

> Our task force called on the US government and the UN to 'affirm that every sovereign government has a "responsibility to protect" its citizens and those within its jurisdiction from genocide, mass killing, and massive and sustained human rights violations.' World leaders endorsed this general principle, which is a very significant step in light of past international resistance to any provision that would seem to endorse interference in a state's 'sovereign internal affairs.' It is critical that this principle be understood broadly to encompass mass killings and massive and sustained human rights violations, whether or not they meet technical legal standards for genocide ... In certain circumstances, a government's abnegation of its responsibilities to protect is so severe that the failure of the Security Council to act must not be used as an excuse for the world to stand by as atrocities continue.[2]

For students of international politics, this is a surprising remark, given its provenance. The United States is not known for the argument that sovereignty is derogable on the basis of human rights concerns. Resistance to this notion is particularly strong on the Republican right, of which Gingrich is a prominent member.

Their discussion of the 'responsibility to protect' points to an element of the relationship between security and rights that tends to be underplayed in the current context of the war on terror. Current discussion focuses largely on the extent to which security concerns might (or might not) justify the infringement of

---

[1] See Task Force on the United Nations, *The Imperative for Action: An Update of the Report of the Task Force on American Interests and UN Reform* (Washington, DC, United States Institute of Peace, December 2005), available at http://www.usip.org.

[2] Gingrich, N and Mitchell, G, 'UN Reform: Report Card from America', *International Herald Tribune*, 26–27 November 2005.

generally recognised individual civil and political rights (from the violation of judicial rights associated with indefinite detention or extraordinary rendition to the limitation on the right to free speech apparent in the prospective UK prohibition on 'glorifying terrorism'). The neglected dimension is that the evolution of the discourse on security may considerably enhance the capacity for international protection of the human rights of individuals and communities at risk from violence perpetrated or tolerated by their states within the territorial jurisdiction of those states. This evolution revolves around the concept of human security. In theory anyway, the 'humanising' of security, and its embedding in international agreements may have a considerable impact on the conceptualisation of state sovereignty in international law and on the rights of states with regard to sovereignty.

This chapter begins with an examination of the conventional meaning of security in traditional international relations theory and discourse on security, and then looks briefly at its relationship to state sovereignty and international norms on domestic jurisdiction. The next section concerns the emergence and meaning of the concept of human security and examines the somewhat ambiguous embedding of the concept in the activity of the international society, with a particular emphasis on the UN Security Council as an authoritative body in the regulation of security matters. The concluding section of the chapter picks up on several analytical and empirical problems with the concept of human security and analyses its implications for international society, notably the qualification of the sovereign rights of states inherent in the focus on the needs of individual human beings for security.

I. SECURITY

The concept of security is essentially contested. Security has something to do with the (relative) absence of threat to the core values of the referents of security. The landscape of threat might include, at a minimum:

- physical threats to the survival of the relevant entity;
- threats to welfare; and
- threats to identity (including values).

One issue that arises immediately is that all good things do not necessarily go together. Given scarce resources, investment in physical security may have a negative impact on welfare.[3] Likewise, a focus on imminent external threat to survival may create threats to established rights, as is evident in the current 'war on terror'. Much of the contestedness of security involves debates about which set of threats should take priority in security policy broadly defined.

Also, it is not immediately obvious whose security counts. Should we focus on humanity, the state, the group or the individual? Focusing on the security of the

---

[3] For an early discussion, see Ullman, R, 'Redefining Security' (1983) 8(1) *International Security* 129–53.

state may damage the security of individuals within it. Conversely, emphasising the security of individuals may make it difficult for states to respond optimally to internal and external threats. Ensuring the security of, say, territorially defined ethnic groups within states may imperil the security of the states. On the other hand, a state's pursuit of national cohesion on security grounds may threaten the identity of groups within it. The pursuit of security by a group within a state may make it difficult for individuals to secure their personal rights where their priorities do not coincide with those of their group; emphasising the rights of individuals may imperil the existence of defined groups within a state.

Traditional international relations analysis of security has focused on externally originating military threats to states.[4] The emphasis has been on national security (the security of sovereign states from the threat of aggression) and international security (the minimisation of interstate violence). This focus is evident in the UN Charter. Although the Charter does not define threats to international peace and security, the relevant Articles (1.1, 2.4 and 39) stress external aggression.

The Charter also makes clear that the rights of states trump those of individuals within them. Although the Charter takes account of human rights (see the Preamble and also Articles 62 and 68 concerning the Economic and Social Council (ECOSOC)) and commits member states to co-operation in their promotion,[5] these have not been obviously binding with regard to the behaviour of member states.

In contrast, Article 2.1 of the Charter strongly embraces the principle of equal sovereignty of states. This was linked closely to a principle of non-intervention, both by states (Article 2.4) and by the UN itself (Article 2.7). The principle of non-intervention was further embedded in declarations of the General Assembly in the 1960s and 1970s, notably those on intervention[6] and friendly relations.[7] The inclusion of these principles in the Charter reflects a long tradition of customary and treaty law in regard to sovereignty and non-intervention, dating back at least to the Peace of Westphalia (1648).[8] Historically, states have been the principal subjects in international public law; individual human beings or groups of human beings have had few international rights.[9]

---

[4] 'Since the early 17th Century, international security has been defined almost exclusively in terms of national survival needs. Security has meant the protection of the state—its boundaries, people, institutions, and values—from external attack': Commission on Global Governance, *Our Global Neighbourhood* (Oxford, Oxford University Press, 1995) 78.

[5] For further discussion, see Farer, TJ and Gaer, F, 'The UN and Human Rights: At the End of the Beginning' in A Roberts (ed), *United Nations, Divided World: The UN's Roles in International Society* (Oxford, Oxford University Press, 1993) 240–96.

[6] 'Declaration on the Inadmissibility of Intervention in the Domestic Affairs of States and the Protection of Their Independence and Sovereignty', United Nations General Assembly Resolution 2131(XX), 21 December 1965.

[7] 'Declaration on Principles of International Law Concerning Friendly Relations and Co-operation among States in Accordance with the Charter of the United Nations', United Nations General Assembly Resolution 2625 (XXV), 24 October 1970.

[8] Hinsley, FH, *Sovereignty*, 2nd edn (Cambridge, Cambridge University Press, 1986); Vincent, RJ, *Non-intervention and International Order* (Princeton, Princeton University Press, 1974).

[9] This is not to say they had none. The emergence of an international legal regime concerning slavery, the protection in treaty of the rights of religious minorities, and the emerging laws of war as they

The (Western) normative logic of the primacy accorded to the state in consideration of security is clear in both absolutist and liberal constitutional theory. In the first (eg, Hobbes), individuals trade their individual sovereignty upwards in return for the protection without which normal life cannot proceed. In liberal constitutionalist theory (eg, Locke), the people choose the character of their state and government, and, consequently, they have obligations to the state. In both instances, the security concerns of individuals are bundled together into the state collectivity. The other side of the bargain is that states provide for the primary security needs of their citizens. As Aristotle pointed out, the *polis* exists first that men should live and then that they should live well.[10]

These normative traditions concerning sovereignty presume that states protect their citizens, further the welfare of citizens and defend citizens' values. To the extent that this is so, it does not make sense to question the sovereignty of states over the affairs of their citizens. And, as the history of the European wars of religion suggests, to act differently could destabilise the pluralist system of international relations while causing incalculable suffering to human beings. For this reason, it has made sense in discourse on security to subordinate the concerns of individuals to those of states. If states could not secure themselves, then individuals within them could not be secure.

This view of the state and its relationship to the security of its citizens is evident in the paucity of international law and practice dealing with individual rights in the period up to 1945. It was also reasonably clear in the activities of the UN Security Council during the Cold War. The Council occupied itself little with the rights of individuals during the first 40 years of its existence.[11] For that matter, it largely ignored events—including wars—within states. The UN rarely intervened in internal conflicts on the basis of Security Council decisions. When it did so, it was largely on the basis of consent by the parties. And such interventions did not involve substantial activity directed at the personal security of civilians in harm's way. This remained true, by and large, through to the end of the Cold War. Massive killings of civilians in civil conflicts, such as those in Nigeria and Bangladesh, and mass murder, as in Kampuchea (now Cambodia), produced little by way of international reaction.[12]

Several aspects of the international history of the twentieth century have drawn these more or less settled understandings of the relationship between the state and the citizen into question:

concerned the wounded, the sick, prisoners, and civilian non-combatants are all examples of the granting of limited rights in international law to human beings. See Bugnion, F, *Le Comité Internationale de la Croix Rouge et la Protection des Victimes de la Guerre* (Geneva, International Committee of the Red Cross, 1994); and Jackson-Preece, J, *National Minorities and the European Nation-state System* (Oxford, Clarendon Press, 1998).

[10] Aristotle, *Politics*, trs William Ellis (London, JM Dent, 1947) 3.

[11] For an extended discussion, see MacFarlane, SN and Yuen, FK, *Human Security and the UN: A Critical History* (Bloomington, Indiana University Press, 2006) 61–95.

[12] For a very useful treatment, see Wheeler, NJ, *Saving Strangers: Humanitarian Intervention in International Society* (Oxford, Oxford University Press, 2000).

- The industrialisation of war made it possible to mobilise ever greater numbers of people into the armed forces. It also greatly increased the lethality of weapons systems. Conscription made military service an obligation for a large portion of the (male) population. The result was rapid growth in the number of citizen casualties in war.
- Technological change (long-range artillery and then the strategic bomber) permitted the application of force well behind the lines upon which armies faced each other. This contributed to a rapid increase in the numbers of civilian casualties in war. The advent of nuclear weapons and the absence of effective means to defend against strategic missiles made it implausible that, *in extremis*, the major powers could actually protect their people. Indeed, the central strategic principle of Cold War stability (mutual assured destruction) presumed that they could not and that they should not attempt to develop the capabilities to do so.
- Over the twentieth century, the proportion of civilians as opposed to soldiers killed in war evolved from one to eight to ten to one. In 2003 the EU noted that 4 million people had died in war since 1990, 90 per cent of them civilians.[13]
- During the twentieth century, more civilians were killed, directly (as in Stalin's purges) or indirectly (as in Mao's Great Leap Forward), by their own governments than were killed in war during the same period. In short, there has been ample evidence that the state, far from being a solution to the security demands of its citizens, may wilfully be a major threat to their security.
- Decolonisation and the collapse of communism produced large numbers of new states that lacked the capacity to exercise effective sovereignty over their territories and those living within them.[14] The state's ability to fulfil its role in contractarian theory is therefore now seriously in question.

These last points raised two significant questions. First, if a state massively violates the rights of its own people, or if it will not or cannot protect them, what is the normative basis of the state's claim to the rights associated with sovereignty in international society?[15] Second, if not the state, then who or what has the responsibility to protect human beings at risk? Serious consideration of these questions was prevented during the Cold War period by the systemic competition between the superpowers. The end of that competition in the late 1980s was a significant permissive condition for the emergence of an alternative discourse on security.

[13] European Council, 'A Secure Europe in a Better World: European Security Strategy', 12 December 2003, available at http://ue.eu.int/cms3_fo/showPage.asp?id=266&lang=en&mode=g. One should note the difficulty, however, of distinguishing soldiers from civilians in much recent conflict.

[14] For a good discussion, see Jackson, RH, *Quasi-states: Sovereignty, International Relations, and the Third World* (Cambridge, Cambridge University Press, 1990). If the ethical basis of the state's claim to hegemony in discourse on security is based on its capacity to protect its citizens, then if it cannot do that, it loses its claim.

[15] In Hobbes' contractarian view of state sovereignty, the contract is deemed more or less absolute and permanent. He did, however, specify two circumstances in which it was void: if the state required the suicide of the individual, and if the state could not deliver on protection.

II. HUMAN SECURITY

The alternative discourse that has emerged since the end of the Cold War focuses on *human* security. Whereas traditional international relations analysis of security focused on military threats to states, human security has expanded the discussion on vertical and horizontal axes. On the vertical one, it has extended the referent of security downward from states to individual human beings. Moreover, human security has extended the substance of security horizontally outwards from its focus on military affairs to embrace other issues, including criminality, the defence of human rights, economic threats, environmental threats and threats to health.[16]

There is substantial disagreement over how broad the category of threats covered under the concept of human security should be.[17] Two general clusters have emerged. One embraces a narrow conception of human security, focusing on violent threats to the survival and integrity of the physical persons.[18] The other takes a much broader and multi-dimensional view of threats to human beings, going well beyond violence.[19] Proponents of this latter, broader view of human security point out that physical violence is far from the most significant threat to the survival and welfare of human beings. Fatalities from violence are dwarfed by those, for example, from disease and from famine.

In another chapter in this volume, Liora Lazarus challenges the amalgamation of specific rights with reasonably clear meaning into an amorphous concept of the right to security. In her view, to move in that direction risks diluting the protections afforded to human beings. The proponents of a narrow view of human security offer an analogous argument: the broader the parameters of security and the fuzzier the boundaries, the less useful the concept of security is as an analytical and policy concept. In contrast, an understanding of security that emphasises freedom from the threat of physical violence avoids the diffusion of attention and of policy that is arguably implicit in broader conceptions. In addition, rolling concepts such as human development and basic rights into an overarching category of human security risks diverting attention and policy focus from those aspirations.

Underlying this conceptual disagreement over the purview of human security is a competition for resources. The word 'security' carries a political and value content that privileges it in resource allocation. It is one thing to say that a policy is a matter of group interest or political preference and quite another to say that it is a matter of security. Appropriating the word, consequently, may enhance access

---

[16] See UNDP, *Human Development Report 1994: New Dimensions of Human Security* (New York, United Nations, 1994); and Commission on Human Security (CHS), *Human Security Now* (Tokyo, CHS, 2003).

[17] For an early treatment, see Hampson, FO, Daudelin, J, Hay, JB, Reid, H and Marting, T, *Madness in the Multitude: Human Security and World Disorder* (Toronto, Oxford University Press, 2001) 17–18.

[18] Eg, International Commission on Intervention and State Sovereignty (ICISS), *The Responsibility to Protect* (Ottawa, International Development Research Council, 2001). See also the contribution by Jennifer Welsh in this volume.

[19] Eg, Commission on Human Security (2003) and UNDP (1994).

to scarce resources. It is not surprising, therefore, that it is in the development community that the economic dimension of security is emphasised, in the health community that disease is highlighted, and so on.

Human security concerns have been translated into numerous normative and legal developments. The acceleration of norm-setting regarding human security issues falls into three categories. In the first, we find a growing number of state treaty commitments regarding the security of civilians, both in conflict and in non-conflict situations. One example is the 1997 treaty banning the deployment, trade and production of anti-personnel landmines;[20] another is the protocol on the recruitment of children into national armed forces;[21] and a third is the earlier International Convention on Torture.[22]

The second category of norm-setting involves recognition by states of the international accountability of individual agents acting in the name of states. The Treaty of Rome, rooted in the Nuremberg precedent and growing out of the International Criminal Tribunals for Yugoslavia and Rwanda, established the International Criminal Court. It also made provision for the international prosecution of individuals accused of war crimes or crimes against humanity when their national authorities either will not or are incapable of adjudicating such cases. In all of these instances, international agreements have limited the discretion of states in the treatment of their own citizens, and the Rome treaty has expanded the jurisdiction of an international tribunal to include cases involving violations of human security.

The third category of norm-setting—and the one most relevant to this analysis—concerns the UN Security Council's changing definition of threats to international peace and security. As already noted, the Charter (in Article 2.7) emphasises that nothing in the document should be construed to permit interference by the United Nations in matters that are 'essentially within the domestic jurisdiction of any State'. However, the Article goes on to note that 'this principle shall not prejudice the application of enforcement measures under Chapter VII'. In other words, the conventional understanding of sovereignty holds, up to the point that the Council decides that what is going on within a country constitutes a threat to international peace and security.

During the Cold War, as already noted, the Council generally took a very narrow view of the meaning of threat. Council actions focused heavily on interstate

---

[20] Convention on the Prohibition of the Use, Stockpiling, Production and Transfer of Anti-personnel Mines and on Their Destruction (Ottawa, 18 September 1997), available at http://www.un.org/ Depts/mine/UNDocs/ban_trty.htm. For a useful discussion of the process leading to the treaty, see Hubert, D, 'The Landmine Ban: A Case Study in Humanitarian Advocacy', Occasional Paper No 42 (Providence, RI, The Thomas J Watson Jr Institute for International Studies, 2000).

[21] Optional Protocol to the Convention on the Rights of the Child on the Involvement of Children in Armed Conflict, UNGA A/RES/263, 25 May 2000, available at http://www.unhchr.ch/html/menu2/ 6/protocolchild.htm.

[22] Convention against Torture and Other Cruel, Inhuman, and Degrading Treatment or Punishment, UNGA A/RES/39/46, 10 December 1984, available at http://www.unhchr.ch/html/ menu3/b/h_cat39.htm. That this Convention was adopted and came into force during the Cold War reminds us of the substantial normative development of relevance to rights during that period.

threats to peace and security, with the exception of resolutions dealing with decolonisation and apartheid. The peacekeeping activities of the UN meanwhile made little provision for the security of human beings and instead focused on the management of conflict and post-conflict situations involving states (the Congo and Cyprus notwithstanding). Forces deployed had no human rights element in their mandates. In this respect, the Council was not a key player in laying the normative framework for human security. The rights and interests of individual human beings seemed much more to be the domain of the General Assembly. It was there that a range of declarations, conventions, covenants and protocols on genocide, torture, civil and political and economic and social rights, the rights of the child, and discrimination on grounds of race or gender were negotiated during the Cold War.

The end of the Cold War period brought significant change in the Council's definition of threat to international peace and security and in its practice vis-à-vis sub-state conflict. In the first place, the volume of Chapter VII resolutions grew rapidly. In the second, they came to focus on responses to internal conflict within recognised states, as opposed to interstate war or conflict associated with decolonisation.

More importantly from our perspective, quite early in the period, the Council came to see the targeting, abuse or neglect of civilians as constituting a threat to international peace and security. This process arguably began with the crisis in Northern Iraq in the spring of 1991. A humanitarian crisis was rapidly developing as Kurds were driven from their homes by advancing Iraqi forces, but Turkey was unwilling to allow displaced persons to cross the border. The Council expressed its grave concern over the repression of Iraqi civilians and the movement of large numbers of civilians towards international frontiers. It noted that the movement of Kurds had occasioned cross-border incursions, which the Council considered to be a threat to international peace and security. It then demanded that Iraq cease its attacks on Iraqi civilians and allow immediate access to humanitarian organisations to meet the needs of the affected civilians.[23]

In terms of the balance between state and human rights and interests, however, it is noteworthy that the Resolution did not invoke Chapter VII and did not contest sovereignty. The Resolution specifically emphasised the Council's respect for Iraq's sovereignty, territorial integrity and political independence. The text suggests that it was not the movement of displaced persons per se that was identified as a threat to peace and security. Instead, it was the problem of cross-border incursion. In other words, at this stage the Council shied away from the notion that an internal humanitarian crisis emanating from the massive violation of citizens' rights by their own state *ipso facto* might fall within its remit. Cross-border incursion and frontier insecurity were much safer grounds because they were inherently international. There was no threat of UN or UN-mandated action to address the root of the problem within Iraq.

---

[23] Security Council Resolution (SCR) 688 (1991).

The rather weak wording of the Resolution and the lack of robust implementation clauses reflected the reluctance of a number of members of the Council to provide a broad power of intervention in domestic jurisdiction on humanitarian grounds. Moreover, the vote indicated that even such a qualified approach was met by considerable reservations: China and India abstained; Yemen, Cuba and Zimbabwe voted against.

The Council's approach to human security evolved further in response to the humanitarian crisis in Somalia in 1992. In this instance, the collapse of the Somali state and the deepening conflict amongst various factions within the country produced mass starvation, yet the situation in the country made it extremely difficult for humanitarian organisations to respond. After several resolutions acknowledging the gravity of the situation, the Council determined that the situation within Somalia constituted a threat to international peace and security. It noted the obstacles to the delivery of humanitarian assistance and the dangers to relief personnel working there. It then declared its determination to create an environment that was conducive to mounting humanitarian operations, and, acting under Chapter VII, it authorised a military action (Unified Task Force (UNITAF)), led by the United States, to foster such conditions.[24] Once UNITAF had achieved a modicum of security in the country, it was replaced by a peacekeeping force (UN Operation in Somalia (UNOSOM) II) operating under Chapter VII with a similar mandate.[25] The unfortunate outcome of the operation notwithstanding, the recognition of 'the magnitude of the human tragedy' as a threat to international peace and security in and of itself, without reference to cross-border implications, was a striking development.

The Council acted in a second case in 1992 to address a humanitarian crisis, this time in Bosnia. Various resolutions in the spring and summer of that year identified the humanitarian crisis there as a threat to international peace and security.[26] The UN deployed a peace operation to assist in the delivery of relief and to protect humanitarian personnel and shipments. In addition, the Council specifically condemned the mass rape of Muslim women in Serb detention camps.[27] As the extent of the crimes against civilians grew clearer, the Council called for the establishment of an International Criminal Tribunal for the former Yugoslavia.[28] Later, UN protection was extended to the Srebrenica 'safe area',[29] and five other such safe areas were added a month later.[30]

The failure of the UN effort to end violence in Bosnia, and US and NATO intervention in the face of the escalation of war in 1995 produced a Security Council mandate for a NATO-led force to enforce the Dayton Agreements ending

---

[24] SCR 794, 3 December 1992.
[25] SCR 814, 26 March 1993.
[26] See, eg, SCR 770.
[27] SCR 798, 18 December 1992.
[28] SCR 808, 20 February 1993.
[29] SCR 819, 16 April 1993.
[30] SCR 824, 6 May 1993.

hostilities in that country.[31] This involved the transfer of significant elements of Bosnia's sovereignty to international authorities, who were charged with the design and implementation of a durable solution to the country's political crisis.

The case of Rwanda, while notable for the indecisiveness and irresponsibility of the Council and Secretariat, also contributed to this evolution. Late in the crisis, the Council, once again determining that humanitarian concerns constituted a threat to international peace and security, acted under Chapter VII to mandate a French-led intervention to protect civilians in the south of the country and to assist in the delivery of humanitarian relief.[32] The Council also established an International Criminal Tribunal for Rwanda to call the principal *génocidaires* to account.

What was striking about the Iraq and Somalia cases, and eventually the response to the Bosnia situation, particularly when compared with earlier peacekeeping operations, was the explicit extension of UN military functions to the protection of civilians, both international personnel involved in humanitarian operations and also, in varying degrees, the victims themselves. The northern Iraq, Bosnia and Rwanda cases—and for that matter, the later case of East Timor—did not obviously raise Article 2.7 concerns because the national authorities consented to UN engagement.[33] However, the Somalia case is particularly notable because it involved intervention for humanitarian purposes without the consent of the state.

The series of decisions just discussed, and others concerning, for example, efforts to restore democratic governance in Haiti and Sierra Leone, do suggest some movement towards privileging the right of civilians to protection in internal conflicts when the right is being grossly abused. This is accompanied by evidence that the Council has sought to hold the agents of states engaging in these gross violations accountable before the law. In a number of instances in the second half of the 1990s (eg, in Kosovo and East Timor), such actions led to the partial or complete suspension of state sovereignty by the United Nations.

However, several caveats are appropriate. First, in almost all of these cases, the unique and non-precedentiary nature of the crisis in question was highlighted in relevant Council documents. This clearly reflected the reluctance of some members (eg, Russia, China and numerous developing countries who are non-permanent members) to move towards general norms, as well as robust rearguard action in defence of the rights and sovereignty of states. In fact, in many instances, the resolutions reaffirmed the sovereign nature of the state in question. Moreover, the unwillingness of the Council to mandate intervention in the case of Kosovo, as well as the widespread concern that greeted NATO's action,[34] suggests the incom-

---

[31] SCR 1031, 15 December 1995.

[32] SCR 929, 29 June 1994.

[33] The East Timor case does, however, raise another important question: if consent is coerced, is it consent?

[34] The Non-aligned Movement, for example, responded by declaring that 'we reject the so-called "right of humanitarian intervention" which has no legal basis in the UN Charter or in the general principles'. The declaration was reproduced at http://www.nam.gov.za/minmeet/newyorkcom.htm. The quotation is at paragraph 171. The 'Declaration of the Summit of the South', Havana G77 summit (April 2000) reiterates the point equally unequivocally.

pleteness of this normative evolution towards the protection of civilians during internal national conflicts, both in the Council and in the broader society of states.

The partial nature of the acceptance of a right and an obligation to protect civilians within the borders of sovereign states is also evident in the selectivity of the Council actions just discussed. The human security grounds for intervention in the civil wars in Sudan and Chechnya were as compelling as those in the cases discussed, but no such forceful action to protect civilians has been forthcoming from the UN. The case of Chechnya, which involves an insurgent region within the territory of a permanent member of the Council, has never even been raised in this forum.

Towards the end of the 1990s and in the context of consideration of UN inaction in Rwanda, the ineffectiveness of intervention in Bosnia and the exit option taken by the NATO states in Kosovo, the Security Council approach to human security evolved further. In response to the massacre at Srebrenica, the General Assembly requested in 1998 that the Secretary-General commission an independent report on the UN's failure to protect.[35] In the case of Rwanda, the Secretary-General himself commissioned a similar report.[36] Both reports indicated that the United Nations and its member states had failed badly in fulfilling their purported responsibility to protect communities in danger of physical destruction.[37]

Partly in reaction to these failures, the Council undertook a broader consideration of protection of human beings in conflict. It held an open meeting to discuss the general issue of protection in February 1999. In the Presidential Statement discussing the meeting, the Council linked the issue of protection directly to its primary responsibility for peace and security and 'expressed its willingness to respond . . . to situations in which civilians, as such, have been targeted or where humanitarian assistance has been deliberately obstructed'.[38] It requested that the Secretary-General produce a report recommending actions it might take to enhance the physical and legal protection of civilians in armed conflict.

In the report that was delivered in September 1999, Kofi Annan outlined several dimensions of the threat, going on to remark—without reference to particular cases—that the Council recognised that 'massive and systematic breaches of human rights law and international humanitarian law constitute threats to international peace and security and therefore demand its attention'.[39] In short, the notion of international responsibility to protect individuals and groups whose security is physically threatened in armed conflict had become, in the mind of the Secretary-General anyway, a generalisable proposition—not limited on an ad hoc

---

[35] United Nations General Assembly Resolution 53/35, 30 November 1998.

[36] See his letter to the Council of 18 March 1999, S/1999/339.

[37] See 'Report of the Secretary-General Pursuant to General Assembly Resolution 53/35: The Fall of Srebrenica', A/54/549, 15 November 1999; and 'Report of the Independent Inquiry into the Actions of the United Nations during the 1994 Genocide in Rwanda', S/1999/1257, 16 December 1999. The report was submitted to the Secretary-General on 15 December 1999.

[38] S/PRST/1999/6, 12 February 1999.

[39] 'Report of the Secretary-General to the Security Council on the Protection of Civilians in Armed Conflict', S/1999/957, 8 September 1999, para 30.

basis to specific crises. Among his recommendations, perhaps the most important was that 'in the face of massive and ongoing abuses, [the Council should] consider the imposition of appropriate enforcement action.'[40]

The Council responded to the Secretary-General's report with two resolutions. In the first, it condemned the targeting of civilians and underlined the importance of safe humanitarian access.[41] The Resolution recommended consideration of how peacekeeping mandates might better take into account the protection of civilians in armed conflict, and noted the special circumstances of women and children. Most importantly from this perspective, the Council responded to the Secretary-General's recommendation concerning intervention by expressing 'its willingness to respond to situations of armed conflict where civilians are being targeted or humanitarian assistance to civilians is being deliberately obstructed'.[42]

The Resolution also established a working group to consider the Council's response in more detail. The working group's efforts were embodied in Resolution 1296, in which the Council noted:

> [T]he deliberate targeting of civilian populations . . . and the committing of systematic, widespread and flagrant violations of international humanitarian and human rights law in situations of armed conflict may constitute a threat to international peace and security, and, in this regard, *reaffirms* [our] readiness to consider such situations and, where necessary, to adopt appropriate steps.[43]

Later in the resolution, it extended this observation to situations in which humanitarian access is deliberately obstructed.[44]

The use of the term 'threat to international peace and security' places these issues potentially within Chapter VII. That in turn raises the possibility of waiving the principle of non-intervention in Article 2.7. Notwithstanding the admonition in the first operative paragraph of SCR 1296 that the Council should approach the issue of protection on a case-by-case basis, these two resolutions appear to suggest the institutionalisation by an authoritative body of a generally accepted norm permitting intervention in the event of grievous lapses in the protection of human beings.

In short, when viewing the matter historically, there does seem to have been a rather substantial shift in the Council's view of security, towards acceptance that the security concerns of human beings within states are a matter of legitimate concern for the body. This is quite significant. It would be unsurprising if it had been

---

[40] 'Report of the Secretary-General to the Security Council on the Protection of Civilians in Armed Conflict', S/1999/957, 8 September 1999, para 40. He was careful, however, to qualify this recommendation by suggesting that before such action were undertaken, the Council should consider the scope of the violation; the inability of local authorities to maintain law and order and their possible complicity in the violations; the exhaustion of peaceful alternatives; Security Council monitoring capacity; and proportionality in the use of force.

[41] SCR 1265 (1999).

[42] *Ibid*, para 10. One Canadian diplomat referred to this paragraph as the Security Council's acceptance of the concept of human security: Interview, 9 November 2002.

[43] SCR 1296 (19 April 2000), para 5.

[44] *Ibid*, para 8.

non-state actors (eg, human rights and humanitarian non-governmental organisations) who had pushed this agenda—their status was not at stake. However, for a body composed of states and dominated by the great powers to take this route, however hesitantly, suggests that many states themselves perceive a need to qualify sovereignty in matters of human security.

III. IMPLICATIONS

The empirical record suggests that the narrow conception of human security as protection from threats associated with physical violence has gained greater traction in international society than has the broader view of the concept. The evolution described above suggests a growing recognition in the Security Council of the principle that human survival and human rights concerns can trump sovereignty and the rights of states associated therewith. The Council is not alone. The UN Secretariat and the General Assembly have both embraced the principle.

Evolving Council practice regarding human security reflects a broad trend in thinking in the advocacy and academic communities on the meaning of sovereignty.[45] It reflects also the thinking of several influential reports of international commissions, not least the International Commission on Intervention and State Sovereignty. This thinking informs the foreign policy of several middle powers (the United Kingdom, Canada, Norway) and is growing in significance in the justification of the US position on a number of key international issues.[46] And this thinking has significant influence on the principles of major regional organisations.[47]

Despite such signs of gradual acceptance, we are still obviously a long way from universal recognition of an international responsibility to protect the rights of people whose human security is jeopardised by conflict within states or by the systematic oppression of their governments. Significant resistance to the responsibility to protect is evident in the declarations and policies of a number of major states, not least Russia and China, not to mention many states in the developing world. This resistance has grown as a result of the manipulation of the discourse

[45] See Deng, FM, Kimaro, S, Lyons, T, Rothchild, D and Zartman, IW, *Sovereignty as Responsibility: Conflict Management in Africa* (Washington, DC, Brookings Institution, 1996).

[46] As Secretary of State Condoleezza Rice said in September 2006 in reference to Sudanese resistance to the deployment of a UN force in Darfur, 'If the notion of the "responsibility to protect" that we all agreed to last year—if the notion of the responsibility to protect the weakest and most powerless among us is ever to be more than an empty promise, then we must take action in Darfur.' 'Remarks before the UN Security Council at the Waldorf Astoria', 22 September 2006, available at http://www.state.gov/secretary/rm/2006/73023.htm.

[47] The need to protect individuals at risk is an important element of the European Union's security strategy. See the European Security Strategy (2003); and also Study Group on Europe's Security Capabilities, 'A Human Security Doctrine for Europe: The Barcelona Report', presented to the EU High Representative for Common Foreign and Security Policy, Barcelona, 15 September 2004. The security protocol of the African Union (AU) makes provision for intervention in the event of significant violations of human rights within states, as do the protocols of the Economic Community of West African States (ECOWAS).

of humanitarian intervention surrounding the invasion of Iraq. It is also paralleled by a rearguard action among some academics who argue that international action in the name of human security handicaps new states in their efforts to consolidate authority within their borders.[48] This reservation is a specific manifestation of a more general concern among many scholars in international relations and international law. Challenges to the principle of equal sovereignty and its corollary, the principle of non-intervention, pose risks to what many see as the underlying structure of what stability there is in international relations.[49] Proponents of human security have no compelling solutions to these objections.

We are no doubt even farther from the consistent practical implementation of such a responsibility, as the case of Darfur daily demonstrates. It is one thing to accept the responsibility to protect in principle. It is another to put one's own citizens at risk to protect others when no direct political or strategic interest is at stake. Moreover, the so-called war on terror has averted attention from these issues to a degree, while raising difficult questions about the balance between individual societal rights.

Nonetheless, the substance of sovereignty and the legal rights attached to it are contested today in a way that they were not two decades ago. The meaning of sovereignty is historically contingent and socially constructed, and as the historical conditions in which states claim and exercise their prerogatives evolve, perceptions of the meaning of sovereignty and the content of the concept change. The evolution of the concept during the last 20 years, which is rooted in a changing understanding of the meaning of security (its humanisation) and is succinctly summarised in the op-ed article cited at the beginning of this chapter, suggests that new ground has been opened for the international protection of human rights in the face of state resistance.

REFERENCES

Aristotle, *Politics*, trs William Ellis (London, JM Dent, 1947).
Ayoob, M, 'Third World Perspectives on Humanitarian Intervention and International Administration' (2004) 10(1) *Global Governance* 99–118.
Bugnion, F, *Le Comité Internationale de la Croix Rouge et la Protection des Victimes de la Guerre* (Geneva, International Committee of the Red Cross, 1994).
Bull, H, *The Anarchical Society: A Study of Order in World Politics* (Cambridge, Cambridge University Press, 1977).
Commission on Global Governance, *Our Global Neighbourhood* (Oxford, Oxford University Press, 1995).
Commission on Human Security (CHS), *Human Security Now* (Tokyo, Commission on Human Security, 2003).

---

[48] See Ayoob, M, 'Third World Perspectives on Humanitarian Intervention and International Administration' (2004) 10(1) *Global Governance* 99–118.
[49] See Bull, H, *The Anarchical Society: A Study of Order in World Politics* (Cambridge, Cambridge University Press, 1977).

Deng, FM, Kimaro, S, Lyons, T, Rothchild, D and Zartman, IW, *Sovereignty as Responsibility: Conflict Management in Africa* (Washington, DC, Brookings Institution, 1996).

European Council, 'A Secure Europe in a Better World: European Security Strategy', 12 December 2003, available at http://ue.eu.int/cms3_fo/showPage.asp?id=266&lang=en&mode=g.

Farer, TJ and Gaer, F, 'The UN and Human Rights: At the End of the Beginning' in A Roberts (ed), *United Nations, Divided World: The UN's Roles in International Society* (Oxford, Oxford University Press, 1993).

Gingrich, N and Mitchell, G, 'UN Reform: Report Card from America', *International Herald Tribune*, 26–27 November 2005.

Hampson, FO, Daudelin, J, Hay, JB, Reid, H and Marting, T, *Madness in the Multitude: Human Security and World Disorder* (Toronto, Oxford University Press, 2001).

Hinsley, FH, *Sovereignty*, 2nd edn (Cambridge, Cambridge University Press, 1986).

Hubert, D, 'The Landmine Ban: A Case Study in Humanitarian Advocacy', Occasional Paper No 42 (Providence, RI, The Thomas J Watson Jr Institute for International Studies, 2000).

International Commission on Intervention and State Sovereignty (ICISS), *The Responsibility to Protect* (Ottawa, International Development Research Council, 2001).

Jackson, RH, *Quasi-states: Sovereignty, International Relations, and the Third World* (Cambridge, Cambridge University Press, 1990).

Jackson-Preece, J, *National Minorities and the European Nation-state System* (Oxford, Clarendon Press, 1998).

MacFarlane, SN and Khong, YF, *Human Security and the UN: A Critical History* (Bloomington, Indiana University Press, 2006).

Study Group on Europe's Security Capabilities, 'A Human Security Doctrine for Europe: The Barcelona Report', presented to the EU High Representative for Common Foreign and Security Policy, Barcelona, 15 September 2004.

Task Force on the United Nations, *The Imperative for Action: An Update of the Report of the Task Force on American Interests and UN Reform* (Washington, DC, United States Institute of Peace, December 2005), available at: www.usip.org.

Ullman, R, 'Redefining Security' (1983) 8(1) *International Security* 129–53.

United Nations Development Programme (UNDP), *Human Development Report 1994: New Dimensions of Human Security* (New York, United Nations, 1994).

Vincent, RJ, *Non-intervention and International Order* (Princeton, Princeton University Press, 1974).

Wheeler, NJ, *Saving Strangers: Humanitarian Intervention in International Society* (Oxford, Oxford University Press, 2000).

16

The Responsibility to Protect: Securing the Individual in International Society

INTRODUCTION

AT THE 2005 Summit marking the sixtieth anniversary of the United Nations, world leaders endorsed in their outcome document the principle of 'the responsibility to protect' (also known as 'R2P').[1] Article 138 of the document recognises the responsibility of individual sovereign states to protect their own populations from genocide, war crimes and ethnic cleansing. However, in what initially appears to be a departure from the original UN Charter, Article 139 endows the international community with the responsibility to take collective action when national authorities 'are manifestly failing to protect their populations' from such atrocities.

This chapter traces the evolution of R2P from its original formulation in the report of the International Commission on Intervention and State Sovereignty (ICISS) in 2001 through to the 2005 World Summit Outcome document. More specifically, it assesses the relationship between R2P and the evolving rules on the use of force in international society, as well as the role of UN Security Council authorisation in legitimating interventions for humanitarian purposes. The argument is in two sections. In the first, I demonstrate that the efforts to shift the debate from rights to responsibilities, while productive in some ways, remain open to challenge both philosophically and legally. Second, I suggest that the articulation of R2P in Articles 138–9 of the Summit Outcome document, despite the hopes of the principle's proponents, represents a weakening of the original notion and circumscribes the international community's obligation to protect individuals from massive human rights violations. Of particular concern is the deference shown to the UN Security Council and the implications that flow from relying on its problematic politics. Thus, while there has been a rhetorical commitment to

---

* An earlier version of this chapter was presented in May 2006 to the Programme for Strategic and International Security Studies, Geneva.
[1] United Nations, '2005 Summit Outcome', General Assembly Document, A/60/L.1, 15 September 2005.

offering international protection for individuals at risk from violence perpetrated (or tolerated) by their own governments, it is not clear that the Summit Outcome document's attempt to 'humanise' security in this way has actually enhanced the capacity of international actors to meaningfully challenge state sovereignty.

THE DEVELOPMENT OF R2P

Debates about the legitimacy of using international military action to address developments in the sovereign jurisdiction of a state have been an integral part of the evolution of modern international society. From the Second World War onward, the debate has focused on the alleged incompatibility of two core principles of the United Nations system: sovereignty and human rights. The former, set out in Articles 2(1), 2(4) and 2(7), suggests that states should enjoy sovereign equality—defined *internally* as exclusive jurisdiction within a territory and *externally* as freedom from outside interference. The latter, identified in the Preamble and Article 1(3) and elaborated in subsequent declarations and conventions, suggests that individual rights are inalienable and transcend sovereign frontiers.

Developments of the past two decades have raised further questions about these seemingly contradictory principles and provided added impetus to those calling for more intervention from 'outsiders': the weakness (or complete failure) of state structures in many conflict-ridden societies, which is often portrayed as opening up opportunities for criminal activity, arms proliferation and terrorism; the increased vulnerability of civilians in the context of civil conflict; the global and instantaneous access to information that can serve to heighten popular awareness of human suffering; the strengthening of human rights norms and proliferation of human rights organisations; the impact of refugee flows across borders; and the search by Western governments for new forms of political legitimacy and 'moral authority' to replace the ideologically driven agenda of the Cold War. Indeed, journalist David Rieff has argued that in the post-Cold War era it has become virtually impossible for Western democracies to wage war 'without describing it to some extent in humanitarian terms'.[2]

What marks today's debate about sovereignty, human rights and the use of force is the relatively permissive context for intervention. This is not to suggest that there is consensus on what constitutes legitimate action. If the international community's failure to act to stop genocide in Rwanda in 1994 provoked condemnation, so too did NATO's military campaign to address the ethnic cleansing of Kosovar Albanians in 1999. China, arguably the most powerful developing country in the contemporary international system, voiced its staunch opposition to the NATO action around the Security Council table. As one Chinese commentator put it at that time:

---

[2] Rieff, D, *A Bed for the Night: Humanitarianism in Crisis* (London, Vintage, 2002) 240.

As a matter of fact, interventionism is not at all 'new'. The Chinese are very familiar with such 'humanitarian intervention' in their past and see it as a tool that was often used by advanced countries to conquer so-called 'barbarous ones' and to impose 'civilized standards'.[3]

For former Secretary-General Kofi Annan, this apparent stalemate over the legitimacy of intervention was unsatisfactory: 'if humanitarian intervention is, indeed, an unacceptable assault on sovereignty, how should we respond to a Rwanda, to a Srebrenica—to gross and systematic violations of human rights that affect every precept of our common humanity?'[4] To put it another way, Annan was searching for a way to make individuals, not just states, more secure (ie, 'no more Rwandas')—but in a way that would command the support of international society as a whole (ie, 'no more Kosovos'). At the General Assembly in 1999, Annan called for a new consensus on the age-old problem of intervention and a plan of action for responding to humanitarian tragedies.

THE INTERNATIONAL COMMISSION ON INTERVENTION
AND STATE SOVEREIGNTY (ICISS)

Canada's response to Annan's challenge, announced at the United Nations Millennium Summit in September 2000, was the establishment of the International Commission on Intervention and State Sovereignty (ICISS). The Commission was tasked with three goals: (1) to promote a comprehensive debate about humanitarian intervention;[5] (2) to foster a new political consensus on how to reconcile the principles of intervention and state sovereignty; and (3) to translate that consensus into action.[6] In the end, its main contributions to the debate on humanitarian intervention were primarily conceptual: in changing the language from a 'right of intervention' to a 'responsibility to protect'; and in setting

---

[3] Zhang, Y, 'China: Whither the World Order after Kosovo?' in A Schnabel and R Thakur (eds), *Kosovo and the Challenge of Humanitarian Intervention* (Tokyo, United Nations University Press, 2000) 122.

[4] Annan, K, 'We the Peoples', *Millennium Report* (New York, United Nations, 2000) 48. It should be noted that the UN Security Council had not been silent on such questions. In cases such as the creation of 'safe havens' for the Kurds in Northern Iraq in 1991, the Council had begun to consider how extreme humanitarian emergencies might constitute threats to international security. Similarly, during the Canadian presidency of the Security Council in 1999, there was a request to the Secretary-General to prepare recommendations on how to improve the physical and legal protection of civilians. These efforts led to Security Council Resolutions 1265 and 1296, which establish that the targeting of civilians and denial of humanitarian assistance can constitute threats to international peace and security.

[5] The task of defining humanitarian intervention is notoriously difficult. For the purposes of this chapter, my definition is as follows: coercive interference in the internal affairs of state, involving the use of armed force, with the purposes of addressing massive human rights violations or preventing widespread human suffering. For more on the debate over definitions, see Welsh, JM, 'Introduction' in JM Welsh (ed), *Humanitarian Intervention and International Relations* (Oxford, Oxford University Press, 2004) 3.

[6] International Commission on Intervention and State Sovereignty (ICISS), 'The Responsibility to Protect: Report of the ICISS' (Ottawa, International Development Research Council, 2001).

out a spectrum of action for the international community, ranging from prevention to military action to post-conflict reconstruction.[7]

The work of the Commission was organised around a central question: 'when,
if ever, it is appropriate for states to take coercive—and in particular military—
action against another state for the purpose of protecting people at risk in that
other state?'[8] Its report offers what at first blush seems an elegant solution to the
dilemma expressed by the Secretary-General: the international community should
view the relationship between sovereignty and intervention as complementary
rather than contradictory. This reconciliation is achieved by reshaping the very
notion of sovereignty and linking it more closely to the responsibility of states to
their citizens.[9] Hence, sovereignty is no longer conceived as undisputed control
over territory but rather as a conditional right dependent upon respect for a minimum standard of human rights. In the words of the ICISS,

> It is acknowledged that sovereignty implies a dual responsibility: externally—to
> respect the sovereignty of other states, and internally, to respect the dignity and basic
> rights of all the people within the state . . . Sovereignty as responsibility has become
> the minimum content of good international citizenship.[10]

For the Commission, it logically followed that intervention is permissible—and
indeed necessary—if it is aimed at protecting civilians and restoring the effective
sovereignty of states.

1. From 'Right' to 'Responsibility'

The central conclusion of the ICISS report is that sovereign states have a responsibility to protect their own citizens from avoidable catastrophe. However, there is
also a residual responsibility that can and must (in certain cases) be borne by the
broader community of states:

> Where a population is suffering serious harm, as a result of internal war, insurgency,
> repression or state failure, and the state in question is unwilling or unable to halt or
> avert it, the principle of non-intervention yields to the international responsibility to
> protect.[11]

The Commissioners suggested that their particular rendering of sovereignty and
responsibility makes this coercive external engagement inside another state more

---

[7] The overview of the ICISS report in the following section draws on Welsh, J, Thielking, C and
MacFarlane, SN, 'The Responsibility to Protect: Assessing the Report of the International Commission
on Intervention and State Sovereignty' in R Thakur, AF Cooper and J English (eds), *International
Commissions and the Power of Ideas* (Tokyo, United Nations University Press, 2005).

[8] ICISS (2001) vii.

[9] For examples of the vast literature on norms associated with sovereignty, see Krasner, SD,
Sovereignty: Organized Hypocrisy? (Princeton, Princeton University Press, 1999); and Jackson, R,
Quasi-states: Sovereignty, International Relations and the Third World (Cambridge, Cambridge
University Press, 1990).

[10] ICISS (2001) 8.

[11] *Ibid*, xi.

legitimate than 'humanitarian intervention' as it has traditionally been conceived. In the words of one Commissioner, Ramesh Thakur,

> R2P is more of a linking concept that bridges the divide between the international community and the sovereign state, whereas the language of the right or duty to intervene is inherently more confrontational . . . The goal of intervention for human protection purposes is not to wage war on a state in order to destroy it and eliminate its statehood but to protect victims of atrocities inside the state, to embed the protection in reconstituted institutions after the intervention, and then to withdraw all foreign troops.[12]

The Commission offered a series of reasons why this formulation, centred on 'responsibility' and 'protection', was more likely to breed agreement in international society. First, it insisted that the notion of protection shifts the focus to where it belongs—on the victims of suffering who seek assistance, rather than on the claims or rights of intervening states.[13] Second, the Commissioners claimed that the narrow, legal concept of intervention fails to consider the importance of prior preventive actions or post-intervention rebuilding, which in their view had to form part of any contemporary approach to military action.[14] Lastly, the Commission's rejection of the term 'humanitarian intervention' responded to concerns by humanitarian organisations that oppose any attempt to militarise the word 'humanitarian'.[15]

Despite these valiant attempts at consensus-building, the ICISS report has not avoided normative and legal controversy. First, it is worth remembering that the terms 'responsibility' and 'protection', like 'humanitarian', are loaded with ethical content. In fact, in the negotiations leading up to the UN Summit in 2005, some developing countries voiced opposition to the phrase 'responsibility to protect' because of neo-colonial connotations.[16] Even if the promoters of R2P have emphasised the protection of civilians rather than the rights of interveners, suspicion on the part of many non-Western states (illustrated most vividly by statements made in the General Assembly and other organisational forums) indicate a lingering fear that sovereign equality will become a chimera if the principle of non-intervention is not vigorously upheld.

In addition, while the Commissioners themselves stayed clear of the word 'duty', the logic of the rights and responsibilities they have drawn upon should lead us to it. According to philosopher David Rodin, if the objective is an *international* responsibility to protect, this implies a prospective responsibility—that is, a duty on the part of international organisations, agencies and outside states to assist citizens if their own state has failed in its primary obligations. But the ICISS articulation of the principle only supports a 'liberty right' for members of the

---

[12] Thakur, R, 'Freedom from Fear' in P Heinbecker and P Goff (eds), *Irrelevant or Indispensable? The United Nations in the 21st Century* (Waterloo, Wilfred Laurier Press, 2005) 123.

[13] ICISS (2001) 15.

[14] *Ibid*, 16.

[15] *Ibid*, 9.

[16] Author's confidential interview with UN official, May 2006.

international community to intervene (whether for prevention, response or rebuilding); by eschewing the notion of duty, it does not offer citizens inside a state a claim against the international community for protection.[17] This results in not only the possibility of unfulfilled expectations, but also a lack of clarity as to who, precisely, in the international community enjoys this 'liberty right'.

Third, there are concerns in legal circles about the merits of a shift from 'right' to 'responsibility'. In 2004, when the UN Human Rights Commission considered whether it should develop an approach on the question of human responsibilities, its membership was split down the middle.[18] In general, Western states were opposed to the idea, fearing that some governments would start to make their fulfilment of human rights contingent on individuals' 'responsible' behaviour, or that international organisations and transnational actors would suddenly be called to take on substantial responsibility for the condition of individuals inside developing or conflict-ridden societies. In the words of Andrew Clapham: 'It is feared that governments that violate human rights will seize the opportunity to reorient the debate around the responsibilities of others.'[19] Such concerns permeate any discussion about creating responsibilities in the human rights context.

Finally, while the ICISS report does not explicitly call for legal reform, it does give a strong impression that the Commissioners believe interventions for humanitarian purposes *should* be undertaken (in extreme cases). This is not the same as saying that states *can* act (that is, that they have a legal right to intervene), but it does raise the question—central for those who had Kosovo in the back of their minds—of whether morality and law should be more closely aligned. Since the end of the Cold War, there has been a legal debate as to whether the general prohibition on the use of force, enshrined in Article 2(4) of the United Nations Charter, should be 'stretched' to accommodate other important principles of the UN, such as human rights (thereby making military intervention for human protection purposes permissible).

Those in favour of such an expansion point to a series of cases from the 1990s (particularly Liberia, Northern Iraq, Somalia and Kosovo) as state practice supportive of a new customary rule, with statements by Western governments articulating humanitarian motives presented as evidence of an accompanying *opinio juris*.[20] The problem with such an approach is that it privileges custom over treaty—a controversial move from the perspective of the Vienna

---

[17] Rodin, D, 'The Responsibility to Protect and the Logic of Rights', Programme for Strategic and International Security Studies, Geneva, May 2006.

[18] 26 voted in favour; 25 voted against; and 2 abstained.

[19] Clapham, A, 'Rights and Responsibilities', Programme for Strategic and International Security Studies, Geneva, May 2006.

[20] See, for example, Cassese, A, '*Ex Iniuria Ius Oritur*: Are We Moving towards International Legitimation of Forcible Humanitarian Countermeasures in the World Community?' (1999) 10(1) *European Journal of International Law* 23–30; Greenwood, C, 'International Law and the NATO Intervention in Kosovo' (2000) 49 *International and Comparative Law Quarterly* 926–34; and Tesón, F, *Humanitarian Intervention: An Inquiry into Law and Morality*, 2nd edn (Irvington-on-Hudson, Transnational Publishers, 1997).

Convention.[21] In addition, non-Western legal opinion tends to oppose this interpretation of the customary law on intervention, since it seems to suggest that certain types of practice 'count' more than others—that is, the actions of Western states versus the stated opposition from those such as China, Russia and India. But above all, the expansionary approach takes us too far beyond the desired intention of the framers of the United Nations, which was to limit the legitimate exceptions to the prohibition on the use of force to those of self-defence and Security Council-authorised acts of collective security. International lawyer Thomas Franck argues that rather than creating new, positive rights and duties of intervention for humanitarian purposes, such acts should be seen as 'mitigated' (even to the point of exoneration) by the context of extreme necessity.[22]

2. A Continuum of Action

A second significant contribution of the Commission's report is its focus on a spectrum of action. According to ICISS, if there is a responsibility to protect, there is also a responsibility to *prevent* and to *rebuild*. In addition, the report insists that when faced with evidence of human suffering inside the domestic jurisdiction of another state, policy makers have a wider array of choices between inaction and military invasion. In so doing, it laments that the resources devoted to preventive measures are dwarfed by the money allocated to war preparation, war fighting, humanitarian assistance to victims of violence, and peacekeeping.

The first part of the spectrum is prevention. Following the Carnegie Commission on Preventing Deadly Conflict, the Commissioners distinguished between two sets of preventive strategies: those directed at so-called root causes of conflict (development assistance and support for good governance and human rights); and those targeted at immediate triggers for violence (good offices and mediation, inducements such as conditional assistance, and punishments such as economic sanctions or suspension of membership in international organisations).[23] The ICISS report also identifies three conditions for successful prevention: effective early warning mechanisms; a well-stocked 'preventive toolbox' that combines political, economic, legal and military measures; and sufficient political

---

[21] As Byers and Chesterman argue: 'Since clear treaty provisions prevail over customary international law, an ordinary customary rule allowing intervention is not sufficient to override Article 2(4). The only way intervention for purposes beyond those of self-defence of collective security could be considered legal is if such interventions had acquired the status of *jus cogens*.' See Byers, M and Chesterman, S, 'Changing the Rules about Rules? Unilateral Humanitarian Intervention and the Future of International Law' in JL Holzgrefe and RO Keohane (eds), *Humanitarian Intervention: Ethical, Legal and Political Dilemmas* (Cambridge, Cambridge University Press, 2003) 180.

[22] Franck, T, 'Interpretation and Change in the Law of Humanitarian Intervention' in JL Holzgrefe and RO Keohane (eds), *Humanitarian Intervention: Ethical, Legal and Political Dilemmas* (Cambridge, Cambridge University Press, 2003). Franck writes: 'It is integral to most national legal systems that an action may be regarded as illegal but that the degree of that illegality should be determined with due regard for extenuating or mitigating factors' (213).

[23] ICISS (2001) 19.

will to act. Nevertheless, the Commission conceded a long-standing thorn in the side of those who have argued for better strategies of prevention: that some states remain reluctant to accept any kind of externally sponsored prevention efforts for fear that internationalising the problem will lead inevitably to intervention.[24]

The second stage on the continuum—protection—kicks in when the situation on the ground places civilians at serious risk. At this point, the Commissioners argued, the option of military action must be considered and evaluated. They employed a 'Just War' framework of six principles to guide decision makers contemplating such action:[25]

1. *Just Cause*: Military intervention is an exceptional measure, to be undertaken only in extreme humanitarian emergencies.
2. *Right Intention*: The primary motive of the military action must be humanitarian.
3. *Last Resort*: All non-military options must be explored before force is used.
4. *Proportional Means*: The nature of the force used must be proportionate to the humanitarian objective and limited in scale and intensity.
5. *Reasonable Prospects*: The operation must have a reasonable chance of success, and negative consequences of force must not outweigh the consequences of inaction.
6. *Right Authority*: Military action should be authorised by the United Nations Security Council (but authorisation can be found elsewhere if the Council fails to act).

Finally, the ICISS report calls upon intervening states to commit to a long-term process of rebuilding once the military phase is complete. Here, the recommended priorities are economic reconstruction, the establishment of legitimate and effective institutions of governance, the restoration of public safety and sustainable development. But the Commissioners also acknowledged that there are benefits and drawbacks to requiring outside actors to stay on in the country in which intervention takes place until sustainable reconstruction and rehabilitation have occurred. In particular, they highlighted the importance of achieving a balance between the responsibilities of international actors and the rights of local 'ownership'. The process of devolving responsibility back to the local community, they insisted, is essential to maintaining the legitimacy of the intervention itself. In what now appears as an understatement (given the problems encountered by international administrations and occupying powers), they concluded:

> A poorly administered occupation which overtly treats the people, or causes them to believe they are being treated, as an 'enemy' will obviously be inimical to the success of any long-term rehabilitation efforts.[26]

---

[24] ICISS (2001) 25.
[25] See *ibid*, xii for the report's synopsis.
[26] *Ibid*, 44.

3. Authorisation

The criteria for action listed above highlight a third contribution of ICISS: its discussion of who should authorise and carry out the responsibilities of the international community. In the wake of the breakdown in diplomacy within the Council in the lead-up to war in Iraq in the spring of 2003, the issue of 'right authority' has become even more contentious. Despite misgivings from some members of the Commission, the ICISS report insists that the UN Security Council is still the appropriate body to authorise intervention for human protection purposes. But the Commissioners were all too aware of the objections to such a recommendation: the slowness of Security Council decision making; the under-representation of key regions; and the political nature of vetoes of the five permanent members. (There is also the more obvious point that by requiring Security Council authorisation, one ensures that R2P will never be applied against a Permanent Five (P5) member.) Nonetheless, they believed recourse to unregulated unilateralism was an even more unpalatable alternative.

The Commissioners' solution was to establish three procedures that would still privilege Chapter VII-authorised intervention but not forbid action if the Council were paralysed by division: states must at least request Council authorisation before acting; a resolution supporting military intervention must have at least majority support in the Council; and if the veto is used in these instances, recourse can be made to the General Assembly (under the 'Uniting for Peace' resolution) or to regional bodies. In addition, to try to counter potential politicisation, the ICISS report recommends that the P5 agree *not* to veto interventions in cases in which their vital interests are not engaged. In the end, the report warns that if the Security Council 'fails to discharge its responsibility to protect in conscience-shocking situations crying out for action, concerned states may not rule out other means to meet the gravity and urgency of that situation—and that the stature and credibility of the United Nations may suffer thereby'.[27]

These three procedures, combined with the Just War criteria on the use of force, suggest that the Commissioners were attempting to establish what Dyzenhaus has elsewhere in this volume called a 'culture of justification' to guide decision making. The hope of the Commission was that Security Council members would have to justify publicly their positions on whether to intervene in humanitarian situations, thereby enabling genuine interventions and preventing abuse. Thus, it was argued that the ICISS recommendations would strengthen the moral authority of those arguing for intervention and would make it much harder for states in the Security Council (particularly the P5) to get away with non-humanitarian objections to using force.[28]

---

[27] *Ibid*, xiii.
[28] Bellamy, AJ, 'Whither the Responsibility to Protect? Humanitarian Intervention and the 2005 World Summit' (2006) 20(2) *Ethics and International Affairs* 143–69, 148–9.

There is a series of challenges, however, to creating such a culture of justification through the current UN framework. The assumption behind the ICISS proposals regarding the Council and the veto is that in today's international system, governments can be persuaded to act in humanitarian crises by the force of international and domestic opinion. But although much is made of the so-called 'CNN effect', and the new-found power of civil society, a close examination of the relevant cases does not provide strong evidence that states intervene in such crises because public opinion has morally shamed them into doing so.[29] Moreover, while the idea of asking the P5 to suspend vetoes in humanitarian situations is an interesting proposition, it does not get around the problem that permanent members have very different views on what constitutes a vital interest.[30] This is partly why, as I will show, the United States, Russia and China have all been lukewarm about implementing key aspects of the ICISS report.

But perhaps the greatest challenge lies in the nature of the deference that is currently shown by members of international society towards the Security Council as the body designated with the power to define what constitutes a threat to international peace and security. Dyzenhaus usefully distinguishes between two kinds of deference towards authority.[31] The first, deference as respect, requires decision makers to provide not only reasons for why they act (or fail to act) but *good* reasons—reasons that satisfy standards of rationality and/or the core principles of a society. In short, there is both a procedural and substantive requirement before deference is given. Submissive deference, on the other hand, requires that we submit to a designated body—whether or not good reasons are given—as long as that body does not overstep its proper role and authority.

While some commentators have questioned the basis for the Security Council's authority in international society and called for substantive principles to have greater play in establishing it, analysis of current practice suggests that states and other actors in international society are more concerned with *the fact* of Security Council authorisation in establishing the legitimacy of an action or decision, by virtue of its powers under the UN Charter.[32] In other words, the Council's designated role as 'proper authority' has generated submissive deference, minimising the need for a more substantive discussion of the principles justifying action or inaction.

---

[29] Bellamy, AJ, 'Whither the Responsibility to Protect? Humanitarian Intervention and the 2005 World Summit' (2006) 20(2) *Ethics and International Affairs* 150–1. Bellamy focuses particularly on the cases of Somalia and East Timor.

[30] Examples include China's use of the veto on extending peacekeeping operations in Guatemala and Macedonia because it objected to the decisions of both countries to establish diplomatic relations with Taiwan, and the threatened use of the veto by the United States over the continuation of the Bosnian mission due to concerns about subjecting American peacekeepers to the jurisdiction of the International Criminal Court.

[31] See the contribution by David Dyzenhaus in this volume.

[32] I have argued elsewhere that the Security Council should be considered not as the 'proper authority' for international society in matters of peace and security, but rather as an entity whose pronouncements are 'authoritative'. See Welsh, JM, 'Authorizing Humanitarian Intervention' in R Price and M Zacher (eds), *The United Nations and Global Security* (New York, Palgrave, 2004).

FROM R2P TO THE WORLD SUMMIT

In Kofi Annan's view, the Commission delivered on its promise of reconciling the principles of intervention and state sovereignty:

> How to protect individual lives while maintaining and even strengthening the sovereignty of States has become clearer with the publication of this report. You are taking away the last excuses of the international community for doing nothing when doing something can save lives. I can offer no higher praise.[33]

But what of the next steps? Those working closely with the Secretary-General insist that his goal was *not* to develop new law but rather to strengthen the implementation of existing international humanitarian law, such as the Genocide Convention.[34] Thus, R2P was to be a new phrase in the lexicon of international relations, calling for implementation of existing commitments.[35]

As part of their strategy for implementing the ICISS report, the Commissioners envisaged a series of initiatives within the United Nations: a General Assembly Resolution embodying the basic framework of the 'responsibility to protect'; Security Council guidelines for responding to military interventions with a humanitarian purpose and Security Council agreement to suspend use of the veto in such situations; and leadership by the Secretary-General to advance the report's findings.[36] To date, only the final area has seen significant activity. By the autumn of 2002, as the pressure for war against Saddam Hussein mounted, the proponents of ICISS had conceded that any formal kind of codification—whether a legally binding convention or amendment to the UN Charter—was both unlikely and unwise in the existing international climate.

THE WAR IN IRAQ

In the summer of 2003, following the end of the military phase of the US-led war in Iraq, Canadian Prime Minister Jean Chrétien once again took up the case of R2P at the Progressive Governance Summit hosted by British Prime Minister Tony Blair in London. But even at this gathering of left-of-centre government leaders—an audience one might think would be amenable to discussions about humanitarian intervention—very little progress was made in moving the debate forward.

---

[33] Annan, K, 'Address to the International Peace Academy Seminar on "The Responsibility to Protect"', Press Release SG/SM/8125, 15 February 2002.

[34] Most states in the international system have accepted, through their ratification of the 1948 Genocide Convention, an obligation to 'prevent and punish' acts of genocide. However, Article VIII of this Convention makes clear that only multilateral responses are legitimate, via the United Nations.

[35] Jones, B, 'Implementing "In Larger Freedom"' in P Heinbecker and P Goff (eds), *Irrelevant or Indispensable? The United Nations in the 21st Century* (Waterloo, Wilfred Laurier Press, 2005) 36.

[36] ICISS (2001) 74–5.

At this time, key developing countries, such as Brazil, continued to express reservations about the international community bypassing the UN system in authorising the use of force—a fear that had particular resonance in the aftermath of the Iraq war. Similarly, the Germans expressed concern that the ICISS concept of the responsibility to protect would be twisted to provide a *post facto* justification for the campaign to unseat Saddam Hussein. Such concerns were not completely unwarranted: as the case for weapons of mass destruction looked weaker and weaker, pro-war Western commentators used the discovery of the mass graves holding Saddam's opponents as further evidence that regime change had been warranted. But for those in favour of a limited right to use military force in cases of genocide and ethnic cleansing, such as ICISS co-chair Gareth Evans, the 'poorly and inconsistently' argued humanitarian justification for the war against Iraq was a huge set-back for efforts to build a new normative consensus around the 'responsibility to protect'.[37] Others such as former British Foreign Office adviser David Clark went even further. For him, the Faustian bargain between liberal proponents of war in Iraq and US neo-conservatives threatened to discredit the concept of humanitarian intervention altogether.[38]

ENSHRINING CRITERIA

Given the debate described above and the wide variety in the practice of humanitarian intervention since the end of the Cold War, does it make sense even to try to enshrine general rules or guidelines for policy makers, along the lines of those proposed by ICISS? For those who answer 'yes', such a checklist would help to establish a robust culture of justification that would both prevent illegitimate interventions and enable action in conscience-shocking situations. In particular, proponents argue that it would make the Security Council more effective and less likely to equivocate, as it did so tragically in the case of Rwanda. Furthermore, codification of criteria would reduce the perceived gap between law and morality with respect to interventions for humanitarian purposes, thereby increasing the legitimacy of international law.

The issue of criteria was picked up by the High-level Panel of experts chosen by Annan in September 2003 to address the growing tensions in the UN's collective security system. The panel's final report, 'A More Secure World' took a holistic approach to security, encompassing the protection of groups and individuals within sovereign frontiers.[39] In defiance of the view, frequently voiced after the

---

[37] Evans, G, 'When is it Right to Fight?' (2004) 46(3) *Survival* 59–81, 63.

[38] Clark, D, 'Iraq has Wrecked our Case for Humanitarian Wars', *The Guardian*, 21 August 2003. Michael Ignatieff, an ICISS Commissioner, was a liberal supporter of the US-led war in Iraq. For a fuller discussion of the Iraq war and debates on humanitarian intervention, see Wheeler, NJ and Morris, J, 'Justifying Iraq as a Humanitarian Intervention: The Cure is Worse than the Disease' in WPS Sidhu and R Thakur (eds), *The Iraq Crisis and World Order: Structural and Normative Challenges* (Tokyo, United Nations University Press, 2006).

[39] United Nations, 'A More Secure World: Our Shared Responsibility', Report of the Secretary-General's High-level Panel on Threats, Challenges and Change, A/59/565, 1 December 2004.

crisis over Iraq, that there are no longer any rules governing the use of force, the report follows ICISS in setting out five criteria to determine whether particular military actions—whether between or within states—would be considered legitimate: seriousness of the threat; proper purpose; last resort; proportional means; and the balance of consequences (ie, that force cannot be justified if it is likely to make matters worse). It is also significant that the panel endorsed the view that 'proper purpose' now encompasses actions designed to save civilians from genocide, ethnic cleansing or other comparable human rights atrocities.

The belief that criteria would enhance the legitimacy of the UN's collective security system was echoed by Annan in his report to the General Assembly in March 2005.[40] This document, which was to serve as the basic for discussion at the September meeting of UN Heads of State in New York, called on the Security Council to adopt a resolution setting out the five criteria listed above and to express its intention to be guided by them when deciding to authorise or mandate the use of force. Paragraph 126 reads:

> By undertaking to make the case for military action in this way, the Council would add transparency to its deliberations and make its decisions more likely to be respected, by both Governments and world public opinion.

If states could not reach a consensus on such questions, the Secretary-General warned, then the UN risked becoming a stage on which to act out differences rather than a forum for resolving them.

While this is an attractive solution for bringing new forms of accountability to decision making around the use of force, there are risks associated with codifying criteria in this way. As more 'restrictionist' international lawyers would argue, *any* exercise that attempts to articulate legitimate instances of intervention could reverse the progress made by the United Nations in outlawing the use of force in international society.[41] Second, criteria that are 'set in stone' diminish the flexibility that currently exists for the P5 to interpret the international security landscape and generate a consensus among them for how to manage it. This is one of the reasons why the current military hegemon in the contemporary international system, the United States, showed little enthusiasm for the ICISS recommendations when they were discussed at a Security Council retreat in May 2002.[42]

---

[40] Annan, K, 'In Larger Freedom: Towards Development, Security and Human Rights for All', Report of the Secretary-General, A/59/2005, 21 March 2005.

[41] Simon Chesterman is representative of this view that establishing further exceptions to Art 2(4), and designing criteria to regulate them, would be detrimental to larger efforts to develop an international rule of law. See Chesterman, S, *Just War or Just Peace? Humanitarian Intervention and International Law* (Oxford, Oxford University Press, 2001) 229–32.

[42] It should be noted that other Security Council members were also concerned about committing to criteria. According to the British and French ambassadors, there was widespread opinion in the meeting that if new situations emerged—for example, in Burundi or the Congo—the five permanent members and broader Council would lack the political will to deliver troops and would restrict themselves to condemnatory resolutions. Similarly, Russia expressed strong reservations about any codified guidelines that would limit its use of the veto. 'La Russie s'oppose à un "usage raisonne" du droit du veto', *Le Monde*, 3 June 2002.

However, it is important to recognise that US reluctance to support any written guidelines for humanitarian intervention derives from two different sets of concerns: its desire to avoid entanglements that do not directly affect its national interests; and its insistence that in cases where US military action is necessary it must be free to interpret notions such as 'last resort' and 'proper authority' on its own terms. During the 2004 presidential election campaign, both George Bush and John Kerry proclaimed that the United States would not give a 'blank cheque' to any organisation that could compromise the sovereign right of the United States to decide when to go to war. Of particular concern for the Bush administration was the Secretary-General's proposal that the preventive use of force by a state must have multilateral sanction to be legitimate. The inability to solve the Iraq crisis through diplomacy or to obtain an additional Security Council resolution explicitly authorising force only strengthened US opposition to those proposing codification.

The United States is similarly unenthusiastic about creating new legal *obligations* in the area of humanitarian intervention. Prior to the September 2005 gathering of world leaders, US ambassador in New York, John Bolton, objected to language in one of the early drafts of the summit document that implied a legal obligation to intervene in humanitarian crises on the part of the Security Council. He conceded:

> [T]he international community has a responsibility to act when the host state allows such atrocities. But the responsibility of the other countries in the international community is not of the same character as the responsibility of the host . . . We do not accept that either the United Nations as a whole, or the Security Council, or individual states, have an obligation to intervene under international law.[43]

Finally, it could be argued that by focusing on establishing firm criteria, attention is diverted from the heart of the problem: how states and organisations operationalise them. Even supposedly clear guidelines such as 'large scale' or 'extreme emergency' are not foolproof; they are ultimately subject to political judgement. In 1999, the situation in Kosovo certainly constituted 'extreme' for some in the international community, although not for others (notably China, India and Russia). Atrocities in Chechnya did not cross the threshold for anyone, despite the fact that the level of abuse of civilians was substantially higher here than it was in Kosovo prior to intervention. And even after former US Secretary of State Colin Powell stated in September 2004 that his government believed genocide had been committed in Darfur, the response of the Security Council remained limited to monitoring and implementing an arms embargo.[44] In short, checklists can only represent necessary, and not sufficient, conditions for a decision to inter-

---

[43] Letter from Ambassador John Bolton, Permanent Representative of the United States of America to the UN, to the United Nations, 30 August 2005, available at http://www.reformtheun.org. I am grateful to Nicholas Wheeler for pointing out this statement to me.

[44] For more on the relevance of R2P to the situation in Sudan, see Williams, PD and Bellamy, AJ, 'The Responsibility to Protect and the Crisis in Darfur' (2005) 36(1) *Security Dialogue* 27–47.

vene.[45] Despite the wishes of political scientists, lawyers, and civil servants to establish constraints and guidelines, the unpredictable and highly politicised processes of bargaining within the Security Council and within the military councils of individual states, remain the dominant factors determining the future incidences of interventions for humanitarian purposes.

It is perhaps not surprising then that the UN Summit of World Leaders, held in September 2005, failed to endorse the set of criteria for the use of force set out in the Secretary-General's March report. (Indeed, the section on peace and security in the Summit Outcome document is conspicuously short when compared to other parts of the document and to Annan's report.) It is also significant that the document dropped the notion of asking the P5 to limit recourse to the veto in humanitarian circumstances. One of the strongest opponents to reforms of this kind was the United States, under the leadership of Bolton. But the United States was not the only party concerned about making explicit those conditions under which military force can be used by UN members. Many developing countries—echoing the concerns of international lawyers outlined earlier—expressed unease about potentially expanding the legitimate exceptions to Article 2(4). For these countries, most vocally represented by India, Iran and China, such an expansion would simply open the door to further military actions by the strong against the weak in international society. There were also concerns expressed about the need to build capacity in weak states to prevent uses of force—ie, helping states under stress *before* intervention-generating crises develop.

The Summit did succeed in enshrining the 'responsibility to protect' as a new principle of international conduct. But it is worth noting where this principle appears in the document. Whereas the earlier High-level Panel report had endorsed the notion of a 'collective international responsibility to protect' in its discussion of collective security and Chapter VII,[46] the Summit Outcome document (following the Secretary-General's report) discusses it under the rubric of human rights. This suggests an aversion on the part of member states to consider intervention for human protection purposes as part of the UN's 'standard' practice of collective security.

What is more noteworthy about the new principle is precisely how it is articulated. It is preceded by Article 138, which acknowledges that each individual state bears the responsibility to protect its population from atrocities such as war crimes and ethnic cleansing. The key clause, Article 139, goes on to state:

> The international community, through the United Nations, also has the responsibility to use appropriate diplomatic, humanitarian and other peaceful means, in accordance with Chapter VI and VII of the Charter, to help protect populations from genocide, war crimes, ethnic cleansing and crimes against humanity. In this context, we are prepared to take collective action, in a timely and decisive manner, through

[45] Roberts, A, 'Intervention: Suggestions for Moving the Debate Forward', Submission to the International Commission on Intervention and State Sovereignty, Roundtable, London, 3 February 2001.
[46] See para 203.

the Security Council, in accordance with the UN Charter, including Chapter VII, on a case by case basis and in cooperation with relevant regional organizations as appropriate, should peaceful means be inadequate and national authorities manifestly failing to protect their populations.

For the original ICISS proponents of R2P, the language on when and how the responsibility should shift to the international community must look weaker. The idea that responsibility for protecting citizens transfers if a host state proves itself 'unable or unwilling' has been replaced by the much stronger idea of 'manifest failure'. Both the United States and developing country members of the General Assembly wanted this less expansive language.[47]

The text is interesting in a number of other ways. First, the clause places the specific entity of the United Nations at the heart of this new responsibility. In other words, the law remains largely the same; the document does not endorse a new and specific responsibility on the part of states to take action to halt the slaughter of civilians. While ICISS and the High-level Panel spoke of the international community or collective responsibility, this document makes clear that the processes of the UN will be employed to decide when intervention takes place. This notion of a 'UN responsibility to protect' was likely designed to alleviate the fears of some developing countries that powerful states will intervene unilaterally. But it also moves away from the boldness of the ICISS report in terms of its willingness to entertain alternatives, should there be failure by the P5 in the Security Council to agree on military action. Submissive deference to the Security Council remains.

In this respect, it is worth contrasting the Summit Outcome document with the other major attempt to enshrine a right or responsibility to intervene for humanitarian purposes. In its founding document, the African Union (AU) both qualifies the principle of non-intervention and asserts 'the right of the Union to intervene in a Member State pursuant to a decision of the Assembly in respect of grave circumstances, namely: war crimes, genocide and crimes against humanity'.[48] Like the Summit Outcome document, this Constitutive Act does not indicate any requirement for host-state consent for intervention—a remarkable development given the previous record of African states in upholding traditional norms of sovereignty.[49] More significantly, and unlike the Summit Outcome document, the Act does not explicitly mention the need for Security Council authorisation for its action. According to some legal scholars, this omission means that Article 4(h) could both change the traditional, hierarchical relationship between the Security Council and regional organisations (as outlined in Chapter VIII of the UN Charter) and challenge the UN Charter's prohibition on the use of

---

[47] For a discussion of the evolution of language from the preliminary to final drafts, see Bellamy (2006) 164–5.

[48] Article 4(h), Constitutive Act of the African Union, 2000. This Act entered into force on 26 May 2001, thereby replacing the Charter of the older Organisation of African Unity (OAU).

[49] OAU members condemned the NATO's intervention over Kosovo in 1999 in their Algiers Declaration, and many African states signed on to the Non-aligned Movement's statement of September 1999, firmly rejecting 'the so-called "right of humanitarian intervention"'.

force.[50] It is beyond the scope of this chapter to analyse *why* the AU formulated its clause on intervention for humanitarian purposes in the way that it did.[51] What is important for our purposes is the suggestion by African states that intervention for humanitarian purposes can be legitimate even when implemented outside the formal structures of the UN.

Second, against the wishes of opponents such as Pakistan, Syria, Egypt and Iran, Article 139 explicitly mentions Chapter VII of the UN Charter. For those states concerned with enshrining the 'responsibility to protect', such as Canada and members of the EU, the principle would have lacked teeth without this link to enforcement by the Security Council. On the other hand, this reference to Chapter VII suggests that states remain reluctant to assert that a human rights violation by a government against its own people is, *in itself*, a sufficient justification for the use of force by outsiders; instead, the Council must determine that such actions some-how represent a threat to international peace and security. Again, the deference to the Council is firmly maintained. During the last 15 years, the Security Council has made such determinations by referring in its resolutions to the flow of refugees or regional instability.

Third, the scope of the paragraph is carefully delineated. While ICISS set as its threshold for intervention 'large scale loss of life, actual or apprehended, with genocidal intent or not' and 'large scale ethnic cleansing, actual or apprehended', the Summit Outcome document delimits a more specific set of actions. Interestingly, with the exception of ethnic cleansing, it is identical to the acts mentioned in Article 4(h) of the Constitutive Act of the AU. In the negotiations leading up to the signing of this Act, the question of thresholds generated much debate. Egypt's Foreign Minister Amre Moussa (who would later become a mem-ber of the Secretary-General's High-level Panel) was particularly concerned that a general formulation, referring to gross violations of human rights, would open up too wide a door for action by outsiders. His preference, echoed by others, was to use the less controversial Rome Statute of the International Criminal Court as a reference point for determining what constitutes legitimate grounds for interven-tion.[52] It is plausible to suggest that the diplomats negotiating the Summit Outcome document took the same approach.

---

[50] See, for example, Allain, J, 'The True Challenge to the United Nations System of the Use of Force: The Failures of Kosovo and Iraq and the Emergence of the African Union' (2004) 8 *Max Planck Yearbook of International Law* 238–89. Article 53 of Chapter VIII of the UN Charter states: 'No regional enforcement action should be taken under regional arrangements or by regional agencies without the authorization of the Security Council.'

[51] A persuasive analysis is offered by Haggis, C, 'The African Union and Intervention: The Origins and Implications of Article 4(h) of the Constitutive Act', unpublished MPhil thesis, University of Oxford, April 2005. Haggis argues that the precedent of Rwanda, when Western states did not inter-vene, was very much on the minds of African diplomats. In addition, however, Libyan leader Muammar Quaddafi was determined to create a legal text that would make it more difficult for non-African states to intervene on the African continent.

[52] *Ibid.* The Rome Statute lists genocide, crimes against humanity, war crimes and the crime of aggression as the most serious actions of concern to the international community as a whole.

Fourth, Article 139 attempts to clarify the ways in which the UN will fulfil its responsibility—most notably through co-operation with regional organisations. While this statement aligns with the text of Chapter VIII of the original UN Charter, it also reflects the practice of interventions in the 1990s, where organisations such as NATO, ECOWAS and the AU have been authorised by the Council to take action for the protection of civilians. In addition, by emphasising that the UN will operate on a 'case-by-case basis', the Article appears to resist any temptation to enshrine a blanket right of humanitarian intervention. Each instance will be deliberated within the context of the highest political organ of the UN, the Security Council. There is no provision mentioned for what would occur should the members of the Council fail to agree.

Finally, the fact that the 'responsibility to protect' is preceded by Article 138 gives states the opportunity to argue about proper sequencing. As Paul Williams and Alex Bellamy have argued, those states that in 2004 opposed the application of sanctions against Sudan over the humanitarian catastrophe in Darfur reiterated that it is sovereign states who remain the first 'port of call', and that the crisis had not reached the point where it could be definitively concluded that Sudan had failed to live up to its responsibilities.[53] This is an interesting example of how developing norms have a capacity to enable as well as to constrain, and can be used by participants in global politics in ways not intended or anticipated by their promoters. Thus, while the phrase 'manifestly failing' strives to inject an element of objective fact into arguments about the appropriate trigger for intervention, states may still disagree on whether the target state has been given sufficient time to address the crisis on its own.

CONCLUSION

So does the inclusion of the 'responsibility to protect' in the 2005 World Summit Outcome document represent a victory for human security and for the more specific aim of protecting civilians against oppressive governments? Much depends on one's view of the importance of words in international politics. 2005 did see a declared commitment on the part of states to act in ways not explicitly provided for in the UN Charter.[54] But R2P as it was formulated at the Summit weakens that commitment in significant ways, contains important ambiguities and reinforces submissive deference toward the Security Council. These concessions were the price to be paid for a minimum consensus among member states. Moreover, as with all UN statements and resolutions, international lawyers will continue to debate the Article's status as a source of law.[55] The principle itself is clearly still

---

[53] Williams and Bellamy (2005).

[54] It is also significant that the language of the document was echoed in a recent Security Council Resolution on the Protection of Civilians in Armed Conflict. See SCR 1674, 28 April 2006.

[55] Some have argued that a document of this kind generates 'soft law'. See Chinkin, C, 'The Challenge of Soft Law: Development and Change in International Law' (1989) 38 *International and*

seen by many as a licence to intervene, despite the wishes of its proponents to change the parameters of global discourse. The fall-out from the Iraq war did much to perpetuate this suspicion.

Most problematic is the fact that the bearer of the international responsibility to protect remains contentious, as the slowness of action in Darfur sharply illustrates. It is the lack of clarity about who will lead international action, and when, that is the biggest drawback in the current formulation of R2P, for it threatens to set up a mismatch between the expectations of individuals being oppressed on the one hand, and the capability and willingness of outside actors to provide for their security on the other. As Emma Rothschild pointed out over a decade ago, this disjuncture sets up both a moral and political problem:

> The individual who is 'troubled by violence' does not know who to ask for protection (which agency of the United Nations, which nongovernmental organization, and in what language?), and she has no political recourse if the protection is not provided.[56]

The promoters of R2P should be uncomfortable with this resting place.

REFERENCES

Allain, J, 'The True Challenge to the United Nations System of the Use of Force: The Failures of Kosovo and Iraq and the Emergence of the African Union' (2004) 8 *Max Planck Yearbook of International Law* 238–89.

Annan, K, 'We the Peoples', *Millennium Report* (New York, United Nations, 2000).

—— 'Address to the International Peace Academy Seminar on "The Responsibility to Protect"', Press Release SG/SM/8125, 15 February 2002.

—— 'In Larger Freedom: Towards Development, Security and Human Rights for All', Report of the Secretary-General, A/59/2005, 21 March 2005.

Bellamy, AJ, 'Whither the Responsibility to Protect? Humanitarian Intervention and the 2005 World Summit' (2006) 20(2) *Ethics and International Affairs* 143–69.

Byers, M and Chesterman, S, 'Changing the Rules about Rules? Unilateral Humanitarian Intervention and the Future of International Law' in JL Holzgrefe and RO Keohane (eds), *Humanitarian Intervention: Ethical, Legal and Political Dilemmas* (Cambridge, Cambridge University Press, 2003).

Cassese, A, '*Ex Iniuria Ius Oritur*: Are We Moving towards International Legitimation of Forcible Humanitarian Countermeasures in the World Community?' (1999) 10(1) *European Journal of International Law* 23–30.

Chesterman, S, *Just War or Just Peace? Humanitarian Intervention and International Law* (Oxford, Oxford University Press, 2001).

Chinkin, C, 'The Challenge of Soft Law: Development and Change in International Law' (1989) 38 *International and Comparative Law Quarterly* 850–66.

Comparative Law Quarterly 850–66. According to Chinkin, rather than setting out precise obligations or rights, soft law is written in general—and sometimes qualified—language, which leaves interpretation open to political contestation.

[56] Rothschild, E, 'What is Security?' (1995) 124(3) *Daedalus* 53–98, 71.

Clapham, A, 'Rights and Responsibilities', Programme for Strategic and International Security Studies, Geneva, May 2006.

Clark, D, 'Iraq has Wrecked our Case for Humanitarian Wars', *The Guardian*, 21 August 2003.

Evans, G, 'When is it Right to Fight?' (2004) 46(3) *Survival* 59–81.

Franck, T, 'Interpretation and Change in the Law of Humanitarian Intervention' in JL Holzgrefe and RO Keohane (eds), *Humanitarian Intervention: Ethical, Legal and Political Dilemmas* (Cambridge, Cambridge University Press, 2003).

Greenwood, C, 'International Law and the NATO Intervention in Kosovo' (2000) 49 *International and Comparative Law Quarterly* 926–34.

Haggis, C, 'The African Union and Intervention: The Origins and Implications of Article 4(h) of the Constitutive Act', unpublished MPhil thesis, University of Oxford, April 2005.

International Commission on Intervention and State Sovereignty (ICISS), 'The Responsibility to Protect' (Ottawa, International Development Research Council, 2001).

Jackson, R, *Quasi-states: Sovereignty, International Relations and the Third World* (Cambridge, Cambridge University Press, 1990).

Jones, B, 'Implementing "In Larger Freedom"' in P Heinbecker and P Goff (eds), *Irrelevant or Indispensable? The United Nations in the 21st Century* (Waterloo, Wilfred Laurier Press, 2005).

Krasner, SD, *Sovereignty: Organized Hypocrisy?* (Princeton, Princeton University Press, 1999).

Le Monde, 'La Russie s'oppose à un "usage raisonne" du droit du veto', 3 June 2002.

Rieff, D, *A Bed for the Night: Humanitarianism in Crisis* (London, Vintage, 2002).

Roberts, A, 'Intervention: Suggestions for Moving the Debate Forward', Submission to the International Commission on Intervention and State Sovereignty, Roundtable, London, 3 February 2001.

Rodin, D, 'The Responsibility to Protect and the Logic of Rights', Programme for Strategic and International Security Studies, Geneva, May 2006.

Rothschild, E, 'What is Security?' (1995) 124(3) *Daedulus* 53–98.

Tesón, F, *Humanitarian Intervention: An Inquiry into Law and Morality*, 2nd edn (Irvington-on-Hudson, Transnational Publishers, 1997).

Thakur, R, 'Freedom from Fear' in P Heinbecker and P Goff (eds), *Irrelevant or Indispensable? The United Nations in the 21st Century* (Waterloo, Wilfred Laurier Press, 2005).

United Nations, '2005 Summit Outcome', General Assembly Document, A/60/L.1, 15 September 2005.

United Nations, 'A More Secure World: Our Shared Responsibility', Report of the Secretary-General's High-level Panel on Threats, Challenges and Change, A/59/565, 1 December 2004.

Welsh, JM, 'Authorizing Humanitarian Intervention' in R Price and M Zacher (eds), *The United Nations and Global Security* (New York, Palgrave, 2004).

—— 'Introduction' in JM Welsh (ed), *Humanitarian Intervention and International Relations* (Oxford, Oxford University Press, 2004).

Welsh, J, Thielking, C and MacFarlane, SN, 'The Responsibility to Protect: Assessing the Report of the International Commission on Intervention and State Sovereignty' in R Thakur, AF Cooper and J English (eds), *International Commissions and the Power of Ideas* (Tokyo, United Nations University Press, 2005).

Wheeler, NJ and Morris, J, 'Justifying Iraq as a Humanitarian Intervention: The Cure is Worse than the Disease' in WPS Sidhu and R Thakur (eds), *The Iraq Crisis and World Order: Structural and Normative Challenges* (Tokyo, United Nations University Press, 2006).

Williams, PD and Bellamy, AJ, 'The Responsibility to Protect and the Crisis in Darfur' (2005) 36(1) *Security Dialogue* 27–47.

Zhang, Y, 'China: Whither the World Order after Kosovo?' in A Schnabel and R Thakur (eds), *Kosovo and the Challenge of Humanitarian Intervention* (Tokyo, United Nations University Press, 2000).

Index